Computer Science:
A Problem-Solving Approach

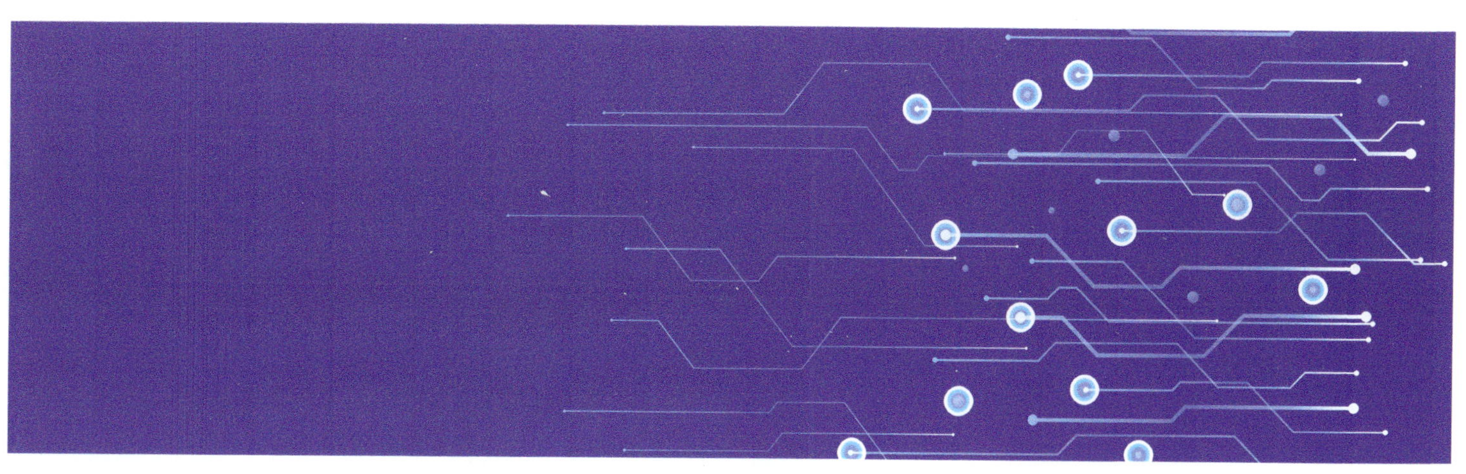

Cover art: halfpoint/123rf.com; BEST-BACKGROUNDS/Shutterstock; Roman Samborskyi/Shutterstock; DC Studio/Shutterstock; DC Studio/Shutterstock; Yusuf Ismail/Alamy Stock Photo; Gorodenkoff/Shutterstock

Library of Congress Cataloging-in-Publication Data

Cataloging-in-Publication Data is available on file at the Library of Congress

2 2023

ISBN-10: 0-13-804307-8
ISBN-13: 978-0-13-804307-0

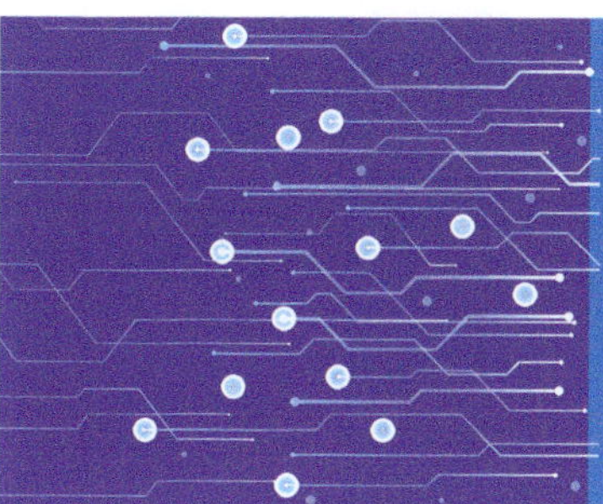

Contents

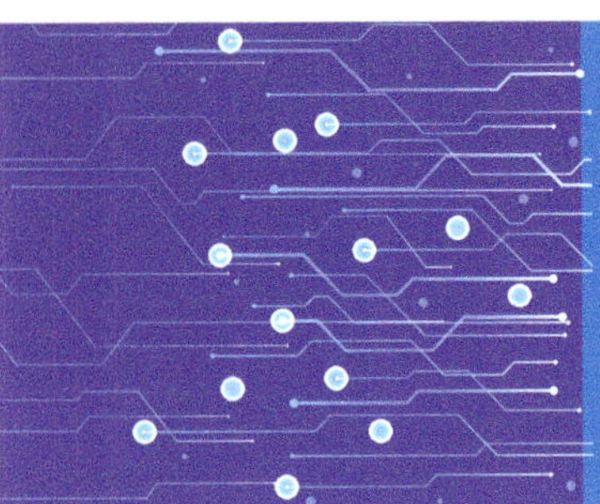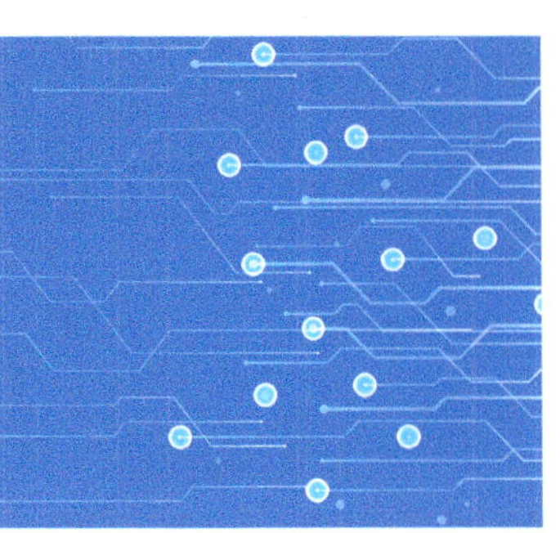

Contents

Contents

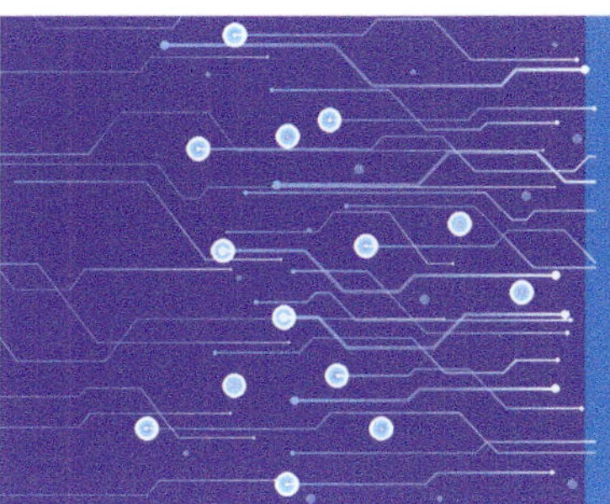

To the Student

Computer Science: A Problem Solving Approach uses the Python language to teach programming concepts and problem-solving skills, without assuming any previous programming experience. With easy-to-understand examples, pseudocode, flowcharts, and other tools, you will learn how to design the logic of programs, and then implement those programs using Python.

You will gain an understanding of the principles of computer science and positive digital citizenship through the study of operations, systems, and concepts. You will explore careers in computer science and the skills that will help you succeed. The text also provides you with the opportunity to collaborate with other students and digital communities to think critically, analyze data, and solve unique challenges using a variety of technologies.

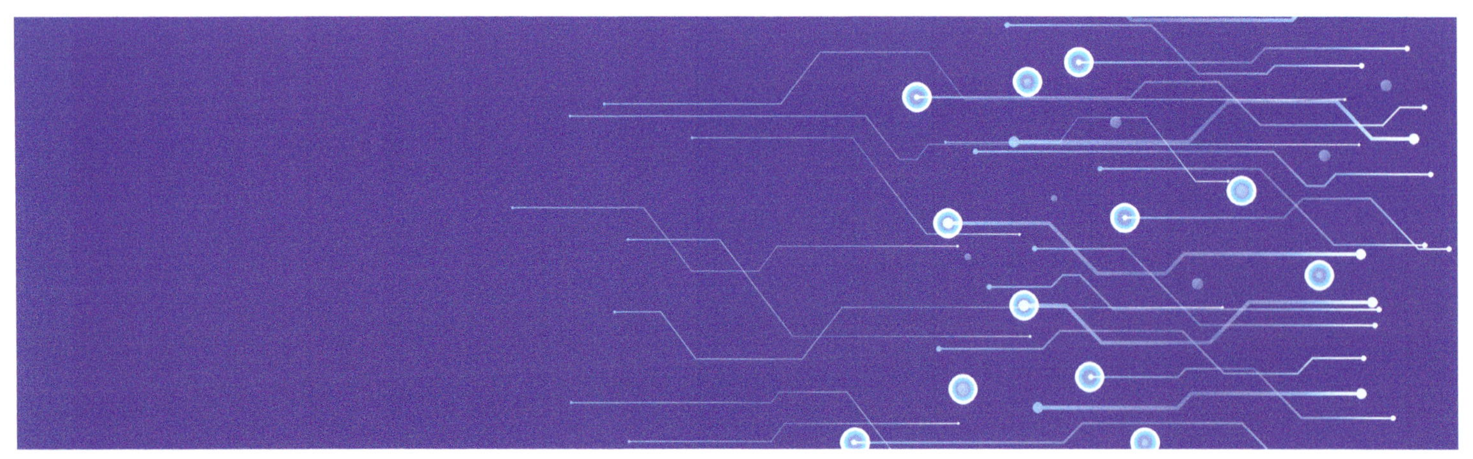

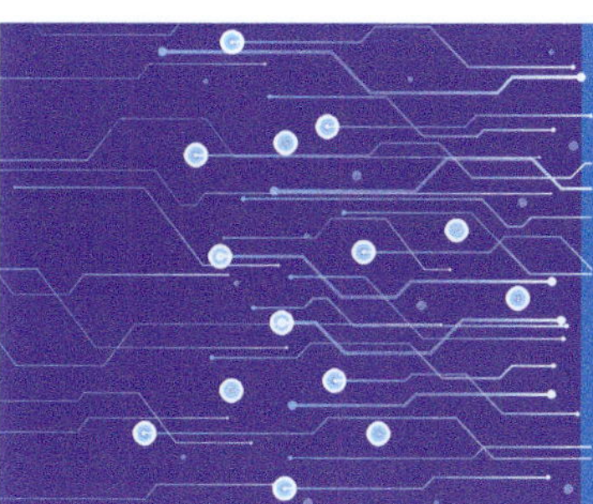

Chapter Overviews

Chapter 1   Introduction to Computer Systems
Chapter 1 covers basic computer concepts, including hardware, software, programming tools, and using an operating system for file management.

Chapter 2   Preparing for a Career in Computer Science
In this chapter you will explore computer science careers. You will learn how to plan for a computer science career while in school and how to develop the skills you will need to succeed in your chosen career.

Chapter 3   How Computers Store and Process Data
Chapter 3 introduces the concepts of binary, ASCII, and Unicode systems. You will learn to convert decimal numbers to binary and binary to decimal. You will also explore how to represent data using ASCII or Unicode.

Chapter 4   Programs and Programming Languages
How does a program work? In Chapter 4, you will learn how program code is processed by a computer. You will explore the differences and similarities of programming languages, learn what a compiler does, and be introduced to syntax.

Chapter 5   Getting Started with Python
In this chapter you learn how to code with Python. You learn about the IDLE programming environment and try your hand at creating lines and shapes with the Python turtle graphics system.

Chapter 6   Processing Input and Output
In Chapter 6 you explore input and output. You use the Print function and learn about comments, variables and constants. This chapter also includes information about reading input from the keyboard and how to display formatted output with f-strings.

Chapter 7   Math Calculations and Boolean Logic
Chapter 7 introductions mathematical operations in Python and how to use Boolean logic. It also introduces math libraries.

Chapter 8   Algorithms and Computational Thinking
Programming requires a problem-solving approach. In this chapter, you learn how to use a problem-solving process to design and test algorithms. You also learn about some common algorithms you can use and reuse in different programming problems.

Chapter 9   Taking a Program from Design to Code
Chapter 9 steps you through the process of designing a program and a solution, including how to use flowcharts and pseudocode. You learn how to use analysis tools and how to document your code. You also learn how to use style conventions and comments to make your code more readable.

Chapter 10   Using Decision Structures

In this chapter you learn how to use conditional statements, logical operators, and Boolean variables. You explore different types of decision structures that you can use to build your algorithms and find solutions for your coding challenges.

Chapter 11   Working with Characters and Strings

Chapter 11 takes you into how to use and manipulate strings. In addition to basic string operations, you explore string slicing and how to test and search strings.

Chapter 12   Using Loop Statements

Programming requires a lot of repetition. In Chapter 12, you learn about repetitive structures in the form of loop statements. It covers the `while` loop and the `for` loop, and you learn how to use a loop statement to calculate a running total.

Chapter 13   Using Lists

Chapter 13 covers lists. You learn about list slicing and how to use the `in` operator to find items in lists. You also learn about using Python's list methods and some built-in functions.

Chapter 14   Testing and Debugging Your Code

In this chapter you learn about common coding errors, including logic, runtime, and syntax. You learn how to find errors and fix them, and how to avoid them. You also learn about exception handling.

Chapter 15   Using Functions

Chapter 15 covers functions. You learn how to design a program to use a function. You explore some common functions and you learn how to use local and global variables with functions.

Chapter 16   Introduction to Object-Oriented Programming

In this chapter you learn the difference between procedural and object-oriented programming. You also learn how to use classes and instances in object-oriented programming.

Chapter 17   Digital Citizenship

Using technology responsibly is a key skill for computer science professionals. In Chapter 17, you learn how technology can pose legal and ethical challenges to individuals and to society. You learn how you can prevent cybercrime and maintain digital privacy, and what role you have in making sure technology is safe and accessible to all.

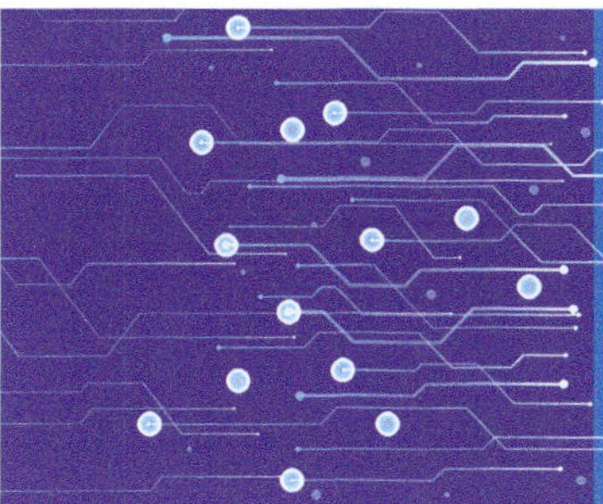

Chapter Overviews

Appendix A   Installing Python
Appendix A provides instructions for downloading and installing Python on your computer system.

Appendix B   Introduction to IDLE
Appendix B introduces the IDLE integrated development environment that comes with Python. You will learn how to start IDLE and then create, save, and run a program. You will also learn about some of the benefits of using IDLE.

Appendix C   Python Keywords
Appendix C provides a list of the words that are reserved and cannot be used as a variable name, function name, or an identifier in a Python program.

Appendix D   Predefined Named Colors
Appendix D is a list of defined color names that you can use with the turtle graphics library.

Appendix E   ASCII Character Set with Decimal and Binary Codes
Appendix E lists the decimal and binary codes for the ASCII character set for easy reference.

Appendix F   Formatting Numeric Output with the format() Function
Appendix F provides a tutorial on how to use the format () Function to format numbers.

Glossary

Index

Using Your Text

The text is organized into 17 chapters and five appendices. Each chapter is organized into sections. Within the text you will find the following features.

Keypoint   Each major section of the text starts with a concept statement that summarizes the main point of the section.

Program 1-1   **Programs**   Within each chapter, concepts and coding skills are illustrated with complete and partial example programs. .py files that you can open in Python are available for download for most of these programs.

Chapter Overviews

In the Spotlight

In the Spotlight case studies provide detailed, step-by-step analysis of problems. These case studies provide the opportunity for you to test your knowledge and skills by working through the problem on your own or with a partner, before viewing the solution provided in the text.

VideoNote

VideoNotes

A VideoNotes icons indicates that a customized video is available online for the topic.

Notes

Notes appear throughout the text. They are short explanations of interesting or often misunderstood points relevant to the current topic.

Tips

Tips advise you on the best techniques for approaching different programming problems.

Warnings

Warnings caution you about programming techniques or practices that can lead to malfunctioning programs or lost data.

Checkpoints

Checkpoints are questions at the end of each main section in each chapter. They are designed to reinforce concepts from the section.

Chapter Review

Each chapter includes a set of review questions and exercises. They include Multiple Choice, True/ False, and Short Answer.

Exercises

Each chapter offers a pool of exercises designed to reinforce your knowledge of the chapter topics. Some exercises let you work alone or with others to research and report on related topics, while Programming Exercises give you the opportunity to practice your Python coding skills. Many chapters also include Algorithm Workbench and Debugging exercises for using algorithms and problem-solving to analyze and solve programming problems.

1.1 Introduction to Computer Science

KEY POINT An understanding of computers and how they work creates a solid foundation for studying computer science.

How do people use computers? Students write papers, conduct research, and participate in online classes. At work, people analyze data, make presentations, conduct business transactions, communicate with customers and coworkers, control machines in manufacturing facilities, and much more. At home, people pay bills, shop online, communicate with friends and family, and play games. And don't forget all the smart devices that connect to the internet, like televisions, audio speakers, lights, automobiles, and doorbells.

Computers can perform such a wide variety of tasks because they can be programmed. This means that computers are not designed to do just one job, but to do any job that their programs tell them to do. A **program** is a set of instructions that a computer follows to perform a task. For example, Figure 1-1 shows screens using Microsoft Word and PowerPoint, two commonly used programs.

Programs are **software**. Software is essential because it controls everything the computer does. All of the software that we use to make our computers useful is created by individuals working in the field of computer science as programmers or software developers. A **programmer**, or **software developer**, is a person with the training and skills necessary to design, create, and test computer programs.

Computer science is the study of computers and computing. It covers a wide range of topics including how computer hardware works to how networks enable devices to connect and communicate. By studying computer science, you can learn how to design, create, improve, repair,

Figure 1-1   A word processing program and a presentation program

Microsoft Corporation   Microsoft Corporation

and use computer systems. This book introduces you to the fundamental concepts of computer programming using the Python language. The Python language is a good choice for beginners because it is easy to learn and programs can be written quickly using it. Python is also a powerful language, popular with professional software developers. In fact, it has been reported that Python is used by Google, NASA, YouTube, various game companies, the New York Stock Exchange, and many others.

Before we begin exploring the concepts of programming, you need to understand a few basic things about computers and how they work. This chapter will build a solid foundation of knowledge that you will continually rely on as you study computer science.

1.2   Hardware Basics

KEY POINT   **The physical devices of which a computer is made are referred to as the computer's hardware.**

Hardware

The term **hardware** refers to all of the physical devices, or **components**, of which a computer is made. A computer is not one single device, but a system of devices that all work together. Like the different instruments in a symphony orchestra, each device in a computer plays its own part.

If you have ever shopped for a computer, you've probably seen sales literature listing components such as microprocessors, random-access memory, and graphics cards, which are found inside the case. It might also list **peripheral** devices, such as video displays, keyboards, and printers, which are found outside the case. As shown in Figure 1-2, a typical computer system consists of the following major components:

- The central processing unit (CPU)
- Primary memory

Figure 1-2   Typical components of a computer system

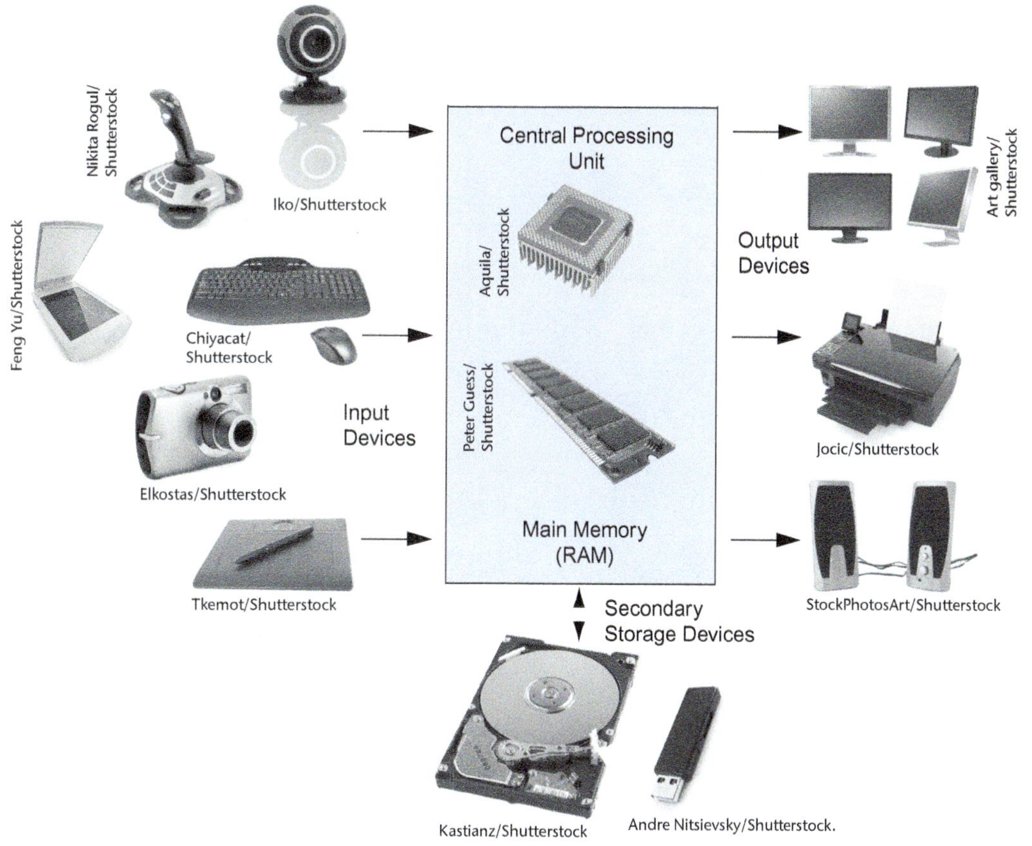

- Secondary memory (storage devices)
- Input devices
- Output devices

Let's take a closer look at each of these components.

The CPU

When a computer is performing the tasks that a program tells it to do, we say that the computer is **running** or **executing** the program. The **central processing unit (CPU)**, is the part of a computer that actually runs programs. The CPU is the most important component in a computer because without it, the computer could not run software.

In the earliest computers, CPUs were huge devices made of electrical and mechanical components such as vacuum tubes and switches. Figure 1-3 shows such a device. The two people in the photo are working with the historic ENIAC computer. The ENIAC, which is considered by many to be the world's first programmable electronic computer, was built in 1945 to calculate artillery ballistic tables for the U.S. Army. This machine, which was primarily one big CPU, was 8 feet tall, 100 feet long, and weighed 30 tons.

Figure 1-3   The ENIAC computer

US Army Center of Military History

Figure 1-4   A lab technician holds a microprocessor

Creativa/Shutterstock

Today, CPUs are small chips known as **microprocessors**. Figure 1-4 shows a photo of a lab technician holding a modern microprocessor. In addition to being much smaller than the old electromechanical CPUs in early computers, microprocessors are also much more powerful.

Primary Memory

Primary memory, or **main memory**, is the computer's work area. This is where the computer stores a program while the program is running, as well as the data that the program is working with. For example, suppose you are using a word processing program to write an essay for one of your classes. While you do this, both the word processing program and the essay are stored in main memory.

One type of primary memory is called **random-access memory (RAM)**. It is called this because the CPU is able to quickly access data stored at any random location in RAM. RAM is usually a **volatile** type of memory that is used only for temporary storage while a program is running.

Figure 1-5   Memory chips

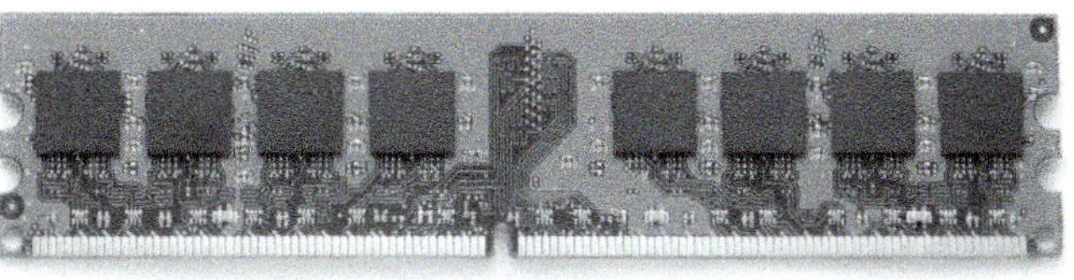

Garsya/Shutterstock

When the computer is turned off, the contents of RAM are erased. Inside your computer, RAM is stored in chips, similar to the ones shown in Figure 1-5.

Another type of primary memory is called **read-only memory (ROM)**. ROM chips store instructions for starting the computer. ROM is **nonvolatile** memory. It stores data permanently, even when the power to the computer is off.

Secondary Memory

Secondary memory is a type of memory that can hold data for long periods of time, even when there is no power to the computer. Secondary memory is what most people think of as **storage**, or **secondary storage**. Programs are normally stored in secondary memory and loaded into main memory as needed. Important data, such as word processing documents, payroll data, and inventory records, is saved to secondary storage, as well.

The most common type of secondary storage device is the **disk drive**. A traditional disk drive stores data by magnetically encoding it onto a spinning circular disk. **Solid-state drives** store data in solid-state memory. A solid-state drive has no moving parts and operates faster than a traditional disk drive. Most computers have some sort of secondary storage device, either a traditional disk drive or a solid-state drive, mounted inside their case. Even cell phones have internal storage, and can perform as external storage devices, as well. External storage devices, which connect to one of the computer's communication ports, can be used to create backup copies of important data or to move data to another computer.

In addition to external storage devices, many types of devices have been created for copying data and for moving it to other computers. For example, **USB drives** are small devices that plug into the computer's USB (universal serial bus) port and appear to the system as a disk drive. These drives do not actually contain a disk, however. They store data in a special type of memory known as **flash memory**. USB drives, which are also known as **memory sticks** and **flash drives**, are inexpensive, reliable, and small enough to be carried in your pocket.

Cloud storage, or **online storage**, is storage space on a network **server** at a remote location. You use a software application program to upload and download files to the server over a network. Examples of cloud storage are Google Drive, Microsoft OneDrive, and Apple iCloud.

Input Devices

Input is any data the computer collects from people and from other devices. The component, or peripheral device, that collects the data and sends it to the computer is called an **input device**. You use common input devices such as a keyboard, mouse, touchscreen, scanner, microphone, and digital camera. Disk drives and optical drives can also be considered input devices, because programs and data are retrieved from them and loaded into the computer's memory.

Output Devices

Output is any data the computer produces for people or for other devices. It might be a sales report, a list of names, or a graphic image. The data is sent to a peripheral **output device**, which formats and presents it. You use common output devices such as video displays and printers. Disk drives can also be considered output devices because the system sends data to them in order to be saved.

 **Checkpoint**

1.1   What is a program?

1.2   What is hardware?

1.3   Identify the five major components of a computer system and their functions.

1.4   What part of the computer actually runs programs?

1.5   What type of memory serves as a work area to store a program and its data while the program is running?

1.6   What type of memory holds data even when there is no power to the computer?

1.7   What type of peripheral device collects data from people and from other devices?

1.8   What type of peripheral device formats and presents data for people or other devices?

1.3　Software Basics

 **The programs that run on a computer are referred to as software.**

For a computer to function, it needs software. Everything a computer does, from the time you turn the power switch on until you shut the system down, is under the control of software. There are two general categories of software: **system software**, which are the programs that control and manage the basic operations of the computer, and **application software**, which are the programs that make a computer useful for everyday tasks. Most computer programs clearly fit into one of these two categories. Let's take a closer look at each.

System Software

System software typically includes the operating system, utility programs, and software development tools.

Operating Systems

An **operating system** is the most fundamental set of programs on a computer. The operating system provides the instructions that control the internal operations of the computer's hardware. It manages all of the devices connected to the computer, allows data to be saved to and retrieved from storage devices, and allows other programs to run on the computer.

Popular operating systems for laptop and desktop computers include Windows, macOS, and Linux. Some version of macOS runs all Apple Macintosh computers. Microsoft Windows runs on most non-Apple personal computers. Linux is an open-source operating system, which means the source code used to create it is available to the public. Google's Chrome OS is based on Linux. Popular operating systems for mobile devices include Android and iOS. iOS is used exclusively on Apple mobile devies. Android runs on devices manufactured by many companies. Android is considered to be more open and customizable.

Utility Programs

A **utility program** performs a specialized task that enhances the computer's operation or safeguards data. Examples of utility programs are virus scanners, file compression programs, and data backup programs.

Probably the most important utilities are file managers, which let you work with data stored on your computer. The operating system, programs, and data are all stored in files, each with a name. Files can be grouped together into folders. Folders are also called directories. A folder can be divided into subfolders.

Software Development Tools

Software development tools are the programs that programmers use to create, modify, and test software. These programs may be called **software development applications.** Along with the hardware they run on, they are referred to as a **development environment.** Assemblers, compilers, interpreters, and debuggers are examples of software development applications.

There are two basic categories of programming and programming tools: procedural and object-oriented. **Procedural programming** uses step-by-step instructions to tell a computer what to do. Procedural programming languages include C, Fortran, Pascal, and Basic. **Object-oriented programming** provides rules for creating and managing **objects**, which are items that include both data and how to process the data. Object-oriented programming languages include Python, Java, Alice, and VBScript. Some programming combines the two. C++ is an example of a **programming language** that uses both procedural and object-oriented programming.

Special programs called **compilers** translate the source code into binary form using only 0s and 1s. The result, called **object code**, can be read and acted on by a computer. Sometimes programs called **interpreters** are used to translate the source code directly into actions, bypassing the need for a compiler. Interpreters are able to immediately follow the instructions in the binary code while compilers must first wait and translate the binary. Even though the compilers take longer to get started, they are able to complete tasks much faster than interpreters.

Some programming languages require the programmer to assign a **data type** to variable data. Some common, or **primitive**, data types include **string**, which is a sequence of characters that does not contain numbers used for calculations; **numeric**, which is numbers or amounts that are used in calculations; **character**, which is text; **integers**, which represent whole numbers; and **date**, which is the method of coding dates.

Application Software

Programs that make a computer useful for everyday tasks are known as **application software**. These are the programs that people normally spend most of their time running on their computers. Figure 1-1, at the beginning of this chapter, shows screens from two commonly used applications: Microsoft Word, a word processing program, and PowerPoint, a presentation program. Some other examples of application software are spreadsheet programs, email programs, web browsers, and game programs. **App** is an abbreviation for the term **application**. The term app is usually used for programs developed specifically for smartphones, tablet computers, and other handheld devices.

In the past, applications were written to run on a specific operating system. Now, most applications can be used on many operating systems. For example, versions of Microsoft Office applications are available for PCs running Windows, Macs running macOS, mobile devices running iOS, Chromebooks running Chrome OS, and mobile devices running Android OS. In addition, most programs include a Save As command that lets you save files in different formats and an Open command that lets you open files saved in a different format. There are also utility programs that can translate files that previously may have been unreadable so they can be used on devices running a different OS.

 **Checkpoint**

   1.9   What fundamental set of programs control the internal operations of the computer's hardware?

   1.10   What operating system runs on all Apple Macintosh computers?

   1.11   What operating system has a source code that is available to the public?

   1.12   What do you call a program that performs a specialized task, such as a virus scanner, a file compression program, or a data backup program?

1.13 Python is an example of what type of programming language?

1.14 Word processing programs, spreadsheet programs, email programs, web browsers, and game programs belong to what category of software?

1.4) File Management Basics

Operating systems have a file manager system utility that you use to manage data stored in files on a computer.

Among the most important system utilities is the file manager, called File Explorer in Windows, Files in Chrome OS, and Finder in macOS. This utility allows you to organize, view, copy, move, rename, and delete files.

Directories and Folders

Most operating systems manage file storage using a multilevel, or **hierarchical**, filing system called a **directory**. At the top is the main storage location, called the **root directory**. Root directories are labeled with letters followed by a colon. On most Windows computers, the root directory is C:, and external hard drives may be D:, E:, and so on. Within the root are subdirectories called folders, which may contain subfolders and files. Figure 1-6 shows an example of hierarchical file system.

Navigating the File System

You navigate through the file system by expanding and collapsing folders to show or hide their contents. You use a **path** to identify the specific location of a folder or file. The path lists each location in the directory hierarchy beginning with the root. Each specific location is separated by a \ character. So, the path C:\Documents\Schoolwork\Report.doc is the storage location for a document file named Report, stored in the Schoolwork subfolder, stored in the Documents folder, in the root directory C:.

Figure 1-6   A hierarchical file system is like the roots of a tree extending out into folders, subfolders, and files.

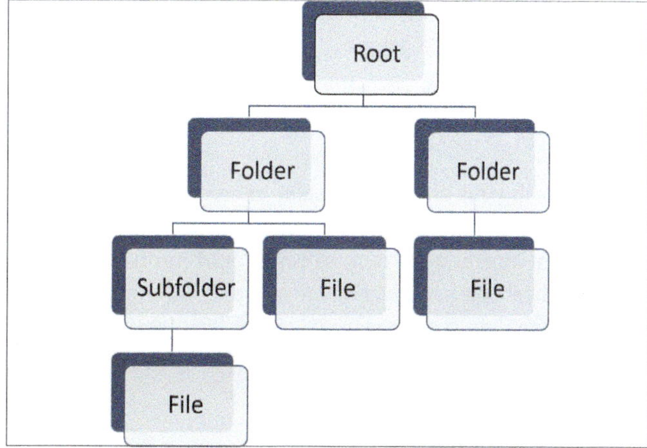

Most operating systems come with some folders already set up. Windows comes with folders set up for each user, including folders for Documents, Pictures, and Downloads. Android devices have a Files or My Files folder with subfolders for Images, Downloads, Audio, Video, and so on.

Use your file manager to identify and change the default storage locations. For example, to find the default Downloads storage location in Windows, open File Explorer, right-click the Downloads folder in the navigation pane on the left of the window, select Properties, and then select the Location tab. The path to the folder displays. For example, the default Downloads storage location for a user named Sam might be C:\Users\Sam\Downloads. The default Documents storage location for the same user might be C:\Users\Sam\Documents.

Naming Files and Folders

When you create a new file or folder, you give it a **file name**. Using descriptive names helps you identify the contents and keep your data organized. For example, the name *Second Semester Grades* is more descriptive than *Grades*. It also helps keep you from accidentally deleting or overwriting files and folders that have the same name. Most operating systems have specific file and folder naming conventions. They usually let you use file and folder names with up to 255 characters, including spaces and punctuation. You cannot use <, >, :, ", /, \, |, ?, or *.

File Type

Operating systems add a period and a file extension to file names. A **file extension** is a short series of letters that indicate the application used to create the file and the **file format**, or **file type**. For example, a Microsoft Word document has the extension .doc or .docx. You can set options to display file types when you view a file list, as shown in Figure 1-7. By default, the operating system uses the program associated with the file type to open the file. So, a file with an .xlsx extension opens in Microsoft Excel and a file with a .pdf extension opens in Adobe Reader or Acrobat.

Cross-Platform Compatibility

Cross-platform compatibility is the ability to use a file on any device no matter what operating system is in use. This is possible because the OS associates files with specific programs, not with an OS. So, a word processing document created with a word processor on a macOS system can be opened on any device running the same word processing application, such as a Windows notebook, iOS tablet, or Android OS phone.

File and Folder Management

You use the file manager in your operating system to create, view, copy, move, rename, and delete files, folders, and subfolders. For example, you can open a file simply by double-clicking it in the file manager window. The operating system stores a lot of information called **metadata** with a file so it can find the file when you need it. For most users, the most important piece of information for identifying files and folders is the name. If you want to remember what a folder contains and what file you need, you should use logical, recognizable names that describe the contents.

Figure 1-7   You can display file types when viewing files with Windows

Desktop ❯ Work in Progress

Name	Type	Size
Current Projects	File folder	
Book Report Compressed.zip	Compressed (zipped) Folder	4,770 KB
IMG_1519.JPG	JPG File	3,888 KB
Data.xlsx	Microsoft Excel Worksheet	7 KB
Book Report Presentation.pptx	Microsoft PowerPoint Presentation	893 KB
New Microsoft Publisher Document.pub	Microsoft Publisher Document	59 KB
Book Report.docx	Microsoft Word Document	14 KB
Book Report Video.mp4	MP4 File	3,760 KB
audiobook.png	PNG File	12 KB

 **Checkpoint**

1.15   What is the file manager called in Chrome OS?

1.16   What is the main storage location in a hierarchical filing system?

1.17   What is the maximum number of characters allowed for a file name in most operating systems?

1.18   What type of file usually has a .docx extension?

1.19   What is metadata?

❓ Chapter Review

Multiple Choice

1. A(n) ___________ is a set of instructions that a computer follows to perform a task.
   a. compiler
   b. program
   c. interpreter
   d. programming language

2. The physical devices that a computer is made of are referred to as ___________.
   a. hardware
   b. software
   c. the operating system
   d. tools

3. The part of a computer that runs programs is called ___________.
   a. RAM
   b. secondary storage
   c. main memory
   d. the CPU

4. Today, CPUs are small chips known as ___________.
   a. ENIACs
   b. microprocessors
   c. memory chips
   d. operating systems

5. The computer stores a program while the program is running, as well as the data that the program is working with, in ___________.
   a. secondary memory
   b. the CPU
   c. main memory
   d. the microprocessor

6. This is a volatile type of memory that is used only for temporary storage while a program is running.
   a. RAM
   b. secondary storage
   c. the disk drive
   d. the USB drive

7. A type of memory that can hold data for long periods of time, even when there is no power to the computer, is called ___________.
    a. RAM
    b. secondary memory
    c. secondary storage
    d. CPU storage

8. A peripheral that collects data from people or other devices and sends it to the computer is called ___________.
    a. an output device
    b. an input device
    c. a secondary storage device
    d. main memory

9. A video display is a(n) ___________ device.
    a. output
    b. input
    c. secondary storage
    d. main memory

10. A ___________ is a secondary storage device with no moving parts.
    a. solid-state drive
    b. magnetic disk drive
    c. CD drive
    d. DVD drive

11. ___________ is nonvolatile primary memory.
    a. RAM
    b. CPU
    c. compiler
    d. ROM

12. ___________ is secondary storage on a network server.
    a. Flash storage
    b. Cloud storage
    c. Peripheral storage
    d. RAM

13. ___________ is an operating system for mobile devices.
    a. iOS
    b. Windows
    c. Linux
    d. MacOS

14. ___________ is an operating system based on Linux.
    a. Windows
    b. Chrome
    c. iOS
    d. MacOs

15. An example of a system utility is ___________.
    a. word processing
    b. spreadsheet
    c. procedural
    d. antivirus program

16. The type of programming that uses step-by-step instructions to tell a computer what to do is ___________.
    a. object-oriented
    b. procedural
    c. VBScript
    d. Python

17. Programs used for every day tasks are called ___________.
    a. utilities
    b. debuggers
    c. applications
    d. viruses

18. Spreadsheet programs, email programs, web browsers, and game programs are examples of ___________.
    a. utilities
    b. file managers
    c. operating systems
    d. applications

19. The term ___________ is usually used for programs developed specifically for smartphones, tablet computers, and other handheld devices.
    a. files
    b. apps
    c. macs
    d. docs

20. The system utility that lets you copy a file from one storage device to another is called a ___________.
    a. scanner
    b. copier
    c. file manager
    d. decoder

21. The file manager in macOS is called ___________.
    a. Mac Explorer
    b. Finder
    c. File Explorer
    d. Files

22. On Windows computers, the root directory is usually called ___________.
    a. A:
    b. B:
    c. C:
    d. D:

23. You cannot use the character ___________ in a file name.
    a. 2
    b. c
    c. /
    d. -

24. The file extension for an Adobe Reader file is ___________.
    a. pdf
    b. xlsx
    c. pptx
    d. pdfx

25. A file with a .doc file extension will probably open in a(n)___________ application.
    a. spreadsheet
    b. slide manager
    c. word processor
    d. image editing

True or False

1. Today, CPUs are huge devices made of electrical and mechanical components such as vacuum tubes and switches.

2. Volatile primary memory is called RAM.

3. A flash drive is volatile primary memory.

4. A peripheral device is connected inside the computer case.

5. A mouse is an output device.

6. A printer is an output device.

7. An antivirus program is an example of an application.

8. You use a system utility to copy or move files and folders.

9. Microsoft PowerPoint is an example of a software development application.

10. Word processing programs, spreadsheet programs, email programs, web browsers, and games are all examples of utility programs.

Short Answer

1. Identify the function of a CPU.
2. What is the difference between primary and secondary memory?
3. Compare three different operating systems.
4. What is the difference between an operating system and an application program?
5. Choose two input devices and explain how to use them.
6. Choose two output devices and explain how to use them.
7. What is RAM?
8. What is a software development application? Give two examples.
9. Analyze and explain the concept of a primitive variable.

Exercises

1. Working alone or with a partner or small team, examine a computer system to identify the major internal and external hardware components. Look at how the different components are connected. Create a five-column chart to record your observations. In the first column, list all the hardware components that you can identify, including primary and secondary memory, the CPU, and peripheral devices. Include the components you think are inside the computer box. In the remaining columns, state the function of each item and whether it is used for inputting, processing, outputting, or storage. With your teacher's permission, unplug and replug all of the computer components, including external drives, a printer, mouse, keyboard, monitor, projector, and the power supply. Start the system. Use the operating system to locate the system specifications and add them to your column chart. Discuss your findings as a class.

2. Working alone or with a partner or small team, write a one-page report that explains the desktop on your computer to someone who has never used a computer before. Describe each icon, and explain what happens when you click, double-click, or right-click it. Identify files or programs that are represented on the desktop, and explain what they are used for, and what file formats they use. Finally, explain how the desktop helps you manage your work on the computer. Share your report with others.

3. Open a word-processing program. Name and save the new, blank file. Use the keyboard to input the definition of five terms you learned in this chapter. Save the changes to the file and close it. Use the file manager to make a copy of the file on a different storage device, and then delete the original file. Rename the copied file. Discuss the process with a partner, or with the class.

4. With your teacher's permission, use the internet to research two or three computer operating systems. As you work, take notes and keep track of your sources. Evaluate the information you find and only use it if it is accurate, relevant, and valid. Create a column chart comparing and contrasting the operating systems. Share the chart with a partner or with the class.

5. With your teacher's permission, use the internet to research two or three software development applications. As you work, take notes and keep track of your sources. Evaluate the information you find and only use it if it is accurate, relevant, and valid. To demonstrate your knowledge, create a column chart comparing and contrasting types of software development applications. Present the chart to a partner or to the class.

2 Preparing for a Career in Computer Science

TOPICS

2.1 Exploring Computer Science Careers

KEY POINT Careers in computer science involve designing and developing computers and computer programs.

The Information Technology Career Cluster

A career is a chosen field of work in which you try to advance over time by gaining responsibility and earning more money. The career you choose has a major impact on the kind of life you will lead. It determines the type of training and education you will need. It might impact where you live and the type of lifestyle you achieve.

The U.S. Department of Education organizes careers into 16 clusters, or groups. Career clusters help you sort career possibilities so you can pursue one that suits your interests and abilities. Information Technology is one of the career clusters. People with careers in information technology design, develop, support, and manage hardware, software, multimedia and systems integration services.

Within each of the 16 career clusters are related job, industry, and occupation types called pathways. Each pathway offers a variety of careers you might choose. The pathways in Information Technology include:

- Information Support and Services
- Network Systems
- Programming and Software Development
- Web and Digital Communications

People interested in computer science careers usually choose the programming and software development pathway. Careers in this pathway involve the design, development, implementation, and maintenance of computer systems and software. When you complete a course of study in the programming and software development pathway, you learn how to research, design, develop, and test operating systems-level software, compilers, and network distribution software. You also learn about creating, modifying, and testing the codes, forms, and scripts that allow computer applications to run. You can go on to use your skills in a wide range of industries such as medical, industrial, military, communications, aerospace, business, scientific, and general computer applications.

People who find satisfaction working in programming and software development take pride in designing, creating, and seeing projects through to completion. Some personal qualities that are helpful for success in computer science careers include:

- Independent
- Organized
- Analytical

Programming and software development professionals must have effective communication skills, a strong sense of self, and the ability to analyze and solve problems. Developing these qualities and skills will help you succeed in a computer science career.

Careers in Computer Science

Every industry that uses computer technology needs computer science professionals. Entry-level positions generally require a bachelor's degree. A master's degree may be required for advancement. According to the U.S. Bureau of Labor Statistics (BLS), in 2021, the median annual salary for computer programmers was about $93,000. The median annual salary for computer and information research scientists was about $131,500.

Knowledge of computer science can help you succeed in many careers. Even if you do not work as a programmer or computer scientist, the logic and problem-solving skills you learn in this course of study are highly valued by employers in many industries and will make you a strong candidate for other positions.

Some careers in computer science include:

- Computer programmer
- Computer system analyst
- Health informatics specialist
- Software developer
- Game designer
- Applications software developer
- Software application specialist
- Computer and information research scientist

 Checkpoint

2.1   What is a career?

2.2   What pathway do people interested in computer science careers choose?

2.3   What are three personal qualities that are helpful for success in computer science careers?

2.4   What was the median annual income for a computer programmer in 2021?

 2.2   Academic Planning for a Computer Science Career

 **There are many things you can do while in school to prepare for a computer science career.**

How Education Affects Employment

Can you name one thing you can do to increase the amount of money you will earn in your lifetime? How about graduating from high school? Even better, graduating from college! (Figure 2-1.)

Figure 2-1   Employers prefer to hire graduates.

Blend Images/Shutterstock

Graduates are more likely to be hired than non-graduates. They earn more money, are healthier, and live better lifestyles. Completing your education is one of the best things you can do for yourself and your career. Academic planning can help you reach that goal.

School also provides an opportunity to prepare for a career. Core subjects such as reading, writing, and math are vital for the career-search process. Science, social studies, music, art, technology, family and consumer sciences, and sports all help you gain knowledge and build skills you will need to succeed at work, such as teamwork, leadership, and problem-solving. School clubs and organizations also help you build skills for future success.

Education teaches you skills and information you need to get and keep a job. Most companies will not hire an employee who has not graduated from high school. Some will not hire an employee who has not graduated from college or university. If a company does hire non-graduates, it usually pays them less than it pays graduates.

Employers assume that graduates have certain characteristics that dropouts don't have. If a graduate and a dropout apply for the same job, the employer thinks that the graduate:

- Knows how to read and write.
- Understands basic math.
- Can communicate with others.
- Knows how to solve problems.
- Has a good work ethic.
- Has a positive attitude.
- Is self-disciplined.
- Is motivated to succeed.

Developing Communications Skills

Almost every employer wants workers who can read, write, and speak effectively. As a computer programmer, you will be called on to read and write documentation as well as emails and text messages with co-workers. You may have to explain your work to teammates and clients, and listen to others explain project goals. In all these situations, you will be expected to demonstrate the use of relevant topics and content, technical concepts, and vocabulary, and to use correct grammar, punctuation, and terminology.

In school, there are many opportunities to develop communications skills. Language Arts classes help you organize written information, understand the things you read, and speak out loud in front of an audience. Clubs and organizations also help you build communications skills. You can join the debate team to learn how to argue politely and effectively. You can write for the school newspaper or website. You can perform with the drama club.

Building Math Skills

Basic math skills such as addition, subtraction, multiplication, and division are vital for success in all careers. For example, you may need basic math to prepare budgets and invoices. You may use time-based mathematics to calculate the number of hours you worked and how much you should be paid. In a computer science career, you will have to apply mathematics knowledge and skill when you write code. You will need an understanding of algorithms to design a program. While in school, you can develop the necessary math skills by taking classes in algebra and geometry. Statistics also provides a good foundation for programming and software development. Other useful math skills include advanced algebra, calculus, trigonometry, and the ability to read and create charts and graphs.

Study Strategies for Success in School

People who do well in school usually work very hard. They know how to use study strategies—careful plans and methods—that improve their ability to remember new things. You can make study strategies part of your academic plan.

- **General strategies.** Sit near the front of the class so you pay attention; take notes; set a daily study goal, such as completing your homework.
- **Strategies for memory.** Study your notes soon after class; make flash cards with a key idea on one side and a definition or explanation on the other side.
- **Strategies for listening and note-taking.** Listen for clues that the speaker is giving a key point; underline or star the main points; use abbreviations for commonly used words.
- **Strategies for planning and organization.** Keep a calendar, schedule, or to-do list; write assignments and due dates in an assignment notebook and on a calendar; prioritize your responsibilities and tasks; break a large project into smaller steps, and set a deadline for each step.
- **Strategies for tests.** Ask your teacher what the test will cover and what type of questions it will include; don't wait until the night before to study—study a little bit each evening in the days leading up to the test; read test directions carefully; check your answers; skip questions you are unsure of and go back to them after you have completed the others.

Setting Goals for Postsecondary Education

Is a high school diploma enough education to land you the career of your choice? If not, you will want to start thinking about postsecondary education, or school after high school. For most people, postsecondary education means college or university, but it can also include military training and apprenticeships.

Many careers require a minimum of an associate's degree (two years after high school) and many require a bachelor's degree (four years after high school). Most computer science careers require a Bachelor of Science (BS) degree in a field such as computer science, information technology, or informatics.

Planning for postsecondary education involves:

- Selecting a school or program
- Making sure you have the necessary qualifications
- Applying for admission
- Obtaining financial aid

Goal-setting skills can help you manage the process from start to finish. They can help you stay focused on the educational objectives that you need to achieve your career goals.

Researching Universities

You can find information about different postsecondary opportunities online, in your school guidance center, and at the library. For example, you can look up a university's computer science program on the school's website. You should be able to find a Contact page where you can request information via email or regular mail.

When considering a postsecondary college or university, it is helpful to compare the computer science programs offered at multiple schools. Some things to consider include:

- What are the requirements for acceptance into the program?
- What are the requirements for completing a degree?
- How many years will it take to complete a degree?
- What courses or specialties are offered?
- What percent of students who start the program graduate?
- What percent of students who graduate are hired for a computer science career?

As you research the programs, ask yourself the following:

- **Where is the school located?** Will I live at home or on campus? Is it in a city or a small town?

- **How many students are there?** Will I be more comfortable in a small school or a large school?

- **How much does it cost?** What is the annual **tuition**—cost of education? How much is **room and board**—the cost of a dorm room and meals? Are there additional fees?

- **Am I qualified for admission?** Does my grade point average meet the school standards? Are my admissions scores high enough? Do I have the right extracurricular activities?

Things You Need to Apply to College or University

A college application form asks for information about yourself and your family. Most have space for listing your extracurricular activities and for a personal essay that tells the college about you, your goals, and your abilities. In addition to the application form, you will also need:

- **An official transcript**, which is a record of the courses you took in high school and the grades you earned.

- **An official score report,** which gives the results of the standard college entrance exam, such as the Scholastic Aptitude Test (SAT) or American College Test (ACT). Some states have their own entrance exams for state universities and colleges.

- **Recommendations,** which are forms that you ask one teacher and one counselor to fill out, describing your qualities as a student and a person.

- **Financial aid forms,** which provide information about your ability to pay tuition.

Nondegree Certificates

An alternative to a degree program at a college or university is a **nondegree certificate**. These certificate programs allow you to learn skills that may help advance your career without attending a college or university. For example, you might be able to earn a certificate for completing a course to learn a particular programming tool, such as C++ or Java. When you complete the program, you are awarded a certificate that shows you are qualified for work that requires those skills. You may complete certification programs before applying for a job or while you work to stay up-to-date on new developments in the field.

Some computer science-related certificate programs are sponsored by businesses that develop and sell programming platforms and other related products. For example, Microsoft offers certifications to software developers who use Microsoft products. Other certificate programs are run by educational institutions or professional organizations.

To earn a certificate, you will have to enroll in a training program, which can cost up to $5,000. You will also have to pay to take the exam, which may add up to $500 to your costs.

In most cases, a certificate alone will not guarantee you will be hired. However, when you combine it with other academic and career skills, a certificate may help you stand out from other job candidates and to advance once you are hired.

 **Checkpoint**

2.5   True or false: A high school dropout usually earns as much money as a high school graduate.

2.6   In high school, what classes can help you develop math skills?

2.7   What are three things you can compare when considering computer science programs at colleges and universities?

2.8   What is a computer science-related certificate?

 ## Developing Employability Skills

 **Employability means having and using skills and abilities to get hired and stay hired.**

Career-Ready Practices

You might graduate from college with a bachelor's degree in computer science, but if employers think you are unfriendly, or if they question your confidence, they are unlikely to hire you. Attitude and confidence are part of employability. **Employability** means having and using your life skills and abilities to get hired and stay hired. It is more than just meeting the qualifications for a position. It also means knowing how to:

- Present your positive qualities to an employer.
- Communicate effectively with employers, co-workers, and customers.
- Meet your responsibilities at work.

Having employability skills will give you an advantage when you are ready to apply and interview for a position, no matter what career you choose. Use the following list of career-ready practices as a guide for the types of skills employers look for when hiring and promoting employees:

- Act as a responsible and contributing citizen and employee.
- Apply appropriate academic and technical skills.
- Attend to personal health and financial well-being.
- Communicate clearly and effectively and with reason.
- Consider the environmental, social, and economic impacts of decisions.
- Demonstrate creativity and innovation.
- Employ valid and reliable research strategies.
- Utilize critical thinking to make sense of problems and persevere in solving them.

- Model integrity, ethical leadership, and effective management.
- Plan education and career paths so they align to personal goals.
- Use technology to enhance productivity.
- Work productively in teams while using cultural global competence.

Employability skills can generally be placed into two groups: **hard skills** and **transferable skills**. Employers often look for people with hard skills to fill specific jobs. For example, a mobile app developer looks to hire people skilled at designing and developing software for mobile devices.

Transferable skills can be used on almost any job. They are called transferable skills because you can transfer them from one situation or career to another. They include:

- Problem-solving.
- Time management.
- Professionalism.
- Critical-thinking.
- Effective communication.
- Cooperation.

Solving Problems

Any barrier or obstacle between you and a goal is a **problem**. Problems pop up all the time. Mostly, we come up with a solution without thinking too hard. Knowing how to solve problems at work is a valuable skill. Employers like to hire problem-solvers. Clients and co-workers respect problem-solvers. Programming and software development are based on problem-solving strategies.

One way to solve a problem is to use a process, or **algorithm**, to figure out the best **solution**:

1. Identify the problem.
2. Consider all possible solutions.
3. Identify the consequences of each solution.
4. Select the best solution.
5. Make and implement a plan of action.
6. Evaluate the solution, process, and outcome.

Planning and Time Management Skills

Planning and time management are critical skills for succeeding at work. **Time management** means organizing your schedule so you have time to complete tasks and meet your responsibilities. To achieve your career goals, you will have to manage your time effectively and **prioritize** tasks—decide which tasks must be completed first.

Time management techniques include figuring out exactly how you currently spend your time, creating a schedule, making to-do lists, and ranking list items in order of importance.

- **You can create a time log to figure out how you are currently spending your time.** Simply track how much time you spend each day on specific tasks. The log will help you identify how you can use your time more effectively.
- **Scheduling helps you plan ahead because you know when you will do something and you can be ready for it.** You can schedule by any time period, but the most useful are by month, week, and day. For example, a monthly schedule can help you plan a project. You can schedule the time you need to meet with your team, conduct research, and complete your work. If you don't have a schedule, you might find yourself in the stressful situation of trying to complete the whole project in just a few days.
- **Making a to-do list every morning can help you plan your time for that day.** Prioritize the items on the list by ranking them in order of importance so you know what you should do first. If something doesn't get done, put it at the top of the to-do list for the next day.

You can make use of technology tools to automate some of your time management tasks and increase your **productivity**, which is the amount of work you accomplish. Computer applications can help you organize and meet your responsibilities, as shown in Figure 2-2.

Figure 2-2   Creating a schedule.

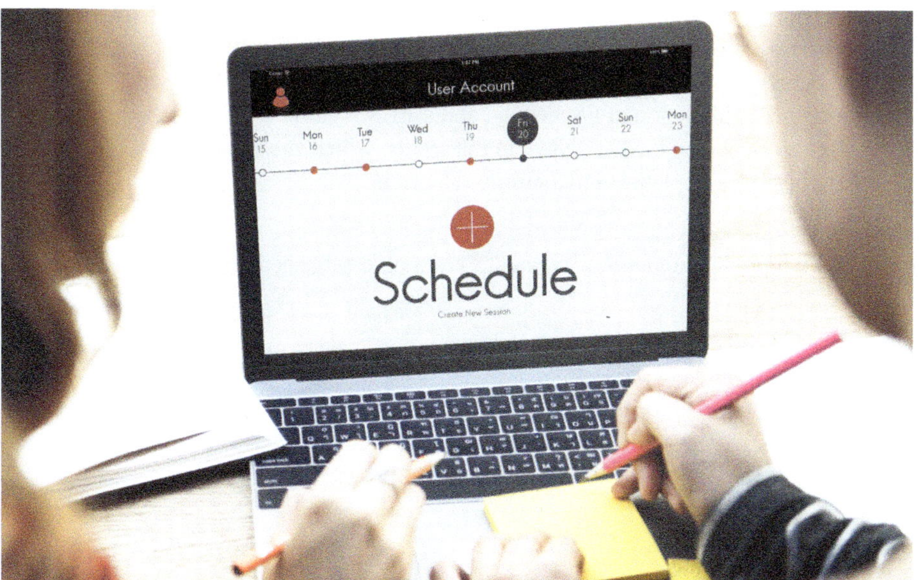

Rawpixel.com/Shutterstock

Make use of the calendar app on your computer or mobile device. You can enter schedules, phone calls, and appointments. Use the tasks list feature to record and prioritize the things you need to accomplish. Set the app to display a message or make a sound to remind you of deadlines. Apps can also help you complete the tasks on your to-do list. The more skilled you are at using applications, the faster and more efficient you will be at completing everyday tasks. Some applications such as Microsoft Excel even include templates for tracking projects or creating a to-do list or schedule.

Project Management

Employers value employees who know how to use project management skills to make sure work is completed on time. **Project management** is a process used to take a project from conception to completion. It helps you design and implement procedures to track trends, set timelines, and evaluate progress for continual improvement. There are four basic parts to the project management process:

1. **Identifying measurable objectives.** An objective is a short-term goal used to keep a project on track for completion. A measurable objective can be evaluated by specific standards.
2. **Identifying deliverables.** A deliverable is a product, or segment of a product, that can be provided to an employer, client, or the public.
3. **Setting a schedule.** The schedule should include a timeline with a final deadline, as well as milestones for achieving each objective. This helps you prioritize your tasks.
4. **Developing supporting plans.** Supporting plans usually specify things like how to allocate resources such as funds and technology, how to identify and manage risk, and develop methods for communication.

Many companies have project management software for scheduling, organizing, coordinating, and tracking project tasks. You can find basic project management templates in programs such as Microsoft Excel. There are also specific tools for project management, such as a **Gantt chart**, which is a horizontal bar chart developed by Henry L. Gantt in 1917, that shows a graphical illustration of a schedule, and a **PERT chart** (Program Evaluation Review Technique), developed by the U.S. Navy in the 1950s, which shows project tasks, the order in which they must be completed, and the time requirements.

These applications help you and your clients evaluate a project's success by tracking both the process and the product under development, based on established criteria, such as deadlines.

Professionalism

Professionalism, or work ethic, is the ability to show respect to everyone around you while you perform your responsibilities as best you can. It includes a basic set of personal qualities that make an employee successful.

These qualities include:

- Integrity
- Courtesy
- Honesty
- Dependability
- Punctuality
- Responsibility
- Cooperativeness
- Positivity
- Open-mindedness
- Flexibility

Professionalism also means you demonstrate positive work behaviors, such as regular attendance. A professional also maintains a clean and safe work environment, performs tasks effectively, shows initiative, and takes pride in their work accomplishments. These behaviors lead to advancement at work, in school, and in everyday life.

Employers and co-workers expect you to honor and respect time in the workplace. You can expect the same thing from them. That means:

- Showing up on time.
- Showing up every day—except vacations and holidays.
- Leaving for lunch and breaks at the scheduled time—not before—and returning promptly—not late.
- Staying until the end of the work day.
- Meeting your deadlines, which means completing all work before it is due.
- Taking care of personal business on your own time, not during work hours.

Respecting time at work shows that you respect your co-workers. It demonstrates to your supervisor that you take your responsibilities seriously. It is one way you prove you are ready for new challenges, such as those that might come from a promotion.

In the Spotlight:

Professional Appearance

Dress standards vary depending on the career that you choose. For example, you wouldn't expect a boom operator to be wearing a suit and tie, and you wouldn't want a business manager to be wearing grease-covered clothing. However, good grooming habits are required in all professions. The following are recommendations for maintaining a well-groomed, professional appearance:

- Wear clothes that are clean, neat, and in good repair.
- Wear clean and appropriate shoes.
- Keep your hair neat and clean.
- Brush your teeth at least twice a day.
- Floss daily.
- Use mouthwash or breath mints.
- Bathe daily.
- Use unscented deodorant.
- Keep makeup light and neutral.
- Keep jewelry to a minimum.
- Do not use perfume or cologne.
- Keep nails clean.

Thinking Critically

Critical thinking can help you evaluate your options in many situations. You can use it when you are making decisions, setting goals, and solving problems, both individually and when you are working with a team. When you think critically, you are honest, rational, and open-minded about your options. You consider all possibilities before rushing to judgment.

- Being honest means acknowledging selfish feelings and preexisting opinions.
- Being rational means relying on reason and thought instead of on emotion or impulse.
- Being open-minded means being willing to evaluate all possible options—even those that are unpopular.

You can think critically about a lot of things, not just decisions and problems. You don't have to believe everything you hear or read. You can question a news report, look deeper into the meaning of a magazine article, or investigate the truth behind a rumor.

When you think critically, you consider all possible options and other points of view. You look objectively at information. **Objective** means fairly, without emotion or prejudice. Then, you use your values, standards, and ethics to interpret the information subjectively. **Subjective** means affected by existing opinions, feelings, and beliefs. Looking at things both objectively and subjectively can help you make choices that are right for you.

 ## Checkpoint

2.9   What is the first step in the problem solving process?

2.10 What is productivity?

2.11 What is project management?

2.12 What are three qualities of professionalism?

 ## 2.4 Developing Communication Skills

Employers hire employees who know how to communicate effectively with clients, co-workers, and managers.

Effective Communication

Communicating is how people connect with others. Communication prevents misunderstandings. It gives you a way to share ideas. It even makes it easier for you to appreciate and respect other people's opinions.

At its most basic, communication is an exchange between a sender and a receiver. The sender transmits the message with a specific intent. The receiver interprets the message and responds.

- **Effective communication** is when the receiver and the sender understand each other.
- **Ineffective communication** is when the receiver and the communicators don't understand each other, whether they're aware of the confusion or not.

You can communicate effectively by using a six-step process:

1. **Be clear.** The receiver is more likely to get your message if you deliver it in a way they can understand. Speak slowly. Consider who you are talking to. You probably use different language when you talk to a client than when you talk to a friend.

2. **Be personal.** Use the other person's name or title so there's no doubt who you are talking to. Use an **"I" statement**—a statement that starts with the word "I"—to frame the statement in terms of you and your goals. An "I" statement indicates that you are taking responsibility for your thoughts and feelings. It helps the receiver understand your point of view and respond to you.

3. **Be positive.** Phrase your message in positive terms. Say what you want, not what you don't want. For example, say, "I want to start shooting at 9:30," instead of saying, "I don't want to start later than 9:30."

4. **Get to the point.** Follow the "I" statement with an explanation of the message you are sending. Explain how or why you feel a certain way, or how or why you think a certain thing. For example, say, "I want to start shooting at 9:30. I think that will give us enough time to get everything done without having to rush."

5. **Listen to the response.** Pay attention and use active listening techniques to make sure you hear the response.

6. **Think before you respond.** Make sure you understand the message. Repeat it, if necessary, and ask questions for clarification. Use critical thinking to make sure you are not letting emotions and preconceived ideas get in the way.

Ways to Communicate

Verbal communication is the exchange of messages by speaking or writing. For most of us, verbal communication is the most common way we stay in touch with other people in our lives. We talk face to face or on the phone. We send text messages, emails, and instant messages. We write blogs, tweet, pass notes, and send cards.

Talking is usually a very effective form of verbal communication. When you speak clearly and use language the receiver understands, they almost always gets the message the way you intend it.

Clear, concise writing is also an effective form of verbal communication, whether it is in a letter, report, email, or text message. However, sometimes the context can be lost through writing, because the receiver cannot hear the sender's tone of voice or see the sender's facial expression.

Nonverbal communication helps put words into context. This form of communication includes visual messages that the receiver can see, such as a smile when you are talking. It also includes physical messages, such as a pat on the back. During a conversation, the tone of your voice and the language you use combine to provide context for the words.

Reading and writing are also verbal communication. Effective writing is simple, clear, and to the point. It is free from spelling and grammatical errors. Effective writing usually uses the active voice rather than the passive voice. In the active voice, the subject takes action. In the passive voice, the subject is acted upon. For example, "She threw the ball." is in the active voice; "The ball was thrown by her." is in the passive voice.

When you write, you lose some of the context, which can make the communication less effective. Exchanging written messages doesn't take place face to face. It might be across great distances. When the receiver can't hear your voice, they might misinterpret the message.

There are different ways to read, depending on what you are reading. Passive reading is the kind of reading you do for entertainment, such as when you read a magazine or a comic book. In this kind of reading, you are just taking in information or following the plot. When you read critically, you take time to really think about what is written and why. Critical reading happens when you are actively engaging the subject as you read.

Critical reading is essential for success. Here are three steps you can use to be sure you are reading critically:

1. Determine the best reading strategy for the text. This means that you need to figure out whether to skim the text, read closely for detail, or read for meaning or critical analysis.
2. As you read, stop and think about what is being said and try to put it in your own words, or rephrase it from your own point of view.
3. Take notes while you are reading to make sure you understand and remember the main points.

Technical Reading and Writing

Technical communication explains technical or specialized information to people who may or may not be familiar with them. Its purpose is to convey very specific information, without extra words or language. In computer science, you will use **technical writing** to communicate your ideas and explain your work to a variety of people, including clients and co-workers. When you write technical information, keep your audience in mind. Be direct and to the point, use the simplest language possible, and define all terms that readers may not know.

Effective technical writing is:

- Clear
- Concise
- Complete
- Logical
- Sequential

Technical reading is a process that uses specific strategies to help you understand technical writing. These include:

- Skimming the document before reading to determine the information it is intended to convey.
- Noting or highlighting headings so you understand how the document is organized.
- Reviewing terminology at the start to make sure you know the meanings.
- Reading to identify key points in each sentence or paragraph.
- Writing an outline or summary to reinforce your understanding. This may include creating a concept map or other diagram that helps you visualize and remember the information.
- Rereading the information.
- Discussing the information with someone else who has read it.

Active Listening

Active listening is an important part of effective communication. When you are an active listener, you mindfully pay attention to the speaker and make sure you hear and understand the message.

Use these skills to be an active listener:

- Show interest using eye contact and positive nonverbal messages.
- Let the other person finish speaking before you respond.
- Ignore distractions such as cell phones and other people.
- Set your predetermined opinions and emotions aside.
- Repeat the message that you hear out loud, to make sure you received it correctly.

Active listening is a sign of respect. It shows you are willing to communicate and that you care about the speaker and the message. When you listen actively, the other person is more likely to listen when you speak, too.

Communicating at Work

Just as you use different types of verbal communication when speaking to your friends and your parents, you use different types of verbal communication when speaking to people with whom you relate on the job, such as your manager, your co-workers, your clients, and your **subordinates**— the people you supervise.

- **Your manager has a higher position in the company than you do and has control over your job.** When communicating with a manager, you usually use a formal style of verbal communication. You show deference—courteous regard or respect—by using their title and refraining from jokes or casual remarks you might use with a friend. You must also recognize that your manager has the final say on most matters, and so you must know when to agree with their decisions, even if you disagree with them personally.
- **Your co-workers, or colleagues, have the same rank in the company that you do.** This does not mean that you should joke around with them as you do with your friends. It also does not mean you should use the same style of verbal communication you would use with your manager. You can speak to them more casually.
- **Your clients are the source of your business.** When communicating with clients, remember the old saying, "The customer is always right." This means that in order to be successful, you must respect your clients and speak with them positively.
- **If you supervise others in the company, you communicate with them using the respect that is due to any worker.** You can also use an assertive or positive style of verbal communication, so that they know exactly what is expected of them.

Not only is what you say important, but so is how you say it. In addition to the different ways you can verbally communicate with others in the workplace, you can use different tones to make your meaning clear. These include:

- **Assertive speech,** which includes action verbs such as "should," "does," and "will."
- **Aggressive speech,** which you should avoid in the workplace, since it can lead to arguments or hurt feelings. An example of aggressive speech would be, "You better help me now!"
- **Passive speech,** which is usually best to use when you also want to show respect or deference. Examples of passive speech include words such as "can," "might," and "could."

Constructive Criticism

Criticism is an analysis and judgement of the positive and negative aspects of something, such as a product, design, work of art, or project. **Constructive criticism** is when the judgement is delivered in a positive way, and includes advice for how to make improvements or solve problems.

In any career, it is important to know how to accept constructive criticism and how to deliver it. Both of these require effective communications skills:

- When you offer constructive criticism, it is important that you deliver your message in a positive, friendly way so the recipient recognizes the value in your advice.
- When you receive constructive criticism, it is important that you listen carefully and consider the message as it is intended—to provide positive feedback to help you improve.

 **Checkpoint**

2.13   What is effective communication?

2.14   What is nonverbal communication?

2.15   What are five qualities of effective technical writing?

2.16   What is one strategy you can use for effective technical reading?

 **2.5**) **Developing Teamwork and Leadership**

Most computer science careers rely on teamwork and leadership to meet project goals.

A **team** is a group of two or more people who work together to achieve a common goal. When you are part of a team, you have access to all the knowledge, experience, and abilities of your teammates. Together, you can have more ideas, achieve more goals, and solve more problems.

A successful team relationship depends on all team members working together. They depend on and trust one another. If one team member does not do their share, the entire team suffers. The challenges of a team relationship come from having different people working together. Even if everyone agrees on a common goal, they may not agree on how to achieve that goal.

Most computer science projects require teamwork. For example, programmers may work with a partner, or with a group of other programmers, usually under the direction of a team leader or project manager. (Figure 2-3). Depending on the size and scope of the project, the team may also include an analyst, senior developer, junior developer, and client/subject matter expert. But, no matter who is on the team and what the team is doing, the interactions between team members will be most productive if the members of the team:

- Listen to each other.
- Respect each other's opinions.
- Recognize each other's skills and abilities.
- Share the work load.
- Share responsibility.

Jacob Lund/Shutterstock

Developing Leadership Characteristics

Even when all members of a team have an equal role in making decisions and solving problems, it is important to have a **leader**. A leader is a type of manager who knows how to use available resources to help others achieve their goals.

Leaders exhibit positive qualities that other people respect, such as self-confidence, honesty, effective listening and speaking skills, decisiveness, respect for others, and open-mindedness. They are organized and supportive of the other team members. Being the leader does not mean you are always right. A strong leader considers the ideas and opinions of the other team members. An effective leader keeps the team on track and focused on achieving its goals.

Although you might have heard that someone is a "born leader," that's not usually the case. Becoming a leader takes time and patience. Leaders have to prove that they can make decisions, set goals, and solve problems. You can develop leadership characteristics by recognizing and modeling positive leadership qualities.

One way to do this is by participating in student leadership and professional development opportunities. For example, you can join clubs and activities such as your school newspaper, yearbook, drama club, or audio-visual club, and volunteer for leadership roles. You might also join a career technical student organization (CTSO) such as SkillsUSA. CTSOs offers members a range of individual and group programs, activities, and competitions designed to build professional skills as well as leadership qualities.

Qualities of an Effective Team Member

While a strong leader is important to the success of a team, team members must also be committed to the group's success. An effective team member helps teammates if they need help, does not blame teammates for problems or mistakes, and offers ideas and suggestions instead of criticism. Effective team members use critical-thinking skills and interpersonal skills to identify and solve problems, overcome conflict, and achieve their goals.

You are a good team member if you are:

- Open-minded
- Willing to compromise
- Cooperative
- Friendly
- Trustworthy

Checkpoint

2.17   What is a team?

2.18   What is a leader?

2.19   What are three qualities of a good team member?

 **Career Search Basics**

Career search documents are your first chance to make a positive impression on a potential employer.

Career Search Documents

As part of a search for a career in computer science, you will need to prepare and organize the materials neccessary for a job search. Every job search requires the following:

- A resume, which is a written summary of your work-related skills, experience, and education. It introduces you to the prospective employer by presenting a snapshot of your qualifications. It should be brief, direct, true, and accurate with no typographical, grammatical, or spelling errors. A good resume attracts the interest of the reader so they want to learn more about you.
- A cover letter, or letter of interest, which is a letter of introduction that you send with a resume.
- A list of references that includes the names and contact information of people who know you and your qualifications and who are willing to speak about you to potential employers.
- A thank-you letter that you send to the employer after an interview to show your interest in the position.
- A portfolio, which is a collection of your best work that you can show a potential employer.

Cover Letter

A **cover letter** is a strong and succinct way to introduce yourself to a potential client or employer. It also helps convince employers to review your resume by focusing attention on specific resume information, such as credentials, skills, or specific projects in your portfolio. The letter should be concise and well-written, with no grammar or spelling mistakes. The cover letter is your first point of contact, so craft one that makes an excellent impression.

Figure 2-4   A resume is necessary to apply for a job

Andrea De Martin/123rf.com

Resume

A **resume**, as shown in Figure 2-4, summarizes your training and experience. It is absolutely necessary when searching for a computer science position. Employers often have to sort through large numbers of resumes, so make yours informative, easy to read, concise, and very specific to the posted position.

Most resumes are first assessed by automated filtering systems that use algorithms to quickly scan hundreds of documents to find a match. That means they look for key terms that indicate the applicant meets the requirements the company is looking for. Make sure you include key terms relevant to the specific job you are seeking. Even when the resume is read by a human, that human is likely to skim the document looking for the same key terms.

In addition to relevant key terms, a resume should list your education, related experience, certificates you have earned, and skills. For a programming resume, you should list specific projects relevant to the job. Make sure to include the coding language and software you used and what you did specifically as a team member or leader on the project. You can even link the projects to your portfolio so employers can actually see the work.

Here are some general best practice guidelines for a professional resume:

- Include a list of schools you attended, with dates and degrees you have earned.
- Include your work history, including internships and volunteer work. Emphasize jobs where you gained relevant experience, summarizing your responsibilities and skills with bullet lists.
- List all licenses and certifications you have earned.
- List relevant work samples, and/or provide links to an online portfolio where employers can view digital versions of your work.
- Use key words specific to the job requirements and qualifications. For example, if a job posting mentions experience with Python, make sure you include "experience with Python" on your resume.
- Make it easy to read. Leave space between lines so it is not crowded or overloaded.
- Use one easy-to-read font, and apply different font styles and sizes for emphasis.
- Emphasize and organize your text with bullet points.
- Use proper spelling, punctuation, grammar, technical terms.
- Keep it to one page, if possible—two pages at the most. (If you use two pages, be sure to put your name in the header or footer on page 2, in case it becomes separated from page 1.)
- If you are printing the document, use plain white paper.

Portfolio

A **portfolio** is your opportunity to show a potential employer what you are capable of. As a high school student, you might keep a portfolio that includes examples of your work from core subjects, along with a transcript of grades and awards you have won. As you begin looking for a computer science career, you will need to develop a portfolio of projects that show off your coding and other programming-related skills.

A **coding portfolio** provides concrete proof that you have the skills you claim on your resume. For example, having the key term "Python" on your resume might get you an interview, but a project that shows you really know how to use Python will get you a job.

If you have the skills, you can create your own portfolio website. Otherwise, there are many online sites where you can create a portfolio. Some sites specialize in portfolios for computer science careers, such as GitHub Pages for coders and Itch.io for game developers.

The portfolio should include information similar to your resume that explains your academic and word-related qualifications. But, the highlight should be the projects. Include at least four, and no more than ten.

Before you include a project in your portfolio, check it to make sure it is quality work. Clean up and improve the code, and add comments that will explain the work to the potential employer.

Filling out a Job Application

A **job application** is a standard form you will fill out when you apply for a job, as shown in Figure 2-5. You might fill it out in person when you visit a potential employer, or you might fill it out online. It requires a lot of the same information that you put on your resume, such as your contact information, as well as details about your education and work experience. It may ask for your Social Security number.

Figure 2-5   A typical job application form

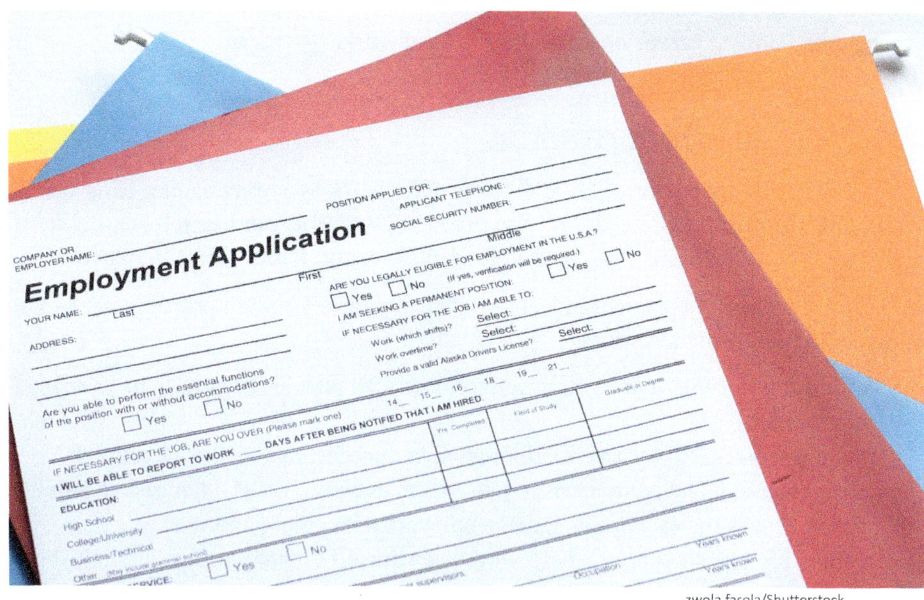

zwola fasola/Shutterstock

Filling out an application form may seem simple, but a lot of people make mistakes or forget important information. A messy or incomplete job application will not make a positive impression on the employer.

- Read the form before you start filling it out.
- Follow all instructions.
- Be truthful and accurate.
- Write neatly.
- Enter N/A for not applicable if there is a question that does not apply to you.
- Check your spelling and grammar.
- If you make a mistake, ask for a new form and start again.

You might find it helpful to bring a personal information card with you when you apply for a job. A personal information card is an index card on which you write the information you might need, such as your Social Security number and the contact information for your past employers.

 **Checkpoint**

2.20   Why is it important to include relevant key terms on a resume?

2.21   True or False: You do not need a portfolio when searching for a computer science career.

2.22   How many projects should you include in a coding portfolio?

2.7 Conducting a Job Search

 **Finding career opportunities is hard work.**

Finding Career Opportunities

The first step in applying for a job is finding out what jobs are available. How can you find opportunities that meet your needs and fit your strengths? You can use **job search resources**— tools designed to help you find **job leads**—to identify opportunities for employment.

You can use a variety of resources to identify available jobs. You will probably need to use more than one of the following resources.

- Networking is using your existing connections with people (friends, family, etc) to find job opportunities.
- Online resources let you access information and job listings on the internet.
- Career counselors help you identify jobs that match your skills, interests, and abilities.
- Employment agencies work to match employers with employees.
- Job fairs provide an opportunity to introduce yourself to many different employers.

Knowing how to make the most out of available job search resources is critical for finding a job.

What Is Networking?

Some studies show that nearly 80 percent of all job openings are never advertised. How can you find out about a job if it isn't advertised? Network! **Networking** in a job search means sharing information about yourself and your career goals with personal contacts—people you know already, or new people you meet in any area of your life. Hopefully, one of the contacts works for a company that is hiring, or knows someone at a company that is hiring. The contact recommends you for the position. Employers like to hire people who come with a recommendation from someone they know and trust.

How Do I Network?

The first step in networking is to tell everyone you know that you are looking for work. Be specific about your career goals. Tell your family, friends, classmates, and teachers. If you volunteer, tell the people at the volunteer organization. If you are a member of a club or organization, tell the other members. Stay in touch with your contacts through regular calls, texts, or email. Set up a networking file to keep track of each contact. Set up the file using index cards or a computer program. In the file, include:

- The name, occupation, mailing address, phone number, and email address of each contact.
- A reminder of how you know the contact. Are they a personal friend? Did you meet through someone else? Did you meet through a club or organization?
- Notes about each time you communicate with the contact. The first time you call a contact, explain who you are and why you are calling.

Do not ask for a job. Instead, ask for:

- Job leads.
- Information about occupations and companies, such as what trends are affecting a certain industry.
- Introductions to people who might become part of your network.

Remember to give the contact your phone number and email address so they can reach you. Always be polite, speak clearly, and say thank you.

Using Online Resources

The internet is the primary means for finding career prospects and job leads. Most companies post jobs online. You can even use the internet to make contacts for networking. Some of the more effective online resources include:

- Company websites. You can learn a lot about a company from its website, including what they do, the backgrounds of the people who work there, and who to contact in each department. Most sites also have a page listing job openings, with information to help you identify the duties and tasks for each job, and how to apply. Even if there are no openings for someone with your skills and abilities, you can contact the human resources department to try to set up an **informational interview**.
- Government sites. Like corporations, government agencies list information and job openings. There are also government websites that provide job listings.
- Industry sites. Many industries and industry associations have websites that list job opportunities. This is particularly true for graphic and web design jobs.
- Social networking sites. You can use social networking to meet contacts and learn about jobs. There are groups for people in certain careers, or who work for specific companies. Employers join these sites, as well. They look for potential employees based on the personal profile you create.

Using a Career Center

A career center is an excellent place to start a job search. Your school might have a career center that you can use free of charge. Career centers have job listings, research resources, and counselors who will help you identify jobs that match your skills and interests. They can also introduce you to former students who are now employed—giving you more opportunities for networking.

Employment offices are similar to career centers. Some are sponsored by the state or local government. They provide job search resources and assistance free of charge.

Private employment agencies charge a fee to match employees with employers. Sometimes you pay the fee, and sometimes the employer pays the fee. Sometimes you pay even if you don't find a job. They all have different policies, so be sure to ask before you sign a contract.

Managing Your Job Search Resources

Keeping your job search resources organized will help you follow up every possibility. When you are actively looking for work at many companies, it is easy to forget who you spoke to and even what you spoke about. An employer might not look favorably on someone who repeats the same conversation, or cannot remember who referred them in the first place.

- Keep a to-do list of tasks you want to accomplish each day, such as people you want to contact, resumes you have to send out, and thank you notes to write. Cross off each item you complete, and add new items as they come up.
- Contact some people in your network every day. Make brief phone calls, or send brief email messages to let them know you are looking for work, and to ask for assistance finding job opportunities.
- Follow up on all leads. Keep a record of the people you contact, including phone numbers, email addresses, and mailing addresses. Include the dates and times, the method of communication, and the result. Did they invite you in for an interview? Did they refer you to someone else?

Set up computer folders for storing document files that relate to your job search. Use the folders to keep track of information you send to each contact or potential employer, and the response you get back. The folder might include copies of the cover letter and work samples (in PDF format, perhaps) that you sent. It might also include notes you took during a phone call or interview, a brochure about the company, and copies of emails you received.

Internship Opportunities

Despite your best job search efforts, as a student or new graduate you might not have the computer science experience an employer is looking for. An **internship** is one way you can work while you build experience and develop skills. An internship is a position in a company in which you learn while you work. For example, an intern in a software development department might participate in team meetings, learn a new programming language, write code, and test software.

You can find internship opportunities the same way you find job opportunities. Use networking, online resources, career counselors, and job fairs. Some companies have formal internship programs that they post on their websites. If not, contact managers or human resources and ask if the company has internship positions, and if you can meet or speak to someone about them.

Most internships do not pay a salary, or pay very little. But, you earn valuable experience. If the intern demonstrates that they can learn and do the work, at the end of the internship they may receive a job offer.

Preparing for a Job Interview

If an employer thinks you have the qualifications for the job, you will be invited for a job interview. A job interview is a meeting between a job seeker and a potential employer—the interviewer. A preliminary interview may be by phone or video conference, but almost all employers will expect a face-to-face meeting at some point. The interview is an opportunity for you and the interviewer to ask questions and decide if the position is right for you.

A job interview is stressful. You are trying to make a good impression. You want to look and sound your best. You want the interviewer to like you and to respect you. You can rehearse how you will act or respond to questions during the interview, to boost your confidence.

Working with a partner is probably the best way to practice. You can take turns being the interviewer and the job seeker. If you are alone, practice in front of a mirror. If possible, record your practice so you can watch yourself.

- Be truthful.
- Pronounce your words in a strong, clear voice.
- Keep your answers brief and to the point.
- Use positive nonverbal communication, such as eye contact, relaxed arms, and good posture.
- Dress as you would for an actual interview.
- Avoid fidgeting or playing with your hair.
- Ask someone to critique your interviewing skills and use their comments to improve your technique.

After the interview, you should write a thank-you note. A thank-you note reminds the interviewer that you are serious about wanting the job. You use a thank-you note to restate your interest in the job and your qualifications and to thank the interviewer for spending time with you. Refer to something specific that you discussed during the interview. Address the note to the person who interviewed you. It may be acceptable to send a thank-you note by email, but mailing an actual printed letter will make a positive impression.

Comparing Job Opportunities

What happens if you are offered a job? A job offer is good news. But, before you accept the offer, make sure you have the information you need to make the best decision. You should evaluate and compare every opportunity to make sure the position is right for you. Some points to consider include:

- What are the responsibilities?
- What is the salary?
- What is the work environment?
- Are there benefits, such as health insurance and vacation time?
- When does the job start, and, for a contract or project-based position, when does it end?
- What are the hours?

When you have all the information you need, use the decision-making process to decide whether to accept the position or not. If you accept the offer, thank the employer and ask when and where you should report to work. You may have to sign a formal letter of acceptance, sign a contract, or write a letter of intent, which states that you are accepting the position.

If you reject the offer, you should still write a letter of intent, thanking the employer and stating that you are not accepting the position.

Checkpoint

2.23   What is networking?

2.24   What is an example of an online job search resource?

2.25   How can you practice for a job interview?

2.8 Ethics in Computer Science Careers

KEY POINT   Ethical behavior is a responsibility for all computer science professionals.

Work Ethics

Recall that ethics are a set of beliefs about what is right and what is wrong. **Work ethics** are beliefs and behaviors about what is right and wrong in a work environment. Ethical behavior includes treating people with respect and also following the law. For example, taking credit for someone else's ideas is not ethical, and taking home office supplies is not ethical—it's stealing.

Ethical employees make ethical decisions, which means they consider how their decisions will impact others, including their employer. Ethical employees respect confidentiality. They do not share client information or sensitive company content with unauthorized individuals. Employers value employees who behave ethically at work. It shows that you are honest and respectful, so others will trust and respect you in return.

Behaving ethically at work also means following the company rules, regulations, and processes. Usually, when you start a new job, you are given an employee handbook. An employee handbook describes company policies and procedures, such as the process for requesting vacation time, and the different benefits that are available. It should also list all rules and policies that you are expected to obey. These might include:

- Maintaining confidentiality of information.
- Respecting copyrights and patents.
- Respecting co-workers' and customers' rights.

Ethics extends beyond the actions and behaviors of individual workers. It also applies to companies and organizations as a whole. A company that ignores the safety of workers, or hides information customers need to make an informed purchasing decision, is not behaving ethically. Sometimes an employee becomes aware that the employer is behaving in an unethical manner. In that case, the employee might be faced with a difficult decision about how to proceed. Options include speaking up in order to try to change the behavior or resigning. In some cases, it may include contacting the police or other law-enforcement agency to report illegal activity.

Legal and Ethical Responsibilities in Computer Science

Computer science professionals, including computer programmers, have many legal and ethical responsibilities. Some are the same as in any industry, such as treating co-workers and clients with respect, obeying all laws and regulations, and calling attention to negligent, illegal, unethical, abusive, or dangerous business practices. Some, however, are unique to computer science.

One of the most significant legal and ethical responsibilities for computer science worker is to stop **software piracy**, which is the act of enabling access to software illegally. This is an area in which computer science workers may be tempted to violate laws and policies for personal gain, but should also recognize the harm it does to their profession.

Another legal and ethical responsibility is to protect **proprietary information**. Computer science workers may have access to a company's trade secrets and other confidential information, such as copyrighted code. Proprietary information includes business information that is generally not available to the public, that has some degree of uniqueness, and that requires cost or effort to develop.

Many companies require employees to sign a **non-disclosure agreement (NDA)** that prohibits them from sharing proprietary information. However, there may be temptations for an employee to break that agreement. They may leave and start working at a competitor, or even be offered money to share the information.

Many computer science workers also have access to employee and client personal information. It is imperative that they follow all security protocols to maintain an individual's right to privacy. **Identity theft** and **fraud** are serious crimes. Computer science workers may be responsible for protecting systems from security breaches which could compromise personal data.

To help computer science professionals recognize and adhere to their legal and ethical responsibilities, some professional associations have developed their own codes of ethics and professional conduct. Both the International Association of Computer Science and Information Technology (IACSIT) and the Association for Computing Machinery (ACM) have their own codes of conduct. These codes include standards such as the following:

- Not misrepresenting or withholding information concerning the capabilities of equipment, software, or systems.
- Not using or taking credit for the work of others without specific acknowledgement and authorization.
- Protecting the privacy and confidentiality of all information.
- Not exploiting the weakness of a computer system for personal gain or personal satisfaction.

Equitable Access to Technology

The **digital divide** refers to the educational and economic divide that exists between people who have access to technology and those who do not. There are different causes for lack of access. It may be geographic—rural areas may not have reliable internet service. It may be physical—websites and programs may not use **accessible color schemes** or **alternate text** for images. Or it may even be content driven—input questions and images may display unintentional bias toward specific groups of people.

As a computer science professional, you may be in a position to influence the impact of technology on society. For example, if you are part of a team developing a database for collecting user input, you can identify and avoid prompts that may show bias. If you are designing a website, you can make sure to use accessible colors and images that reflect all of society.

In fact, your legal and ethical responsibilities include abiding by accessible technology laws and standards. For example,the Americans with Disabilities Act requires equal access to technology for all. The World Wide Web Consortium's Web Content Accessibility Guidelines provide guidance on designing websites that can be used by all.

Checkpoint

2.26   Why is taking credit for someone else's work unethical?

2.27   What is software piracy?

2.28   Why might a company have employees sign a non-disclosure agreement?

2.29   What is the digital divide?

2.30   What is accessible technology?

Chapter Review

Multiple Choice

1. What pathway do people interested in computer science usually choose?
   a. Information Support and Services
   b. Network Systems
   c. Programming and Software Development
   d. Web and Digital Communications

2. What quality will help you succeed in a computer science career?
   a. effective communication skills
   b. strong sense of self
   c. ability to analyze and solve problems
   d. all of the above

3. Which of the following is a career in computer science?
   a. game designer
   b. photojournalist
   c. emergency medical technician
   d. architect

4. When comparing computer science programs offered at universities, what should you consider?
   a. quality of food in the dining hall
   b. percent of graduates who get computer science jobs
   c. record of the football team
   d. school colors

5. Colleges and universities require you to submit a record of the courses you took in high school and the grades you earned, called a ____________.
   a. certificate
   b. resume
   c. transcript
   d. recommendation

6. Companies such as Microsoft offer ____________ to software developers who use Microsoft products.
   a. bonuses
   b. jobs
   c. free computers
   d. certificates

7. Having and using your life skills and abilities to get hired and stay hired is called ____________.
   a. hireability
   b. employability
   c. responsibility
   d. manageability

8. Any barrier between you and a goal is a ____________.
   a. solution
   b. product
   c. problem
   d. algorithm

9. When you ____________ tasks, you decide which ones must be completed first.
   a. prioritize
   b. manage
   c. schedule
   d. identify

10. The amount of work you accomplish is one way to determine your ____________.
    a. productivity
    b. project management
    c. problem-solving
    d. critical-thinking

11. The process used to take a project from conception to completion is called project ____________
    a. productivity
    b. management
    c. solving
    d. responsibility

12. A horizontal bar chart that shows a graphical illustration of a schedule is
    called a _____________
    a. ORG chart
    b. PERT chart
    c. Gantt chart
    d. Venn chart

13. Which of the following demonstrates that you respect time at work?
    a. showing up on time
    b. returning late from lunch
    c. leaving early
    d. missing deadlines

14. _________________ thinking can help you evaluate your options in many situations.
    a. quick
    b. critical
    c. emergency
    d. emotional

15. _________________ communication is when the receiver interprets the message the way
    the sender intended.
    a. verbal
    b. nonverbal
    c. effective
    d. ineffective

16. Computer scientists use _________________ writing to explain their work to a variety
    of people.
    a. scientific
    b. technical
    c. complicated
    d. simplified

17. Most computer science projects require co-workers to work together in a _________.
    a. conference room
    b. online chat room
    c. team
    d. pod

18. A _______ is a type of manager who knows how to use available resources to help others
    achieve their goals.
    a. leader
    b. programmer
    c. executive
    d. teammate

19. On your resume, make sure you include ____________ relevant to the specific job you are seeking.
    a. pictures
    b. key terms
    c. code
    d. locations

20. A coding ____________ provides concrete proof that you have the skills you claim on your resume.
    a. diagram
    b. project
    c. letter
    d. portfolio

21. The act of enabling access to software illegally is called ____________.
    a. software theft
    b. software secrets
    c. software piracy
    d. software larceny

22. A(n) ______________ agreement prohibits employees from sharing proprietary information.
    a. non-disclosure
    b. disclosure
    c. non-discussion
    d. piracy

True or False

1. Careers in the programming and software development pathway involve the design, development, implementation, and maintenance of computer systems and software.
2. Computer system analyst is not a career in the field of computer science.
3. You can look up a university's computer science program online to learn about the requirements for acceptance.
4. You must attend a four-year university program to earn a nondegree certificate in computer science.
5. Time management is a transferable skill.
6. Coding is a transferable skill.
7. You can use an algorithm to solve a problem.
8. Scheduling is a good tool for time management.
9. The four basic parts to the project management process are identifying measureable objectives, identifying deliverables, setting a schedule, and developing supporting plans.
10. Critical thinking helps you rush to judgment.
11. Effective technical writing should be clear and concise.
12. Technical reading is just another way of saying reading technical documents.

13. You should include only one project in a coding portfolio.
14. It is ethical for a computer science professional to share information about clients and co-workers.

Short Answer

1. What are skills you study and develop careers in the programming and software development pathway?
2. Why do high school graduates earn more money than non-graduates?
3. What are four things to consider when you are comparing university computer science programs?
4. How can earning a certificate help you advance in a computer science career?
5. Explain how a schedule can help you with planning and time management.
6. How can you avoid ineffective communication?
7. What is a benefit of working in a team?
8. Why is it important to include key terms on a resume?
9. Examine and explain the importance of a portfolio for someone trying to start a career as a computer science professional.
10. How can you behave ethically at work?
11. How can computing technologies perpetuate inequalities and help to bring about equity in society?

Exercises

1. With your teacher's permission, research programs in computer science at two different universities. You may do this on the internet, in a library, or by contacting the universities directly. Use technical reading strategies to make sure you understand the information you find. Use critical thinking to evaluate the information, and only use content that is valid and accurate. Record and cite all source information. When your research is complete, make a chart comparing the two programs. Write a paragraph explaining which program you would choose and why. Read your paragraph to a partner or to the class.

2. Alone, with a partner, or with a small group, and with your teacher's permission, use the internet or other resources to identify careers in computer science. Employee effective technical reading strategies to make sure you understand the information you find. Use critical thinking to evaluate the information, and only use content that is valid and accurate. Record and cite all source information. When your research is complete, make a three-column chart. In one column, identify at least three jobs available in the programming and software development pathway. In the second column, identify the type of business or industry in which someone in that position might work. In the third column, identify the job duties and tasks. Select one of the careers and employ effective technical writing skills to write a fact sheet explaining the career, including information about job duties and tasks. Share your research with a different group or the class.

3. Using the information on one of the careers you researched in exercise 2, create a cover letter and resume for someone applying for that career. Exchange documents with a classmate. Provide constructive criticism to your classmate, and use the feedback you receive to improve your documents. Write a paragraph examining the role of resumes for computer science professionals.

4. Use the techniques described in this chapter to identify companies or organizations that hire computer science professionals. Identify career and internship opportunities by contacting at least two of the companies. Locate or request information about the education and experience they look for when hiring. Ask if they have internship programs and if you could meet with someone for an informational interview. Share what you learn with a partner or with the class.

5. Alone, with a partner, or with a small group, and with your teacher's permission, use the internet to research certificates in the computer science field. Employ effective technical reading strategies to make sure you understand the information you find. Use critical thinking to evaluate the information, and only use content that is valid and accurate. Record and cite all source information. When your research is complete, create a presentation examining the role of certification in computer science professions and explaining why earning certificates can be an important part of a career in computer science. Deliver your presentation to another group or to the class.

6. Working in small teams, plan a presentation about legal and ethical responsibilities in relation to the field of computer science. Demonstrate problem-solving, planning, and time-management skills such as project management to organize the project. You may want to use a project management template in a program such as Excel. Take turns so each team member has the opportunity to demonstrate team leadership skills and function effectively as a team member.. With your teacher's permission, use the internet to research the topic using effective technical reading skills. Use critical thinking to evaluate the information that you find online, and only use content that is valid and accurate. Record and cite all source information. When your research is complete, compile the information into a presentation that communicates your understanding of legal and ethical responsibilities in relation to the field of computer science. Employ effective writing skills to develop a script to accompany the slides. Take turns employing effective verbal and nonverbal communications skills to read the script out loud and deliver the presentation.

3 How Computers Store and Process Data

TOPICS

3.1 How Computers Store Data

KEY POINT **All data that is stored in a computer is converted to sequences of 0s and 1s.**

A computer's memory is divided into tiny storage locations known as **bytes**. One byte is only enough memory to store a letter of the alphabet or a small number. In order to do anything meaningful, a computer has to have lots of bytes. Most computers today have millions, or even billions, of bytes of memory.

Each byte is divided into eight smaller storage locations known as bits. The term **bit** stands for **binary digit**. Computer scientists usually think of bits as tiny switches that can be either on or off. Bits aren't actual "switches," however, at least not in the conventional sense. In most computer systems, bits are tiny electrical components that can hold either a positive or a negative charge. Computer scientists think of a positive charge as a switch in the *on* position, and a negative charge as a switch in the off position. Figure 3-1 shows the way that a computer scientist might think of a byte of memory: as a collection of switches that are each flipped to either the on or off position.

Figure 3-1 Think of a byte as eight switches

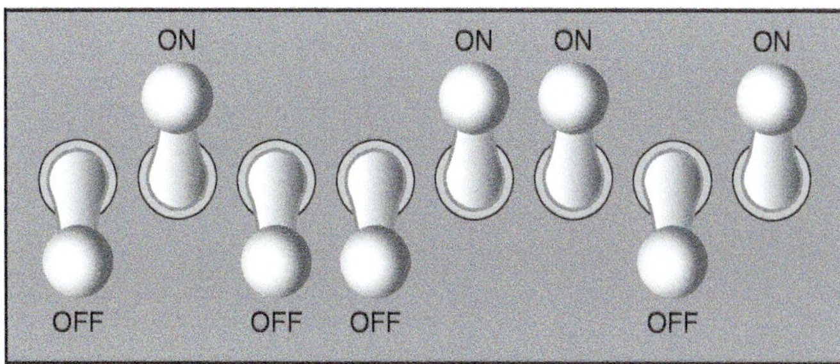

When a piece of data is stored in a byte, the computer sets the eight bits to an on/off pattern that represents the data. For example, the pattern on the left in Figure 3-2 shows how the number 77 would be stored in a byte, and the pattern on the right shows how the letter A would be stored in a byte.

Figure 3-2   Bit patterns for the number 77 and the letter A

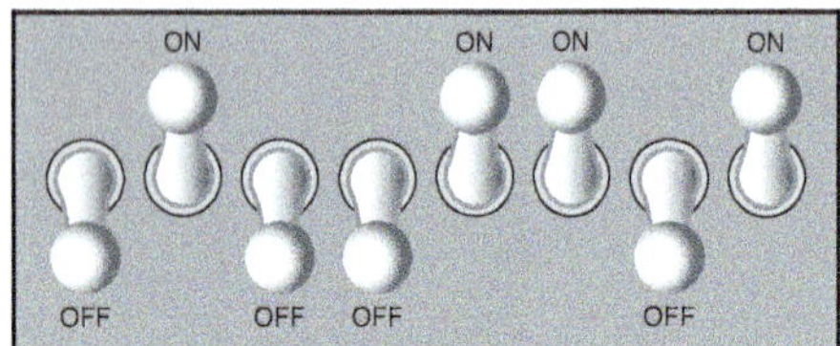

The number 77 stored in a byte.

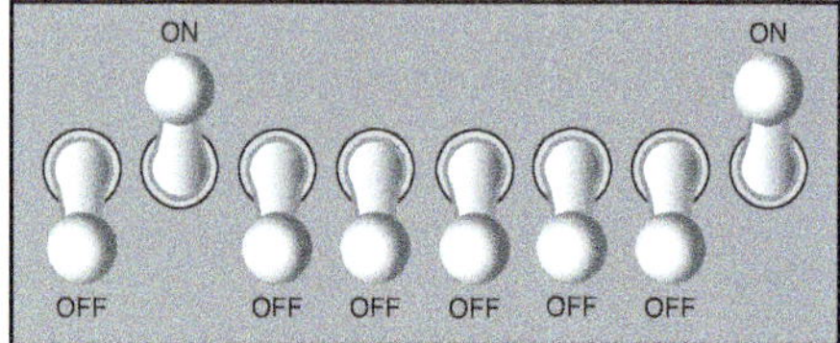

The letter A stored in a byte.

Storing Numbers

A bit can be used in a very limited way to represent numbers. Depending on whether the bit is turned on or off, it can represent one of two different values. In computer systems, a bit that is turned off represents the number 0, and a bit that is turned on represents the number 1. This corresponds perfectly to the **binary numbering system**. In the binary numbering system (or **binary**, as it is usually called), all numeric values are written as sequences of 0s and 1s. Here is an example of a number that is written in binary:

    10011101

The position of each digit in a binary number has a value assigned to it. Starting with the rightmost digit and moving left, the position values are 2^0, 2^1, 2^2, 2^3, and so forth, as shown in Figure 3-3. Figure 3-4 shows the same diagram with the position values calculated. Starting with the rightmost digit and moving left, the position values are 1, 2, 4, 8, and so forth.

Figure 3-3   The values of binary digits as powers of 2

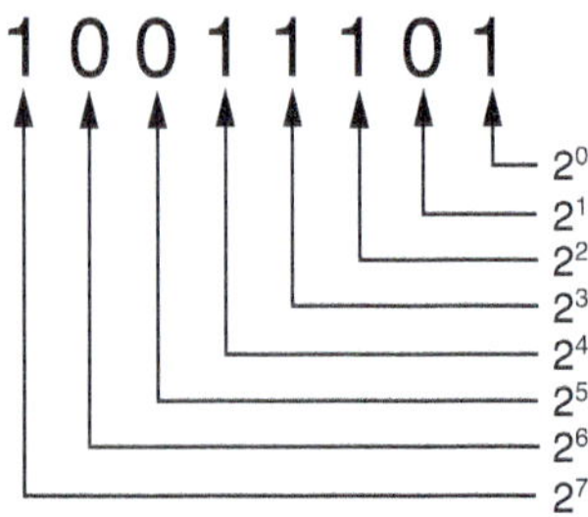

Figure 3-4   The values of binary digits

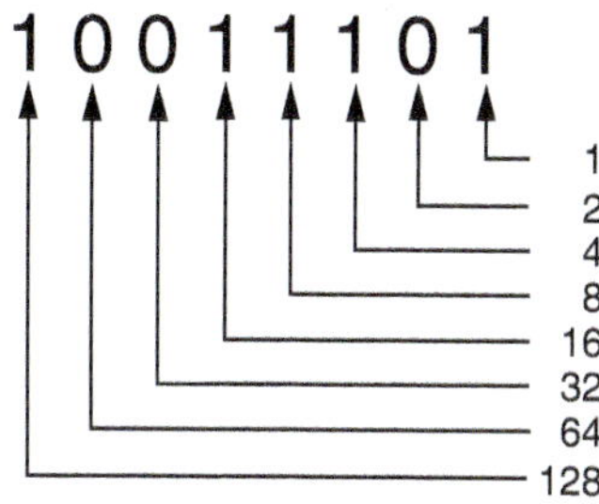

To determine the value of a binary number, you simply add up the position values of all the 1s. For example, in the binary number 10011101, the position values of the 1s are 1, 4, 8, 16, and 128. This is shown in Figure 3-5. The sum of all of these position values is 157. So, the value of the binary number 10011101 is 157.

Figure 3-5   Determining the value of 10011101

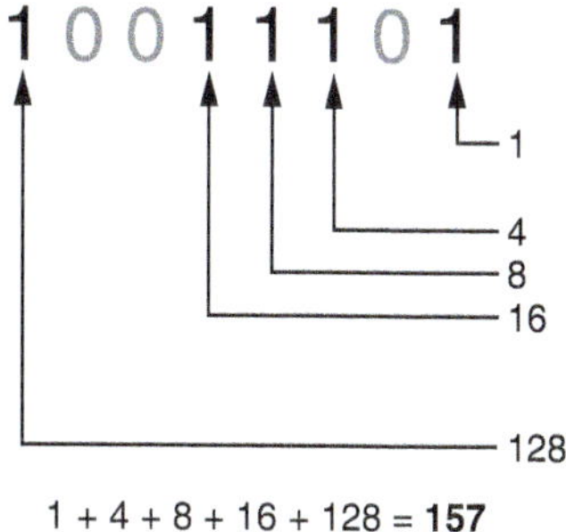

Figure 3-6 shows how you can picture the number 157 stored in a byte of memory. Each 1 is represented by a bit in the on position, and each 0 is represented by a bit in the off position.

Figure 3-6   The bit pattern for 157

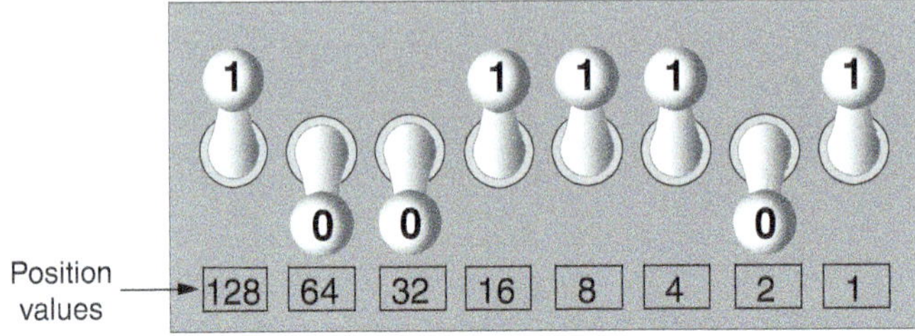

128 + 16 + 8 + 4 + 1 = **157**

When all of the bits in a byte are set to 0 (turned off), then the value of the byte is 0. When all of the bits in a byte are set to 1 (turned on), then the byte holds the largest value that can be stored in it. The largest value that can be stored in a byte is 1 + 2 + 4 + 8 + 16 + 32 + 64 + 128 = 255. This limit exists because there are only eight bits in a byte.

What if you need to store a number larger than 255? The answer is simple: use more than one byte. For example, suppose we put two bytes together. That gives us 16 bits. The position values of those 16 bits would be 2^0, 2^1, 2^2, 2^3, and so forth, up through 2^{15}. As shown in Figure 3-7, the maximum value that can be stored in two bytes is 65,535. If you need to store a number larger than this, then more bytes are necessary.

Figure 3-7   Two bytes used for a large number

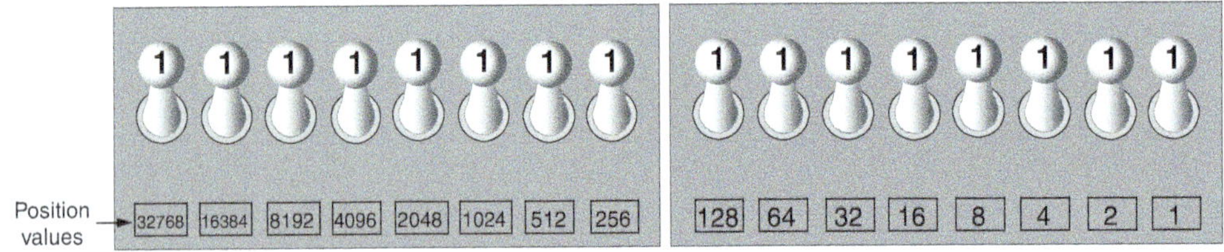

32768 + 16384 + 8192 + 4096 + 2048 + 1024 + 512 + 256 + 128 + 64 + 32 + 16 + 8 + 4 + 2 + 1 = **65535**

TIP: In case you're feeling overwhelmed by all this, relax! You will not have to actually convert numbers to binary while programming. Knowing that this process is taking place inside the computer will help you as you learn, and in the long term, this knowledge will make you a better programmer.

Storing Characters

Any piece of data that is stored in a computer's memory must be stored as a binary number. That includes nonnumeric characters, such as letters and punctuation marks. When a character is stored in memory, it is first converted to a numeric code. The numeric code is then stored in memory as a binary number.

Over the years, different coding schemes have been developed to represent characters in computer memory. Historically, the most important of these coding schemes is **ASCII**, which stands for the **American Standard Code for Information Interchange**. ASCII is a set of 128 numeric codes that represent the English letters, various punctuation marks, and other characters. For example, the ASCII code for the uppercase letter A is 65. When you type an uppercase A on your computer keyboard, the number 65 is stored in memory (as a binary number, of course). This is shown in Figure 3-8.

Figure 3-8   The letter A is stored in memory as the number 65

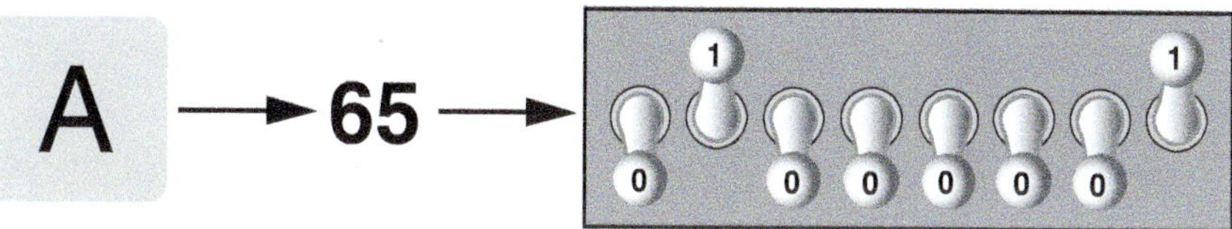

TIP: The acronym ASCII is pronounced "askee."

The ASCII character set was developed in the early 1960s and was eventually adopted by almost all computer manufacturers. ASCII is limited, however, because it defines codes for only 128 characters. To remedy this, the Unicode character set was developed in the early 1990s. **Unicode** is an extensive encoding scheme that is compatible with ASCII, but can also represent characters for many of the languages in the world. Today, Unicode is quickly becoming the standard character set used in the computer industry. Section 3.4 provides more information on working with ASCII and Unicode.

Advanced Number Storage

Earlier, you read about numbers and how they are stored in memory. While reading that section, perhaps it occurred to you that the binary numbering system can be used to represent only integer numbers, beginning with 0. Negative numbers and real numbers (such as 3.14159) cannot be represented using the simple binary numbering technique we discussed.

Computers are able to store negative numbers and real numbers in memory, but to do so, they use encoding schemes along with the binary numbering system. Negative numbers are encoded using a technique known as **two's complement**, and real numbers are encoded in **floating-point notation**. You don't need to know how these encoding schemes work, only that they are used to convert negative numbers and real numbers to binary format.

Other Types of Data

Computers are often referred to as digital devices. The term **digital** can be used to describe anything that uses binary numbers. **Digital data** is data that is stored in binary format, and a **digital device** is any device that works with binary data. In this section, we have discussed how numbers and characters are stored in binary, but computers also work with many other types of digital data.

For example, consider the pictures that you take with your digital camera or mobile phone. These images are composed of tiny dots of color known as **pixels**. (The term pixel stands for **picture element**.) As shown in Figure 3-9, each pixel in an image is converted to a numeric code that represents the pixel's color. The numeric code is stored in memory as a binary number.

Figure 3-9   A digital image is stored in binary format

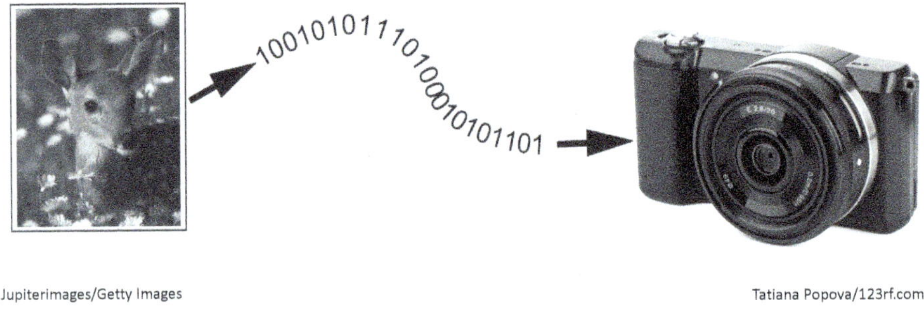

Jupiterimages/Getty Images   Tatiana Popova/123rf.com

The music that you stream or download is also digital. A digital song is broken into small pieces known as samples. Each sample is converted to a binary number, which can be stored in memory. The more samples that a song is divided into, the more it sounds like the original music when it is played back.

 **Checkpoint**

3.1   What amount of memory is enough to store a letter of the alphabet or a small number?

3.2   What do you call a tiny "switch" that can be set to either on or off?

3.3   In what numbering system are all numeric values written as sequences of 0s and 1s?

3.4   What is the purpose of ASCII?

3.5   What encoding scheme is extensive enough to represent the characters of many of the languages in the world?

3.6   What do the terms "digital data" and "digital device" mean?

3.2) Converting Decimal Numbers to Binary

Knowing how to convert from decimal to binary will help you understand the difference between the two numbering systems.

Binary vs. Decimal

While the binary numbering system is base 2, using just 0 and 1, the decimal numbering system is base ten. That means it uses ten digits: 0, 1, 2, 3, 4, 5, 6, 7, 8, and 9. It is easier for people to use decimal numbers, because you need fewer digits to represent a number. For example, 500 in binary is 111110100. A computer does not care how many digits there are in a number; it just needs simple, logical rules, like a two base numbering system where a switch can be either on or off.

As a programmer, when you write a number such as 40 in a program, the computer assumes it is a decimal number. Internally, computer software converts between decimal and binary numbers.

Counting in Binary

How do you count when you only have 1s and 0s? In a decimal system, when you reach 9, you add a place and start again. In binary, you start again when you reach 1. So, starting at zero and counting to 10 in binary looks like this: 0, 1, 10, 11, 100, 101, 110, 111, 1000, 1001, 1010.

Converting from Decimal to Binary

You can convert a decimal number to binary by drawing a simple chart, and then performing repeated subtraction. The following steps show how to convert the decimal number 162 to binary.

1. Make a two-row chart. The top row should list all of the numbers that are powers of two, up to but not greater than the number you are trying to convert. (Powers of two are $2^0 = 1$, $2^1 = 2$, $2^2 = 4$, $2^3 = 8$, and so forth.) The numbers should be listed from right to left.

   To convert the decimal number 162 to binary, you would make the following chart. (The chart stops at 128 because the next power of two would be 256, which is greater than the number we are trying to convert.)

128	64	32	16	8	4	2	1

2. Find the greatest number in the chart (in this case it is 128), and write a 1 below it in the second row. Then, subtract the greatest number in the chart from the number you are trying to convert. In this problem, the result is 34. This is your new number. Your workspace should look something like this:

128	64	32	16	8	4	2	1
1							

$$\begin{array}{r} 162 \\ -\ 128 \\ \hline 34 \end{array}$$

3. Find the greatest number in the chart that is not greater than the new number you calculated in Step 2. In this problem, we are looking for the greatest number that is not greater than 34. The number we are looking for is 32. Write a 1 below that number in the second row. Then, subtract this new "greatest number" from the number you are currently working with. In this problem, the result is 2. This is your new number. Your workspace should look something like this:

128	64	32	16	8	4	2	1
1		1					

$$\begin{array}{r} 162 \\ -\,128 \\ \hline 34 \\ -\,32 \\ \hline 2 \end{array}$$

4. Find the greatest number in the chart that is not greater than the new number you calculated in Step 3. In this problem, we are looking for the greatest number that is not greater than 2. The number we are looking for is 2. Write a 1 below that number in the second row. Then, subtract this new "greatest number" from the number you are currently working with. In this problem, the result is 0. This is your new number. Your workspace should look something like this:

128	64	32	16	8	4	2	1
1		1				1	

$$\begin{array}{r} 162 \\ -\,128 \\ \hline 34 \\ -\,32 \\ \hline 2 \\ -\,2 \\ \hline 0 \end{array}$$

5. When you reach 0 as your new value, you have converted the number. Go back to the chart and write a 0 in each empty slot in the second row. Your chart should look like this:

128	64	32	16	8	4	2	1
1	0	1	0	0	0	1	0

The second row now shows the binary number that is equivalent to 162: 10100010

Checkpoint

3.6 What base is the binary numbering system?

3.7 What base is the decimal numbering system?

3.8 What mathematical operation do you use to convert decimal numbers to binary?

3.3 Converting Binary Numbers to Decimal

KEY POINT ➞ **To easily read large binary numbers, convert them to decimal.**

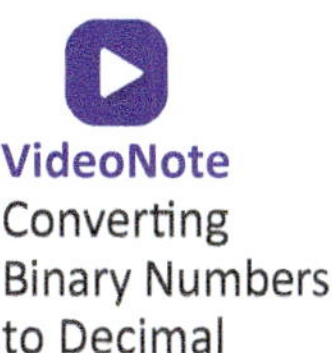

VideoNote
Converting
Binary Numbers
to Decimal

Now that you understand how to convert a decimal number to binary, you can reverse the process and convert a binary number to a decimal number. This might come in handy if you encounter a large binary number. It will be much easier to read if you convert it to decimal.

The following steps show how to convert the binary number 1011 to its equivalent decimal number.

1. Draw a two-row, eight-column chart similar to the one you used in the previous section. For very large binary numbers, you will need more columns, but eight columns is a good place to start. Place the binary number you want to convert in the bottom row, listed from right to left.

To convert the binary number 1011, your chart should look like this:

				1	0	1	1

2. In the top row, place the decimals numbers that are powers of two of the numbers you are going to convert. Begin by placing the first number in the top-right block, then work from right to left. As a reminder, the powers of two are: $2^0 = 1$, $2^1 = 2$, $2^2 = 4$, $2^3 = 8$, $2^4 = 16$, $2^5 = 32$, and so on.

Your chart should look like this:

				8	4	2	1
				1	0	1	1

3. To determine the equivalent decimal number, add together all the top row numbers that have a 1 in the row below them.

$$8 + 2 + 1 = 11$$

4. The total is the equivalent decimal number:
   The binary number 1011 = the decimal number 11

Checkpoint

3.9 Why might you need to convert a binary number to decimal?

3.10 What do you place in the top row of your conversion chart?

3.11 What numbers do you add in the top row to get the equivalent decimal number of the binary number in the bottom row?

3.4 Representing Data using ASCII or Unicode

For a computer to understand alphanumeric characters, it converts ASCII or Unicode to binary.

Using the ASCII Standard

The ASCII standard is an arbitrary decimal numeric code assigned to each letter in the English alphabet and to other symbols, such as punctuation marks. Once you have the ASCII decimal code, you can convert any alphanumeric character to a binary representation.

The table below is a list of standard ASCII codes that represent a corresponding character.

Character	Code	Character	Code	Character	Code
!	33	A	65	a	97
"	34	B	66	b	98
#	35	C	67	c	99
$	36	D	68	d	100
%	37	E	69	e	101
&	38	F	70	f	102
'	39	G	71	g	103
(	40	H	72	h	104
)	41	I	73	i	105
*	42	J	74	j	106
+	43	K	75	k	107
,	44	L	76	l	108
-	45	M	77	m	109
.	46	N	78	n	110
/	47	O	79	o	111
0	48	P	80	p	112
1	49	Q	81	q	113
2	50	R	82	r	114
3	51	S	83	s	115
4	52	T	84	t	116
5	53	U	85	u	117
6	54	V	86	v	118
7	55	W	87	w	119
8	56	X	88	x	120
9	57	Y	89	y	121
:	58	Z	90	z	122
;	59	[	91	{	123
<	60	\	92	|	124
=	61	]	93	}	125
>	62	^	94	~	126
?	63	_	95	DEL	127
@	64	`	96		

Because the ASCII codes are decimal, you can convert them to binary. The table below adds a column to the ASCII table to show the corresponding binary value. The binary value is what the computer will ultimately understand.

Character	Decimal Code	Binary Code	Character	Decimal Code	Binary Code	Character	Decimal Code	Binary Code
!	33	100001	A	65	1000001	a	97	1100001
"	34	100010	B	66	1000010	b	98	1100010
#	35	100011	C	67	1000011	c	99	1100011
$	36	100100	D	68	1000100	d	100	1100100
%	37	100101	E	69	1000101	e	101	1100101
&	38	100110	F	70	1000110	f	102	1100110
'	39	100111	G	71	1000111	g	103	1100111
(	40	101000	H	72	1001000	h	104	1101000
)	41	101001	I	73	1001001	i	105	1101001
*	42	101010	J	74	1001010	j	106	1101010
+	43	101011	K	75	1001011	k	107	1101011
,	44	101100	L	76	1001100	l	108	1101100
-	45	101101	M	77	1001101	m	109	1101101
.	46	101110	N	78	1001110	n	110	1101110
/	47	101111	O	79	1001111	o	111	1101111
0	48	110000	P	80	1010000	p	112	1110000
1	49	110001	Q	81	1010001	q	113	1110001
2	50	110010	R	82	1010010	r	114	1110010
3	51	110011	S	83	1010011	s	115	1110011
4	52	110100	T	84	1010100	t	116	1110100
5	53	110101	U	85	1010101	u	117	1110101
6	54	110110	V	86	1010110	v	118	1110110
7	55	110111	W	87	1010111	w	119	1110111
8	56	111000	X	88	1011000	x	120	1111000
9	57	111001	Y	89	1011001	y	121	1111001
:	58	111010	Z	90	1011010	z	122	1111010
;	59	111011	[	91	1011011	{	123	1111011
<	60	111100	\	92	1011100	|	124	1111100
=	61	111101	]	93	1011101	}	125	1111101
>	62	111110	^	94	1011110	~	126	1111110
?	63	111111	_	95	1011111	DEL	127	1111111
@	64	1000000	`	96	1100000			

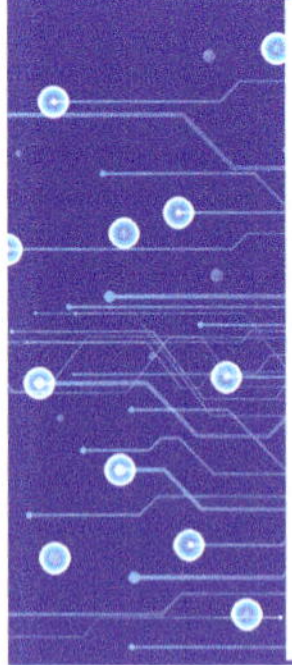

In the Spotlight:

Using a code to represent something else is actually a practice you do all the time. Consider the symbol '4.' If you have a shopping list that says 4 apples, you know to put four apples in your shopping cart. You recognize that the symbol '4' represents four items. The symbol itself has no meaning, but it is a standard symbol that represents four items in our counting system.

TIP: While it is not necessary to memorize the ASCII table, it is helpful to notice the sequential numeric pattern. For instance, the letter A = 65, followed by B = 66, C = 67, and so on. The lowercase letters also have a sequential pattern of ASCII code values beginning with a = 97, b = 98, c = 99, and so on.

Using the Unicode Standard

ASCII represents 128 different alphanumeric characters of the English language. Unicode is a newer encoding standard developed in 1991. Like ASCII, Unicode assigns a unique decimal value to each character. The decimal value can then be converted to binary.

Unicode includes the 128 characters in the ASCII character set, as well as letters and symbols for other major languages such as Greek, Arabic, Urdu, and Hindu. It also includes emojis and math symbols. In Unicode version 15.0, there are nearly 150,000 unique symbols and codes. Unicode continues to evolve, adding new characters with each release.

Appendix E includes a table with ASCII codes, which align with the first 128 Unicode symbols. You can search online for a Unicode table to learn more about the Unicode standard.

Checkpoint

3.12 How many characters are represented by the ASCII standard?

3.13 Identify the ASCII code for a lowercase k character.

3.14 What is the difference between ASCII and Unicode?

3.15 Identify the binary equivalent of the Unicode code for an uppercase Q character.

Chapter Review

Multiple Choice

1. Each byte is divided into eight smaller storage locations known as __________.
    a. bots
    b. bats
    c. bits
    d. bets

2. Computer scientists think of a positive charge as a switch in the __________ position.
    a. on
    b. off
    c. go
    d. stop

3. Computer scientists think of a negative charge as a switch in the __________ position.
    a. on
    b. off
    c. go
    d. stop

4. In computer systems, a bit that is turned off represents the number 0, and a bit that is turned on represents the number _______________.
    a. 1
    b. 10
    c. 100
    d. 1,000

5. The rightmost digit in a binary number has a position value of__________.
    a. 2^3
    b. 2^0
    c. 21
    d. 22

6. What is the value of a byte when all of the bits are set to 0?
    a. 0
    b. 1
    c. 8
    d. 10

7. What is the largest value that can be stored in a byte?
    a. 1
    b. 8
    c. 155
    d. 255

8. ASCII defines codes for how many characters?
    a. 78
    b. 128
    c. 278
    d. 328

9. Computers encode negative numbers using a technique known as _____________.
    a. ten's complement
    b. one's complement
    c. five's complement
    d. two's complement

10. Each pixel in an image is converted to a numeric code that represents its __________.
    a. size
    b. color
    c. position
    d. name

True or False

1. 12002001 is an example of a binary number.

2. Any piece of data that is stored in a computer's memory must be stored as a binary number.

3. The binary number system is base 2.

4. The decimal numbering system is base ten.

5. The binary system uses fewer digits to represent a number than the decimal system.

6. Unicode has the same number of codes as ASCII.

7. ASCII codes are binary.

8. ASCII includes codes for punctuation marks.

Short Answer

1. Explain the relationship between bits and bytes.

2. Why do computer scientists think of bits as switches that can be off or on?

3. Compare a binary numbering system with a decimal numbering system.

4. Explain what you would do if you need a to store a number larger than 255 while using a binary numbering system.

5. Explain the difference between ASCII and Unicode?

6. What is 20 in the binary numbering system?

Exercises

1. Convert binary number 1011101 to its decimal equivalent.

    1. Create a chart with two rows and eight columns.

    2. Working from right to left, place the binary number in the bottom row.

    3. Working from right to left, place the decimal numbers that are powers of two in the top row.

    4. Add the values of the top row that have a 1 in the row below it.

    5. Your solution should look like this:

	64	32	16	8	4	2	1
	1	0	1	1	1	0	1

2. Convert the decimal number 54 to its binary equivalent.

    1. Create a chart with two rows and eight columns.

    2. Working from right to left, place the decimal numbers that are a power of two in the top row. (1, 2, 4, 8, 16, 32, 64, 128)

    3. Perform the steps to fill in the 1's in the bottom row.

    4. When your remainder is 0, you are finished identifying the 1's.

    5. Fill in all empty blocks on the bottom row with a 0.

    Your workspace to find the solution should look similar to the following

128	64	32	16	8	4	2	1
0	0	1	1	0	1	1	0

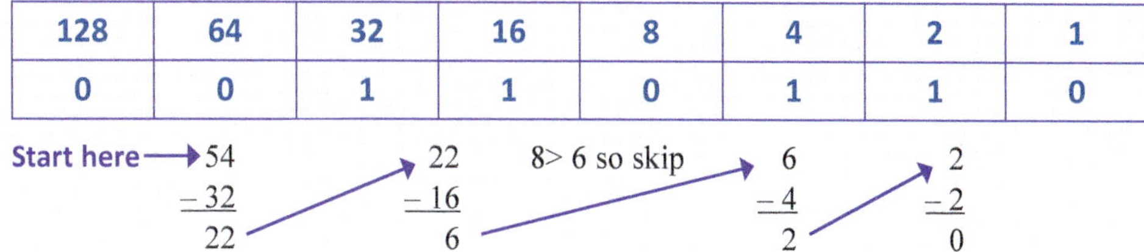

3. Using the ASCII table, identify the ASCII code assigned to the uppercase letter A.

4. Using the ASCII table, identify the binary code for an exclamation point.

5. With a partner or a small team, write a sentence in ASCII. Exchange coded sentences with another team. Decode the other team's sentence.

6. Try writing a two- or three-word phrase in binary. Then, exchange your work with a partner, and see if you can convert it so you can read what it says.

7. With a partner, make a chart counting from 1 to 50 in decimal and in binary.

4   Programs and Programming Languages

TOPICS

4.1   How a Program Works

KEY POINT   **A computer's CPU can only understand instructions that are written in machine language. Because people find it very difficult to write entire programs in machine language, other programming languages have been invented.**

Earlier, we stated that the CPU is the most important component in a computer because it is the part of the computer that runs programs. Sometimes the CPU is called the "computer's brain" and is described as being "smart." Although these are common metaphors, you should understand that the CPU is not a brain, and it is not smart. The CPU is an electronic device that is designed to do specific things. In particular, the CPU is designed to perform operations such as the following:

- Reading a piece of data from main memory
- Adding two numbers
- Subtracting one number from another number
- Multiplying two numbers
- Dividing one number by another number
- Moving a piece of data from one memory location to another
- Determining whether one value is equal to another value

As you can see from this list, the CPU performs simple operations on pieces of data. The CPU does nothing on its own, however. It has to be told what to do, and that's the purpose of a program. A program is nothing more than a list of instructions that cause the CPU to perform operations.

Each instruction in a program is a command that tells the CPU to perform a specific operation. Here's an example of an instruction that might appear in a program:

```
10110000
```

To you and me, this is only a series of 0s and 1s. To a CPU, however, this is an instruction to perform an operation. It is written in 0s and 1s because CPUs only understand instructions that are written in **machine language**, and machine language instructions always have an underlying binary structure.

A machine language instruction exists for each operation that a CPU is capable of performing. For example, there is an instruction for adding numbers, there is an instruction for subtracting one number from another, and so forth. The entire set of instructions that a CPU can execute is known as the CPU's **instruction set.**

The machine language instruction that was previously shown is an example of only one instruction. It takes a lot more than one instruction, however, for the computer to do anything meaningful. Because the operations that a CPU knows how to perform are so basic in nature, a meaningful task can be accomplished only if the CPU performs many operations. For example, if you want your computer to calculate how many hours you must work to earn enough money to buy a new pair of shoes, the CPU will have to perform a large number of instructions, carried out in the proper sequence. It is not unusual for a program to contain thousands or even millions of machine language instructions.

Programs may be stored on a secondary storage device such as a disk drive, or they may be stored on a network server.. When you install a program on your computer, the program is typically downloaded from a website or installed from an online app store.

Although a program can be stored on a secondary storage device such as a disk drive, it has to be copied into main memory, or RAM, each time the CPU executes it. For example, suppose you have a word processing program on your computer's disk. To execute the program, you use the mouse to double-click the program's icon. This causes the program to be copied from the disk into main memory. Then, the computer's CPU executes the copy of the program that is in main memory. This process is illustrated in Figure 4-1.

Figure 4-1 A program is copied into main memory and then executed

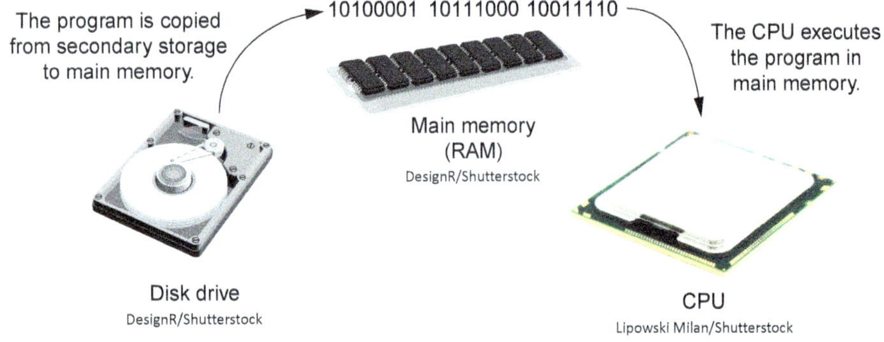

When a CPU executes the instructions in a program, it is engaged in a process that is known as the **fetch-decode-execute cycle**. This cycle, which consists of three steps, is repeated for each instruction in the program. The steps are:

1. **Fetch.** A program is a long sequence of machine language instructions. The first step of the cycle is to fetch, or read, the next instruction from memory into the CPU.

2. **Decode.** A machine language instruction is a binary number that represents a command that tells the CPU to perform an operation. In this step, the CPU decodes the instruction that was just fetched from memory, to determine which operation it should perform.

3. **Execute.** The last step in the cycle is to execute, or perform, the operation.

Figure 4-2 illustrates these steps.

Figure 4-2   The fetch-decode-execute cycle

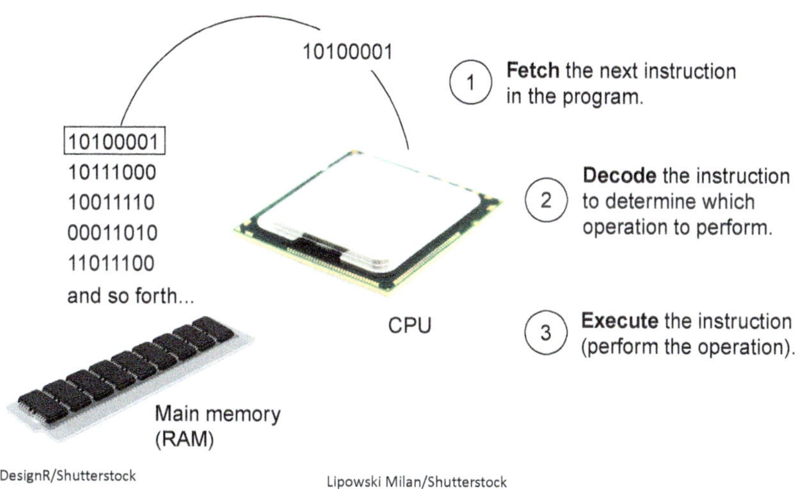

From Machine Language to Assembly Language

Computers can only execute programs that are written in machine language. As previously mentioned, a program can have thousands or even millions of binary instructions, and writing such a program would be very tedious and time consuming. Programming in machine language would also be very difficult, because putting a 0 or a 1 in the wrong place will cause an error.

Although a computer's CPU only understands machine language, it is impractical for people to write programs in machine language. For this reason, **assembly language** was created in the early days of computing as an alternative to machine language. Instead of using binary numbers for instructions, assembly language uses short words that are known as **mnemonics**. For example, in assembly language, the mnemonic add typically means to add numbers, mul typically means to multiply numbers, and mov typically means to move a value to a location in memory. When a programmer uses assembly language to write a program, they can write short mnemonics instead of binary numbers.

NOTE: There are many different versions of assembly language. It was mentioned earlier that each brand of CPU has its own machine language instruction set. Each brand of CPU typically has its own assembly language, as well.

Assembly language programs cannot be executed by the CPU, however. The CPU only understands machine language, so a special program known as an **assembler** is used to translate an assembly language program to a machine language program. This process is shown in Figure 4-3. The machine language program that is created by the assembler can then be executed by the CPU.

Figure 4-3 An assembler translates an assembly language program to a machine language program

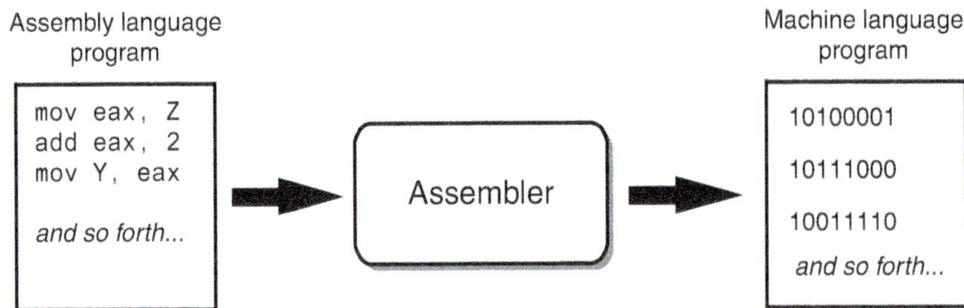

High-Level Languages

Assembly language makes it unnecessary to write binary machine language instructions, but it has complexities of its own. Assembly language is primarily a direct substitute for machine language, and like machine language, it requires that you know a lot about the CPU. Assembly language also requires that you write a large number of instructions for even the simplest program. Because assembly language is so close in nature to machine language, it is referred to as a **low-level language.**

In the 1950s, a new generation of programming languages known as **high-level languages** began to appear. A high-level language allows you to create powerful and complex programs without knowing how the CPU works and without writing large numbers of low-level instructions. In addition, most high-level languages use words that are easy to understand. For example, if a programmer were using COBOL (which was one of the early high-level languages created in the 1950s), they would write the following instruction to display the message *Hello world* on the computer screen:

```
DISPLAY "Hello world"
```

Python is a modern, high-level programming language that we will use in this book. In Python, you would display the message *Hello world* with the following instruction:

```
print('Hello world')
```

Doing the same thing in assembly language would require several instructions and an intimate knowledge of how the CPU interacts with the computer's output device. As you can see from this example, high-level languages allow programmers to concentrate on the tasks they want to perform with their programs, rather than the details of how the CPU will execute those programs.

Keywords, Operators, and Syntax: An Overview

Each high-level language has its own set of predefined words that the programmer must use to write a program. The words that make up a high-level programming language are known as **keywords** or **reserved words**. Each keyword has a specific meaning and cannot be used for any other purpose. Table 4-1 shows Python keywords. (See Appendix C for more information.)

Table 4-1 The Python keywords

and	continue	finally	is	raise
as	def	for	lambda	return
assert	del	from	None	True
async	elif	global	nonlocal	try
await	else	if	not	while
break	except	import	or	with
class	False	in	pass	yield

In addition to keywords, programming languages have **operators** that perform various operations on data. For example, all programming languages have math operators that perform arithmetic. In Python, as well as most other languages, the + sign is an operator that adds two numbers. The following adds 12 and 75:

```
12 + 75
```

There are numerous other operators in the Python language, many of which you will learn about as you progress through this text.

Each language also has its own **syntax,** which is a set of rules that must be strictly followed when writing a program. The syntax rules dictate how keywords, operators, and various punctuation characters must be used in a program. When you are learning a programming language, you must learn the syntax rules for that particular language.

The individual instructions that you use to write a program in a high-level programming language are called **statements**. A programming statement can consist of keywords, operators, punctuation, and other allowable programming elements, arranged in the proper sequence to perform an operation.

Compilers and Interpreters

Because the CPU understands only machine language instructions, programs that are written in a high-level language must be translated into machine language. Depending on the language in which a program has been written, the programmer will use either a compiler or an interpreter to make the translation.

A **compiler** is a program that translates a high-level language program into a separate machine language program. The machine language program can then be executed any time it is needed. This is shown in Figure 4-4. As shown in the figure, compiling and executing are two different processes.

Figure 4-4   Compiling a high-level program and executing it

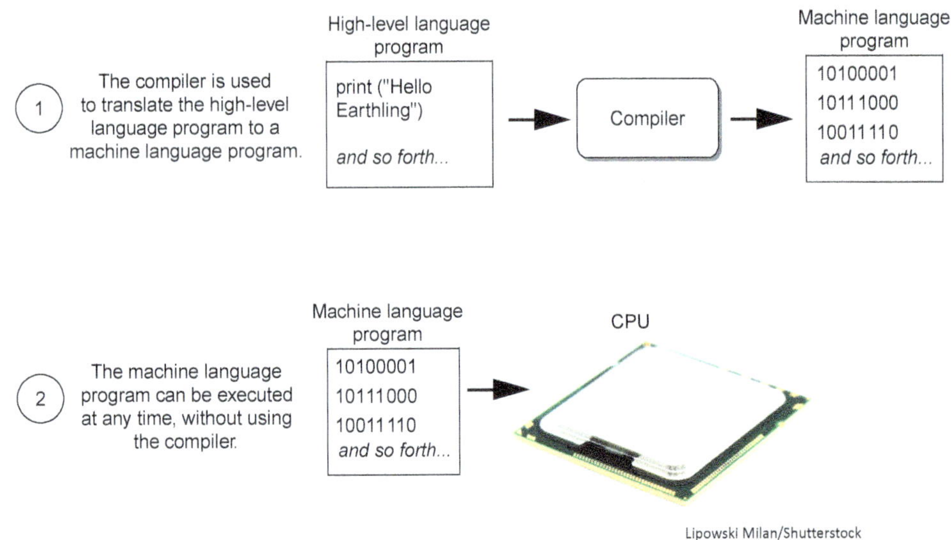

The Python language uses an **interpreter**, which is a program that both translates and executes the instructions in a high-level language program. As the interpreter reads the individual instructions in the program, it converts them to machine language instructions and immediately executes them. This process repeats for every instruction in the program. This process is illustrated in Figure 4-5. Because interpreters combine translation and execution, they typically do not create separate machine language programs.

Figure 4-5   Executing a high-level program with an interpreter

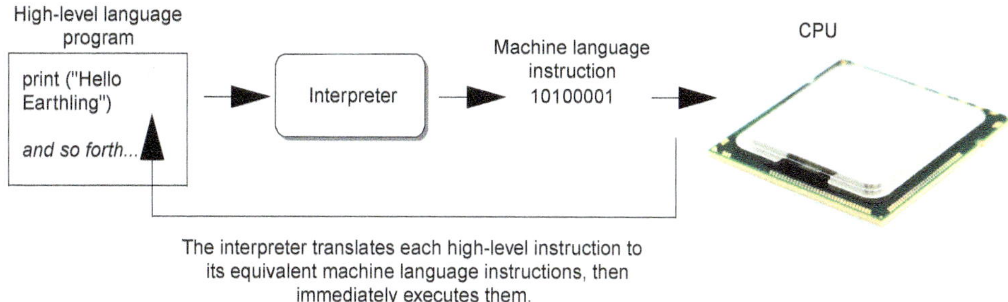

Lipowski Milan/Shutterstock

The statements that a programmer writes in a high-level language are called **source code**, or simply **code**. Typically, the programmer types a program's code into a text editor, then saves the code in a file on the computer's disk. Next, the programmer uses a compiler to translate the code into a machine language program, or an interpreter to translate and execute the code. If the code contains a syntax error, however, it cannot be translated. A **syntax error** is a mistake such as a misspelled keyword, a missing punctuation character, or the incorrect use of an operator. When this happens, the compiler or interpreter displays an error message indicating that the program contains a syntax error. The programmer corrects the error, then attempts once again to translate the program.

NOTE: Human languages also have syntax rules. Do you remember when you took your first English class, and you learned all those rules about commas, apostrophes, capitalization, and so forth? You were learning the syntax of the English language.

Although people commonly violate the syntax rules of their native language when speaking and writing, other people usually understand what they mean. Unfortunately, compilers and interpreters do not have this ability. If even a single syntax error appears in a program, the program cannot be compiled or executed. When an interpreter encounters a syntax error, it stops executing the program.

Checkpoint

4.1   A CPU understands instructions that are written only in what language?

4.2   A program has to be copied into what type of memory each time the CPU executes it?

4.3   When a CPU executes the instructions in a program, it is engaged in what process?

4.4   What is assembly language?

4.5   What type of programming language allows you to create powerful and complex programs without knowing how the CPU works?

4.6 Each language has a set of rules that must be strictly followed when writing a program. What is this set of rules called?

4.7 What do you call a program that translates a high-level language program into a separate machine language program?

4.8 What do you call a program that both translates and executes the instructions in a high-level language program?

4.9 What type of mistake is usually caused by a misspelled keyword, a missing punctuation character, or the incorrect use of an operator?

4.2 Comparing Programming Languages

There are hundreds of different high-level programming languages, and they are constantly evolving. Having a general understanding of the major languages will help you get started. If you learn the fundamentals of coding in one language, it is easier to learn additional languages later.

Similarities and Differences between Languages

While the focus of this course is Python, it is helpful to understand the similarities and differences between languages. Below is a comparison of code in the popular languages of C, C#, Java, Python, and JavaScript. All code segments accomplish the same task of printing "Hello World!" to the screen. Note that each code segment includes comments that begin with either '//' or '#'.

C Code :

```
// C program to display Hello World!

// include an external file
#include <stdio.h>

// main function -
int main()
{

    // prints hello world!
    printf("Hello World!");

    return 0;
}
```

C# Code:

```csharp
// C# program to display Hello World!

using System;

// namespace declaration
namespace HelloWorldApp {

// Class declaration
class HelloWorld
    // Main Method
    static void Main(string[] args)
    {

            // prints Hello World!
            Console.WriteLine("Hello World!");

            // To prevent the program from
            // from closing
            Console.ReadKey();
    }
}
}
```

Java Code:

```java
// Java program to display Hello World!
class HelloWorld {

    public static void main(
            String args[])
    {
            System.out.println("Hello World!");
    }
}
```

Python Code:

```python
# Python program to display Hello World!
print("Hello World!")
```

JavaScript Code:

```
// JavaScript program to display Hello World!
<script>
  console.log('Hello World!');
</script>
```

Output for all Code Segments:

```
Hello World!
```

Notice that the syntax is different across the languages. For instance, some languages encase segments of code in brackets { } , while others do not. The method name used to print to the screen is different across languages. For instance, JavaScript uses console.log() and Python uses print(). Despite these differences, all the code arrives at the same output.

Popular Languages and their Uses

Some languages are used to develop specific types of applications. Others, such as Python and Java, are general-purpose languages used for a variety of applications. In these cases, the decision on which language to use may be a personal preference. Your school or company policy can also influence the language you will use.

Table 4-2 lists several well-known languages, a brief history, and their typical uses.

Table 4-2 Programming languages

Language	Description
Ada	Ada was created in the 1970s, primarily for applications used by the U.S. Department of Defense. The language is named in honor of Countess Ada Lovelace, an influential and historic figure in the field of computing.
BASIC	**B**eginners **A**ll-purpose **S**ymbolic **I**nstruction **C**ode is a general-purpose language that was originally designed in the early 1960s to be simple enough for beginners to learn. Today, there are many different versions of BASIC.
FORTRAN	**FOR**mula **TRAN**slator was the first high-level programming language. It was designed in the 1950s for performing complex mathematical calculations. It is used in science and engineering. Other languages are more popular today, but there are many legacy applications that still require updates using FORTRAN.
COBOL	**CO**mmon **B**usiness-**O**riented Language was created in the 1950s and was designed for business applications.

Table 4-2 Programming languages *(continued)*

Language	Description
Pascal	Pascal was created in 1970 and was originally designed for teaching programming. The language was named in honor of the mathematician, physicist, and philosopher Blaise Pascal.
C and C++	C and C++ (pronounced "c plus plus") are powerful, general-purpose languages developed at Bell Laboratories. The C language was created in 1972, and the C++ language was created in 1983. These languages are often used to create operating systems, graphical user interfaces, and functionality for embedded devices such as smart watches, thermostats, or traffic lights.
C#	Pronounced "c sharp." This language was created by Microsoft around the year 2000 for developing applications based on the Microsoft .NET platform.
Java	Java was created by Sun Microsystems in the early 1990s. It can be used to develop programs that run on a single computer or over the internet from a web server. It is a popular multi-purpose language widely used to create business applications.
JavaScript	JavaScript, created in the 1990s, can be used in web pages. Despite its name, JavaScript is not related to Java. It is a very popular language to create interactive websites and mobile applications.
Python	Python, the language we use in this book, is a general-purpose language created in the early 1990s. It is a very popular language used in business applications, artificial intelligence, and data science. Several social media sites such as Instagram are written in Python. It is often used to teach programming because the syntax is easy to understand.
Ruby	Ruby is a general-purpose language that was created in the 1990s. It is increasingly becoming a popular language for programs that run on web servers.

Strongly-Typed versus Loosely-Typed Languages

One trait that differentiates languages from one another is whether the language is strongly typed or loosely typed. **Strongly-typed languages**, which may be called strong or typed, require you to explicitly declare the type of data you plan to store in a variable. Examples of data types are integers, strings, and floating-point numbers. Once declared, that variable can only store the designated type of data. An error occurs if the rule is violated.

Loosely-typed languages, which may be called weak or untyped, are more flexible. They allow you to store data in variables without explicitly declaring what type of data you plan to store.

There are pros and cons to both approaches. A loosely-typed language gives you more flexibility to code and make changes more quickly. JavaScript is an example of a loosely-typed language. A strongly-typed language provides more structure and prevents you from inadvertently storing the wrong type of data, which can potentially cause unforeseen errors in your application. It is an excellent choice if you are collaborating with a team of programmers as it forces everyone to use the intended data type. Java and C++ are examples of strongly-typed languages.

Python is generally considered a strongly-typed language, because the interpreter keeps track of variable types and will only perform operations on the variable that are suitable for that type. It is also considered a loosely-typed language because in Python, a variable is a value attached to a name. The value has a data type, but the variable does not. That gives the programmer flexibility to change the variable in the future by assigning a different data type.

The following is a Java code example to explicitly declare a variable:

Java Code:

```
//declare a variable called num of an integer data type
int number;

//assign the value of 100 to a variable named number
number = 100;
```

The following is a Python code example to implicitly declare a variable:

Python Code:

```
#assign the numeric value of 100 to a variable named number
number = 100

#easily change the value to a string
number = 'hello'
```

 Checkpoint

4.10 What method name does JavaScript use to print to the screen?

4.11 What does BASIC stand for?

4.12 What powerful languages are often used to create operating systems, graphical user interfaces, and functionality for embedded devices such as smart watches, thermostats, or traffic lights?

4.13 Why is Python often used to teach programming?

4.14 What is a strongly-typed programming language?

? Chapter Review

Multiple Choice

1. If you were to look at a machine language program, you would see __________.
    a. Python code
    b. a stream of binary numbers
    c. English words
    d. circuits

2. In the __________ part of the fetch-decode-execute cycle, the CPU determines which operation it should perform.
    a. fetch
    b. decode
    c. execute
    d. deconstruct

3. Computers can only execute programs that are written in __________.
    a. Java
    b. assembly language
    c. machine language
    d. Python

4. The __________ translates an assembly language program to a machine language program.
    a. assembler
    b. compiler
    c. translator
    d. interpreter

5. The words that make up a high-level programming language are called __________.
    a. binary instructions
    b. mnemonics
    c. commands
    d. keywords

6. The rules that must be followed when writing a program are called __________.
    a. syntax
    b. punctuation
    c. keywords
    d. operators

7. A(n) __________ program translates a high-level language program into a separate machine language program.
    a. assembler
    b. compiler
    c. translator
    d. utility

8. What method name does Python use to print to the screen?
   a. console.log()
   b. print()
   c. console.log{}
   d. print {}

9. What was the first high-level programming language?
   a. Python
   b. BASIC
   c. FORTRAN
   d. Ruby

10. What is an example of a loosely-typed programming language?
   a. JavaScript
   b. BASIC
   c. C++
   d. COBOL

True or False

1. Machine language is the only language that a CPU understands.
2. Assembly language is considered a high-level language.
3. An interpreter is a program that both translates and executes the instructions in a high-level language program.
4. A syntax error does not prevent a program from being compiled and executed.
5. C++ is considered a loosely-typed programming language.

Short Answer

1. What are the words that make up a high-level programming language called?
2. What are the short words that are used in assembly language called?
3. What is the difference between a compiler and an interpreter?
4. Differentiate between Python, JavaScript, and C++. Discuss the general purpose of each.
5. Compare the pros and cons of a strongly-typed language and a loosely-typed language, giving examples of each.

Exercises

1. With your teacher's permission, use the internet to research the history of the Python programming language. Employ technical reading strategies to make sure you understand the information you find. Use critical thinking to evaluate the information, and only use content that is valid and accurate. Record and cite all source information. When your research is complete, answer the following questions:

   1. Who was the creator of Python?
   2. When was Python created?
   3. In the Python programming community, the person who created Python is commonly referred to as the "BDFL." What does this mean?

2. Choose a high-level compiled programming language and an interpreted language. With your teacher's permission, research the two languages online. Make a two-column chart differentiating between the two. Share your chart with a partner or with the class.

3. On your own or with a partner, create a flowchart or process diagram that illustrates the fetch - decode - execute process. Explain your illustration to a partner or to the class.

4. With your teacher's permission, use the internet to look for job listings for software programmers. You might look on a site such as Indeed.com or LinkedIn or you might look on a company's website for programming careers. Take notes on the types of programming projects and the languages they list. Do you notice any trends? Is there one language mentioned more often than others? Share your findings with a partner or with the class.

5 Getting Started with Python

TOPICS

5.1 The Python Language
5.2 Using Python
5.3 Creating Lines and Shapes using Turtle Graphics

5.1 The Python Language

KEY POINT Python is a popular general purpose programming language you can use to write many types of applications.

Python is a general-purpose programming language. It is used to write many types of applications such as web applications, games, data analysis, and artificial intelligence. Python is also a popular language used to learn programming because it uses simple syntax that is easy to read and write. Python is not only a good language to learn programming, but also a good skill to have for today's job market. For example, Python is the most popular language used in the rapidly growing field of data science.

Python is an interpreted language which means the code is executed one line at a time. This is different than compiled languages, such as Java, where all lines of code are compiled as a unit, converted to machine language, and then executed. Like most other programming languages, Python has keywords. **Keywords** are designated words that have special meaning to the interpreter. They serve as a building block for you to write code, and their meaning cannot be changed. An example of a Python keyword is `import`, which you will use later in this chapter. You can find a list of other Python keywords in Appendix C.

Python is free to use and is maintained by a large group of volunteers. This book uses the latest 3.0 version of Python.

Checkpoint

5.1 What is a difference between Python and Java?

5.2 How much does Python cost to use?

5.3 What is a keyword?

5.2   Using Python

Python includes tools for writing, running, executing, and testing programs, including the Python interpreter and IDLE.

Choosing a Development Environment

Before you can try any of the programs shown in this book, or write any programs of your own, you need to choose a Python **development environment** to write your code. There are two ways you can do this. The first method is to install Python on your computer. If you are working in a computer lab, this has probably been done already. If you are using your own computer, you can follow the instructions in Appendix A to download and install Python.

The second method is to use an **online environment** to write and test your code. The online option does not require an installation but you must be connected to the internet. There are many online environments, such as Replit, that are geared to student learning.

NOTE: Your instructor may tell you which development environment to use.

The Python Interpreter

Recall that Python is an interpreted language. If you choose to install the Python language on your computer, one of the items that is installed is the Python interpreter. The **Python interpreter** is a program that can read Python programming statements and execute them. (Sometimes, we will refer to the Python interpreter simply as the interpreter.)

You can use the interpreter in two modes: interactive mode and script mode. In **interactive mode,** the interpreter waits for you to type Python statements on the keyboard. Once you type a statement, the interpreter executes it and then waits for you to type another statement. In **script mode,** the interpreter reads the contents of a file that contains Python statements. Such a file is known as a **Python program** or a **Python script.** The interpreter executes each statement in the Python program as it reads it.

Interactive Mode

Once Python has been installed and set up on your system, you start the interpreter in interactive mode by going to the operating system's command line and typing the following command:

```
python
```

If you are using Windows, you can type **python** in the Windows search box. Click the Python Run command, or click Open. Clicking this item will start the Python interpreter in interactive mode.

> **NOTE: When the Python interpreter is running in interactive mode, it is commonly called the Python shell.**

When the Python interpreter starts in interactive mode, you will see something like the following displayed in a console window:

```
Python 3.10.5 (tags/v3.10.5:f377153, Jun 6 2022, 16:14:13)
[MSC v.1929 64 bit (AMD64)] on win32
Type "help", "copyright", "credits" or "license"
for more information.
>>>
```

The >>> that you see is a prompt that indicates the interpreter is waiting for you to type a Python statement. Let's try it out. One of the simplest things that you can do in Python is print a message on the screen. For example, the following statement prints the message *Python programming is fun!* on the screen:

```
print('Python programming is fun!')
```

You can think of this as a command that you are sending to the Python interpreter. If you type the statement exactly as it is shown, the message *Python programming is fun!* is printed on the screen. Here is an example of how you type this statement at the interpreter's prompt:

```
>>> print('Python programming is fun!') Enter
```

After typing the statement, you press the Enter key, and the Python interpreter executes the statement, as shown here:

```
>>> print('Python programming is fun!') Enter
Python programming is fun!
>>>
```

After the message is displayed, the >>> prompt appears again, indicating the interpreter is waiting for you to enter another statement. Let's look at another example. In the following sample session, we have entered two statements:

```
>>> print('To be or not to be') Enter
To be or not to be
>>> print('That is the question.') Enter
That is the question.
>>>
```

If you incorrectly type a statement in interactive mode, the interpreter will display an error message. This will make interactive mode useful to you while you learn Python. As you learn new parts of the Python language, you can try them out in interactive mode and get immediate feedback from the interpreter.

To quit the Python interpreter in interactive mode on a Windows computer, press Ctrl-Z (pressing both keys together) followed by Enter. On a Mac, Linux, or UNIX computer, press Ctrl-D.

Writing Python Programs and Running Them in Script Mode

Although interactive mode is useful for testing code, the statements that you enter in interactive mode are not saved as a program. They are simply executed and their results displayed on the screen. If you want to save a set of Python statements as a program, you save those statements in a file. Then, to execute the program, you use the Python interpreter in script mode.

For example, suppose you want to write a Python program that displays the following three lines of text:

```
Nudge nudge
Wink wink
Know what I mean?
```

To write the program start a simple text editor like Notepad (which is installed on all Windows computers) and type in the following statements:

```
print('Nudge nudge')
print('Wink wink')
print('Know what I mean?')
```

> NOTE: It is possible to use a word processor to create a Python program, but you must save the program as a plain text file.

Then, choose the File > Save As command and save and name the file as `test.py`. When you save a Python program, you give it a name that ends with the `.py` extension, which identifies it as a Python program. To run the program, open the operating system command line (Command Prompt, in Windows) change to the directory or folder where you saved the file, and at the prompt, type:

```
python test.py
```

This starts the Python interpreter in script mode and causes it to execute the statements in the file `test.py`. When the program finishes executing, the Python interpreter exits.

The IDLE Programming Environment

The previous sections described how the Python interpreter can be started in interactive mode or script mode at the operating system command line. As an alternative, you can use an **integrated development environment,** which is a single program that gives you all of the tools you need to write, execute, and test a program.

Recent versions of Python include a program named **IDLE**, which is automatically installed when the Python language is installed. (IDLE stands for **I**ntegrated **D**evelopment **L**earning **E**nvironment.)

When you run IDLE, the window shown in Figure 5-1 appears. Notice the >>> prompt appears in the IDLE window, indicating that the interpreter is running in interactive mode. You can type Python statements at this prompt and see them executed in the IDLE window.

Figure 5-1   The IDLE Shell window

Python Software Foundation

IDLE also has a built-in text editor with features specifically designed to help you write Python programs. For example, the IDLE editor "colorizes" code so keywords and other parts of a program are displayed in their own distinct colors. This helps make programs easier to read. In IDLE, you can write programs, save them to disk, and execute them. Appendix B provides a quick introduction to IDLE and leads you through the process of creating, saving, and executing a Python program.

> **NOTE:** Although IDLE is installed with Python, there are several other Python IDEs available, such as PyCharm and Replit. Your instructor might prefer that you use a specific one in class.

Participating in a Learning Community

As part of a **learning community**, you have the opportunity to work with others to develop skills and knowledge that will help you succeed in school, career, and life. Your role may take on various forms such as learning, helping others, leading the project, designing the solution, writing code, analyzing code, or documenting code.

Throughout the book, some projects and coding exercises suggest that you work with a partner or as a team. These provide the opportunity for you to participate as a **learner**, **initiator**, **contributor**, teacher, or **mentor** to practice what you have learned and develop new skills.

Your learning community also provides the opportunity for you to seek feedback from others, including your peers, teachers, and business professionals. You can seek advice on the quality and accuracy of your work. Then, you can respond to the advice by making improvements.

Checkpoint

5.4 What is the Python interpreter?

5.5 What are the two modes for the Python interpreter?

5.6 What does >>> mean in the Python interpreter?

5.7 What extension do you give to a file name to identify it as a Python program?

5.8 What is IDLE?

5.9 List and explain five ways you can participate in a learning community.

5.3 Creating Lines and Shapes using Turtle Graphics

The Python turtle graphics system simulates a "turtle" that obeys commands to draw simple graphics.

VideoNote
Introduction
to Turtle
Graphics

In the late 1960s, MIT professor Seymour Papert used a robotic "turtle" to teach programming. The turtle was tethered to a computer where a student could enter commands, causing the turtle to move. The turtle also had a pen that could be raised and lowered, so it could be placed on a sheet of paper and programmed to draw images. Python has a **turtle graphics** system that simulates a robotic turtle. The system displays a small cursor (the turtle) on the screen. You can use Python statements to move the turtle around the screen to draw lines and shapes.

The first step in using Python's turtle graphics system is to write the following statement:

```
import turtle
```

This statement is necessary because the turtle graphics system is not built into the Python interpreter. Instead, it is stored in a file known as the turtle module. The import turtle statement loads the turtle module into memory so the Python interpreter can use it.

If you are writing a Python program that uses turtle graphics, you will write the `import` statement at the top of the program. If you want to experiment with turtle graphics in interactive mode, you can type the statement into the Python shell, as shown here:

```
>>> import turtle
>>>
```

NOTE: Some online development environments provide a program template that automatically imports in the Turtle library. As an example, if you are using replit.com, you should choose the Python (with Turtle) template when you create your program.

Drawing Lines

The Python turtle is initially positioned in the center of a graphics window that serves as its canvas. In interactive mode, you can enter the `turtle.showturtle()` command to display the turtle in its window. Here is an example session that imports the `turtle` module, and then shows the turtle:

```
>>> import turtle
>>> turtle.showturtle()
```

This causes a graphics window similar to the one shown in Figure 5-2 to appear. Notice the turtle doesn't look like a turtle at all. Instead, it looks like an arrowhead (➤). This is important, because it points in the direction that the turtle is currently facing. If we instruct the turtle to move forward, it will move in the direction that the arrowhead is pointing.

Let's try it out. You can use the `turtle.forward(n)` command to move the turtle forward *n* **pixels**. (Just type the desired number of pixels in place of *n*.) For example, the command `turtle.forward(200)` moves the turtle forward 200 pixels. Here is an example of a complete session in the Python shell:

```
>>> import turtle
>>> turtle.forward(200)
>>>
```

Figure 5-3 shows the output of this interactive session. Notice a line was drawn by turtle as it moved forward.

Figure 5-2   The turtle's graphics window

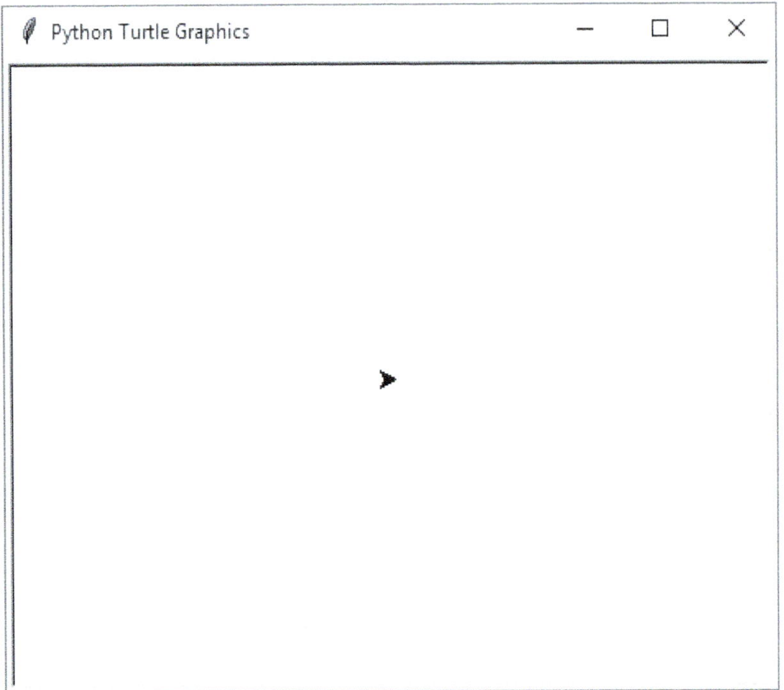

Python Software Foundation

Figure 5-3   The turtle moving forward 200 pixels

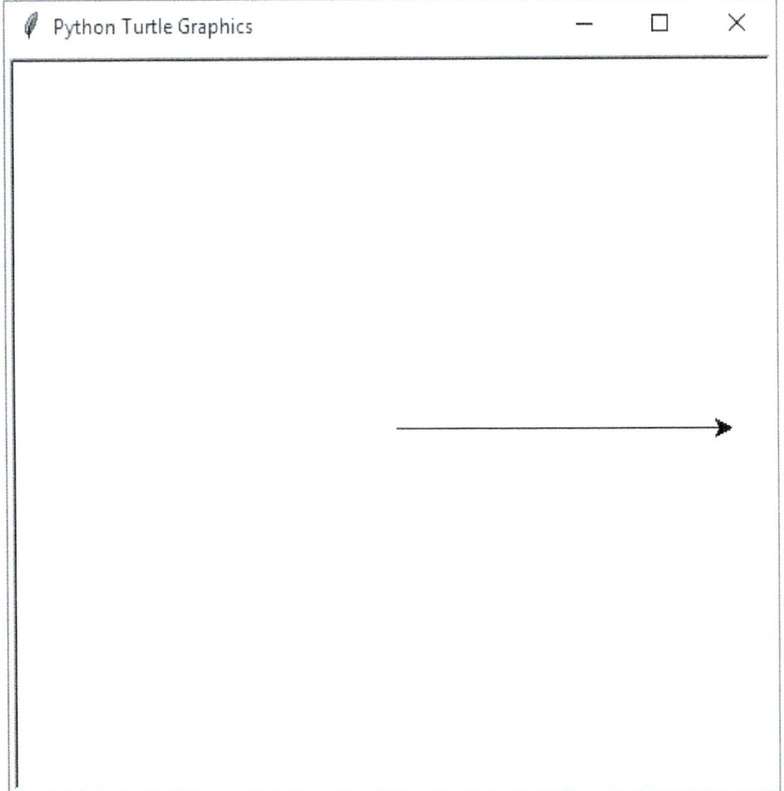

Python Software Foundation

Changing Line Direction

When the turtle first appears, its default heading is 0 degrees (east). This is shown in Figure 5-4.

You can turn the turtle so it faces a different direction by using either the `turtle.right(angle)` command, or the `turtle.left(angle)` command. The `turtle.right(angle)` command turns the turtle right by *angle* degrees, and the `turtle.left(angle)` command turns the turtle left by *angle* degrees. Here is an example session that uses the `turtle.right(angle)` command:

```
>>> import turtle
>>> turtle.forward(200)
>>> turtle.right(90)
>>> turtle.forward(200)
>>>
```

This session first moves the turtle forward 200 pixels. Then it turns the turtle right by 90 degrees (the turtle will be pointing down). Then it moves the turtle forward by 200 pixels. The session's output is shown in Figure 5-5.

Here is an example session that uses the `turtle.left(angle)` command:

```
>>> import turtle
>>> turtle.forward(100)
>>> turtle.left(120)
>>> turtle.forward(150)
>>>
```

Figure 5-4   The turtle's heading

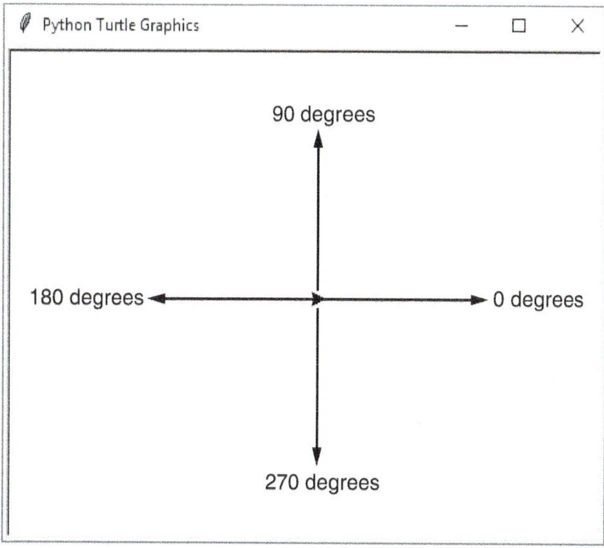

Python Software Foundation

Figure 5-5 The turtle turns right

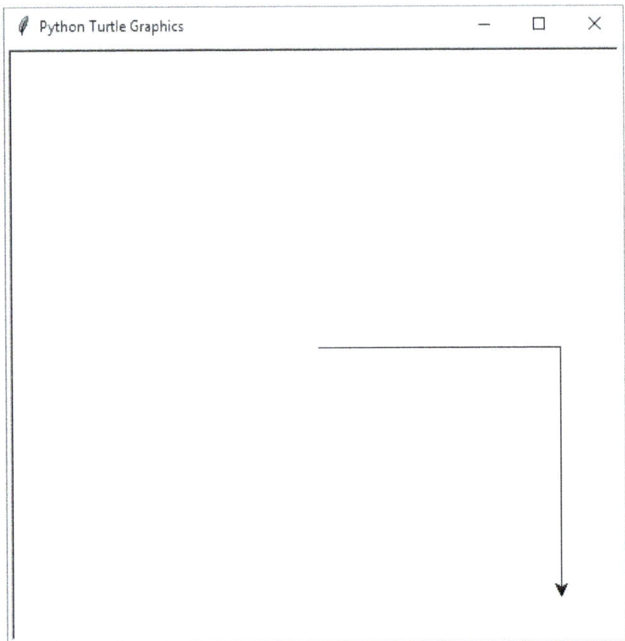

Python Software Foundation

This session first moves the turtle forward 100 pixels. Then it turns the turtle left by 120 degrees (the turtle will be pointing in a northwestern direction). Then it moves the turtle forward by 150 pixels. The session's output is shown in Figure 5-6.

Figure 5-6 The turtle turns left

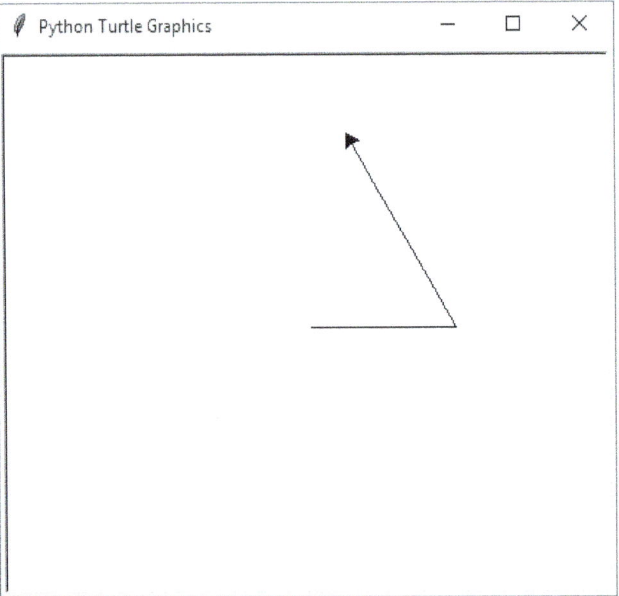

Python Software Foundation

Keep in mind that the `turtle.right` and `turtle.left` commands turn the turtle *by* a specified angle. For example, the turtle's current heading is 90 degrees (due north). If you enter the command `turtle.left(20)`, then the turtle will be turned left by 20 degrees. This means the turtle's heading will be 110 degrees. For another example, look at the following interactive session:

```
>>> import turtle
>>> turtle.forward(50)
>>> turtle.left(45)
>>> turtle.forward(50)
>>> turtle.left(45)
>>> turtle.forward(50)
>>> turtle.left(45)
>>> turtle.forward(50)
>>>
```

Figure 5-7 shows the session's output. At the beginning of this session, the turtle's heading is 0 degrees. In the third line, the turtle is turned left by 45 degrees. In the fifth line, the turtle is turned left again by an additional 45 degrees. In the seventh line, the turtle is once again turned left by 45 degrees. After all of these 45 degree turns, the turtle's heading will finally be 135 degrees.

Figure 5-7 Turning the turtle by 45 degree angles

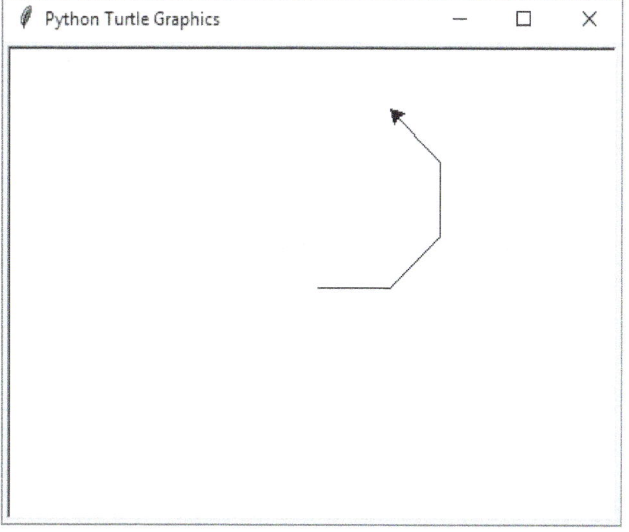

Setting the Turtle's Heading to a Specific Angle

You can use the `turtle.setheading(angle)` command to set the turtle's heading to a specific angle. Simply specify the desired angle as the *angle* **argument**. The following interactive session shows an example:

```
>>> import turtle
>>> turtle.forward(50)
>>> turtle.setheading(90)
>>> turtle.forward(100)
>>> turtle.setheading(180)
>>> turtle.forward(50)
>>> turtle.setheading(270)
>>> turtle.forward(100)
>>>
```

As usual, the turtle's initial heading is 0 degrees. In the third line, the turtle's heading is set to 90 degrees. Then, in the fifth line, the turtle's heading is set to 180 degrees. Then, in the seventh line, the turtle's heading is set to 270 degrees. The session's output is shown in Figure 5-8.

Figure 5-8   Setting the turtle's heading

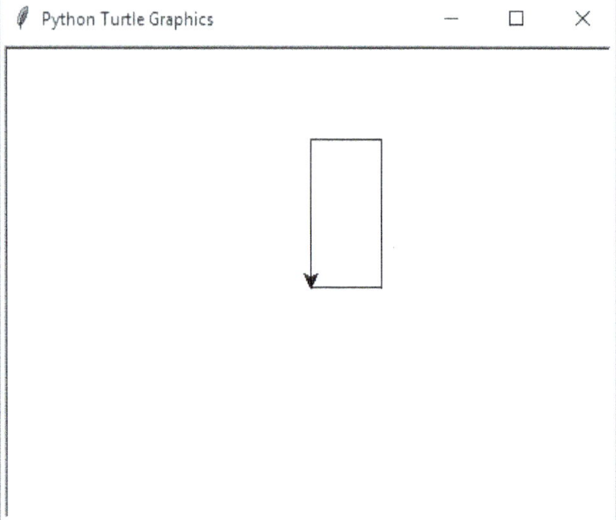

Python Software Foundation

Getting the Turtle's Current Heading

In an interactive session, you can use the `turtle.heading()` command to display the turtle's current heading. Here is an example:

```
>>> import turtle
>>> turtle.heading()
0.0
>>> turtle.setheading(180)
>>> turtle.heading()
180.0
>>>
```

Moving the Pen Up and Down

The original robotic turtle sat on a large sheet of paper, and had a pen that could be raised and lowered. When the pen was down, it was in contact with the paper and would draw a line as the turtle moved. When the pen was up, it was not touching the paper, so the turtle could move without drawing a line.

In Python, you can use the `turtle.penup()` command to "raise the pen," and the `turtle.pendown()` command to "lower the pen." When the pen is up, you can move the turtle without drawing a line. When the pen is down, the turtle leaves a line when it is moved. (By default, the pen is down.) The following session shows an example. The session's output is shown in Figure 5-9.

```
>>> import turtle
>>> turtle.forward(50)
>>> turtle.penup()
>>> turtle.forward(25)
>>> turtle.pendown()
>>> turtle.forward(50)
>>> turtle.penup()
>>> turtle.forward(25)
>>>
```

Figure 5-9   Raising and lowering the pen

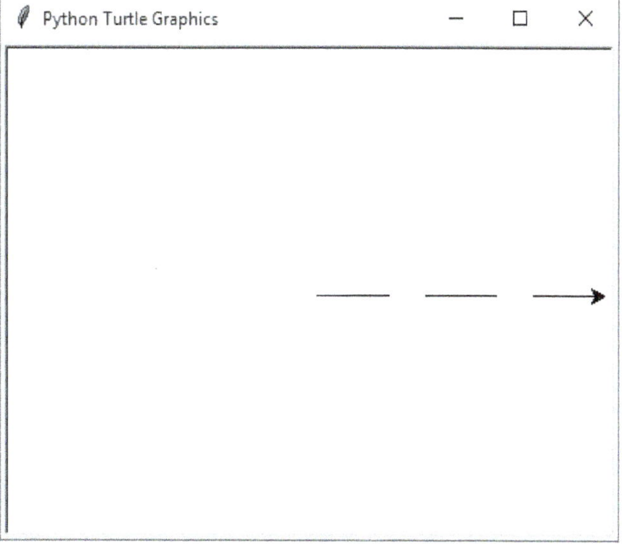

Python Software Foundation

Drawing Circles and Dots

You can use the `turtle.circle(`*`radius`*`)` command to make the turtle draw a circle with a radius of *radius* pixels. For example, the command `turtle.circle(100)` causes the turtle to draw a circle with a radius of 100 pixels. The following interactive session displays the output shown in Figure 5-10:

```
>>> import turtle
>>> turtle.circle(100)
>>>
```

You can use the `turtle.dot()` command to make the turtle draw a simple dot. For example, the following interactive session produces the output shown in Figure 5-11:

```
>>> import turtle
>>> turtle.dot()
>>> turtle.forward(50)
>>> turtle.dot()
>>> turtle.forward(50)
>>> turtle.dot()
>>> turtle.forward(50)
>>>
```

Changing the Pen Size

You can use the `turtle.pensize(`*`width`*`)` command to change the width of the turtle's pen, in pixels. The *width* argument is an integer specifying the pen's width. For example, the following interactive session sets the pen's width to 5 pixels, then draws a circle:

```
>>> import turtle
>>> turtle.pensize(5)
>>> turtle.circle(100)
>>>
```

Figure 5-10   A circle

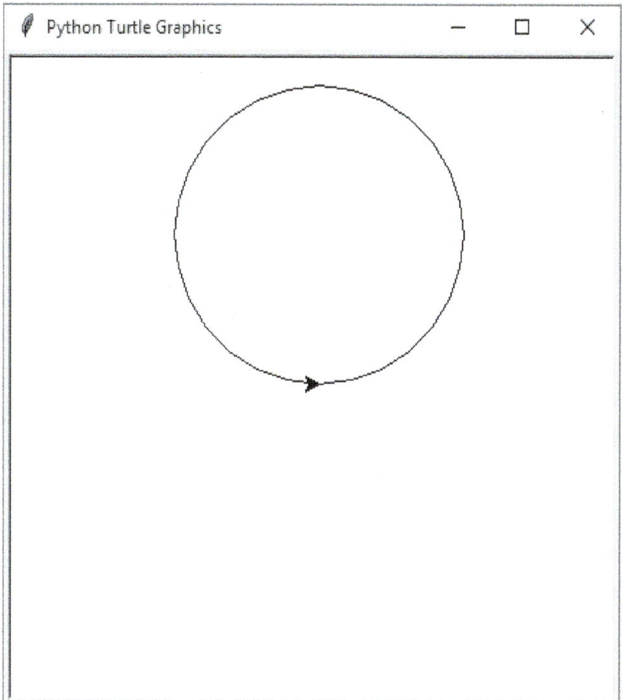

Python Software Foundation

Figure 5-11   Drawing dots

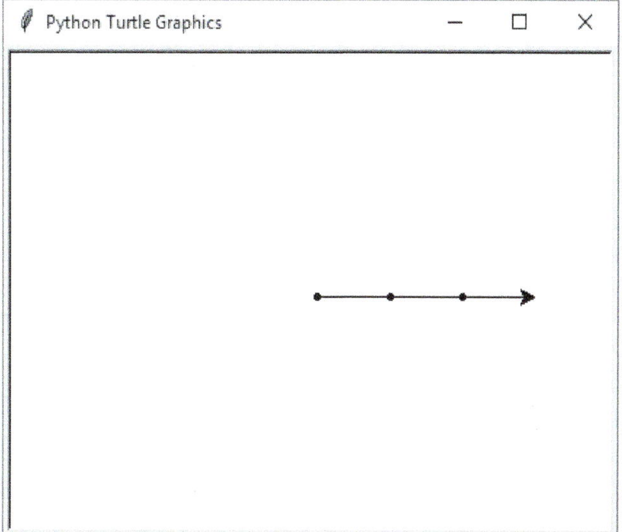

Python Software Foundation

Changing the Drawing Color

You can use the `turtle.pencolor(color)` command to change the turtle's drawing color. The *color* argument is the name of a color, as a string. For example, the following interactive session changes the drawing color to red, then draws a circle:

```
>>> import turtle
>>> turtle.pencolor('red')
>>> turtle.circle(100)
>>>
```

There are numerous predefined color names that you can use with the `turtle.pencolor` command, and Appendix D shows the complete list. Some of the more common colors are `'red'`, `'green'`, `'blue'`, `'yellow'`, and `'cyan'`.

Changing the Background Color

You can use the `turtle.bgcolor(color)` command to change the background color of the turtle's graphics window. The *color* argument is the name of a color, as a **string**, or sequence of characters. For example, the following interactive session changes the background color to gray, changes the drawing color to red, then draws a circle:

```
>>> import turtle
>>> turtle.bgcolor('gray')
>>> turtle.pencolor('red')
>>> turtle.circle(100)
>>>
```

See Appendix D for a complete list of predefined color names.

Resetting the Screen

There are three commands that you can use to reset the turtle's graphics window: `turtle.reset()`, `turtle.clear()`, and `turtle.clearscreen()`. Here is a summary of the commands:

- The `turtle.reset()` command erases all drawings that currently appear in the graphics window, resets the drawing color to black, and resets the turtle to its original position in the center of the screen. This command does not reset the graphics window's background color.

- The `turtle.clear()` command simply erases all drawings that currently appear in the graphics window. It does not change the turtle's position, the drawing color, or the graphics window's background color.

- The `turtle.clearscreen()` command erases all drawings that currently appear in the graphics window, resets the drawing color to black, reset the graphics window's background color to white, and resets the turtle to its original position in the center of the graphics window.

Specifying the Size of the Graphics Window

You can use the `turtle.setup(width, height)` command to specify a size for the graphics window. The *width* and *height* arguments are the width and height, in pixels. For example, the following interactive session creates a graphics window that is 640 pixels wide and 480 pixels high:

```
>>> import turtle
>>> turtle.setup(640, 480)
>>>
```

Moving the Turtle to a Specific Location

A **Cartesian coordinate system** is used to identify the position of each pixel in the turtle's graphics window, as illustrated in Figure 5-12. Each pixel has an X coordinate and a Y coordinate. The X coordinate identifies the pixel's horizontal position, and the Y coordinate identifies its vertical position. Here are the important things to know:

- The pixel in the center of the graphics window is at the position (0, 0), which means that its X coordinate is 0 and its Y coordinate is 0.
- The X coordinates increase in value as we move toward the right side of the window, and they decrease in value as we move toward the left side of the window.
- The Y coordinates increase in value as we move toward the top of the window, and decrease in value as we move toward the bottom of the window.
- Pixels that are located to the right of the center point have positive X coordinates, and pixels that are located to the left of the center point have negative X coordinates.
- Pixels that are located above the center point have positive Y coordinates, and pixels that are located below the center point have negative Y coordinates.

Figure 5-12   Cartesian coordinate system

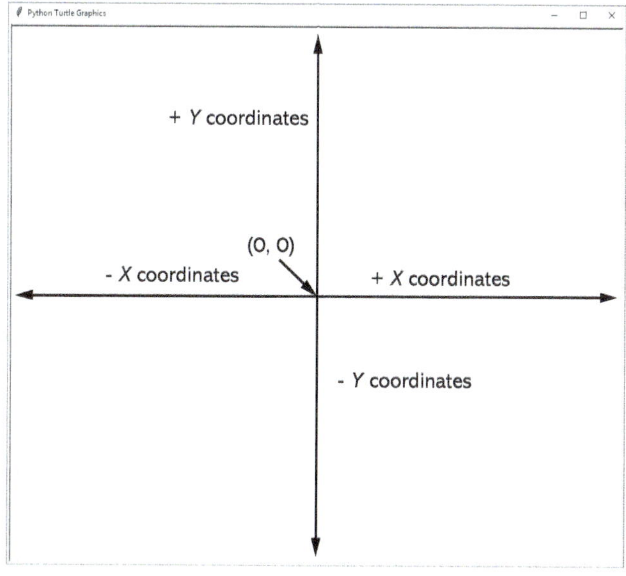

Python Software Foundation

You can use the `turtle.goto(x, y)` command to move the turtle from its current location to a specific position in the graphics window. The *x* and *y* arguments are the coordinates of the position to which to move the turtle. If the turtle's pen is down, a line will be drawn as the turtle moves. For example, the following interactive session draws the lines shown in Figure 5-13:

```
>>> import turtle
>>> turtle.goto(0, 100)
>>> turtle.goto(-100, 0)
>>> turtle.goto(0, 0)
>>>
```

Figure 5-13   Moving the turtle

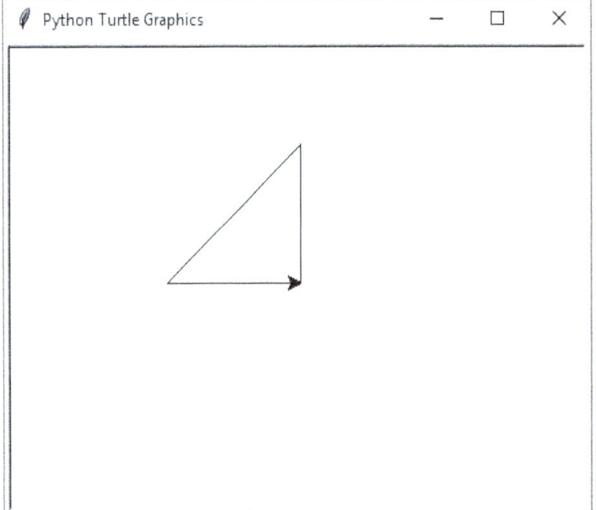

Python Software Foundation

Getting the Turtle's Current Position

In an interactive session, you can use the `turtle.pos()` command to display the turtle's current position. Here is an example:

```
>>> import turtle
>>> turtle.goto(100, 150)
>>> turtle.pos()
(100.00, 150.00)
>>>
```

You can also use the `turtle.xcor()` command to display the turtle's *X* coordinate, and the `turtle.ycor()` command to display the turtle's *Y* coordinate. Here is an example:

```
>>> import turtle
>>> turtle.goto(100, 150)
>>> turtle.xcor()
100
>>> turtle.ycor()
150
>>>
```

Controlling the Turtle's Animation Speed

You can use the `turtle.speed(speed)` command to change the speed at which the turtle moves. The *speed* argument is a number in the range of 0 through 10. If you specify 0, then the turtle will make all of its moves instantly (animation is disabled). For example, the following interactive session disables the turtle's animation, then draws a circle. As a result, the circle will be instantly drawn:

```
>>> import turtle
>>> turtle.speed(0)
>>> turtle.circle(100)
>>>
```

If you specify a *speed* value in the range of 1 through 10, then 1 is the slowest speed, and 10 is the fastest speed. The following interactive session sets the animation speed to 1 (the slowest speed) then draws a circle:

```
>>> import turtle
>>> turtle.speed(1)
>>> turtle.circle(100)
>>>
```

You can get the current animation speed with the `turtle.speed()` command (do not specify a *speed* argument). Here is an example:

```
>>> import turtle
>>> turtle.speed()
3
>>>
```

Hiding the Turtle

If you don't want the turtle to be displayed, you can use the `turtle.hideturtle()` command to hide it. This command does not change the way graphics are drawn, it simply hides the turtle icon. When you want to display the turtle again, use the `turtle.showturtle()` command.

Displaying Text in the Graphics Window

You can use the `turtle.write(text)` command to display text in the graphics window. The *text* argument is a string that you want to display. When the string is displayed, the lower-left corner of the first character will be positioned at the turtle's X and Y coordinates. The following interactive session demonstrates this. The session's output is shown in Figure 5-14.

```
>>> import turtle
>>> turtle.write('Hello World')
>>>
```

Figure 5-14   Text displayed in the graphics window

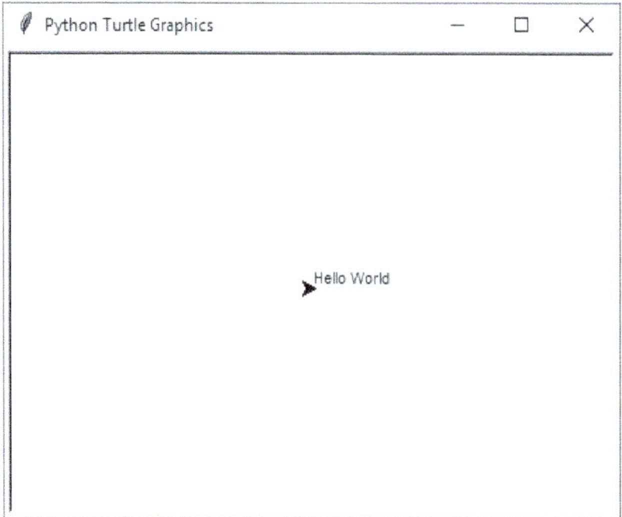

Python Software Foundation

The following interactive session shows another example in which the turtle is moved to specific locations to display text. The session's output is shown in Figure 5-15.

```
>>> import turtle
>>> turtle.setup(300, 300)
>>> turtle.penup()
>>> turtle.hideturtle()
>>> turtle.goto(-120, 120)
>>> turtle.write("Top Left")
>>> turtle.goto(70, -120)
>>> turtle.write("Bottom Right")
>>>
```

Filling Shapes

To fill a shape with a color, you use the `turtle.begin_fill()` command before drawing the shape, then you use the `turtle.end_fill()` command after the shape is drawn. When the `turtle.end_fill()` command executes, the shape will be filled with the current fill color. The following interactive session demonstrates this. The session's output is shown in Figure 5-16.

```
>>> import turtle
>>> turtle.hideturtle()
>>> turtle.begin_fill()
>>> turtle.circle(100)
>>> turtle.end_fill()
>>>
```

Figure 5-15   Text displayed at specific locations in the graphics window

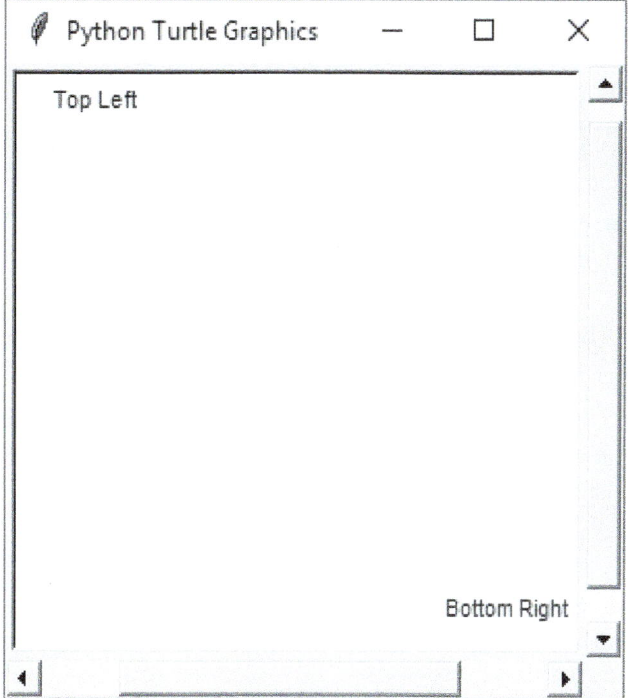

Python Software Foundation

Figure 5-16   A filled circle

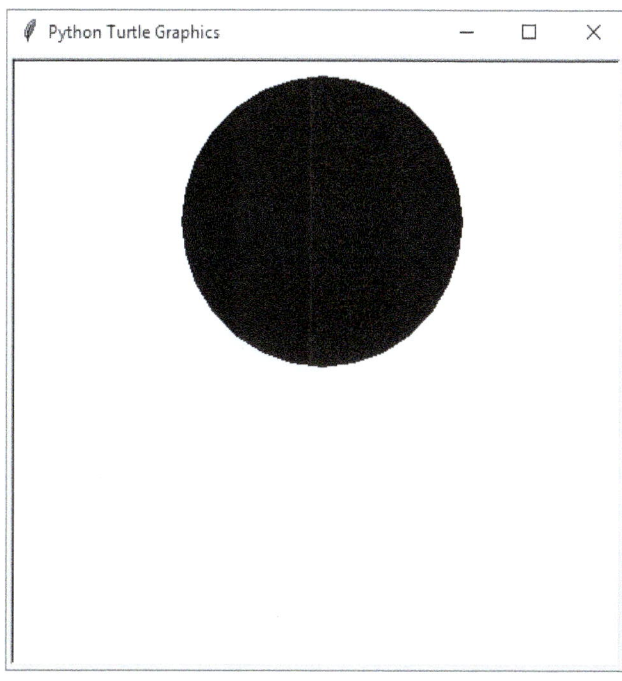

Python Software Foundation

The circle that is drawn in Figure 5-16 is filled with black, which is the default color. You can change the fill color with the `turtle.fillcolor(color)` command. The *color* argument is the name of a color, as a string. For example, the following interactive session changes the drawing color to red, then draws a circle:

```
>>> import turtle
>>> turtle.hideturtle()
>>> turtle.fillcolor('red')
>>> turtle.begin_fill()
>>> turtle.circle(100)
>>> turtle.end_fill()
>>>
```

There are numerous predefined color names that you can use with the `turtle.fillcolor` command, and Appendix D shows the complete list. Some of the more common colors are 'red', 'green', 'blue', 'yellow', and 'cyan'.

The following interactive session demonstrates how to draw a square that is filled with the color blue. The session's output is shown in Figure 5-17.

```
>>> import turtle
>>> turtle.hideturtle()
>>> turtle.fillcolor('blue')
>>> turtle.begin_fill()
>>> turtle.forward(100)
>>> turtle.left(90)
>>> turtle.forward(100)
>>> turtle.left(90)
>>> turtle.forward(100)
>>> turtle.left(90)
>>> turtle.forward(100)
>>> turtle.end_fill()
>>>
```

Figure 5-17   A square filled with the color blue

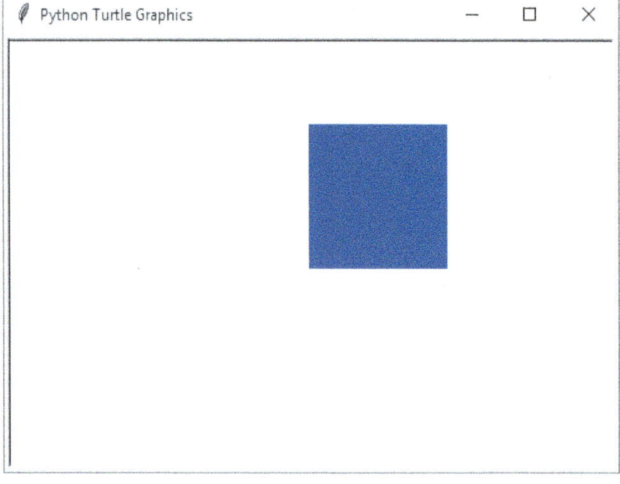

Python Software Foundation

If you fill a shape that is not enclosed, the shape will be filled as if you had drawn a line connecting the starting point with the ending point. For example, the following interactive session draws two lines. The first is from (0, 0) to (120, 120), and the second is from (120, 120) to (200, −100). When the `turtle.end_fill()` command executes, the shape is filled as if there were a line from (0, 0) to (200, −120). Figure 5-18 shows the session's output.

```
>>> import turtle
>>> turtle.hideturtle()
>>> turtle.begin_fill()
>>> turtle.goto(120, 120)
>>> turtle.goto(200, -100)
>>> turtle.end_fill()
>>>
```

Figure 5-18   Shape filled

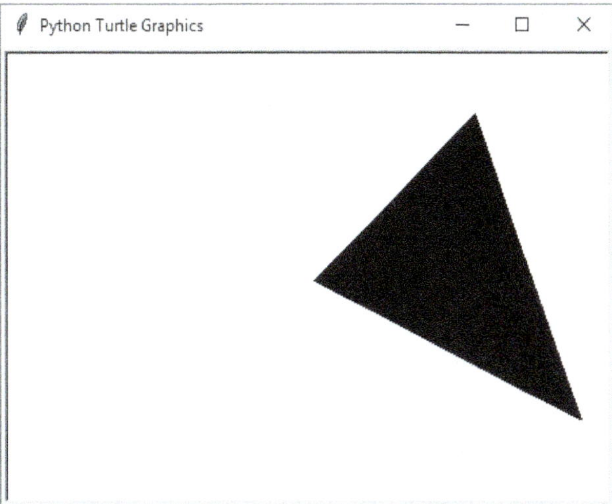

Python Software Foundation

Getting User Input with a Dialog Box

You can use the `turtle.numinput` command to get numeric input from the user and assign it to a **variable**. The `turtle.numinput` command displays a small graphical window known as a **dialog box**. The dialog box provides an area for the user to type input, as well as an OK button and a Cancel button. A dialog box that prompts for user input is a common feature of a **graphical user interface (GUI)**. Figure 5-19 shows an example.

Figure 5-19   A dialog box

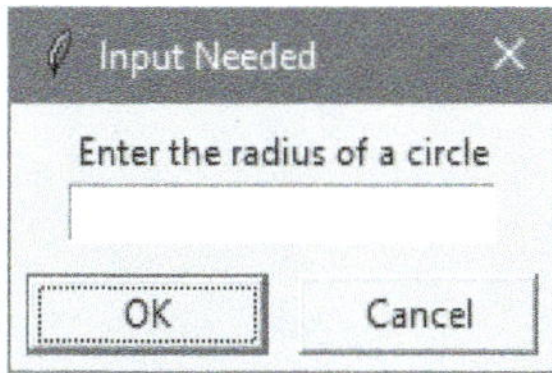

Python Software Foundation

Here is the general format of a statement that uses the `turtle.numinput` command:

```
variable = turtle.numinput(title, prompt)
```

In the general format, *variable* is the name of a variable that will be assigned the value that the user enters. The *title* argument is a string that is displayed in the dialog box's title bar (the bar at the top of the window), and the *prompt* argument is a string that is displayed inside the dialog box. The purpose of the *prompt* string is to instruct the user to enter some data. When the user clicks the OK button, the command returns the number (as a floating-point value) that the user entered into the dialog box. The number is then assigned to *variable*.

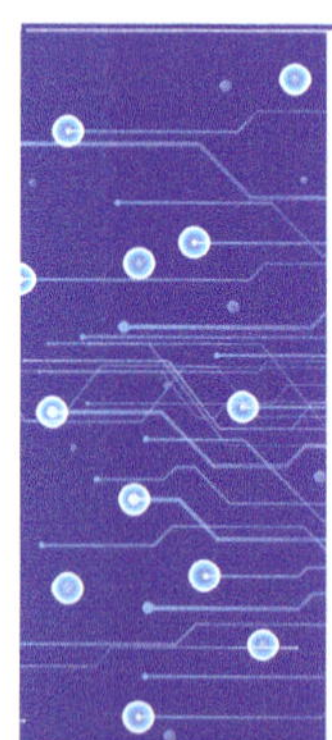

In the Spotlight:

Prompting for User Input

How would you command the turtle to draw a circle with a radius determined by user input?

On Your Own: Alone or with a partner, try writing the commands you would need to accomplish this task. Then, read on to see if your work matches the work shown below.

The following interactive session demonstrates how to command the turtle to draw a circle using user input for the radius. The session's output is shown in Figure 5-20.

```
>>> import turtle
>>> radius = turtle.numinput('Input Needed', 'Enter the radius of a
circle')
>>> turtle.circle(radius)
>>>
```

The second statement shown in the interactive session displays the dialog box shown on the left in Figure 5-20. In the example session, the user enters 100 into the dialog box and clicks the OK button. As a result, the `turtle.numinput` command returns the value 100.0, which is assigned to the `radius` variable. The next statement in the session executes the `turtle.circle` command, passing the `radius` variable as its argument. This causes a circle with a radius of 100 to be drawn, as shown on the right in Figure 5-20.

If the user clicks the Cancel button instead of the OK button, the `turtle.numinput` command returns the special value None, which indicates that the user entered no input.

Figure 5-20 Prompting the user for the radius of a circle

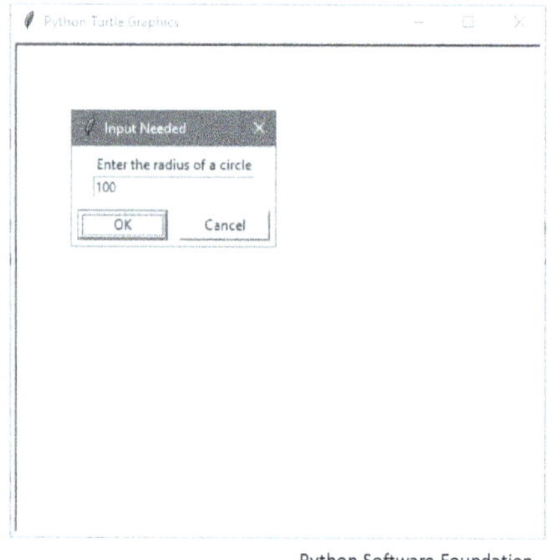

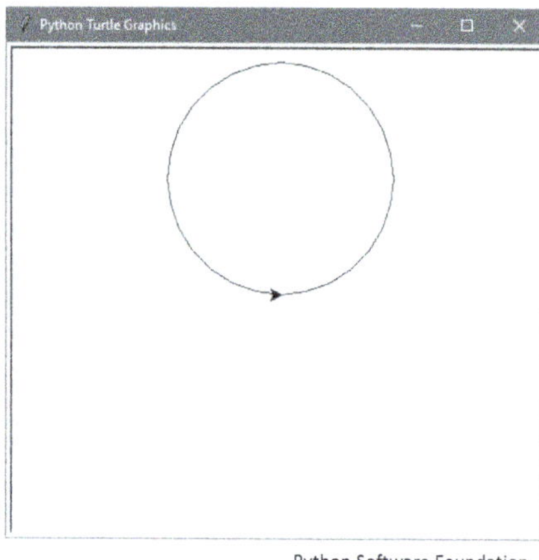

In addition to the *title* and *prompt* arguments, there are three optional arguments that you can use with the `turtle.numinput` command, as shown in the following general format:

```
variable = turtle.numinput(title, prompt, default=x, minval=y,
maxval=z)
```

- The `default=x` argument specifies that you want the default value x displayed in the input box. This makes it easy for the user to simply click the OK button and accept the default value.

- The `minval=y` argument specifies that you want to reject any number entered by the user that is less than y. If the user enters a number less than y, an error message will be displayed and the dialog box will remain open.

- The `maxval=z` argument specifies that you want to reject any number entered by the user that is greater than z. If the user enters a number greater than z, an error message will be displayed and the dialog box will remain open.

Here is an example of a statement that uses all the optional arguments:

```
num = turtle.numinput('Input Needed', 'Enter a value in the range 1-10',
                      default=5, minval=1, maxval=10)
```

This statement specifies a default value of 5, a minimum value of 1, and a maximum value of 10. Figure 5-21 shows the dialog box displayed by this statement. If the user enters a value less than 1 and clicks OK, the system will display a message similar to the one shown on the left in Figure 5-22. If the user enters a value greater than 10 and clicks OK, the system will display a message similar to the one shown on the right in Figure 5-31.

Figure 5-21　Dialog box with a default value displayed

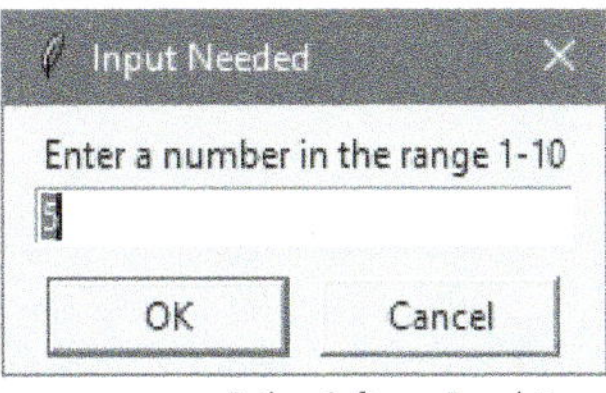

Python Software Foundation

Figure 5-22　Error messages for input out of range

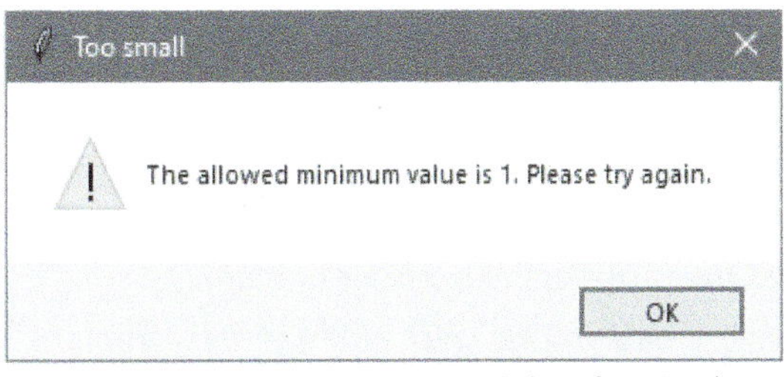

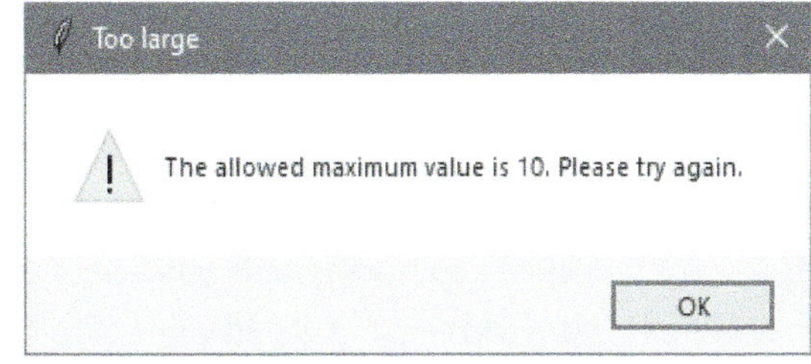

Python Software Foundation　　　　　　　　　　　　Python Software Foundation

Getting String Input with the `turtle.textinput` Command

You can also use the `turtle.textinput` command to get string input from the user. Here is the general format of a statement that uses the `turtle.textinput` command:

```
variable = turtle.textinput(title, prompt)
```

The `turtle.textinput` command works like the `turtle.numinput` command, except the `turtle.textinput` command returns the user's input as a string. The following interactive session demonstrates. The dialog box displayed by the second statement is shown in Figure 5-23.

```
>>> import turtle
>>> name = turtle.textinput('Input Needed', 'Enter your name')
>>> print(name)
Jess Klaus
>>>
```

Figure 5-23   Dialog box asking for the user's name

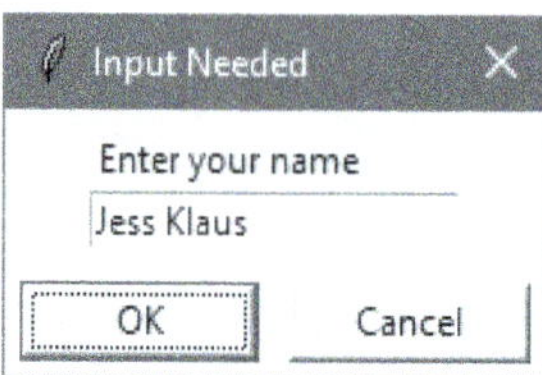

Python Software Foundation

Using `turtle.done()` to Keep the Graphics Window Open

If you are running a Python turtle graphics program from an environment other that IDLE (for example, at the command line), you may notice the graphics window disappears as soon as your program ends. To prevent the window from closing after the program ends, you will need to add the `turtle.done()` statement to the very end of your turtle graphics programs. This will cause the graphics window to remain open, so you can see its contents after the program finishes executing. To close the window, simply click the window's standard "close" button.

If you are running your programs from IDLE, it is not necessary to have the `turtle.done()` statement in your programs. It may not be necessary for some online coding environments.

 **Checkpoint**

5.10   What is the turtle's default heading when it first appears?

5.11   How do you move the turtle forward?

5.12   How would you turn the turtle right by 45 degrees?

5.13   How would you move the turtle to a new location without drawing a line?

5.14   What command would you use to display the turtle's current heading?

5.15   What command would you use to draw a circle with a radius of 100 pixels?

5.16   What command would you use to change the turtle's pen size to 8 pixels?

5.17   What command would you use to change the turtle's drawing color to blue?

5.18   What command would you use to change the background color of the turtle's graphics window to black?

5.19   What command would you use to set the size of the turtle's graphics window to 500 pixels wide by 200 pixels high?

5.20   What command would you use to move the turtle to the location (100, 50)?

5.21   What command would you use to display the coordinates of the turtle's current position?

5.22   Which of the following commands will make the animation speed faster? turtle. speed(1) or turtle.speed(10)

5.23   What command would you use to disable the turtle's animation?

5.24   Describe how to draw a shape that is filled with a color.

5.25   How do you display text in the turtle's graphics window?

5.26   Create a turtle graphics statement that displays a dialog box that gets a number from the user. The text Enter a Value should appear in the dialog box's title bar. The dialog box should display the prompt What is the radius of the circle? The value that the user enters into the dialog box should be assigned to a variable named radius.

Chapter Review
Multiple Choice

1. The Python ________ is a program that can read Python programming statements and execute them.
   - a. Interpreter
   - b. Statement
   - c. Program
   - d. Keyword

2. In ________ mode, the interpreter waits for you to type Python statements on the keyboard.
   - a. Script
   - b. Windows
   - c. Language
   - d. Interactive (shell)

3. In ________ mode, the interpreter reads the contents of a file that contains Python statements.
   - a. Script
   - b. Windows
   - c. Language
   - d. Interactive (shell)

4. >>> is a prompt that indicates:
   - a. You incorrectly typed a command.
   - b. The interpreter is waiting for you to type a Python statement.
   - c. You are using a word processor.
   - d. You have not installed Python on your computer.

5. Which command can you use to display the following: Python programming is fun!
   - a. turtle.setheading(180)
   - b. turtle.bgcolor('Python programming is fun!')
   - c. print('Python programming is fun!')
   - d. turtle.clearscreen()

6. What does the command turtle.goto(0, 100) do?
   - a. It moves the turtle from its current location to 0, 100 in the graphics window.
   - b. It displays the turtle's current location.
   - c. It specifies the size of the graphics window.
   - d. It turns the turtle left by 100 degrees.

7. Which command can you use to display the turtle's current heading?
   - a. turtle.setheading(180)
   - b. import turtle
   - c. turtle.goto(0, 0)
   - d. turtle.heading()

8. What colors can you use with the turtle graphics system?
   - a. Any color you can think of.
   - b. Predefined color names.
   - c. Only black and white.
   - d. Only the three primary colors.

9. The ________ command displays a small graphical window known as a dialog box.
   - a. turtle.numinput
   - b. turtle turtle.circle(100)
   - c. turtle.write('Dialog Box')
   - d. turtle.clearscreen()

10. To prevent the graphics window from closing after the program ends, you will need to add the ________ statement to the very end of your turtle graphics programs.
    - a. turtle.clearscreen()
    - b. turtle.hideturtle()
    - c. turtle.begin_fill()
    - d. turtle.done()

True or False

1. You can write a Python program in a simple text editor like Notepad.

2. When the pen is up, you can move the turtle without drawing a line.

3. You cannot display text in the turtle graphics window — you can only draw shapes.

4. The turtle.clear() command erases all drawings that currently appear in the graphics window, but it does not change the turtle's position, the drawing color, or the graphics window's background color.

5. You cannot specify a size for the graphics window.

Short Answer

1. Name two ways that you can use the turtle graphics program to create a filled shape.

2. What is the difference between the statements turtle.bgcolor('gray') and turtle.pencolor('gray')?

3. What is the difference between interactive mode and script mode?

4. What can you do in IDLE (integrated development environment)?

5. What would the command turtle.setup(640, 480) do?

Algorithm Workbench

1. Write a turtle graphics statement that displays a circle with a radius of 75 pixels.

2. Write the turtle graphics statements to display a square that is 100 pixels wide on each side and filled with the color blue.

3. Write the turtle graphics statements to display a square that is 100 pixels wide on each side and a circle that is centered inside the square. The circle's radius should be 80 pixels. The circle should be filled with the color red. (The square should not be filled with a color.)

Exercises

1. With your instructor's permission, download and install Python. Open it and use print to display a sentence on the screen. Open and explore IDLE.

2. Working in pairs or small teams as participants in a learning community, brainstorm programs you would like to write using Python. You might take turns acting as initiators who lead and manage the session and contributors who participate and support the leader to achieve the team goals. Write down every idea that you have in five minutes. Together, decide which one is the most realistic and satisfying. Seek advice by asking another group to evaluate the quality and accuracy of your idea and provide feedback. Respond to the feedback by improving your idea.

3. For this exercise, work with a partner or small team as participants in a learning community. Take turns being the learner, teacher, and mentor. The teacher should provide instructions; the learner should write the code; the mentor should review the learner's work and provide feedback, constructive criticism, and support. If you are learning Python on your own, you can find online communities of learners like yourself. Ask your instructor for guidance on selecting a tool and joining or participating an online learning community. Use the turtle graphics library to write programs that display each of the designs shown in Figure 5-24. When you have completed the programs, seek advice by asking another group or your instructor to evaluate the quality and accuracy of your work. Respond to the feedback you receive to improve the quality and accuracy of the designs.

Figure 5-24   Designs

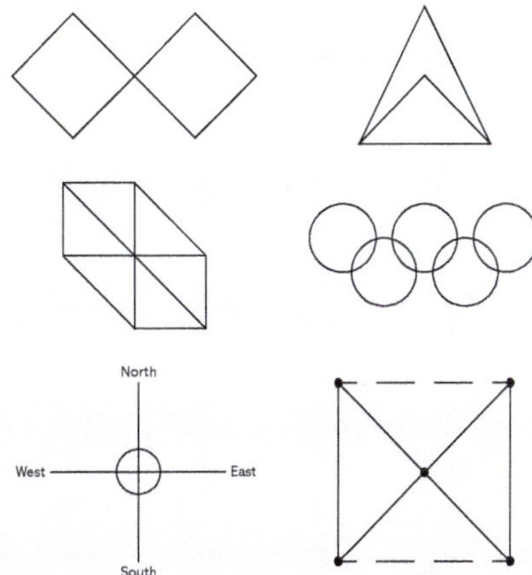

6 Input, Processing, and Output

TOPICS

6.1 Input, Processing, and Output

KEY POINT **Input is data that the program receives. When a program receives data, it usually processes the data by performing some operation with it. The result of the operation is sent out of the program as output.**

Computer programs typically perform the following three-step process:

1. Input is received.

2. Some process is performed on the input.

3. Output is produced.

Recall that input is any data that the program receives while it is running. One common form of input is data that is typed on the keyboard. The program receives the data and then performs some process on it, such as a mathematical calculation. The results of the process are then sent out of the program as output.

Figure 6.1 illustrates these three steps in a pay calculating program. The number of hours worked and the hourly pay rate are provided as input. The program processes this data by multiplying the hours worked by the hourly pay rate. The results of the calculation are then displayed on the screen as output.

Figure 6-1 The input, processing, and output of the pay calculating program

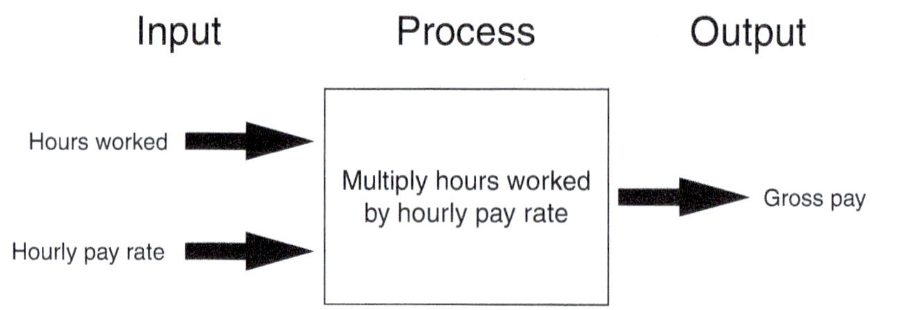

In this chapter, we will discuss basic ways that you can perform input, processing, and output using Python.

 **Checkpoint**

6.1 What is an example of input?

6.2 What is an example of a process a computer program might perform?

6.3 What is an example of output?

6.2 Displaying Output with the `print` Function

 **You use the `print` function to display output in a Python program.**

A **function** is a piece of prewritten code that performs an operation. Python has numerous built-in functions that perform various operations. Perhaps the most fundamental built-in function is the `print` function, which displays output on the screen. Here is an example of a statement that executes the `print` function:

```
print('Hello world')
```

In interactive mode, if you type this statement and press the Enter key, the message *Hello world* is displayed. Here is an example:

```
>>> print('Hello world') Enter
Hello world
>>>
```

When programmers execute a function, they say that they are **calling** the function. When you call the `print` function, you type the word `print`, followed by a set of parentheses. Inside the parentheses, you type an **argument**, which is the data that you want displayed as output on the screen. In the previous example, the argument is `'Hello world'`. Notice the quote marks are not displayed when the statement executes. The quote marks simply label the beginning and the end of the text that you wish to output.

Suppose your instructor tells you to write a program that displays your name and address on the computer screen. Program 6-1 shows an example of such a program, with the output that it will produce when it runs. (The line numbers that appear in a program listing in this book are *not* part of the program. We use the line numbers in our discussion to refer to parts of the program.)

Program 6-1   (`output.py`)

```
1  print('Kate Austen')
2  print('123 Full Circle Drive')
3  print('Asheville, NC 28899')
```

Program Output

```
Kate Austen
123 Full Circle Drive
Asheville, NC 28899
```

It is important to understand that the statements in this program execute in the order that they appear, from the top of the program to the bottom. When you run this program, the first statement will execute, followed by the second statement, and followed by the third statement.

NOTE: Throughout the text, a Python file name in parentheses indicates that the file is available for download.

Strings and String Literals

Programs almost always work with data of some type. For example, Program 6-1 uses the following three pieces of data:

```
'Kate Austen'
'123 Full Circle Drive
'Asheville, NC 28899'
```

These pieces of data are sequences of characters. In programming terms, a sequence of characters that is used as data is called a **string**. When a string appears in the actual code of a program, it is called a **string literal**. In Python code, string literals must be enclosed in quote marks. As mentioned earlier, the quote marks simply label where the string data begins and ends.

In Python, you can enclose string literals in a set of single-quote marks (`'`) or a set of double-quote marks (`"`). The string literals in Program 6-1 are labeled using single-quote marks, but the program could also be written using double-quote marks, as shown in Program 6-2.

Program 6-2   (`double_quotes.py`)

```
1  print("Kate Austen")
2  print("123 Full Circle Drive")
3  print("Asheville, NC 28899")
```

Program Output

```
Kate Austen
123 Full Circle Drive
Asheville, NC 28899
```

If you want a string literal to contain either a single-quote or an apostrophe as part of the string, you can label the string literal in double-quote marks. For example, Program 6-3 prints two strings that contain apostrophes.

Program 6-3   (`apostrophe.py`)

```
1  print("Don't fear!")
2  print("I'm here!")
```

Program Output

```
Don't fear!
I'm here!
```

Likewise, you can use single-quote marks to label a string literal that contains double-quotes as part of the string. Program 6-4 shows an example.

Program 6-4   (`display_quote.py`)

```
1  print('Your assignment is to read "Hamlet" by tomorrow.')
```

Program Output

```
Your assignment is to read "Hamlet" by tomorrow.
```

Python also allows you to label string literals in triple quotes (either `"""` or `'''`). Triple-quoted strings can contain both single quotes and double quotes as part of the string. The following statement shows an example:

```
print("""I'm reading "Hamlet" tonight.""")
```

This statement will print

```
I'm reading "Hamlet" tonight.
```

Triple quotes can also be used to surround **multiline strings** when single and double quotes cannot be used. Here is an example:

```
print("""One
Two
Three""")
```

This statement will print

```
One
Two
Three
```

Checkpoint

6.4 Create a statement that displays your name as output.

6.5 Create a statement that displays the following text as output:

```
Python's the best!
```

6.6 Write a statement that displays the following text as output:

```
The cat said "meow."
```

6.3 Comments

Comments are notes of explanation that document lines or sections of a program. Comments are part of the program, but the Python interpreter ignores them. They are intended for people who may be reading the source code.

Comments are short notes placed in different parts of a program, explaining how those parts of the program work. Although comments are a critical part of a program, they are ignored by the Python interpreter. Comments are intended for any person reading a program's code, not the computer.

In Python, you begin a comment with the # character. When the Python interpreter sees a # character, it ignores everything from that character to the end of the line. For example, look at Program 6-5. Lines 1 and 2 are comments that briefly explain the program's purpose.

Program 6-5   (`comment1.py`)

```
1   # This program displays a person's
2   # name and address.
3   print('Kate Austen')
4   print('123 Full Circle Drive')
5   print('Asheville, NC 28899')
```

Program Output

```
Kate Austen
123 Full Circle Drive
Asheville, NC 28899
```

Programmers commonly write end-line comments in their code. An **end-line comment** is a comment that appears at the end of a line of code. It usually explains the statement that appears in that line. Program 6-6 shows an example. Each line ends with a comment that briefly explains what the line does.

Program 6-6   (`comment2.py`)

```
1   print('Kate Austen')              # Display the name.
2   print('123 Full Circle Drive')    # Display the address.
3   print('Asheville, NC 28899')      # Display the city, state, and ZIP.
```

Program Output

```
Kate Austen
123 Full Circle Drive
Asheville, NC 28899
```

As a beginning programmer, you might be resistant to the idea of writing lots of comments in your programs. After all, it can seem more productive to write code that actually does something! It is crucial that you take the extra time to write comments, however. They will almost certainly save you and others time in the future when you have to modify or debug the program. Large and complex programs can be almost impossible to read and understand if they are not properly commented.

 **Checkpoint**

6.7 What is a comment?

6.8 In Python, what character do you use to begin a comment?

6.9 What is an end-line comment?

6.4 Variables

A variable is a name that represents a storage location in the computer's memory.

Programs usually store data in the computer's memory and perform operations on that data. For example, consider the typical online shopping experience: you browse a website and add the items that you want to purchase to the shopping cart. As you add items to the shopping cart, data about those items is stored in memory. Then, when you click the checkout button, a program running on the website's computer calculates the cost of all the items you have in your shopping cart, applicable sales taxes, shipping costs, and the total of all these charges. When the program performs these calculations, it stores the results in the computer's memory.

Programs use variables to store data in memory. A **variable** is a name that represents a value in the computer's memory. For example, a program that calculates the sales tax on a purchase might use the variable name `tax` to represent that value in memory. And a program that calculates the distance between two cities might use the variable name `distance` to represent that value in memory. When a variable represents a value in the computer's memory, we say that the variable **references** the value. In some languages (but not Python) a variable must be assigned a data type. A **primitive variable** is assigned to a basic data type, such as integer or float.

Creating Variables with Assignment Statements

You use an **assignment statement** to create a variable and make it reference a piece of data. Here is an example of an assignment statement:

```
age = 25
```

After this statement executes, a variable named `age` will be created, and it will reference the value 25. This concept is shown in Figure 6-4. In the figure, think of the value 25 as being stored somewhere in the computer's memory. The arrow that points from `age` to the value 25 indicates

Figure 6-2 The age variable references the value 25

that the variable name `age` references the value.

An assignment statement is written in the following general format:
```
variable = expression
```

The equal sign (=) is known as the **assignment operator**. In the general format, *variable* is the name of a variable and *expression* is a value, or any piece of code that results in a value. After an assignment statement executes, the variable listed on the left side of the = operator will reference the value given on the right side of the = operator.

To experiment with variables, you can type assignment statements in interactive mode, as shown here:

```
>>> width = 10 Enter
>>> length = 5 Enter
>>>
```

The first statement creates a variable named `width` and assigns it the value 10. The second statement creates a variable named `length` and assigns it the value 5. Next, you can use the `print` function to display the values referenced by these variables, as shown here:

```
>>> print(width) Enter
10
>>> print(length) Enter
5
>>>
```

When you pass a variable as an argument to the `print` function, you do not enclose the variable name in quote marks. If you do, it is labeled as a string for output. Look at the following interactive session:

```
>>> print('width') Enter
width
>>> print(width) Enter
10
>>>
```

In the first statement, we passed `'width'` as an argument to the `print` function, and the function printed the string: width. In the second statement, we passed width (with no quote marks) as an argument to the `print` function, and the function displayed the value referenced by the `width` variable.

In an assignment statement, the variable that is receiving the assignment must appear on the left side of the = operator. As shown in the following interactive session, an error occurs if the item on the left side of the = operator is not a variable:

```
>>> 25 = age Enter
SyntaxError: can't assign to literal
>>>
```

The code in Program 6-7 demonstrates a variable. Line 2 creates a variable named `room` and assigns it the value 503. The statements in lines 3 and 4 display a message. Notice line 4 displays the value that is referenced by the `room` variable.

Program 6-7   `(variable_demo.py)`

```
1   # This program demonstrates a variable.
2   room = 503
3   print('I am staying in room number')
4   print(room)
```

Program Output
```
I am staying in room number
503
```

Program 6-8 shows a sample program that uses two variables. Line 2 creates a variable named `top_speed`, assigning it the value 160. Line 3 creates a variable named `distance`, assigning it the value 300. This is illustrated in Figure 6-3.

Program 6-8   `(variable_demo2.py)`

```
1   # Create two variables: top_speed and distance.
2   top_speed = 160
3   distance = 300
4
5   # Display the values referenced by the variables.
6   print('The top speed is')
7   print(top_speed)
8   print('The distance traveled is')
9   print(distance)
```

Program Output
```
The top speed is
160
The distance traveled is
300
```

Figure 6-3 Two variables

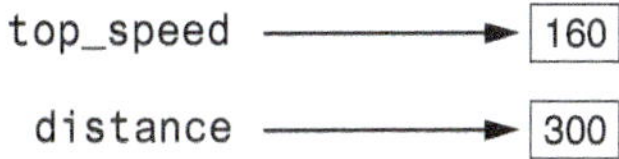

WARNING! You cannot use a variable until you have assigned a value to it. An error will occur if you try to perform an operation on a variable, such as printing it, before it has been assigned a value.

Sometimes a simple typing mistake will cause this error. One example is a misspelled variable name, as shown here:

```
temperature = 74.5   # Create a variable
print(tempereture)   # Error! Misspelled variable name
```

In this code, the variable temperature is created by the assignment statement. The variable name is spelled differently in the print statement, however, which will cause an error. Another example is the inconsistent use of uppercase and lowercase letters in a variable name. Here is an example:

```
temperature = 74.5   # Create a variable
print(Temperature)   # Error! Inconsistent use of case
```

In this code, the variable temperature (in all lowercase letters) is created by the assignment statement. In the print statement, the name Temperature is spelled with an uppercase T. This will cause an error because variable names are case sensitive in Python.

NOTE: Internally, Python variables work differently than variables in most other programming languages. In most programming languages, a variable is a memory location that holds a value. In those languages, when you assign a value to a variable, the value is stored in the variable's memory location.

In Python, however, a variable is a memory location that holds the **address** of another memory location. When you assign a value to a Python variable, that value is stored in a location that is separate from the variable. The variable will hold the address of the memory location that holds the value. That is why, in Python, instead of saying that a variable "holds" a value, we say that a variable "references" a value.

Variable Naming Rules

Although you are allowed to make up your own names for variables, you must follow these rules:

- You cannot use one of Python's keywords as a variable name. (See Appendix C for a list of Python keywords.)
- A variable name cannot contain spaces.

- The first character must be one of the letters a through z, A through Z, or an underscore character (_).
- After the first character, you may use the letters a through z or A through Z, the digits 0 through 9, or underscores.
- Python is **case-sensitive**, which means uppercase and lowercase characters are distinct. This means the variable name `ItemsOrdered` is not the same as `itemsordered`.

In addition to following these rules, you should always choose descriptive identifiers as names for your variables. Descriptive identifiers give readers information about what they are used for and make your code more functional. For example, a variable that references the temperature might be named `temperature`, and a variable that references a car's speed might be named `speed`. You may be tempted to give variables names such as `x` and `b2`, but names like these are not descriptive and give no clue as to what the variable's purpose is.

Because a variable's name should reflect the variable's purpose, programmers often find themselves creating names that are made of multiple words. For example, consider the following variable names:

```
grosspay
payrate
hotdogssoldtoday
```

Unfortunately, these names are not easily read by the human eye because the words aren't separated. Because we can't have spaces in variable names, we need to find another way to separate the words in a multiword variable name and make it more readable.

One way to do this is to use the underscore character to represent a space. For example, the following variable names are easier to read than those previously shown:

```
gross_pay
pay_rate
hot_dogs_sold_today
```

This style of naming variables is popular among Python programmers and is the style we will use in this book. There are other popular styles, however, such as the **camelCase** naming convention. camelCase names are written in the following manner:

- The variable name begins with lowercase letters.
- The first character of the second and subsequent words is written in uppercase.

For example, the following variable names are written in camelCase:

```
grossPay
payRate
hotDogsSoldToday
```

NOTE: This style of naming is called camelCase because the uppercase characters that appear in a name may suggest a camel's humps.

Table 6-1 lists several sample variable names and indicates whether each is legal or illegal in Python

Table 6-1   Sample variable names

Variable Name	Legal or Illegal?
units_per_day	Legal
dayOfWeek	Legal
3dGraph	Illegal. Variable names cannot begin with a digit.
June1997	Legal
Mixture#3	Illegal. Variable names may only use letters, digits, or underscores.

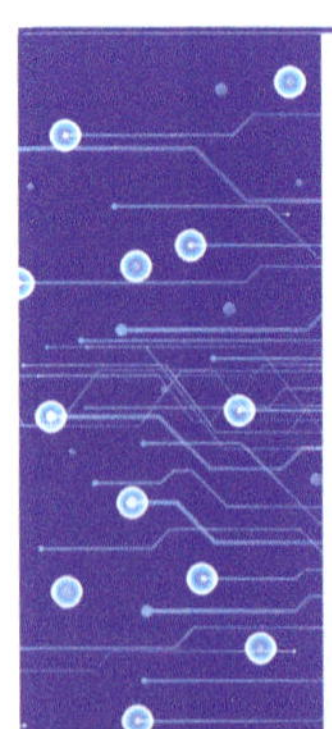

In the Spotlight:

Displaying Multiple Items with the **print** Function

If you refer to Program 6-7, you will see that we used the following two statements in lines 3 and 4:

```
print('I am staying in room number')
print(room)
```

We called the print function twice because we needed to display two pieces of data. Line 3 displays the string literal 'I am staying in room number', and line 4 displays the value referenced by the room variable.

This program can be simplified, however, because Python allows us to display multiple items with one call to the print function. We simply have to separate the items with commas as shown in Program 6-9.

On Your Own: How would you do it? Alone or with a partner, see if you can write a program that displays the same information without calling the print function twice. When you are ready, compare your work to Program 6-9.

Program 6-9   (variable_demo3.py)

```
1  # This program demonstrates a variable.
2  room = 503
3  print('I am staying in room number', room)
```

Program Output

```
I am staying in room number 503
```

In line 3, we passed two arguments to the print function. The first argument is the string literal 'I am staying in room number', and the second argument is the room variable. When the print function executed, it displayed the values of the two arguments in the order that we passed them to the function. Notice the print function automatically printed a space separating the two items. When multiple arguments are passed to the print function, they are automatically separated by a space when they are displayed on the screen.

Variable Reassignment

Variables are called "variable" because they can reference different values while a program is running. When you assign a value to a variable, the variable will reference that value until you assign it a different value. For example, look at Program 6-10. The statement in line 3 creates a variable named `dollars` and assigns it the value 2.75. This is shown in the top part of Figure 6-4. Then, the statement in line 8 assigns a different value, 99.95, to the `dollars` variable. The bottom part of Figure 6-4 shows how this changes the `dollars` variable. The old value, 2.75, is still in the computer's memory, but it can no longer be used because it isn't referenced by a variable. When a value in memory is no longer referenced by a variable, the Python interpreter automatically removes it from memory through a process known as **garbage collection**.

Program 6-10   `(variable_demo4.py)`

```
1   # This program demonstrates variable reassignment.
2   # Assign a value to the dollars variable.
3   dollars = 2.75
4   print('I have', dollars, 'in my account.')
5
6   # Reassign dollars so it references
7   # a different value.
8   dollars = 99.95
9   print('But now I have', dollars, 'in my account!')
```

Program Output

```
I have 2.75 in my account.
But now I have 99.95 in my account!
```

Figure 6-4   Variable reassignment in Program 2-10

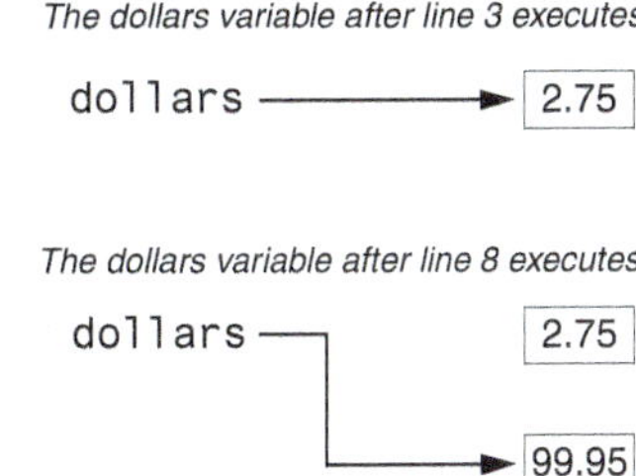

Numeric Data Types and Literals

Because different types of numbers are stored and manipulated in different ways, Python uses **data types** to categorize values in memory. You must choose, identify, and use the appropriate data type when you write program solutions. When an integer is stored in memory, it is classified as an `int`, and when a **real number** (a number with a fractional part) is stored in memory, it is classified as a `float`.

Let's look at how Python determines the data type of a number. Several of the programs that you have seen so far have numeric data written into their code. For example, the following statement, which appears in Program 6-9, has the number 503 written into it:

```
room = 503
```

This statement causes the value 503 to be stored in memory, and it makes the `room` variable reference it. The following statement, which appears in Program 6-10, has the number 2.75 written into it:

```
dollars = 2.75
```

This statement causes the value 2.75 to be stored in memory, and it makes the `dollars` variable reference it. A number that is written into a program's code is called a **numeric literal**. When the Python interpreter reads a numeric literal in a program's code, it determines its data type according to the following rules:

- A numeric literal that is written as a whole number with no decimal point is considered an `int`. Examples are 7, 124, and −9.
- A numeric literal that is written with a decimal point is considered a `float`. Examples are 1.5, 3.14159, and 5.0.

So, the following statement causes the number 503 to be stored in memory as an `int`:

```
room = 503
```

And the following statement causes the number 2.75 to be stored in memory as a `float`:

```
dollars = 2.75
```

When you store an item in memory, it is important for you to be aware of the item's data type. As you will see, some operations behave differently depending on the type of data involved, and some operations can only be performed on values of a specific data type.

As an experiment, you can use the built-in `type` function in interactive mode to determine the data type of a value. For example, look at the following session:

```
>>> type(1) Enter
<class 'int'>
>>>
```

In this example, the value 1 is passed as an argument to the `type` function. The message that is displayed on the next line, `<class 'int'>`, indicates that the value is an `int`. Here is another example:

```
>>> type(1.0) Enter
<class 'float'>
>>>
```

In this example, the value 1.0 is passed as an argument to the `type` function. The message that is displayed on the next line, `<class 'float'>`, indicates that the value is a `float`.

WARNING! You cannot write currency symbols, spaces, or commas in numeric literals. For example, the following statement will cause an error:

```
value = $4,567.99
```

This statement must be written as:

```
value = 4567.99
```

Storing Strings with the `str` Data Type

In addition to the `int` and `float` data types, Python also has a data type named `str`, which is used for storing strings in memory. The code in Program 6-11 shows how strings can be assigned to variables.

Program 6-11   (`string_variable.py`)

```
1  # Create variables to reference two strings.
2  first_name = 'Kathryn'
3  last_name = 'Marino'
4
5  # Display the values referenced by the variables.
6  print(first_name, last_name)
```

Program Output

```
Kathryn Marino
```

Reassigning a Variable to a Different Type

Keep in mind that in Python, a variable is just a name that refers to a piece of data in memory. It is a mechanism that makes it easy for you, the programmer, to store and retrieve data. Internally, the Python interpreter keeps track of the variable names that you create and the pieces of data to which those variable names refer. Any time you need to retrieve one of those pieces of data, you simply use the variable name that refers to it.

A variable in Python can refer to items of any type. After a variable has been assigned an item of one type, it can be reassigned an item of a different type. To demonstrate, look at the following interactive session. (We have added line numbers for easier reference.)

```
1  >>> x = 99 Enter
2  >>> print(x) Enter
3  99
4  >>> x = 'Take me to your leader' Enter
5  >>> print(x) Enter
6  Take me to your leader
7  >>>
```

The statement in line 1 creates a variable named x and assigns it the `int` value 99. Figure 6-5 shows how the variable x references the value 99 in memory. The statement in line 2 calls the `print` function, passing x as an argument. The output of the `print` function is shown in line 3. Then, the statement in line 4 assigns a string to the x variable. After this statement executes, the x variable no longer refers to an `int`, but to the string `'Take me to your leader'`. This is shown in Figure 6-6. Line 5 calls the `print` function again, passing x as an argument. Line 6 shows the `print` function's output.

Figure 6-5 The variable x references an integer

x ⟶ | 99 |

Figure 6-6 The variable **x** references a string

 **Checkpoint**

6.10 What is a variable?

6.11 Which of the following are illegal variable names in Python, and why?

```
x
99bottles
july2009
theSalesFigureForFiscalYear
r&d
grade_report
```

6.12 Is the variable name `Sales` the same as `sales`? Why or why not?

6.13 Is the following assignment statement valid or invalid? If it is invalid, why?

```
72 = amount
```

6.14 What will the following code display?

```
val = 99
print('The value is', 'val')
```

6.15 Look at the following assignment statements:

```
value1 = 99
value2 = 45.9
value3 = 7.0
value4 = 7
value5 = 'abc'
```

After these statements execute, what is the Python data type of the values referenced by each variable?

6.16 What will be displayed by the following program?

```
my_value = 99
my_value = 0
print(my_value)
```

6.5 Reading Input from the Keyboard

Use Python functions to have a program read input typed by the user on the keyboard.

VideoNote
Reading Input
from the
Keyboard

Most of the programs that you will write will need to read input and then perform an operation on that input. In this section, we will discuss a basic input operation: reading data that has been typed on the keyboard. When a program reads data from the keyboard, usually it stores that data in a variable so it can be used later by the program.

We will use Python's built-in input function to read input from the keyboard. The input function reads a piece of data that has been entered at the keyboard and returns that piece of data, as a string, back to the program. You normally use the input function in an assignment statement that follows this general format:

 variable = input(*prompt*)

In the general format, *prompt* is a string that is displayed on the screen. The string's purpose is to instruct the user to enter a value; *variable* is the name of a variable that references the data that was entered on the keyboard. Here is an example of a statement that uses the input function to read data from the keyboard:

 name = input('What is your name? ')

When this statement executes, the following things happen:

- The string 'What is your name? ' is displayed on the screen.
- The program pauses and waits for the user to type something on the keyboard and then to press the Enter key.
- When the Enter key is pressed, the data that was typed is returned as a string and assigned to the name variable.

To demonstrate, look at the following interactive session:

```
>>> name = input('What is your name? ') Enter
What is your name?  Holly   Enter
>>> print(name) Enter
Holly
>>>
```

When the first statement was entered, the interpreter displayed the prompt 'What is your name?' and waited for the user to enter some data. The user entered **Holly** and pressed the Enter key. As a result, the string 'Holly' was assigned to the name variable. When the second statement was entered, the interpreter displayed the value referenced by the name variable.

Program 6-12 shows a complete program that uses the input function to read two strings as input from the keyboard.

Program 6-12 **(string_input.py)**

```
1  # Get the user's first name.
2  first_name = input('Enter your first name: ')
3
4  # Get the user's last name.
5  last_name = input('Enter your last name: ')
6
7  # Print a greeting to the user.
8  print('Hello', first_name, last_name)
```

Program Output (with input shown in bold)
```
Enter your first name: Vinny Enter
Enter your last name: Brown Enter
Hello Vinny Brown
```

Take a closer look in line 2 at the string we used as a prompt:

```
'Enter your first name: '
```

Notice the last character in the string, inside the quote marks, is a space. The same is true for the following string, used as a prompt in line 5:

```
'Enter your last name: '
```

We put a space character at the end of each string because the input function does not automatically display a space after the prompt. When the user begins typing characters, they appear on the screen immediately after the prompt. Making the last character in the prompt a space visually separates the prompt from the user's input on the screen.

Reading Numbers with the `input` Function

The input function always returns the user's input as a string, even if the user enters numeric data. For example, suppose you call the input function, type the number 72, and press the Enter key. The value that is returned from the input function is the string '72'. This can be a problem if you want to use the value in a math operation. Math operations can be performed only on numeric values, not strings.

Fortunately, Python has built-in functions that you can use to convert a string to a numeric type. Table 6-2 summarizes two of these functions.

Table 6-2 Data conversion functions

Function	Description
int(*item*)	You pass an argument to the int() function and it returns the argument's value converted to an int.
float(*item*)	You pass an argument to the float() function and it returns the argument's value converted to a float.

For example, suppose you are writing a payroll program and you want to get the number of hours that the user has worked. Look at the following code:

```
string_value = input('How many hours did you work? ')
hours = int(string_value)
```

The first statement gets the number of hours from the user and assigns that value as a string to the string_value variable. The second statement calls the int() function, passing string_value as an argument. The value referenced by string_value is converted to an int and assigned to the hours variable.

This example illustrates how the int() function works, but it is inefficient because it creates two variables: one to hold the string that is returned from the input function, and another to hold the integer that is returned from the int() function. The following code shows a better approach. This one statement does all the work that the previously shown statements do, and it creates only one variable:

```
hours = int(input('How many hours did you work? '))
```

This one statement uses **nested function** calls. The value that is returned from the input function is passed as an argument to the int() function. This is how it works:

- It calls the input function to get a value entered at the keyboard.
- The value that is returned from the input function (a string) is passed as an argument to the int() function.
- The int value that is returned from the int() function is assigned to the hours variable.

After this statement executes, the hours variable is assigned the value entered at the keyboard, converted to an int.

Let's look at another example. Suppose you want to get the user's hourly pay rate. The following statement prompts the user to enter that value at the keyboard, converts the value to a float, and assigns it to the pay_rate variable:

```
pay_rate = float(input('What is your hourly pay rate? '))
```

This is how it works:

- It calls the input function to get a value entered at the keyboard.
- The value that is returned from the input function (a string) is passed as an argument to the float() function.
- The float value that is returned from the float() function is assigned to the pay_rate variable.

After this statement executes, the pay_rate variable is assigned the value entered at the keyboard, converted to a float.

Program 6-13 shows a complete program that uses the input function to read a string, an int, and a float, as input from the keyboard.

Program 6-13   (input.py)

```
 1  # Get the user's name, age, and income.
 2  name = input('What is your name? ')
 3  age = int(input('What is your age? '))
 4  income = float(input('What is your income? '))
 5
 6  # Display the data.
 7  print('Here is the data you entered:')
 8  print('Name:', name)
 9  print('Age:', age)
10  print('Income:', income)
```

Program Output (with input shown in bold)
```
What is your name? Chris [Enter]
What is your age? 25 [Enter]
What is your income? 75000.0
Here is the data you entered:
Name: Chris
Age: 25
Income: 75000.0
```

Let's take a closer look at the code:

- Line 2 prompts the user to enter their name. The value that is entered is assigned, as a string, to the `name` variable.
- Line 3 prompts the user to enter their age. The value that is entered is converted to an `int` and assigned to the `age` variable.
- Line 4 prompts the user to enter their income. The value that is entered is converted to a `float` and assigned to the `income` variable.
- Lines 7 through 10 display the values that the user entered.

The `int()` and `float()` functions work only if the item that is being converted contains a valid numeric value. If the argument cannot be converted to the specified data type, an error known as an exception occurs. An **exception** is an unexpected error that occurs while a program is running, causing the program to halt if the error is not properly dealt with. For example, look at the following interactive mode session:

```
>>> age = int(input('What is your age? ')) Enter
What is your age?  xyz  Enter
Traceback (most recent call last):
    File "<pyshell#81>", line 1, in <module>
        age = int(input('What is your age? '))
ValueError: invalid literal for int() with base 10: 'xyz'
>>>
```

NOTE: In this section, we mentioned the user. The *user* is simply any hypothetical person that is using a program and providing input for it. The user is sometimes called the *end user*.

Checkpoint

6.17 You need the user of a program to enter a customer's last name. Write a statement that prompts the user to enter this data and assigns the input to a variable.

6.18 You need the user of a program to enter the amount of sales for the week. Write a statement that prompts the user to enter this data and assigns the input to a variable.

6.6) String Concatenation

  **String concatenation is the appending of one string to the end of another.**

A common operation that is performed on strings is **concatenation**, which means to append one string to the end of another string. In Python, we use the + operator to concatenate strings. The + operator produces a string that is the combination of the two strings used as its operands. The following interactive session shows an example:

```
>>> message = 'Hello ' + 'world' (Enter)
>>> print(message) (Enter)
Hello world
>>>
```

The first statement combines the strings 'Hello ' and 'world' to produce the string 'Hello world'. The string 'Hello world' is then assigned to the message variable. The second statement displays the string.

Program 6-14 further demonstrates string concatenation.

Program 6-14   **(concatenation.py)**

```
1  # This program demonstrates string concatenation.
2  first_name = input('Enter your first name: ')
3  last_name = input('Enter your last name: ')
4
5  # Combine the names with a space between them.
6  full_name = first_name + ' ' + last_name
7
8  # Display the user's full name.
9  print('Your full name is ' + full_name)
```

Program Output (with input shown in bold)

```
Enter your first name: Alex (Enter)
Enter your last name: Morgan (Enter)
Your full name is Alex Morgan
```

Let's take a closer look at the program. Lines 2 and 3 prompt the user to enter his or her first and last names. The user's first name is assigned to the first_name variable and the user's last name is assigned to the last_name variable.

Line 6 assigns the result of a string concatenation to the full_name variable. The string that is assigned to the full_name variable begins with the value of the first_name variable, followed by a space (' '), followed by the value of the last_name variable. In the example program output, the user entered *Alex* for the first name and *Morgan* for the last name. As a result, the string 'Alex Morgan' was assigned to the full_name variable. The statement in line 9 displays the value of the full_name variable.

String concatenation can be useful for breaking up a string literal so a lengthy call to the `print` function can span multiple lines. Here is an example:

```
print('Enter the amount of ' +
      'sales for each day and ' +
      'press Enter.')
```

This statement will display the following:

```
Enter the amount of sales for each day and press Enter.
```

Implicit String Literal Concatenation

When two or more string literals are written adjacent to each other, separated only by spaces, tabs, or newline characters, Python will implicitly concatenate them into a single string. For example, look at the following interactive session:

```
>>> my_str = 'one' 'two' 'three'
>>> print(my_str)
onetwothree
```

In the first line, the string literals `'one'`, `'two'`, and `'three'` are separated only by a space. As a result, Python concatenates them into the single string `'onetwothree'`. The string is then assigned to the `my_str` variable.

Implicit string literal concatenation is commonly used to break up long string literals across multiple lines. Here is an example:

```
print('Enter the amount of '
      'sales for each day and '
      'press Enter.')
```

This statement will display the following:

```
Enter the amount of sales for each day and press Enter.
```

 ## Checkpoint

6.19 Explain string concatenation and give an example of how you would use it to represent text data.

6.20 After the follow statement executes, what value will be assigned to the `result` variable?

```
result = '1' + '2'
```

6.21 After the follow statement executes, what value will be assigned to the `result` variable?

```
result = 'h' 'e' 'l' 'l' 'o'
```

6.7 More About the `print` Function

  **Learning to use the print function will give you more control over how output displays.**

So far, we have discussed only basic ways to display data. Eventually, you will want to exercise more control over the way data appear on the screen. In this section, you will learn more details about the Python `print` function, and you'll see techniques for formatting output in specific ways.

Suppressing the `print` Function's Ending Newline

The `print` function normally displays a line of output. For example, the following three statements will produce three lines of output:

```
print('One')
print('Two')
print('Three')
```

Each of the statements shown here displays a string and then prints a **newline character**. You do not see the newline character, but when it is displayed, it causes the output to advance to the next line. (You can think of the newline character as a special command that causes the computer to start a new line of output.)

If you do not want the `print` function to start a new line of output when it finishes displaying its output, you can pass the special argument end=' ' to the function, as shown in the following code:

```
print('One', end=' ')
print('Two', end=' ')
print('Three')
```

Notice in the first two statements, the argument end=' ' is passed to the `print` function. This specifies that the `print` function should print a space instead of a newline character at the end of its output. Here is the output of these statements:

```
One Two Three
```

Sometimes, you might not want the `print` function to print anything at the end of its output, not even a space. If that is the case, you can pass the argument end='' to the `print` function, as shown in the following code:

```
print('One', end='')
print('Two', end='')
print('Three')
```

Notice in the argument end='' there is no space between the quote marks. This specifies that the `print` function should print nothing at the end of its output. Here is the output of these statements:

```
OneTwoThree
```

Specifying an Item Separator

When multiple arguments are passed to the `print` function, they are automatically separated by a space when they are displayed on the screen. Here is an example, demonstrated in interactive mode:

```
>>> print('One', 'Two', 'Three') Enter
One Two Three
>>>
```

If you do not want a space printed between the items, you can pass the argument `sep=''` to the `print` function, as shown here:

```
>>> print('One', 'Two', 'Three', sep='') Enter
OneTwoThree
>>>
```

You can also use this special argument to specify a character other than the space to separate multiple items. Here is an example:

```
>>> print('One', 'Two', 'Three', sep='*') Enter
One*Two*Three
>>>
```

Notice in this example, we passed the argument `sep='*'` to the `print` function. This specifies that the printed items should be separated with the * character. Here is another example:

```
>>> print('One', 'Two', 'Three', sep='~~~') Enter
One~~~Two~~~Three
>>>
```

Escape Characters

An **escape character** is a special character that is preceded with a backslash (\), appearing inside a string literal. When a string literal that contains escape characters is printed, the escape characters are treated as special commands that are embedded in the string.

For example, \n is the newline escape character. When the \n escape character is printed, it isn't displayed on the screen. Instead, it causes output to advance to the next line. For example, look at the following statement:

```
print('One\nTwo\nThree')
```

When this statement executes, it displays

```
One
Two
Three
```

Python recognizes several escape characters, some of which are listed in Table 6-3.

Table 6-3 Some of Python's escape characters

Escape Character	Effect
\n	Causes output to be advanced to the next line.
\t	Causes output to skip over to the next horizontal tab position.
\'	Causes a single quote mark to be printed.
\"	Causes a double quote mark to be printed.
\\	Causes a backslash character to be printed.

The \t escape character advances the output to the next horizontal tab position. (A tab position normally appears after every eighth character.) The following statements are illustrative:

```
print('Mon\tTues\tWed')
print('Thur\tFri\tSat')
```

This statement prints Monday, then advances the output to the next tab position, then prints Tuesday, then advances the output to the next tab position, then prints Wednesday. The output will look like this:

```
Mon     Tues    Wed
Thur    Fri     Sat
```

You can use the \' and \" escape characters to display quotation marks. The following statements are illustrative:

```
print("Your assignment is to read \"Hamlet\" by tomorrow.")
print('I\'m ready to begin.')
```

These statements display the following:

```
Your assignment is to read "Hamlet" by tomorrow.
I'm ready to begin.
```

You can use the \\ escape character to display a backslash, as shown in the following:

```
print('The path is C:\\temp\\data.')
```

This statement will display

```
The path is C:\temp\data.
```

Checkpoint

6.22 How do you suppress the print function's ending newline?

6.23 How can you change the character that is automatically displayed between multiple items that are passed to the print function?

6.24 What is the '\n' escape character?

6.8 Displaying Formatted Output with F-strings

KEY POINT F-strings are a special type of string literal that allow you to format values in a variety of ways.

> NOTE: F-strings were introduced in Python 3.6. If you are using an earlier version of Python, consider using the `format` function instead. See Appendix F for more information.

F-strings, or **formatted string literals**, give you an easy way to format the output that you want to display with the `print` function. With an f-string, you can create messages that contain the contents of variables, and you can format numbers in a variety of ways.

An f-string is a string literal that is enclosed in quotation marks and prefixed with the letter `f`. Here is a very simple example of an f-string:

```
f'Hello world'
```

This looks like an ordinary string literal, except that it is prefixed with the letter `f`. If we want to display an f-string, we pass it to the `print` function as shown in the following interactive session:

```
>>> print(f'Hello world') Enter
Hello world
```

F-strings are much more powerful than regular string literals, however. An f-string can contain placeholders for variables and other expressions. An **expression** is a statement that represents a value or calls a procedure. For example, look at the following interactive session:

```
>>> name = 'Johnny' Enter
>>> print(f'Hello {name}.') Enter
Hello Johnny.
```

In the first statement, we assign `'Johnny'` to the `name` variable. Then, in the second statement, we pass an f-string to the `print` function. Inside the f-string, `{name}` is a placeholder for the `name` variable. When the statement is executed, the placeholder is replaced with the value of the `name` variable. As a result, the statement prints *Hello Johnny*.

Here is another example:

```
>>> temperature = 45 Enter
>>> print(f'It is currently {temperature} degrees.') Enter
It is currently 45 degrees.
```

In the first statement, we assign the value 45 to the `temperature` variable. In the second statement, we pass an f-string to the `print` function. Inside the f-string, `{temperature}` is a placeholder for the `temperature` variable. When the statement is executed, the placeholder is replaced with the value of the `temperature` variable.

Placeholder Expressions

In the previous f-string examples, we used placeholders to display the values of variables. In addition to variable names, placeholders can contain any valid expression. Here is an example:

```
>>> print(f'The value is {10 + 2}.') Enter
The value is 12.
```

In this example, {10 + 2} is the placeholder. When the statement is executed, the placeholder is replaced with the value of the expression 10 + 2. Here is an example:

```
>>> val = 10 Enter
>>> print(f'The value is {val + 2}.') Enter
The value is 12.
```

In the first statement, we assign the value 10 to the val variable. In the second statement, we pass an f-string to the print function. Inside the f-string, {val + 2} is the placeholder. When the statement is executed, the placeholder is replaced with the value of the expression val + 2.

It is important to understand that in the previous example, the val variable is not changed. The expression val + 2 simply gives us the value 12. It does not change the value of the val variable in any way.

Formatting Values

Placeholders in an f-string can include a **format specifier** that causes the placeholder's value to be formatted when it is displayed. For example, with a format specifier, you can round values to a specified number of decimal places and display numbers with comma separators. You can also left-, right-, or center-align values with a format specifier. In fact, you can use format specifiers to control many of the ways that values are displayed.

Here is the general format for writing a placeholder with a format specifier:

```
{placeholder:format-specifier}
```

Notice that in the general format, the placeholder and the format specifier are separated by a colon. Let's look at a few specific ways to use format specifiers.

Rounding Floating-Point Numbers

You might not always be happy with the way that floating-point numbers are displayed on the screen. When a floating-point number is displayed by the print function, it can appear with up to 17 significant digits. This is shown in the output of Program 6-15.

Program 6-15   (f_string_no_formatting.py)

```
1  # This program demonstrates how a floating-point
2  # number is displayed with no formatting.
3  amount_due = 5000.0
4  monthly_payment = amount_due / 12.0
5  print(f'The monthly payment is {monthly_payment}.')
```

Program Output *(continued)*
```
The monthly payment is 416.6666666666667.
```

Because this program displays a dollar amount, it would be nice to see that amount rounded to two decimal places. We can accomplish that with the following format specifier:

```
.2f
```

In the format specifier, .2 is a *precision designator* that indicates the number should be rounded to two decimal places. The letter f is a *type designator*, and it indicates that the value should be displayed with a fixed number of digits after the decimal point. When we add this format specifier to the f-string placeholder in line 5, it will appear as:

```
{monthly_payment:.2f}
```

This will cause the value of the monthly_payment variable to appear as 416.67 in the program's output. Program 6-16 demonstrates this.

Program 6-16   (f_string_rounding.py)

```
1   # This program demonstrates how a floating-point
2   # number can be rounded.
3   amount_due = 5000.0
4   monthly_payment = amount_due / 12.0
5   print(f'The monthly payment is {monthly_payment:.2f}.')
```

Program Output
```
The monthly payment is 416.67.
```

The following interactive session demonstrates how to round a number 3 decimal places:

```
>> pi = 3.1415926535  Enter
>> print(f'{pi:.3f}')  Enter
3.142
>>>
```

The following interactive session demonstrates how to round the value of a placeholder expression to 1 decimal point:

```
>> a = 2  Enter
>> b = 3  Enter
>> print(f'{a / b:.1f}')  Enter
0.7
>>>
```

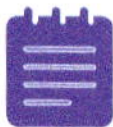

> **NOTE:** The fixed-point type designator may be written in either lowercase (f) or uppercase (F).

Inserting Comma Separators

It's easier for the human eye to read large numbers if they are displayed with comma separators. You can use a format specifier to insert comma separators into a number, as shown in the following interactive session:

```
>>> number = 1234567890.12345 [Enter]
>>> print(f'{number:,}') [Enter]
1,234,567,890.12345
>>>
```

Here is an example of how we can combine format specifiers to simultaneously round a number and insert comma separators:

```
>>> number = 1234567890.12345 [Enter]
>>> print(f'{number:,.2f}') [Enter]
1,234,567,890.12
>>>
```

In the format specifier, the comma must be written before (to the left of) the precision designator. Otherwise an error will occur when the code executes.

Program 6-17 demonstrates how the comma separator and a precision of two decimal places can be used to format a number as a currency amount.

Program 6-17   (dollar_display.py)

```
1  # This program demonstrates how a floating-point
2  # number can be displayed as currency.
3  monthly_pay = 5000.0
4  annual_pay = monthly_pay * 12
5  print(f'Your annual pay is ${annual_pay:,.2f}')
```

Program Output

```
Your annual pay is $60,000.00
```

Formatting a Floating-Point Number as a Percentage

Instead of using f as the type designator, you can use the % symbol to format a floating-point number as a percentage. The % symbol causes the number to be multiplied by 100 and displayed with a % sign following it. Here is an example:

```
>>> discount = 0.5
>>> print(f'{discount:%}') [Enter]
50.000000%
>>>
```

Here is an example that rounds the output value to 0 decimal places:

```
>>> discount = 0.5
>>> print(f'{discount:.0%}') [Enter]
50%
>>>
```

Formatting in Scientific Notation

If you prefer to display floating-point numbers in scientific notation, you can use the letter e or the letter E instead of f. Here are some examples:

```
>>> number = 12345.6789
>>> print(f'{number:e}')  (Enter)
1.234568e+04
>>> print(f'{number:.2e}')  (Enter)
1.23e+04
>>>
```

The first statement simply formats the number in scientific notation. The number is displayed with the letter e indicating the exponent. (If you use uppercase E in the format specifier, the result will contain an uppercase E indicating the exponent.) The second statement additionally specifies a precision of two decimal places.

Formatting Integers

All the previous examples demonstrated how to format floating-point numbers. You can also use an f-string to format integers. There are two differences to keep in mind when writing a format specifier that will be used to format an integer:

• When you need to use a type designator, use d or D. This indicates that the value should be displayed as a decimal integer.

• You do not use a precision designator.

Let's look at some examples in the interactive interpreter. In the following session, the number 123456 is printed with no special formatting:

```
>>> number = 123456
>>> print(f'{number:d}')  (Enter)
123456
>>>
```

In the following session, the number 123456 is printed with a comma separator:

```
>>> number = 123456
>>> print(f'{number:,d}')  (Enter)
123,456
>>>
```

Specifying a Minimum Field Width

The format specifier can also include a minimum field width, which is the minimum number of spaces that should be used to display the value. The following example displays an integer in a field that is 10 spaces wide:

```
>>> number = 99
>>> print(f'The number is {number:10}')  (Enter)
The number is         99
>>>
```

In this example, the 10 that appears as the format specifier is a *field width designator*. It indicates that the value should be displayed in a field that is a minimum of 10 spaces wide. In this case, the length of the value that is displayed is less than the field width. The number 99 uses only 2 spaces on the screen, but it is displayed in a field that is 10 spaces wide. When this is the case, the number is right justified in the field, as illustrated in Figure 6-7.

Figure 6-7 Field width of displayed item

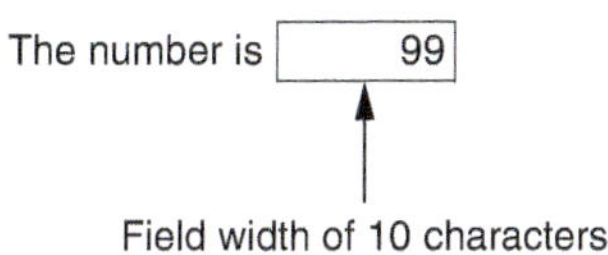

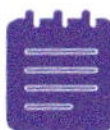
NOTE: If a value is too large to fit in the specified field width, the field width is automatically enlarged to accommodate it.

The following example displays a floating-point value rounded to 2 decimal places, with comma separators, in a field that is 12 spaces wide:

```
>>> number = 12345.6789
>>> print(f'The number is {number:12,.2f}') Enter
The number is    12,345.68
>>>
```

Note that the field width designator is written before (to the left of) the comma separator. Otherwise an error will occur when the code executes. Here is an example that specifies field width and precision, but does not use comma separators:

```
>>> number = 12345.6789
>>> print(f'The number is {number:12.2f}) Enter
The number is    12345.68
>>>
```

Field widths can help when you need to display values aligned in columns. For example, look at Program 6-18. The variables are displayed in two columns that are 10 spaces wide.

Program 6-18   (columns.py)

```
1  # This program displays the following numbers
2  # in two columns.
3  num1 = 127.899
4  num2 = 3465.148
5  num3 = 3.776
6  num4 = 264.821
7  num5 = 88.081
8  num6 = 799.999
```

Program 6-18   *(continued)*

```
 9
10   # Each number is displayed in a field of 10 spaces
11   # and rounded to 2 decimal places.
12   print(f'{num1:10.2f}{num2:10.2f}')
13   print(f'{num3:10.2f}{num4:10.2f}')
14   print(f'{num5:10.2f}{num6:10.2f}')
```

Program Output

```
    127.90    3465.15
      3.78     264.82
     88.08     800.00
```

Aligning Values

When a value is displayed in a field that is wider than the value, the value must be aligned to the right, left, or center of the field. By default, numbers are aligned to the right, as shown in the following interactive session:

```
>>> number = 22
>>> print(f'The number is {number:10}')  Enter
The number is         22
>>>
```

In this example, the number 22 is aligned to the right of a field that is 10 spaces wide. Strings, by default, are aligned to the left as shown in the following interactive session:

```
>>> name = 'Jay'
>>> print(f'Hello {name:10}. Nice to meet you.')  Enter
Hello Jay       . Nice to meet you.
>>>
```

In this example, the string 'Jay' is aligned to the left of a field that is 10 spaces wide. If you want to change the default alignment for a value, you can use one of the **alignment designators** shown in Table 6-4 in the format specifier.

Assume the number variable references an integer. The following f-string left-aligns the variable's value in a field of 10 characters:

```
f'{number}'
```

Assume the total variable references floating-point value. The following f-string right-aligns the variable's value in a field of 20 characters and rounds the value to 2 decimal points:

```
f'{total:>20.2f}'
```

Program 6-19 shows an example of center-aligning strings. The program displays six strings, all center-aligned in a field that is 20 characters wide.

Table 6-4 Alignment Designators

Alignment Designator	Meaning
<	Left-aligns the value
>	Right-aligns the value
^	Center-aligns the value

Program 6-19   `(center_align.py)`

```
 1   # This program demonstrates how to center-align strings.
 2   name1 = 'Gordon'
 3   name2 = 'Smith'
 4   name3 = 'Washington'
 5   name4 = 'Alvarado'
 6   name5 = 'Livingston'
 7   name6 = 'Jones'
 8

 9   # Display the names.
10   print(f'***{name1:^20}***')
11   print(f'***{name2:^20}***')
12   print(f'***{name3:^20}***')
13   print(f'***{name4:^20}***')
14   print(f'***{name5:^20}***')
15   print(f'***{name6:^20}***')
```

Program Output
```
***        Gordon        ***
***        Smith         ***
***      Washington      ***
***       Alvarado       ***
***      Livingston      ***
***         Jones        ***
```

The Order of Designators

When using multiple designators in a format specifier, it's important to write the designators in the proper order, which is:

```
[alignment][width][,][.precision][type]
```

If you get the designators out of order, an error will occur. For example, assume the `number` variable references floating-point value. The following statement displays the variable's value center-aligned in a field of 10 characters, inserts comma separators, and rounds the value to 2 decimal points:

```
print(f'{number:^10,.2f}')
```

However, the following statement will cause an error because the designators are not in the correct order:

```
print(f'{number:10^,.2f}')    # Error
```

Concatenation with F-strings

When you concatenate two or more f-strings, the result will also be an f-string. For example, look at the following interactive session:

```
1  >>> name = 'Abbie Lloyd'
2  >>> department = 'Sales'
3  >>> position = 'Manager'
4  >>> print(f'Employee Name: {name}, ' +
5             f'Department: {department}, ' +
6             f'Position: {position}')
7  Employee Name: Abbie Lloyd, Department: Sales, Position: Manager
8  >>>
```

In lines 4, 5, and 6, we concatenate three f-strings and the result is passed as an argument to the `print` function. Notice that each of the strings that we are concatenating has the `f` prefix. If you leave out the `f` prefix on any of the string literals that you are concatenating, those strings will be treated as regular strings, not f-strings. For example, look at the following, which is a continuation of the previous interactive session:

```
 9  >>> print(f'Employee Name: {name}, ' +
10             'Department: {department}, ' +
11             'Position: {position}')
12 Employee Name: Abbie Lloyd, Department: {department}, Position:
   {position}
13 >>>
```

In this example, the string literals in lines 10 and 11 do not have the `f` prefix, so they are treated as regular strings. As a result, the placeholders that appear in those lines do not function as placeholders. Instead, they are simply printed on the screen as regular text.

You can use implicit concatenation with f-strings, as shown here:

```
print(f'Name: {name}, '
      f'Department: {department}, '
      f'Position: {position}')
```

Checkpoint

6.25 What will the following code display?
```
name = 'Karlie'
print('Hello {name}')
```

6.26 What will the following code display?
```
name = 'Karlie'
print(f'Hello {name}')
```

6.27 What will the following code display?
```
value = 99
print(f'The value is {value + 1}')
```

6.28 What will the following code display?

```
value = 65.4321
print(f'The value is {value:.2f}')
```

6.29 What will the following code display?

```
value = 987654.129
print(f'The value is {value:,.2f}')
```

6.30 What will the following code display?

```
value = 9876543210
print(f'The value is {value:,d}')
```

6.31 In the following statement, what is the purpose of the number 10 in the format specifier?

```
print(f'{name:10}')
```

6.32 In the following statement, what is the purpose of the number 15 in the format specifier?

```
print(f'{number:15,d}')
```

6.33 In the following statement, what is the purpose of the number 8 in the format specifier?

```
print(f'{number:8,.2f}')
```

6.34 In the following statement, what is the purpose of the < character in the format specifier?

```
print(f'{number:<12d}')
```

6.35 In the following statement, what is the purpose of the > character in the format specifier?

```
print(f'{number:>12d}')
```

6.36 In the following statement, what is the purpose of the ^ character in the format specifier?

```
print(f'{number:^12d}')
```

6.9 Named Constants

KEY POINT: A named constant is a name that represents a special value, such as a magic number.

Imagine, for a moment, that you are a programmer working for a bank. You are updating an existing program that calculates data pertaining to loans, and you see the following line of code:

```
amount = balance * 0.069
```

Because someone else wrote the program, you aren't sure what the number 0.069 is. It appears to be an interest rate, but it could be a number that is used to calculate some sort of fee. You simply can't determine the purpose of the number 0.069 by reading this line of code. This is an example of a magic number. A **magic number** is an unexplained value that appears in a program's code.

Magic numbers can be problematic for a number of reasons. First, as illustrated in our example, it can be difficult for someone reading the code to determine the purpose of the number. Second, if the magic number is used in multiple places in the program, it can take painstaking effort to change the number in each location, should the need arise. Third, you take the risk of making a typographical mistake each time you type the magic number in the program's code. For example, suppose you intend to type 0.069, but you accidentally type .0069. This mistake will cause mathematical errors that can be difficult to find.

These problems can be addressed by using named constants to represent magic numbers. A **named constant** is a name that represents a special value. The following is an example of how we will declare named constants in our code:

```
INTEREST_RATE = 0.069
```

This creates a named constant named INTEREST_RATE that is assigned the value 0.069. Notice the named constant is written in all uppercase letters. This is a standard practice in most programming languages because it makes named constants easily distinguishable from regular variables.

One advantage of using named constants is that they make programs more self-explanatory. The following statement:

```
amount = balance * 0.069
```

can be changed to read:

```
amount = balance * INTEREST_RATE
```

A new programmer can read the second statement and know what is happening. It is evident that balance is being multiplied by the interest rate.

Another advantage to using named constants is that widespread changes can easily be made to the program. Let's say the interest rate appears in a dozen different statements throughout the program. When the rate changes, the initialization value in the declaration of the named constant is the only value that needs to be modified. If the rate increases to 7.2 percent, the declaration can be changed to:

```
INTEREST_RATE = 0.072
```

The new value of 0.072 will then be used in each statement that uses the INTEREST_RATE constant.

Another advantage to using named constants is that they help to prevent the typographical errors that are common when using magic numbers. For example, if you accidentally type .0069 instead of 0.069 in a math statement, the program will calculate the wrong value. However, if you misspell INTEREST_RATE, the Python interpreter will display a message indicating that the name is not defined.

 **Checkpoint**

6.37 What are three advantages of using named constants?

6.38 Write a Python statement that defines a named constant for a 10 percent discount.

? Chapter Review

Multiple Choice

1. A __________ is a sequence of characters.
   a. char sequence
   b. character collection
   c. string
   d. text block

2. A __________ is a name that references a value in the computer's memory.
   a. variable
   b. register
   c. RAM slot
   d. byte

3. A __________ is any hypothetical person using a program and providing input for it.
   a. designer
   b. user
   c. guinea pig
   d. test subject

4. A string literal in Python must be enclosed in __________.
   a. parentheses.
   b. single-quotes.
   c. double-quotes.
   d. either single-quotes or double-quotes.

5. Short notes placed in different parts of a program explaining how those parts of the program work are called __________.
   a. comments
   b. reference manuals
   c. tutorials
   d. external documentation

6. A(n) __________ makes a variable reference a value in the computer's memory.
   a. variable declaration
   b. assignment statement
   c. math expression
   d. string literal

7. This symbol marks the beginning of a comment in Python.
   a. &
   b. *
   c. **
   d. #

8. By default, numbers displayed in a field are aligned to the ___________.
   - a. left
   - b. right
   - c. center
   - d. top

9. A magic number is ___________________.
   - a. a number that is mathematically undefined
   - b. an unexplained value that appears in a program's code
   - c. a number that cannot be divided by 1
   - d. a number that causes computers to crash

10. A ___________ is a name that represents a value that does not change during the program's execution.
   - a. named literal
   - b. named constant
   - c. variable signature
   - d. key term

True or False

1. An end-line comment appears at the end of the last line in a program.
2. A string that appears in the actual code of a program is called a string literal.
3. Variable names can have spaces in them.
4. In Python, the first character of a variable name cannot be a number.
5. If you print a variable that has not been assigned a value, the number 0 will be displayed.

Short Answer

1. What does `float` classify?
2. What is the data type str used for?
3. Computer programs typically perform what three steps?
4. What is a magic number? Why are magic numbers problematic?
5. Assume a program uses the named constant `PI` to represent the value 3.14159. The program uses the named constant in several statements. What is the advantage of using the named constant instead of the actual value 3.14159 in each statement?

Algorithm Workbench

1. Using proper programming style for spacing, write Python code including comments that prompts the user to enter their height, assigns the user's input to a variable named `height`, and then properly outputs the user's height. Make sure to choose, identify and use the appropriate data type, such as integer, real, or float.

2. Using proper programming style for spacing, write Python code including comments that prompts the user to enter their favorite color, assigns the user's input to a variable named `color`, and then properly outputs the color.

3. What will the following statement display?
```
print('George', 'John', 'Paul', 'Ringo', sep='@')
```

Programming Exercises

1. Write a program that creates and properly labels and displays each of the following text data as output on a separate line:

   Your name

   Your favorite food

   Your favorite animal

2. Modify the program you wrote in Programming Exercise 1 to concatenate the output into one line. Manipulate the text to separate each item of information with a backslash character.

3. Assemble a team of at least three people. Decide who will be the lead programmer and what roles the other team members will play. As a team, choose a computer science career and then write a program that will display the career title, three job responsibilities, and at least one requirement or skill needed for the career. Present your program to the class or another team. Ask your peers to evaluate your work and provide feedback on the quality and accuracy. Evaluate and provide feedback on another team's work. Meet with your team and discuss the feedback you received, and how you could improve the quality and accuracy of your work.

4. Working alone or with a partner, brainstorm a program that would require comments, user input, at least one variable, string concatenation, and at least one named constant. Be sure to choose, identify, and use the appropriate data types, such as integer, real, or float. Write the program. It should display output using standard formatting styles on the screen. Ask another team to evaluate your work and provide feedback on the quality and accuracy. Evaluate and provide feedback on another team's work. Use the feedback you received to improve your program.

7 Math Calculations and Boolean Logic

TOPICS

7.1 Performing Calculations
7.2 Using Math Libraries
7.3 Using Boolean Logic

7.1 Performing Calculations

KEY POINT **Python has numerous operators that can be used to perform mathematical calculations.**

Most real-world algorithms require calculations to be performed. A programmer's tools for performing calculations are **math operators**. Table 7-1 lists the math operators that are provided by the Python language.

Programmers use the operators shown in Table 7-1 to create math expressions. A **math expression** performs a calculation and gives a value. The following is an example of a simple math expression:

```
12 + 2
```

Table 7-1 Python math operators

Symbol	Operation	Description
+	Addition	Adds two numbers
−	Subtraction	Subtracts one number from another
*	Multiplication	Multiplies one number by another
/	Division	Divides one number by another and gives the result as a floating-point number
/ /	Integer division	Divides one number by another and gives the result as a whole number
%	Remainder	Divides one number by another and gives the remainder
* *	Exponent	Raises a number to a power

The values on the right and left of the + operator are called **operands**. These are values that the + operator adds together. If you type this expression in interactive mode, you will see that it gives the value 14:

```
>>> 12 + 2 [Enter]
14
>>>
```

Variables may also be used in a math expression. For example, suppose we have two variables named hours and pay_rate. The following math expression uses the * operator to multiply the value referenced by the hours variable by the value referenced by the pay_rate variable:

```
hours * pay_rate
```

When we use a math expression to calculate a value, normally we want to save that value in memory so we can use it again in the program. We do this with an assignment statement. Program 7-1 shows an example.

Program 7-1   (simple_math.py)

```
 1  # Assign a value to the salary variable.
 2  salary = 2500.0
 3
 4  # Assign a value to the bonus variable.
 5  bonus = 1200.0
 6
 7  # Calculate the total pay by adding salary
 8  # and bonus. Assign the result to pay.
 9  pay = salary + bonus
10
11  # Display the pay.
12  print('Your pay is', pay)
```

Program Output

```
Your pay is 3700.0
```

Line 2 assigns 2500.0 to the salary variable, and line 5 assigns 1200.0 to the bonus variable. Line 9 assigns the result of the expression salary + bonus to the pay variable. As you can see from the program output, the pay variable holds the value 3700.0.

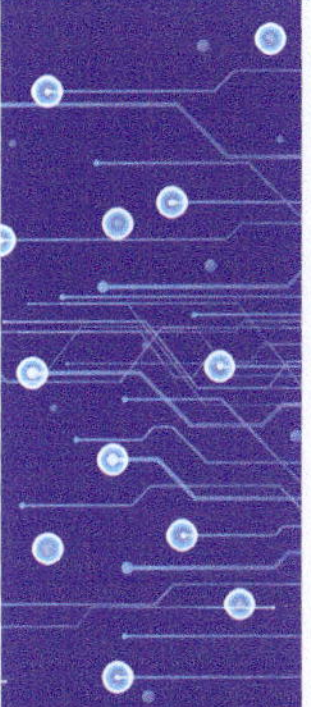

In the Spotlight:

Calculating a Percentage

If you are writing a program that works with a percentage, you have to make sure that the percentage's decimal point is in the correct location before doing any math with the percentage. This is especially true when the user enters a percentage as input. Most users enter the number 50 to mean 50 percent, 20 to mean 20 percent, and so forth. Before you perform any calculations with such a percentage, you have to divide it by 100 to move its decimal point two places to the left.

Let's step through the process of writing a program that calculates a percentage. Suppose a retail business is planning to have a storewide sale where the prices of all items will be 20 percent off. We have been asked to write a program to calculate the sale price of an item after the discount is subtracted. Here is the algorithm:

1. *Get the original price of the item.*
2. *Calculate 20 percent of the original price. This is the amount of the discount.*
3. *Subtract the discount from the original price. This is the sale price.*
4. *Display the sale price.*

In step 1, we get the original price of the item. We will prompt the user to enter this data on the keyboard. In our program, we will use the following statement to do this. Notice the value entered by the user will be stored in a variable named `original_price`.

```
original_price = float(input("Enter the item's original price: "))
```

In step 2, we calculate the amount of the discount. To do this, we multiply the original price by 20 percent. The following statement performs this calculation and assigns the result to the `discount` variable:

```
discount = original_price * 0.2
```

In step 3, we subtract the discount from the original price. The following statement does this calculation and stores the result in the `sale_price` variable:

```
sale_price = original_price - discount
```

Last, in step 4, we will use the following statement to display the sale price:

```
print('The sale price is', sale_price)
```

Program 7-2 shows the entire program, with example output.

Program 7-2   **(sale_price.py)**

```
1  # This program gets an item's original price and
2  # calculates its sale price, with a 20% discount.
3
4  # Get the item's original price.
5  original_price = float(input("Enter the item's original price: "))
6
7  # Calculate the amount of the discount.
```

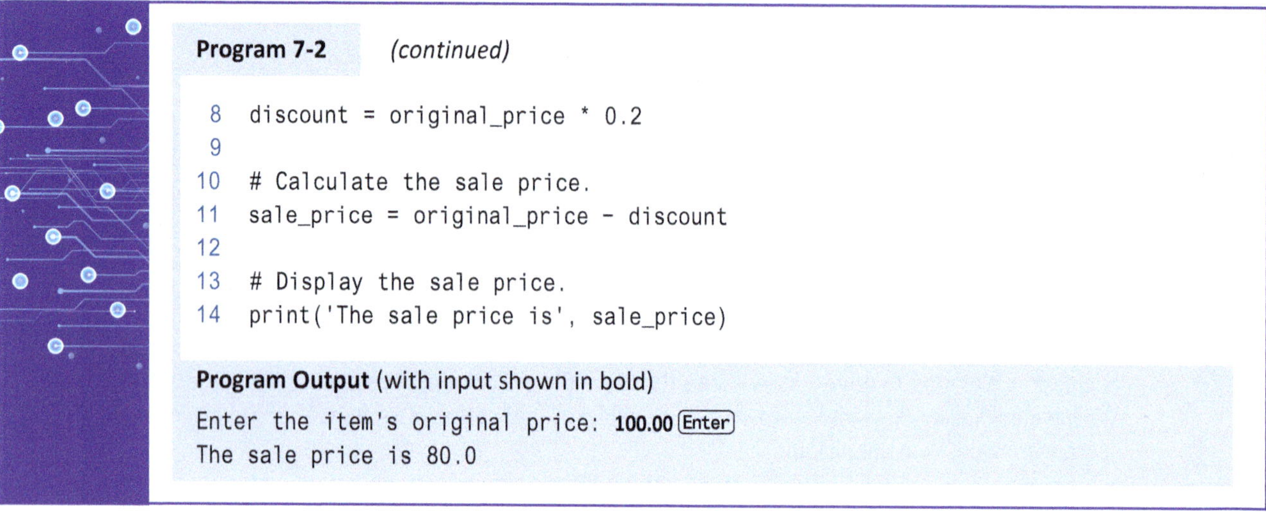


```
 8   discount = original_price * 0.2
 9
10   # Calculate the sale price.
11   sale_price = original_price - discount
12
13   # Display the sale price.
14   print('The sale price is', sale_price)
```

Program Output (with input shown in bold)

```
Enter the item's original price: 100.00 (Enter)
The sale price is 80.0
```

Floating-Point and Integer Division

Notice in Table 7-1 that Python has two different division operators. The / operator performs floating-point division, and the // operator performs integer division. Both operators divide one number by another. The difference between them is that the / operator gives the result as a floating-point value, and the // operator gives the result as a whole number. Let's use the interactive mode interpreter to demonstrate:

```
>>> 5 / 2 (Enter)
2.5
>>>
```

Using the / operator to divide 5 by 2 the result is 2.5. When you use the // operator to perform integer division, as shown here, the result is 2:

```
>>> 5 // 2 (Enter)
2
>>>
```

That's because when the result is positive, it is **truncated**, which means that its fractional part is thrown away. When the result is negative, however, it is rounded away from zero to the nearest integer:

```
>>> -5 // 2 (Enter)
-3
>>>
```

Some numeric data types have finite limits, which means they can only store numbers that fall within a specific range. For example, when a calculation results in an integer that is too large or too small to store, **wrap around**, or overflow, occurs. The stored value becomes a very small or even a negative number. Integer wrap around is used on purpose for applications such as clocks, that loop or wrap from the highest value to the smallest. When not intentional, it can be a security risk.

Operator Precedence

You can write statements that use complex mathematical expressions involving several operators. The following statement assigns the sum of 17, the variable x, 21, and the variable y to the variable answer:

```
answer = 17 + x + 21 + y
```

Some expressions are not that straightforward, however. Consider the following statement:

```
outcome = 12.0 + 6.0 / 3.0
```

What value will be assigned to `outcome`? The number 6.0 might be used as an operand for either the addition or division operator. The `outcome` variable could be assigned either 6.0 or 14.0, depending on when the division takes place. Fortunately, the answer can be predicted because Python follows the same order of operations that you learned in math class.

First, operations that are enclosed in parentheses are performed first. Then, when two operators share an operand, the operator with the higher **precedence** is applied first. The precedence of the math operators, from highest to lowest, are:

1. Exponentiation: `**`
2. Multiplication, division, and remainder: `*  /  //  %`
3. Addition and subtraction: `+ −`

Notice the multiplication (`*`), floating-point division (`/`), integer division (`//`), and remainder (`%`) operators have the same precedence. The addition (`+`) and subtraction (`−`) operators also have the same precedence. When two operators with the same precedence share an operand, the operators execute from left to right.

Now, let's go back to the previous math expression:

```
outcome = 12.0 + 6.0 / 3.0
```

The value that will be assigned to `outcome` is 14.0 because the division operator has a higher precedence than the addition operator. As a result, the division takes place before the addition. The expression can be diagrammed as shown in Figure 7-1.

Figure 7-1 Operator precedence

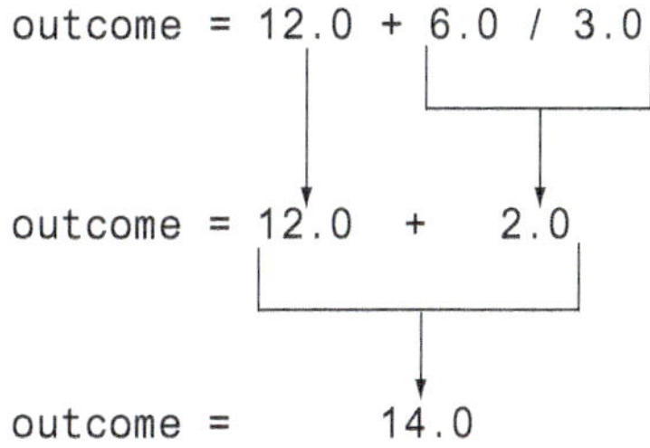

NOTE: There is an exception to the left-to-right rule. When two `**` operators share an operand, the operators execute right-to-left. For example, the expression `2**3**4` is evaluated as `2**(3**4)`.

Table 7-2 shows some other sample expressions with their values.

Table 7-2 Some expressions

Expression	Value
5 + 2 * 4	13
10 / 2 - 3	2.0
8 + 12 * 2 - 4	28
6 - 3 * 2 + 7 - 1	6

Grouping with Parentheses

Parts of a mathematical expression may be grouped with parentheses to force some operations to be performed before others. In the following statement, the variables a and b are added together, and their sum is divided by 4:

```
result = (a + b) / 4
```

Without the parentheses, however, b would be divided by 4 and the result added to a. Table 7-3 shows more expressions and their values.

Table 7-3 More expressions and their values

Expression	Value
(5 + 2) * 4	28
10 / (5 - 3)	5.0
8 + 12 * (6 - 2)	56
(6 - 3) * (2 + 7) / 3	9.0

In the Spotlight:
Calculating an Average

Determining the average of a group of values is a simple calculation: add all of the values, then divide the sum by the number of values. Although this is a straightforward calculation, it is easy to make a mistake when writing a program that calculates an average. For example, let's assume that the variables a, b, and c each hold a value and we want to calculate the average of those values. If we are careless, we might write a statement such as the following to perform the calculation:

```
average = a + b + c / 3.0
```

Can you see the error in this statement? When it executes, the division will take place first. The value in c will be divided by 3, then the result will be added to a + b. That is not the correct way

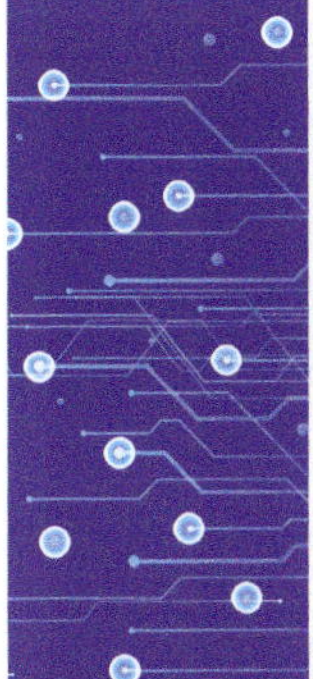

to calculate an average. To correct this error, we need to put parentheses around a + b + c, as shown here:

```
average = (a + b + c) / 3.0
```

Let's step through the process of writing a program that calculates an average. Suppose you have taken three tests in your computer science class, and you want to write a program that will display the average of the test scores. Here is the algorithm:

1. *Get the first test score.*
2. *Get the second test score.*
3. *Get the third test score.*
4. *Calculate the average by adding the three test scores and dividing the sum by 3.*
5. *Display the average.*

In steps 1, 2, and 3, we will prompt the user to enter the three test scores. We will store those test scores in the variables test1, test2, and test3. In step 4, we will calculate the average of the three test scores. We will use the following statement to perform the calculation and store the result in the average variable:

```
average = (test1 + test2 + test3) / 3.0
```

Last, in step 5, we display the average. Program 7-3 shows the program.

Program 7-3   **(test_score_average.py)**

```
 1  # Get three test scores and assign them to the
 2  # test1, test2, and test3 variables.
 3  test1 = float(input('Enter the first test score: '))
 4  test2 = float(input('Enter the second test score: '))
 5  test3 = float(input('Enter the third test score: '))
 6
 7  # Calculate the average of the three scores
 8  # and assign the result to the average variable.
 9  average = (test1 + test2 + test3) / 3.0
10
11  # Display the average.
12  print('The average score is', average)
```

Program Output (with input shown in bold)
```
Enter the first test score: 90 [Enter]
Enter the second test score: 80 [Enter]
Enter the third test score: 100 [Enter]

The average score is 90.0
```

The Exponent Operator

Two asterisks written together (`**`) is the exponent operator, and its purpose is to raise a number to a power. For example, you can use the exponent operator to square a number. To square a number is to multiply the number by itself. For example, to square the value of 4, you could use the following mathematical expression:

```
4 * 4 = 16
```

Raising a number by the power of 2 accomplishes the same thing.

```
4^2 = 16
```

The following statement squares the value of 4 and assigns it to the `area` variable:

```
area = 4**2
```

In addition to using the exponent operator to square numbers, you can use it to raise numbers to any power.

Practice using the exponent operator by typing the following code to show the values of the expressions `4**2`, `5**3`, and `2**10`:

```
>>> 4**2 [Enter]
16
>>> 5**3 [Enter]
125
>>> 2**10 [Enter]
1024
>>>
```

The Remainder Operator

In Python, the `%` symbol is the **remainder operator**. (This is also known as the **modulus operator**.) The remainder operator performs division, but instead of returning the quotient, it returns the remainder. The following statement assigns 2 to `leftover`:

```
leftover = 17 % 3
```

This statement assigns 2 to leftover because 17 divided by 3 is 5 with a remainder of 2. The remainder operator is useful in certain situations. It is commonly used in calculations that convert times or distances, detect odd or even numbers, and perform other specialized operations. For example, Program 7-4 gets a number of seconds from the user, and it converts that number of seconds to hours, minutes, and seconds. For example, it would convert 11,730 seconds to 3 hours, 15 minutes, and 30 seconds.

Program 7-4   (`time_converter.py`)

```python
 1  # Get a number of seconds from the user.
 2  total_seconds = float(input('Enter a number of seconds: '))
 3
 4  # Get the number of hours.
 5  hours = total_seconds // 3600
 6
 7  # Get the number of remaining minutes.
 8  minutes = (total_seconds // 60) % 60
 9
10  # Get the number of remaining seconds.
11  seconds = total_seconds % 60
12
13  # Display the results.
14  print('Here is the time in hours, minutes, and seconds:')
15  print('Hours:', hours)
16  print('Minutes:', minutes)
17  print('Seconds:', seconds)
```

Program Output (with input shown in bold)

```
Enter a number of seconds: 11730 Enter
Here is the time in hours, minutes, and seconds:
Hours: 3.0
Minutes: 15.0
Seconds: 30.0
```

Let's take a closer look at the code:

- Line 2 gets a number of seconds from the user, converts the value to a `float`, and assigns it to the `total_seconds` variable.

- Line 5 calculates the number of hours in the specified number of seconds. There are 3600 seconds in an hour, so this statement divides `total_seconds` by 3600. Notice we used the integer division operator (`//`) operator. This is because we want the number of hours with no fractional part.

- Line 8 calculates the number of remaining minutes. This statement first uses the `//` operator to divide `total_seconds` by 60. This gives us the total number of minutes. Then, it uses the `%` operator to divide the total number of minutes by 60 and get the remainder of the division. The result is the number of remaining minutes.

- Line 11 calculates the number of remaining seconds. There are 60 seconds in a minute, so this statement uses the `%` operator to divide the `total_seconds` by 60 and get the remainder of the division. The result is the number of remaining seconds.

- Lines 14 through 17 display the number of hours, minutes, and seconds.

Converting Math Formulas to Programming Statements

Recall from algebra class that the expression $2xy$ is understood to mean 2 times x times y. In math, you do not always use an operator for multiplication. Python, as well as other programming languages, requires an operator for any mathematical operation. Table 7-4 shows some algebraic expressions that perform multiplication and the equivalent programming expressions.

Table 7-4 Algebraic expressions

Algebraic Expression	Operation Being Performed	Programming Expression
$6B$	6 times B	6 * B
$(3)(12)$	3 times 12	3 * 12
$4xy$	4 times x times y	4 * x * y

When converting some algebraic expressions to programming expressions, you may have to insert parentheses that do not appear in the algebraic expression. For example, look at the following formula:

$$x = \frac{a + b}{c}$$

To convert this to a programming statement, $a + b$ will have to be enclosed in parentheses:

```
x = (a + b)/c
```

Table 7-5 shows additional algebraic expressions and their Python equivalents.

Table 7-5 Algebraic and programming expressions

Algebraic Expression	Python Statement
$y = 3\dfrac{x}{2}$	y = 3 * x / 2
$z = 3bc + 4$	z = 3 * b * c + 4
$a = \dfrac{x + 2}{b - 1}$	a = (x + 2) / (b - 1)

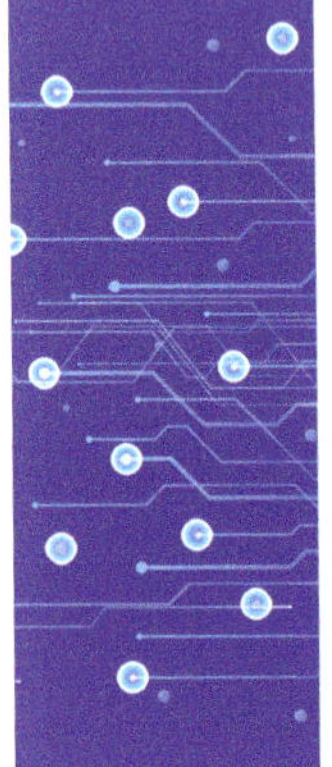

In the Spotlight:

Converting a Math Formula to a Programming Statement

Suppose you want to deposit a certain amount of money into a savings account and leave it alone to draw interest for the next 10 years. At the end of 10 years, you would like to have $10,000 in the account. How much do you need to deposit today to make that happen? You can use the following formula to find out:

$$P = \frac{F}{(1 + r)^n}$$

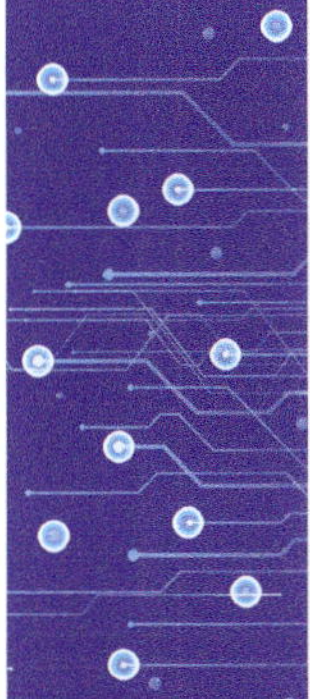

The terms in the formula are as follows:

- P is the present value, or the amount that you need to deposit today.
- F is the future value that you want in the account. (In this case, F is \$10,000.)
- r is the annual interest rate.
- n is the number of years that you plan to let the money sit in the account.

It would be convenient to write a computer program to perform the calculation because then we can experiment with different values for the variables. Here is an algorithm that we can use:

1. *Get the desired future value.*
2. *Get the annual interest rate.*
3. *Get the number of years that the money will sit in the account.*
4. *Calculate the amount that will have to be deposited.*
5. *Display the result of the calculation in step 4.*

In steps 1 through 3, we will prompt the user to enter the specified values. We will assign the desired future value to a variable named `future_value`, the annual interest rate to a variable named `rate`, and the number of years to a variable named `years`.

In step 4, we calculate the present value, which is the amount of money that we will have to deposit. We will convert the formula previously shown to the following statement. The statement stores the result of the calculation in the `present_value` variable.

```
present_value = future_value / (1.0 + rate)**years
```

In step 5, we display the value in the `present_value` variable. Program 7-5 shows the program.

Program 7-5   (`future_value.py`)

```
 1   # Get the desired future value.
 2   future_value = float(input('Enter the desired future value: '))
 3
 4   # Get the annual interest rate.
 5   rate = float(input('Enter the annual interest rate: '))
 6
 7   # Get the number of years that the money will appreciate.
 8   years = int(input('Enter the number of years the money will grow: '))
 9
10   # Calculate the amount needed to deposit.
11   present_value = future_value / (1.0 + rate)**years
12
13   # Display the amount needed to deposit.
14   print('You will need to deposit this amount:', present_value)
```

Program Output (with input shown in bold)
```
Enter the desired future value: 10000.0 [Enter]
Enter the annual interest rate: 0.05 [Enter]
Enter the number of years the money will grow: 10 [Enter]

You will need to deposit this amount: 6139.13253541
```

NOTE: Unlike the output shown for this program, dollar amounts are usually rounded to two decimal places. Later in this chapter, you will learn how to format numbers so they are rounded to a specified number of decimal places.

Mixed-Type Expressions and Data Type Conversion

When you perform a math operation on two operands, the data type of the result will depend on the data type of the operands. Python follows these rules when evaluating mathematical expressions:

- When an operation is performed on two `int` values, the result will be an `int`.
- When an operation is performed on two `float` values, the result will be a `float`.
- When an operation is performed on an `int` and a `float`, the `int` value will be temporarily converted to a `float` and the result of the operation will be a `float`. (An expression that uses operands of different data types is called a **mixed-type expression.**)

The first two situations are straightforward: operations on `int`s produce `int`s, and operations on `float`s produce `float`s. Let's look at an example of the third situation, which involves mixed-type expressions:

```
my_number = 5 * 2.0
```

When this statement executes, the value 5 will be converted to a `float` (5.0), then multiplied by 2.0. The result, 10.0, will be assigned to `my_number`.

The `int` to `float` conversion that takes place in the previous statement happens implicitly. If you need to explicitly perform a conversion, you can use either the `int()` or `float()` functions. For example, you can use the `int()` function to convert a floating-point value to an integer, as shown in the following code:

```
fvalue = 2.6
ivalue = int(fvalue)
```

The first statement assigns the value 2.6 to the `fvalue` variable. The second statement passes `fvalue` as an argument to the `int()` function. The `int()` function returns the value 2, which is assigned to the `ivalue` variable. After this code executes, the `fvalue` variable is still assigned the value 2.6, but the `ivalue` variable is assigned the value 2.

As demonstrated in the previous example, the `int()` function converts a floating-point argument to an integer by truncating it. As previously mentioned, that means it throws away the number's fractional part. Here is an example that uses a negative number:

```
fvalue = -2.9
ivalue = int(fvalue)
```

In the second statement, the value −2 is returned from the `int()` function. After this code executes, the `fvalue` variable references the value −2.9, and the `ivalue` variable references the value −2.

You can use the `float()` function to explicitly convert an `int` to a `float`, as shown in the following code:

```
ivalue = 2
fvalue = float(ivalue)
```

After this code executes, the `ivalue` variable references the integer value 2, and the `fvalue` variable references the floating-point value 2.0.

Breaking Long Statements into Multiple Lines

Most programming statements are written on one line. If a programming statement is too long, however, you will not be able to view all of it in your editor window without scrolling horizontally. In addition, if you print your program code on paper and one of the statements is too long to fit on one line, it will wrap around to the next line and make the code difficult to read.

Python allows you to break a statement into multiple lines by using the **line continuation character**, which is a backslash (\). You simply type the backslash character at the point you want to break the statement, then press the Enter key.

For example, here is a statement that performs a mathematical calculation and has been broken up to fit on two lines:

```
result = var1 * 2 + var2 * 3 + \
         var3 * 4 + var4 * 5
```

The line continuation character that appears at the end of the first line tells the interpreter that the statement is continued on the next line.

Python also allows you to break any part of a statement that is enclosed in parentheses into multiple lines without using the line continuation character. For example, look at the following statement:

```
print("Monday's sales are", monday,
      "and Tuesday's sales are", tuesday,
      "and Wednesday's sales are", wednesday)
```

The following code shows another example:

```
total = (value1 + value2 +
         value3 + value4 +
         value5 + value6)
```

 **Checkpoint**

7.1 Complete the following table by writing the value of each expression in the Value column:

Expression	Value
6 + 3 * 5	______
12 / 2 - 4	______
9 + 14 * 2 - 6	______
(6 + 2) * 3	______
14 / (11 - 4)	______
9 + 12 * (8 - 3)	______

7.2 What value will be assigned to `result` after the following statement executes?
```
result = 9 // 2
```

7.3 What value will be assigned to `result` after the following statement executes?
```
result = 9 % 2
```

7.2) Using math Libraries

 **The Python standard library's math module contains numerous functions that can be used in mathematical calculations.**

Python provides several built-in math functions. As an example, the abs() function can be used to determine the absolute value of a number. The abs() function accepts an argument and returns the absolute value of the argument. Here is an example of how it is used:

```
x = abs(-10)
print(x)
```

The above code segment calls the abs() function, passing the value of -10. The function returns the absolute value and prints **10** to the screen.

Using functions is a powerful way to provide functionality, reuse components, and modularize your code. You learn more about functions in chapter 16. Here, we will explore functions that specifically relate to performing math calculations.

In addition to the built-in functions such as abs(), there are many math libraries available in Python. A **library** is a collection of functions that have already been written and are available for your use. To use a specific library, you simply reference the name of that library using the import keyword. The following code, for example, references the math library.

```
import math
```

The math module in the Python standard library contains several functions that are useful for performing mathematical operations. Table 7-6 lists many of the functions in the math module. These functions typically accept one or more values as arguments, perform a mathematical operation using the arguments, and return the result. (All of the functions listed in Table 7-6 return a float value, except the ceil and floor functions, which return int values.) For example, one of the functions is named sqrt. The sqrt function accepts an argument and returns the square root of the argument. Here is an example of how it is used:

```
result = math.sqrt(16)
```

This statement calls the sqrt function, passing 16 as an argument. The function returns the square root of 16, which is then assigned to the result variable. Program 7-6 demonstrates the sqrt() function. Notice the import math statement in line 2. You need to write this in any program that uses the math module.

Program 7-6   (square_root.py)

```
1   # This program demonstrates the sqrt function.
2   import math
3
4   def main():
5       # Get a number.
6       number = float(input('Enter a number: '))
7
8       # Get the square root of the number.
```

Program 7-6   *(continued)*

```
 9        square_root = math.sqrt(number)
10
11        # Display the square root.
12        print(f'The square root of {number} is {square_root}.')
13
14   # Call the main function.
15   main()
```

Program Output (with input shown in bold)
```
Enter a number: 25 Enter
The square root of 25.0 is 5.0.
```

Program 7-7 shows another example that uses the `math` module. This program uses the `hypot` function to calculate the length of a right triangle's hypotenuse.

Program 7-7   (`hypotenuse.py`)

```
 1   # This program calculates the length of a right
 2   # triangle's hypotenuse.
 3   import math
 4
 5   def main():
 6       # Get the length of the triangle's two sides.
 7       a = float(input('Enter the length of side A: '))
 8       b = float(input('Enter the length of side B: '))
 9
10       # Calculate the length of the hypotenuse.
11       c = math.hypot(a, b)
12
13       # Display the length of the hypotenuse.
14       print(f'The length of the hypotenuse is {c}.')
15
16   # Call the main function.
17   main()
```

Program Output (with input shown in bold)
```
Enter the length of side A: 5.0 Enter
Enter the length of side B: 12.0 Enter
The length of the hypotenuse is 13.0.
```

Table 7-6 Many of the functions in the math module

math Module Function	Description
acos(x)	Returns the arc cosine of x, in radians
asin(x)	Returns the arc sine of x, in radians
atan(x)	Returns the arc tangent of x, in radians
ceil(x)	Returns the smallest integer that is greater than or equal to x
cos(x)	Returns the cosine of x in radians
degrees(x)	Assuming x is an angle in radians, the function returns the angle converted to degrees
exp(x)	Returns e^x
floor(x)	Returns the largest integer that is less than or equal to x
hypot(x, y)	Returns the length of a hypotenuse that extends from (0, 0) to (x, y)
log(x)	Returns the natural logarithm of x
log10(x)	Returns the base-10 logarithm of x
radians(x)	Assuming x is an angle in degrees, the function returns the angle converted to radians
sin(x)	Returns the sine of x in radians
sqrt(x)	Returns the square root of x
tan(x)	Returns the tangent of x in radians

The math.pi and math.e Values

The math module also defines two variables, pi and e, which are assigned mathematical values for *pi* and *e*. You can use these variables in equations that require their values. For example, the following statement, which calculates the area of a circle, uses pi. (Notice we use dot notation to refer to the variable.)

```
area = math.pi * radius**2
```

Checkpoint

7.4 What import statement do you need to write in a program that uses the math module?

7.5 Write a statement that uses a math module function to get the square root of 100 and assigns it to a variable.

7.6 Write a statement that uses a math module function to convert 45 degrees to radians and assigns the value to a variable.

7.3 Using Boolean Logic

VideoNote
The if
Statement

The if **statement is used to create a decision structure, which allows a program to have more than one path of execution. The** if **statement causes one or more statements to execute only when a Boolean expression is true.**

A **control structure** is a logical design that controls the order in which a set of statements execute. So far in this book, we have used only the simplest type of control structure: the sequence, or non-branching, structure. A **sequence structure** is a set of statements that execute in the order in which they appear. For example, the following code is a sequence structure because the statements execute from top to bottom:

```
name = input('What is your name? ')
age = int(input('What is your age? '))
print('Here is the data you entered:')
print('Name:', name)
print('Age:', age)
```

Although the sequence structure is heavily used in programming, it cannot handle every type of task. This is because some problems simply cannot be solved by performing a set of ordered steps, one after the other. For example, consider a pay-calculating program that determines whether an employee has worked overtime. If the employee has worked more than 40 hours, they get paid extra for all the hours over 40. Otherwise, the overtime calculation should be skipped. Programs like this require a different type of control structure: one that can execute a set of statements only under certain circumstances. This can be accomplished with a **decision structure**. (Decision structures are also known as branching or **selection structures**.)

In a decision structure's simplest form, a specific action is performed only if a certain **condition** exists. If the condition does not exist, the action is not performed. The flowchart shown in Figure 7-2 shows how the logic of an everyday decision can be diagrammed as a decision structure. The diamond symbol represents a true/false condition. If the condition is true, the flowchart branches to follow one path, which leads to an action being performed. If the condition is false, the flowchart branches to follow another path, which skips the action.

Figure 7-2 A simple decision structure

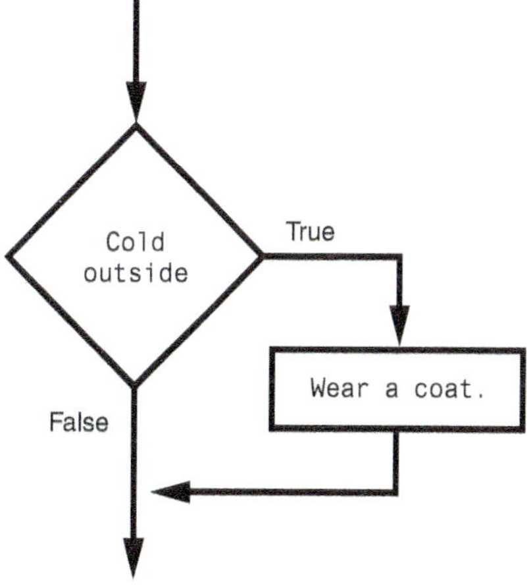

In the flowchart, the diamond symbol indicates some condition that must be tested. In this case, we are determining whether the condition `Cold outside` is true or false. If this condition is true, the action `Wear a coat` is performed. If the condition is false, the action is skipped. The action is **conditionally executed** because it is performed only when a certain condition is true.

Programmers call the type of decision structure shown in Figure 7-2 a **single alternative decision structure**. This is because it provides only one alternative path of execution. If the condition in the diamond symbol is true, we take the alternative path. Otherwise, we exit the structure. Figure 7-3 shows a more elaborate example, where three actions are taken only when it is cold outside. It is still a single alternative decision structure, because there is one alternative path of execution.

In Python, we use the **`if` statement** to write a single alternative decision structure. Here is the general format of the `if` statement:

```
if condition:
    statement
    statement
    etc.
```

Figure 7-3 A decision structure that performs three actions if it is cold outside

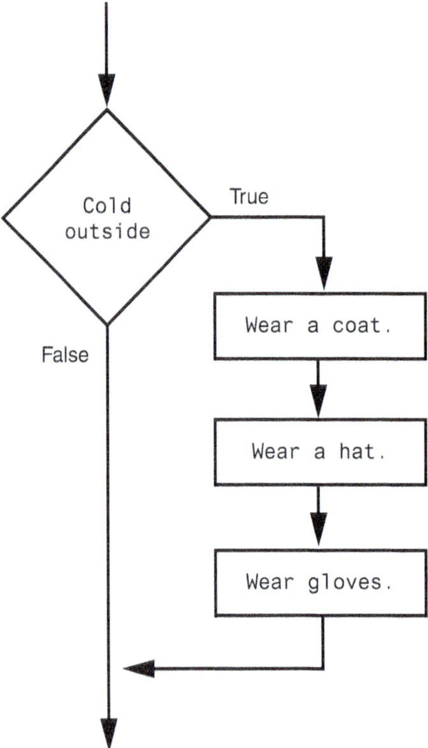

For simplicity, we will refer to the first line as the *if clause*. The if clause begins with the word if, followed by a *condition*, which is an expression that will be evaluated as either true or false. A colon appears after the *condition*. Beginning at the next line is a block of statements. A **block** is simply a set of statements that belong together as a group. Notice in the general format that all of the statements in the block are indented. This indentation is required because the Python interpreter uses it to tell where the block begins and ends.

When the if statement executes, the *condition* is tested. If the *condition* is true, the statements that appear in the block following the if clause are executed. If the condition is false, the statements in the block are skipped.

Boolean Expressions and Relational Operators

As previously mentioned, the if statement tests an expression to determine whether it is true or false. The expressions that are tested by the if statement are called **Boolean expressions**, named in honor of the English mathematician George Boole. In the 1800s, Boole invented a system of mathematics in which the abstract concepts of true and false can be used in computations.

Typically, the Boolean expression that is tested by an if statement is formed with a relational operator. A **relational operator** determines whether a specific relationship exists between two values. For example, the greater than operator (>) determines whether one value is greater than another. The equal to operator (==) determines whether two values are equal. Table 7-7 lists the relational operators that are available in Python.

Table 7-7 Relational operators

Operator	Meaning
>	Greater than
<	Less than
>=	Greater than or equal to
<=	Less than or equal to
==	Equal to
!=	Not equal to

The following is an example of an expression that uses the greater than (>) operator to compare two variables, length and width:

```
length > width
```

This expression determines whether the value referenced by length is greater than the value referenced by width. If length is greater than width, the value of the expression is true. Otherwise, the value of the expression is false. The following expression uses the less than operator to determine whether length is less than width:

```
length < width
```

Table 7-8 shows examples of several Boolean expressions that compare the variables x and y.

Table 7-8 Boolean expressions using relational operators

Expression	Meaning
x > y	Is x greater than y?
x < y	Is x less than y?
x >= y	Is x greater than or equal to y?
x <= y	Is x less than or equal to y?
x == y	Is x equal to y?
x != y	Is x not equal to y?

You can use the Python interpreter in interactive mode to experiment with these operators. If you type a Boolean expression at the >>> prompt, the interpreter will evaluate the expression and display its value in a Boolean data type as either `True` or `False`. For example, look at the following interactive session. (We have added line numbers for easier reference.)

```
1   >>> x = 1 (Enter)
2   >>> y = 0 (Enter)
3   >>> x > y (Enter)
4   True
5   >>> y > x (Enter)
6   False
7   >>>
```

The statement in line 1 assigns the value 1 to the variable x. The statement in line 2 assigns the value 0 to the variable y. In line 3, we type the Boolean expression x > y. The value of the expression (`True`) is displayed in line 4. Then, in line 5, we type the Boolean expression y > x. The value of the expression (`False`) is displayed in line 6.

The following interactive session demonstrates the < operator:

```
1   >>> x = 1 (Enter)
2   >>> y = 0 (Enter)
3   >>> y < x (Enter)
4   True
5   >>> x < y (Enter)
6   False
7   >>>
```

The statement in line 1 assigns the value 1 to the variable x. The statement in line 2 assigns the value 0 to the variable y. In line 3, we type the Boolean expression y < x. The value of the expression (`True`) is displayed in line 4. Then, in line 5, we type the Boolean expression x < y. The value of the expression (`False`) is displayed in line 6.

The >= and <= Operators

Two of the operators, >= and <=, test for more than one relationship. The >= operator determines whether the operand on its left is greater than *or* equal to the operand on its right. The <= operator determines whether the operand on its left is less than *or* equal to the operand on its right.

For example, look at the following interactive session:

```
1   >>> x = 1 (Enter)
2   >>> y = 0 (Enter)
3   >>> z = 1 (Enter)
4   >>> x >= y (Enter)
5   True
6   >>> x >= z (Enter)
7   True
8   >>> x <= z (Enter)
9   True
10  >>> x <= y (Enter)
11  False
12  >>>
```

In lines 1 through 3, we assign values to the variables x, y, and z. In line 4, we enter the Boolean expression x >= y, which is True. In line 6, we enter the Boolean expression x >= z, which is True. In line 8, we enter the Boolean expression x <= z, which is True. In line 10, we enter the Boolean expression x <= y, which is False.

The == Operator

The == operator determines whether the operand on its left is equal to the operand on its right. If the values referenced by both operands are the same, the expression is true. Assuming a is 4, the expression a == 4 is true, and the expression a == 2 is false.

The following interactive session demonstrates the == operator:

```
1   >>> x = 1 (Enter)
2   >>> y = 0 (Enter)
3   >>> z = 1 (Enter)
4   >>> x == y (Enter)
5   False
6   >>> x == z (Enter)
7   True
8   >>>
```

NOTE: The equality operator is two = symbols together. Don't confuse this operator with the assignment operator, which is one = symbol.

The != Operator

The != operator is the not-equal-to operator. It determines whether the operand on its left is not equal to the operand on its right, which is the opposite of the == operator. As before, assuming a is 4, b is 6, and c is 4, both a != b and b != c are true because a is not equal to b and b is not equal to c. However, a != c is false because a is equal to c.

The following interactive session demonstrates the != operator:

```
1   >>> x = 1 (Enter)
2   >>> y = 0 (Enter)
3   >>> z = 1 (Enter)
4   >>> x != y (Enter)
5   True
6   >>> x != z (Enter)
7   False
8   >>>
```

Putting It All Together

Let's look at the following example of the if statement:

```
if sales > 50000:
    bonus = 500.0
```

This statement uses the > operator to determine whether sales is greater than 50,000. If the expression sales > 50000 is true, the variable bonus is assigned 500.0. If the expression is false, however, the assignment statement is skipped. Figure 7-4 shows a flowchart for this section of code.

Figure 7-4 Example decision structure

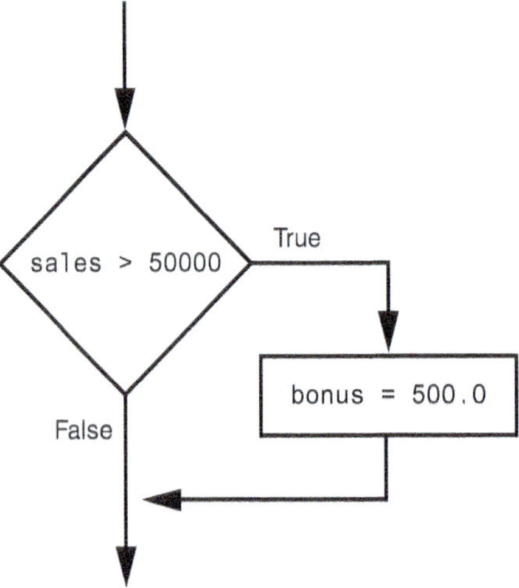

The following example conditionally executes a block containing three statements. Figure 7-5 shows a flowchart for this section of code:

```
if sales > 50000:
    bonus = 500.0
    commission_rate = 0.12
    print('You met your sales quota!')
```

Figure 7-5 Example decision structure for a block containing three statements

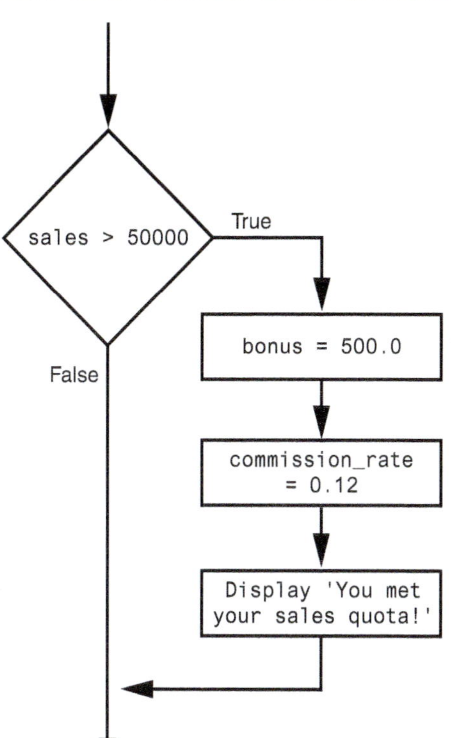

The following code uses the == operator to determine whether two values are equal. The expression balance == 0 will be true if the balance variable is assigned 0. Otherwise, the expression will be false.

```
if balance == 0:
    # Statements appearing here will
    # be executed only if balance is
    # equal to 0.
```

The following code uses the != operator to determine whether two values are *not* equal. The expression choice != 5 will be true if the choice variable does not reference the value 5. Otherwise, the expression will be false.

```
if choice != 5:
    # Statements appearing here will
    # be executed only if choice is
    # not equal to 5.
```

In the Spotlight:
Using the `if` Statement

Kathryn teaches a science class and her students are required to take three tests. She wants to write a program that her students can use to calculate their average test score. She also wants the program to congratulate the student enthusiastically if the average is greater than 95.

On Your Own: Before reading on, working alone or with a partner, see if you can write an algorithm and the code for Kathryn's program. Then, continue reading. Your work does not have to match the solution here, but the result should be the same.

Here is the algorithm in pseudocode:

1. Get the first test score.

2. Get the second test score.

3. Get the third test score.

4. Calculate the average.

5. Display the average.

6. If the average is greater than 95:
Congratulate the user.

Program 7-8 shows the code for the program.

Program 7-8   **(test_average.py)**

```
 1   # This program gets three test scores and displays
 2   # their average. It congratulates the user if the
 3   # average is a high score.
 4
 5   # The HIGH_SCORE named constant holds the value that is
 6   # considered a high score.
 7   HIGH_SCORE = 95
 8
 9   # Get the three test scores.
10   test1 = int(input('Enter the score for test 1: ' ))
11   test2 = int(input('Enter the score for test 2: ' ))
12   test3 = int(input('Enter the score for test 3: ' ))
13
14   # Calculate the average test score.
15   average = (test1 + test2 + test3) / 3
16
17   # Print the average.
18   print(f'The average score is {average}.')
19
20   # If the average is a high score,
21   # congratulate the user.
```

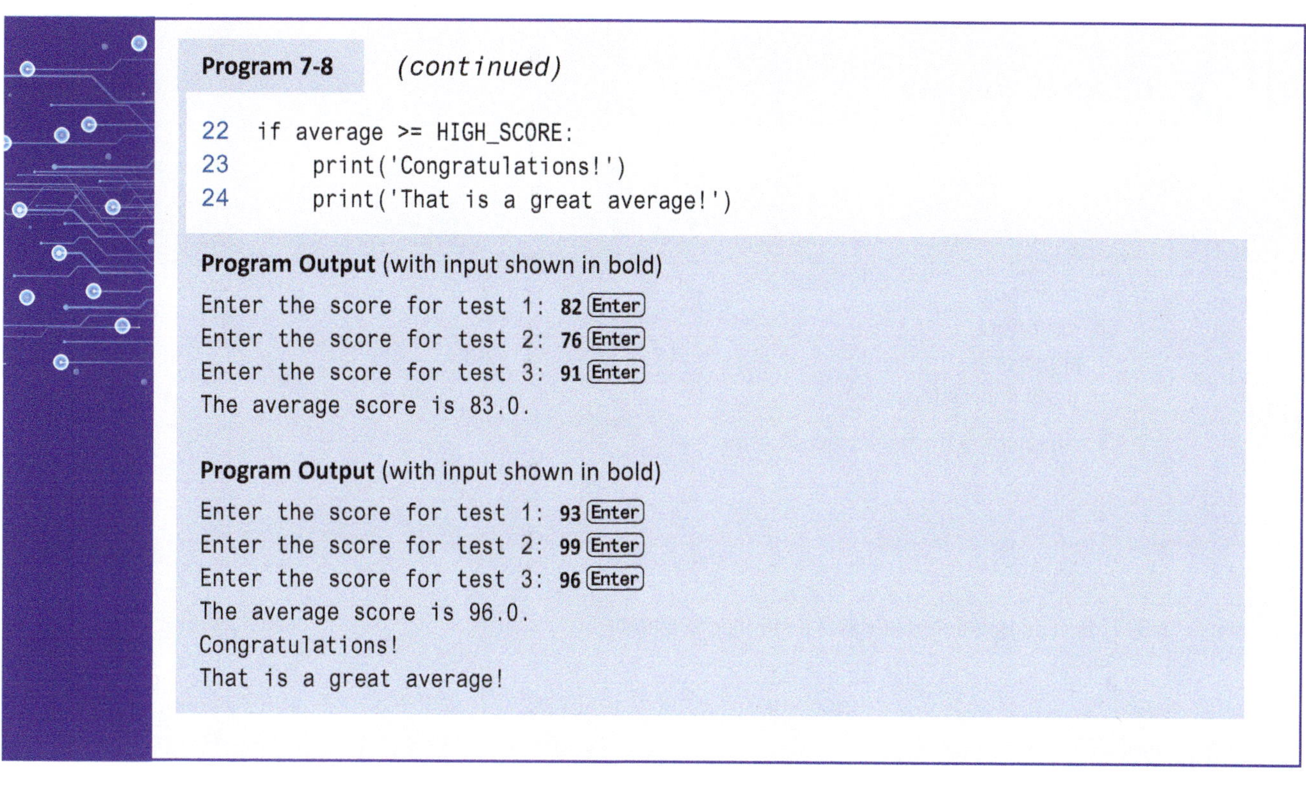

Program 7-8   *(continued)*

```
22  if average >= HIGH_SCORE:
23      print('Congratulations!')
24      print('That is a great average!')
```

Program Output (with input shown in bold)
```
Enter the score for test 1: 82 [Enter]
Enter the score for test 2: 76 [Enter]
Enter the score for test 3: 91 [Enter]
The average score is 83.0.
```

Program Output (with input shown in bold)
```
Enter the score for test 1: 93 [Enter]
Enter the score for test 2: 99 [Enter]
Enter the score for test 3: 96 [Enter]
The average score is 96.0.
Congratulations!
That is a great average!
```

 **Checkpoint**

7.7   What is a control structure?

7.8   What is a decision structure?

7.9   What is a single alternative decision structure?

7.10 What is a Boolean expression?

7.11 What values can be stored in a Boolean data type?

7.12 What types of relationships between values can you test with relational operators?

7.13 Write an `if` statement that assigns 0 to x if y is equal to 20.

7.14 Write an `if` statement that assigns 0.2 to `commissionRate` if `sales` is greater than or equal to 10000.

Chapter Review

Multiple Choice

1. In the expression 12 + 7, the values on the right and left of the + symbol are
   called ___________.
   a. operands
   b. operators
   c. arguments
   d. math expressions

2. This operator performs integer division.
   a. //
   b. %
   c. **
   d. /

3. This is an operator that raises a number to a power.
   a. %
   b. *
   c. **
   d. /

4. This operator performs division, but instead of returning the quotient, it returns the remainder.
   a. %
   b. *
   c. **
   d. /

5. Suppose the following statement is in a program: price = 99.0. After this statement
   executes, the price variable will reference a value of which data type?
   a. int
   b. float
   c. currency
   d. str

6. When using the // operator, when the result is positive, it is _____________.
   a. rounded up
   b. rounded down
   c. truncated
   d. hidden

7. What math module function returns the tangent of x in radians?
   a. tan(x)
   b. sine(x)
   c. log(x)
   d. sqrt(x)

True or False

1. In a math expression, multiplication and division take place before addition and subtraction.

2. Variables may not be used in a math expression.

3. Operations that are enclosed in parentheses are performed first.

4. The purpose of the exponent operator is to divide a number by 2.

5. The algebraic expression 8A is the same as the programming expression 8 * A.

Short Answer

1. Explain the difference between the / operator and the // operator.

2. Explain and demonstrate how to use a function to find the absolute value of a number.

3. Explain and demonstrate how to save a calculated value in memory so you can use it again in a program.

4. What is a mixed-typed expression?

5. Explain Boolean data type and demonstrate how to use a Boolean expression to determine if the value of y is greater than or equal to the value of x.

6. Explain the phrase finite limits of numeric data. Identify an example.

Algorithm Workbench

1. Write assignment statements that perform the following operations with the variables a, b, and c:
   a. Adds 2 to a and assigns the result to b
   b. Multiplies b times 4 and assigns the result to a
   c. Divides a by 3.14 and assigns the result to b
   d. Subtracts 8 from b and assigns the result to a

2. Assume the variables result, w, x, y, and z are all integers, and that w = 5, x = 4, y = 8, and z = 2. What value will be stored in result after each of the following statements execute?

   a. result = x + y
   b. result = z * 2
   c. result = y / x
   d. result = y − z
   e. result = w // z

3. Write a Python statement that assigns the sum of 10 and 14 to the variable total.

4. Write a Python statement that subtracts the variable down_payment from the variable total and assigns the result to the variable due.

5. Write a Python statement that multiplies the variable subtotal by 0.15 and assigns the result to the variable total.

6. What would the following display?

   num = 99
   num = 5
   print(num)

7. Assume the variable sales references a float value. Write a statement that displays the value rounded to two decimal points.

8. Assume the following statement has been executed:

   number = 1234567.456

   Write a Python statement that displays the value referenced by the number variable formatted as 1,234,567.5

Programming Exercises

1. Sales Prediction

A company has determined that its annual profit is typically 23 percent of total sales. Write a program that asks the user to enter the projected amount of total sales, then displays the profit that will be made from that amount.
Hint: Use the value 0.23 to represent 23 percent.

2. Land Calculation

One acre of land is equivalent to 43,560 square feet. Write a program that asks the user to enter the total square feet in a tract of land and calculates the number of acres in the tract.
Hint: Divide the amount entered by 43,560 to get the number of acres.

3. Total Purchase

A customer in a store is purchasing five items. Write a program that asks for the price of each
item, then displays the subtotal of the sale, the amount of sales tax, and the total.
Assume the sales tax is 7 percent.

4. Miles-per-Gallon

A car's miles-per-gallon (MPG) can be calculated with the following formula:

   MPG = Miles driven ÷ Gallons of gas used

Write a program that asks the user for the number of miles driven and the gallons of gas used. It
should calculate the car's MPG and display the result.

5. Tip, Tax, and Total

Write a program that calculates the total amount of a meal purchased at a restaurant. The
program should ask the user to enter the charge for the food, then calculate the amounts of
a 18 percent tip and 7 percent sales tax. Display each of these amounts and the total.

6. Celsius to Fahrenheit Temperature Converter

Write a program that converts Celsius temperatures to Fahrenheit temperatures. The formula is
as follows:

   $F = (C \times (9/5)) + 32$

The program should ask the user to enter a temperature in Celsius, then display the temperature
converted to Fahrenheit.

7. Ingredient Adjuster

A cookie recipe calls for the following ingredients:

- 1.5 cups of sugar
- 1 cup of butter
- 2.75 cups of flour

The recipe produces 48 cookies with this amount of the ingredients. Write a program that
asks the user how many cookies they want to make, then displays the number of cups of each
ingredient needed for the specified number of cookies.

8. Male and Female Percentages

Write a program that asks the user for the number of males and the number of females registered
in a class. The program should display the percentage of males and females in the class.

*Hint: Suppose there are 8 males and 12 females in a class. There are 20 students in the class.
The percentage of males can be calculated as 8 ÷ 20 = 0.4, or 40%. The percentage of females
can be calculated as 12 ÷ 20 = 0.6, or 60%.*

9. Planting Grapevines

A vineyard owner is planting several new rows of grapevines, and needs to know how many grapevines to plant in each row. The owner has determined that after measuring the length of a future row, they can use the following formula to calculate the number of vines that will fit in the row, along with the trellis end-post assemblies that will need to be constructed at each end of the row:

$$V = \frac{R - 2E}{S}$$

The terms in the formula are:

- V is the number of grapevines that will fit in the row.
- R is the length of the row, in feet.
- E is the amount of space, in feet, used by an end-post assembly.
- S is the space between vines, in feet.

Write a program that makes the calculation for the vineyard owner. The program should ask the user to input the following:

- The length of the row, in feet
- The amount of space used by an end-post assembly, in feet
- The amount of space between the vines, in feet

Once the input data has been entered, the program should calculate and display the number of grapevines that will fit in the row.

10. Compound Interest

When a bank account pays compound interest, it pays interest not only on the principal amount that was deposited into the account, but also on the interest that has accumulated over time. Suppose you want to deposit some money into a savings account, and let the account earn compound interest for a certain number of years. The formula for calculating the balance of the account after a specified number of years is:

$$A 5 P(1 + r/n)nt$$

The terms in the formula are:

- A is the amount of money in the account after the specified number of years.
- P is the principal amount that was originally deposited into the account.
- r is the annual interest rate.
- n is the number of times per year that the interest is compounded.

- *t* is the specified number of years.

Write a program that makes the calculation for you. The program should ask the user to input the following:

- The amount of principal originally deposited into the account
- The annual interest rate paid by the account
- The number of times per year that the interest is compounded (For example, if interest is compounded monthly, enter 12. If interest is compounded quarterly, enter 4.)
- The number of years the account will be left to earn interest
  Once the input data has been entered, the program should calculate and display the amount of money that will be in the account after the specified number of years.

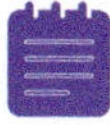

NOTE: The user should enter the interest rate as a percentage. For example, 2 percent would be entered as 2, not as .02. The program will then have to divide the input by 100 to move the decimal point to the correct position.

8 Algorithms and Computational Thinking

TOPICS

8.1 Problem-Solving Concepts

8.2 Algorithmic Thinking

8.3 Exploring Common Algorithms

8.1 Problem-Solving Concepts

You can use a six-step process to identify and solve problems.

A **problem**, or challenge, is something that gets between you and a **goal**. People make decisions every day to solve problems that affect their lives. The problems may be as unimportant as what to eat for breakfast or as important as choosing a new profession. If they make a good decision, they will overcome the problem and achieve their goal. If they make a bad decision, they waste time and resources and might never achieve their goal.

There are six steps you can follow to make a good decision to solve a problem. If you complete all six steps, you should come up with an effective solution. If any of the six steps are not completed well, you are unlikely to solve the problem. You can use these steps to solve your own problems, or as part of your work as a computer scientist. In computer science, solving problems is key to meeting the needs of clients and producing effective programming.

Six Steps of Problem-Solving

These six steps are:

1. **Identify the problem.** This includes identifying the goal the problem is interfering with. If you don't know what the problem is, you cannot solve it.

2. **Understand the problem.** This includes understanding how the problem is interfering with the goal. It also means understanding the **knowledge base** of the person or machine for whom you are solving the problem.

   • When you are setting up a solution for a person—yourself or a client—then you must know what that person knows. You will want to customize the solution based on this knowledge base. For example, you would use a more detailed set of instructions to tell someone how to find a restaurant in your city if they have a limited knowledge of the city than if they know the city well.

- When you are working with a computer, its knowledge base is the limited instructions the computer can understand in the particular language or application you are using to solve the problem. Knowing the knowledge base is very important since you cannot use any instructions outside this base.

- You also must know your own knowledge base. You cannot solve a problem if you do not know the subject. For example, to solve a problem involving accounting, you must know accounting. Knowing your knowledge base lets you communicate with your client and understand how to solve the problem.

3. **Identify ways to solve the problem.** Make a list of all possible solutions. This list should be as complete as possible. Do not stop thinking of solutions until you run out of ideas. You can even talk to other people such as co-workers, teammates, and professionals in related fields to find solutions you did not think of. All solutions must be reasonable and acceptable ways to solve the problem without creating new problems. For example, you could travel from Denver to Los Angeles by way of New York, but this would probably not be an acceptable solution to your travel needs.

4. **Select the best solution from your list.** Set criteria for your solutions. For example, you may want the fastest solution or the least expensive solution. Evaluate the pros and cons of each possible solution based on the criteria, and then select the best solution. Keep in mind that the solution should fall within the knowledge base set in step 2.

5. **Write an action plan for putting the solution into effect.** This means listing complete instructions in a logical sequence of steps that enable you to solve the problem using the selected solution. These numbered, step-by-step instructions must fall within the knowledge base set in step 2. That means that no instruction can be used unless the individual or the machine can understand it. This can be very limiting, especially when working with computers.

6. **Evaluate the solution.** To evaluate or test a solution means to check its result to see if it is correct, and to see if it satisfies the needs of the person(s) with the problem. For example, if a person needs a piece of furniture to sleep on, buying them a cot may be a correct solution, but it may not be satisfactory. If the result is either incorrect or unsatisfactory, then the problem solver must review the list of instructions to see if they are correct or start the process all over again.

Problem-Solving in Action

People solve problems daily at home, or work, or wherever they go. Problems at home include such things as what to cook for dinner, what to do on family night, which car to buy, or how to sell the house. At work, the problems might involve dealing with fellow employees, work policies, management, or customers. The better the decisions an employee can make, the more valuable that person will be to the company. In each case, the six steps in problem-solving can be followed. Most people use them without even knowing it. Here is an example:

1. **Identify the problem.** What to do on family night?

2. **Understand the problem.** With this simple problem, also, the knowledge base of the participants must be considered. The only solutions that should be selected are ones that everyone involved would know how to do. You probably would not select playing a game of chess as a possible solution if only one person in the family knows how to play.

3. **Identify alternatives.** The alternatives might include: a. Watch television. b. Play a board game. c. Play video games. d. Go to the movies. e. Go to play miniature golf. f. Go to the amusement park. g. Go visit a relative. The list is complete only when you can think of no more alternatives.

4. **Select the best way to solve the problem.** Set criteria and evaluate the solutions. Criteria might be what costs the least or how long would it take to get someplace. Based on your criteria, identify the pros and cons of each alternative. For example, going to the movies is expensive but close by. Miniature golf is less expensive and nearby. Based on the pros and cons, select the best solution.

5. **Prepare an action plan for achieving the solution.** For example, if you select miniature golf, the action plan might include the time you will meet, the location you will meet, and who will drive.

6. **Evaluate the solution.** Is it correct and satisfactory? In this case, does it meet the needs of everyone in the family, and will everyone have a good time? If not, review the criteria you used to select a solution and the action plan to see if you should have made a different choice.

Types of Solutions

Some problems, such as baking a cake, have a pretty straight-forward solution. They can be solved with a series of actions called an **algorithm**. These solutions are called **algorithmic solutions.** Using the baking example, once you choose the type of cake, the recipe is your algorithmic solution. You can diagram the algorithmic solution as a flowchart, like the one in Figure 8-1. You follow the steps to an acceptable and satisfying solution.

Figure 8-1   An algorithm for baking a cake.

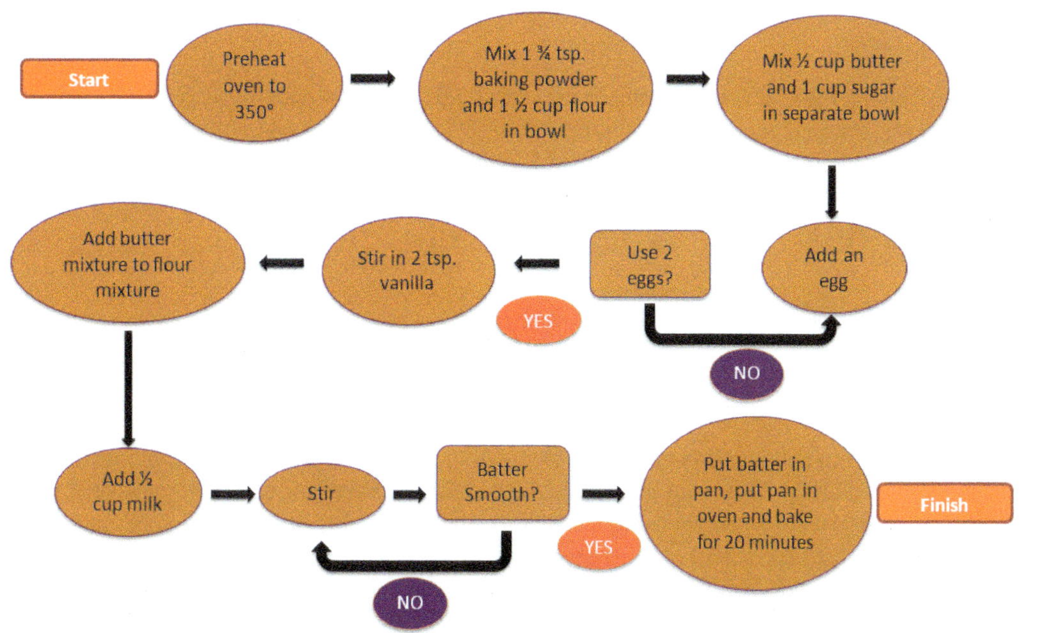

The solutions of other problems, such as how to buy the best stock or whether to expand a company, are not so straightforward. These solutions require reasoning built on knowledge and experience, and a process of trial and error. Solutions that cannot be reached through a direct set of steps are called **heuristic solutions.**

As a problem solver, you can use the six-step process for both algorithmic and heuristic solutions. However, Step 6 (evaluating the solution) is much harder with heuristic solutions. It's easy to tell pretty quickly if your completed cake or a computer program you wrote is correct and satisfactory, but it might take a long time to know if you have bought the best stock. With heuristic solutions, the problem solver will often need to follow the six steps more than once, carefully evaluating each possible solution before deciding which is best.

Furthermore, the same solution you choose may not be correct and satisfactory at another time, or for a different client. In that case, you may have to reevaluate and resolve the same problem later. The stock that did well in January may do poorly in June. Most problems require a combination of the two kinds of solutions.

Problem-solving with Computers

Computers are built to deal with algorithmic solutions, which are often difficult or very time consuming for humans. People are better than computers at developing heuristic solutions. Solving a complicated calculus problem or alphabetizing 10,000 names is an easy task for the computer, but the problem of how to throw a ball or how to speak English is not.

The difficulty lies in the programming. How can problems such as how to throw a ball or speak English be solved in a set of steps that the computer can understand? The field of computers that deals with heuristic types of problems is called **artificial intelligence**. Artificial intelligence enables a computer to do things like build its own knowledge bank and speak in a human language. Using artificial intelligence, the computer's problem-solving abilities are similar to those of a human being.

Artificial intelligence is an expanding computer field, especially with the increased use of robotics. However, until computers can be built to think like humans, people will process most heuristic solutions and computers will process mostly algorithmic solutions. Heuristic problem-solving can help determine alternative solutions. However, for computer use, they must be transformed into an algorithmic format.

Difficulties with Problem-solving

People have many problems with problem-solving. Some people have never been taught how to solve problems. Others are afraid to make a decision for fear it will be the wrong one.

Often, when people go through the problem-solving process, they complete one or more of the steps inadequately. They may not define the problem correctly or may not generate a sufficient list of alternatives. When choosing the best alternative, they may eliminate good alternatives or list the pros and cons too hastily. They may not use a logical sequence of steps in their action plan, or they may focus on details before the framework for the solution is in place. Finally, they may incorrectly or haphazardly evaluate the solution. The problem-solving process is not easy. It takes practice and time to perfect, but in the long run, the process proves to be of great benefit.

When solving problems on the computer, one of the most difficult tasks for the problem solver is writing the instructions. Take the task of deciding which number is the largest from a group of three numbers. Almost anyone can immediately tell which is the largest, but many cannot explain the steps they followed to arrive at it. Most people will say, "I can't explain how I know, I just know it!" This explanation is not good enough for the computer. The computer is a tool that will perform only tasks that the user can explain.

The computer has a specific system of communication that programmers and users must learn. This system demands that no step in the solution to a problem be left unstated and that all steps be in the proper order. You must assume the computer knows nothing except what you tell it. You must think of it as an ignorant but efficient aid to problem-solving.

Branching and Iteration

Some problems require branching in order to achieve a solution. **Branching** is when you—or the computer—moves to the next step in the algorithm based on certain conditions. For example, if you have enough money, you will go to the movies; if not, you will stay home and stream a show. A **non-branching** problem is strictly sequential. No conditions are required for the algorithm to go through the steps to a solution.

An **iterative** solution is a process that repeats and fine-tunes the algorithm until the desired solution is achieved. When you use an iterative process, you continually test and improve your algorithms throughout the development cycle. A **non-iterative** solution is a process where you put in the effort of designing up-front, so when you finally create and test the algorithm, it works as intended.

 **Checkpoint**

8.1   How many steps are in the problem-solving process?

8.2   What is an algorithmic solution?

8.3   What is a heuristic solution?

8.4   What are two things that could go wrong with the problem-solving process?

8.2 Algorithmic Thinking

An algorithm is a precise, systematic method for producing a specified result.

Recall that computers must be given instructions for everything they do, so all they do is run algorithms. We normally call them programs, which are algorithms customized to do a specific task. Naturally, programmers and software developers care a lot about algorithms. But, they matter to the rest of us, too.

Many of the problems we must solve personally are solved by algorithms, from describing how to achieve a clever effect editing a video on a smartphone to correcting mistakes in a term paper. Algorithms are solutions. And the best part is that by writing out the method carefully, some other agent—another person or a computer—can do the work. Of course, that is the reason computers are such powerful and useful tools.

In this section, we familiarize ourselves with algorithms and become more adept at reading them, writing them, and evaluating them. We start by learning about Jean-Dominique Bauby, a man whose hospital care required the use of algorithms. Next, we review algorithms we already know— how we learn them and how we use them. After that, we consider some defining characteristics of algorithms. Then, we study an algorithm we use every day; because it is an "industrial-strength" algorithm, it illustrates how an algorithm can exist in different forms, and why we prefer some algorithms over others. Finally, we consider how we know an algorithm does what it claims. Again, a simple illustration makes the point.

Algorithms

The book (and movie) The Diving Bell and the Butterfly tells the true story of a French man who became paralyzed from his chin down. He couldn't write. He couldn't talk. He couldn't even swallow. All he could do was turn his head a few degrees and blink his left eyelid. But he could think. And amazingly, he wrote the book about himself just by blinking his left eyelid!

The man, Jean-Dominique Bauby, wrote in The Diving Bell and the Butterfly that to be so paralyzed was like wearing the heavy suit and metal helmet deep sea divers wore in the days before SCUBA gear. He suffered from a condition called Locked-In Syndrome: His body was useless but his mind was active. He compared his thoughts to a butterfly, flitting quickly from one topic to the next. The idea became the title of his book.

Before he was paralyzed, Bauby was editor-in-chief at the fashion magazine Elle and an accomplished writer. So, it is not surprising that he wrote a book. What is surprising is that simply by blinking his left eye, he was able to communicate well enough to write at all. His problem— writing by blinking—will give us a situation to study algorithms.

Homemade Algorithms

Whenever Bauby wanted to say something, he had to spell it out letter by letter. To assist him, his nurses and visitors would say the alphabet, or point to the letters of the alphabet listed on a card in the order shown in Figure 8-2. When they got to the correct letter, he blinked. Then, they would go on to the next letter, starting over with the alphabet (see Figure 8-2).

Figure 8-2   Alphabet listing shown to Jean-Dominque Bauby. When the nurse pointed to the correct letter, he blinked his left eyelid.

E	S	A	R	I	N	T	U	L
O	M	D	P	C	F	B	V	
H	G	J	Q	Z	Y	X	K	W

The Stanford University InfoLab: infolab.stanford.edu/~backrub/google.html

This process is an algorithm invented by his nurses. It illustrates important points about algorithms:

- We use and invent algorithms all the time to solve our problems; it doesn't take a degree in computer science to create algorithms.

- Although the algorithm doesn't seem to compute in the popular imagination of computing—where are the numbers, the mathematical formulas?—it does; it creates the content for a document, namely Bauby's book.

- The agent running the algorithm is not a computer. It's a nurse, and Bauby is the user. Often the agent that "runs" the algorithm is a person rather than a computer.

As we are about to see, there are better and worse variations of this algorithm.

These observations emphasize the point that an algorithm is not an exotic creation requiring years of study and deep scientific knowledge, but rather a familiar concept that we use all the time without realizing it or thinking about it.

Speeding Up the Process

Blink-communication is slow. But, the speed could be improved using "word completion," in which the attendant said the word she guessed Bauby was trying to spell. This familiar autocomplete technique—for example, URL completion on the Web and word completion when texting—can save a lot of effort if you're blinking letters. Another way to speed up blink-communication. is to use frequency order.

Notice that the letters in Figure 8-2 are not listed in alphabetical order. You might guess that because Bauby is French, the order **e s a r i n t u l o m d p c f b v h g j q z y x k w** is how the French say the alphabet, but it's not. Like all people who use the Latin alphabet, the French use the standard **a b c** ... sequence, too. The letters are listed by how often they are used in written French—most to least. So, e is the most frequently used letter in French, **s** is next most frequent, then **a, r, i,** and so forth

Asking—or pointing to—the letters in frequency order was faster, because it meant that Bauby's assistant usually tried fewer letters. There is no guarantee, of course. The frequency ordering is an average, found by counting the number of times each letter occurs on thousands and thousands of pages of French text. Not every collection of French words has the same frequency, but it works pretty well.

Let's give an example

The famous French saying, "the more things change, the more they stay the same," *Plus ça change, plus c'est la même chose,* can be communicated by the algorithm just described. We illustrate how well the frequency ordering works by counting how many letters a person must ask to communicate the saying compared to communicating it using the normal alphabetical ordering. How do they compare?

To begin, we start with the first word, *plus*. To find **p**, we ask **e s a r i n t u l o m d p,** and determine that **p** is located after pointing to 13 letters. Next, we look for l, asking **e s a r i n t u l**, so **l** takes 9 letters. We find that u takes 8, and s is the second letter.

So, to communicate the first word, plus, requires us to ask $13 + 9 + 8 + 2 = 32$ letters. A computer program can finish the process for us, and finds that the total for the whole sentence is 247.

Now, we run the same experiment using the normal alphabetical order **a b c** . . . . Repeating the process from before, we ask **a b c d e f g h i j k l m n o p** to find that in this order **p** is letter 16, l is 12, u is 21, and **s** is 19. So, communicating *plus* using the normal alphabetical ordering takes $16 + 12 + 21 + 19 = 68$, which is more than twice the 32 letters needed when using the French frequency ordering. The computer program finds that for the whole sentence, the normal alphabetical order requires 324 tries.

So, asking in frequency order required 247 letters compared to 324 for alphabetical order. Claude Mendibil and the other people assisting Bauby were very smart to use the frequency ordering. It saved him many, many blinks, which shortened the time it took to write *The Diving Bell and the Butterfly*. Such ideas are used in text compression.

Writing the book was a **computation** in which Bauby was the user and the assistant pointing to or asking the letters was the "agent," the person or thing following the instructions. In this case, the instructions were simple: Repeatedly ask the alphabet in frequency order, and each time Bauby blinks, write down the letter.

Spelling it Out

For a method to be precise enough for a computer to follow, *everything* needs to be spelled out. Programmers make algorithms perfectly precise for computers by writing them in a programming language.

People can figure things out from context, so many things can be left out of the explanation; for example, after finding a letter, a computer has to be told to go back to the beginning of the letter sequence to start looking for the next letter. People figure that out by themselves.

Algorithms Versus Programs

Programs are algorithms that have been specialized to a specific set of conditions and assumptions, and are (usually) written in a specific programming language.

The original explanation of an assistant asking the letters and Bauby blinking at the right moment was a *Letter Search* algorithm. You could use the same *Letter Search* algorithm specialized to search for a letter based on frequency order or one specialized to search on alphabetical order. This doesn't seem like a big difference, and it's not. We could write a letter search program that inputs the letter sequence to follow before it starts. It would be a different program but it would still use the *Letter Search* algorithm.

So, programs are algorithms, and now you know the small difference between the two. In most cases, however, we do not need to make the distinction and can use the terms interchangeably.

Every computational task has many ways of being solved. Computer professionals spend much of their time figuring out how well a solution works, or how to improve it. And it's important that they find a fast solution: When you're waiting for a computer to finish its task, you don't want to wait longer than necessary.

Experience with Algorithms

Because programs are algorithms and all of the applications you use daily are programs, you obviously use algorithms all the time. But, you regularly learn algorithms, too.

NOTE: Algorithm is a strange word. (It's an anagram of logarithm!) It comes from the name of a famous Arabic textbook author, Abu Ja'far Mohammed ibn Mûsâ al-Khowârizmî (780–840 AD). He was a Persian scientist, mathematician, and astronomer, but he didn't invent the word "algorithm." The end of his name, al-Khowârizmî, means native of Khowârism (today it is Khiva, Uzbekistan). Over the centuries, references to his famous book corrupted the end of his name into algorithm.

Inventing Algorithms

You developed most of the algorithms you know by yourself simply by thinking through what is required to achieve your goal. For example, think of all of the things you know how to do with your phone, or with complex applications like video editing software. When someone asks your help with a "How do I . . . " question, you will likely answer with an algorithm. For your answer to be successful, it is important that your algorithm have a few basic properties.

Writing Algorithms

An algorithm must have five properties:

- **Input specified**
- **Output specified**
- **Definiteness**
- **Effectiveness**
- **Finiteness**

Input Specified. The **input** is the data to be transformed during the computation to produce the output. We specify the type of data, the amount of data, and the form of the data that the algorithm expects.

Output Specified. The **output** is the data resulting from the computation, the intended result. Often the output description is given in the name of the algorithm, as in "Algorithm to compute a batting average." As with input, we must specify the type, amount, and the form the output will have. A possible output for some computations is a statement that there is no output—that is, there is no possible solution.

Definiteness. Algorithms must specify every step and the order to perform them. **Definiteness** means specifying the sequence of operations for transforming the input into the output. Details of each step must be spelled out, including how to handle errors. Definiteness ensures that if the algorithm is performed at different times or by different agents (people or computers) using the same data, the output is the same.

Effectiveness. It must be possible for the agent to execute the algorithm mechanically without any further input, special talent, clairvoyance, creativity, help from Superman, and so on. Whereas definiteness specifies which operations to do, in what order, and when, **effectiveness** means that they are doable.

Finiteness. An algorithm must have **finiteness**; it must eventually stop, either with the right output or with a statement that no solution is possible. If no answer comes back, we can't tell whether the agent is still working on an answer or is just plain "stuck." Finiteness is not usually an issue for noncomputer algorithms because they typically don't repeat instructions. But, as you will see, computer algorithms often repeat instructions with different data.

Query Evaluation

To discuss key ideas about algorithms, let's begin with an algorithm you probably use every day: the Google query evaluation algorithm.

A **query processor** makes an ordered list of the pages that hit on the keywords of your search query. Query evaluation makes that list; ordering that list so it is most convenient for you is a separate task and not considered here. Figure 8-3 shows the query evaluation algorithm invented by Sergey Brin and Larry Page and presented in their original paper, *The Anatomy of a Large-Scale Hypertextual Web Search Engine*.

The first thing we notice about this algorithm is that it is not written in a programming language. It uses "normal" English—specifically, "tech speak" English.

So, for example, the term "doclist" is the list of URLs associated with each keyword. The term "rank" means "page rank"; "seek" means to go to a position in a list (stored as a file on a disk). If we read the whole paper, we would not know what "short barrels" and "full barrels" are, but even without those definitions, tech speak is easier to understand than, say, ancient Greek.

 NOTE: When the Brin/Page algorithm was finally written in a programming language, it doubtless took tens of thousands of lines of code, explaining why humans prefer this seven-step description.

Figure 8-3   Original query evaluation algorithm developed by Brin and Page to find the hits for a Google search; from their original paper, The Anatomy of a Large-Scale Hypertextual Web Search Engine

1. Parse the query.
2. Convert words into wordIDs.
3. Seek to the start of the doclist in the short barrel for every word.
4. Scan through the doclists until there is a document that matches all the search terms.
5. Compute the rank of that document for the query.
6. If we are in the short barrels and at the end of any doclist, seek to the start of the doclist in the full barrel for every word and go to step 4.
7. If we are not at the end of any doclist go to step 4.

   Sort the documents that have matched by rank and return the top k.

infolab.stanford.edu/~backrub/google.html

The paper initially presents its algorithm in tech speak for a few reasons. Firstly, only computers prefer to read code—humans have an easier time reading English. Secondly, humans do not need all the specifics of the actual program to understand query evaluation; Brin and Page left out a lot of details that a computer would need, simplifying the algorithm for a human audience.

Here are some facts about algorithms that are illustrated by query evaluation:

Algorithmic Fact 1. Algorithms can be specified at different levels of detail. It is only necessary that the agent know the terms and operations used in the specification, and that they be within the agent's capability to perform (that is, effective).

The Brin/Page algorithm is written for technically-trained people, so it meets the criterion. When you explain smartphone video editing or other complicated operations to your friends, you use terms you know they know and operations you know they can perform.

Programs are usually written in a programming language (PL), which is compiled into assembly language (AL), which is assembled into binary form. All three —PL, AL, and binary—are different forms of the same thing. Each one is more detailed than its predecessor and is understandable to anyone or anything fluent in that language.

NOTE: English or any natural language is a very imprecise way to give an algorithm. Among its sources of imprecision are pronouns—he, she, they, them, and so on—and among them "it" is the worst, because we can't always be sure what it refers to. (The only pronoun Brin and Page used in their algorithm is the "royal we.") Using nouns instead of pronouns won't win any writing awards, but your algorithm will be more understandable.

Algorithms always use functions to simplify the algorithmic description. For example, Step 4 of the Brin/Page algorithm states, "Scan through the doclists until there is a document that matches all the search terms." They don't give instructions for performing a "scan through," but it's an operation that is critical to their solution; they assumed the agent's capability includes knowing how to do this right. Notice that this is not a case of an undefined word. "Scan" has its obvious meaning, but when it is necessary to match items on each list, the exact operation of the scan matters a lot.

The functionality Brin and Page assumed in their algorithm was Step 3, moving through the lists in a particular way.

Algorithmic Fact 2. Algorithms always build on functionality previously defined and known to the agent.

In our case, readers of the Brin/Page paper would know that the most efficient way to "scan through" looking for matches is to alphabetize the lists and proceed as specified in the *Intersecting Alphabetized Lists* (IAL) algorithm.

Let's be clear about what their readers knew by giving an example of an algorithm that should not be used.

Another way to implement "scan" to find the needed matches—we call it No Alphabetized Lists (NAL)—starts with any lists and works like an odometer. (The lists can be alphabetized or not; the algorithm will ignore the ordering.) It places the arrow pointers at the start of each list, and then advances the pointer of one of the lists all the way to the end, looking for a match at each step; it then advances the next list one position and repeats what it has done up to this point. (Think of the odometer as starting at 00000 and finding the 10 hits, 00000, 11111, . . . , 99999.) This is an algorithm. It checks every combination of URLs and finds the same ones that the IAL does. But it's MUCH slower.

How much slower? An example will convince you that it's a lot slower. Consider five 10-item lists. The IAL moves the pointer past each item of each list once, giving a worst-case number of steps as

IAL: $10 + 10 + 10 + 10 + 10 = 50$

(We don't know what order the pointers will be advanced in, but it doesn't matter when we're only counting up how many advancements there are: At most, there are ten for each list.)

But the non-alphabetized lists solution repeatedly visits the same items. Because it works like an odometer, our sample lists will require as many steps as sweeping through a five-digit odometer:

NAL: $10 \times 10 \times 10 \times 10 \times 10 = 100{,}000$

Both solutions work. One solution is very efficient compared to the other.

So, when Brin and Page said "scan through the doclists," they knew that readers would use the IAL approach to find each match.

Algorithmic Fact 3. Different algorithms can solve the same problem differently, and the different solutions can take different amounts of time. The feature that makes IAL better than NAL is obviously the alphabetical order. It allows us to skip many, many checks for matching that would fail.

Different Solutions

An important point to emphasize is that the IAL and NAL algorithms are *not* different versions of the same solution. They are *different solutions* that solve one problem differently. This is clear because they each require a different form of the input and rely on that input's characteristics. For the IAL, the doclists must be alphabetized. The NAL doesn't care if the doclists are alphabetized or not because it ignores the order when it runs. Using the added information allows the IAL to bypass unproductive tests.

The difference in running times for the IAL and NAL algorithms also points to the fact that they are different solutions: Different forms of the same algorithm will have the same running time.

Understanding Why IAL Works

We (and computer scientists generally) believe that the IAL solution is good in the sense of being clear and simple, and we've just argued that it is efficient. There is one main remaining question: How do we know that the algorithm works? That is, how do we know if it finds all of the hits?

Sometimes when we develop an algorithm to solve a problem, the solution doesn't have any loops in it. This makes it particularly easy to test—run it and see if the result is right. Done. But, most algorithms have loops and so they need a little bit of analysis to be sure they are right. Specifically, trying the program might reveal an error, but it might not.

If the error involves a larger problem—and therefore, more looping—the small problem may work fine. Programs containing loops cannot be verified exhaustively, that is, by trying all cases, because there are infinitely many. We must be smarter.

Discovering why an algorithm works might seem difficult, but usually it is not. As its creator, we will know why because we gave the algorithm the "correct" properties when we developed it.

So, our strategy for "knowing why it works" is as follows:

1. Find one or more properties that ensure the algorithm works.

2. Explain, using the program, why they make it work.

In the case of the Intersecting Alphabetized Lists problem, we need to be sure that if there are hits to be found, the algorithm will find them. (If there are no hits, then Step 2 will always fail, meaning the algorithm "works" in that case.) So, we assume that one or more hits are among the URLs in the lists we are given. That means that the same URL is in all of the lists.

Checkpoint

8.5   What do you call the practice of listing items by how often they are used?

8.6   What are the five properties of an algorithm?

8.7   How many steps are in the original query evaluation algorithm developed to find the hits for a Google search?

8.3 Exploring Common Algorithms

There are common algorithms used often in programming that you can learn and save for future use.

Algorithmic thinking is used throughout the software development lifecycle. In this section, you will create common algorithms used often in programming. In later chapters, you will practice using these algorithms to write code.

We will examine three common algorithms:

- **Finding the greatest common divisor**
- **Finding the largest of three values**
- **Finding a prime number**

As you read this section, practice creating and testing the algorithms. You may work on your own, or with a partner or small group. Save your practice solutions. They will be a good reference as you begin designing programs and writing code in later chapters. Your instructor may have provided time to discuss your solution with others, receive feedback, and implement any changes to your solution based on the feedback.

Finding the Greatest Common Divisor

The greatest common divisor of two numbers is the largest number that divides them both. That means that the greatest common divisor (gcd) of the two integers **4** and **2** is **2**.

The greatest common divisor of the two integers **16** and **24** is **8**.

How would you write a program to find the greatest common divisor? Would you immediately begin to write the code? No. It is important to th*ink before you code.* Thinking enables you to generate a logical solution for the problem even before you know how to write the code.

Start by writing the steps on paper. Let the two input integers be **a** and **b.**

You know that number **1** is a common divisor, but it may not be the greatest common divisor. So, you can check whether **k** (where **k** is **2**, then **3**, then **4**, and so on) is a common divisor for **a** and **b**.

Keep incrementing **k** by **1** number until **k** is greater than **a** or **b**. Store the common divisor in a variable named **gcd**. Initially, **gcd** is **1**. Whenever a new common divisor is found, it becomes the new gcd. When you have checked all the possible common divisors from **2** up to **a** or **b**, the value in variable **gcd** is the greatest common divisor.

Finding the Largest of Three Values

Suppose you have a list of three numbers, and you need to determine which of the three numbers is the largest, then print the largest number to the screen.

Start by writing out the steps on paper. You will discover that there is usually more than one right answer to writing an algorithm.

Your steps may look like Example 1:

```
Example 1
Step 1: Compare number1 to number2
Step 2: If number1 > number2, then number1 = largestnumber
Step 3: if number2 > number1, then number2 = largestnumber
Step 4: If number3 > largestnumber, then number3 = largestnumber
Step 5: Print largestnumber
```

Or your steps may look like Exampe 2:

```
Example 2
Step1: Store the values in x,y,z
Step2: If x > y and x > z, print x
Step3: Otherwise, if y > z and y > x, print y
Step4: Otherwise, print z
```

Both solutions provide the correct answer. More advanced topics of computer science discuss how some algorithms are more efficient than others. For now, we will focus on developing an accurate solution and understanding that your solution may look slightly different from other solutions.

It is helpful to test your algorithm by plugging in actual values, stepping through the algorithm, and evaluating the results. Perform the following steps to test the accuracy of Example 1:

1. Replace the words number1, number2, and number3 with the numbers 2, 4, and 6.
2. Step through the algorithm. Is the output correct?
   (*Hint*: The output should be: 6.)
3. Change the order of the numbers and test again. Is the output correct?
4. Try an entirely different set of numbers, such as 54, 120, 18. Is the output correct?
5. Your testing should confirm that the solution works for any set of three numbers.

Repeat the process for Example 2. Are both solutions accurate?

Finding a Prime Number

A prime number is any whole number greater than 1 that is only divisible by 1 or itself. For example, 2, 3, 5, and 7 are prime numbers. The numbers 4, 6, 8, and 9 are not prime numbers.

Write the steps to find the first 10 prime numbers, then display them to the screen. They should each be displayed on a separate line.

```
Example
Step1: For numbers 2, 3, 4, 5, 6, 7 …. And so on, test each
       number to see if it is prime.
Step2: Count the number of prime numbers found. When you
       reach 10, stop testing.
Step3: Print a prime number, then go to the next line.
Step4: Repeat step 3 until all 10 prime numbers are displayed
       to the screen.
```

Remember, this is an example of a possible solution. Your solution may look different.

Checkpoint

8.8   Why should you think before writing code?

8.9   Why might the algorithms you write look different from the ones your classmates write?

8.10 How might you test the algorithm for finding a prime number?

Chapter Review

Multiple Choice

1. You can diagram an algorithm using a _______________.
   a. Venn diagram
   b. an organizational chart
   c. a flowchart
   d. a column chart

2. What type of solution requires a process of trial and error?
   a. algorithmic
   b. heuristic
   c. flowchart
   d. computational

3. What is a common term for an algorithm that is customized to do a specific task?
   a. solution
   b. computer
   c. function
   d. program

4. An algorithm is a(n) _____________.
   a. list of general nonspecific steps to produce an output.
   b. logarithm.
   c. systematic method for producing a specified result.
   d. math problem.

5. Algorithms are used by __________.
   a. only computers.
   b. only humans.
   c. various agents.
   d. no one, they are not real.

6. Algorithms must always ________________.
   a. produce output.
   b. produce output or state that there is no solution.
   c. produce input or state that there is no solution.
   d. state that there is no solution.

7. Algorithms are guaranteed to work _____________.
   a. 99.9 percent of the time.
   b. 100 percent of the time.
   c. depends on the computers they are running on.
   d. 50 percent of the time.

8. When writing an algorithm in a natural language, it is helpful to use _________ instead of _________.

   a. programming language, natural language

   b. nouns, pronouns

   c. abbreviations, actual words

   d. nouns, adjectives

9. If an algorithm is performed with the same data, at different times with different agents, the output will be _______________.

   a. the same.

   b. different.

   c. sometimes different and sometimes the same.

   d. impossible to tell.

True or False

1. Programs containing loops cannot be verified exhaustively.

2. A program is an algorithm that has been customized.

3. Algorithms should not be finite.

4. There is only one algorithm for solving any given problem.

5. A recipe is an example of an algorithm.

Short Answer

1. What are the six steps of problem-solving?

2. Name three current problems in your life that could be solved through an algorithmic process. Explain why each of these problems is algorithmic in nature.

3. Name three current problems in your life that might be solved through a heuristic approach. Explain why each of these problems is heuristic in nature.

4. Name three problems that might arise at home, at school, or in a business that could be solved more efficiently with computer assistance. Do these problems require an algorithmic or heuristic solution? Why?

5. What makes IAL (intersect an alphabetized list) faster than NAL (no alphabetized lists)?

Algorithm Workbench

1. Create a flowchart showing the steps in an algorithm for checking your email inbox.

2. Explain the five properties of the algorithm you created in exercise 1 (input specified, output specified, definiteness, effectiveness, and finiteness).

3. Develop an algorithm for brushing your teeth. Then explain the correctness of your algorithm, detailing why it works.

Programming Exercises

1. Choose one of the problems you identified in Short Answer question 2. Complete the six problem-solving steps to develop a sequential (non-branching) algorithm solve the problem.

   Step 1: Identify the problem.

   Step 2: Understand the problem.

       a. Include comments about the problem to aid in understanding it.

       b. Write a description of the knowledge base (this list would include what you would be expected to know to follow the solution).

   Step 3: Identify alternative solutions.

   Step 4: Select the best solution. Why did you select this solution?

   Step 5: Write a set of numbered step-by-step instructions to achieve the solution.

   Step 6: Test the solution. Does this solution work? If not, how might you change the solution so it will work?

2. Select one of the following tasks. Working alone or with a partner, write a set of numbered, step-by-step instructions (a solution) that another person could use to perform the task without asking questions. Define the knowledge base of this person by listing what you expect the person to know in order to follow your directions. For example, for task "a" (below), make a cup of cocoa, the knowledge base might include such things as knowledge of milk or water, a refrigerator, pan, spoon, cocoa, cup, range top or microwave, and so forth.

       a. Make a cup of cocoa.

       b. Sharpen a pencil.

       c. Walk from the classroom to the cafeteria.

       d. Get a glass of water from your kitchen.

       f. Start your computer.

3. Test your solution for Programming Exercise 2 by giving your instructions to a classmate to see whether they can accomplish the task without your help. If they can't, modify your solution so that the person can accomplish the task. Check the solution again by giving the instructions to another person.

4. With a partner or a small group, share the practice solutions you created in Section 8.3. (If you did not create any, do so now.) Analyze the code and identify any components you might be able to reuse in other problem-solving algorithms. Did you all come up with the same solutions? If necessary, make changes to your solutions based on the feedback you receive from your peers.

5. With a partner or a small group, create an algorithm for finding the average of a series of numbers. Write the steps on paper and then test them. Try your hand at using Python to implement your solution. Ask a classmate to check your Python program and evaluate it for accuracy and efficiency, then respond to the feedback by improving your work.

6. Another common algorithm is called "Making Change." It solves the problem: What is the minimum number of coins I need to make a specific total? With a partner or small group, create an algorithm for making change. Write the steps on paper and then test them. For example, your friend owes you $9.35 and gives you a $10 bill. What is the minimum number of coins you need to pay them back? Try your hand at using Python to implement your solution. Ask a classmate to check your Python program and evaluate it for accuracy and efficiency, then respond to the feedback by improving your work.

9 Taking a Program From Design to Code

TOPICS

9.1 Designing a Program

Programs must be carefully designed before they are written. During the design process, programmers use tools such as pseudocode and flowcharts to create models of programs.

The Program Development Cycle

Recall that programmers typically use high-level languages such as Python to create programs. There is much more to creating a program than writing code, however. The process of creating a program that works correctly typically requires the five phases shown in Figure 9-1. The entire process is known as the **program development cycle**.

Figure 9-1   The program development cycle

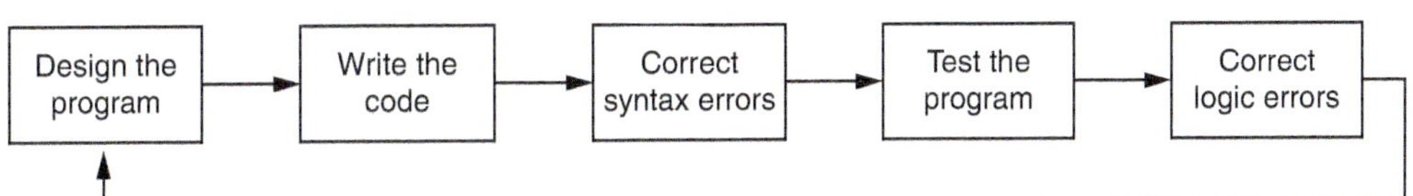

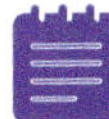

NOTE: If the program development cycle sounds familiar, it is because it is similar to the problem-solving process you learned in Chapter 8. The similarities will become even more clear as we move through this chapter.

Let's take a closer look at each stage in the cycle.

1. **Design the Program.** All professional programmers will tell you that a program should be carefully designed before the code is actually written. When programmers begin a new project, they should never jump right in and start writing code as the first step. They start by creating a design of the program. There are several ways to design a program, and later in this section, we will discuss some techniques that you can use to design your Python programs.

2. **Write the Code.** After designing the program, the programmer begins writing code in a high-level language such as Python. Recall that each language has its own rules, known as syntax, that must be followed when writing a program. A language's syntax rules dictate things such as how keywords, operators, and punctuation characters can be used. A syntax error occurs if the programmer violates any of these rules.

3. **Correct Syntax Errors.** If the program contains a syntax error, or even a simple mistake such as a misspelled keyword, the compiler or interpreter will display an error message indicating what the error is. Virtually all code contains syntax errors when it is first written, so the programmer will typically spend some time correcting these. Once all of the syntax errors and simple typing mistakes have been corrected, the program can be compiled and translated into a machine language program (or executed by an interpreter, depending on the language being used).

4. **Test the Program.** Once the code is in an executable form, it is then tested to determine whether any logic errors exist. A **logic error** is a mistake that does not prevent the program from running, but causes it to produce incorrect results. (Mathematical mistakes are common causes of logic errors.)

5. **Correct Logic Errors.** If the program produces incorrect results, the programmer **debugs** the code. This means that the programmer finds and corrects logic errors in the program. Sometimes during this process, the programmer discovers that the program's original design must be changed. In this event, the program development cycle starts over and continues until no errors can be found.

More About the Design Process

The process of designing a program is arguably the most important part of the cycle. You can think of a program's design as its foundation. If you build a house on a poorly constructed foundation, eventually you will find yourself doing a lot of work to fix the house! A program's design should be viewed no differently. If your program is designed poorly, eventually you will find yourself doing a lot of work to fix the program.

The process of designing a program can be summarized in the following two steps:

1. Understand the task that the program is to perform.
2. Determine the steps that must be taken to perform the task.

Let's take a closer look at each of these steps.

Understand the Task That the Program Is to Perform

It is essential that you understand what a program is supposed to do before you determine the steps that the program will perform. Typically, a professional programmer gains this understanding by working directly with the customer. We use the term **customer** to describe the person, group, or organization that is asking you to write a program. This could be a customer in the traditional sense of the word, meaning someone who is paying you to write a program. It could also be your boss, or the manager of a department within your company. Regardless of whom it is, the customer will be relying on your program to perform an important task.

To get a sense of what a program is supposed to do, the programmer usually interviews the customer.

> **TIP:** If you choose to become a professional software developer, your customer will be anyone who asks you to write programs as part of your job. As long as you are a student, however, your customer is your instructor! In every programming class that you will take, it's practically guaranteed that your instructor will assign programming problems for you to complete. For your academic success, make sure that you understand your instructor's requirements for those assignments and write your programs accordingly.

During the interview, the customer will describe the task that the program should perform, and the programmer will ask questions to uncover as many details as possible about the task. A follow-up interview is usually needed because customers rarely mention everything they want during the initial meeting, and programmers often think of additional questions.

The programmer studies the information that was gathered from the customer during the interviews and creates a list of different software requirements. A **software requirement** is simply a single task that the program must perform in order to satisfy the customer. Once the customer agrees that the list of requirements is complete, the programmer can move to the next phase.

Determine the Steps That Must Be Taken to Perform the Task

Once you understand the task that the program will perform, you begin by breaking down the task into a series of steps. This is similar to the way you would break down a task into a series of steps that another person can follow. For example, suppose someone asks you how to boil water. You might break down that task into a series of steps as follows:

1. Pour the desired amount of water into a pot.
2. Put the pot on a stove burner.
3. Turn the burner to high.
4. Watch the water until you see large bubbles rapidly rising. When this happens, the water is boiling.

This should sound familiar, as it is an example of an algorithm. Recall that an algorithm is a set of well-defined logical steps that must be taken to perform a task. Notice the steps in this algorithm are sequentially ordered. Step 1 should be performed before step 2, and so on. If a person follows these steps exactly as they appear, and in the correct order, they should be able to boil water successfully.

A programmer breaks down the task that a program must perform in a similar way. An algorithm is created, which lists all of the logical steps that must be taken. For example, suppose you have been asked to write a program to calculate and display the gross pay for an hourly paid employee.

Here are the steps that you would take:

1. Get the number of hours worked.
2. Get the hourly pay rate.
3. Multiply the number of hours worked by the hourly pay rate.
4. Display the result of the calculation that was performed in step 3.

Of course, this algorithm isn't ready to be executed on the computer. The steps in this list have to be translated into code. Programmers commonly use two tools to help them accomplish this: pseudocode and flowcharts. Let's look at each of these in more detail.

Pseudocode

Because small mistakes like misspelled words and forgotten punctuation characters can cause syntax errors, programmers have to be mindful of such small details when writing code. For this reason, programmers find it helpful to write a program in **pseudocode** (pronounced "sue doe code") before they write it in the actual code of a programming language such as Python.

The word "pseudo" means fake, so pseudocode is fake code. It is an informal language that has no syntax rules and is not meant to be compiled or executed. Instead, programmers use pseudocode to create models, or "mock-ups," of programs. Because programmers don't have to worry about syntax errors while writing pseudocode, they can focus all of their attention on the program's design. Once a satisfactory design has been created with pseudocode, the pseudocode can be translated directly to actual code. Here is an example of how you might write pseudocode for the pay calculating program that we discussed earlier:

> *Input the hours worked*
> *Input the hourly pay rate*
> *Calculate gross pay as hours worked multiplied by pay rate*
> *Display the gross pay*

Each statement in the pseudocode represents an operation that can be performed in Python. For example, Python can read input that is typed on the keyboard, perform mathematical calculations, and display messages on the screen.

Flowcharts

Flowcharting is another tool that programmers use to design programs. Recall that a flowchart is a diagram that graphically depicts the steps that take place in a program. Figure 9-2 shows how you might create a flowchart for the pay calculating program.

Notice there are three types of symbols in the flowchart: ovals, parallelograms, and a rectangle. Each of these symbols represents a step in the program, as described here:

- The ovals, which appear at the top and bottom of the flowchart, are called **terminal symbols**. The **Start** terminal symbol marks the program's starting point, and the **End** terminal symbol marks the program's ending point.
- Parallelograms are used as **input symbols** and **output symbols**. They represent steps in which the program reads input or displays output.
- Rectangles are used as **processing symbols**. They represent steps in which the program performs some process on data, such as a mathematical calculation.

The symbols are connected by arrows that represent the "flow" of the program. To step through the symbols in the proper order, you begin at the *Start* terminal and follow the arrows until you reach the *End* terminal.

Figure 9-2 Flowchart for the pay calculating program

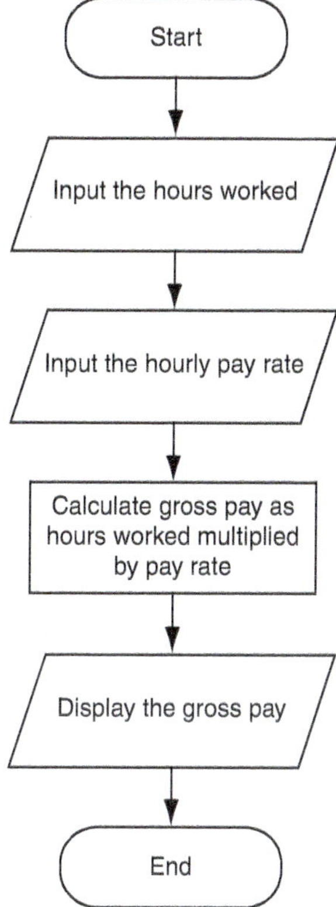

 **Checkpoint**

9.1 Who is a programmer's customer?

9.2 What is a software requirement?

9.3 What is an algorithm?

9.4 What is pseudocode?

9.5 What is a flowchart?

9.6 What do each of the following symbols mean in a flowchart?

- Oval
- Parallelogram
- Rectangle

9.2 Using Analysis Tools to Design a Solution

KEY POINT Using tools such as a problem analysis chart will help you plan and organize your program design.

Certain organizational tools will help you learn to solve problems on the computer. Some of these tools include:

- Problem analysis chart (PAC), which shows a beginning analysis of the problem.
- Structure chart or interactivity chart, which shows the overall layout or structure of the solution.
- IPO chart, which shows the input, the processing, and the output.
- Algorithms, which show the sequence of instructions comprising the solution.
- Flowcharts, which are graphic representations of the algorithms and pseudocode.

To analyze a problem and set up the most efficient solution, a programmer organizes the solution by using all or some of these tools. When the programmer does not use these tools during the problem-solving process, the solution takes longer to program, and the final program is less efficient, lacks readability, and increases programmer frustration.

Analyzing the Problem

To organize a solution, the programmer first has to understand and analyze the requirements of the problem. A good way to analyze a problem is to separate it into four parts, shown in the problem analysis chart (PAC) in Figure 9-3:

1. The given data
2. The required results
3. The processing that is required in the problem
4. A list of solution alternatives

Figure 9-3 Problem Analysis Chart

Given Data	Required Results
Section 1: Data given in the problem or provided by the user. These can be known values or general names for data, such as price, quantity, and so forth.	**Section 2:** Requirements for the output reports. This includes the information needed and the format required.
Processing Required	**Solution Alternatives**
Section 3: List of processing required. This includes equations or other types of processing, such as sorting, searching, and so forth.	**Section 4:** List of ideas for the solution of the problem.

You can make your own PAC by setting up a two-column chart with four rows. As a problem unfolds, you can use this form to sort it into the sections, as follows:

- Data, constants and variables, would be entered in Section 1, under Given Data. Variable data are the input values.
- Requirements for the output reports would be entered in Section 2, under Required Results.
- Any equations or other processing requirements would be entered in Section 3, under Processing Required.
- Finally, the programmer would write any other ideas that spring to mind concerning the solution in Section 4, under Solution Alternatives.

The following problem illustrates how to use a PAC:

Suppose you must calculate the gross pay of an employee given the hours worked and the rate of pay. The gross pay is calculated by multiplying the hours worked by the rate of pay. Figure 9-4 shows how the problem solver would fill in the PAC for this problem.

1. **Given Data.** The hours worked and the pay rate are the given data, so you enter them into Section 1.

2. **Required Results.** You need to calculate the gross pay and display that information for the user, so you enter that into Section 2.

3. **Processing Required.** The formula for calculating the Gross Pay is:
   GrossPay = Hours x PayRate
   You enter the formula into Section 3.

4. **Solution Alternatives,** which you enter into Section 4, are:
   1. Define the hours worked and the pay rate as constants.
   2. Define the hours worked and the pay rate as input values.

Figure 9-4 Problem Analysis Chart for the Payroll Problem

Given Data	Required Results
Hours Pay Rate	Gross Pay
Processing Required	**Solution Alternatives**
GrossPay = Hours x PayRate	1. Define the hours worked and pay rate as constants. *2. Define the hours worked and pay rate as input values.

Now, you can look at the information in the PAC to analyze the problem and determine a solution. Consider all the solution alternatives to find the one that is most efficient.

Note the asterisk next to solution 2 in Section 4. For this problem, that is the best solution option because the program will not need to be changed in order to calculate the gross pay for other employees.

The problem analysis chart is an aid to clear thinking because it helps you, as the problem solver, to identify the essential data and information in a problem and to disregard the nonessentials. Most problems programmers work with are word problems. This is true whether they are working in a classroom situation or out on the job. The PAC helps to pare down the words so you can easily identify and select the best solution.

Checkpoint

9.5   What is a problem analysis chart used for?

9.6   What is a structure chart used for?

9.7   What are the four parts in a PAC?

9.3 Documenting Your Code

A program's external documentation describes aspects of the program for the user. The internal documentation is for the programmer and explains how parts of the program work.

A program's documentation explains various details about the program. There are usually two types of program documentation: external and internal. **External documentation** is typically designed for the user. It consists of documents such as a reference guide that describes the program's features, and tutorials that teach the user how to operate the program.

Sometimes the programmer is responsible for writing all or part of a program's external documentation. This might be the case in a small organization, or in a company that has a relatively small programming staff. Some organizations, particularly large companies, will employ a staff of technical writers whose job is to produce external documentation. These documents might be in printed manuals, or in files that can be viewed on the computer. In recent years, it has become common for software companies to provide all of a program's external documentation in PDF (Portable Document Format) files.

Internal documentation appears as **comments** in a program's code. Recall from Chapter 6 that comments are short notes placed in different parts of a program, explaining how those parts of the program work. Although comments are a critical part of a program, they are ignored by the compiler or interpreter. Comments are intended for human readers of a program's code, not the computer.

Programming languages provide special symbols or words for writing comments. In several languages, including Java, C, and C++, you begin a comment with two forward slashes (/ /). In Python, you begin a comment with a hashmark (#) and a space. Everything that you write on the same line as the comment symbol is ignored by the compiler. Here is an example of a comment in Java:

```
// Get the number of hours worked.
```

Python uses the # symbol. Here is an example of a comment in Python:

```
# Get the number of hours worked.
```

Psuedocode is intended to represent an algorithm that can be programmed in any language. Because both the forward slashes (//) and the hashtag (#) are universal symbols used to represent comments, you will see them used interchangeability in pseudocode.

Block Comments and Line Comments

Programmers generally write two types of comments in a program: block comments and line comments. **Block comments** take up several lines and are used when lengthy explanations are required. For example, a block comment often appears at the beginning of a program, explaining what the program does, listing the name of the author, giving the date that the program was last modified, and any other necessary information. The following is an example of a block comment:

```
# This program calculates an employee's gross pay.
# Written by Kiran Sharma.
# Last modified on 12/14/2021
```

NOTE: Some programming languages provide special symbols to mark the beginning and ending of a block comment.

Line comments are comments that occupy a single line and explain a short section of the program. The following statements show an example:

```
# Calculate the interest.
Set interest = balance * interest_Rate
# Add the interest to the balance.
Set balance = balance + interest
```

A line comment does not have to occupy an entire line. Anything from the # symbol, to the end of the line, is ignored, so a comment can appear after an executable statement. Here is an example:

```
Input age      # Get the user's age.
```

TIP: Take the time to learn how to write comments. Using comments will almost certainly save you time in the future when you have to modify or debug a program. Even large and complex programs can be made easy to read and understand if they are properly commented.

 Checkpoint

9.8   Explain external and internal documentation.

9.9   What symbol do you use to start a comment in Python?

9.10 What are the two general types of comments that programmers write in a program's code? Describe each.

9.4 Using Style Conventions and Comments

Understanding how style conventions and comments are used in code will help you and your teammates develop effective programming solutions.

Suppose we have been given the following programming problem: Scientists have determined that the world's ocean levels are currently rising at about 1.5 millimeters per year. Write a program to display the following:

- The number of millimeters that the oceans will rise in five years.
- The number of millimeters that the oceans will rise in seven years.
- The number of millimeters that the oceans will rise in ten years.

Here is the algorithm:

1. Calculate the amount that the oceans will rise in five years.
2. Display the result of the calculation in Step 1.
3. Calculate the amount that the oceans will rise in seven years.
4. Display the result of the calculation in Step 3.
5. Calculate the amount that the oceans will rise in ten years.
6. Display the result of the calculation in Step 5.

This program is straightforward. It performs three calculations and displays the results of each. The calculations should give the amount the oceans will rise in five, seven, and ten years. Each of these values can be calculated with the following formula:

$$Amount\ of\ yearly\ rise \times Number\ of\ years$$

On Your Own: Before reading on, work with a partner or a small group to design and create the program or pseudocode for this problem. You may want to use a PAC to analyze the problem and select a solution, then use a flowchart to illustrate it. When you are finished, compare your flowchart to the one in Figure 9-5 and your pseudocode to Program 9-1.

The amount of yearly rise is the same for each calculation, so we will create a constant to represent that value. Program 9-1 shows the pseudocode for the program.

Program 9-1

```
 1  # Declare the variables
 2  Declare Real fiveYears
 3  Declare Real sevenYears
 4  Declare Real tenYears
 5
 6  # Create a constant for the yearly rise
 7  Constant Real YEARLY_RISE = 1.5
 8
 9  # Display the amount of rise in five years
10  Set fiveYears = YEARLY_RISE * 5
11  Display "The ocean levels will rise ", fiveYears,
12          " millimeters in five years."
```

Program 9-1   *(continued)*

```
13
14  # Display the amount of rise in seven years
15  Set sevenYears = YEARLY_RISE * 7
16  Display "The ocean levels will rise ", sevenYears,
17          " millimeters in seven years."
18
19  # Display the amount of rise in ten years
20  Set tenYears = YEARLY_RISE * 10
21  Display "The ocean levels will rise ", tenYears,
22          " millimeters in ten years."
```

Program Output

```
The ocean levels will rise 7.5 millimeters in five years.
The ocean levels will rise 10.5 millimeters in seven years.
The ocean levels will rise 15 millimeters in ten years.
```

Three variables, fiveYears, sevenYears, and tenYears, are declared in lines 2 through 4. These variables will hold the amount that the ocean levels will rise in five, seven, and ten years.

Line 7 creates a constant, YEARLY_RISE, which is set to the value 1.5. This is the amount that the oceans rise per year. This constant will be used in each of the program's calculations.

Lines 10 through 12 calculate and display the amount that the oceans will rise in five years. The same values for seven years and ten years are calculated and displayed in lines 15 through 17 and 20 through 22.

This program illustrates the following standardized programming **style conventions**, which are recommended guidelines and best practices for writing code:

- Several blank lines appear throughout the program (see lines 5, 8, 13, and 18). These blank lines do not affect the way the program works, but make the pseudocode easier to read. Leaving blank lines in code for readability is called **whitespacing**.
- Line comments are used in various places to explain what the program is doing.
- Notice that each of the Display statements is too long to fit on one line. (See lines 11 and 12, 16 and 17, 21 and 22.) Most programming languages allow you to write long statements across several lines. When we do this in pseudocode, we will indent the second and subsequent lines. This will give a visual indication that the statement spans more than one line.

Figure 9-5 shows a flowchart for the program.

Figure 9-5 Flowchart for Program 9-1

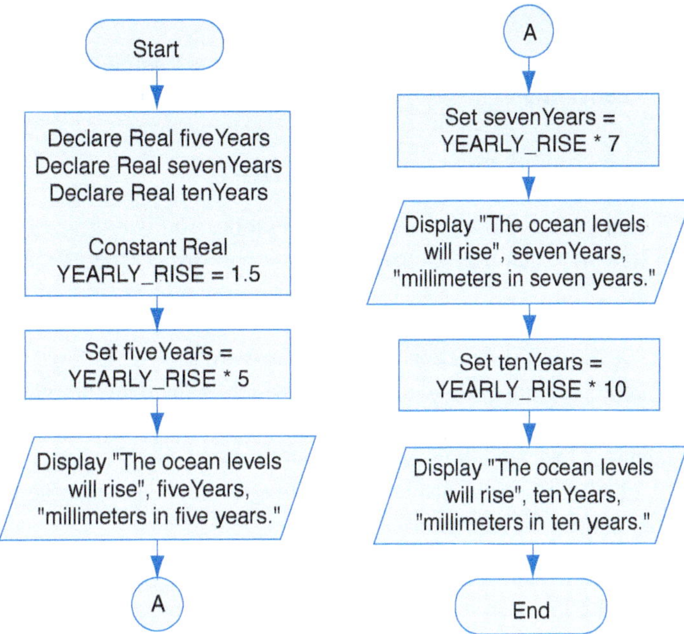

Checkpoint

9.11 Explain the benefits of using standard programming style conventions.

9.12 What is whitespacing?

9.13 In pseudocode, how can you indicate that a statement spans more than one line?

9.5 Input and Output Standards in Python

To write readable, efficient code, you must know how to use standards and conventions.

Displaying Screen Output in Python

To display output on the computer's screen in Python, you use the `print` function. Here is an example of a statement that uses the `print` function to display the message *Hello world.*

```
print('Hello world')
```

Recall that to use the `print` function, you type the word `print`, followed by a set of parentheses. Inside the parentheses, you type an **argument**, which is the data that you want displayed on the screen. In this example, the argument is `'Hello world'`. The quote marks will not be displayed when the statement executes, however. The quote marks simply specify the beginning and the end of the text that we wish to display. Program 9-2 shows an example of a complete program that displays output on the screen.

TIP: Remember, the line numbers are NOT part of the program! Don't type the line numbers when you are entering program code. The line numbers are shown for reference purposes only.

Program 9-2   **(output.py)**

```
1  print('My major is Computer Science.')
2  print('I plan to be a software developer.')
3  print('Programming is fun!')
```

Program Output

```
My major is Computer Science.
I plan to be a software developer.
Programming is fun!
```

In Chapter 6, you learned that in Python, you can enclose string literals in a set of single-quote marks (') or a set of double-quote marks ("). The string literals in Program 9-3 are enclosed in single-quote marks, but the program could also be written as shown here:

```
print("My major is Computer Science.")
print("I plan to be a software developer.")
print("Programming is fun!")
```

Python Variables

Recall that you do not declare variables in Python. Instead, you use an **assignment statement** to create a variable. Here is an example of an assignment statement:

```
age = 25
```

After this statement executes, a variable named `age` will be created and it will be assigned the integer value 25. Here is another example:

```
title = 'Vice President'
```

After this statement executes, a variable named `title` will be created and it will be assigned the string `'Vice President'`.

Variable Names in Python

Recall, also, that you may choose your own variable names in Python, as long as you do not use any of the Python keywords. (See Appendix C for a complete list of Python keywords.) Let's review the additional rules you must follow when naming variables in Python:

- A variable name cannot contain spaces.
- The first character must be one of the letters a through z, A through Z, or an underscore character (_).
- After the first character you may use the letters a through z or A through Z, the digits 0 through 9, or underscores.
- Uppercase and lowercase characters are distinct. This means the variable name `ItemsOrdered` is not the same as `itemsordered`.

Displaying Multiple Items with the `print` Function in Python

Recall that you can pass multiple arguments to the print function, and Python will print each argument's value on the screen, separated by a space. Review the example in Program 9-3.

Program 9-3   **(print_multiple.py)**

```
1 room = 503
2 print('I am staying in room number', room)
```

Program Output

```
I am staying in room number 503
```

The statement in line 1 creates a variable named `room` and assigns it the integer value 503. The statement in line 2 displays two items: a string literal followed by the value of the `room` variable. Notice that Python automatically displayed a space between these two items.

Reading Input from the Keyboard in Python

Recall that you can use Python's built-in `input` function to read input from the keyboard. The `input` function reads a piece of data that has been entered at the keyboard and returns that piece of data, as a string, back to the program. You normally use the `input` function in an assignment statement that follows this general format:

```
variable = input(prompt)
```

In the general format, *prompt* is a string that is displayed on the screen. The string's purpose is to instruct the user to enter a value. *variable* is the name of a variable that will reference the data that was entered on the keyboard. Here is an example of a statement that uses the `input` function to read data from the keyboard:

```
name = input('What is your name? ')
```

When this statement executes, the following things happen:

- The string `'What is your name? '` is displayed on the screen.
- The program pauses and waits for the user to type something on the keyboard, waits for the user to type something on the keyboard, then press the Enter key.
- When the Enter key is pressed, the data that was typed is returned as a string and assigned to the `name` variable.

Program 9-4 shows a complete program that uses the `input` function to read two strings as input from the keyboard.

Program 9-4   **(string_input.py)**

```
1 first_name = input('Enter your first name: ')
2 last_name = input('Enter your last name: ')
3 print('Hello', first_name, last_name)
```

Program Output (with input shown in bold)

```
Enter your first name:  Vinny [Enter]
Enter your last name:  Brown [Enter]
Hello Vinny Brown
```

Reading Numbers with the `input` Function in Python

In Chapter 6, you learned that the `input` function always returns the user's input as a string, even if the user enters numeric data. For example, suppose you call the `input` function and the user types the number 72 and pressed the Enter key. The value that is returned from the `input` function is the string `'72'`. This can be a problem if you want to use the value in a math operation. Math operations can be performed only on numeric values, not strings.

Recall that Python has built-in functions that you can use to convert a string to a numeric type. Table 9-1 summarizes two of these functions.

Table 9-1 Python Data Conversion Functions

Function	Description
int(*item*)	You pass an argument to the int() function and it returns the argument's value converted to an integer.
float(*item*)	You pass an argument to the float() function and it returns the argument's value converted to a floating-point number.

For example, the following code gets an integer and a floating-point number from the user:

```
hours = int(input('How many hours did you work? '))
pay_rate = float(input('What is your hourly pay rate? '))
```

Performing Calculations in Python

The Python arithmetic operators are shown in Table 9-2.

Table 9-2 Python Arithmetic Operators

+	Addition
–	Subtraction
*	Multiplication
/	Division
%	Modulus
**	Exponent

Here are some examples of Python statements that use an arithmetic operator to calculate a value, then assign that value to a variable:

```
total = price + tax
sale = price – discount
population = population * 2
half = number / 2
leftOver = 17 % 3
result = 4**2
```

Program 9-5 shows an example program that performs mathematical calculations.

Program 9-5   **(sale_price.py)**

```
1  original_price = float(input("Enter the item's original price: "))
2  discount = original_price * 0.2
3  sale_price = original_price – discount
4  print('The sale price is', sale_price)
```

Program Output (with input shown in bold)

```
Enter the item's original price:  100.00 Enter
The sale price is 80.0
```

Checkpoint

9.14   What function do you use to display output on screen in Python?

9.15   What should you type in Python to display the text "Goodnight." on screen?

9.16   In Python, what do you do instead of declaring a variable?

9.17   What function do you use in Python to read input from the keyboard?

9.6   Code a Solution

Breaking a main task into subtasks makes it faster and easier to define and solve a problem.

Before diving into coding, you should take the time to refine your algorithms and design. Recall that the software development lifecycle is an **iterative** process. That means you continually test and improve your work. Start simple, and then iteratively refine the design. It is tempting to jump right into coding, but spending time in the planning phase will save you time in the long run. The job of coding will be easier.

In Chapter 8, you designed an algorithm to find the largest of three values. Working alone or with a partner or small group, use the following three steps to refine that algorithm, then code the solution.

Step 1: Define the problem.

When defining the problem, you should first identify and define the main task. Then, you should break down the larger problem into **subtasks**. This method of problem-solving is sometimes referred to as the **divide and conquer method**.

Working with subtasks makes it easier to achieve your goal. First, each subtask is probably more manageable and faster to complete than the main task. Second, you can divide the subtasks among teammates so that you can work on multiple tasks at the same time.

Main task: Given any three integers, find the largest of the three values.

Subtasks: Retrieve user input as x,y,z of integer data types; use relational operators to determine the largest number; output the largest value to the screen.

If you have trouble identifying what the subtasks should be, start by thinking about what the input, process, and output of the program should look like. This helps you identify the data types and objects, such as variables, that you need. For this problem, we can list input, process, output as follows:

- Input: x, y, and z values of integer data type
- Process: The program must determine the largest number of three values.
- Output: Display the largest integer value to screen.

Step 2: Describe the steps with pseudocode.

Our initial algorithm from Chapter 8 looked like the following:

```
Step1: Store the values in x, y, z
Step2: If x > y and x > z print x
Step3: Otherwise, if y > z and y > x print y
Step4: Otherwise print z
```

Next, we use the initial algorithm steps, and refine it to pseudocode. There is more than one way to writing pseudocode. Your design may look different.

```
declare x,y,z as integer values
declare max as integer value
assign values to x,y,z
if x > y and x > z then max is x
elseif y > z and y > x then max is y
else max is z
print max
```

Step 3: Code the solution

Evaluating the pseudocode helps determine the programming construct that best solves the problem. A **programming construct** is a structure used to control the flow of code execution. We need to perform a task if some condition is met. Therefore, a conditional statement is the best construct to use. The following is a solution to the problem.

```python
# Given any three integers, this program
# determines the largest of the three.

# Assign values to x,y,z,max
x = 5
y = 3
z = 9
max = 0

# Use a conditional construct
# and relational operators to find max.
if (x > y) and (x > z):
    max = x
elif (y > z) and (y > x):
    max = y
else:
    max = z

# Display the result.
print('The largest number is ', max)

Solution output:
The largest number is 9
```

You can use this simple solution to test your code by assigning various values to x, y, z and running the program. Does the solution work for any given set of values?

Once you've tested the code, you are ready to add additional functionality to the solution. For instance, the project definition states that x, y, z values should be retrieved from the user. The following code satisfies the main task and subtasks of the problem definition.

```python
# Declare and assign values to x,y,z,max.
x = 0
y = 0
z = 0
max = 0

# Retrieve input from user.
x = int(input('What is your first number? '))
y = int(input('What is your second number? '))
z = int(input('What is your third number? '))

# Use relational operators to find max.
if (x > y) and (x > z):
    max = x
elif (y > x) and (y > z):
    max = y
else:
    max = z

# Display the result.
print('The largest number is ', max)
```

Checkpoint

9.18   Explain the problem-solving technique: Divide and Conquer.

9.19   What three things should you identify to help define the subtasks of a program?

9.20   Recall the algorithm used in Chapter 8 for Finding a Prime Number. Refine the algorithm and code the solution.

? Chapter Review

Multiple Choice

1. What type of error does not prevent the program from running, but causes it to produce incorrect results?
   a. syntax
   b. hardware
   c. logic
   d. fatal

2. A single function that the program must perform in order to satisfy the customer is called a __________.
   a. task
   b. software requirement
   c. prerequisite
   d. predicate

3. A set of well-defined logical steps that must be taken to perform a task is called a(n) __________.
   a. logarithm
   b. plan of action
   c. logic schedule
   d. algorithm

4. An informal language that has no syntax rules and is not meant to be compiled or executed is called __________.
   a. faux code
   b. pseudocode
   c. Python
   d. a flowchart

5. What type of diagram graphically depicts the steps that take place in a program?
   a. flowchart
   b. step chart
   c. code graph
   d. program graph

6. What do you call the ovals that appear at the top and bottom of a flowchart?
   a. processing symbols
   b. terminal symbols
   c. input symbols
   d. output symbols

7. What type of chart can you use to begin analysis of a problem?
   a. IPO chart
   b. flowchart
   c. interactivity chart
   d. problem analysis chart

8. What is an example of external program documentation?
   a. comments
   b. reference guide
   c. variables
   d. functions

9. What symbol do you use to start a comment line in Python?
   a. //
   b. /
   c. #
   d. *

10. What function do you use to display output onscreen in Python?
    a. output
    b. display
    c. print
    d. copy

11. In Python, what characters do you use to enclose string literals?
    a. single-quote marks
    b. hashtags
    c. slashes
    d. carets

12. In Python, what string instructs the user to enter a value?
    a. enter
    b. type
    c. input
    d. prompt

13. To make it easier and faster to solve a problem, divide the main task into ________.
    a. goals
    b. subtasks
    c. mini-problems
    d. solutions

True or False

1. Programmers must be careful not to make syntax errors when writing pseudocode programs.

2. When using a PAC, put the list of processing required in Section 2.

3. In Python, use // to start a comment line.

4. Display statements must always fit on a single line.

5. You do not declare variables in Python.

6. In Python, you must enclose string literals in single-quote marks.

7. In Python, a variable name cannot contain spaces.

8. In Python, the input function always returns user input as a string.

Short Answer

1. What does a professional programmer usually do first to gain an understanding of a problem?

2. What is pseudocode?

3. How does whitespacing improve the readability and functionality of code?

4. Explain how you might use a block comment when coding.

5. What would you type if you want to display the text "I want to be a computer scientist." on the screen?

6. What is a programming construct?

Algorithm Workbench

1. Select the most appropriate construct and design an algorithm that prompts the user to enter the temperature and stores the user's input in a variable named temperature. Use the processes you have learned in this chapter to define and analyze the problem. For example, identify the main task and subtasks. Identify the data type(s) and objects you will need. Demonstrate the processes using charts and graphic organizers, such as a flowchart and PAC. Share your work with a partner or with the class, and improve it based on feedback.

2. Select the most appropriate construct and design an algorithm that prompts the user to enter their favorite color and stores the user's input in a variable named color. Use the processes you have learned in this chapter to define and analyze the problem. For example, identify the main task and subtasks. Identify the data type(s) and objects you will need. Demonstrate the processes using charts and graphic organizers, such as a flowchart and PAC. Share your work with a partner or with the class, and improve it based on feedback.

3. Write assignment statements that perform the following operations with the variables a and b.
   a. Adds 2 to a and stores the result in b
   b. Multiplies b times 4 and stores the result in a
   c. Divides a by 3.14 and stores the result in b
   d. Subtracts 8 from b and stores the result in a

4. Assume the variables result, x, y, and z are all integers, and that x = 4, y = 8, and z = 2. What value will be stored in result in each of the following statements?
   a. Set result = x + y
   b. Set result = z * 2
   c. Set result = y / x
   d. Set result = y − z

5. Write a pseudocode statement that declares the variable cost so it can hold real numbers.

6. Write a pseudocode statement that declares the variable total so it can hold integers. Initialize the variable with the value 0.

7. Write a pseudocode statement that assigns the value 27 to the variable count.

8. Write a pseudocode statement that assigns the sum of 10 and 14 to the variable total.

9. Write a pseudocode statement that subtracts the variable downPayment from the variable total and assigns the result to the variable due.

10. Write a pseudocode statement that multiplies the variable subtotal by 0.15 and assigns the result to the variable totalFee.

11. If the following pseudocode were an actual program, what would it display?
```
Declare Integer a = 5
Declare Integer b = 2
Declare Integer c = 3
Declare Integer result
Set result = a + b * c
Display result
```

12. If the following pseudocode were an actual program, what would it display?
```
Declare Integer num = 99
Set num = 5
Display num
```

Programming Exercises

1. Land Calculation

One acre of land is equivalent to 43,560 square feet. Using the processes you have learned in this chapter, write a program that asks the user to enter the total square feet in a tract of land and calculates the number of acres in the tract.

Hint: Divide the amount entered by 43,560 to get the number of acres.

Demonstrate the processes using charts and graphic organizers, such as a flowchart and PAC. For example, identify the main task and break it into subtasks. Identify the data type(s) and objects you will need. Use standard programming style conventions such as whitespacing to enhance the readability and functionality of the code.

Share your work with a partner or with the class, and improve it based on feedback.

2. Total Purchase

A customer in a store is purchasing five items. Given the cost of each item and the sales tax, select the most appropriate construct for a program that will calculate the subtotal of the sale, the amount of sales tax, and the total cost. Using the processes you have learned in this chapter, design the solution to the problem. Using the design, write the code for a program that asks for the price of each item, and then displays the subtotal of the sale, the amount of sales tax, and the total. Assume the sales tax is 6 percent.

Demonstrate the processes using charts and graphic organizers, such as a flowchart and PAC. Share your work with a partner or with the class, and improve it based on feedback.

3. Distance Traveled

Assuming there are no accidents or delays, the distance that a car travels down the interstate can be calculated with the following formula:

$$Distance = Speed \times Time$$

A car is traveling at a constant 60 miles per hour. Using the processes you have learned in this chapter, write a program that displays the following:

- The distance the car will travel in 5 hours
- The distance the car will travel in 8 hours
- The distance the car will travel in 12 hours

Demonstrate the processes using charts and graphic organizers, such as a flowchart and PAC. For example, identify the main task and break it into subtasks. Identify the data type(s) and objects you will need. Use standard programming style conventions such as whitespacing to enhance the readability and functionality of the code. Share your work with a partner or with the class, and improve it based on feedback.

4. Miles-per-Gallon

A car's miles-per-gallon (MPG) can be calculated with the following formula:

MPG = Miles driven / Gallons of gas used

Using the processes you have learned in this chapter, design a program that asks the user for the number of miles driven and the gallons of gas used. It should calculate the car's miles-per-gallon and display the result on the screen.

Demonstrate the processes using charts and graphic organizers, such as a flowchart and PAC. Share your work with a partner or with the class, and improve it based on feedback.

5. Tip, Tax, and Total

Using the processes you have learned in this chapter, design a program that calculates the total amount of a meal purchased at a restaurant. The program should ask the user to enter the charge for the food, and then calculate the amount of a 15 percent tip and 7 percent sales tax. Display each of these amounts and the total.

Demonstrate the processes using charts and graphic organizers, such as a flowchart and PAC. Share your work with a partner or with the class, and improve it based on feedback.

6. Leftover Pizza

You're planning a pizza party and you plan to give each person three slices of pizza. Using the processes you have learned in this chapter, create a program that displays the number of slices that will be leftover.

The program should ask for the following input:

- The number of pizzas you will have
- The number of slices that each pizza is cut into
- The number of people that will be attending

The program should display the number of slices that will be left over.

Demonstrate the processes using charts and graphic organizers, such as a flowchart and PAC. For example, identify the main task and break it into subtasks. Identify the data type(s) and objects you will need. Use standard programming style conventions such as whitespacing to enhance the readability and functionality of the code. Share your work with a partner or with the class, and improve it based on feedback.

7. Celsius to Fahrenheit Temperature Converter

Using the processes you have learned in this chapter, design a program that converts Celsius temperatures to Fahrenheit temperatures.

The formula is as follows:

$$F = \frac{9}{5} C + 32$$

The program should ask the user to enter a temperature in Celsius, and then display the temperature converted to Fahrenheit.

Demonstrate the processes using charts and graphic organizers, such as a flowchart and PAC. Share your work with a partner or with the class, and improve it based on feedback.

8. Ingredient Adjuster

A cookie recipe calls for the following ingredients:

- 1.5 cups of sugar
- 1 cup of butter
- 2.75 cups of flour

The recipe produces 48 cookies with these amounts of the ingredients. Using the processes you have learned in this chapter, assemble a team of at least three people to design a program that asks the user how many cookies they want to make, and then displays the number of cups of each ingredient needed for the specified number of cookies. Decide who will be the lead programmer and what roles the other team members will play, and work together using professionalism and teamwork.

Demonstrate the processes using charts and graphic organizers, such as a flowchart and PAC. Break the main task into subtasks, as necessary. Present your work to another team or to the class, and improve it based on feedback.

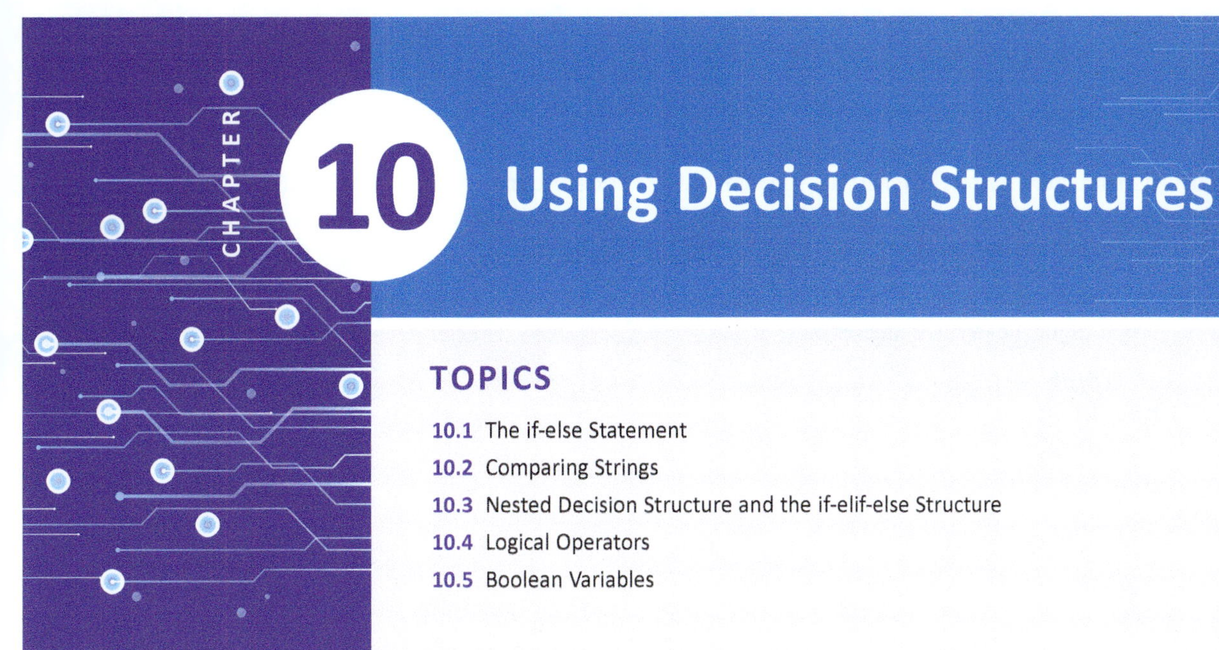

10 Using Decision Structures

TOPICS

10.1 The if-else Statement

10.2 Comparing Strings

10.3 Nested Decision Structure and the if-elif-else Structure

10.4 Logical Operators

10.5 Boolean Variables

10.1 The IF-ELSE Statement

VideoNote
The if-else
Statement

KEY POINT An `if-else` statement will execute one block of statements if its condition is true, or another block if its condition is false.

Chapter 7 introduced the single alternative decision structure (the `if` statement), which has one alternative branch, or path of execution. Now, we will look at the **dual alternative decision structure**, which has two possible branches, or paths of execution—one path is taken if a condition is true, and the other path is taken if the condition is false. Figure 10-1 shows a flowchart for a dual alternative decision structure.

Figure 10-1   A dual alternative decision structure

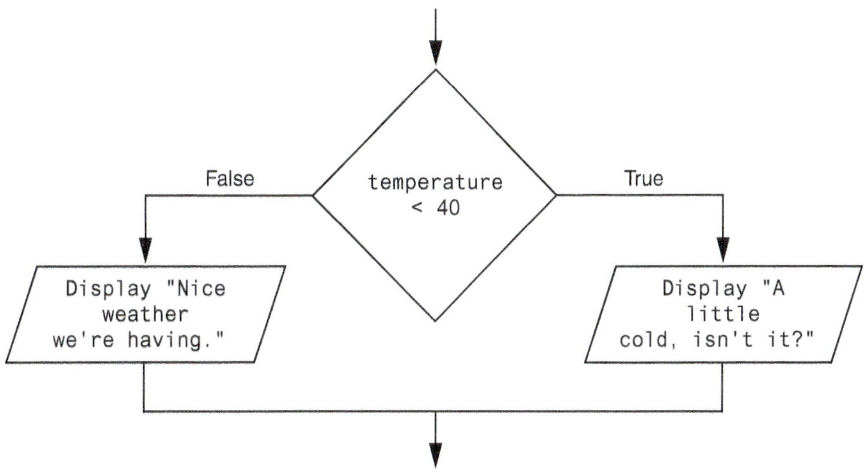

The decision structure in the flowchart tests the condition `temperature < 40`. If this condition is true, the message "`A little cold, isn't it?`" is displayed. If the condition is false, the statement message "`Nice weather we're having.`" is displayed.

In code, we write a dual alternative decision structure as an **if-else statement**. Here is the general format of the `if-else` statement:

```
if condition:
    statement
    statement
    etc.
else:
    statement
    statement
    etc.
```

When this statement executes, the condition is tested. If it is true, the block of indented statements following the `if` clause is executed, then control of the program jumps to the statement that follows the `if-else` statement. If the condition is false, the block of indented statements following the `else` clause is executed, then control of the program jumps to the statement that follows the `if-else` statement. This action is described in Figure 10-2.

Figure 10-2   Conditional execution in an `if-else` statement

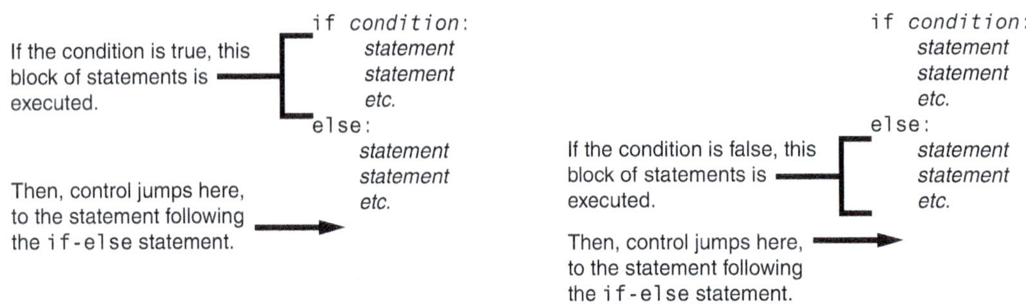

The following code shows an example of an `if-else` statement. This code matches the flowchart that was shown in Figure 10-1.

```
if temperature < 40:
    print("A little cold, isn't it?")
else:
    print("Nice weather we're having.")
```

Indentation in the `if-else` Statement

When you write an `if-else` statement, follow these guidelines for indentation:

- Make sure the `if` clause and the `else` clause are aligned.
- The `if` clause and the `else` clause are each followed by a block of statements. Make sure the statements in the blocks are consistently indented.

This is shown in Figure 10-3.

Figure 10-3   Indentation with an `if-else` statement

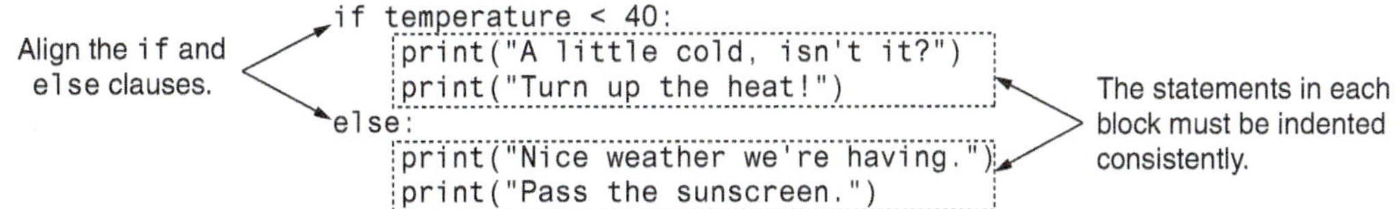

In the Spotlight:

Using the `if-else` Statement

Chris owns an auto repair business and has several employees. If any employee works over 40 hours in a week, he pays them 1.5 times their regular hourly pay rate for all hours over 40. He has asked you to design a simple payroll program that calculates an employee's gross pay, including any overtime wages.

On Your Own: Working alone or with a partner, see if you can design an algorithm to solve the problem. Use problem-solving strategies to select the most appropriate construct, such as identifying the main task and subtasks. When you have completed your work, continue reading to see a solution.

You design the following algorithm:
1. *Get the number of hours worked.*
2. *Get the hourly pay rate.*
3. *If the employee worked more than 40 hours:*
    Calculate and display the gross pay with overtime.
4. *Else:*
    Calculate and display the gross pay as usual.

The code for the program is shown in Program 3-2. Notice two variables are created in lines 3 and 4. The BASE_HOURS named constant is assigned 40, which is the number of hours an employee can work in a week without getting paid overtime. The OT_MULTIPLIER named constant is assigned 1.5, which is the pay rate multiplier for overtime hours. This means that the employee's hourly pay rate is multiplied by 1.5 for all overtime hours.

Program 10-1   **(auto_repair_payroll.py)**

```
 1   # Named constants to represent the base hours and
 2   # the overtime multiplier.
 3   BASE_HOURS = 40      # Base hours per week
 4   OT_MULTIPLIER = 1.5  # Overtime multiplier
 5
 6   # Get the hours worked and the hourly pay rate.
 7   hours = float(input('Enter the number of hours worked: '))
 8   pay_rate = float(input('Enter the hourly pay rate: '))
 9
10   # Calculate and display the gross pay.
```

Program 10-1   *(continued)*

```
11   if hours > BASE_HOURS:
12       # Calculate the gross pay with overtime.
13       # First, get the number of overtime hours worked.
14       overtime_hours = hours - BASE_HOURS
15
16       # Calculate the amount of overtime pay.
17       overtime_pay = overtime_hours * pay_rate * OT_MULTIPLIER
18
19       # Calculate the gross pay.
20       gross_pay = BASE_HOURS * pay_rate + overtime_pay
21   else:
22       # Calculate the gross pay without overtime.
23       gross_pay = hours * pay_rate
24
25   # Display the gross pay.
26   print(f'The gross pay is ${gross_pay:,.2f}.')
```

Program Output (with input shown in bold)

```
Enter the number of hours worked: 40 Enter
Enter the hourly pay rate: 20 Enter
The gross pay is $800.00.
```

Program Output (with input shown in bold)

```
Enter the number of hours worked: 50 Enter
Enter the hourly pay rate: 20 Enter
The gross pay is $1,100.00.
```

Checkpoint

10.1   How does a dual alternative decision structure work?

10.2   What statement do you use in Python to write a dual alternative decision structure?

10.3   When you write an if-else statement, under what circumstances do the statements that appear after the else clause execute?

10.2 Comparing Strings

Python allows you to compare strings. This allows you to create decision structures that test the value of a string.

You saw in the preceding examples how numbers can be compared in a decision structure. You can also compare strings. Recall that a string is a sequence of characters. For example, look at the following code:

```python
name1 = 'Mary'
name2 = 'Mark'
if name1 == name2:
    print('The names are the same.')
else:
    print('The names are NOT the same.')
```

The `==` operator compares `name1` and `name2` to determine whether they are equal. Because the strings `'Mary'` and `'Mark'` are not equal, the `else` clause will display the message `'The names are NOT the same.'`

Let's look at another example. Assume the `month` variable references a string. The following code uses the `!=` operator to determine whether the value referenced by `month` is not equal to `'October'`:

```python
if month != 'October':
    print('This is the wrong time for Octoberfest!')
```

Program 10-2 is a complete program demonstrating how two strings can be compared. The program prompts the user to enter a password, then determines whether the string entered is equal to `'prospero'`.

Program 10-2   (password.py)

```python
 1  # This program compares two strings.
 2  # Get a password from the user.
 3  password = input('Enter the password: ')
 4
 5  # Determine whether the correct password
 6  # was entered.
 7  if password == 'prospero':
 8      print('Password accepted.')
 9  else:
10      print('Sorry, that is the wrong password.')
```

Program Output (with input shown in bold)
```
Enter the password: ferdinand [Enter]
Sorry, that is the wrong password.
```

Program Output (with input shown in bold)
```
Enter the password: prospero [Enter]
Password accepted.
```

String comparisons are case sensitive. For example, the strings `'saturday'` and `'Saturday'` are not equal because the `"s"` is lowercase in the first string, but uppercase in the second string. The following sample session with Program 10-2 shows what happens when the user enters `Prospero` as the password (with an uppercase P).

Program Output (with input shown in bold)
```
Enter the password: Prospero (Enter)
Sorry, that is the wrong password.
```

TIP: In Chapter 12, you will learn how to manipulate strings so case-insensitive comparisons can be performed.

Other String Comparisons

In addition to determining whether strings are equal or not equal, you can also determine whether one string is greater than or less than another string. This is a useful capability because programmers commonly need to design programs that sort strings in some order.

Recall that computers do not actually store characters, such as A, B, C, and so on, in memory. Instead, they store numeric codes that represent the characters. Chapter 1 mentioned that ASCII (the American Standard Code for Information Interchange) is a commonly-used character coding system. You can see the set of ASCII codes in Appendix C, but here are some facts about it:

- The uppercase characters A through Z are represented by the numbers 65 through 90.
- The lowercase characters a through z are represented by the numbers 97 through 122.
- When the digits 0 through 9 are stored in memory as characters, they are represented by the numbers 48 through 57. (For example, the string `'abc123'` would be stored in memory as the codes 97, 98, 99, 49, 50, and 51.)
- A blank space is represented by the number 32.

In addition to establishing a set of numeric codes to represent characters in memory, ASCII also establishes an order for characters. The character "A" comes before the character "B", which comes before the character "C", and so on.

When a program compares characters, it actually compares the codes for the characters. For example, look at the following `if` statement:

```
if 'a' < 'b':
    print('The letter a is less than the letter b.')
```

This code determines whether the ASCII code for the character `'a'` is less than the ASCII code for the character `'b'`. The expression `'a' < 'b'` is true because the code for `'a'` is less than the code for `'b'`. So, if this were part of an actual program, it would display the message `'The letter a is less than the letter b.'`

Let's look at how strings containing more than one character are typically compared. Suppose a program uses the strings `'Mary'` and `'Mark'` as follows:

```
name1 = 'Mary'
name2 = 'Mark'
```

Figure 10-4 shows how the individual characters in the strings `'Mary'` and `'Mark'` would actually be stored in memory, using ASCII codes.

Figure 10-4 Character codes for the strings `'Mary'` and `'Mark'`

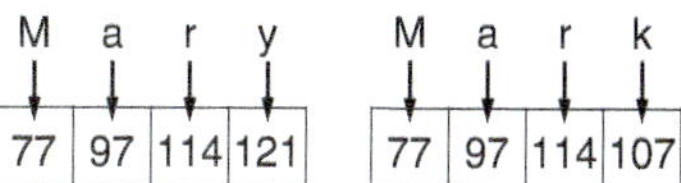

When you use relational operators to compare these strings, the strings are compared character-by-character. For example, look at the following code:

```
name1 = 'Mary'
name2 = 'Mark'
if name1 > name2:
    print('Mary is greater than Mark')
else:
    print('Mary is not greater than Mark')
```

The > operator compares each character in the strings `'Mary'` and `'Mark'`, beginning with the first, or leftmost, characters. This is shown in Figure 10-5.

Figure 10-5 Comparing each character in a string

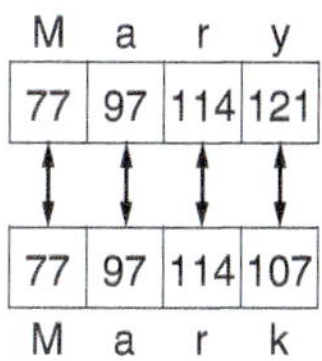

Here is how the comparison takes place:

1. The `'M'` in `'Mary'` is compared with the `'M'` in `'Mark'`. Since these are the same, the next characters are compared.
2. The `'a'` in `'Mary'` is compared with the `'a'` in `'Mark'`. Since these are the same, the next characters are compared.
3. The `'r'` in `'Mary'` is compared with the `'r'` in `'Mark'`. Since these are the same, the next characters are compared.
4. The `'y'` in `'Mary'` is compared with the `'k'` in `'Mark'`. Since these are not the same, the two strings are not equal. The character `'y'` has a higher ASCII code (121) than `'k'` (107), so it is determined that the string `'Mary'` is greater than the string `'Mark'`.

If one of the strings in a comparison is shorter than the other, only the corresponding characters will be compared. If the corresponding characters are identical, then the shorter string is considered less than the longer string. For example, suppose the strings `'High'` and `'Hi'` were being compared.

The string `'Hi'` would be considered less than `'High'` because it is shorter.

Program 10-3 shows a simple demonstration of how two strings can be compared with the < operator. The user is prompted to enter two names, and the program displays those two names in alphabetical order.

Program 10-3   (`sort_names.py`)

```
 1   # This program compares strings with the < operator.
 2   # Get two names from the user.
 3   name1 = input('Enter a name (last name first): ')
 4   name2 = input('Enter another name (last name first): ')
 5
 6   # Display the names in alphabetical order.
 7   print('Here are the names, listed alphabetically.')
 8
 9   if name1 < name2:
10       print(name1)
11       print(name2)
12   else:
13       print(name2)
14       print(name1)
```

Program Output (with input shown in bold)
```
Enter a name (last name first): Jones, Richard Enter
Enter another name (last name first) Costa, Joan Enter
Here are the names, listed alphabetically:
Costa, Joan
Jones, Richard
```

Checkpoint

10.4 What would the following code display?

```
if 'z' < 'a':
    print('z is less than a.')
else:
    print('z is not less than a.')
```

10.5 What would the following code display?

```
s1 = 'New York'
s2 = 'Boston'
if s1 > s2:
    print(s2)
    print(s1)
else:
    print(s1)
    print(s2)
```

10.3 Nested Decision Structures and the `if-elif-else` Statement

KEY POINT To test more than one condition, a decision structure can be nested inside another decision structure.

A **control structure** determines the order in which a set of statements executes. Programs are usually designed as combinations of different control structures. For example, Figure 10-6 shows a flowchart that combines a **decision structure** with two **sequence structures**.

Figure 10-6   Combining sequence structures with a decision structure

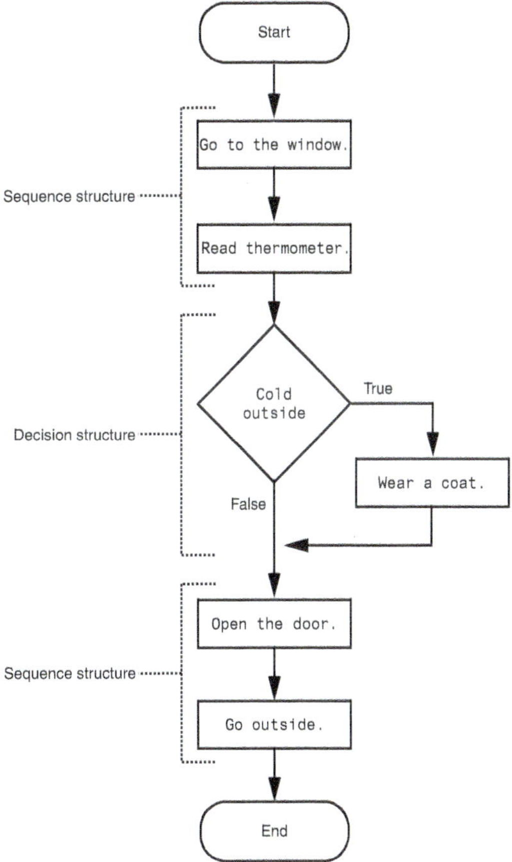

The flowchart in the figure starts with a sequence structure. Assuming you have an outdoor thermometer in your window, the first step is Go to the window, and the next step is Read thermometer. A decision structure appears next, testing the condition Cold outside. If this is true, the action Wear a coat is performed. Another sequence structure appears next. The step Open the door is performed, followed by Go outside.

Quite often, structures must be nested inside other structures. For example, look at the partial flowchart in Figure 10-7. It shows a decision structure with a sequence structure nested inside it. The decision structure tests the condition Cold outside. If that condition is true, the steps in the sequence structure are executed.

Figure 10-7   A sequence structure nested inside a decision structure

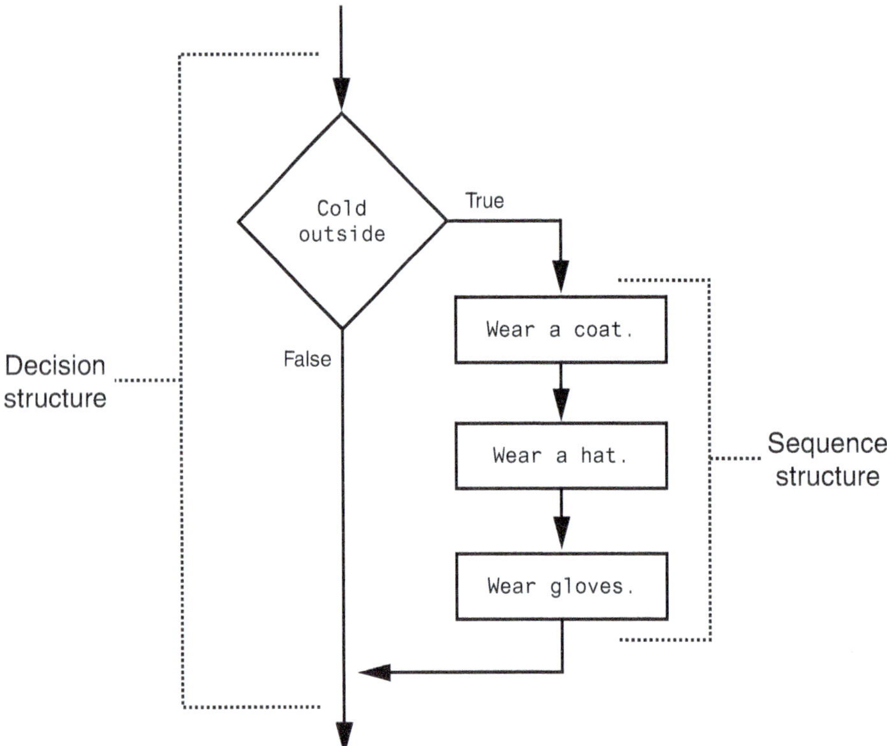

You can also nest decision structures inside other decision structures. In fact, this is a common requirement in programs that need to test more than one condition. For example, consider a program that determines whether a bank customer qualifies for a loan. To qualify, two conditions must exist: (1) the customer must earn at least $30,000 per year, and (2) the customer must have been employed for at least two years. Figure 10-8 shows a flowchart for an algorithm that could be used in such a program. Assume the salary variable is assigned the customer's annual salary, and the years_on_job variable is assigned the number of years that the customer has worked on his or her current job.

Figure 10-8   A nested decision structure

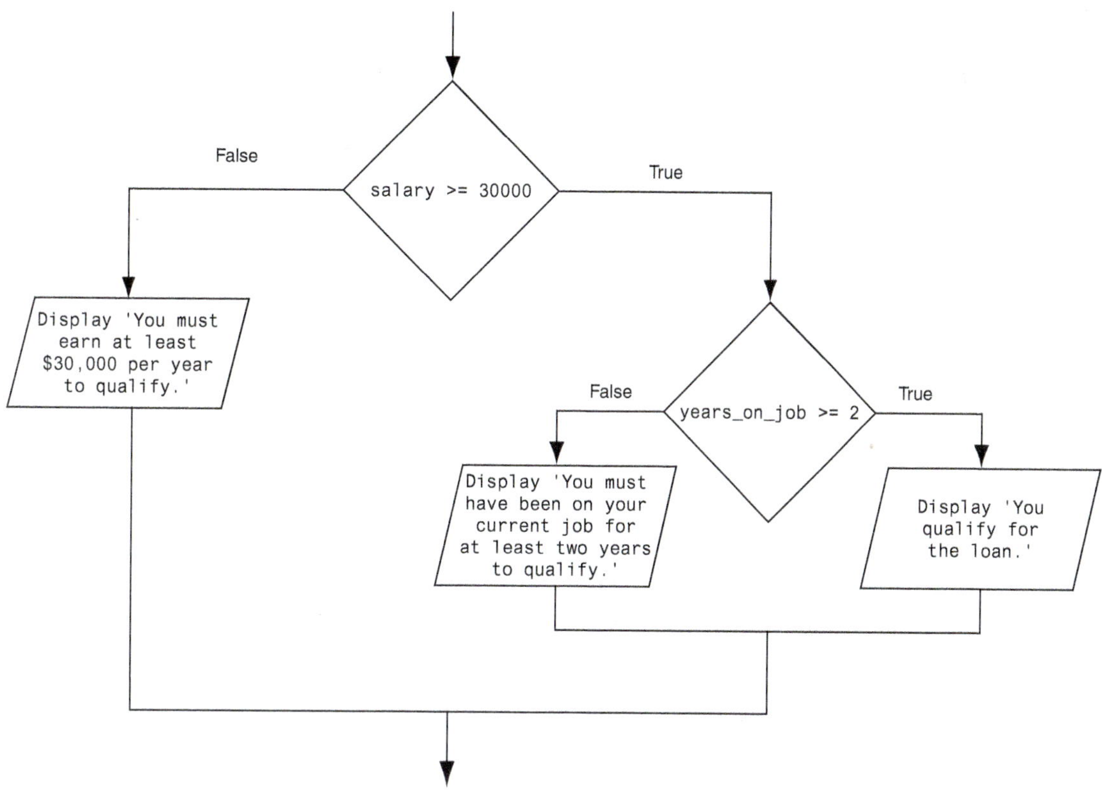

If we follow the flow of execution, we see that the condition `salary >= 30000` is tested. If this condition is false, there is no need to perform further tests; we know the customer does not qualify for the loan. If the condition is true, however, we need to test the second condition. This is done with a nested decision structure that tests the condition `years_on_job >= 2`. If this condition is true, then the customer qualifies for the loan. If this condition is false, then the customer does not qualify. Program 10-4 shows the code for the complete program.

Program 10-4   (`loan_qualifier.py`)

```
 1  # This program determines whether a bank customer
 2  # qualifies for a loan.
 3
 4  MIN_SALARY = 30000.0    # The minimum annual salary
 5  MIN_YEARS = 2           # The minimum years on the job
 6
 7  # Get the customer's annual salary.
 8  salary = float(input('Enter your annual salary: '))
 9
10  # Get the number of years on the current job.
```

Program 10-4   *(continued)*

```
11   years_on_job = int(input('Enter the number of ' +
12                             'years employed: '))
13
14   # Determine whether the customer qualifies.
15   if salary >= MIN_SALARY:
16       if years_on_job >= MIN_YEARS:
17           print('You qualify for the loan.')
18       else:
19           print(f'You must have been employed '
20                 f'for at least {MIN_YEARS} '
21                 f'years to qualify.')
22   else:
23       print(f'You must earn at least $'
24             f'{MIN_SALARY:,.2f} '
25             f'per year to qualify.')
```

Program Output (with input shown in bold)

```
Enter your annual salary: 35000 Enter
Enter the number of years employed: 1 Enter
You must have been employed for at least 2 years to qualify.
```

Program Output (with input shown in bold)

```
Enter your annual salary: 25000 Enter
Enter the number of years employed: 5 Enter
You must earn at least $30,000.00 per year to qualify.
```

Program Output (with input shown in bold)

```
Enter your annual salary: 35000 Enter
Enter the number of years employed: 5 Enter
You qualify for the loan.
```

Look at the if-else statement that begins in line 15. It tests the condition salary >= MIN_SALARY. If this condition is true, the if-else statement that begins in line 16 is executed. Otherwise, the program jumps to the else clause in line 22 and executes the statement in lines 23 through 25.

To function properly, the Python interpreter requires proper indentation in a nested decision structure. Proper indentation also makes it easier for a reader to see which actions are performed by each part of the structure. Follow these rules when writing nested if statements:

• Make sure each else clause is aligned with its matching if clause. This is shown in Figure 10-9.

• Make sure the statements in each block are consistently indented. The shaded parts of Figure 10-10 show the nested blocks in the decision structure. Notice each statement in each block is indented the same amount.

Figure 10-9   Alignment of `if` and `else` clauses

Figure 10-10   Nested blocks

```
if salary >= MIN_SALARY:
    if years_on_job >= MIN_YEARS:
        print('You qualify for the loan.')
    else:
        print(f'You must have been employed '
              f'for at least {MIN_YEARS} '
              f'years to qualify.')
else:
    print(f'You must earn at least $'
          f'{MIN_SALARY:,.2f} '
          f'per year to qualify.')
```

Testing a Series of Conditions

In the previous example, you saw how a program can use nested decision structures to test more than one condition. It is not uncommon for a program to have a series of conditions to test, then perform an action depending on which condition is true. One way to accomplish this is to have a decision structure with numerous other decision structures nested inside it. For example, consider the program presented in the following *In the Spotlight* section.

In the Spotlight:

Multiple Nested Decision Structures

Dr. Suarez teaches a literature class and uses the following 10-point grading scale for all of his exams:

Test Score	Grade
90 and above	A
80–89	B
70–79	C
60–69	D
Below 60	F

He has asked you to write a program that will allow a student to enter a test score and then display the grade for that score.

On Your Own: Working alone or with a partner, see if you can design an algorithm to solve this problem. Use problem-solving strategies to select the most appropriate construct, such as identifying the main task and subtasks. When you have completed your work, continue reading to see a solution.

Here is the algorithm that you will use:

      1. Ask the user to enter a test score.
      2. Determine the grade in the following manner:

If the score is greater than or equal to 90, then the grade is A.
   Else, if the score is greater than or equal to 80, then the grade is B.
     Else, if the score is greater than or equal to 70, then the grade is C.
       Else, if the score is greater than or equal to 60, then the grade is D.
        Else, the grade is F.

You decide that the process of determining the grade will require several nested decision structures, as shown in Figure 10-11. Program 10-5 shows the code for the program. The code for the nested decision structures is in lines 14 through 26.

Figure 10-11   Nested decision structure to determine a grade

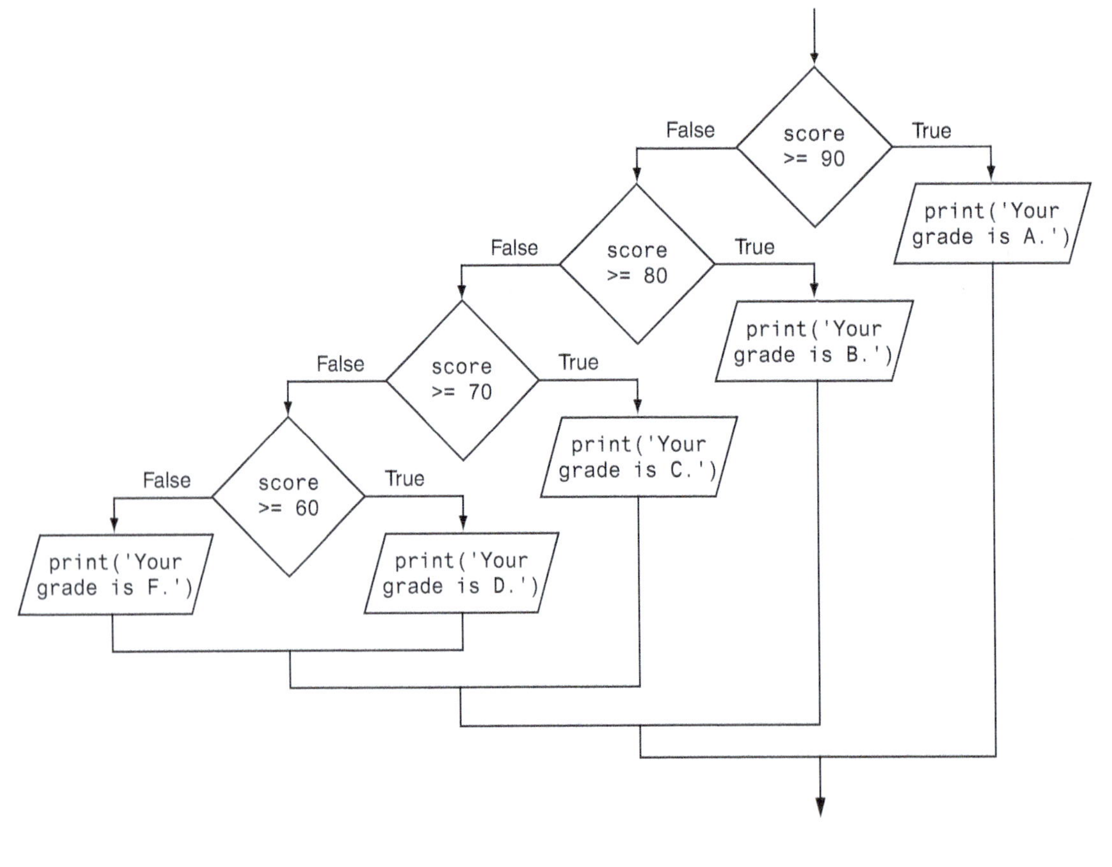

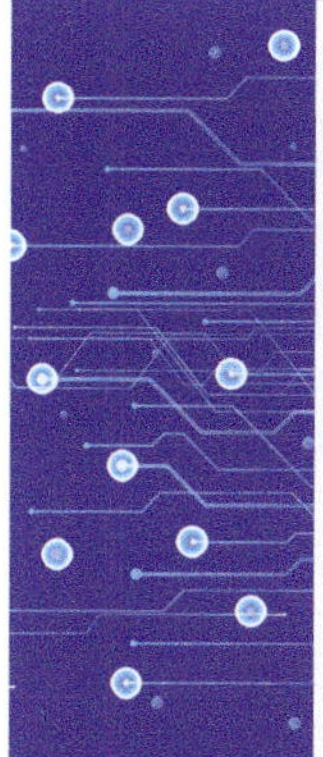

Program 10-5   (`grader.py`)

```python
 1   # This program gets a numeric test score from the
 2   # user and displays the corresponding letter grade.
 3
 4   # Named constants to represent the grade thresholds
 5   A_SCORE = 90
 6   B_SCORE = 80
 7   C_SCORE = 70
 8   D_SCORE = 60
 9
10   # Get a test score from the user.
11   score = int(input('Enter your test score: '))
12
13   # Determine the grade.
14   if score >= A_SCORE:
15       print('Your grade is A.')
16   else:
17       if score >= B_SCORE:
18           print('Your grade is B.')
19       else:
20           if score >= C_SCORE:
21               print('Your grade is C.')
22           else:
23               if score >= D_SCORE:
24                   print('Your grade is D.')
25               else:
26                   print('Your grade is F.')
```

Program Output (with input shown in bold)
```
Enter your test score: 78 Enter
Your grade is C.
```

Program Output (with input shown in bold)
```
Enter your test score: 84 Enter
Your grade is B.
```

The `if-elif-else` Statement

Even though Program 10-5 is a simple example, the logic of the nested decision structure is fairly complex. Python provides a special version of the decision structure known as the **if-elif-else statement**, which makes this type of logic simpler to write. Here is the general format of the `if-elif-else` statement:

```
if condition_1:
    statement
    statement
    etc.
elif condition_2:
    statement
    statement
    etc.
```
Insert as many elif clauses as necessary . . .
```
else:
    statement
    statement
    etc.
```

When the statement executes, `condition_1` is tested. If `condition_1` is true, the block of statements that immediately follow is executed, up to the `elif` clause. The rest of the structure is ignored. If `condition_1` is false, however, the program jumps to the very next `elif` clause and tests `condition_2`. If it is true, the block of statements that immediately follow is executed, up to the next `elif` clause. The rest of the structure is then ignored. This process continues until a condition is found to be true, or no more `elif` clauses are left. If no condition is true, the block of statements following the `else` clause is executed.

The following is an example of the `if-elif-else` statement. This code works the same as the nested decision structure in lines 14 through 26 of Program 10-5.

```
if score >= A_SCORE:
    print('Your grade is A.')
elif score >= B_SCORE:
    print('Your grade is B.')
elif score >= C_SCORE:
    print('Your grade is C.')
elif score >= D_SCORE:
    print('Your grade is D.')
else:
    print('Your grade is F.')
```

Notice the alignment and indentation that is used with the `if-elif-else` statement: The `if`, `elif`, and `else` clauses are all aligned, and the conditionally executed blocks are indented.

The `if-elif-else` statement is never required because its logic can be coded with nested `if-else` statements. However, a long series of nested `if-else` statements has two particular disadvantages when you are debugging code:

- The code can grow complex and become difficult to understand.
- Because of the required indentation, a long series of nested `if-else` statements can become too long to be displayed on the computer screen without horizontal scrolling. Also, long statements tend to "wrap around" when printed on paper, making the code even more difficult to read.

The logic of an `if-elif-else` statement is usually easier to follow than a long series of nested `if-else` statements. And, because all of the clauses are aligned in an `if-elif-else` statement, the lengths of the lines in the statement tend to be shorter.

Checkpoint

10.6 Convert the following code to an `if-elif-else` statement:

```
if number == 1:
    print('One')
else:
    if number == 2:
        print('Two')
    else:
        if number == 3:
            print('Three')
        else:
            print('Unknown')
```

10.4) Logical Operators

The logical and operator and the logical or operator allow you to connect multiple Boolean expressions to create a compound expression. The logical not operator reverses the truth of a Boolean expression.

Python provides a set of operators known as **logical operators**, which you can use to create complex Boolean expressions. Recall that Boolean expressions are a logical statement that is either true or false, and can be tested using an if statement. Table 10-1 describes these operators.

Table 10-1   Logical operators

Operator	Meaning
and	The and operator connects two Boolean expressions into one compound expression. Both subexpressions must be true for the compound expression to be true.
or	The or operator connects two Boolean expressions into one compound expression. One of the two subexpressions must be true for the compound expression to be true, and it does not matter which. It is also possible for both subexpressions to be true.
not	The not operator is a unary operator, meaning it works with only one operand. The operand must be a Boolean expression. The not operator reverses the truth of its operand. If it is applied to an expression that is true, the operator returns false. If it is applied to an expression that is false, the operator returns true.

Table 10-2 shows examples of several compound Boolean expressions that use logical operators.

Table 10-2   Compound Boolean expressions using logical operators

Expression	Meaning
x > y and a < b	Is x greater than y AND is a less than b?
x == y or x == z	Is x equal to y OR is x equal to z?
not (x > y)	Is the expression x > y NOT true?

The and Operator

The and operator takes two Boolean expressions as **operands** and creates a compound Boolean expression that is true only when both subexpressions are true. The following is an example of an if statement that uses the and operator:

```
if temperature < 20 and minutes > 12:
    print('The temperature is in the danger zone.')
```

In this statement, the two Boolean expressions temperature < 20 and minutes > 12 are combined into a compound expression. The print function will be called only if temperature is less than 20 and `minutes` is greater than 12. If either of the Boolean subexpressions is false, the compound expression is false and the message is not displayed.

Table 10-3 shows a truth table for the and operator. The truth table lists expressions showing all the possible combinations of true and false connected with the and operator. The resulting values of the expressions are also shown.

Table 10-3   Truth table for the and operator

Expression	Value of the Expression
true and false	false
false and true	false
false and false	false
true and true	true

As the table shows, both sides of the and operator must be true for the operator to return a true value.

The or Operator

The or operator takes two Boolean expressions as operands and creates a compound Boolean expression that is true when either of the subexpressions is true. The following is an example of an `if` statement that uses the or operator:

```
if temperature < 20 or temperature > 100:
    print('The temperature is too extreme')
```

The print function will be called only if `temperature` is less than 20 or `temperature` is greater than 100. If either subexpression is true, the compound expression is true. Table 10-4 shows a truth table for the or operator.

Table 10-4   Truth table for the or operator

Expression	Value of the Expression
true or false	true
false or true	true
false or false	false
true or true	true

All it takes for an or expression to be true is for one side of the or operator to be true. It doesn't matter if the other side is false or true.

Short-Circuit Evaluation

Both the and and or operators perform **short-circuit evaluation** which means the evaluation stops as soon as the first condition which satisfies or negates the expression is found. Here's how it works with the and operator: If the expression on the left side of the and operator is false, the expression on the right side will not be checked. Because the compound expression will be false if only one of the subexpressions is false, it would waste CPU time to check the remaining expression. So, when the and operator finds that the expression on its left is false, it short-circuits and does not evaluate the expression on its right.

Here's how short-circuit evaluation works with the or operator: If the expression on the left side of the or operator is true, the expression on the right side will not be checked. Because it is only necessary for one of the expressions to be true, it would waste CPU time to check the remaining expression.

The not Operator

The not operator is a unary operator that takes a Boolean expression as its operand and reverses its logical value. In other words, if the expression is true, the not operator returns false, and if the expression is false, the not operator returns true. The following is an if statement using the not operator:

```
if not(temperature > 100):
    print('This is below the maximum temperature.')
```

First, the expression (temperature > 100) is tested and a value of either true or false is the result. Then the not operator is applied to that value. If the expression (temperature > 100) is true, the not operator returns false. If the expression (temperature > 100) is false, the not operator returns true. The previous code is equivalent to asking: "Is the temperature not greater than 100?"

> **NOTE: In this example, we have put parentheses around the expression** temperature > 100. **This is to make it clear that we are applying the** not **operator to the value of the expression** temperature > 100, **not just to the** temperature **variable.**

Table 10-5 shows a truth table for the not operator.

Table 10-5   Truth table for the not operator

Expression	Value of the Expression
not true	false
not false	true

The Loan Qualifier Program Revisited

In some situations, the and operator can be used to simplify nested decision structures. For example, recall that the loan qualifier program in Program 10-4 uses the following nested if-else statements:

```python
if salary >= MIN_SALARY:
    if years_on_job >= MIN_YEARS:
        print('You qualify for the loan.')
    else:
        print(f'You must have been employed '
              f'for at least {MIN_YEARS} '
              f'years to qualify.')
else:
    print(f'You must earn at least $'
          f'{MIN_SALARY:,.2f} '
          f'per year to qualify.')
```

The purpose of this decision structure is to determine that a person's salary is at least $30,000 and that they have been at their current job for at least two years. Program 10-6 shows a way to perform a similar task with simpler code.

Program 10-6   **(loan_qualifier2.py)**

```python
 1  # This program determines whether a bank customer
 2  # qualifies for a loan.
 3
 4  MIN_SALARY = 30000.0 # The minimum annual salary
 5  MIN_YEARS = 2        # The minimum years on the job
 6
 7  # Get the customer's annual salary.
 8  salary = float(input('Enter your annual salary: '))
 9
10  # Get the number of years on the current job.
11  years_on_job = int(input('Enter the number of ' +
12                           'years employed: '))
13
14  # Determine whether the customer qualifies.
15  if salary >= MIN_SALARY and years_on_job >= MIN_YEARS:
16      print('You qualify for the loan.')
17  else:
18      print('You do not qualify for this loan.')
```

Program Output (with input shown in bold)
```
Enter your annual salary: 35000 (Enter)
Enter the number of years employed: 1 (Enter)
You do not qualify for this loan.
```

Program Output (with input shown in bold) *(continued)*
```
Enter your annual salary: 25000 Enter
Enter the number of years employed: 5 Enter
You do not qualify for this loan.
```

Program Output (with input shown in bold)
```
Enter your annual salary: 35000 Enter
Enter the number of years employed: 5 Enter
You qualify for the loan.
```

The if-else statement in lines 15 through 18 tests the compound expression salary >= MIN_SALARY and years_on_job >= MIN_YEARS. If both subexpressions are true, the compound expression is true and the message "You qualify for the loan" is displayed. If either of the subexpressions is false, the compound expression is false and the message "You do not qualify for this loan" is displayed.

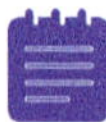

NOTE: A careful observer will realize that Program 10-6 is similar to Program 10-4, but it is not equivalent. If the user does not qualify for the loan, Program 10-6 displays only the message "You do not qualify for this loan" whereas Program 10-4 displays one of two possible messages explaining why the user did not qualify.

Yet Another Loan Qualifier Program

Suppose the bank is losing customers to a competing bank that isn't as strict about to whom it loans money. In response, the bank decides to change its loan requirements. Now, customers have to meet only one of the previous conditions, not both. Program 10-7 shows the code for the new loan qualifier program. The compound expression that is tested by the if-else statement in line 15 now uses the or operator.

Program 10-7   (loan_qualifier3.py)

```
 1   # This program determines whether a bank customer
 2   # qualifies for a loan.
 3
 4   MIN_SALARY = 30000.0 # The minimum annual salary
 5   MIN_YEARS = 2        # The minimum years on the job
 6
 7   # Get the customer's annual salary.
 8   salary = float(input('Enter your annual salary: '))
 9
10   # Get the number of years on the current job.
11   years_on_job = int(input('Enter the number of ' +
12                            'years employed: '))
13
```

Program 10-7   *(continued)*

```
14   # Determine whether the customer qualifies.
15   if salary >= MIN_SALARY or years_on_job >= MIN_YEARS:
16       print('You qualify for the loan.')
17   else:
18       print('You do not qualify for this loan.')
```

Program Output (with input shown in bold)
```
Enter your annual salary: 35000 Enter
Enter the number of years employed: 1 Enter
You qualify for the loan.
```

Program Output (with input shown in bold)
```
Enter your annual salary: 25000 Enter
Enter the number of years employed: 5 Enter
You qualify for the loan.
```

Program Output (with input shown in bold)
```
Enter your annual salary 12000 Enter
Enter the number of years employed:  1 Enter
You do not qualify for this loan.
```

Checking Numeric Ranges with Logical Operators

Sometimes you will need to design an algorithm that determines whether a numeric value is within a specific range of values or outside a specific range of values. When determining whether a number is inside a range, it is best to use the and operator. For example, the following if statement checks the value in x to determine whether it is in the range of 20 through 40:

```
if x >= 20 and x <= 40:
    print('The value is in the acceptable range.')
```

The compound Boolean expression being tested by this statement will be true only when x is greater than or equal to 20 and less than or equal to 40. The value in x must be within the range of 20 through 40 for this compound expression to be true.

When determining whether a number is outside a range, it is best to use the or operator. The following statement determines whether x is outside the range of 20 through 40:

```
if x < 20 or x > 40:
    print('The value is outside the acceptable range.')
```

It is important not to get the logic of the logical operators confused when testing for a range of numbers. For example, the compound Boolean expression in the following code would never test true:

```
# This is an error!
if x < 20 and x > 40:
    print('The value is outside the acceptable range.')
```

Obviously, x cannot be less than 20 and at the same time be greater than 40.

Checkpoint

10.7   What is a compound Boolean expression?

10.8   The following truth table shows various combinations of the values true and false connected by a logical operator. Complete the table by choosing whether the result of such a combination is true or false.

Logical Expression	Result	
True and False	T	F
True and True	T	F
False and True	T	F
False and False	T	F
True or False	T	F
True or True	T	F
False or True	T	F
False or False	T	F
not True	T	F
not False	T	F

10.9   Assume the variables a = 2, b = 4, and c = 6. Are the following conditions true or false?

```
a == 4 or b > 2          T   F
6 <= c and a > 3         T   F
1 != b and c != 3        T   F
a >= -1 or a <= b        T   F
not (a > 2)              T   F
```

10.10   Explain how short-circuit evaluation works with the and and or operators.

10.11   Write an if statement that displays the message "The number is valid" if the value referenced by speed is within the range 0 through 200.

10.12   Write an if statement that displays the message "The number is not valid" if the value referenced by speed is outside the range 0 through 200.

10.5 Boolean Variables

A Boolean variable can reference one of two values: True or False. Boolean variables are commonly used as flags, which indicate whether specific conditions exist.

So far, we have worked with `int`, `float`, and `str` (string) variables. In addition to these data types, Python also provides a bool data type. The bool data type allows you to create variables that may reference one of two possible values: `True` or `False`. Here are examples of how we assign values to a `bool` variable:

```
hungry = True
sleepy = False
```

Boolean variables are most commonly used as flags. A **flag** is a variable that signals when some condition exists in the program. When the flag variable is set to `False`, it indicates the condition does not exist. When the flag variable is set to `True`, it means the condition does exist.

For example, suppose a salesperson has a quota of $50,000. Assuming `sales` references the amount that the salesperson has sold, the following code determines whether the quota has been met:

```
if sales >= 50000.0:
    sales_quota_met = True
else:
    sales_quota_met = False
```

As a result of this code, the `sales_quota_met` variable can be used as a flag to indicate whether the sales quota has been met. Later in the program, we might test the flag in the following way:

```
if sales_quota_met:
    print('You have met your sales quota!')
```

This code displays `'You have met your sales quota!'` if the bool variable `sales_quota_met` is True. Notice we did not have to use the `==` operator to explicitly compare the `sales_quota_met` variable with the value True. This code is equivalent to the following:

```
if sales_quota_met == True:
    print('You have met your sales quota!')
```

Checkpoint

10.13 What values can you assign to a `bool` variable?

10.14 What is a flag variable?

Chapter Review

Multiple Choice

1. A(n) __________ structure tests a condition and then takes one path if the condition is true, or another path if the condition is false.
    a. `if` statement
    b. single alternative decision
    c. dual alternative decision
    d. sequence

2. You use a(n) __________ statement to write a single alternative decision structure.
    a. `test-jump`
    b. `if`
    c. `if-else`
    d. `if-call`

3. You use a(n) __________ statement to write a dual alternative decision structure.
    a. `test-jump`
    b. `if`
    c. `if-else`
    d. `if-call`

4. and, or, and not are __________ operators.
    a. relational
    b. logical
    c. conditional
    d. ternary

5. A compound Boolean expression created with the __________ operator is true only if both of its subexpressions are true.
    a. `and`
    b. `or`
    c. `not`
    d. `both`

6. A compound Boolean expression created with the __________ operator is true if either of its subexpressions is true.
    a. `and`
    b. `or`
    c. `not`
    d. `either`

7. The __________ operator takes a Boolean expression as its operand and reverses its logical value.
    a. `and`
    b. `or`
    c. `not`
    d. `either`

8. A ___________ is a Boolean variable that signals when some condition exists in the program.
   a. flag
   b. signal
   c. sentinel
   d. siren

True or False

1. You can write any program using only sequence structures.

2. A program can be made of only one type of control structure. You cannot combine structures.

3. A single alternative decision structure tests a condition and then takes one path if the condition is true, or another path if the condition is false.

4. A decision structure can be nested inside another decision structure.

5. A compound Boolean expression created with the and operator is true only when both subexpressions are true.

Short Answer

1. Explain what is meant by the term "conditionally executed."

2. You need to test a condition, then execute one set of statements if the condition is true. If the condition is false, you need to execute a different set of statements. What structure will you use?

3. Briefly describe how the and operator works.

4. Briefly describe how the or operator works.

5. When determining whether a number is inside a range, which logical operator is it best to use?

6. What is a flag and how does it work?

Algorithm Workbench

1. Write an `if` statement that assigns 20 to the variable y and assigns 40 to the variable z if the variable x is greater than 100.

2. Write an `if` statement that assigns 0 to the variable b and assigns 1 to the variable c if the variable a is less than 10.

3. Write an `if-else` statement that assigns 0 to the variable b if the variable a is less than 10. Otherwise, it should assign 99 to the variable b.

4. The following code contains several nested `if-else` statements. Unfortunately, it was written without proper alignment and indentation. Rewrite the code using standard programming style for alignment and indentation to enhance functionality and readability.

```
if score >= A_score:
print('Your grade is A.')
else:
if score >= B_score:
print('Your grade is B.')
else:
if score >= C_score:
print('Your grade is C.')
else:
if score >= D_score:
print('Your grade is D.')
else:
print('Your grade is F.')
```

5. Write nested decision structures that perform the following: If `amount1` is greater than 10 and `amount2` is less than 100, display the greater of `amount1` and `amount2`.

6. Write an `if-else` statement that displays `'Speed is normal'` if the speed variable is within the range of 24 to 56. If the speed variable's value is outside this range, display `'Speed is abnormal'`.

7. Write an `if-else` statement that determines whether the `points` variable is outside the range of 9 to 51. If the variable's value is outside this range, it should display "Invalid points." Otherwise, it should display "Valid points."

Programming Exercises

1. Day of the Week
Write a program that asks the user for a number in the range of 1 through 7. The program should display the corresponding day of the week, where 1 = Monday, 2 = Tuesday, 3 = Wednesday, 4 = Thursday, 5 = Friday, 6 = Saturday, and 7 = Sunday. The program should display an error message if the user enters a number that is outside the range of 1 through 7.

VideoNote
The Areas of
Rectangles
Problem

2. Areas of Rectangles
The area of a rectangle is the rectangle's length times its width. Write a program that asks for the length and width of two rectangles. The program should tell the user which rectangle has the greater area, or if the areas are the same.

3. Age Classifier
Write a program that asks the user to enter a person's age. The program should display a message indicating whether the person is an infant, a child, a teenager, or an adult. Following are the guidelines:

- If the person is 1 year old or less, they are an infant.
- If the person is older than 1 year, but younger than 13 years, they are a child.
- If the person is at least 13 years old, but less than 20 years old, they are a teenager.
- If the person is at least 20 years old, they are an adult.

4. Roman Numerals

Write a program that prompts the user to enter a number within the range of 1 through 10. The program should display the Roman numeral version of that number. If the number is outside the range of 1 through 10, the program should display an error message. The following table shows the Roman numerals for the numbers 1 through 10:

Number	Roman Numeral
1	I
2	II
3	III
4	IV
5	V
6	VI
7	VII
8	VIII
9	IX
10	X

5. Mass and Weight

Scientists measure an object's mass in kilograms and its weight in newtons. If you know the amount of mass of an object in kilograms, you can calculate its weight in newtons with the following formula:

weight = mass x 9.8

Write a program that asks the user to enter an object's mass, then calculates its weight. If the object weighs more than 500 newtons, display a message indicating that it is too heavy. If the object weighs less than 100 newtons, display a message indicating that it is too light.

6. Magic Dates

The date June 10, 1960, is special because when it is written in the following format, the month times the day equals the year:

6/10/60

Design a program that asks the user to enter a month (in numeric form), a day, and a two-digit year. The program should then determine whether the month times the day equals the year. If so, it should display a message saying the date is magic. Otherwise, it should display a message saying the date is not magic.

7. Color Mixer

The colors red, blue, and yellow are known as the primary colors because they cannot be made by mixing other colors. When you mix two primary colors, you get a secondary color, as shown here:

- When you mix red and blue, you get purple.
- When you mix red and yellow, you get orange.
- When you mix blue and yellow, you get green.

Design a program that prompts the user to enter the names of two primary colors to mix. If the user enters anything other than "red," "blue," or "yellow," the program should display an error message. Otherwise, the program should display the name of the secondary color that results.

8. Hot Dog Cookout Calculator

Assume hot dogs come in packages of 10 and hot dog buns come in packages of 8. Write a program that calculates the number of packages of hot dogs and the number of packages of hot dog buns needed for a cookout, with the minimum amount of leftovers. The program should ask the user for the number of people attending the cookout and the number of hot dogs each person will be given. The program should display the following details:

- The minimum number of packages of hot dogs required
- The minimum number of packages of hot dog buns required
- The number of hot dogs that will be left over
- The number of hot dog buns that will be left over

9. Money Counting Game

Create a change-counting game that gets the user to enter the number of coins required to make exactly one dollar. The program should prompt the user to enter the number of pennies, nickels, dimes, and quarters. If the total value of the coins entered is equal to one dollar, the program should congratulate the user for winning the game. Otherwise, the program should display a message indicating whether the amount entered was more than or less than one dollar.

10. Book Club Points

Serendipity Booksellers has a book club that awards points to its customers based on the number of books purchased each month. The points are awarded as follows:

- If a customer purchases 0 books, they earn 0 points.
- If a customer purchases 2 books, they earn 5 points.
- If a customer purchases 4 books, they earn 15 points.
- If a customer purchases 6 books, they earn 30 points.
- If a customer purchases 8 or more books, they earn 60 points.

Write a program that asks the user to enter the number of books that they have purchased this month, then displays the number of points awarded.

11. Software Sales

A software company sells a package that retails for $99. Quantity discounts are given according to the following table:

Quantity	Discount
10–19	10%
20–49	20%
50–99	30%
100 or more	40%

Write a program that asks the user to enter the number of packages purchased. The program should then display the amount of the discount (if any) and the total amount of the purchase after the discount.

12. Shipping Charges

The Fast Freight Shipping Company charges the following rates:

Weight of Package	Rate per Pound
2 pounds or less	$1.50
Over 2 pounds but not more than 6 pounds	$3.00
Over 6 pounds but not more than 10 pounds	$4.00
Over 10 pounds	$4.75

Write a program that asks the user to enter the weight of a package, then displays the shipping charges.

13. Time Calculator

Write a program that asks the user to enter a number of seconds and works as follows:

- There are 60 seconds in a minute. If the number of seconds entered by the user is greater than or equal to 60, the program should convert the number of seconds to minutes and seconds.
- There are 3,600 seconds in an hour. If the number of seconds entered by the user is greater than or equal to 3,600, the program should convert the number of seconds to hours, minutes, and seconds.
- There are 86,400 seconds in a day. If the number of seconds entered by the user is greater than or equal to 86,400, the program should convert the number of seconds to days, hours, minutes, and seconds.

14. February Days

The month of February normally has 28 days. But if it is a *leap year*, February has 29 days. Write a program that asks the user to enter a year. The program should then display the number of days in February that year. Use the following criteria to identify leap years:

1. Determine whether the year is divisible by 100. If it is, then it is a leap year if and only if it is also divisible by 400. For example, 2000 is a leap year, but 2100 is not.
2. If the year is not divisible by 100, then it is a leap year if and only if it is divisible by 4. For example, 2008 is a leap year, but 2009 is not.

Here is a sample run of the program:

```
Enter a year: 2008 Enter
In 2008 February has 29 days.
```

15. Wi-Fi Diagnostic Tree

Figure 10-12 shows a simplified flowchart for troubleshooting a bad Wi-Fi connection. Use the flowchart to create a program that leads a person through the steps of fixing a bad Wi-Fi connection. Here is an example of the program's output:

```
Reboot the computer and try to connect.
Did that fix the problem? no [Enter]
Reboot the router and try to connect.
Did that fix the problem? yes [Enter]
```

Notice the program ends as soon as a solution is found to the problem. Here is another example of the program's output:

```
Reboot the computer and try to connect.
Did that fix the problem? no [Enter]
Reboot the router and try to connect.
Did that fix the problem? no [Enter]
Make sure the cables between the router and modem are plugged in firmly.
Did that fix the problem? no [Enter]
Move the router to a new location.
Did that fix the problem? no [Enter]
Get a new router.
```

16. Restaurant Selector

You have a group of friends coming to visit for your high school reunion, and you want to take them out to eat at a local restaurant. You aren't sure if any of them have dietary restrictions, but your restaurant choices are as follows:

Joe's Gourmet Burgers—Vegetarian: No, Vegan: No, Gluten-Free: No
Main Street Pizza Company—Vegetarian: Yes, Vegan: No, Gluten-Free: Yes
Corner Café—Vegetarian: Yes, Vegan: Yes, Gluten-Free: Yes
Mama's Fine Italian—Vegetarian: Yes, Vegan: No, Gluten-Free: No
The Chef's Kitchen—Vegetarian: Yes, Vegan: Yes, Gluten-Free: Yes

Write a program that asks whether any members of your party are vegetarian, vegan, or gluten-free, to which then displays only the restaurants to which you may take the group. Here is an example of the program's output:

```
Is anyone in your party a vegetarian? yes [Enter]
Is anyone in your party a vegan? no [Enter]
Is anyone in your party gluten-free? yes [Enter]
Here are your restaurant choices:
    Main Street Pizza Company
    Corner Cafe
    The Chef's Kitchen
```

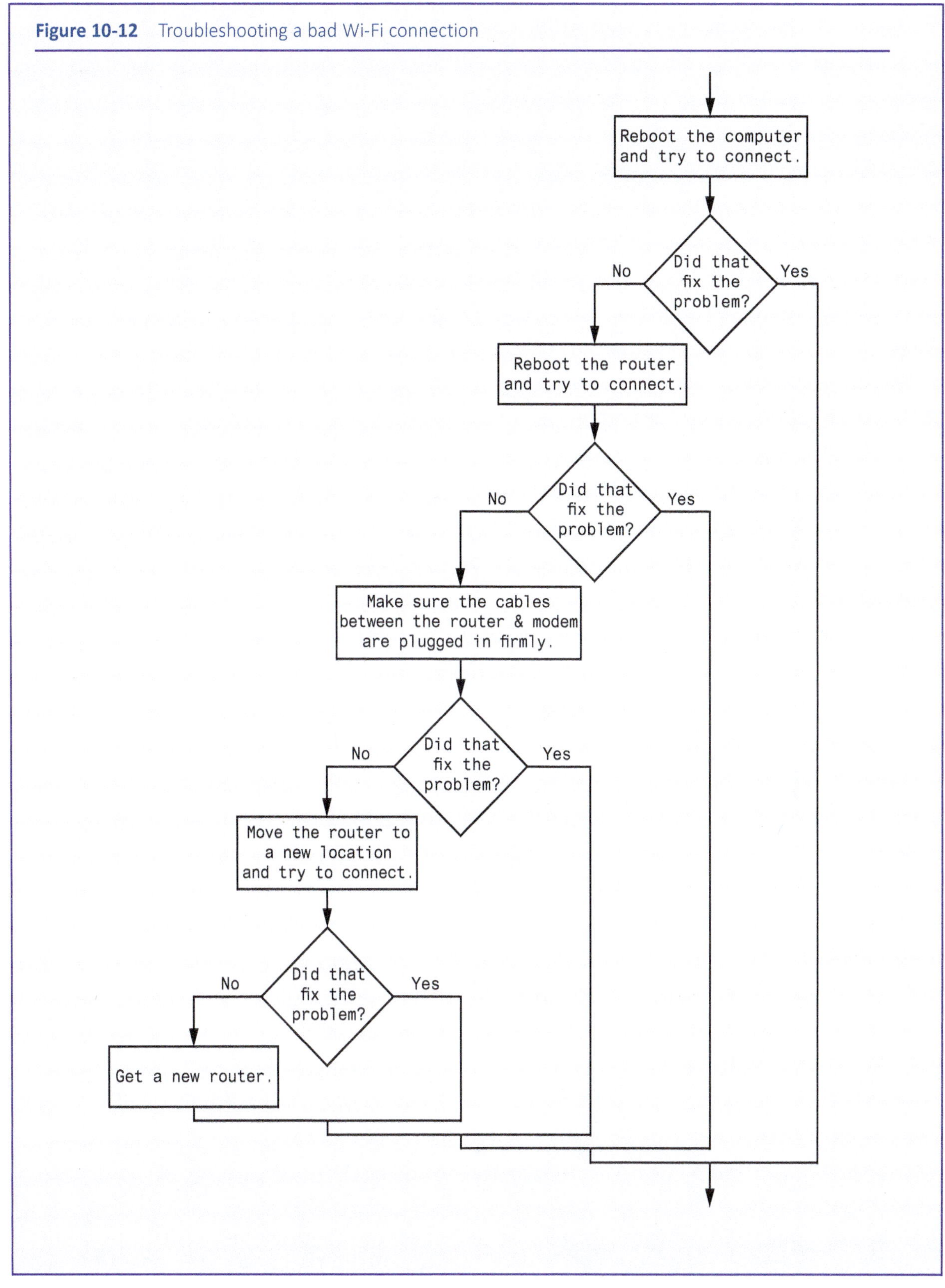

Figure 10-12 Troubleshooting a bad Wi-Fi connection

11 More About Strings

TOPICS

11.1 Basic String Operations

11.2 String Slicing

11.3 Testing, Searching, and Manipulating Strings

11.1 Basic String Operations

  **Python provides several ways to access the individual characters in a string. Strings also have methods that allow you to perform operations on them.**

Many of the programs that you have written so far have worked with strings, but only in a limited way. The operations that you have performed with strings so far have primarily involved only input and output. For example, you have read strings as input from the keyboard and from files, and sent strings as output to the screen and to files.

There are many types of programs that not only read strings as input and write strings as output, but also perform operations on strings. Word processing programs, for example, manipulate large amounts of text and thus work extensively with strings. Email programs and search engines are other examples of programs that perform operations on strings.

Python provides a wide variety of tools and programming techniques that you can use to examine and manipulate strings.

 **NOTE: Strings are a type of sequence. Sequences are covered in more depth in Chapter 13.**

Accessing the Individual Characters in a String

Some programming tasks require that you access the individual characters in a string. For example, you are probably familiar with websites that require you to set up a password. For security reasons, many sites require that your password have at least one uppercase letter, at least one lowercase letter, and at least one digit. When you set up your password, a program examines each character to ensure that the password meets these qualifications. (Later in this chapter, you will see an example of a program that does this sort of thing.) In this section, we will look at two techniques that you can use in Python to access the individual characters in a string: using the `for` loop and indexing.

Iterating over a String with the `for` Loop

One of the easiest ways to access the individual characters in a string is to use the `for` loop. Here is the general format:

```
for variable in string:
    statement
    statement
    etc.
```

In the general format, *variable* is the name of a variable, and *string* is either a string literal or a variable that references a string. Each time the loop iterates, *variable* will reference a copy of a character in *string*, beginning with the first character. We say that the loop iterates over the characters in the string. Here is an example:

```
name = 'Juliet'
for ch in name:
    print(ch)
```

The `name` variable references a string with six characters, so this loop will iterate six times. The first time the loop iterates, the ch variable will reference `'J'`, the second time the loop iterates, the ch variable will reference `'u'`, and so forth. This is illustrated in Figure 11-1. When the code executes, it will display the following:

```
J
u
l
i
e
t
```

Figure 11-1   Iterating over the string `'Juliet'`

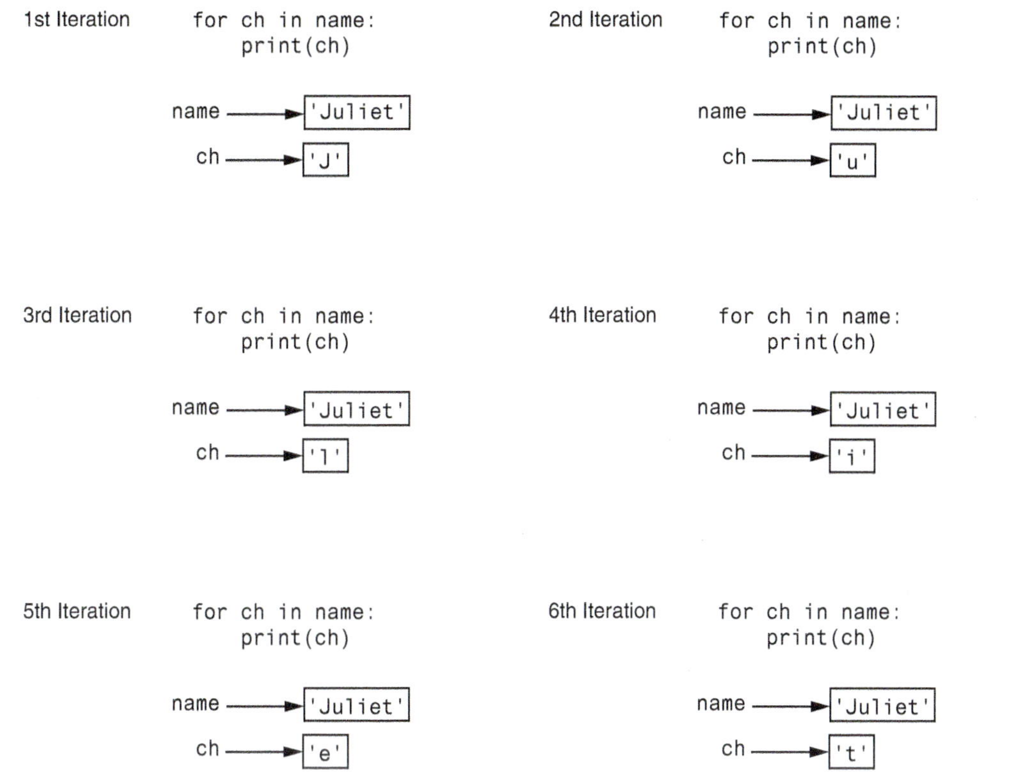

NOTE: Figure 11-1 illustrates how the ch variable references a copy of a character from the string as the loop iterates. If we change the value that ch references in the loop, it has no effect on the string referenced by name. To demonstrate, look at the following:

```
1   name = 'Juliet'
2   for ch in name:
3        ch = 'X'
4   print(name)
```

The statement in line 3 merely reassigns the ch variable to a different value each time the loop iterates. It has no effect on the string `'Juliet'` that is referenced by name, and it has no effect on the number of times the loop iterates. When this code executes, the statement in line 4 will print:

```
Juliet
```

Program 11-1 shows another example. This program asks the user to enter a string. It then uses a `for` loop to iterate over the string, counting the number of times that the letter T (uppercase or lowercase) appears.

Program 11-1   (count_Ts.py)

```
 1  # This program counts the number of times
 2  # the letter T (uppercase or lowercase)
 3  # appears in a string.
 4
 5  def main():
 6      # Create a variable to use to hold the count.
 7      # The variable must start with 0.
 8      count = 0
 9
10      # Get a string from the user.
11      my_string = input('Enter a sentence: ')
12
13      # Count the Ts.
14      for ch in my_string:
15          if ch == 'T' or ch == 't':
16              count += 1
17
18      # Print the result.
19      print(f'The letter T appears {count} times.')
20
21  # Call the main function.
22  if __name__ == '__main__':
23      main()
```

Program Output (with input shown in bold)
```
Enter a sentence: Today we sold twenty-two toys. Enter
The letter T appears 5 times.
```

Indexing

Another way that you can access the individual characters in a string is with an **index**. Each character in a string has an index that specifies its position in the string. Indexing starts at 0, so the index of the first character is 0, the index of the second character is 1, and so forth. The index of the last character in a string is 1 less than the number of characters in the string. Figure 11-2 shows the indexes for each character in the string 'Roses are red'. The string has 13 characters, so the character indexes range from 0 through 12.

Figure 11-2   String indexes

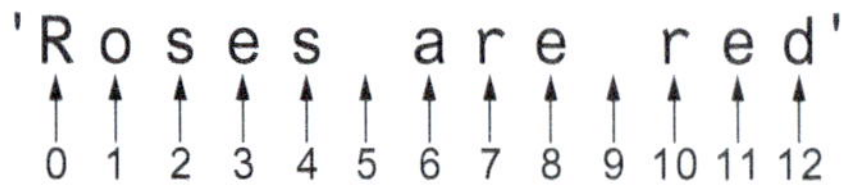

'Roses are red'
0 1 2 3 4 5 6 7 8 9 10 11 12

You can use an index to retrieve a copy of an individual character in a string, as shown here:

```
my_string = 'Roses are red'
ch = my_string[6]
```

The expression `my_string[6]` in the second statement returns a copy of the character at index 6 in `my_string`. After this statement executes, `ch` will reference `'a'` as shown in Figure 11-3.

Figure 11-3   Getting a copy of a character from a string

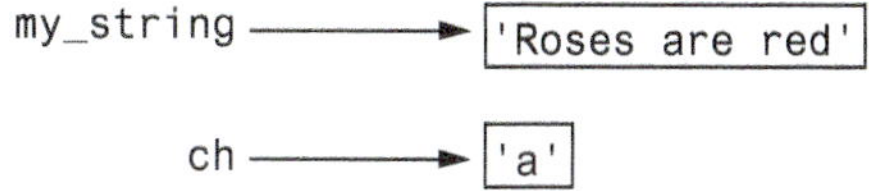

Here is another example:

```
my_string = 'Roses are red'
print(my_string[0], my_string[6], my_string[10])
```

This code will print the following:

```
R a r
```

You can also use negative numbers as indexes, to identify character positions relative to the end of the string. The Python interpreter adds negative indexes to the length of the string to determine the character position. The index −1 identifies the last character in a string, −2 identifies the next to last character, and so forth. The following code shows an example:

```
my_string = 'Roses are red'
print(my_string[-1], my_string[-2], my_string[-13])
```

This code will print the following:

```
d e R
```

IndexError Exceptions

An `IndexError` exception will occur if you try to use an index that is out of range for a particular string. For example, the string `'Boston'` has 6 characters, so the valid indexes are 0 through 5. (The valid negative indexes are −1 through −6.) The following is an example of code that causes an `IndexError` exception:

```
city = 'Boston'
print(city[6])
```

This type of error is most likely to happen when a loop incorrectly iterates beyond the end of a string, as shown here:

```
city = 'Boston'
index = 0
while index < 7:
    print(city[index])
    index += 1
```

The last time that this loop iterates, the `index` variable will be assigned the value 6, which is an invalid index for the string `'Boston'`. As a result, the `print` function will cause an `IndexError` exception to be raised.

The len Function

The len function returns the length of a sequence. (You learn more about len in Chapter 13.) The len function can also be used to get the length of a string. The following code demonstrates:

```
city = 'Boston'
size = len(city)
```

The second statement calls the len function, passing the city variable as an argument. The function returns the value 6, which is the length of the string 'Boston'. This value is assigned to the size variable.

The len function is especially useful to prevent loops from iterating beyond the end of a string, as shown here:

```
city = 'Boston'
index = 0
while index < len(city):
    print(city[index])
    index += 1
```

Notice the loop iterates as long as index is *less than* the length of the string. This is because the index of the last character in a string is always 1 less than the length of the string.

String Concatenation

A common operation that performed on strings is **concatenation**, or appending one string to the end of another string. You have seen examples in earlier chapters that use the + operator to concatenate strings. The + operator produces a string that is the combination of the two strings used as its operands. The following interactive session demonstrates:

```
1  >>> message = 'Hello ' + 'world' (Enter)
2  >>> print(message) (Enter)
3  Hello world
4  >>>
```

Line 1 concatenates the strings 'Hello' and 'world' to produce the string 'Hello world'. The string 'Hello world' is then assigned to the message variable. Line 2 prints the string that is referenced by the message variable. The output is shown in line 3.

Here is another interactive session that demonstrates concatenation:

```
1  >>> first_name = 'Emily' (Enter)
2  >>> last_name = 'Yeager' (Enter)
3  >>> full_name = first_name + ' ' + last_name (Enter)
4  >>> print(full_name) (Enter)
5  Emily Yeager
6  >>>
```

Line 1 assigns the string 'Emily' to the first_name variable. Line 2 assigns the string 'Yeager' to the last_name variable. Line 3 produces a string that is the concatenation of first_name, followed by a space, followed by last_name. The resulting string is assigned to the full_name variable. Line 4 prints the string referenced by full_name. The output is shown in line 5.

You can also use the += operator to perform concatenation. The following interactive session demonstrates:

```
1  >>> letters = 'abc' Enter
2  >>> letters += 'def' Enter
3  >>> print(letters) Enter
4  abcdef
5  >>>
```

The statement in line 2 performs string concatenation. It works the same as

```
letters = letters + 'def'
```

After the statement in line 2 executes, the letters variable will reference the string 'abcdef'. Here is another example:

```
>>> name = 'Kelly' Enter           # name is 'Kelly'
>>> name += ' ' Enter              # name is 'Kelly '
>>> name += 'Yvonne' Enter         # name is 'Kelly Yvonne'
>>> name += ' ' Enter              # name is 'Kelly Yvonne '
>>> name += 'Smith' Enter          # name is 'Kelly Yvonne Smith'
>>> print(name) e
Kelly Yvonne Smith
>>>
```

Keep in mind that the operand on the left side of the += operator must be an existing variable. If you specify a nonexistent variable, an exception is raised.

Strings Are Immutable

In Python, strings are **immutable**, which means once they are created, they cannot be changed. Some operations, such as concatenation, give the impression that they modify strings, but in reality they do not. For example, look at Program 11-2.

Program 11-2   **(concatenate.py)**

```
1   # This program concatenates strings.
2
3   def main():
4       name = 'Carmen'
5       print(f'The name is: {name}')
6       name = name + ' Brown'
7       print(f'Now the name is: {name}')
8
9   # Call the main function.
10  if __name__ == '__main__':
11      main()
```

Program Output

```
The name is: Carmen
Now the name is: Carmen Brown
```

The statement in line 4 assigns the string `'Carmen'` to the name variable, as shown in Figure 8-4. The statement in line 6 concatenates the string `' Brown'` to the string `'Carmen'` and assigns the result to the name variable, as shown in Figure 11-5. As you can see from the figure, the original string `'Carmen'` is not modified. Instead, a new string containing `'Carmen Brown'` is created and assigned to the name variable. (The original string, `'Carmen'` is no longer usable because no variable references it. The Python interpreter will eventually remove the unusable string from memory.)

Figure 11-4   The string 'Carmen' assigned to name

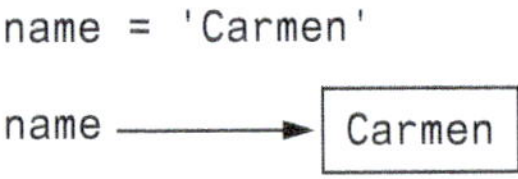

Figure 11-5   The string 'Carmen Brown' assigned to name

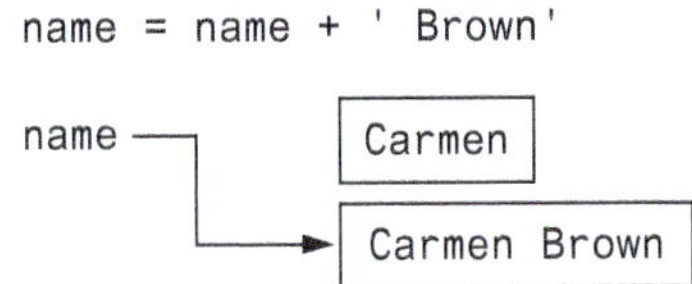

Because strings are immutable, you cannot use an expression in the form *string[index]* on the left side of an assignment operator. For example, the following code will cause an error:

```python
# Assign 'Bill' to friend.
friend = 'Bill'
# Can we change the first character to 'J'?
friend[0] = 'J'    # No, this will cause an error!
```

The last statement in this code will raise an exception because it attempts to change the value of the first character in the string `'Bill'`.

Checkpoint

11.1   Assume the variable name references a string. Write a for loop that prints each character in the string.

11.2   What is the index of the first character in a string?

11.3   If a string has 10 characters, what is the index of the last character?

11.4   What happens if you try to use an invalid index to access a character in a string?

11.5   How do you find the length of a string?

11.6   What is wrong with the following code?

```python
animal = 'Tiger'
animal[0] = 'L'
```

11.2 String Slicing

KEY POINT You can use slicing expressions to select a range of characters from a string.

A **slice** is a span of items that are taken from a sequence. (Slices are covered in more depth in Chapter 13.) When you take a slice from a string, you get a span of characters from within the string. String slices are also called **substrings.**

To get a slice of a string, you write an expression in the following general format:

```
string[start : end]
```

In the general format, *start* is the index of the first character in the slice, and *end* is the index marking the end of the slice. The expression will return a string containing a copy of the characters from *start* up to (but not including) *end*. For example, suppose we have the following:

```
full_name = 'Patty Lynn Smith'
middle_name = full_name[6:10]
```

The second statement assigns the string 'Lynn' to the middle_name variable. If you leave out the *start* index in a slicing expression, Python uses 0 as the starting index. Here is an example:

```
full_name = 'Patty Lynn Smith'
first_name = full_name[:5]
```

The second statement assigns the string 'Patty' to first_name. If you leave out the *end* index in a slicing expression, Python uses the length of the string as the *end* index. Here is an example:

```
full_name = 'Patty Lynn Smith'
last_name = full_name[11:]
```

The second statement assigns the string 'Smith' to last_name. What do you think the following code will assign to the my_string variable?

```
full_name = 'Patty Lynn Smith'
my_string = full_name[:]
```

The second statement assigns the entire string 'Patty Lynn Smith' to my_string. The statement is equivalent to:

```
my_string = full_name[0 : len(full_name)]
```

The slicing examples we have seen so far get slices of consecutive characters from strings. Slicing expressions can also have step value, which can cause characters to be skipped in the string. Here is an example of code that uses a slicing expression with a step value:

```
letters = 'ABCDEFGHIJKLMNOPQRSTUVWXYZ'
print(letters[0:26:2])
```

The third number inside the brackets is the step value. A step value of 2, as used in this example, causes the slice to contain every second character from the specified range in the string. The code will print the following:

```
ACEGIKMOQSUWY
```

You can also use negative numbers as indexes in slicing expressions to reference positions relative to the end of the string. Here is an example:

```
full_name = 'Patty Lynn Smith'
last_name = full_name[-5:]
```

Recall that Python adds a negative index to the length of a string to get the position referenced by that index. The second statement in this code assigns the string `'Smith'` to the `last_name` variable.

> **NOTE:** Invalid indexes do not cause slicing expressions to raise an exception. For example:
> - If the *end* index specifies a position beyond the end of the string, Python will use the length of the string instead.
> - If the *start* index specifies a position before the beginning of the string, Python will use 0 instead.
> - If the *start* index is greater than the *end* index, the slicing expression will return an empty string.

In the Spotlight:

Extracting Characters from a String

At a university, each student is assigned a system login name, which the student uses to log into the campus computer system. As part of your internship with the university's Information Technology department, you have been asked to write the code that generates system login names for students.

On Your Own: Working alone or with a partner, see if you can design an algorithm to solve the problem. Use problem-solving strategies to select the most appropriate construct, such as identifying the main task and subtasks. When you have completed your work, continue reading to see a solution.

You will use the following algorithm to generate a login name:

1. *Get the first three characters of the student's first name. (If the first name is less than three characters in length, use the entire first name.)*

2. *Get the first three characters of the student's last name. (If the last name is less than three characters in length, use the entire last name.)*

3. *Get the last three characters of the student's ID number. (If the ID number is less than three characters in length, use the entire ID number.)*

4. *Concatenate the three sets of characters to generate the login name.*

For example, if a student's name is Amanda Spencer, and her ID number is ENG6721, her login name would be AmaSpe721. You decide to write a function named `get_login_name` that accepts a student's first name, last name, and ID number as arguments, and returns the student's login name as a string. You will save the function in a module named `login.py`. This module can then be imported into any Python program that needs to generate a login name. Program 11-3 shows the code for the `login.py` module.

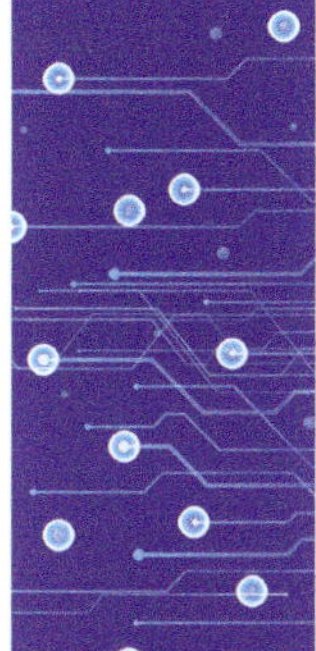

Program 11-3   (`login.py`)

```
 1  # The get_login_name function accepts a first name,
 2  # last name, and ID number as arguments. It returns
 3  # a system login name.
 4
 5  def get_login_name(first, last, idnumber):
 6      # Get the first three letters of the first name.
 7      # If the name is less than 3 characters, the
 8      # slice will return the entire first name.
 9      set1 = first[0 : 3]
10
11      # Get the first three letters of the last name.
12      # If the name is less than 3 characters, the
13      # slice will return the entire last name.
14      set2 = last[0 : 3]
15
16      # Get the last three characters of the student ID.
17      # If the ID number is less than 3 characters, the
18      # slice will return the entire ID number.
19      set3 = idnumber[-3 :]
20
21      # Put the sets of characters together.
22      login_name = set1 + set2 + set3
23
24      # Return the login name.
25      return login_name
```

The `get_login_name` function accepts three string arguments: a first name, a last name, and an ID number. The statement in line 9 uses a slicing expression to get the first three characters of the string referenced by `first` and assigns those characters, as a string, to the `set1` variable. If the string referenced by `first` is less than three characters long, then the value 3 will be an invalid ending index. If this is the case, Python will use the length of the string as the ending index, and the slicing expression will return the entire string.

The statement in line 14 uses a slicing expression to get the first three characters of the string referenced by last. Then it assigns those characters, as a string, to the `set2` variable. The entire string referenced by `last` will be returned if it is less than three characters.

The statement in line 19 uses a slicing expression to get the last three characters of the string referenced by `idnumber` and assigns those characters, as a string, to the `set3` variable. If the string referenced by `idnumber` is less than three characters, then the value −3 will be an invalid starting index. If this is the case, Python will use 0 as the starting index.

The statement in line 22 assigns the concatenation of `set1`, `set2`, and `set3` to the `login_name` variable. The variable is returned in line 25. Program 11-4 shows a demonstration of the function.

Program 11-4   `(generate_login.py)`

```python
 1  # This program gets the user's first name, last name, and
 2  # student ID number. Using this data, it generates a
 3  # system login name.
 4
 5  import login
 6
 7  def main():
 8      # Get the user's first name, last name, and ID number.
 9      first = input('Enter your first name: ')
10      last = input('Enter your last name: ')
11      idnumber = input('Enter your student ID number: ')
12
13      # Get the login name.
14      print('Your system login name is:')
15      print(login.get_login_name(first, last, idnumber))
16
17  # Call the main function.
18  if __name__ == '__main__':
19      main()
```

Program Output (with input shown in bold)
```
Enter your first name: Holly [Enter]
Enter your last name: Gaddis [Enter]
Enter your student ID number: CSC34899 [Enter]
Your system login name is:
HolGad899
```

Program Output (with input shown in bold)
```
Enter your first name: Jo [Enter]
Enter your last name: Cusimano [Enter]
Enter your student ID number: BIO4497 [Enter]
Your system login name is:
JoCus497
```

 ### Checkpoint

11.7 What will the following code display?
```python
mystring = 'abcdefg'
print(mystring[2:5])
```

11.8 What will the following code display?
```python
mystring = 'abcdefg'
print(mystring[3:])
```

11.9 What will the following code display?
```python
mystring = 'abcdefg'
print(mystring[:3])
```

11.10 What will the following code display?
```python
mystring = 'abcdefg'
print(mystring[:])
```

11.3 Testing, Searching, and Manipulating Strings

Python provides operators and methods for testing strings, searching the contents of strings, and getting modified copies of strings.

Testing Strings with `in` and `not in`

In Python, you can use the `in` operator to determine whether one string is contained in another string. Here is the general format of an expression using the `in` operator with two strings:

```
string1 in string2
```

string1 and *string2* can be either string literals or variables referencing strings. The expression returns true if *string1* is found in *string2*. For example, look at the following code:

```
text = 'Four score and seven years ago'
if 'seven' in text:
    print('The string "seven" was found.')
else:
    print('The string "seven" was not found.')
```

This code determines whether the string `'Four score and seven years ago'` contains the string `'seven'`. If we run this code, it will display:

```
The string "seven" was found.
```

You can use the `not in` operator to determine whether one string is *not* contained in another string. Here is an example:

```
names = 'Bill Joanne Susan Chris Juan Katie'
if 'Pierre' not in names:
    print('Pierre was not found.')
else:
    print('Pierre was found.')
```

If we run this code, it will display:

```
Pierre was not found.
```

String Methods

A **method** is a function that belongs to an object and performs some operation on that object. Strings in Python have numerous methods. In this section, we will discuss several string methods for performing the following types of operations:

- Testing the values of strings
- Performing various modifications
- Searching for substrings and replacing sequences of characters

Here is the general format of a string method call:

```
stringvar.method(arguments)
```

In the general format, *stringvar* is a variable that references a string, *method* is the name of the method that is being called, and *arguments* is one or more arguments being passed to the method. Let's look at some examples.

String Testing Methods

The string methods shown in Table 11-1 test a string for specific characteristics. For example, the isdigit method returns true if the string contains only numeric digits. Otherwise, it returns false. Here is an example:

```
string1 = '1200'
if string1.isdigit():
    print(f'{string1} contains only digits.')
else:
    print(f'{string1} contains characters other than digits.')
```

This code will display

```
1200 contains only digits.
```

Here is another example:

```
string2 = '123abc'
if string2.isdigit():
    print(f'{string2} contains only digits.')
else:
    print(f'{string2} contains characters other than digits.')
```

This code will display

```
123abc contains characters other than digits.
```

Table 11-1 Some string testing methods

Method	Description
isalnum()	Returns true if the string contains only alphabetic letters or digits and is at least one character in length. Returns false otherwise.
isalpha()	Returns true if the string contains only alphabetic letters and is at least one character in length. Returns false otherwise.
isdigit()	Returns true if the string contains only numeric digits and is at least one character in length. Returns false otherwise.
islower()	Returns true if all of the alphabetic letters in the string are lowercase and the string contains at least one alphabetic letter. Returns false otherwise.
isspace()	Returns true if the string contains only whitespace characters and is at least one character in length. Returns false otherwise. (Whitespace characters are newlines (\n), tabs (\t), and spaces.)
isupper()	Returns true if all of the alphabetic letters in the string are uppercase and the string contains at least one alphabetic letter. Returns false otherwise.

Program 11-5 demonstrates several of the string testing methods. It asks the user to enter a string, then displays various messages about the string, depending on the return value of the methods.

Program 11-5   (string_test.py)

```
 1  # This program demonstrates several string testing methods.
 2
 3  def main():
 4      # Get a string from the user.
 5      user_string = input('Enter a string: ')
 6
 7      print('This is what I found about that string:')
 8
 9      # Test the string.
10      if user_string.isalnum():
11          print('The string is alphanumeric.')
12      if user_string.isdigit():
13          print('The string contains only digits.')
14      if user_string.isalpha():
15          print('The string contains only alphabetic characters.')
16      if user_string.isspace():
17          print('The string contains only whitespace characters.')
18      if user_string.islower():
19          print('The letters in the string are all lowercase.')
20      if user_string.isupper():
21          print('The letters in the string are all uppercase.')
22
23  # Call the string.
24  if __name__ == '__main__':
25      main()
```

Program Output (with input shown in bold)
```
Enter a string: abc Enter
This is what I found about that string:
The string is alphanumeric.
The string contains only alphabetic characters.
The letters in the string are all lowercase.
```

Program Output (with input shown in bold)
```
Enter a string: 123 Enter
This is what I found about that string:
The string is alphanumeric.
The string contains only digits.
```

Program Output (with input shown in bold)
```
Enter a string: 123ABC Enter
This is what I found about that string:
The string is alphanumeric.
The letters in the string are all uppercase.
```

String Modification Methods

Although strings are immutable, meaning they cannot be modified, they do have a number of methods that return modified versions of themselves. Table 11-2 lists several of these methods.

Table 11-2   String Modification Methods

Method	Description
lower()	Returns a copy of the string with all alphabetic letters converted to lowercase. Any character that is already lowercase, or is not an alphabetic letter, is unchanged.
lstrip()	Returns a copy of the string with all leading whitespace characters removed. Leading whitespace characters are spaces, newlines (\n), and tabs (\t) that appear at the beginning of the string.
lstrip(*char*)	The *char* argument is a string containing a character. Returns a copy of the string with all instances of *char* that appear at the beginning of the string removed.
rstrip()	Returns a copy of the string with all trailing whitespace characters removed. Trailing whitespace characters are spaces, newlines (\n), and tabs (\t) that appear at the end of the string.
rstrip(*char*)	The *char* argument is a string containing a character. The method returns a copy of the string with all instances of *char* that appear at the end of the string removed.
strip()	Returns a copy of the string with all leading and trailing whitespace characters removed.
strip(*char*)	Returns a copy of the string with all instances of *char* that appear at the beginning and the end of the string removed.
upper()	Returns a copy of the string with all alphabetic letters converted to uppercase. Any character that is already uppercase, or is not an alphabetic letter, is unchanged.

For example, the lower method returns a copy of a string with all of its alphabetic letters converted to lowercase. Here is an example:

```
letters = 'WXYZ'
print(letters, letters.lower())
```

This code will print

```
WXYZ wxyz
```

The upper method returns a copy of a string with all of its alphabetic letters converted to uppercase. Here is an example:

```
letters = 'abcd'
print(letters, letters.upper())
```

This code will print

```
abcd ABCD
```

The lower and upper methods are useful for making case-insensitive string comparisons. String comparisons are **case-sensitive**, which means the uppercase characters are distinguished from the lowercase characters. For example, in a case-sensitive comparison, the string `'abc'` is not considered the same as the string `'ABC'` or the string `'Abc'` because the case of the characters is different. Sometimes it is more convenient to perform a **case-insensitive** comparison, in which the case of the characters is ignored. In a case-insensitive comparison, the string `'abc'` is considered the same as `'ABC'` and `'Abc'`.

For example, look at the following code:

```
again = 'y'
while again.lower() == 'y':
    print('Hello')
    print('Do you want to see that again?')
    again = input('y = yes, anything else = no: ')
```

Notice the last statement in the loop asks the user to enter y to see the message displayed again. The loop iterates as long as the expression `again.lower() =='y'` is true. The expression will be true if the `again` variable references either `'y'` or `'Y'`.

Similar results can be achieved by using the upper method, as shown here:

```
again = 'y'
while again.upper() == 'Y':
    print('Hello')
    print('Do you want to see that again?')
    again = input('y = yes, anything else = no: ')
```

Searching and Replacing

Programs commonly need to search for **substrings**, or strings that appear within other strings. For example, suppose you have a document opened in your word processor, and you need to search for a word that appears somewhere in it. The word that you are searching for is a substring that appears inside a larger string, the document.

Table 11-3 lists some of the Python string methods that search for substrings, as well as a method that replaces the occurrences of a substring with another string.

Table 11-3 Search and replace methods

Method	Description
endswith(*substring*)	The *substring* argument is a string. The method returns true if the string ends with *substring*.
find(*substring*)	The *substring* argument is a string. The method returns the lowest index in the string where *substring* is found. If *substring* is not found, the method returns −1.
replace(*old, new*)	The *old* and *new* arguments are both strings. The method returns a copy of the string with all instances of *old* replaced by *new*.
startswith(*substring*)	The *substring* argument is a string. The method returns true if the string starts with *substring*.

The `endswith` method determines whether a string ends with a specified substring. Here is an example:

```python
filename = input('Enter the filename: ')
if filename.endswith('.txt'):
    print('That is the name of a text file.')
elif filename.endswith('.py'):
    print('That is the name of a Python source file.')
elif filename.endswith('.doc'):
    print('That is the name of a word processing document.')
else:
    print('Unknown file type.')
```

The `startswith` method works like the `endswith` method, but determines whether a string begins with a specified substring.

The `find` method searches for a specified substring within a string. The method returns the lowest index of the substring, if it is found. If the substring is not found, the method returns −1. Here is an example:

```python
string = 'Four score and seven years ago'
position = string.find('seven')
if position != -1:
    print(f'The word "seven" was found at index {position}.')
else:
    print('The word "seven" was not found.')
```

This code will display

```
The word "seven" was found at index 15.
```

The `replace` method returns a copy of a string, where every occurrence of a specified substring has been replaced with another string. For example, look at the following code:

```python
string = 'Four score and seven years ago'
new_string = string.replace('years', 'days')
print(new_string)
```

This code will display

```
Four score and seven days ago
```

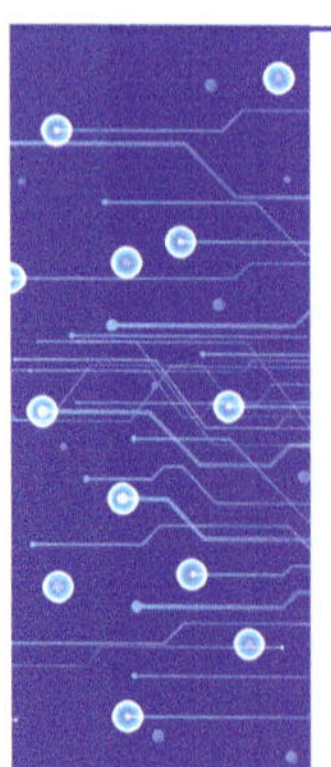

In the Spotlight:

Validating the Characters in a Password

Passwords for the campus computer system must meet the following requirements:
- The password must be at least seven characters long.
- It must contain at least one uppercase letter.
- It must contain at least one lowercase letter.
- It must contain at least one numeric digit.

When a student sets up their password, the password must be validated to ensure it meets these requirements. You have been asked to write the code that performs this validation.

On Your Own: Working alone or with a partner, see if you can design an algorithm to solve the problem. Use problem-solving strategies to select the most appropriate construct, such as identifying the main task and subtasks. When you are finished, continue reading to see a solution.

You decide to write a function named `valid_password` that accepts the password as an argument and returns either true or false, to indicate whether it is valid. Here is the function, in pseudocode:

valid_password function:
       Set the correct_length variable to false
       Set the has_uppercase variable to false
       Set the has_lowercase variable to false
       Set the has_digit variable to false
       If the password's length is seven characters or greater:
         Set the correct_length variable to true
         for each character in the password:
           if the character is an uppercase letter:
             Set the has_uppercase variable to true
           if the character is a lowercase letter:
             Set the has_lowercase variable to true
           if the character is a digit:
             Set the has_digit variable to true

       If correct_length and has_uppercase and has_lowercase and has_digit:
         Set the is_valid variable to true
       else:
         Set the is_valid variable to false

       Return the is_valid variable

Earlier (in the previous *In the Spotlight* section), you created a function named `get_login_name` and stored that function in the `login` module. Because the `valid_password` function's purpose is related to the task of creating a student's login account, you decide to store the `valid_password` function in the `login` module, as well. Program 11-6 shows the login module with the `valid_password` function added to it. The function begins at line 34.

Program 11-6   (`login.py`)

```
1   # The get_login_name function accepts a first name,
2   # last name, and ID number as arguments. It returns
3   # a system login name.
4
5   def get_login_name(first, last, idnumber):
6       # Get the first three letters of the first name.
7       # If the name is less than 3 characters, the
8       # slice will return the entire first name.
9       set1 = first[0 : 3]
10
```

Program 11-6   *(continued)*

```
11       # Get the first three letters of the last name.
12       # If the name is less than 3 characters, the
13       # slice will return the entire last name.
14       set2 = last[0 : 3]
15
16       # Get the last three characters of the student ID.
17       # If the ID number is less than 3 characters, the
18       # slice will return the entire ID number.
19       set3 = idnumber[-3 :]
20
21       # Put the sets of characters together.
22       login_name = set1  + set2 + set3
23
24       # Return the login name.
25       return login_name
26
27   # The valid_password function accepts a password as
28   # an argument and returns either true or false to
29   # indicate whether the password is valid. A valid
30   # password must be at least 7 characters in length,
31   # have at least one uppercase letter, one lowercase
32   # letter, and one digit.
33
34   def valid_password(password):
35       # Set the Boolean variables to false.
36       correct_length = False
37       has_uppercase = False
38       has_lowercase = False
39       has_digit = False
40
41       # Begin the validation. Start by testing the
42       # password's length.
43       if len(password) >= 7:
44           correct_length = True
45
46           # Test each character and set the
47           # appropriate flag when a required
48           # character is found.
49           for ch in password:
50               if ch.isupper():
51                   has_uppercase = True
52               if ch.islower():
53                   has_lowercase = True
54               if ch.isdigit():
55                   has_digit = True
56
```

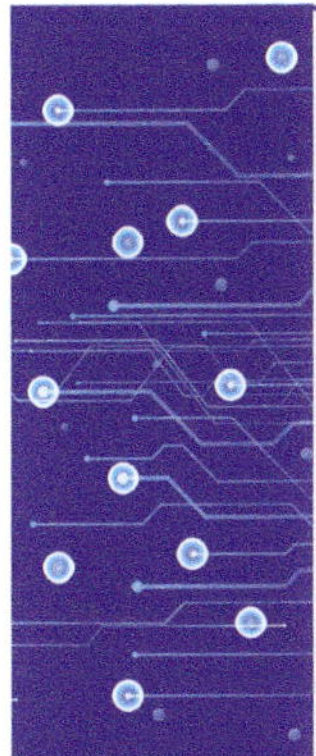

Program 11-6   *(continued)*

```
57          # Determine whether all of the requirements
58          # are met. If they are, set is_valid to true.
59          # Otherwise, set is_valid to false.
60          if correct_length and has_uppercase and \
61             has_lowercase and has_digit:
62             is_valid = True
63          else:
64             is_valid = False
65
66          # Return the is_valid variable.
67          return is_valid
```

Program 11-7 imports the login module and demonstrates the `valid_password` function.

Program 11-7   **(validate_password.py)**

```
 1  # This program gets a password from the user and
 2  # validates it.
 3
 4  import login
 5
 6  def main():
 7      # Get a password from the user.
 8      password = input('Enter your password: ')
 9
10      # Validate the password.
11      while not login.valid_password(password):
12          print('That password is not valid.')
13          password = input('Enter your password: ')
14
15      print('That is a valid password.')
16
17  # Call the main function.
18  if __name__ == '__main__':
19      main()
```

Program Output (with input shown in bold)
```
Enter your password: bozo Enter
That password is not valid.
Enter your password: kangaroo Enter
That password is not valid.
Enter your password: Tiger9 Enter
That password is not valid.
Enter your password: Leopard6 Enter
That is a valid password.
```

The Repetition Operator

The repetition operator (*) makes multiple copies of an object, such as a **list** or string, and combines them together. Here is the general format for using the repetition operator with strings:

*string_to_copy * n*

The repetition operator creates a string that contains *n* repeated copies of *string_to_copy*. Here is an example:

```
my_string = 'w' * 5
```

After this statement executes, my_string will reference the string 'wwwww'. Here is another example:

```
print('Hello' * 5)
```

This statement will print:

```
HelloHelloHelloHelloHello
```

Program 11-8 demonstrates the repetition operator.

Program 11-8 (repetition_operator.py)

```
 1  # This program demonstrates the repetition operator.
 2
 3  def main():
 4      # Print nine rows increasing in length.
 5      for count in range(1, 10):
 6          print('Z' * count)
 7
 8      # Print nine rows decreasing in length.
 9      for count in range(8, 0, -1):
10          print('Z' * count)
11
12  # Call the main function.
13  if __name__ == '__main__':
14      main()
```

Program Output
```
Z
ZZ
ZZZ
ZZZZ
ZZZZZ
ZZZZZZ
ZZZZZZZ
ZZZZZZZZ
ZZZZZZZZZ
ZZZZZZZZ
```

Program Output   *(continued)*

```
ZZZZZZZ
ZZZZZZ
ZZZZZ
ZZZZ
ZZZ
ZZ
Z
```

Splitting a String

Strings in Python have a method named `split` that returns a list containing the words in the string. Program 11-9 shows an example.

Program 11-9   (`string_split.py`)

```
 1   # This program demonstrates the split method.
 2
 3   def main():
 4       # Create a string with multiple words.
 5       my_string = 'One two three four'
 6
 7       # Split the string.
 8       word_list = my_string.split()
 9
10       # Print the list of words.
11       print(word_list)
12
13   # Call the main function.
14   if __name__ == '__main__':
15       main()
```

Program Output

```
['One', 'two', 'three', 'four']
```

By default, the split method uses spaces as separators (that is, it returns a list of the words in the string that are separated by spaces). You can specify a different separator by passing it as an argument to the split method. For example, suppose a string contains a date, as shown here:

```
date_string = '11/26/2024'
```

If you want to break out the month, day, and year as items in a list, you can call the `split` method using the `'/'` character as a separator, as shown here:

```
date_list = date_string.split('/')
```

After this statement executes, the `date_list` variable will reference this list:

```
['11', '26', '2024']
```

Program 11-10 demonstrates this.

Program 11-10   (`split_date.py`)

```
 1  # This program calls the split method, using the
 2  # '/' character as a separator.
 3
 4  def main():
 5      # Create a string with a date.
 6      date_string = '11/26/2024'
 7
 8      # Split the date.
 9      date_list = date_string.split('/')
10
11      # Display each piece of the date.
12      print(f'Month: {date_list[0]}')
13      print(f'Day: {date_list[1]}')
14      print(f'Year: {date_list[2]}')
15
16  # Call the main function.
17  if __name__ == '__main__':
18      main()
```

Program Output

```
Month: 11
Day: 26
Year: 2024
```

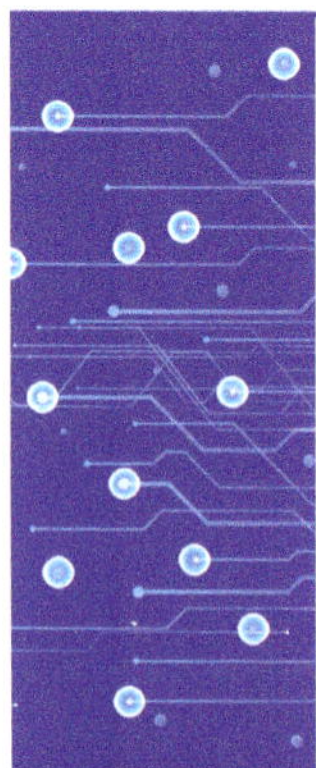

In the Spotlight:
String Tokens

Sometimes a string will contain a series of words or other items of data separated by spaces or other characters. For example, look at the following string:

```
'peach raspberry strawberry vanilla'
```

This string contains the following four items of data: peach, raspberry, strawberry, and vanilla. In programming terms, items such as these are known as *tokens*. Notice a space appears between the items. The character that separates tokens is known as a *delimiter*. Here is another example:

```
'17;92;81;12;46;5'
```

This string contains the following tokens: 17, 92, 81, 12, 46, and 5. Notice a semicolon appears between each item. In this example, the semicolon is used as a delimiter. Some programming problems require you to read a string that contains a list of items, then extract all the tokens from the string for processing. For example, look at the following string that contains a date:

```
'3-22-2024'
```

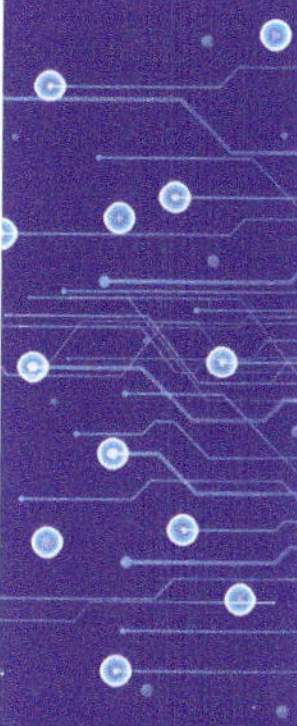

The tokens in this string are 3, 22, and 2024, and the delimiter is the hyphen character. Perhaps a program needs to extract the month, day, and year from such a string. Another example is an operating system pathname, such as the following:

```
'/home/rsullivan/data'
```

The tokens in this string are `home`, `rsullivan`, and `data`, and the delimiter is the `/` character. Perhaps a program needs to extract all the directory names from such a pathname. The process of breaking a string into tokens is known as **tokenizing** a string. In Python, you use the `split` method to tokenize strings. Program 11-11 demonstrates.

Program 11-11 (`tokens.py`)

```
 1   # This program demonstrates how to tokenize strings.
 2
 3   def main():
 4       # Strings to tokenize
 5       str1 = 'one two three four'
 6       str2 = '10:20:30:40:50'
 7       str3 = 'a/b/c/d/e/f'
 8
 9       # Display the tokens in each string.
10       display_tokens(str1, ' ')
11       print()
12       display_tokens(str2, ':')
13       print()
14       display_tokens(str3, '/')
15
16   # The display_tokens function displays the tokens
17   # in a string. The data parameter is the string
18   # to tokenize and the delimiter parameter is the
19   # delimiter.
20   def display_tokens(data, delimiter):
21       tokens = data.split(delimiter)
22       for item in tokens:
23           print(f'Token: {item}')
24
25   # Execute the main function.
26   if __name__ == '__main__':
27       main()
```

Program Output

```
Token: one
Token: two
Token: three
Token: four
```

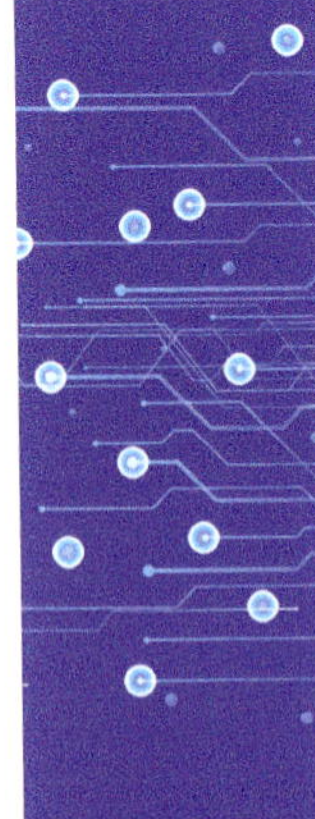

Program Output   *(continued)*
```
Token: 10
Token: 20
Token: 30
Token: 40
Token: 50

Token: a
Token: b
Token: c
Token: d
Token: e
Token: f
```

Let's take a closer look at the program. First, look at the `display_tokens` function in lines 20-23. The purpose of the function is to display the tokens in a string. The function has two parameters, `data` and `delimiter`. The `data` parameter will contain the string that we want to tokenize, and the `delimiter` parameter will contain the character that is used as the delimiter. Line 21 calls the `data` variable's `split` method, passing `delimiter` as an argument. The `split` method returns a list of the tokens, which is assigned to the `tokens` variable. The `for loop` in lines 22-23 displays the tokens.

In the `main` function, lines 5-7 define three strings that contain data items separated by delimiters:

- `str1` contains data items that are delimited by spaces (`' '`).
- `str2` contains data items that are delimited by colons (`':'`).
- `str3` contains data items that are delimited by forward-slashes (`'/'`).

Line 10 calls the `display_tokens` function passing `str1` and `' '` as arguments. The function will tokenize the string using the `' '` character as the delimiter. Line 12 calls the `display_tokens` function passing `str2` and `':'` as arguments. The function will tokenize the string using the `':'` character as the delimiter. Line 14 calls the `display_tokens` function passing `str3` and `'/'` as arguments. The function will tokenize the string using the `'/'` character as the delimiter.

In the Spotlight:
Reading CSV Files

Most spreadsheet and database applications can export data to a file format known as *CSV*, which stands for *comma-separated values*. Each line in a CSV file contains a row of data items that are separated by commas. For example, suppose an instructor keeps her students' test scores in the spreadsheet shown in Figure 11-6. Each row in the spreadsheet holds the test scores for one student, and each student has five test scores.

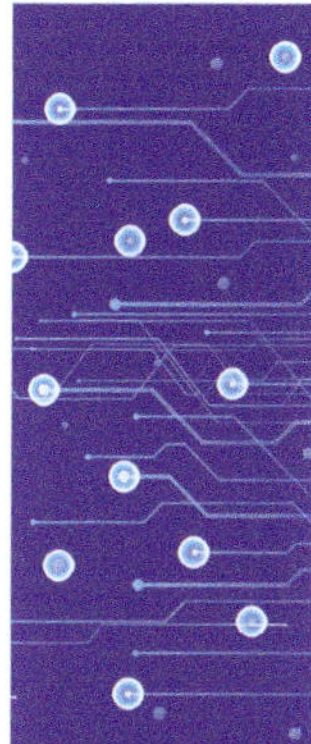

Figure 11-6   Data in a spreadsheet application

	A	B	C	D	E	F
1	87	79	91	82	94	
2	72	79	81	74	88	
3	94	92	81	89	96	
4	77	56	67	81	79	
5	79	82	85	81	90	
6						

Microsoft Corporation

Suppose we want to write a Python program to read the test scores and perform operations with them. The first step is to export the data from the spreadsheet to a CSV file. When the data is exported, it will be written in the following format:

```
87,79,91,82,94
72,79,81,74,88
94,92,81,89,96
77,56,67,81,79
79,82,85,81,90
```

The next step is to write a Python program that reads each line from the file, tokenizing the line using the comma character as the delimiter. Once you have extracted the tokens from a line, you can perform any type of operation you need using the tokens.

On Your Own: Working alone or with a partner, see if you can design and write a program to read the test scores from a CSV file and calculate each student's average. When you have completed your work, continue reading to see a solution.

Let's assume the test scores are stored in a CSV file named test_scores.csv. Program 11-12 shows how to read the test scores from the file and calculate each student's average.

Program 11-12   (test_averages.py)

```
 1   # This program reads test scores from a CSV file
 2   # and calculates each student's test average.
 3
 4   def main():
 5       # Open the file.
 6       csv_file = open('test_scores.csv', 'r')
 7
 8       # Read the file's lines into a list.
 9       lines = csv_file.readlines()
10
11       # Close the file.
12       csv_file.close()
13
14       # Process the lines.
15       for line in lines:
16           # Get the test scores as tokens.
```

Program 11-12   *(continued)*

```
17              tokens = line.split(',')
18
19              # Calculate the total of the test scores.
20              total = 0.0
21              for token in tokens:
22                  total += float(token)
23
24              # Calculate the average of the test scores.
25              average = total / len(tokens)
26              print(f'Average: {average}')
27
28  # Execute the main function.
29   if __name__ == '__main__':
30        main()
```

Program Output

```
Average: 86.6
Average: 78.8
Average: 90.4
Average: 72.0
Average: 83.4
```

Let's take a closer look at the program. Line 6 opens the CSV file. Line 9 calls the file object's readlines method. The readlines method returns a file's entire contents as a list. Each element of the list will be a line from the file. Line 12 closes the file.

The for loop that begins in line 15 iterates over each element of the lines list. Inside the loop, line 17 tokenizes the current line, using the comma character as a delimiter. A list containing the tokens is assigned to the tokens variable. Line 20 initializes the total variable with 0.0. (We will use the total variable as an accumulator.) The for loop that begins in line 21 iterates over each element of the tokens list. Inside the loop, line 22 converts the current token to a float and adds it to the total variable. When this loop finishes, the total variable will contain the sum of the tokens in the current line. Line 25 calculates the average of the tokens, and line 26 displays the average.

 **Checkpoint**

11.11   Write code using the `in` operator that determines whether `'d'` is in `mystring`.

11.12   Assume the variable `big` references a string. Write a statement that converts the string it references to lowercase and assigns the converted string to the variable `little`.

11.13   Write an `if` statement that displays "Digit" if the string referenced by the variable `ch` contains a numeric digit. Otherwise, it should display "No digit."

11.14   What is the output of the following code?

```
ch = 'a'
ch2 = ch.upper()
print(ch, ch2)
```

11.15   Write a loop that asks the user "Do you want to repeat the program or quit? (R/Q)". The loop should repeat until the user has entered an R or Q (either uppercase or lowercase).

11.16   What will the following code display?

```
var = '$'
print(var.upper())
```

11.17   Write a loop that counts the number of uppercase characters that appear in the string referenced by the variable `mystring`.

11.18   Assume the following statement appears in a program:

```
days = 'Monday Tuesday Wednesday'
```

Write a statement that splits the string, creating the following list:

```
['Monday', 'Tuesday', 'Wednesday']
```

11.19   Assume the following statement appears in a program:

```
values = 'one$two$three$four'
```

Write a statement that splits the string, creating the following list:

```
['one', 'two', 'three', 'four']
```

Chapter Review

Multiple Choice

1. This is the first index in a string.
   - a. –1
   - b. 1
   - c. 0
   - d. The size of the string minus one

2. This is the last index in a string.
   - a. 1
   - b. 99
   - c. 0
   - d.   The size of the string minus one

3. This will happen if you try to use an index that is out of range for a string.
   - a. A `ValueError` exception will occur.
   - b. An `IndexError` exception will occur.
   - c. The string will be erased and the program will continue to run.
   - d. Nothing—the invalid index will be ignored.

4. This function returns the length of a string.
   - a. `length`
   - b. `size`
   - c. `len`
   - d. `lengthof`

5. This string method returns a copy of the string with all leading whitespace characters removed.
   - a. `lstrip`
   - b. `rstrip`
   - c. `remove`
   - d. `strip_leading`

6. This string method returns the lowest index in the string where a specified substring is found.
   - a. `first_index_of`
   - b. `locate`
   - c. `find`
   - d. `index_of`

7. This operator determines whether one string is contained inside another string.
   - a. `contains`
   - b. `is_in`
   - c. `==`
   - d. `in`

8. This string method returns true if a string contains only alphabetic characters and is at least one character in length.
   - a. the `isalpha` method
   - b. the `alpha` method
   - c. the `alphabetic` method
   - d. the `isletters` method

9. This string method returns true if a string contains only numeric digits and is at least one character in length.
   - a. the `digit` method
   - b. the `isdigit` method
   - c. the `numeric` method
   - d. the `isnumber` method

10. This string method returns a copy of the string with all leading and trailing whitespace characters removed.
   - a. `clean`
   - b. `strip`
   - c. `remove_whitespace`
   - d. `rstrip`

True or False

1. Once a string is created, it cannot be changed.

2. You can use the `for` loop to iterate over the individual characters in a string.

3. The `isupper` method converts a string to all uppercase characters.

4. The repetition operator (*) works with strings as well as with lists.

5. When you call a string's `split` method, the method divides the string into two substrings.

Short Answer

1. What does the following code display?
```
mystr = 'yes'
mystr += 'no'
mystr += 'yes'
print(mystr)
```

2. What does the following code display?
```
mystr = 'abc' * 3
print(mystr)
```

3. What will the following code display?
```
mystring = 'abcdefg'
print(mystring[2:5])
```

4. What does the following code display?
```
numbers = [1, 2, 3, 4, 5, 6, 7]
print(numbers[4:6])
```

5. What does the following code display?
```
name = 'joe'
print(name.lower())
print(name.upper())
print(name)
```

Algorithm Workbench

1. Assume `choice` references a string. The following `if` statement determines whether `choice` is equal to 'Y' or 'y':
```
if choice == 'Y' or choice == 'y':
```
Rewrite this statement so it only makes one comparison and does not use the `or` operator. *(Hint: use either the upper or lower methods.)*

2. Write a loop that counts the number of space characters that appear in the string referenced by `mystring`.

3. Write a loop that counts the number of digits that appear in the string referenced by `mystring`.

4. Write a loop that counts the number of lowercase characters that appear in the string referenced by `mystring`.

5. Write a function that accepts a string as an argument and returns true if the argument ends with the substring `'.com'`. Otherwise, the function should return false.

6. Write code that makes a copy of a string with all occurrences of the lowercase letter `'t'` converted to uppercase.

7. Write a function that accepts a string as an argument and displays the string backwards.

8. Assume `mystring` references a string. Write a statement that uses a slicing expression and displays the first 3 characters in the string.

9. Assume `mystring` references a string. Write a statement that uses a slicing expression and displays the last 3 characters in the string.

10. Look at the following statement:
```
mystring = 'cookies>milk>fudge>cake>ice cream'
```
Write a statement that splits this string, creating the following list:
```
['cookies', 'milk', 'fudge', 'cake', 'ice cream']
```

Programming Exercises

1. Initials

Write a program that gets a string containing a person's first, middle, and last names, and displays their first, middle, and last initials. For example, if the user enters John William Smith, the program should display J. W. S.

2. Sum of Digits in a String

Write a program that asks the user to enter a series of single-digit numbers with nothing separating them. The program should display the sum of all the single digit numbers in the string. For example, if the user enters 2514, the method should return 12, which is the sum of 2, 5, 1, and 4.

3. Date Printer

Write a program that reads a string from the user containing a date in the form mm/dd/yyyy. It should print the date in the format March 12, 2024.

4. Morse Code Converter

Morse code is a code where each letter of the English alphabet, each digit, and various punctuation characters are represented by a series of dots and dashes. Table 11-4 shows part of the code.

Write a program that asks the user to enter a string, then converts that string to Morse code.

Table 11-4   Morse code

Character	Code	Character	Code	Character	Code	Character	Code
space	*space*	6	−....	G	−−.	Q	−−.−
comma	−−..−−	7	−−...	H	....	R	.−.
period	.−.−.−	8	−−−..	I	..	S	...
question mark	..−−..	9	−−−−.	J	.−−−	T	−
0	−−−−−	A	.−	K	−.−	U	..−
1	.−−−−	B	−...	L	.−..	V	...−
2	..−−−	C	−.−.	M	−−	W	.−−
3	...−−	D	−..	N	−.	X	−..−
4	....−	E	.	O	−−−	Y	−.−
5	.....	F	..−.	P	.−−.	Z	−−..

5. Alphabetic Telephone Number Translator

Many companies use telephone numbers like 555-GET-FOOD so the number is easier for their customers to remember. On a standard telephone, the alphabetic letters are mapped to numbers in the following fashion:

A, B, and C = 2
D, E, and F = 3
G, H, and I = 4
J, K, and L = 5
M, N, and O = 6
P, Q, R, and S = 7
T, U, and V = 8
W, X, Y, and Z = 9

Write a program that asks the user to enter a 10-character telephone number in the format XXX-XXX-XXXX. The application should display the telephone number with any alphabetic characters that appeared in the original translated to their numeric equivalent. For example, if the user enters 555-GET-FOOD, the application should display 555-438-3663.

6. Sentence Capitalizer

Write a program with a function that accepts a string as an argument and returns a copy of the string with the first character of each sentence capitalized. For instance, if the argument is "hello. my name is Joe. what is your name?" the function should return the string "Hello. My name is Joe. What is your name?" The program should let the user enter a string and then pass it to the function. The modified string should be displayed.

VideoNote
The
Vowels and
Consonants
Problem

7. Vowels and Consonants

Write a program with a function that accepts a string as an argument and returns the number of vowels that the string contains. The application should have another function that accepts a string as an argument and returns the number of consonants that the string contains. The application should let the user enter a string and should display the number of vowels and the number of consonants it contains.

8. Most Frequent Character

Write a program that lets the user enter a string and displays the character that appears most frequently in the string.

9. Word Separator

Write a program that accepts as input a sentence in which all of the words are run together, but the first character of each word is uppercase. Convert the sentence to a string in which the words are separated by spaces and only the first word starts with an uppercase letter. For example, the string "`StopAndSmellTheRoses`." would be converted to "`Stop and smell the roses`."

10. Pig Latin

Write a program that accepts a sentence as input and converts each word to "Pig Latin." In one version, to convert a word to Pig Latin, you remove the first letter and place that letter at the end of the word. Then, you append the string "ay" to the word. Here is an example:

English:	I SLEPT MOST OF THE NIGHT
Pig Latin:	IAY LEPTSAY OSTMAY FOAY HETAY IGHTNAY

12 Using Loop Statements

TOPICS

12.1 Introduction to Loop Statements

  **A repetition structure, such as a loop, causes a statement or set of statements to execute repeatedly.**

Programmers commonly have to write code that performs the same task over and over. For example, suppose you have been asked to write a program that calculates a 10 percent sales commission for several salespeople. Although it would not be a good design, one approach would be to write the code to calculate one salesperson's commission, and then repeat that code for each salesperson. For example, look at the following:

```
# Get a salesperson's sales and commission rate.
sales = float(input('Enter the amount of sales: '))
comm_rate = float(input('Enter the commission rate: '))

# Calculate the commission.
commission = sales * comm_rate

# Display the commission.
print('The commission is $', format(commission, ',.2f'), sep='')

# Get another salesperson's sales and commission rate.
sales = float(input('Enter the amount of sales: '))
comm_rate = float(input('Enter the commission rate: '))

# Calculate the commission.
commission = sales * comm_rate
```

```
# Display the commission.
print('The commission is $', format(commission, ',.2f'), sep='')

# Get another salesperson's sales and commission rate.
sales = float(input('Enter the amount of sales: '))
comm_rate = float(input('Enter the commission rate: '))

# Calculate the commission.
commission = sales * comm_rate
# Display the commission.

print('The commission is $', format(commission, ',.2f'), sep='')
```

And this code goes on and on . . .

As you can see, this code is one long sequence structure containing a lot of duplicated code. There are several disadvantages to this approach, including the following:

- The duplicated code makes the program large.
- Writing a long sequence of statements can be time-consuming.
- If part of the duplicated code has to be corrected or changed, then the correction or change has to be done many times.

Instead of writing the same sequence of statements over and over, a better way to repeatedly perform an operation is to write the code for the operation once, then place that code in a structure that makes the computer repeat it as many times as necessary. This can be done with a **repetition structure**, which repeats a set of statements. A repetition structure is also known as an **iterative** structure, or a **loop**.

Condition-Controlled and Count-Controlled Loops

In this chapter, we will look at two broad categories of loops: condition-controlled and count-controlled. A **condition-controlled loop** uses a true/false condition to control the number of times that it repeats. A **count-controlled loop** repeats a specific number of times. In Python, you use the `while` statement to write a condition-controlled loop, and you use the `for` statement to write a count-controlled loop. In this chapter, we will demonstrate how to write both types of loops.

Checkpoint

12.1 What is a repetition structure?

12.2 What is a condition-controlled loop?

12.3 What is a count-controlled loop?

12.2 The while Loop: A Condition-Controlled Loop

A condition-controlled loop causes a statement or set of statements to repeat as long as a condition is true. In Python, you use the while statement to write a condition-controlled loop.

The while loop gets its name from the way it works: *while a condition is true, do some task.* The loop has two parts: (1) a condition that is tested for a true or false value, and (2) a statement or set of statements that is repeated as long as the condition is true. Figure 12-1 shows the logic of a while loop.

Figure 12-1   The logic of a while loop

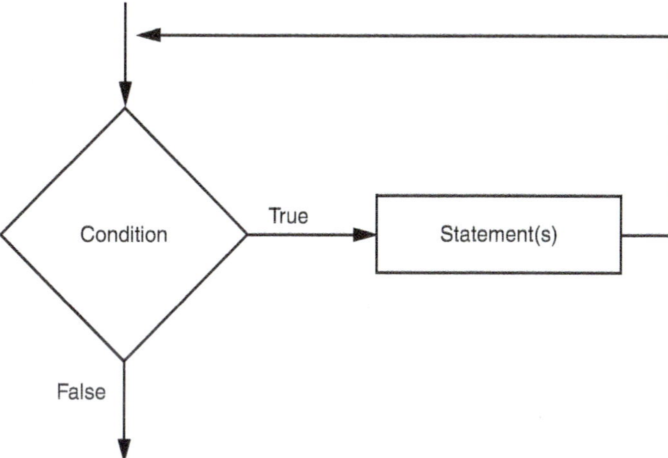

The diamond symbol represents the condition that is tested. Notice what happens if the condition is true: one or more statements are executed, and the program's execution flows back to the point just above the diamond symbol. The condition is tested again, and if it is true, the process repeats. If the condition is false, the program exits the loop. In a flowchart, you will always recognize a loop when you see a flow line going back to a previous part of the flowchart.

Here is the general format of the while loop in Python:

```
while condition:
    statement
    statement
    etc.
```

For simplicity, we will refer to the first line as the *while clause.* The while clause begins with the word while, followed by a Boolean *condition* that will be evaluated as either true or false. A colon appears after the *condition.* Beginning at the next line is a block of statements. Note that all of the statements in a block must be consistently indented. This indentation is required because the Python interpreter uses it to tell where the block begins and ends.

When the while loop executes, the *condition* is tested. If the *condition* is true, the statements that appear in the block following the while clause are executed, and the loop starts over. If the *condition* is false, the program exits the loop. Program 12-1 shows how we might use a `while` loop to write the commission-calculating program that was described at the beginning of this chapter.

Program 12-1   (`commission.py`)

```
 1  # This program calculates sales commissions.
 2
 3  # Create a variable to control the loop.
 4  keep_going = 'y'
 5
 6  # Calculate a series of commissions.
 7  while keep_going == 'y':
 8      # Get a salesperson's sales and commission rate.
 9      sales = float(input('Enter the amount of sales: '))
10      comm_rate = float(input('Enter the commission rate: '))
11
12      # Calculate the commission.
13      commission = sales * comm_rate
14
15      # Display the commission.
16      print(f'The commission is ${commission:,.2f}.')
17
18      # See if the user wants to do another one.
19      keep_going = input('Do you want to calculate another ' +
20                         'commission (Enter y for yes): ')
```

Program Output (with input shown in bold)
```
Enter the amount of sales: 10000.00 [Enter]
Enter the commission rate: 0.10 [Enter]
The commission is $1,000.00.
Do you want to calculate another commission (Enter y for yes): y [Enter]
Enter the amount of sales: 20000.00 [Enter]
Enter the commission rate: 0.15 [Enter]
The commission is $3,000.00.
Do you want to calculate another commission (Enter y for yes): y [Enter]
Enter the amount of sales: 12000.00 [Enter]
Enter the commission rate: 0.10 [Enter]
The commission is $1,200.00.
Do you want to calculate another commission (Enter y for yes): n [Enter]
```

In line 4, we use an assignment statement to create a variable named `keep_going`. Notice the variable is assigned the value `'y'`. This initialization value is important, and in a moment, you will see why.

Line 7 is the beginning of a `while` loop, which starts like this:

```
while keep_going == 'y':
```

Notice the condition that is being tested: keep_going =='y'. The loop tests this condition, and if it is true, the statements in lines 8 through 20 are executed. Then, the loop starts over at line 7. It tests the expression keep_going =='y' and if it is true, the statements in lines 8 through 20 are executed again. This cycle repeats until the expression keep_going =='y' is tested in line 7 and found to be false. When that happens, the program exits the loop. This is illustrated in Figure 12-2.

Figure 12-2   The while loop

```
                                This condition is tested.
                                          |
                                 ┌────────┴────────┐
                          while keep_going == 'y':

                              # Get a salesperson's sales and commission rate.
                              sales = float(input('Enter the amount of sales: '))
  If the condition is true,    comm_rate = float(input('Enter the commission rate: '))
  these statements are
  executed, and then the       # Calculate the commission.
  loop starts over.            commission = sales * comm_rate

  If the condition is false,   # Display the commission.
  these statements are         print(f'The commission is ${commission:,.2f}.')
  skipped, and the
  program exits the loop.      # See if the user wants to do another one.
                              keep_going = input('Do you want to calculate another ' +
                                                 'commission (Enter y for yes): ')
```

In order for this loop to stop executing, something has to happen inside the loop to make the expression keep_going == 'y' false. The statement in lines 19 through 20 takes care of this. This statement displays the prompt "Do you want to calculate another commission (Enter y for yes)." The value that is read from the keyboard is assigned to the keep_going variable. If the user enters y (and it must be a lowercase y), then the expression keep_going == 'y' will be true when the loop starts over. This will cause the statements in the body of the loop to execute again. But if the user enters anything other than lowercase y, the expression will be false when the loop starts over, and the program will exit the loop.

Now that you have examined the code, look at the program output in the sample run. First, the user entered 10000.00 for the sales and 0.10 for the commission rate. Then, the program displayed the commission for that amount, which is $1,000.00. Next the user is prompted "Do you want to calculate another commission? (Enter y for yes)." The user entered y, and the loop started the steps over. In the sample run, the user went through this process three times. Each execution of the body of a loop is known as an **iteration**. In the sample run, the loop iterated three times.

Figure 12-3 shows a flowchart for the main function. In the flowchart, we have a repetition structure, which is the while loop. The condition keep_going =='y' is tested, and if it is true, a series of statements is executed and the flow of execution returns to the point just above the conditional test.

Figure 12-3   Flowchart for Program 12-1

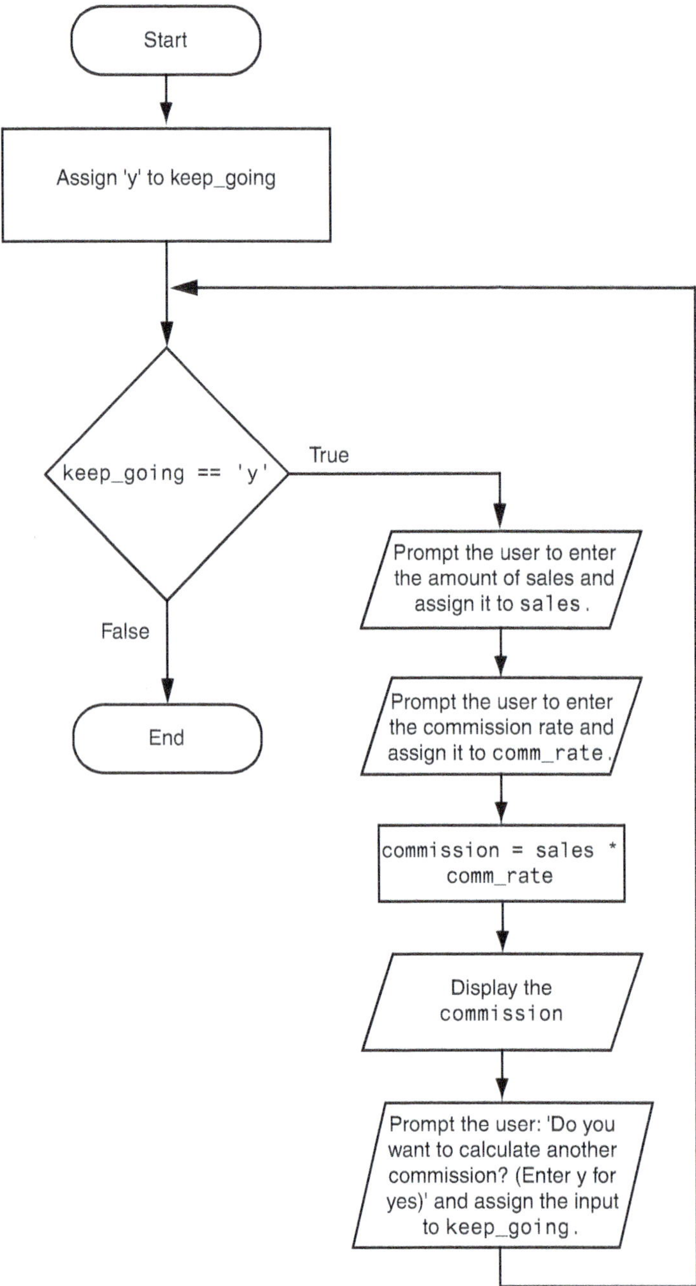

The `while` Loop Is a Pretest Loop

The `while` loop is known as a **pretest** loop, which means it tests its condition *before* performing an iteration. Because the test is done at the beginning of the loop, you usually have to perform some steps prior to the loop to make sure that the loop executes at least once. For example, the loop in Program 12-1 starts like this:

```
while keep_going == 'y':
```

The loop will perform an iteration only if the expression `keep_going ==`'y' is true. This means that (a) the `keep_going` variable has to exist, and (b) it has to reference the value 'y'. To make sure the expression is true the first time that the loop executes, we assigned the value 'y' to the `keep_going` variable in line 4 as follows:

```
keep_going = 'y'
```

By performing this step, we know that the condition `keep_going ==`'y' will be true the first time the loop executes. This is an important characteristic of the while loop: it will never execute if its condition is false to start with. In some programs, this is exactly what you want. The following *In the Spotlight* section gives an example.

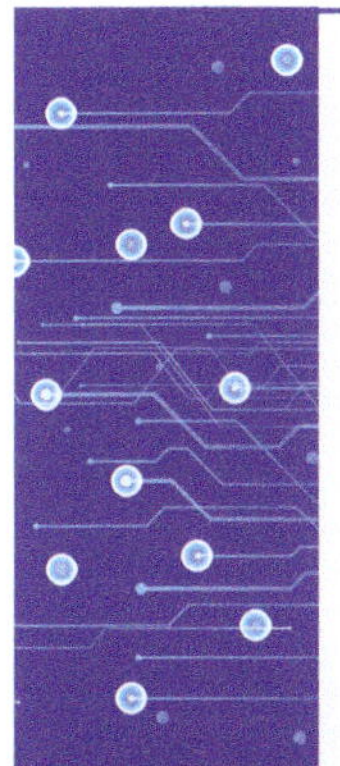

In the Spotlight:

Designing a Program with a `while` Loop

A project currently underway at Chemical Labs, Inc. requires that a substance be continually heated in a vat. A technician must check the substance's temperature every 15 minutes. If the substance's temperature does not exceed 102.5 degrees Celsius, then the technician does nothing. However, if the temperature is greater than 102.5 degrees Celsius, the technician must turn down the vat's thermostat, wait 5 minutes, and check the temperature again. The technician repeats these steps until the temperature does not exceed 102.5 degrees Celsius. The director of engineering has asked you to write a program that guides the technician through this process.

On Your Own: Working alone or with a partner, see if you can design an algorithm and write a program to solve the problem. Use problem-solving strategies to select the most appropriate construct, such as identifying the main task and subtasks. When you have completed your work, continue reading to see a solution.

Here is the algorithm:

1. Get the substance's temperature.
2. Repeat the following steps as long as the temperature is greater than 102.5 degrees Celsius:
    a. Tell the technician to turn down the thermostat, wait 5 minutes, and check the temperature again.
    b. Get the substance's temperature.
3. After the loop finishes, tell the technician that the temperature is acceptable and to check it again in 15 minutes.

After reviewing this algorithm, you realize that steps 2(a) and 2(b) should not be performed if the test condition (temperature is greater than 102.5) is false to begin with. The `while` loop will work

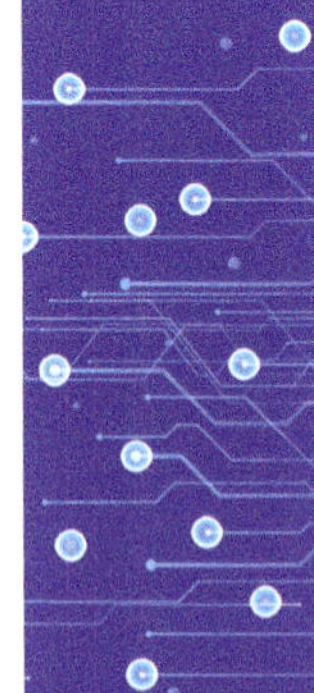

well in this situation, because it will not execute even once if its condition is false. Program 12-2 shows the code for the program.

Program 12-2   (`temperature.py`)

```
 1   # This program assists a technician in the process
 2   # of checking a substance's temperature.
 3
 4   # Named constant to represent the maximum
 5   # temperature.
 6   MAX_TEMP = 102.5
 7
 8   # Get the substance's temperature.
 9   temperature = float(input("Enter the substance's Celsius temperature: "))
10
11   # As long as necessary, instruct the user to
12   # adjust the thermostat.
13   while temperature > MAX_TEMP:
14       print('The temperature is too high.')
15       print('Turn the thermostat down and wait')
16       print('5 minutes. Then take the temperature')
17       print('again and enter it.')
18       temperature = float(input('Enter the new Celsius temperature: '))
19
20   # Remind the user to check the temperature again
21   # in 15 minutes.
22   print('The temperature is acceptable.')
23   print('Check it again in 15 minutes.')
```

Program Output (with input shown in bold)
```
Enter the substance's Celsius temperature: 104.7 [Enter]
The temperature is too high.
Turn the thermostat down and wait
5 minutes. Take the temperature
again and enter it.
Enter the new Celsius temperature: 103.2 [Enter]
The temperature is too high.
Turn the thermostat down and wait
5 minutes. Take the temperature
again and enter it.
Enter the new Celsius temperature: 102.1 [Enter]
The temperature is acceptable.
Check it again in 15 minutes.
```

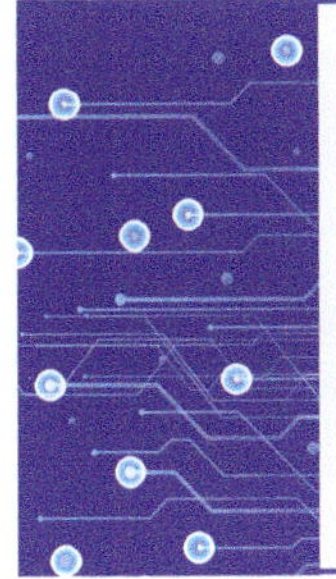

Program 12-2   *(continued)*

Program Output (with input shown in bold)
```
Enter the substance's Celsius temperature: 102.1 Enter
The temperature is acceptable.
Check it again in 15 minutes.
```

Infinite Loops

In all but rare cases, loops must contain within themselves a way to terminate. This means that something inside the loop must eventually make the test condition false. The loop in Program 12-1 stops when the expression keep_going == 'y' is false. If a loop does not have a way of stopping, it is called an infinite loop. An **infinite loop** continues to repeat until the program is interrupted. Infinite loops usually occur when the programmer forgets to write code inside the loop that makes the test condition false. In most circumstances, you should avoid writing infinite loops.

Program 12-3 demonstrates an infinite loop. This is a modified version of the commission-calculating program shown in Program 12-1. In this version, we have removed the code that modifies the keep_going variable in the body of the loop. Each time the expression keep_going == 'y' is tested in line 6, keep_going will reference the string 'y'. As a consequence, the loop has no way of stopping. (The only way to stop this program is to press Ctrl+C on the keyboard to interrupt it.)

Program 12-3   (infinite.py)

```
 1   # This program demonstrates an infinite loop.
 2   # Create a variable to control the loop.
 3   keep_going = 'y'
 4
 5   # Warning! Infinite loop!
 6   while keep_going == 'y':
 7       # Get a salesperson's sales and commission rate.
 8       sales = float(input('Enter the amount of sales: '))
 9       comm_rate = float(input('Enter the commission rate: '))
10
11       # Calculate the commission.
12       commission = sales * comm_rate
13
14       # Display the commission.
15       print(f'The commission is ${commission:,.2f}.')
```

Checkpoint

12.4 What is a loop iteration?

12.5 Does the `while` loop test its condition before or after it performs an iteration?

12.6 How many times will `'Hello World'` be printed in the following program?

```
count = 10
while count < 1:
        print('Hello World')
```

12.7 What is an infinite loop?

12.3 The `for` Loop: A Count-Controlled Loop

VideoNote
The for
Loop

A count-controlled loop iterates a specific number of times. In Python, you use the for statement to write a count-controlled loop.

As mentioned at the beginning of this chapter, a count-controlled loop iterates a specific number of times. Count-controlled loops are commonly used in programs. For example, suppose a business is open six days per week, and you are going to write a program that calculates the total sales for a week. You will need a loop that iterates exactly six times. Each time the loop iterates, it will prompt the user to enter the sales for one day.

You use the `for` statement to write a count-controlled loop. In Python, the `for` statement is designed to work with a sequence of data items. When the statement executes, it iterates once for each item in the sequence. Here is the general format:

```
for variable in [value1, value2, etc.]:
    statement
    statement
    etc.
```

We will refer to the first line as the *for clause*. In the for clause, *variable* is the name of a variable. Inside the brackets, a sequence of values appears, with a comma separating each value. (In Python, a comma-separated sequence of data items enclosed in brackets is called a **list**. In Chapter 13, you will learn more about lists.) Beginning at the next line is a block of statements that is executed each time the loop iterates.

The `for` statement executes in the following manner: The *variable* is assigned the first value in the list, then the statements that appear in the block are executed. Then, *variable* is assigned the next value in the list, and the statements in the block are executed again. This continues until *variable* has been assigned the last value in the list. Program 12-4 shows a simple example that uses a `for` loop to display the numbers 1 through 5.

Program 12-4   (`simple_loop1.py`)

```
1   # This program demonstrates a simple for loop
2   # that uses a list of numbers.
3
4   print('I will display the numbers 1 through 5.')
5   for num in [1, 2, 3, 4, 5]:
6       print(num)
```

Program Output
```
I will display the numbers 1 through 5.
1
2
3
4
5
```

The first time the for loop iterates, the num variable is assigned the value 1 and then the statement in line 6 executes (displaying the value 1). The next time the loop iterates, num is assigned the value 2, and the statement in line 6 executes (displaying the value 2). This process continues, as shown in Figure 12-4, until num has been assigned the last value in the list. Because the list contains five values, the loop will iterate five times.

Figure 12-4   The for loop

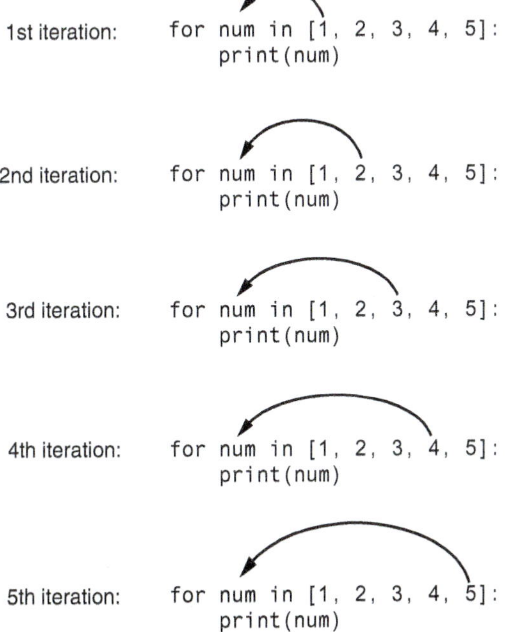

Python programmers commonly refer to the variable that is used in the `for` clause as the **target variable** because it is the target of an assignment at the beginning of each loop iteration.

The values that appear in the list do not have to be a consecutively-ordered series of numbers. For example, Program 12-5 uses a `for` loop to display a list of odd numbers. There are five numbers in the list, so the loop iterates five times.

Program 12-5   (`simple_loop2.py`)

```
1   # This program also demonstrates a simple for
2   # loop that uses a list of numbers.
3
4   print('I will display the odd numbers 1 through 9.')
5   for num in [1, 3, 5, 7, 9]:
6       print(num)
```

Program Output
```
I will display the odd numbers 1 through 9.
1
3
5
7
9
```

Program 12-6 shows another example. In this program, the `for` loop iterates over a list of strings. Notice the list (in line 4) contains the three strings 'Winken', 'Blinken', and 'Nod'. As a result, the loop iterates three times.

Program 12-6   (`simple_loop3.py`)

```
1   # This program also demonstrates a simple for
2   # loop that uses a list of strings.
3
4   for name in ['Winken', 'Blinken', 'Nod']:
5       print(name)
```

Program Output
```
Winken
Blinken
Nod
```

Using the `range` Function with the `for` Loop

Python provides a built-in function named `range` that simplifies the process of writing a count-controlled `for` loop. The range function creates a type of object known as an iterable. An **iterable** is an object that is similar to a list. It contains a sequence of values that can be iterated over with something like a loop. Here is an example of a `for` loop that uses the `range` function:

```
for num in range(5):
    print(num)
```

Notice instead of using a list of values, we call to the `range` function, passing 5 as an argument. In this statement, the `range` function will generate an iterable sequence of integers from 0 up to (but not including) 5. This code works the same as the following:

```
for num in [0, 1, 2, 3, 4]:
    print(num)
```

As you can see, the list contains five numbers, so the loop will iterate five times. Program 12-7 uses the `range` function with a `for` loop to display "Hello world" five times.

Program 12-7   (`simple_loop4.py`)

```
1   # This program demonstrates how the range
2   # function can be used with a for loop.
3
4   # Print a message five times.
5   for x in range(5):
6       print('Hello world')
```

Program Output
```
Hello world
Hello world
Hello world
Hello world
Hello world
```

If you pass one argument to the `range` function, as demonstrated in Program 12-7, that argument is used as the ending limit of the sequence of numbers. If you pass two arguments to the `range` function, the first argument is used as the starting value of the sequence, and the second argument is used as the ending limit. Here is an example:

```
for num in range(1, 5):
    print(num)
```

This code will display the following:

```
1
2
3
4
```

By default, the `range` function produces a sequence of numbers that increase by 1 for each successive number in the list. If you pass a third argument to the `range` function, that argument is used as a **step value**. Instead of increasing by 1, each successive number in the sequence will increase by the step value. Here is an example:

```
for num in range(1, 10, 2):
    print(num)
```

In this `for` statement, three arguments are passed to the `range` function:

- The first argument, 1, is the starting value for the sequence.
- The second argument, 10, is the ending limit of the list. This means that the last number in the sequence will be 9.
- The third argument, 2, is the step value. This means that 2 will be added to each successive number in the sequence.

This code will display the following:

```
1
3
5
7
9
```

Using the Target Variable Inside the Loop

In a `for` loop, the purpose of the target variable is to reference each item in a sequence of items as the loop iterates. In many situations, it is helpful to use the target variable in a calculation or other task within the body of the loop. For example, suppose you need to write a program that displays the numbers 1 through 10 and their respective squares, in a table similar to the following:

Number	Square
1	1
2	4
3	9
4	16
5	25
6	36
7	49
8	64
9	81
10	100

This can be accomplished by writing a `for` loop that iterates over the values 1 through 10. During the first iteration, the target variable will be assigned the value 1; during the second iteration, it will be assigned the value 2, and so forth. Because the target variable will reference the values 1 through 10 during the loop's execution, you can use it in the calculation inside the loop. Program 12-8 shows how this is done.

Program 12-8   (`squares.py`)

```
 1  # This program uses a loop to display a
 2  # table showing the numbers 1 through 10
 3  # and their squares.
 4
 5  # Print the table headings.
 6  print('Number\tSquare')
 7  print('--------------')
 8
 9  # Print the numbers 1 through 10
10  # and their squares.
11  for number in range(1, 11):
12      square = number**2
13      print(f'{number}\t{square}')
```

Program Output
```
Number  Square
--------------
1       1
2       4
3       9
4       16
5       25
6       36
7       49
8       64
9       81
10      100
```

First, take a closer look at line 6, which displays the table headings:

```
print('Number\tSquare')
```

Notice the \t escape sequence between the words Number and Square. Recall that the \t escape sequence is like pressing the Tab key; it causes the output cursor to move over to the next tab position. This causes the space that you see between the words Number and Square in the sample output.

The for loop that begins in line 11 uses the range function to produce a sequence containing the numbers 1 through 10. During the first iteration, number will reference 1; during the second iteration, number will reference 2, and so forth, up to 10. Inside the loop, the statement in line 12 raises number to the power of 2 (recall that ** is the exponent operator) and assigns the result to the square variable. The statement in line 13 prints the value referenced by number, tabs over, then prints the value referenced by square. (Tabbing over with the \t escape sequence causes the numbers to be aligned in two columns in the output.)

Figure 12-5 shows how we might draw a flowchart for this program.

Figure 12-5 Flowchart for Program 12-8

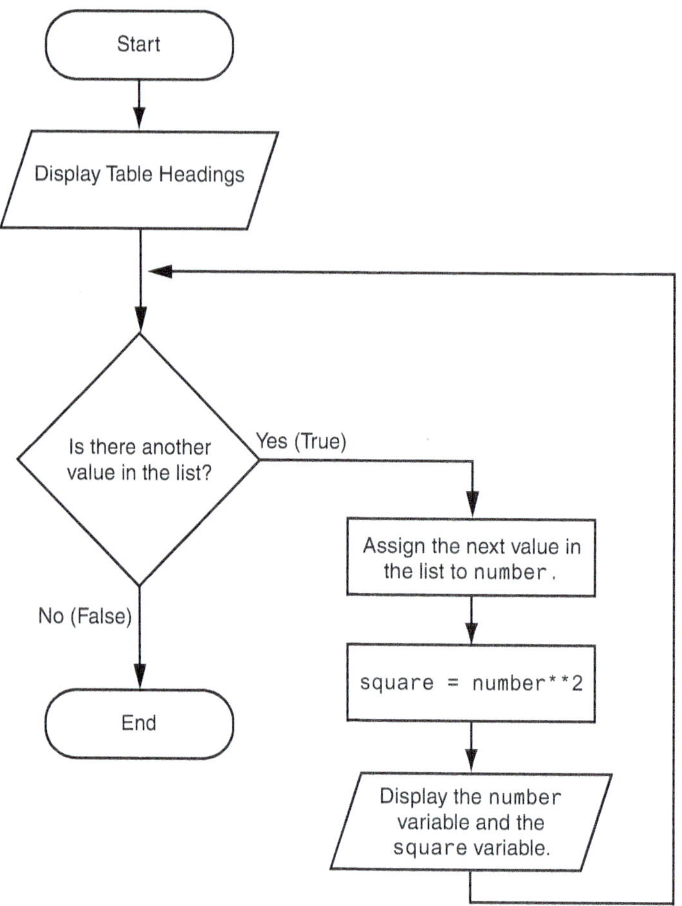

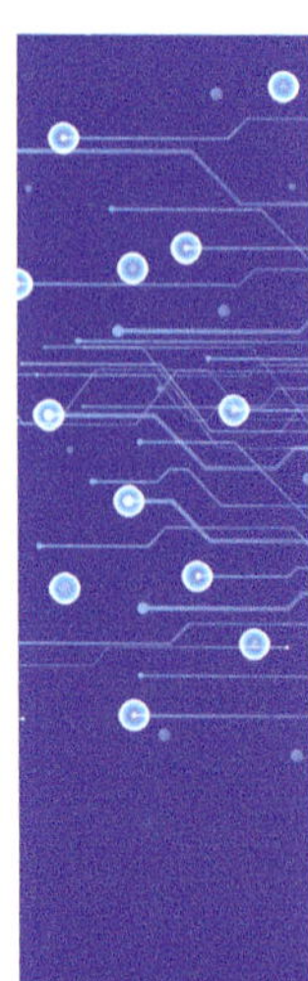

In the Spotlight:

Designing a Count-Controlled Loop with the **for** Statement

Your friend Amanda just inherited a European sports car from her uncle. Amanda lives in the United States, and she is afraid she will get a speeding ticket because the car's speedometer indicates kilometers per hour (KPH). She has asked you to write a program that displays a table of speeds in KPH with their values converted to miles per hour (MPH). The formula for converting KPH to MPH is:

$$MPH = KPH \times 0.6214$$

In the formula, *MPH* is the speed in miles per hour, and *KPH* is the speed in kilometers per hour.

On Your Own: Working alone or with a partner, see if you can design an algorithm and write a program to solve the problem. Use problem-solving strategies to select the most appropriate construct, such as identifying the main task and subtasks. When you have completed your work, continue reading to see a solution.

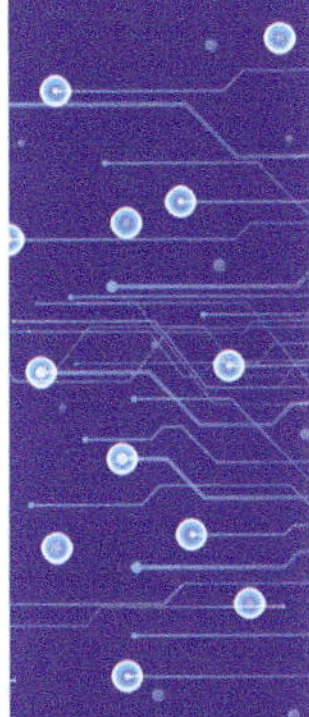

The table that your program displays should show speeds from 60 KPH through 130 KPH, in increments of 10, along with their values converted to MPH. The table should look something like this:

KPH	MPH
60	37.3
70	43.5
80	49.7
etc. . . .	
130	80.8

After thinking about this table of values, you decide that you will write a for loop. The list of values that the loop will iterate over will be the kilometer-per-hour speeds. In the loop, you will call the range function like this:

```
range(60, 131, 10)
```

The first value in the sequence will be 60. Notice the third argument specifies 10 as the step value. This means the numbers in the list will be 60, 70, 80, and so forth. The second argument specifies 131 as the sequence's ending limit, so the last number in the sequence will be 130.

Inside the loop, you will use the target variable to calculate a speed in miles per hour. Program 12-9 shows the program.

Program 12-9   (speed_converter.py)

```
 1   # This program converts the speeds 60 kph,
 2   # through 130 kph (in 10 kph increments)
 3   # to mph.
 4
 5   START_SPEED = 60                # Starting speed
 6   END_SPEED = 131                 # Ending speed
 7   INCREMENT = 10                  # Speed increment
 8   CONVERSION_FACTOR = 0.6214   # Conversion factor
 9
10   # Print the table headings.
11   print('KPH\tMPH')
12   print('--------------')
13
14   # Print the speeds.
15   for kph in range(START_SPEED, END_SPEED, INCREMENT)
16       mph = kph * CONVERSION_FACTOR
17       print(f'{kph}\t{mph:.1f}')
```

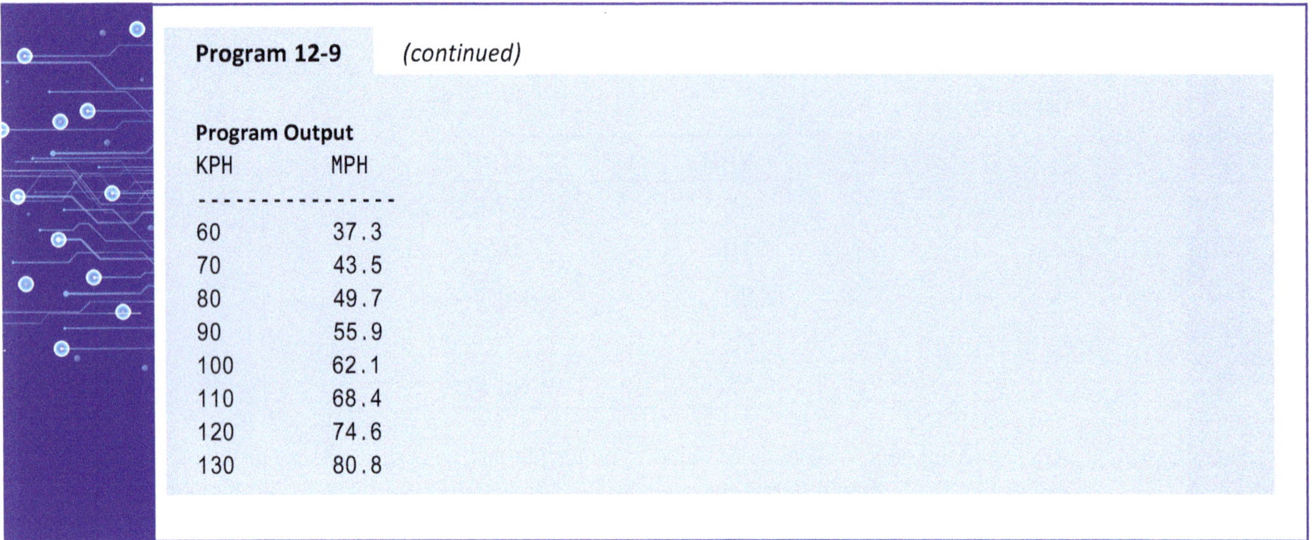

Program 12-9   *(continued)*

Program Output

```
KPH         MPH
---------------
60          37.3
70          43.5
80          49.7
90          55.9
100         62.1
110         68.4
120         74.6
130         80.8
```

Letting the User Control the Loop Iterations

In many cases, the programmer knows the exact number of iterations that a loop must perform. For example, recall Program 12-8, which displays a table showing the numbers 1 through 10 and their squares. When the code was written, the programmer knew that the loop had to iterate over the values 1 through 10.

Sometimes, the programmer needs to let the user control the number of times that a loop iterates. For example, what if you want Program 12-8 to be a bit more versatile by allowing the user to specify the maximum value displayed by the loop? Program 12-10 shows how you can accomplish this.

Program 12-10   (user_squares1.py)

```python
 1  # This program uses a loop to display a
 2  # table of numbers and their squares.
 3
 4  # Get the ending limit.
 5  print('This program displays a list of numbers')
 6  print('(starting at 1) and their squares.')
 7  end = int(input('How high should I go? '))
 8
 9  # Print the table headings.
10  print()
11  print('Number\tSquare')
12  print('--------------')
13
14  # Print the numbers and their squares.
15  for number in range(1, end + 1):
16      square = number**2
17        print(f'{number}\t{square}')
```

Program 12-10   *(continued)*

Program Output (with input shown in bold)
```
This program displays a list of numbers
(starting at 1) and their squares.
How high should I go? 5 Enter

Number    Square
-----------------
1         1
2         4
3         9
4         16
5         25
```

This program asks the user to enter a value that can be used as the ending limit for the list. This value is assigned to the end variable in line 7. Then, the expression end + 1 is used in line 15 as the second argument for the range function. (We have to add one to end because otherwise the sequence would go up to, but not include, the value entered by the user.)

Program 12-11 shows an example that allows the user to specify both the starting value and the ending limit of the sequence.

Program 12-11   **(user_squares2.py)**

```
 1   # This program uses a loop to display a
 2   # table of numbers and their squares.
 3
 4   # Get the starting value.
 5   print('This program displays a list of numbers')
 6   print('and their squares.')
 7   start = int(input('Enter the starting number: '))
 8
 9   # Get the ending limit.
10   end = int(input('How high should I go? '))
11
12   # Print the table headings.
13   print()
14   print('Number\tSquare')
15   print('--------------')
16
17   # Print the numbers and their squares.
18   for number in range(start, end + 1):
19       square = number**2
20       print(f'{number}\t{square}')
```

Program 12-11   *(continued)*

Program Output (with input shown in bold)
```
This program displays a list of numbers and their squares.
Enter the starting number: 5 Enter
How high should I go? 10 Enter

Number Square
---------------
5          25
6          36
7          49
8          64
9          81
10         100
```

Generating an Iterable Sequence that Ranges from Highest to Lowest

In the examples you have seen so far, the range function was used to generate a sequence with numbers that go from lowest to highest. Alternatively, you can use the range function to generate sequences of numbers that go from highest to lowest. Here is an example:

```
range(10, 0, -1)
```

In this function call, the starting value is 10, the sequence's ending limit is 0, and the step value is −1. This expression will produce the following sequence:

```
10, 9, 8, 7, 6, 5, 4, 3, 2, 1
```

Here is an example of a for loop that prints the numbers 5 down to 1:

```
for num in range(5, 0, -1):
    print(num)
```

 **Checkpoint**

12.8 Rewrite the following code so it calls the range function instead of using the list
`[0, 1, 2, 3, 4, 5]`:
```
for x in [0, 1, 2, 3, 4, 5]:
    print('I love to program!')
```

12.9 What will the following code display?
```
for number in range(6):
    print(number)
```

12.10 What will the following code display?
```
for number in range(2, 6):
    print(number)
```

12.11 What will the following code display?
```
for number in range(0, 501, 100):
    print(number)
```

12.12 What will the following code display?
```
for number in range(10, 5, -1):
    print(number)
```

12.4 Calculating a Running Total

**A running total is a sum of numbers that accumulates with each
iteration of a loop. The variable used to keep the running total
is called an accumulator.**

Many programming tasks require you to calculate the total of a series of numbers. For example, suppose you are writing a program that calculates a business's total sales for a week. The program would read the sales for each day as input and calculate the total of those numbers.

Programs that calculate the total of a series of numbers typically use two elements:

- A loop that reads each number in the series.
- A variable that accumulates the total of the numbers as they are read.

The variable that is used to accumulate the total of the numbers is called an **accumulator**. It is often said that the loop keeps a **running total** because it accumulates the total as it reads each number in the series. Figure 12-6 shows the general logic of a loop that calculates a running total.

Figure 12-6   Logic for calculating a running total

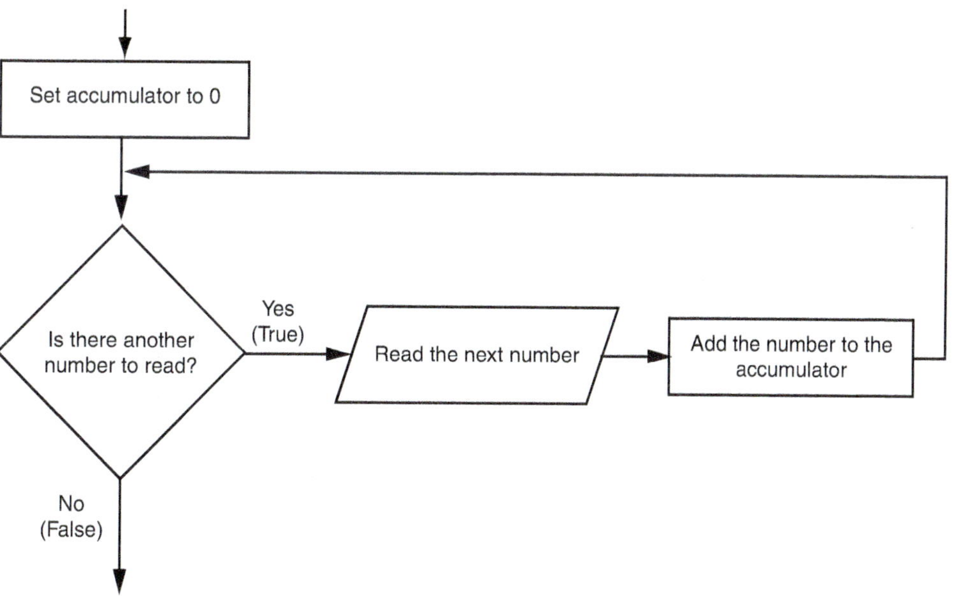

When the loop finishes, the accumulator will contain the total of the numbers that were read by the loop. Notice the first step in the flowchart is to set the accumulator variable to 0. This is a critical step. Each time the loop reads a number, it adds it to the accumulator. If the accumulator starts with any value other than 0, it will not contain the correct total when the loop finishes.

Let's look at a program that calculates a running total. Program 12-12 allows the user to enter five numbers and displays the total of the numbers entered.

Program 12-12   (`sum_numbers.py`)

```
 1   # This program calculates the sum of a series
 2   # of numbers entered by the user.
 3
 4   MAX = 5 # The maximum number
 5
 6   # Initialize an accumulator variable.
 7   total = 0.0
 8
 9   # Explain what we are doing.
10   print('This program calculates the sum of ', end='')
11   print(f'{MAX} numbers you will enter.')
12
13   # Get the numbers and accumulate them.
14   for counter in range(MAX):
15       number = int(input('Enter a number: '))
16       total = total + number
17
18   # Display the total of the numbers.

19   print(f'The total is {total}.')
```

Program Output (with input shown in bold)
```
This program calculates the sum of 5 numbers you will enter.
Enter a number: 1 Enter
Enter a number: 2 Enter
Enter a number: 3 Enter
Enter a number: 4 Enter
Enter a number: 5 Enter
The total is 15.0.
```

The `total` variable, created by the assignment statement in line 7, is the accumulator. Notice it is initialized with the value 0.0. The `for` loop, in lines 14 through 16, does the work of getting the numbers from the user and calculating their total. Line 15 prompts the user to enter a number, then assigns the input to the number variable. Then, the following statement in line 16 adds `number` to `total`:

```
total = total + number
```

After this statement executes, the value referenced by the `number` variable will be added to the value in the `total` variable. It's important that you understand how this statement works. First, the interpreter gets the value of the expression on the right side of the = operator, which is `total` + `number`. Then, that value is assigned by the = operator to the `total` variable. The effect of the statement is that the value of the `number` variable is added to the `total` variable. When the loop finishes, the `total` variable will hold the sum of all the numbers that were added to it. This value is displayed in line 19.

The Augmented Assignment Operators

Quite often, programs have assignment statements in which the variable that is on the left side of the = operator also appears on the right side of the = operator. Here is an example:

```
x = x + 1
```

On the right side of the assignment operator, 1 is added to x. The result is then assigned to x, replacing the value that x previously referenced. Effectively, this statement adds 1 to x. You saw another example of this type of statement in Program 12-13:

```
total = total + number
```

This statement assigns the value of total + number to total. As mentioned before, the effect of this statement is that number is added to the value of total. Here is one more example:

```
balance = balance - withdrawal
```

This statement assigns the value of the expression balance - withdrawal to balance. The effect of this statement is that withdrawal is subtracted from balance.

Table 12-1 shows other examples of statements written this way.

Table 12-1 Various assignment statements (assume x = 6 in each statement)

Statement	What It Does	Value of x after the Statement
x = x + 4	Add 4 to x	10
x = x − 3	Subtracts 3 from x	3
x = x * 10	Multiplies x by 10	60
x = x / 2	Divides x by 2	3
x = x % 4	Assigns the remainder of x / 4 to x	2

These types of operations are common in programming. For convenience, Python offers a special set of operators designed specifically for these jobs. Table 12-2 shows the **augmented assignment operators.**

Table 12-2 Augmented assignment operators

Operator	Example Usage	Equivalent To
+=	x += 5	x = x + 5
−=	y −= 2	y = y − 2
*=	z *= 10	z = z * 10
/=	a /= b	a = a / b
%=	c %= 3	c = c % 3
//=	x //= 3	x = x // 3
**=	y **= 2	y = y**2

As you can see, the augmented assignment operators do not require the programmer to type the variable name twice. The following statement:

```
total = total + number
```

could be rewritten as

```
total += number
```

Similarly, the statement

```
balance = balance - withdrawal
```

could be rewritten as

```
balance -= withdrawal
```

Checkpoint

12.13   What is an accumulator?

12.14   Should an accumulator be initialized to any specific value? Why or why not?

12.15   What will the following code display?
```
total = 0
for count in range(1, 6):
    total = total + count
print(total)
```

12.16   What will the following code display?
```
number1 = 10
number2 = 5
number1 = number1 + number2
print(number1)
print(number2)
```

12.17   Rewrite the following statements using augmented assignment operators:
```
a) quantity = quantity + 1
b) days_left = days_left - 5
c) price = price * 10
d) price = price / 2
```

Chapter Review

Multiple Choice

1. A common name for a repetition structure is_______________.
   - a. input
   - b. cycle
   - c. loop
   - d. string

2. A ___________ -controlled loop uses a true/false condition to control the number of times that it repeats.
   - a. Boolean
   - b. condition
   - c. decision
   - d. count

3. A ___________ -controlled loop repeats a specific number of times.
   - a. Boolean
   - b. condition
   - c. decision
   - d. count

4. Each repetition of a loop is known as a(n) ___________.
   - a. cycle
   - b. revolution
   - c. orbit
   - d. iteration

5. The `while` loop is a ___________ type of loop.
   - a. pretest
   - b. no-test
   - c. prequalified
   - d. post-iterative

6. A(n) ___________ loop has no way of ending and repeats until the program is interrupted.
   - a. indeterminate
   - b. interminable
   - c. infinite
   - d. timeless

7. The `-=` operator is an example of a(n) ___________ operator.
   - a. relational
   - b. augmented assignment
   - c. complex assignment
   - d. reverse assignment

8. A(n) ___________ variable keeps a running total.
   a. sentinel
   b. sum
   c. total
   d. accumulator

True or False

1. A condition-controlled loop always repeats a specific number of times.
2. The `while` loop is a pretest loop.
3. The following statement subtracts 1 from x : x = x − 1
4. It is not necessary to initialize accumulator variables.
5. In a nested loop, the inner loop goes through all of its iterations for every single iteration of the outer loop.
6. To calculate the total number of iterations of a nested loop, add the number of iterations of all the loops.

Short Answer

1. What is a condition-controlled loop?
2. What is a count-controlled loop?
3. What is an infinite loop? Write the code for an infinite loop.
4. Explain the logic of a while loop.
5. Why is it critical that accumulator variables are properly initialized?

Algorithm Workbench

1. Write a `while` loop that lets the user enter a number. The number should be multiplied by 10, and the result assigned to a variable named `product`. The loop should iterate as long as `product` is less than 100.

2. Write a `while` loop that asks the user to enter two numbers. The numbers should be added and the sum displayed. The loop should ask the user if they want to perform the operation again. If so, the loop should repeat; otherwise, it should terminate.

3. Write a `for` loop that displays the following set of numbers:

   ```
   0, 10, 20, 30, 40, 50 . . . 1000
   ```

4. Write a loop that asks the user to enter a number. The loop should iterate 10 times and keep a running total of the numbers entered.

5. Write a loop that calculates the total of the following series of numbers:

$$\frac{1}{30} + \frac{2}{29} + \frac{3}{28} + \ldots \frac{30}{1}$$

6. Rewrite the following statements using augmented assignment operators.

   a. `x = x + 1`
   b. `x = x * 2`
   c. `x = x / 10`
   d. `x = x - 100`

7. Write a set of nested loops that display 10 rows of # characters. There should be 15 # characters in each row.

8. Write code that prompts the user to enter a positive nonzero number and validates the input.

9. Write code that prompts the user to enter a number in the range of 1 through 100 and validates the input.

Programming Exercises

VideoNote
The Bug
Collector
Problem

1. Bug Collector

A bug collector collects bugs every day for five days. Develop an algorithm and write a program that keeps a running total of the number of bugs collected during the five days. The loop should ask for the number of bugs collected for each day, and when the loop is finished, the program should display the total number of bugs collected.

2. Calories Burned

Running on a particular treadmill, you burn 4.2 calories per minute. Develop an algorithm and write a program that uses a loop to display the number of calories burned after 10, 15, 20, 25, and 30 minutes.

3. Budget Analysis

Develop an algorithm and write a program that asks the user to enter the amount that they have budgeted for a month. A loop should then prompt the user to enter each of their expenses for the month and keep a running total. When the loop finishes, the program should display the amount that the user is over or under budget.

4. Distance Traveled

The distance a vehicle travels can be calculated as follows:

$$distance = speed \times time$$

For example, if a train travels 40 miles per hour for three hours, the distance traveled is 120 miles. Develop an algorithm and write a program that asks the user for the speed of a vehicle (in miles per hour) and the number of hours it has traveled. It should then use a loop to display the distance the vehicle has traveled for each hour of that time period. Here is an example of the desired output:

```
What is the speed of the vehicle in mph? 40 Enter

How many hours has it traveled? 3 Enter

Hour            Distance Traveled
1                      40
2                      80
3                     120
```

5. Average Rainfall
Develop an algorithm and write a program that uses nested loops to collect data and calculate the average rainfall over a period of years. The program should first ask for the number of years. The outer loop will iterate once for each year. The inner loop will iterate twelve times, once for each month. Each iteration of the inner loop will ask the user for the inches of rainfall for that month. After all iterations, the program should display the number of months, the total inches of rainfall, and the average rainfall per month for the entire period.

6. Celsius to Fahrenheit Table
Develop an algorithm and write a program that displays a table of the Celsius temperatures 0 through 20 and their Fahrenheit equivalents. The formula for converting a temperature from Celsius to Fahrenheit is

$$F = \frac{9}{5} C + 32$$

where F is the Fahrenheit temperature and C is the Celsius temperature. Your program must use a loop to display the table.

7. Pennies for Pay
Develop an algorithm and write a program that calculates the amount of money a person would earn over a period of time if his or her salary is one penny the first day, two pennies the second day, and continues to double each day. The program should ask the user for the number of days. Display a table showing what the salary was for each day, then show the total pay at the end of the period. The output should be displayed in a dollar amount, not the number of pennies.

8. Sum of Numbers
Develop an algorithm and write a program with a loop that asks the user to enter a series of positive numbers. The user should enter a negative number to signal the end of the series. After all the positive numbers have been entered, the program should display their sum.

9. Ocean Levels
Assuming the ocean's level is currently rising at about 1.6 millimeters per year. Develop an algorithm and write a program that displays the number of millimeters that the ocean will have risen each year for the next 25 years.

10. Calculating the Factorial of a Number
In mathematics, the notation $n!$ represents the factorial of the nonnegative integer n. The factorial of n is the product of all the nonnegative integers from 1 to n. For example,

$$7! \times 1 \times 2 \times 3 \times 4 \times 5 \times 6 \times 7 = 5,040$$

and

$$4! = 1 \times 2 \times 3 \times 4 = 24$$

Write a program that lets the user enter a nonnegative integer, then uses a loop to calculate the factorial of that number. Display the factorial.

11. Population

Develop an algorithm and write a program that predicts the approximate size of a population of organisms. The application should use text boxes to allow the user to enter the starting number of organisms, the average daily population increase (as a percentage), and the number of days the organisms will be left to multiply. For example, assume the user enters the following values:

Starting number of organisms: 2
Average daily increase: 30%
Number of days to multiply: 10

The program should display the following table of data:

Day Approximate	Population
1	2
2	2.6
3	3.38
4	4.394
5	5.7122
6	7.42586
7	9.653619
8	12.5497
9	16.31462
10	21.209

12. Draw a Pattern #1

Write a program that uses nested loops to draw this pattern:

```
* * * * * * *
* * * * * *
* * * * *
* * * *
* * *
* *
*
```

13. Draw a Pattern #2

Write a program that uses nested loops to draw this pattern:

```
##
#  #
#    #
#      #
#        #
#          #
```

13 Using Lists

TOPICS

13.1 Sequences

KEY POINT A sequence is an object that holds multiple items of data, stored one after the other. You can perform operations on a sequence to examine and manipulate the items stored in it .

A **sequence** is an object that contains multiple items of data. The items that are in a sequence are stored one after the other. In most programming languages these are called **arrays**; in Python, they are called lists. Python provides various ways to perform operations on the items that are stored in a sequence.

There are several different types of sequence objects in Python. Two of the fundamental sequence data types are lists and **tuples**. Both lists and tuples are sequences that can hold various types of data. The difference between lists and tuples is simple: a list is **mutable**, which means that a program can change its contents, but a tuple is **immutable**, which means that once it is created, its contents cannot be changed. In this chapter, we will look at lists. We will explore some of the operations that you may perform on lists, including ways to access and manipulate their contents.

Checkpoint

13.1 What is a sequence?

13.2 What are two types of sequences in Python?

13.3 Explain the term *immutable*.

13.2 Introduction to Lists

Lists are dynamic data structures, meaning that items may be added to them or removed from them.

Recall that a **list** is an object that contains multiple data items. Each item that is stored in a list is called an **element**. Here is a statement that creates a list of integers:

```
even_numbers = [2, 4, 6, 8, 10]
```

The items that are enclosed in brackets and separated by commas are the list elements. After this statement executes, the variable even_numbers will reference the list, as shown in Figure 13-1.

Figure 13-1   A list of integers

The following is another example:

```
names = ['Molly', 'Steven', 'Will', 'Alicia', 'Adriana']
```

This statement creates a list of five strings. After the statement executes, the name variable will reference the list as shown in Figure 13-2.

Figure 13-2   A list of strings

A list can hold items of different types, as shown in the following example:

```
info = ['Alicia', 27, 1550.87]
```

This statement creates a list containing a string, an integer, and a floating-point number. After the statement executes, the info variable will reference the list as shown in Figure 13-3.

Figure 13-3   A list holding different types

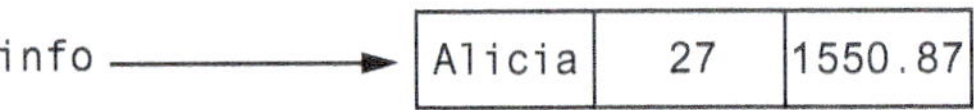

You can use the print function to display an entire list, as shown here:

```
numbers = [5, 10, 15, 20]
print(numbers)
```

In this example, the print function will display the elements of the list like this:

```
[5, 10, 15, 20]
```

Python also has a built-in list() function that can convert certain types of objects to lists. For example, recall that the range function returns an *iterable*, which is an object that holds a series of values that can be iterated over. You can use a statement such as the following to convert the range function's iterable object to a list:

```
numbers = list(range(5))
```

When this statement executes, the following things happen:

- The range function is called with 5 passed as an argument. The function returns an iterable containing the values 0, 1, 2, 3, 4.
- The iterable is passed as an argument to the list() function. The list() function returns the list [0, 1, 2, 3, 4].
- The list [0, 1, 2, 3, 4] is assigned to the numbers variable.

Here is another example:

```
numbers = list(range(1, 10, 2))
```

Recall that when you pass three arguments to the range function, the first argument is the starting value, the second argument is the ending limit, and the third argument is the step value. This statement will assign the list [1, 3, 5, 7, 9] to the numbers variable.

The Repetition Operator

You learned that the * symbol multiplies two numbers. However, when the operand on the left side of the * symbol is a sequence (such as a list) and the operand on the right side is an integer, it becomes the **repetition operator.** The repetition operator makes multiple copies of a list and joins them all together. Here is the general format:

```
list * n
```

In the general format, *list* is a list, and *n* is the number of copies to make. The following interactive session demonstrates:

```
1   >>> numbers = [0] * 5 Enter
2   >>> print(numbers) Enter
3   [0, 0, 0, 0, 0]
4   >>>
```

Let's take a closer look at each statement:

In line 1, the expression [0] * 5 makes five copies of the list [0] and joins them all together in a single list. The resulting list is assigned to the numbers variable.

In line 2, the numbers variable is passed to the print function. The function's output is shown in line 3.

Here is another interactive mode demonstration:

```
1   >>> numbers = [1, 2, 3] * 3 Enter
2   >>> print(numbers) Enter
3   [1, 2, 3, 1, 2, 3, 1, 2, 3]
4   >>>
```

> NOTE: Most programming languages allow you to create sequence structures known as *arrays*, which are similar to lists, but are much more limited in their capabilities. You cannot create traditional arrays in Python because lists serve the same purpose and provide many more built-in capabilities.

Iterating over a List with the `for` Loop

You can **traverse** a list in order to find and work with individual elements. The easiest way is to use the `for` loop. Here is the general format:

```
for variable in list:
    statement
    statement
    etc.
```

In the general format, *variable* is the name of a variable, and *list* is the name of a list. Each time the loop iterates, *variable* will reference a copy of an element in *list*, beginning with the first element. We say that the loop iterates, or traverses, over the elements in the list. Here is an example:

```
numbers = [1, 2, 3, 4]
for num in numbers:
    print(num)
```

The `numbers` variable references a list with four elements, so this loop will iterate four times. The first time the loop iterates, the `num` variable will reference the value 1; the second time the loop iterates, the `num` variable will reference the value 2, and so forth. This is illustrated in Figure 13-4. When the code executes, it will display the following:

```
1
2
3
4
```

Figure 13-4   Iterating over the list `[1, 2, 3, 4]`

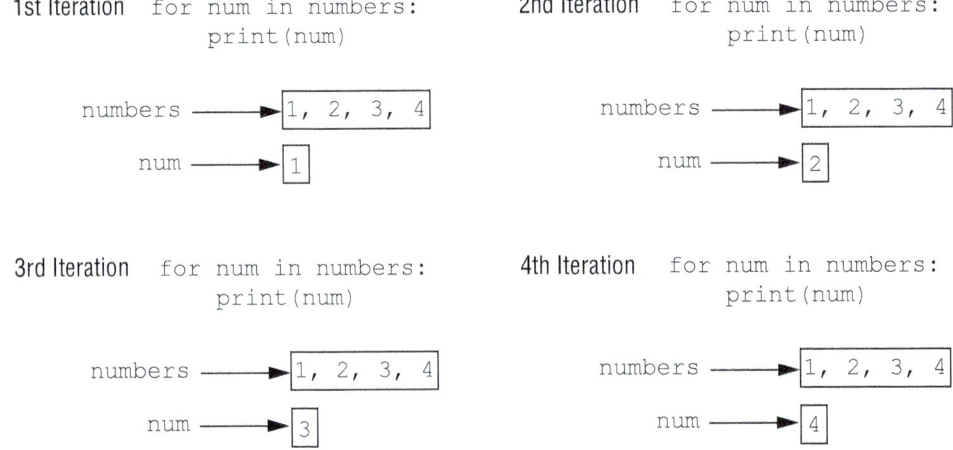

Figure 13-4 illustrates how the num variable references a copy of an element from the numbers list as the loop iterates. It is important to realize that we cannot use the num variable to change the contents of an element in the list. If we change the value that num references in the loop, it has no effect on the list. To demonstrate, look at the following code:

```
1   numbers = [1, 2, 3, 4]
2   for num in numbers:
3       num = 99
4   print(numbers)
```

The statement in line 3 merely reassigns the num variable to the value 99 each time the loop iterates. It has no effect on the list that is referenced by numbers. When this code executes, the statement in line 4 will print:

```
[1, 2, 3, 4]
```

Indexing

Another way that you can search for and access the individual elements in a list is with an **index**. Each element in a list has an index that specifies its position in the list. Indexing starts at 0, so the index of the first element is 0, the index of the second element is 1, and so forth. The index of the last element in a list is 1 less than the number of elements in the list.

For example, the following statement creates a list with 4 elements:

```
my_list = [10, 20, 30, 40]
```

The indexes of the elements in this list are 0, 1, 2, and 3. We can print the elements of the list with the following statement:

```
print(my_list[0], my_list[1], my_list[2], my_list[3])
```

The following loop also prints the elements of the list:

```
index = 0
while index < 4:
    print(my_list[index])
    index += 1
```

You can also use negative indexes with lists to identify element positions relative to the end of the list. The Python interpreter adds negative indexes to the length of the list to determine the element position. The index −1 identifies the last element in a list, −2 identifies the next to last element, and so forth. The following code shows an example:

```
my_list = [10, 20, 30, 40]
print(my_list[-1], my_list[-2], my_list[-3], my_list[-4])
```

In this example, the print function will display:

```
40    30    20    10
```

An IndexError exception will be raised if you use an invalid index with a list. For example, look at the following code:

```
# This code will cause an IndexError exception.
my_list = [10, 20, 30, 40]
```

```
index = 0
while index < 5:
    print(my_list[index])
    index += 1
```

The last time that this loop begins an iteration, the `index` variable will be assigned the value 4, which is an invalid index for the list. As a result, the statement that calls the `print` function will cause an `IndexError` exception to be raised.

The `len` Function

Python has a built-in function named `len` that returns the length of a sequence, such as a list. The following code demonstrates:

```
my_list = [10, 20, 30, 40]
size = len(my_list)
```

The first statement assigns the list [10, 20, 30, 40] to the `my_list` variable. The second statement calls the `len` function, passing the `my_list` variable as an argument.

The function returns the value 4, which is the number of elements in the list. This value is assigned to the `size` variable.

The `len` function can be used to prevent an `IndexError` exception when iterating over a list with a loop. Here is an example:

```
my_list = [10, 20, 30, 40]
index = 0
while index < len(my_list):
    print(my_list[index])
    index += 1
```

Using a `for` Loop to Iterate by Index Over a List

You can use the `len` function along with the `range` function to get the indexes for a list. For example, suppose we have the following list of strings:

```
names = ['Jenny', 'Kelly', 'Chloe', 'Aubrey']
```

The expression `range(len(names))` will give us the values 0, 1, 2, and 3. Because these values are the valid indexes for the list, we can use the expression in a `for` loop, as shown in the following code:

```
1  names = ['Jenny', 'Kelly', 'Chloe', 'Aubrey']
2  for index in range(len(names)):
3      print(names[index])
```

As the `for` loop iterates, the `index` variable will be assigned the values 0, 1, 2, and 3. The code will display the following:

```
Jenny
Kelly
Chloe
Aubrey
```

Lists Are Mutable

Lists in Python are mutable, which means their elements can be changed. Consequently, an expression in the form list[index] can appear on the left side of an assignment operator. The following code shows an example:

```
1   numbers = [1, 2, 3, 4, 5]
2   print(numbers)
3   numbers[0] = 99
4   print(numbers)
```

The statement in line 2 will display

```
[1, 2, 3, 4, 5]
```

The statement in line 3 assigns 99 to numbers[0]. This changes the first value in the list to 99. When the statement in line 4 executes, it will display

```
[99, 2, 3, 4, 5]
```

When you use an indexing expression to assign a value to a list element, you must use a valid index for an existing element or an IndexError exception will occur. For example, look at the following code:

```
numbers = [1, 2, 3, 4, 5]      # Create a list with 5 elements.
numbers[5] = 99                # This raises an exception!
```

The numbers list that is created in the first statement has five elements, with the indexes 0 through 4. The second statement will raise an IndexError exception because the numbers list has no element at index 5.

If you want to use indexing expressions to fill a list with values, you have to create the list first, as shown here:

```
1   # Create a list with 5 elements.
2   numbers = [0] * 5
3
4   # Fill the list with the value 99.
5   for index in range(len(numbers)):
6       numbers[index] = 99
```

The statement in line 2 creates a list with five elements, each element assigned the value 0. The loop in lines 5 through 6 then steps through the list elements, assigning 99 to each one.

Program 13-1 shows an example of how user input can be assigned to the elements of a list. This program gets sales amounts from the user and assigns them to a list.

Program 13-1   (sales_list.py)

```
1   # The NUM_DAYS constant holds the number of
2   # days that we will gather sales data for.
3   NUM_DAYS = 5
4
```

Program 13-1   *(continued)*

```
 5   def main():
 6       # Create a list to hold the sales for each day.
 7       sales = [0] * NUM_DAYS
 8
 9       print('Enter the sales for each day.')
10
11       # Get the sales for each day.
12       for index in range(len(sales)):
13           sales[index] = float(input(f'Day #{index + 1}: '))
14
15       # Display the values entered.
16       print('Here are the values you entered:')
17       for value in sales:
18           print(value)
19
20   # Call the main function.
21   if __name__ == '__main__':
22       main()
```

Program Output (with input shown in bold)
```
Enter the sales for each day.
Day #1: 1000 Enter
Day #2: 2000 Enter
Day #3: 3000 Enter
Day #4: 4000 Enter
Day #5: 5000 Enter
Here are the values you entered:
1000.0
2000.0
3000.0
4000.0
5000.0
```

The statement in line 3 creates the variable NUM_DAYS, which is used as a constant for the number of days. The statement in line 7 creates a list with five elements, with each element assigned the value 0.

The loop in lines 12 through 13 iterates 5 times. The first time it iterates, index references the value 0, so the statement in line 13 assigns the user's input to sales[0]. The second time the loop iterates, index references the value 1, so the statement in line 13 assigns the user's input to sales[1]. This continues until input values have been assigned to all the elements in the list.

Concatenating Lists

To **concatenate** means to join two things together. You can use the + operator to concatenate two lists. Here is an example:

```
list1 = [1, 2, 3, 4]
list2 = [5, 6, 7, 8]
list3 = list1 + list2
```

After this code executes, list1 and list2 remain unchanged, and list3 references the following list:

```
[1, 2, 3, 4, 5, 6, 7, 8]
```

The following interactive mode session also demonstrates list concatenation:

```
>>> girl_names = ['Joanne', 'Karen', 'Lori'] Enter
>>> boy_names = ['Chris', 'Jerry', 'Will'] Enter
>>> all_names = girl_names + boy_names Enter
>>> print(all_names) Enter
['Joanne', 'Karen', 'Lori', 'Chris', 'Jerry', 'Will']
```

You can also use the += augmented assignment operator to concatenate one list to another. Here is an example:

```
list1 = [1, 2, 3, 4]
list2 = [5, 6, 7, 8]
list1 += list2
```

The last statement appends list2 to list1. After this code executes, list2 remains unchanged, but list1 references the following list:

```
[1, 2, 3, 4, 5, 6, 7, 8]
```

The following interactive mode session also demonstrates the += operator used for list concatenation:

```
>>> girl_names = ['Joanne', 'Karen', 'Lori'] Enter
>>> girl_names += ['Jenny', 'Kelly'] Enter
>>> print(girl_names) Enter
['Joanne', 'Karen', 'Lori', 'Jenny', 'Kelly']
>>>
```

NOTE: You can concatenate lists only with other lists. If you try to concatenate a list with something that is not a list, an exception will be raised.

Checkpoint

13.4   What will the following code display?

```
numbers = [1, 2, 3, 4, 5]
numbers[2] = 99
print(numbers)
```

13.5   What will the following code display?

```
numbers = list(range(3))
print(numbers)
```

13.6   What will the following code display?

```
numbers = [10] * 5
print(numbers)
```

13.7   What will the following code display?

```
numbers = list(range(1, 10, 2))
for n in numbers:
    print(n)
```

13.8   What will the following code display?

```
numbers = [1, 2, 3, 4, 5]
print(numbers[-2])
```

13.9   How do you find the number of elements in a list?

13.10   What will the following code display?

```
numbers1 = [1, 2, 3]
numbers2 = [10, 20, 30]
numbers3 = numbers1 + numbers2
print(numbers1)
print(numbers2)
print(numbers3)
```

13.11   What will the following code display?

```
numbers1 = [1, 2, 3]
numbers2 = [10, 20, 30]
numbers2 += numbers1
print(numbers1)
print(numbers2)
```

13.3 List Slicing

A slicing expression selects a range of elements from a sequence.

VideoNote
List Slicing

You have seen how indexing allows you to select a specific element in a sequence. Sometimes you want to select more than one element from a sequence. In Python, you can write expressions that select subsections of a sequence, known as slices.

Recall that a slice is a span of items that are taken from a sequence. When you take a slice from a list, you get a span of elements from within the list. To get a slice of a list, you write an expression in the following general format:

```
list_name[start : end]
```

In the general format, *start* is the index of the first element in the slice, and *end* is the index marking the end of the slice. The expression returns a list containing a copy of the elements from *start* up to (but not including) *end*. For example, suppose we create the following list:

```
days = ['Sunday', 'Monday', 'Tuesday', 'Wednesday',
        'Thursday', 'Friday', 'Saturday']
```

The following statement uses a slicing expression to get the elements from indexes 2 up to, but not including, 5:

```
mid_days = days[2:5]
```

After this statement executes, the `mid_days` variable references the following list:

```
['Tuesday', 'Wednesday', 'Thursday']
```

You can quickly use the interactive mode interpreter to see how slicing works. For example, look at the following session. (We have added line numbers for easier reference.)

```
1   >>> numbers = [1, 2, 3, 4, 5] (Enter)
2   >>> print(numbers) (Enter)
3   [1, 2, 3, 4, 5]
4   >>> print(numbers[1:3]) (Enter)
5   [2, 3]
6   >>>
```

Here is a summary of each line:

- In line 1, we created the list [1, 2, 3, 4, 5] and assigned it to the `numbers` variable.
- In line 2, we passed `numbers` as an argument to the `print` function. The `print` function displayed the list in line 3.
- In line 4, we sent the slice `numbers[1:3]` as an argument to the `print` function. The `print` function displayed the slice in line 5.

If you leave out the *start* index in a slicing expression, Python uses 0 as the starting index. The following interactive mode session shows an example:

```
1   >>> numbers = [1, 2, 3, 4, 5] (Enter)
2   >>> print(numbers) (Enter)
3   [1, 2, 3, 4, 5]
4   >>> print(numbers[:3]) (Enter)
5   [1, 2, 3]
6   >>>
```

Notice line 4 sends the slice `numbers[:3]` as an argument to the `print` function. Because the starting index was omitted, the slice contains the elements from index 0 up to 3.

If you leave out the *end* index in a slicing expression, Python uses the length of the list as the *end* index. The following interactive mode session shows an example:

```
1   >>> numbers = [1, 2, 3, 4, 5] (Enter)
2   >>> print(numbers) (Enter)
3   [1, 2, 3, 4, 5]
4   >>> print(numbers[2:]) (Enter)
5   [3, 4, 5]
6   >>>
```

Notice line 4 sends the slice `numbers[2:]` as an argument to the `print` function. Because the ending index was omitted, the slice contains the elements from index 2 through the end of the list.

If you leave out both the *start* and *end* index in a slicing expression, you get a copy of the entire list. The following interactive mode session shows an example:

```
1  >>> numbers = [1, 2, 3, 4, 5] Enter
2  >>> print(numbers) Enter
3  [1, 2, 3, 4, 5]
4  >>> print(numbers[:]) Enter
5  [1, 2, 3, 4, 5] 6  >>>
```

The slicing examples we have seen so far get slices of consecutive elements from lists. Slicing expressions can also have step value, which can cause elements to be skipped in the list. The following interactive mode session shows an example of a slicing expression with a step value:

```
1  >>> numbers = [1, 2, 3, 4, 5, 6, 7, 8, 9, 10] Enter
2  >>> print(numbers) Enter
3  [1, 2, 3, 4, 5, 6, 7, 8, 9, 10]
4  >>> print(numbers[1:8:2]) Enter
5  [2, 4, 6, 8] 6  >>>
```

In the slicing expression in line 4, the third number inside the brackets is the step value. A step value of 2, as used in this example, causes the slice to contain every second element from the specified range in the list.

You can also use negative numbers as indexes in slicing expressions to reference positions relative to the end of the list. Python adds a negative index to the length of a list to get the position referenced by that index. The following interactive mode session shows an example:

```
1  >>> numbers = [1, 2, 3, 4, 5, 6, 7, 8, 9, 10] Enter
2  >>> print(numbers) Enter
3  [1, 2, 3, 4, 5, 6, 7, 8, 9, 10]
4  >>> print(numbers[-5:]) Enter
5  [6, 7, 8, 9, 10]
6  >>>
```

NOTE: Invalid indexes do not cause slicing expressions to raise an exception. For example:

- If the *end* index specifies a position beyond the end of the list, Python will use the length of the list instead.
- If the *start* index specifies a position before the beginning of the list, Python will use 0 instead.
- If the *start* index is greater than the *end* index, the slicing expression will return an empty list.

Checkpoint

13.12 What will the following code display?

```
numbers = [1, 2, 3, 4, 5]
my_list = numbers[1:3]
print(my_list)
```

13.13 What will the following code display?

```
numbers = [1, 2, 3, 4, 5]
my_list = numbers[1:]
print(my_list)
```

13.14 What will the following code display?

```
numbers = [1, 2, 3, 4, 5]
my_list = numbers[:1]
print(my_list)
```

13.15 What will the following code display?

```
numbers = [1, 2, 3, 4, 5]
my_list = numbers[:]
print(my_list)
```

13.16 What will the following code display?

```
numbers = [1, 2, 3, 4, 5]
my_list = numbers[-3:]
print(my_list)
```

13.4 Finding Items in Lists with the in Operator

KEY POINT You can search for an item in a list using the in operator.

In Python, you can use the `in` operator to determine whether an item is contained in a list. Here is the general format of an expression written with the `in` operator to search for an item in a list:

```
item in list
```

In the general format, *item* is the item for which you are searching, and *list* is a list. The expression returns true if *item* is found in the *list*, or false otherwise. Program 13-2 shows an example.

Program 13-2   (in_list.py)

```
1   # This program demonstrates the in operator
2   # used with a list.
3
4   def main():
```

Program 13-2 *(continued)*

```
 5        # Create a list of product numbers.
 6        prod_nums = ['V475', 'F987', 'Q143', 'R688']
 7
 8        # Get a product number to search for.
 9        search = input('Enter a product number: ')
10
11        # Determine whether the product number is in the list.
12        if search in prod_nums:
13            print(f'{search} was found in the list.')
14        else:
15            print(f'{search} was not found in the list.')
16
17   # Call the main function.
18   if __name__ == '__main__':
19       main()
```

Program Output (with input shown in bold)
```
Enter a product number: Q143 [Enter]
Q143 was found in the list.
```

Program Output (with input shown in bold)
```
Enter a product number: B000 [Enter]
B000 was not found in the list.
```

The program gets a product number from the user in line 9 and assigns it to the search variable. The if statement in line 12 determines whether search is in the prod_nums list.

You can use the not in operator to determine whether an item is *not* in a list. Here is an example:

```
if search not in prod_nums:
    print(f'{search} was not found in the list.')
else:
    print(f'{search} was found in the list.')
```

Checkpoint

13.17 What will the following code display?

```
names = ['Jim', 'Jill', 'John', 'Jasmine']
if 'Jasmine' not in names:
    print('Cannot find Jasmine.')
else:
    print("Jasmine's family:")
    print(names)
```

13.5 List Methods and Useful Built-in Functions

Lists have numerous methods that allow you to work with the elements that they contain. Python also provides some built-in functions that are useful for working with lists.

Lists have numerous methods that allow you to add elements, remove elements, change the ordering of elements, and so forth. We will look at a few of these methods, which are listed in Table 13-1. (For a description of all of the list methods, see the Python documentation at www.python.org.)

Table 13-1   A few of the list methods

Method	Description
`append(item)`	Adds *item* to the end of the list.
`index(item)`	Returns the index of the first element whose value is equal to *item*. A ValueError exception is raised if item is not found in the list.
`insert(index, item)`	Inserts *item* into the list at the specified *index*. When an *item* is inserted into a list, the list is expanded in size to accommodate the new item. The item that was previously at the specified index, and all the items after it, are shifted by one position toward the end of the list. No exceptions will occur if you specify an invalid index. If you specify an index beyond the end of the list, the item will be added to the end of the list. If you use a negative index that specifies an invalid position, the item will be inserted at the beginning of the list.
`sort()`	Sorts the items in the list so they appear in ascending order (from the lowest value to the highest value).
`remove(item)`	Removes the first occurrence of *item* from the list. A ValueError exception is raised if item is not found in the list.
`reverse()`	Reverses the order of the items in the list.

The append Method

The append method is commonly used to add items to a list. The item that is passed as an argument is appended to the end of the list's existing elements. Program 13-3 shows an example.

Program 13-3   (`list_append.py`)

```
1   # This program demonstrates how the append
2   # method can be used to add items to a list.
3
4   def main():
5       # First, create an empty list.
6       name_list = []
```

Program 13-3 *(continued)*

```
 7
 8          # Create a variable to control the loop.
 9          again = 'y'
10
11          # Add some names to the list.
12          while again == 'y':
13              # Get a name from the user.
14              name = input('Enter a name: ')
15
16              # Append the name to the list.
17              name_list.append(name)
18
19              # Add another one?
20              print('Do you want to add another name?')
21              again = input('y = yes, anything else = no: ')
22              print()
23
24          # Display the names that were entered.
25          print('Here are the names you entered.')
26
27          for name in name_list:
28              print(name)
29
30   # Call the main function.
31   if __name__ == '__main__':
32       main()
```

Program Output (with input shown in bold)
```
Enter a name: Kathryn [Enter]
Do you want to add another name?
y = yes, anything else = no: y [Enter]

Enter a name: Chris [Enter]
Do you want to add another name?
y = yes, anything else = no: y [Enter]

Enter a name: Kenny [Enter]
Do you want to add another name?
y = yes, anything else = no: y [Enter]

Enter a name: Renee [Enter]
Do you want to add another name?
y = yes, anything else = no: n [Enter]

Here are the names you entered.
Kathryn
Chris
Kenny
Renee
```

Notice the statement in line 6:

```
name_list = []
```

This statement creates an empty list (a list with no elements) and assigns it to the
`name_list` variable. Inside the loop, the append method is called to build the list. The first
time the method is called, the argument passed to it will become element 0. The second time the
method is called, the argument passed to it will become element 1. This continues until the user
exits the loop.

The `index` Method

Earlier, you saw how the `in` operator can be used to determine whether an item is in a list.
Sometimes you need to know not only whether an item is in a list, but where it is located. The
`index` method is useful in these cases. You pass an argument to the `index` method, and it returns
the index of the first element in the list containing that item. If the item is not found in the list, the
method raises a `ValueError` exception. Program 13-4 demonstrates the `index` method.

Program 13-4   **(`index_list.py`)**

```
 1   # This program demonstrates how to get the
 2   # index of an item in a list and then replace
 3   # that item with a new item.
 4
 5   def main():
 6       # Create a list with some items.
 7       food = ['Pizza', 'Burgers', 'Chips']
 8
 9       # Display the list.
10       print('Here are the items in the food list:')
11       print(food)
12
13       # Get the item to change.
14       item = input('Which item should I change? ')
15
16       try:
17           # Get the item's index in the list.
18           item_index = food.index(item)
19
20           # Get the value to replace it with.
21           new_item = input('Enter the new value: ')
22
23           # Replace the old item with the new item.
24           food[item_index] = new_item
25
26           # Display the list.
27           print('Here is the revised list:')
```

Program 13-4   *(continued)*

```
28              print(food)
29         except ValueError:
30              print('That item was not found in the list.')
31
32   # Call the main function.
33   if __name__ == '__main__':
34       main()
```

Program Output (with input shown in bold)
```
Here are the items in the food list:
['Pizza', 'Burgers', 'Chips']
Which item should I change? Burgers [Enter]
Enter the new value: Pickles [Enter]
Here is the revised list:
['Pizza', 'Pickles', 'Chips']
```

The elements of the food list are displayed in line 11, and in line 14, the user is asked which item they want to change. Line 18 calls the index method to get the index of the item. Line 21 gets the new value from the user, and line 24 assigns the new value to the element holding the old value.

The insert Method

The insert method allows you to insert an item into a list at a specific position. You pass two arguments to the insert method: an index specifying where the item should be inserted and the item that you want to insert. Program 13-5 shows an example.

Program 13-5   (insert_list.py)

```
1    # This program demonstrates the insert method.
2
3    def main():
4        # Create a list with some names.
5        names = ['James', 'Kathryn', 'Bill']
6
7        # Display the list.
8        print('The list before the insert:')
9        print(names)
10
11       # Insert a new name at element 0.
12       names.insert(0, 'Joe')
13
14       # Display the list again.
15       print('The list after the insert:')
```

Program 13-5   *(continued)*

```
16        print(names)
17
18  # Call the main function.
19  if __name__ == '__main__':
20        main()
```

Program Output
```
The list before the insert:
['James', 'Kathryn', 'Bill']
The list after the insert:
['Joe', 'James', 'Kathryn', 'Bill']
```

The sort Method

The sort method rearranges the elements of a list so they appear in ascending order (from the lowest value to the highest value). Here is an example:

```
my_list = [9, 1, 0, 2, 8, 6, 7, 4, 5, 3]
print('Original order:', my_list)
my_list.sort()
print('Sorted order:', my_list)
```

When this code runs, it will display the following:

```
Original order: [9, 1, 0, 2, 8, 6, 7, 4, 5, 3]
Sorted order: [0, 1, 2, 3, 4, 5, 6, 7, 8, 9]
```

Here is another example:

```
my_list = ['beta', 'alpha', 'delta', 'gamma']
print('Original order:', my_list)
my_list.sort()
print('Sorted order:', my_list)
```

When this code runs, it will display the following:

```
Original order: ['beta', 'alpha', 'delta', 'gamma']
Sorted order: ['alpha', 'beta', 'delta', 'gamma']
```

The remove Method

The remove method removes an item from the list. You pass an item to the method as an argument, and the first element containing that item is removed. This reduces the size of the list by one element. All of the elements after the removed element are shifted one position toward the beginning of the list. A ValueError exception is raised if the item is not found in the list. Program 13-6 demonstrates the method.

Program 13-6 `(remove_item.py)`

```
 1   # This program demonstrates how to use the remove
 2   # method to remove an item from a list.
 3
 4   def main():
 5       # Create a list with some items.
 6       food = ['Pizza', 'Burgers', 'Chips']
 7
 8       # Display the list.
 9       print('Here are the items in the food list:')
10       print(food)
11
12       # Get the item to change.
13       item = input('Which item should I remove? ')
14
15       try:
16           # Remove the item.
17           food.remove(item)
18
19           # Display the list.
20           print('Here is the revised list:')
21           print(food)
22
23       except ValueError:
24           print('That item was not found in the list.')
25
26   # Call the main function.
27   if __name__ == '__main__':
28       main()
```

Program Output (with input shown in bold)
```
Here are the items in the food list:
['Pizza', 'Burgers', 'Chips']
Which item should I remove? Burgers Enter
Here is the revised list:
['Pizza', 'Chips']
```

The reverse Method

The reverse method simply reverses the order of the items in the list. Here is an example:

```
my_list = [1, 2, 3, 4, 5]
print('Original order:', my_list)
my_list.reverse()
print('Reversed:', my_list)
```

This code will display the following:

```
Original order: [1, 2, 3, 4, 5]
Reversed: [5, 4, 3, 2, 1]
```

The del Statement

The remove method you saw earlier removes a specific item from a list, if that item is in the list. Some situations might require you remove an element from a specific index, regardless of the item that is stored at that index. This can be accomplished with the del statement. Here is an example of how to use the del statement:

```
my_list = [1, 2, 3, 4, 5]
print('Before deletion:', my_list)
del my_list[2]
print('After deletion:', my_list)
```

This code will display the following:

```
Before deletion: [1, 2, 3, 4, 5]
After deletion: [1, 2, 4, 5]
```

The min and max Functions

Python has two built-in functions named min and max that work with sequences. The min function accepts a sequence, such as a list, as an argument and returns the item that has the lowest value in the sequence. Here is an example:

```
my_list = [5, 4, 3, 2, 50, 40, 30]
print('The lowest value is', min(my_list))
```

This code will display the following:

```
The lowest value is 2
```

The max function accepts a sequence, such as a list, as an argument and returns the item that has the highest value in the sequence. Here is an example:

```
my_list = [5, 4, 3, 2, 50, 40, 30]
print('The highest value is', max(my_list))
```

This code will display the following:

```
The highest value is 50
```

 **Checkpoint**

13.18   What is the difference between calling a list's remove method and using the del statement to remove an element?

13.19   How do you find the lowest and highest values in a list?

13.20   Assume the following statement appears in a program:

```
names = []
```

Which of the following statements would you use to add the string 'Wendy' to the list at index 0? Why would you select this statement instead of the other?

a. `names[0] = 'Wendy'`
b. `names.append('Wendy')`

13.21   Describe the following list methods:

a. `index`
b. `insert`
c. `sort`
d. `reverse`

Chapter Review

Multiple Choice

1. This term refers to an individual item in a list.
   a. element
   b. bin
   c. cubbyhole
   d. slot

2. This is a number that identifies an item in a list.
   a. element
   b. index
   c. bookmark
   d. identifier

3. This is the first index in a list.
   a. –1
   b. 1
   c. 0
   d. The size of the list minus one

4. This is the last index in a list.
   a. 1
   b. 99
   c. 0
   d. The size of the list minus one

5. This will happen if you try to use an index that is out of range for a list.
   a. A `ValueError` exception will occur.
   b. An `IndexError` exception will occur.
   c. The list will be erased and the program will continue to run.
   d. Nothing—the invalid index will be ignored.

6. This function returns the length of a list.
   a. `length`
   b. `size`
   c. `len`
   d. `lengthof`

7. When the * operator's left operand is a list and its right operand is an integer, the operator becomes this.
   a. The multiplication operator
   b. The repetition operator
   c. The initialization operator
   d. Nothing—the operator does not support those types of operands.

8. This list method adds an item to the end of an existing list.
   a. add
   b. add_to
   c. increase
   d. append

9. This removes an item at a specific index in a list.
   a. the remove method
   b. the delete method
   c. the del statement
   d. the kill method

10. Assume the following statement appears in a program:

    ```
    mylist = []
    ```
    Which of the following statements would you use to add the string 'Labrador' to the list at index 0?
    a. mylist[0] = 'Labrador'
    b. mylist.insert(0, 'Labrador')
    c. mylist.append('Labrador')
    d. mylist.insert('Labrador', 0)

11. If you call the index method to locate an item in a list and the item is not found, this happens.
    a. A ValueError exception is raised.
    b. An InvalidIndex exception is raised.
    c. The method returns −1.
    d. Nothing happens. The program continues running at the next statement.

12. This built-in function returns the highest value in a list.
    a. highest
    b. max
    c. greatest
    d. best_of

True or False

1. Lists in Python are immutable.

2. Tuples in Python are immutable.

3. The del statement deletes an item at a specified index in a list.

4. Assume list1 references a list. After the following statement executes, list1 and list2 will reference two identical but separate lists in memory:

   ```
   list2 = list1
   ```

5. You can use the + operator to concatenate two lists.

6. A list can be an element in another list.

Short Answer

1. Look at the following statement:

```
numbers = [10, 20, 30, 40, 50]
```

a. How many elements does the list have?

b. What is the index of the first element in the list?

c. What is the index of the last element in the list?

2. Look at the following statement:

```
numbers = [1, 2, 3]
```

a. What value is stored in `numbers[2]`?

b. What value is stored in `numbers[0]`?

c. What value is stored in `numbers[-1]`?

3. What will the following code display?

```
values = [2, 4, 6, 8, 10]
print(values[1:3])
```

4. What does the following code display?

```
numbers = [1, 2, 3, 4, 5, 6, 7]
print(numbers[5:])
```

5. What does the following code display?

```
numbers = [1, 2, 3, 4, 5, 6, 7, 8]
print(numbers[-4:])
```

6. What does the following code display?

```
values = [2] * 5
print(values)
```

Algorithm Workbench

1. Write a statement that creates a list with the following strings: `'Einstein'`, `'Newton'`, `'Copernicus'`, and `'Kepler'`.

2. Assume `names` references a list. Write a `for` loop that displays each element of the list.

3. Draw a flowchart showing the general logic for totaling the values in a list.

4. Write a function that accepts a list as an argument (assume the list contains integers) and returns the total of the values in the list.

5. Assume the `names` variable references a list of strings. Write code that determines whether `'Ruby'` is in the `names` list. If it is, display the message `'Hello Ruby'`. Otherwise, display the message `'No Ruby'`.

6. What will the following code print?

```
list1 = [40, 50, 60]
list2 = [10, 20, 30]
list3 = list1 + list2
print(list3)
```

Programming Exercises

1. Total Sales

Design a program that asks the user to enter a store's sales for each day of the week. The amounts should be stored in a list. Use a loop to calculate the total sales for the week and display the result.

2. Rainfall Statistics

Design a program that lets the user enter the total rainfall for each of 12 months into a list. The program should calculate and display the total rainfall for the year, the average monthly rainfall, and the months with the highest and lowest amounts.

3. Number Analysis Program

Design a program that asks the user to enter a series of 20 numbers. The program should store the numbers in a list, then display the following data:

- The lowest number in the list
- The highest number in the list
- The total of the numbers in the list
- The average of the numbers in the list

4. Larger Than n

In a program, write a function that accepts two arguments: a list, and a number *n*. Assume that the list contains numbers. The function should display all of the numbers in the list that are greater than the number *n*.

5. Driver's License Exam

The local driver's license office has asked you to create an application that grades the written portion of the driver's license exam. The exam has 20 multiple-choice questions. Here are the correct answers:

1. A	6. B	11. A	16. C
2. C	7. C	12. D	17. B
3. A	8. A	13. C	18. B
4. A	9. C	14. A	19. D
5. D	10. B	15. D	20. A

Your program should store these correct answers in a list. The program should read the student's answers for each of the 20 questions from a text file and store the answers in another list. (Create your own text file to test the application.) After the student's answers have been read from the file, the program should display a message indicating whether the student passed or failed the exam. (A student must correctly answer 15 of the 20 questions to pass the exam.) It should then display the total number of correctly-answered questions, the total number of incorrectly-answered questions, and a list showing the question numbers of the incorrectly-answered questions.

14 Testing and Debugging Your Code

TOPICS

14.1 Types of Errors

Programming errors can be categorized into three types: syntax errors, runtime errors, and logic errors.

Syntax Errors

Errors that are detected by the interpreter are called **syntax errors** or **compile errors**. Syntax errors result from errors in code construction, such as mistyping a keyword, omitting some necessary punctuation, or using an uppercase or lowercase character in the wrong place. Python is a case-sensitive language. This means that it sees an uppercase character different than a lowercase character. For example, 'A' is not the same as 'a'. These errors are usually easy to detect because the information about the error displays in an error message when you try to run the program.

For example, try entering the following code. When you run it, a syntax error displays.

```
1   # Add two numbers and assign to total.
2   total = 3 + 4
3   print(Total)
```

In most cases, you will be able to use the line number reported in the error message to identify and fix the error. A closer examination of your code reveals that 'total' was referenced using an uppercase 'T'. It should be changed to lowercase 't' to match the spelling of the variable declared in line 2. Try making the change and running the program. It should execute correctly.

Since a single error will often display many lines of compile errors, it is a good practice to fix errors from the top line and work downward. Fixing errors that occur earlier in the program may also fix additional errors that occur later.

TIP: If you don't know how to correct an error, compare your program closely, character by character, with similar examples in the text. As you gain experience fixing syntax errors, you will soon be able to find and fix them quickly—or not make them at all!

Runtime Errors

Runtime errors are errors that cause a program to terminate abnormally. They occur while a program is running if the environment detects an operation that is impossible to carry out.

Input mistakes typically cause runtime errors. An **input error** occurs when the program is waiting for the user to enter a value, but the user enters a value that the program cannot handle. For example, if the program expects to read in a number, but instead the user enters a string, this causes a data type mismatch and a runtime error occurs.

Another example of a runtime error is division by zero. This happens when the divisor is zero for integer divisions. For instance, try entering and running the following program. It will result in a runtime error that causes the program to terminate abnormally.

```
1   # If the user inputs zero, a runtime error occurs.
2   total = 10
3   num = int(input("Enter a value: "))
4   total = total/num
5   print(total)
```

Logic Errors

Logic errors occur when a program does not perform the way it was intended to. Errors of this kind occur for many different reasons and can be harder to find than syntax and runtime errors. This is demonstrated in the following code, which is supposed to determine if a user is eligible to vote, based on being 18 years old. Can you find the logic error?

```
1   # An 18 year old is eligible to vote.
2   # This code causes a logic error printing "you cannot vote".

3   voting_age = 18
4   age = 18
5   if age > voting_age:
6       print("you can vote")
7   else:
8       print("you cannot vote")
```

This program will print "you cannot vote' when the age=18. This is wrong because we have stated that an 18 year old is eligible to vote. To get the correct result, you need to change line 5 operator from '>' to '>=' so that all ages greater than or equal to 18 will display a message "you can vote".

Finding Errors

In general, syntax errors are easy to find and easy to correct because the compiler gives error messages as to where the errors came from and why they are wrong. Runtime errors are not difficult to find, either, since the reasons and locations for the errors are displayed in a message on the console when the program aborts. Finding logic errors, on the other hand, can be very challenging. In the next section, you will learn the techniques of tracing programs and finding logic errors.

Checkpoint

14.1 What are syntax errors (compile errors), runtime errors, and logic errors?

14.2 Give examples of syntax errors, runtime errors, and logic errors.

14.3 If you forget to put a closing quotation mark on a string, what kind of error will be raised?

14.4 Suppose you write a program for computing the perimeter of a rectangle, and you mistakenly write your program so that it computes the area of a rectangle. What kind of error is this?

14.2 Hand Tracing a Program

Hand tracing is a simple debugging process for locating hard-to-find errors in a program.

Hand tracing is a debugging process where you imagine that you are the computer executing a program. (This process is also known as **desk checking**.) You step through each of the program's statements one by one. As you carefully look at a statement, you record the contents that each variable will have after the statement executes. This process is often helpful in finding mathematical mistakes and other logic errors. Once you find the problems, you can take steps to solve them.

To hand trace a program, you construct a chart that has a column for each variable and a row for each line in the program. For example, Figure 14-1 shows how we would construct a hand trace chart for the program that you saw in the previous section. The chart has a column for each of the four variables: test1, test2, test3, and average. The chart also has nine rows, one for each line in the program.

Figure 14.1   A program with a hand trace chart

```
1  Declare Real test1
2  Declare Real test2
3  Declare Real test3
4  Declare Real average
5
6  Set test1 = 88.0
7  Set test2 = 92.5
8  Set average = (test1 + test2 + test3) / 3
9  Display "Your average test score is ", average
```

	test1	test2	test3	average
1				
2				
3				
4				
5				
6				
7				
8				
9				

To hand trace this program, you step through each statement, observing the operation that is taking place, and then record the value that each variable will hold after the statement executes. When the process is complete, the chart will appear as shown in Figure 14-2. We have written question marks in the chart to indicate that a variable is uninitialized.

Figure 14-2   Program with the hand trace chart completed

```
1   Declare Real test1
2   Declare Real test2
3   Declare Real test3
4   Declare Real average
5
6   Set test1 = 88.0
7   Set test2 = 92.5
8   Set average = (test1 + test2 + test3) / 3
9   Display "Your average test score is ", average
```

	test1	test2	test3	average
1	?	?	?	?
2	?	?	?	?
3	?	?	?	?
4	?	?	?	?
5	?	?	?	?
6	88	?	?	?
7	88	92.5	?	?
8	88	92.5	?	undefined
9	88	92.5	?	undefined

When we get to line 8, we will carefully do the math. This means we look at the values of each variable in the expression. At that point, we discover that one of the variables, test3, is uninitialized. Because it is uninitialized, we have no way of knowing the value that it contains. Consequently, the result of the calculation will be undefined. After making this discovery, we can correct the problem by adding a line that assigns a value to test3.

Hand tracing is a simple process that focuses your attention on each statement in a program. Often, this helps you locate errors that are not obvious.

Checkpoint

14.5   What is hand tracing?

14.6   How many columns and rows do you have in a hand trace chart?

14.7   Explain the process of using a hand trace chart.

14.3 Handling Exceptions

An exception is an error that occurs while a program is running, causing the program to abruptly halt. You can use the `try`/`except` statement to gracefully handle exceptions.

An **exception** is an error that occurs while a program is running. In most cases, an exception causes a program to abruptly halt. For example, look at Program 14-1. This program gets two numbers from the user, then divides the first number by the second number. In the sample running of the program, however, a ZeroDivisionError exception occurred because the user entered 0 as the second number. Division by zero causes an exception because it is mathematically impossible.

Program 14-1   **(division.py)**

```
 1   # This program divides a number by another number.
 2
 3   def main():
 4       # Get two numbers.
 5       num1 = int(input('Enter a number: '))
 6       num2 = int(input('Enter another number: '))
 7
 8       # Divide num1 by num2 and display the result.
 9       result = num1 / num2
10       print(f'{num1} divided by {num2} is {result}')
11
12   # Call the main function.
13   if _ _name_ _ == '_ _main_ _':
14       main()
```

Program Output (with input shown in bold)
```
Enter a number: 10 [Enter]
Enter another number: 0 [Enter]
Traceback (most recent call last):
  File "C:\Python\division.py," line 13, in <module>
      main()
  File "C:\Python\division.py," line 9, in main
      result = num1 / num2
ZeroDivisionError: integer division or modulo by zero
```

The error message that is shown in the sample run is called a **traceback**. It gives information regarding the line number(s) that caused the exception. The last line of the error message shows the name of the exception (`ZeroDivisionError`) and a brief description of the error that caused the exception (`integer division or modulo by zero`). You use the information to solve the problem by fixing the code.

You can prevent many exceptions from being raised by carefully coding your program. For example, Program 14-2 shows how division by 0 can be prevented with a simple `if` statement. Rather than allowing the exception to be raised, the program tests the value of `num2`, and displays an error message if the value is 0. This is an example of gracefully avoiding an exception.

Program 14-2   (`division2.py`)

```python
 1  # This program divides a number by another number.
 2
 3  def main():
 4      # Get two numbers.
 5      num1 = int(input('Enter a number: '))
 6      num2 = int(input('Enter another number: '))
 7
 8      # If num2 is not 0, divide num1 by num2
 9      # and display the result.
10      if num2 != 0:
11          result = num1 / num2
12          print(f'{num1} divided by {num2} is {result}')
13      else:
14          print('Cannot divide by zero.')
15
16  # Call the main function.
17  if __name__ == '__main__':
18      main()
```

Program Output (with input shown in bold)
```
Enter a number: 10 [Enter]
Enter another number: 0 [Enter]
Cannot divide by zero.
```

Some exceptions cannot be avoided regardless of how carefully you write your program. For example, look at Program 14-3. This program calculates gross pay. It prompts the user to enter the number of hours worked and the hourly pay rate. It gets the user's gross pay by multiplying these two numbers and displays that value on the screen.

Program 14-3   (`gross_pay1.py`)

```python
 1  # This program calculates gross pay.
 2
 3  def main():
 4      # Get the number of hours worked.
 5      hours = int(input('How many hours did you work? '))
 6
 7      # Get the hourly pay rate.
 8      pay_rate = float(input('Enter your hourly pay rate: '))
 9
10      # Calculate the gross pay.
11      gross_pay = hours * pay_rate
12
13      # Display the gross pay.
```

Program 14-3 *(continued)*

```
14       print(f'Gross pay: ${gross_pay:,.2f}')
15
16   # Call the main function.
17   if _ _name_ _ == '_ _main_ _':
18       main()
```

Program Output (with input shown in bold)
```
How many hours did you work? forty Enter
Traceback (most recent call last):
  File "C:\Users\Tony\Documents\Python\Source
Code\Chapter 06\gross_pay1.py", line 17, in <module>
    main()
  File "C:\Users\Tony\Documents\Python\Source
Code\Chapter 06\gross_pay1.py", line 5, in main
    hours = int(input('How many hours did you work? '))
ValueError: invalid literal for int() with base 10: 'forty'
```

Look at the Program Output. An exception occurred because the user entered the string `'forty'` instead of the number 40 when prompted for the number of hours worked. Because the string `'forty'` cannot be converted to an integer, the `int()` function raised an exception in line 5, and the program halted. Look carefully at the last line of the traceback message, and you will see that the name of the exception is `ValueError`, and its description is: `invalid literal for int() with base 10: 'forty'`.

Python, like most modern programming languages, allows you to write code that responds to exceptions when they are raised and prevents the program from abruptly crashing. Such code is called an **exception handler** and is written with the `try/except` statement. There are several ways to write a `try/except` statement, but the following general format shows the simplest variation:

```
try:
   statement
   statement
   etc.
except  ExceptionName:
   statement
   statement
   etc.
```

First, the keyword `try` appears, followed by a colon. Next, a code block appears, which we will refer to as the **try suite.** The try suite is one or more statements that can potentially raise an exception.

After the try suite, an *except clause* appears. The except clause begins with the keyword `except`, optionally followed by the name of an exception and ending with a colon. Beginning on the next line is a block of statements that we will refer to as a **handler.**

When the `try/except` statement executes, the statements in the try suite begin to execute. The following describes what happens next:

- If a statement in the try suite raises an exception that is specified by the *ExceptionName* in an `except` clause, then the handler that immediately follows the `except` clause executes. Then, the program resumes execution with the statement immediately following the `try/except` statement.

- If a statement in the try suite raises an exception that is *not* specified by the `ExceptionName` in an `except` clause, then the program will halt with a traceback error message.

- If the statements in the try suite execute without raising an exception, then any `except` clauses and handlers in the statement are skipped, and the program resumes execution with the statement immediately following the `try/except` statement.

Program 14-4 shows how we can write a `try/except` statement to gracefully respond to a `ValueError` exception.

Program 14-4   **(gross_pay2.py)**

```
 1  # This program calculates gross pay.
 2
 3  def main():
 4      try:
 5          # Get the number of hours worked.
 6          hours = int(input('How many hours did you work? '))
 7
 8          # Get the hourly pay rate.
 9          pay_rate = float(input('Enter your hourly pay rate: '))
10
11          # Calculate the gross pay.
12          gross_pay = hours * pay_rate
13
14          # Display the gross pay.
15          print(f'Gross pay: ${gross_pay:,.2f}')
16      except ValueError:
17          print('ERROR: Hours worked and hourly pay rate must')
18          print('be valid numbers.')
19
20  # Call the main function.
21  if __name__ == '__main__':
22      main()
```

Program Output (with input shown in bold)
```
How many hours did you work? forty [Enter]
ERROR: Hours worked and hourly pay rate must
be valid numbers.
```

Let's look at what happened in the sample run. The statement in line 6 prompts the user to enter the number of hours worked, and the user enters the string `'forty'`. Because the string `'forty'` cannot be converted to an integer, the `int()` function raises a `ValueError` exception. As a result, the program jumps immediately out of the try suite to the `except ValueError` clause in line 16 and begins executing the handler block that begins in line 17. This is illustrated in Figure 14-3.

Figure 14-3   Handling an exception

```
                    # This program calculates gross pay.

                    def main():
                        try:
                            # Get the number of hours worked.
                            hours = int(input('How many hours did you work? '))

                            # Get the hourly pay rate.
                            pay_rate = float(input('Enter your hourly pay rate: '))

                            # Calculate the gross pay.
                            gross_pay = hours * pay_rate

                            # Display the gross pay.
                            print(f'Gross pay: ${gross_pay:,.2f}')
                        except ValueError:
                            print('ERROR: Hours worked and hourly pay rate must')
                            print('be valid integers.')

                    # Call the main function.
                    if __name__ == '__main__':
                        main()
```


Let's look at another example in Program 14-5. This program, which does not use exception handling, gets the name of a file from the user, then displays the contents of the file. The program works as long as the user enters the name of an existing file. An exception will be raised, however, if the file specified by the user does not exist. This is what happened in the sample run.

Program 14-5   (display_file.py)

```
 1  # This program displays the contents
 2  # of a file.
 3
 4  def main():
 5      # Get the name of a file.
 6      filename = input('Enter a filename: ')
 7
 8      # Open the file.
 9      infile = open(filename, 'r')
10
11      # Read the file's contents.
12      contents = infile.read()
13
14      # Display the file's contents.
```

Program 14-5   *(continued)*

```
15        print(contents)
16
17        # Close the file.
18        infile.close()
19
20   # Call the main function.
21   if _ _name_ _ == '_ _main_ _':
22        main()
```

Program Output (with input shown in bold)
```
Enter a filename: bad_file.txt Enter
Traceback (most recent call last):
File "C:\Python\display_file.py," line 21, in <module>
main()
File "C:\Python\display_file.py," line 9, in main
infile = open(filename, 'r')
IOError: [Errno 2] No such file or directory: 'bad_file.txt'
```

The statement in line 9 raised the exception when it called the open function. Notice in the traceback error message that the name of the exception that occurred is IOError. This is an exception that is raised when a file I/O operation fails. You can see in the traceback message that the cause of the error was No such file or directory: 'bad_file.txt'.

Program 14-6 shows how we can modify Program 14-5 with a try/except statement that gracefully responds to an IOError exception. In the sample run, assume the file bad_file.txt does not exist.

Program 14-6   (display_file2.py)

```
 1   # This program displays the contents
 2   # of a file.
 3
 4   def main():
 5       # Get the name of a file.
 6       filename = input('Enter a filename: ')
 7
 8       try:
 9           # Open the file.
10           infile = open(filename, 'r')
11
12           # Read the file's contents.
13           contents = infile.read()
14
15           # Display the file's contents.
16           print(contents)
```

Program 14-6   *(continued)*

```
17
18          # Close the file.
19          infile.close()
20      except IOError:
21          print('An error occurred trying to read')
22          print('the file', filename)
23
24  # Call the main function.
25  if _ _name_ _ == '_ _main_ _':
26      main()
```

Program Output (with input shown in bold)
```
Enter a filename: bad_file.txt Enter
An error occurred trying to read
the file bad_file.txt
```

Let's look at what happened in the sample run. When line 6 executed, the user entered bad_file.txt, which was assigned to the filename variable. Inside the try suite, line 10 attempts to open the file bad_file.txt. Because this file does not exist, the statement raises an IOError exception. When this happens, the program exits the try suite, skipping lines 11 through 19. Because the except clause in line 20 specifies the IOError exception, the program jumps to the handler that begins in line 21.

Handling Multiple Exceptions

In many cases, the code in a try suite will be capable of throwing more than one type of exception. In such a case, you need to write an except clause for each type of exception that you want to handle. For example, Program 14-7 reads the contents of a file named sales_data.txt. Each line in the file contains the sales amount for one month, and the file has several lines. Here are the contents of the file:

```
24987.62
26978.97
32589.45
31978.47
22781.76
29871.44
```

Program 14-7 reads all of the numbers from the file and adds them to an accumulator variable.

Program 14-7   (sales_report1.py)

```
1  # This program displays the total of the
2  # amounts in the sales_data.txt file.
3
4  def main():
5      # Initialize an accumulator.
6      total = 0.0
```

Program 14-7 (continued)

```
 7
 8      try:
 9          # Open the sales_data.txt file.
10          infile = open('sales_data.txt', 'r')
11
12          # Read the values from the file and
13          # accumulate them.
14          for line in infile:
15              amount = float(line)
16              total += amount
17
18          # Close the file.
19          infile.close()
20
21          # Print the total.
22          print(f'{total:,.2f}')
23
24      except IOError:
25          print('An error occured trying to read the file.')
26
27      except ValueError:
28          print('Non-numeric data found in the file.')
29
30      except:
31          print('An error occured.')
32
33  # Call the main function.
34  if _ _name_ _ == '_ _main_ _':
35      main()
```

The try suite contains code that can raise different types of exceptions. For example:

- The statement in line 10 can raise an IOError exception if the sales_data.txt file does not exist. The for loop in line 14 can also raise an IOError exception if it encounters a problem reading data from the file.
- The float function in line 15 can raise a ValueError exception if the line variable references a string that cannot be converted to a floating-point number (an alphabetic string, for example).

Notice the try/except statement has three except clauses:

- The except clause in line 24 specifies the IOError exception. Its handler in line 25 will execute if an IOError exception is raised.
- The except clause in line 27 specifies the ValueError exception. Its handler in line 28 will execute if a ValueError exception is raised.
- The except clause in line 30 does not list a specific exception. Its handler in line 31 will execute if an exception that is not handled by the other except clauses is raised.

If an exception occurs in the try suite, the Python interpreter examines each of the `except` clauses, in the `try/except` statement from top to bottom. When it finds an `except` clause that specifies a type that matches the type of exception that occurred, it branches to that `except` clause. If none of the `except` clauses specifies a type that matches the exception, the interpreter branches to the except clause in line 30.

Using One except Clause to Catch All Exceptions

The previous example demonstrated how multiple types of exceptions can be handled individually in a `try/except` statement. Sometimes you might want to write a `try/except` statement that simply catches any exception that is raised in the try suite and, regardless of the exception's type, responds the same way. You can accomplish that in a `try/except` statement by writing one except clause that does not specify a particular type of exception. Program 14-8 shows an example.

Program 14-8   (`sales_report2.py`)

```
 1  # This program displays the total of the
 2  # amounts in the sales_data.txt file.
 3
 4  def main():
 5      # Initialize an accumulator.
 6      total = 0.0
 7
 8      try:
 9          # Open the sales_data.txt file.
10          infile = open('sales_data.txt', 'r')
11
12          # Read the values from the file and
13          # accumulate them.
14          for line in infile:
15              amount = float(line)
16              total += amount
17
18          # Close the file.
19          infile.close()
20
21          # Print the total.
22          print(f'{total:,.2f}')
23      except:
24          print('An error occurred.')
25
26  # Call the main function.
27  if _ _name_ _ == '_ _main_ _':
28      main()
```

Notice the try/except statement in this program has only one except clause, in line 23. The except clause does not specify an exception type, so any exception that occurs in the try suite (lines 9 through 22) causes the program to branch to line 23 and execute the statement in line 24.

Displaying an Exception's Default Error Message

When an exception is thrown, an object known as an **exception object** is created in memory. The exception object usually contains a default error message pertaining to the exception. (In fact, it is the same error message that you see displayed at the end of a traceback when an exception goes unhandled.) When you write an except clause, you can optionally assign the exception object to a variable, as shown here:

```
except ValueError as err:
```

This except clause catches ValueError exceptions. The expression that appears after the except clause specifies that we are assigning the exception object to the variable err. (There is nothing special about the name err. That is simply the name that we have chosen for the examples. You can use any name that you wish.) After doing this, you can pass the err variable to the print function in the exception handler to display the default error message that Python provides for that type of error. Program 14-9 shows an example of how this is done.

Program 14-9   (gross_pay3.py)

```
 1  # This program calculates gross pay.
 2
 3  def main():
 4      try:
 5          # Get the number of hours worked.
 6          hours = int(input('How many hours did you work? '))
 7
 8          # Get the hourly pay rate.
 9          pay_rate = float(input('Enter your hourly pay rate: '))
10
11          # Calculate the gross pay.
12          gross_pay = hours * pay_rate
13
14          # Display the gross pay.
15          print(f'Gross pay: ${gross_pay:,.2f}')
16      except ValueError as err:
17          print(err)
18
19  # Call the main function.
20  if _ _name_ _ == '_ _main_ _':
21      main()
```

Program Output (with input shown in bold)
```
How many hours did you work? forty Enter
invalid literal for int() with base 10: 'forty'
```

When a `ValueError` exception occurs inside the try suite (lines 5 through 15), the program branches to the `except` clause in line 16. The expression `ValueError as err` in line 16 causes the resulting exception object to be assigned to a variable named `err`. The statement in line 17 passes the `err` variable to the `print` function, which causes the exception's default error message to be displayed.

If you want to have just one `except` clause to catch all the exceptions that are raised in a try suite, you can specify `Exception` as the type. Program 14-10 shows an example.

Program 14-10   (sales_report3.py)

```python
 1   # This program displays the total of the
 2   # amounts in the sales_data.txt file.
 3
 4   def main():
 5       # Initialize an accumulator.
 6       total = 0.0
 7
 8       try:
 9           # Open the sales_data.txt file.
10           infile = open('sales_data.txt', 'r')
11
12           # Read the values from the file and
13           # accumulate them.
14           for line in infile:
15               amount = float(line)
16               total += amount
17
18           # Close the file.
19           infile.close()
20
21           # Print the total.
22           print(f'{total:,.2f}')
23       except Exception as err:
24           print(err)
25
26   # Call the main function.
27   if _ _name_ _ == '_ _main_ _':
28       main()
```

The `else` Clause

The `try`/`except` statement may have an optional `else` clause, which appears after all the `except` clauses. Here is the general format of a `try`/`except` statement with an `else` clause:

```
try:
    statement
    statement
    etc.
except ExceptionName:
    statement
    statement
    etc.
else:
    statement
    statement
    etc.
```

The block of statements that appears after the `else` clause is known as the **else suite**. The statements in the else suite are executed after the statements in the try suite, only if no exceptions were raised. If an exception is raised, the else suite is skipped. Program 14-11 shows an example.

Program 14-11   (`sales_report4.py`)

```
 1  # This program displays the total of the
 2  # amounts in the sales_data.txt file.
 3
 4  def main():
 5      # Initialize an accumulator.
 6      total = 0.0
 7
 8      try:
 9          # Open the sales_data.txt file.
10          infile = open('sales_data.txt', 'r')
11
12          # Read the values from the file and
13          # accumulate them.
14          for line in infile:
15              amount = float(line)
16              total += amount
17
18          # Close the file.
19          infile.close()
20      except Exception as err:
21          print(err)
22      else:
23          # Print the total.
```

<table>
<tr><td>Program 14-11</td><td>(continued)</td></tr>
</table>

```
24              print(f'{total:,.2f}')
25
26  # Call the main function.
27  if _ _name_ _ == '_ _main_ _':
28      main()
```

In Program 14-11, the statement in line 24 is executed only if the statements in the try suite (lines 9 through 19) execute without raising an exception.

The `finally` Clause

The `try`/`except` statement may have an optional `finally` clause, which must appear after all the except clauses. Here is the general format of a `try`/`except` statement with a `finally` clause:

```
try:
    statement
    statement
    etc.
except ExceptionName:
    statement
    statement
    etc.
finally:
    statement
    statement
    etc.
```

The block of statements that appears after the `finally` clause is known as the **finally suite**. The statements in the finally suite are always executed after the try suite and any exception handlers have executed. The statements in the finally suite execute whether an exception occurs or not. The purpose of the finally suite is to perform cleanup operations, such as closing files or other resources. Any code that is written in the finally suite will always execute, even if the try suite raises an exception.

What If an Exception Is Not Handled?

Unless an exception is handled, it will cause the program to halt. There are two possible ways for a thrown exception to go unhandled. The first possibility is for the `try`/`except` statement to contain no `except` clauses specifying an exception of the right type. The second possibility is for the exception to be raised from outside a try suite. In either case, the exception will cause the program to halt.

In this section, you've seen examples of programs that can raise `ZeroDivisionError` exceptions, `IOError` exceptions, and `ValueError` exceptions. There are many different types of exceptions that can occur in a Python program. When you are designing `try`/`except` statements, one way you can learn about the exceptions that you need to handle is to consult **reference materials**, such as the Python documentation.

Reference materials, Python documentation (or documentation for whatever language you are using), and error messages, are all effective strategies you can use to identify and solve problems with your code.

Another effective strategy is experimentation. You can run a program and deliberately perform actions that will cause errors. By watching the traceback error messages that are displayed, you will see the names of the exceptions that are raised. You can then write `except` clauses to handle these exceptions.

 **Checkpoint**

14.8   Briefly describe what an exception is.

14.9   If an exception is raised and the program does not handle it with a try/except statement, what happens?

14.10 What type of exception does a program raise when it tries to open a nonexistent file?

14.11 What type of exception does a program raise when it uses the float function to convert a non-numeric string to a number?

 14.4 Avoiding Common Errors

 **Avoiding common errors is the best way to develop clean code that executes properly.**

Writing code to handle exceptions will help prevent your application from crashing. Additionally, you can implement standard coding practices that will reduce the number of runtime and logic errors. The three most effective practices for avoiding errors are:

- Being mindful of spelling.
- Using proper white spacing.
- Indenting your code in the right places.

While comments do not prevent errors, they help you find them. If you develop the habit of commenting your code now, it will be very helpful later as your project size grows. Likewise, using descriptive identifiers does not prevent errors, but may make it easier to avoid them or find them when they do occur.

In the rest of this section, we will look at some ways you can avoid common errors.

Pay Attention to Indentation

Indenting in the right places is very important in Python. In other languages, indenting code is simply a way to make your code easier to read. In Python, it has a specific purpose. All lines of code with the same indentation are executed as a single block of code. Improper indentation can cause both syntax and logic errors. Can you figure out why the following code generates a syntax error?

```
1 # While count is less than 20.
2 # Print count.
3 # Print a final message when finished.
4 count = 0
5 while (count < 20):
6 print(count)
7   count = count + 3
8 print("finished")
```

If you enter and run the code, you will get an error message that there is an unexpected indent on line 6.

The following code generates a logic error. The message 'finished" is printed seven times rather than once. Can you figure out why?

```
1 # Loop while count is less than 20.
2 # Print count.
3 # Print a final message when finished.
4 count = 0
5 while (count < 20):
6   print(count)
7   count = count + 3
8   print("finished")
```

Output:
```
0
finished
3
finished
6
finished
9
finished
12
finished
15
finished
18
finished
```

Don't Forget the Colon ':'

Forgetting to end conditional and looping statements with the colon symbol is a common mistake. The following code generates a syntax error because the colon is missing at the end of line 2.

```
1 count = 0
2 while (count < 20)
3   print(count)
4   count = count + 3
5 print("finished")
```

Don't Forget to Place Begin and End Quotes Around a String

When you are troubleshooting errors, look for missing begin and end quotes around strings. The following code generates a syntax error because the end quote around the output string is missing from line 3.

```
1 count = 0
2 while (count < 20):
3   print("Your count value is:, count)
4   count = count + 3
5 print("finished")
```

Use the Correct Character Case

Recall that Python is a case-sensitive language. Using the wrong character case creates a syntax error. Each programming language has its own set of rules about case sensitivity. It's a common mistake that even the best of software developers who program in multiple languages make. It's a bothersome mistake, but easy to fix!

In Python, keywords are all lowercase. The following code generates an error because the keyword import is capitalized in line 1.

```
Line1:    Import turtle
Line2:    turtle.forward(100)
Line3:    turtle.right(90)
```

Watch for Lexical Errors

Lexical errors are simply misspellings and invalid characters that the interpreter does not recognize. The following code generates an error because an incorrect character was typed on line 2.

```
Line1:    Import turtle
Line2:    turtle,forward(100)
Line3:    turtle.right(90)
```

 **Checkpoint**

14.12 Correct each of the above code samples. Type in each code segment and run the code to test the results.

14.13 What is wrong with the following line of code?
```
Turtle.forward(45)
```

14.14 What is wrong with the following line of code?
```
turtle.forward(10%)
```

14.15 Does adding comments to your code prevent errors? Explain your answer.

Chapter Review

Multiple Choice

1. What type of error occurs when you use the incorrect character?
    a. logic
    b. lexical
    c. exception
    d. variable

2. What type of error occurs when a program does not perform the way it was intended to?
    a. logic
    b. lexical
    c. exception
    d. input

3. What type of error occurs if the computer expects user input to be a number but the user enters a string?
    a. logic
    b. lexical
    c. runtime
    d. exception

4. A debugging process in which you imagine that you are the computer executing a program is called ___________.
    a. imaginative computing
    b. role playing
    c. mental simulation
    d. hand tracing

5. Another term for hand tracing is ___________.
    a. desk checking
    b. code tracing
    c. bug checking
    d. elbow tracing

6. A hand trace chart should have one column for each ___________ in the program.
    a. line
    b. variable
    c. comment
    d. string

7. In most cases, an exception causes a program to ___________.
   a. run faster
   b. display the incorrect output
   c. abruptly halt
   d. request user input

8. What is a term for one or more statements that can potentially raise an exception?
   a. run handler
   b. except clause
   c. try suite
   d. else suite

9. What is created in memory when an exception is thrown?
   a. exception handler
   b. logic error
   c. exception statement
   d. exception object

10. The block of statements that appears after the finally clause in a try/except statement is called:
   a. try suite
   b. else suite
   c. finally suite
   d. except suite

True or False

1. Logic errors are easier to find than syntax errors.

2. Hand tracing is the process of translating a pseudocode program into machine language by hand.

3. Indentation does not matter in Python.

4. You must have a colon to end conditional and looping statements in Python.

5. In Python, you only need quotes to identify the beginning of a string.

6. Python is case-sensitive.

Short Answer

1. What happens when a computer encounters a runtime error while trying to execute a program?

2. Explain why syntax errors are usually easier to find than logic errors.

3. What is a traceback?

4. Explain how to use one except clause to catch all exceptions.

5. What are two ways a thrown exception might not be handled?

Debugging Exercises

1. If the following pseudocode were an actual program, why would it not display the output that the programmer expects?

```
Declare String favoriteFood
Display "What is the name of your favorite food?"
Input favoriteFood
Display "Your favorite food is "
Display "favoriteFood"
```

2. If the programmer translates the following pseudocode to an actual programming language, a syntax error is likely to occur. Can you find the error?

```
Declare String 1stPrize
Display "Enter the award for first prize."
Input 1stPrize
Display "The first prize winner will receive ", 1stPrize
```

3. The following code will not display the results expected by the programmer. Can you find the error?

```
Declare Real lowest, highest, average
Display "Enter the lowest score."
Input lowest
Display "Enter the highest score."
Input highest
Set average = low + high / 2
Display "The average is ", average, "."
```

4. Find the error in the following pseudocode.

```
Display "Enter the length of the room."
Input length
Declare Integer length
```

5. Find the error in the following pseudocode.

```
Declare Integer value1, value2, value3, sum
Set sum = value1 + value2 + value3
Display "Enter the first value."
Input value1
Display "Enter the second value."
Input value2
Display "Enter the third value."
Input value3
Display "The sum of numbers is ", sum
```

6. Find the error in the following pseudocode.

```
Declare Real pi
Set 3.14159265 = pi
Display "The value of pi is ", pi
```

7. Find the error in the following pseudocode.

```
Constant Real GRAVITY = 9.81
Display "Rates of acceleration of an object in free fall:"
Display "Earth: ", GRAVITY, " meters per second every second."
Set GRAVITY = 1.63
Display "Moon: ", GRAVITY, " meters per second every second."
```

Programming Exercises

1. Wear a Sweater

Working alone or with a partner, brainstorm, design a sequential algorithm, and write a program that tells users to wear a sweater if the temperature is 50 degrees Fahrenheit or below. Write a version of the code using proper programming style so there are no errors, and write a version that has at least one error. Exchange the version of the code that includes errors with a classmate or other team. Analyze the other team's code. Use error messages and other effective strategies including reference materials and Python language documentation to identify and solve the problems in the code. Debug the code. Exchange code back, and compare your original error-free code with the code the other team debugged. Discuss how they are the same, and how they are different.

2. Bedtime

Working alone or with a partner, brainstorm, design, and write a program that tells users to go to sleep if it is 10 p.m. or later. Write a version of the code using proper programming style so there are no errors, and write a version that has at least error. Exchange the version of the code that includes errors with a classmate or other team. Analyze the other team's code. Use error messages and other effective strategies including reference materials and Python language documentation to identify and solve the problems in the code. Debug the code. Exchange code back, and compare your original error-free code with the code the other team debugged. Discuss how they are the same, and how they are different.

3. Handling Errors

Working alone or with a partner, brainstorm, design, and write a program that uses error handling techniques that you learned in this chapter to prevent common errors such as division by zero or data type mismatch. Exchange your code with a classmate or other team. Analyze the code. If necessary, use reference materials and Python language documentation to find information on any techniques you do not recognize. Write a paragraph explaining how the other team used error handling techniques to produce error-free code.

15 Functions

TOPICS

15.1 Introduction to Functions

A function is a group of statements that exist within a program for the purpose of performing a specific task.

In Chapters 6 and 9, we described simple algorithms for calculating an employee's pay. In the algorithm, the number of hours worked is multiplied by an hourly pay rate. A more realistic payroll algorithm, however, would do much more than this. In a real-world application, the overall task of calculating an employee's pay would consist of several subtasks, such as the following:

- Getting the employee's hourly pay rate
- Getting the number of hours worked
- Calculating the employee's gross pay
- Calculating overtime pay
- Calculating withholdings for taxes and benefits
- Calculating the net pay
- Printing the paycheck

Most programs perform tasks that are large enough to be broken down into several subtasks. For this reason, programmers usually break down their programs into small manageable pieces known as functions. A **function** is a group of statements that exist within a program for the purpose of performing a specific task. Instead of writing a large program as one long sequence of statements, it can be written as several small functions, each one performing a specific part of the task. These small functions can then be executed in the desired order to perform the overall task.

This approach is sometimes called **divide and conquer** because a large task is divided into several smaller tasks that are easily performed. Figure 15-1 illustrates this idea by comparing two programs:

one that uses a long complex sequence of statements to perform a task, and another that divides a task into smaller tasks, each of which is performed by a separate function. In some programs, a function may be called a **subroutine**, a procedure, or a method.

When using functions in a program, you generally isolate each task within the program in its own function. For example, for a realistic pay calculating program you might create the following functions:

- A function that gets the employee's hourly pay rate
- A function that gets the number of hours worked
- A function that calculates the employee's gross pay
- A function that calculates the overtime pay
- A function that calculates the withholdings for taxes and benefits
- A function that calculates the net pay
- A function that prints the paycheck

A program that has been written with each task in its own function is called a **modularized program**.

Figure 15-1 Using functions to divide and conquer a large task

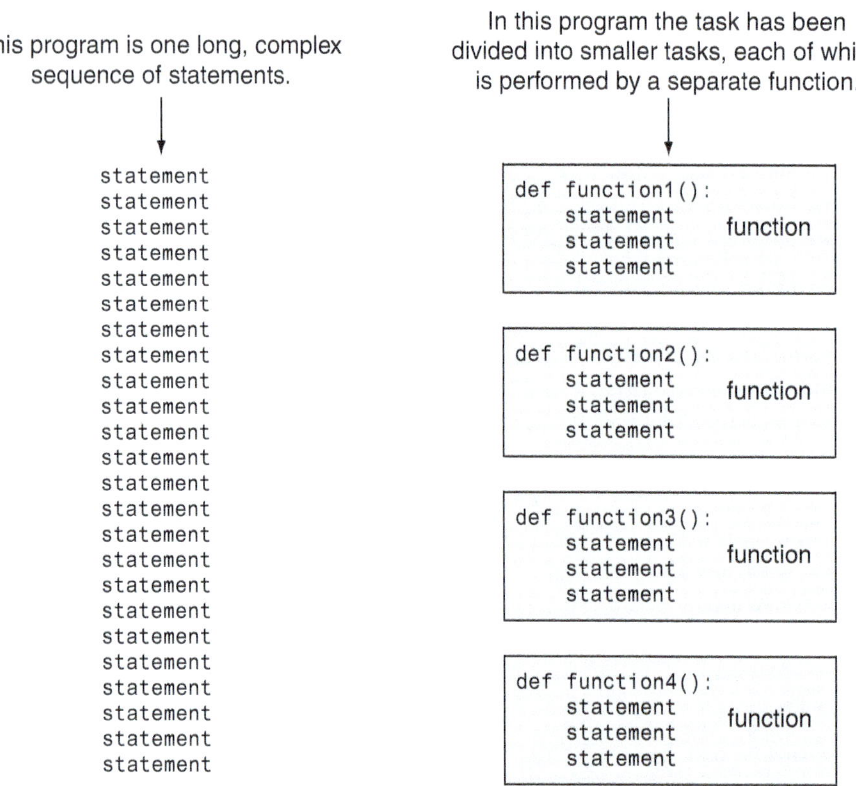

Benefits of Modularizing a Program with Functions

A program benefits in the following ways when it is broken down into subroutines or functions:

1. **Simpler code.** A program's code tends to be simpler and easier to understand when it is broken down into functions. Several small functions are much easier to read than one long sequence of statements.

2. **Code reuse.** Functions also reduce the duplication of code within a program. If a specific operation is performed in several places in a program, a function can be written once to perform that operation, then be executed any time it is needed. This benefit of using functions is known as **code reuse** because you are writing the code to perform a task once, then reusing it each time you need to perform the task.

3. **Better testing.** When each task within a program is contained in its own function, testing and debugging becomes simpler. Programmers can test each function in a program individually, to determine whether it correctly performs its operation. This makes it easier to isolate and fix errors.

4. **Faster development.** Suppose a programmer or a team of programmers is developing multiple programs. They discover that each of the programs performs several common tasks, such as asking for a username and a password, displaying the current time, and so on. It doesn't make sense to write the code for these tasks multiple times. Instead, functions can be written for the commonly-needed tasks, and those functions can be incorporated into each program that needs them.

5. **Easier facilitation of teamwork.** Functions also make it easier for programmers to work in teams. When a program is developed as a set of functions that each performs an individual task, then different programmers can be assigned the job of writing different functions.

Void Functions and Value-Returning Functions

In this chapter, you will learn to write two types of functions: void functions and value-returning functions. When you call a **void function**, it simply executes the statements it contains and then terminates. When you call a **value-returning function,** it executes the statements that it contains, then returns a value back to the statement that called it. The input function is an example of a value-returning function. When you call the input function, it gets the data that the user types on the keyboard and returns that data as a string. The int and float functions are also examples of value-returning functions. You pass an argument to the int function, and it returns that argument's value converted to an integer. Likewise, you pass an argument to the float function, and it returns that argument's value converted to a floating-point number.

In Python, a void function actually returns the value None. The print function is an example of a void function. Note that in some programming languages, void functions are not considered functions at all, because they do not return a value. They may be called procedures.

Checkpoint

15.1   What is a function?

15.2   What is meant by the phrase "divide and conquer"?

15.3   How do functions help you reuse code in a program?

15.4   How can functions make the development of multiple programs faster?

15.5   How can functions make it easier for programs to be developed by teams of programmers?

15.2 Defining and Calling a Void Function

KEY POINT   Although in most programming languages a void function does not return a value, in Python it returns the value None.

Function Names

Before we discuss the process of creating and using functions, we should mention a few things about function names. Just as you name the variables that you use in a program, you also name the functions. A function's name should be descriptive enough so that anyone reading your code can reasonably guess what the function does.

Python requires that you follow the same rules that you follow when naming variables, which we recap here:

- You cannot use one of Python's keywords as a function name. (See Appendix C for a list of the keywords.)
- A function name cannot contain spaces.
- The first character must be one of the letters a through z, A through Z, or an underscore character (_).
- After the first character, you may use the letters a through z or A through Z, the digits 0 through 9, or underscores.
- Uppercase and lowercase characters are distinct.

Because functions perform actions, most programmers prefer to use verbs in function names. For example, a function that calculates gross pay might be named `calculate_gross_pay`. This name would make it evident to anyone reading the code that the function calculates something. What does it calculate? The gross pay, of course. Other examples of good function names would be `get_hours`, `get_pay_rate`, `calculate_overtime`, `print_check`, and so on. Each function name describes what the function does.

Defining and Calling a Function

To create a function, you write its **definition**. Here is the general format of a function definition in Python:

```
def function_name():
    statement
    statement
    etc.
```

The first line is known as the **function header**. It marks the beginning of the function definition. The function header begins with the keyword `def`, followed by the name of the function, followed by a set of parentheses, followed by a colon.

Beginning at the next line is a set of statements known as a block. A **block** is simply a set of statements that belong together as a group. These statements are performed any time the function is executed. Notice in the general format that all of the statements in the block are indented. This indentation is required, because the Python interpreter uses it to tell where the block begins and ends. You can name the block, which makes it a subroutine that can be called in different places within code.

Let's look at an example of a function. Keep in mind that this is not a complete program. We will show the entire program in a moment.

```python
def message():
    print('I am Arthur,')
    print('King of the Britons.')
```

This code defines a function named `message`. The `message` function contains a block with two statements. Executing the function will cause these statements to execute.

Calling a Function

A function definition specifies what a function does, but it does not cause the function to execute. To execute a function, you must **call** it. This is how we would call the `message` function:

```python
message()
```

When a function is called, the interpreter jumps to that function and executes the statements in its block. Then, when the end of the block is reached, the interpreter jumps back to the part of the program that called the function, and the program resumes execution at that point. When this happens, we say that the function **returns.** To fully demonstrate how function calling works, we will look at Program 15-1.

Program 15-1   (`function_demo.py`)

```python
1   # This program demonstrates a function.
2   # First, we define a function named message.
3   def message():
4       print('I am Arthur,')
5       print('King of the Britons.')
6
7   # Call the message function.
8   message()
```

Program Output
```
I am Arthur,
King of the Britons.
```

Let's step through this program and examine what happens when it runs. First, the interpreter ignores the comments that appear in lines 1 and 2. Then, it reads the `def` statement in line 3. This causes a function named `message` to be created in memory, containing the block of statements in lines 4 and 5. (Remember, a function definition creates a function, but it does not cause the function to execute.) Next, the interpreter encounters the comment in line 7, which is ignored. Then it executes the statement in line 8, which is a function call. This causes the `message` function to execute, which prints the two lines of output. Figure 15-2 illustrates the parts of this program.

Figure 15-2   The function definition and the function call

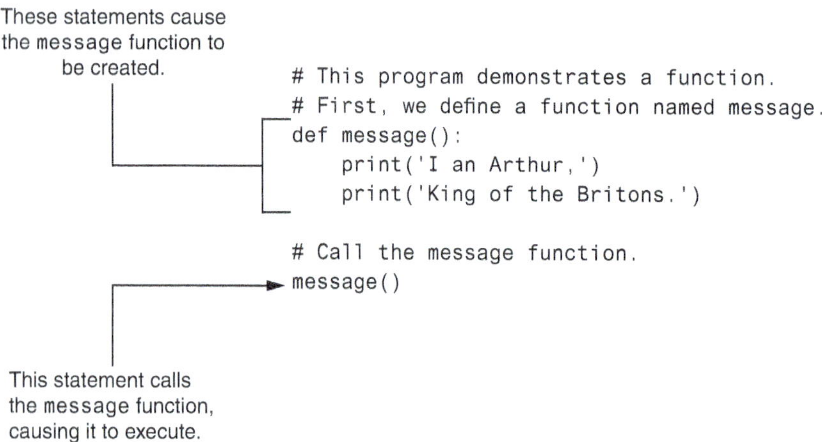

Program 15-1 has only one function, but it is possible to define many functions in a program. In fact, it is common for a program to have a `main` function that is called when the program starts. The `main` function then calls other functions in the program as they are needed. It is often said that the `main` function contains a program's **mainline logic,** which is the overall logic of the program. Program 15-2 shows an example of a program with two functions: `main` and `message`.

Program 15-2   (two_functions.py)

```
 1  # This program has two functions. First we
 2  # define the main function.
 3  def main():
 4      print('I have a message for you.')
 5      message()
 6      print('Goodbye!')
 7
 8  # Next we define the message function.
 9  def message():
10      print('I am Arthur,')
11      print('King of the Britons.')
12
13  # Call the main function.
14  main()
```

Program 15-2	*(continued)*

Program Output

```
I have a message for you.
I am Arthur,
King of the Britons.
Goodbye!
```

The definition of the `main` function appears in lines 3 through 6, and the definition of the `message` function appears in lines 9 through 11. The statement in line 14 calls the `main` function, as shown in Figure 15-3.

Figure 15-3   Calling the `main` function

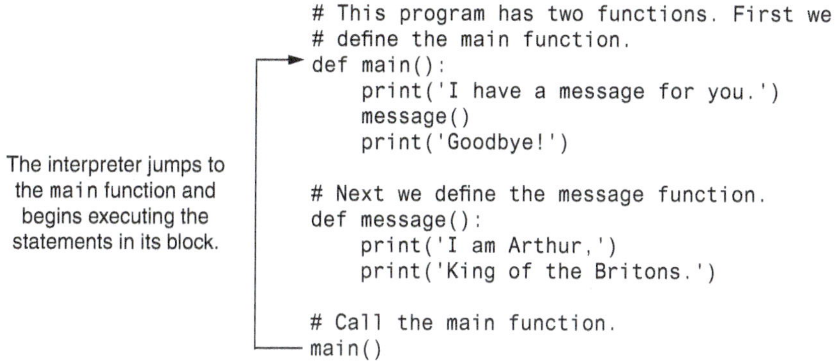

The interpreter jumps to the `main` function and begins executing the statements in its block.

```
# This program has two functions. First we
# define the main function.
def main():
    print('I have a message for you.')
    message()
    print('Goodbye!')

# Next we define the message function.
def message():
    print('I am Arthur,')
    print('King of the Britons.')

# Call the main function.
main()
```

The first statement in the `main` function calls the `print` function in line 4. It displays the string `'I have a message for you'`. Then, the statement in line 5 calls the `message` function. This causes the interpreter to jump to the `message` function, as shown in Figure 15-4. After the statements in the `message` function have executed, the interpreter returns to the `main` function and resumes with the statement that immediately follows the function call. As shown in Figure 15-5, this is the statement that displays the string `'Goodbye!'`.

Figure 15-4   Calling the `message` function

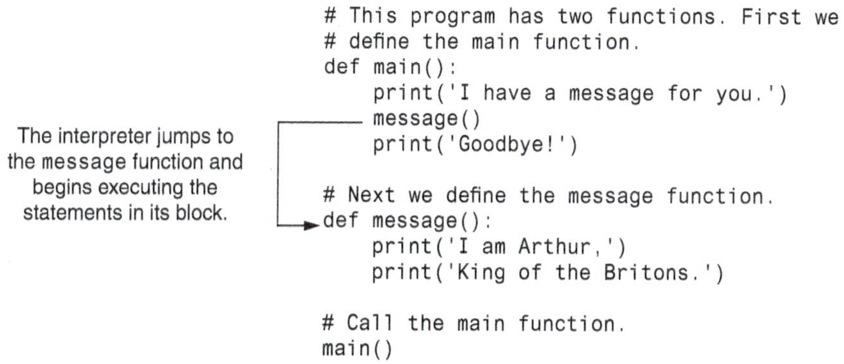

The interpreter jumps to the `message` function and begins executing the statements in its block.

```
# This program has two functions. First we
# define the main function.
def main():
    print('I have a message for you.')
    message()
    print('Goodbye!')

# Next we define the message function.
def message():
    print('I am Arthur,')
    print('King of the Britons.')

# Call the main function.
main()
```

Figure 15-5 The message function returns

When the message function ends, the interpreter jumps back to the part of the program that called it and resumes execution from that point.

```
# This program has two functions. First we
# define the main function.
def main():
    print('I have a message for you.')
    message()
    print('Goodbye!')

# Next we define the message function.
def message():
    print('I am Arthur,')
    print('King of the Britons.')

# Call the main function.
main()
```

That is the end of the `main` function, so the function returns as shown in Figure 15-6. There are no more statements to execute, so the program ends.

Figure 15-6 The main function returns

When the `main` function ends, the interpreter jumps back to the part of the program that called it. There are no more statements, so the program ends.

```
# This program has two functions. First we
# define the main function.
def main():
    print('I have a message for you.')
    message()
    print('Goodbye!')

# Next we define the message function.
def message():
    print('I am Arthur,')
    print('King of the Britons.')

# Call the main function.
main()
```

NOTE: When a program calls a function, programmers commonly say that the control of the program transfers to that function. This simply means that the function takes control of the program's execution.

Indentation in Python

In Python, each line in a block must be indented. As shown in Figure 15-7, the last indented line after a function header is the last line in the function's block.

Figure 15-7 All of the statements in a block are indented

The last indented line is the last line in the block.

These statements are not in the block.

```
def greeting():
    print('Good morning!')
    print('Today we will learn about functions.')

print('I will call the greeting function.')
greeting()
```

When you indent the lines in a block, make sure each line begins with the same number of spaces. Otherwise, an error will occur. For example, the following function definition will cause an error because the lines are all indented with different numbers of spaces:

```
def my_function():
   print('And now for')
print('something completely')
     print('different.')
```

In an editor, there are two ways to indent a line: (1) by pressing the Tab key at the beginning of the line, or (2) by using the spacebar to insert spaces at the beginning of the line. You can use either tabs or spaces when indenting the lines in a block, but don't use both. Doing so may confuse the Python interpreter and cause an error.

IDLE, as well as most other Python editors, automatically indents the lines in a block. When you type the colon at the end of a function header, all of the lines typed afterward will automatically be indented. After you have typed the last line of the block, you press the Backspace key to get out of the automatic indentation.

TIP: Python programmers customarily use four spaces to indent the lines in a block. You can use any number of spaces you wish, as long as all the lines in the block are indented by the same amount.

NOTE: Blank lines that appear in a block are ignored.

Checkpoint

15.6   A function definition has what two parts?

15.7   What does the phrase "calling a function" mean?

15.8   When a function is executing, what happens when the end of the function's block is reached?

15.9   Why must you indent the statements in a block?

15.3 Designing a Program to Use Functions

Programmers commonly use a technique known as top-down design to break down an algorithm into functions.

Flowcharting a Program with Functions

Recall that flowcharts are a tool for designing programs. In a flowchart, a function call is shown with a rectangle that has vertical bars at each side, as shown in Figure 15-8. The name of the function that is being called is written on the symbol. The example shown in Figure 15-8 shows how we would represent a call to the `message` function.

Figure 15-8 Function call symbol

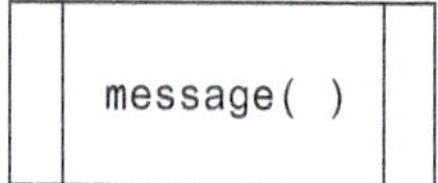

Programmers typically draw a separate flowchart for each function in a program. For example, Figure 15-9 shows how the `main` function and the `message` function in Program 15-2 would be flowcharted. When drawing a flowchart for a function, the starting terminal symbol usually shows the name of the function and the ending terminal symbol usually reads `Return`.

Figure 15-9 Flowchart for Program 15-2

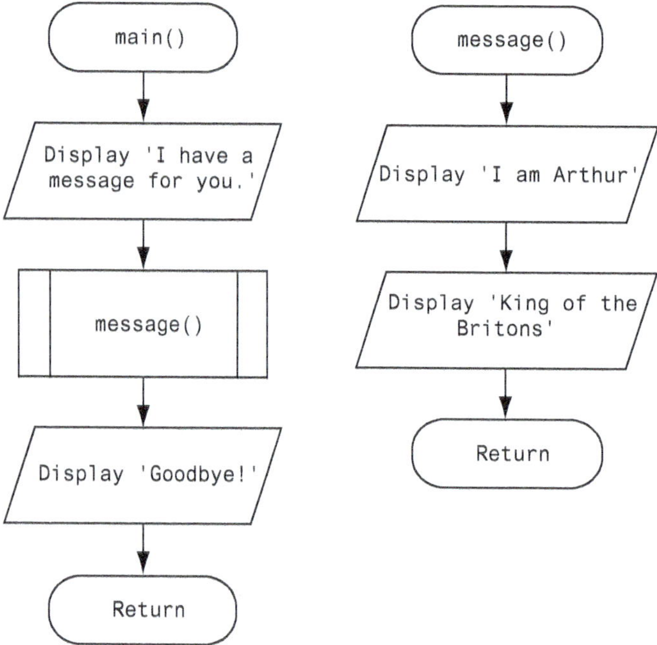

Top-Down Design

In this section, we have discussed and demonstrated how functions work. You've seen how control of a program is transferred to a function when it is called, then returns to the part of the program that called the function when the function ends. It is important that you understand these mechanical aspects of functions.

Just as important as understanding how functions work is understanding how to design a program that uses functions. Programmers commonly use a technique known as **top-down design** to break down an algorithm into functions. The process of top-down design is performed in the following manner:

- The overall task that the program is to perform is broken down into a series of subtasks.
- Each of the subtasks is examined to determine whether it can be further broken down into more subtasks. This step is repeated until no more subtasks can be identified.
- Once all of the subtasks have been identified, they are written in code.

This process is called top-down design because the programmer begins by looking at the topmost level of tasks that must be performed and then breaks down those tasks into lower levels of subtasks.

Hierarchy Charts

Flowcharts are good tools for graphically depicting the flow of logic inside a function, but they do not give a visual representation of the relationships between functions. Programmers commonly use **hierarchy charts** for this purpose. A hierarchy chart, which is also known as a **structure chart,** shows boxes that represent each function in a program. The boxes are connected in a way that shows which functions call other functions. Figure 15-10 shows an example of a hierarchy chart for a hypothetical pay calculating program.

Figure 15-10   A hierarchy chart

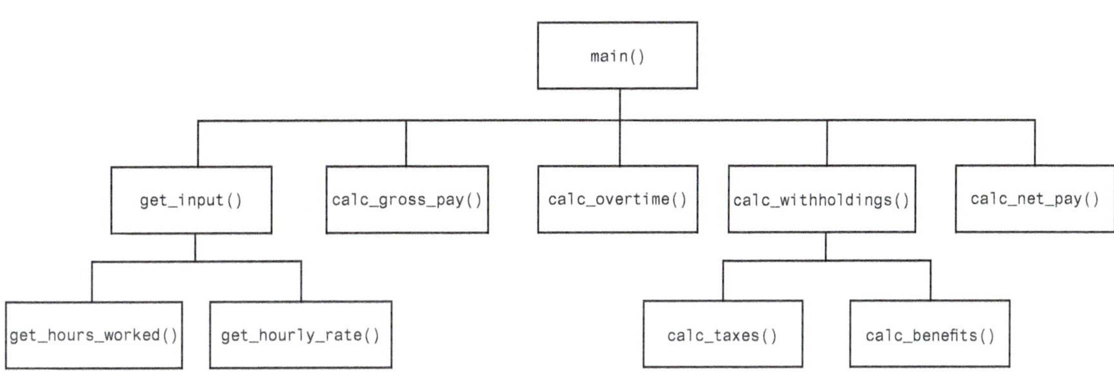

The chart shown in Figure 15-10 shows the `main` function as the topmost function in the hierarchy. The `main` function calls five other functions: `get_input`, `calc_gross_pay`, `calc_overtime`, `calc_withholdings`, and `calc_net_pay`. The `get_input` function calls two additional functions: `get_hours_worked` and `get_hourly_rate`. The `calc_withholdings` function also calls two functions: `calc_taxes` and `calc_benefits`.

Notice the hierarchy chart does not show the steps that are taken inside a function. Because they do not reveal any details about how functions work, they do not replace flowcharts or pseudocode.

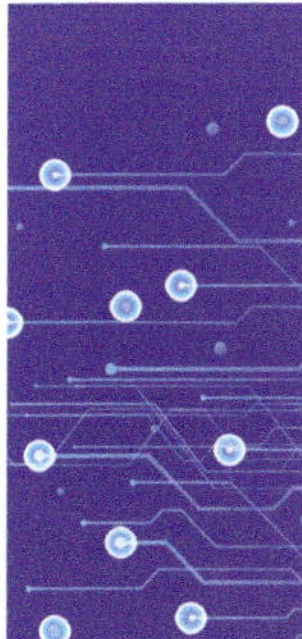

In the Spotlight:

Defining and Calling Functions

Professional Appliance Service, Inc. offers maintenance and repair services for household appliances. The owner wants to give each of the company's service technicians a small handheld computer that displays step-by-step instructions for many of the repairs that they perform. To see how this might work, the owner has asked you to develop a program that displays the following instructions for disassembling an Acme laundry dryer:

Step 1: Unplug the dryer and move it away from the wall.
Step 2: Remove the six screws from the back of the dryer.
Step 3: Remove the dryer's back panel.
Step 4: Pull the top of the dryer straight up.

On Your Own: Working alone or with a partner, see if you can design an algorithm to solve the problem, and illustrate it with a hierarchy chart. When you have completed your work, continue reading to see a solution.

During your interview with the owner, you determine that the program should display the steps one at a time. You decide that after each step is displayed, the user will be asked to press the Enter key to see the next step. Here is the algorithm in pseudocode:

1. Display a starting message, explaining what the program does.
2. Ask the user to press Enter to see step 1.
3. Display the instructions for step 1.
4. Ask the user to press Enter to see the next step.
5. Display the instructions for step 2.
6. Ask the user to press Enter to see the next step.
7. Display the instructions for step 3.
8. Ask the user to press Enter to see the next step.
9. Display the instructions for step 4.

This algorithm lists the top level of tasks that the program needs to perform and becomes the basis of the program's `main` function. Figure 15-11 shows the program's structure in a hierarchy chart.

Figure 15-11   Hierarchy chart for the program

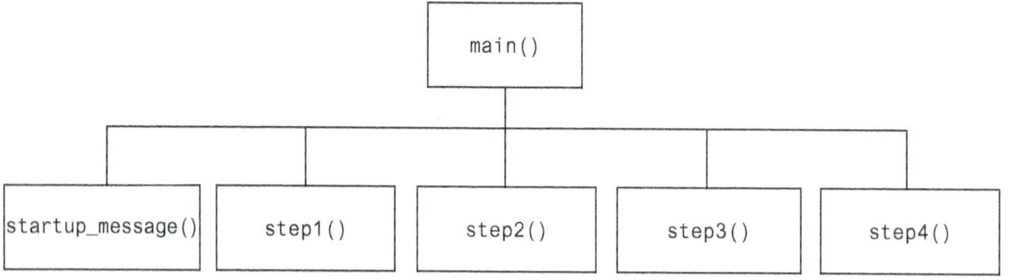

As you can see from the hierarchy chart, the `main` function will call several other functions. Here are summaries of those functions:

- `startup_message`. This function will display the starting message that tells the technician what the program does.
- `step1`. This function will display the instructions for step 1.
- `step2`. This function will display the instructions for step 2.
- `step3`. This function will display the instructions for step 3.
- `step4`. This function will display the instructions for step 4.

Between calls to these functions, the `main` function will instruct the user to press a key to see the next step in the instructions. Program 15-3 shows the code for the program.

Program 15-3   (acme_dryer.py)

```python
 1   # This program displays step-by-step instructions
 2   # for disassembling an Acme dryer.
 3   # The main function performs the program's main logic.
 4   def main():
 5       # Display the start-up message.
 6       startup_message()
 7       input('Press Enter to see Step 1.')
 8       # Display step 1.
 9       step1()
10       input('Press Enter to see Step 2.')
11       # Display step 2.
12       step2()
13       input('Press Enter to see Step 3.')
14       # Display step 3.
15       step3()
16       input('Press Enter to see Step 4.')
17       # Display step 4.
18       step4()
19
20   # The startup_message function displays the
21   # program's initial message on the screen.
22   def startup_message():
23       print('This program tells you how to')
24       print('disassemble an ACME laundry dryer.')
25       print('There are 4 steps in the process.')
26       print()
27
28   # The step1 function displays the instructions
29   # for step 1.
30   def step1():
31       print('Step 1: Unplug the dryer and')
32       print('move it away from the wall.')
33       print()
34
35   # The step2 function displays the instructions
36   # for step 2.
37   def step2():
38       print('Step 2: Remove the six screws')
39       print('from the back of the dryer.')
40       print()
41
42   # The step3 function displays the instructions
43   # for step 3.
44   def step3():
45       print('Step 3: Remove the back panel')
```

Program 15-3   (continued)

```
46        print('from the dryer.')
47        print()
48
49   # The step4 function displays the instructions
50   # for step 4.
51   def step4():
52        print('Step 4: Pull the top of the')
53        print('dryer straight up.')
54
55   # Call the main function to begin the program.
56   main()
```

Program Output

```
This program tells you how to
disassemble an ACME laundry dryer.
There are 4 steps in the process.

Press Enter to see Step 1. Enter
Step 1: Unplug the dryer and
move it away from the wall.

Press Enter to see Step 2. Enter
Step 2: Remove the six screws
from the back of the dryer.

Press Enter to see Step 3. Enter
Step 3: Remove the back panel
from the dryer.

Press Enter to see Step 4. Enter
Step 4: Pull the top of the
dryer straight up.
```

Pausing Execution Until the User Presses Enter

Sometimes you want a program to pause so the user can read information that has been displayed on the screen. When the user is ready for the program to continue execution, they press the Enter key and the program resumes. In Python, you can use the `input` function to cause a program to pause until the user presses the Enter key. Line 7 in Program 15-3 is an example:

```
input('Press Enter to see Step 1.')
```

This statement displays the prompt `'Press Enter to see Step 1.'` and pauses until the user presses the Enter key. The program also uses this technique in lines 10, 13, and 16.

Using the pass Keyword

Sometimes when you are initially writing a program's code, you know the names of the functions you plan to use, but you might not know all the details of the code that will be in those functions. When this is the case, you can use the `pass` keyword to create empty functions. Later, when the details of the code are known, you can come back to the empty functions and replace the `pass` keyword with meaningful code.

For example, when we were writing the code for Program 15-3, we could have initially written empty function definitions for the `step1`, `step2`, `step3`, and `step4` functions, as shown here:

```
def step1():
    pass

def step2():
    pass

def step3():
    pass

def step4():
    pass
```

The `pass` keyword is ignored by the Python interpreter, so this code creates four functions that do nothing.

> **TIP:** The `pass` keyword can be used as a placeholder anywhere in your Python code. For example, it can be used in an `if` statement, as shown here:
>
> ```
> if x > y:
>     pass
> else:
>     pass
> ```
>
> Here is an example of a `while` loop that uses the `pass` keyword:
>
> ```
> while x < 100:
>     pass
> ```

15.4 Local Variables

A local variable is created inside a function and cannot be accessed by statements that are outside the function. Different functions can have local variables with the same names because the functions cannot see each other's local variables.

Anytime you assign a value to a variable inside a function, you create a *local variable*. A local variable belongs to the function in which it is created, and only statements inside that function can access the variable. (The term *local* means that the variable can only be used locally, within the function in which it is created.)

An error will occur if a statement in one function tries to access a local variable that belongs to another function. For example, look at Program 15-4.

Program 15-4 (bad_local.py)

```
 1  # Definition of the main function.
 2  def main():
 3      get_name()
 4      print(f'Hello {name}.')       # This causes an error!
 5
 6  # Definition of the get_name function.
 7  def get_name():
 8      name = input('Enter your name: ')
 9
10  # Call the main function.
11  main()
```

This program has two functions: main and get_name. In line 8, the name variable is assigned a value that is entered by the user. This statement is inside the get_name function, so the name variable is local to that function. This means that the name variable cannot be accessed by statements outside the get_name function.

The main function calls the get_name function in line 3. Then, the statement in line 4 tries to access the name variable. This results in an error because the name variable is local to the get_name function, and statements in the main function cannot access it.

Scope and Local Variables

A variable's scope is the part of a program in which the variable may be accessed. A variable is visible only to statements in the variable's scope. A local variable's scope is the function in which the variable is created. As you saw demonstrated in Program 15-4, no statement outside the function may access the variable.

In addition, a local variable cannot be accessed by code that appears inside the function at a point before the variable has been created. For example, look at the following function. It will cause an error because the print function tries to access the val variable, but this statement appears before the val variable has been created. Moving the assignment statement to a line before the print statement will fix this error.

```
def bad_function():
    print(f'The value is {val}.')     # This will cause an error!
    val = 99
```

Because a function's local variables are hidden from other functions, the other functions may have their own local variables with the same name. For example, look at Program 15-5. In addition to the `main` function, this program has two other functions: `texas` and `california`. These two functions each have a local variable named `birds`.

Program 15-5   (`birds.py`)

```
 1  # This program demonstrates two functions that
 2  # have local variables with the same name.
 3
 4  def main():
 5      # Call the texas function.
 6      texas()
 7      # Call the california function.
 8      california()
 9
10  # Definition of the texas function. It creates
11  # a local variable named birds.
12  def texas():
13      birds = 5000
14      print(f'texas has {birds} birds.')
15
16  # Definition of the california function. It also
17  # creates a local variable named birds.
18  def california():
19      birds = 8000
20      print(f'california has {birds} birds.')
21
22  # Call the main function.
23  main()
```

Program Output
```
texas has 5000 birds.
california has 8000 birds.
```

Although there are two separate variables named `birds` in this program, only one of them is visible at a time because they are in different functions. This is illustrated in Figure 15-12. When the `texas` function is executing, the `birds` variable that is created in line 13 is visible. When the `california` function is executing, the `birds` variable that is created in line 19 is visible.

Figure 15-12   Each function has its own birds variable

```
def texas():
    birds = 5000
    print(f'texas has {birds} birds.')


birds ──────────▶  5000
```

```
def california():
    birds = 8000
    print(f'california has {birds} birds.')


birds ──────────▶  8000
```

 **Checkpoint**

15.10 What is a local variable? How is access to a local variable restricted?

15.11 What is a variable's scope?

15.12 Is it permissible for a local variable in one function to have the same name as a local variable in a different function?

15.5 Passing Arguments to Functions

VideoNote
Passing
Arguments to
a Function

KEY POINT   **An argument is any piece of data that is passed into a function when the function is called. A parameter is a variable that receives an argument that is passed into a function.**

Sometimes it is useful not only to call a function, but also to send one or more pieces of data into the function. Pieces of data that are sent into a function are known as **arguments**. The function can use its arguments in calculations or other operations.

If you want a function to receive arguments when it is called, you must equip the function with one or more parameter variables. A **parameter variable**, often simply called a **parameter**, is a special variable that is assigned the value of an argument when a function is called. Here is an example of a function that has a parameter variable:

```
def show_double(number):
    result = number * 2
    print(result)
```

This function's name is show_double. Its purpose is to accept a number as an argument and display the value of that number doubled. Look at the function header and notice the word number that appears inside the parentheses. This is the name of a parameter variable. This variable will be assigned the value of an argument when the function is called. Program 15-6 demonstrates the function in a complete program.

Program 15-6   **(pass_arg.py)**

```
 1  # This program demonstrates an argument being
 2  # passed to a function.
 3
 4  def main():
 5      value = 5
 6      show_double(value)
 7
 8  # The show_double function accepts an argument
 9  # and displays double its value.
10  def show_double(number):
11      result = number * 2
12      print(result)
13
14  # Call the main function.
15  main()
```

Program Output

```
10
```

When this program runs, the `main` function is called in line 15. Inside the `main` function, line 5 creates a local variable named `value`, assigned the value 5. Then the following statement in line 6 calls the `show_double` function:

```
show_double(value)
```

Notice `value` appears inside the parentheses. This means that `value` is being passed as an argument to the `show_double` function, as shown in Figure 15-13 When this statement executes, the `show_double` function will be called, and the `number` parameter will be assigned the same value as the `value` variable. This is shown in Figure 15-14.

Let's step through the `show_double` function. As we do, remember that the `number` parameter variable will be assigned the value that was passed to it as an argument. In this program, that number is 5.

Figure 15-13   The value variable is passed as an argument

```
def main():
    value = 5
    show_double(value)



def show_double(number):
    result = number * 2
    print(result)
```

Figure 15-14 The value variable and the number parameter reference the same value

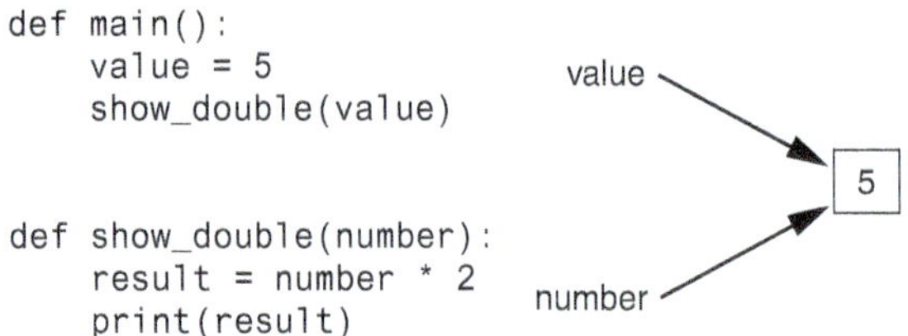

Line 11 assigns the value of the expression number * 2 to a local variable named result. Because number references the value 5, this statement assigns 10 to result. Line 12 displays the result variable.

The following statement shows how the show_double function can be called with a numeric literal passed as an argument:

```
show_double(50)
```

This statement executes the show_double function, assigning 50 to the number parameter. The function will print 100.

Parameter Variable Scope

Earlier in this chapter, you learned that a variable's scope is the part of the program in which the variable may be accessed. A variable is visible only to statements inside the variable's scope. A parameter variable's scope is the function in which the parameter is used. All of the statements inside the function can access the parameter variable, but no statement outside the function can access it.

In the Spotlight:

Passing an Argument to a Function

Your friend Michael runs a catering company. Some of the ingredients that his recipes require are measured in cups. When he goes to the grocery store to buy those ingredients, however, they are sold only by the fluid ounce. He has asked you to write a simple program that converts cups to fluid ounces.

On Your Own: Working alone or with a partner, see if you can design an algorithm to solve the problem. Then, illustrate it with a hierarchy chart. You might even try writing the program itself. When you have completed your work, continue reading to see a solution.

You design the following algorithm:

1. *Display an introductory screen that explains what the program does.*
2. *Get the number of cups.*
3. *Convert the number of cups to fluid ounces and display the result.*

This algorithm lists the top level of tasks that the program needs to perform and becomes the basis of the program's main function. Figure 15-15 shows the program's structure in a hierarchy chart.

Figure 15-15   Hierarchy chart for the program

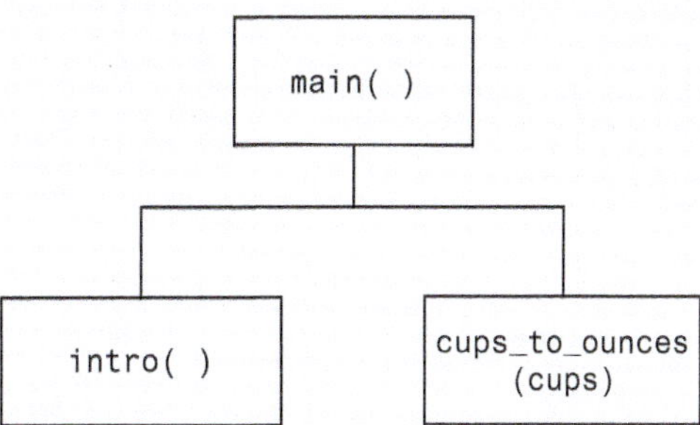

As shown in the hierarchy chart, the main function will call two other functions.

Here are summaries of those functions:

- intro. This function will display a message on the screen that explains what the program does.

- cups_to_ounces. This function will accept the number of cups as an argument and calculate and display the equivalent number of fluid ounces.

In addition to calling these functions, the main function will ask the user to enter the number of cups. This value will be passed to the cups_to_ounces function. The code for the program is shown in Program 15-7.

Program 15-7   **(cups_to_ounces.py)**

```
 1   # This program converts cups to fluid ounces.
 2
 3   def main():
 4       # display the intro screen.
 5       intro()
 6       # Get the number of cups.
 7       cups_needed = int(input('Enter the number of cups: '))
 8       # Convert the cups to ounces.
 9       cups_to_ounces(cups_needed)
10
11   # The intro function displays an introductory screen.
12   def intro():
13       print('This program converts measurements')
14       print('in cups to fluid ounces. For your')
15       print('reference the formula is:')
16       print(' 1 cup = 8 fluid ounces')
17       print()
18
19   # The cups_to_ounces function accepts a number of
20   # cups and displays the equivalent number of ounces.
21   def cups_to_ounces(cups):
```

Program 15-7   *(continued)*

```
22       ounces = cups * 8
23       print(f'That converts to {ounces} ounces.')
24
25   # Call the main function.
26   main()
```

Program Output (with input shown in bold)

```
This program converts measurements
in cups to fluid ounces. For your
reference the formula is:
    1 cup = 8 fluid ounces
Enter the number of cups: 4 (Enter)
That converts to 32 ounces.
```

Passing Multiple Arguments

Often it's useful to write functions that can accept multiple arguments. Program 15-8 shows a function named show_sum that accepts two arguments. The function adds the two arguments and displays their sum.

Program 15-8   **(multiple_args.py)**

```
 1   # This program demonstrates a function that accepts
 2   # two arguments.
 3
 4   def main():
 5       print('The sum of 12 and 45 is')
 6       show_sum(12, 45)
 7
 8   # The show_sum function accepts two arguments
 9   # and displays their sum.
10   def show_sum(num1, num2):
11       result = num1 + num2
12       print(result)
13
14   # Call the main function.
15   main()
```

Program Output

```
The sum of 12 and 45 is
57
```

Notice two parameter variable names, num1 and num2, appear inside the parentheses in the show_sum function header. This is often referred to as a **parameter list.** Also notice a comma separates the variable names.

The statement in line 6 calls the show_sum function and passes two arguments: 12 and 45. These arguments are **passed by position** to the corresponding parameter variables in the function. In other words, the first argument is passed to the first parameter variable, and the second argument is passed to the second parameter variable. So, this statement causes 12 to be assigned to the num1 parameter and 45 to be assigned to the num2 parameter, as shown in Figure 15-16.

Figure 15-16   Two arguments passed to two parameters

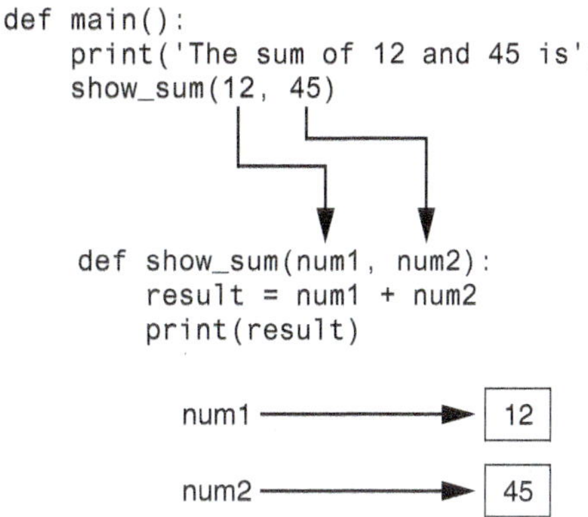

Suppose we were to reverse the order in which the arguments are listed in the function call, as shown here:

```
show_sum(45, 12)
```

This would cause 45 to be passed to the num1 parameter, and 12 to be passed to the num2 parameter. The following code shows another example. This time, we are passing variables as arguments.

```
value1 = 2
value2 = 3
show_sum(value1, value2)
```

When the show_sum function executes as a result of this code, the num1 parameter will be assigned the value 2, and the num2 parameter will be assigned the value 3.

Program 15-9 shows one more example, in which the arguments are **passed by type**. This program passes two strings as arguments to a function.

Program 15-9   (string_args.py)

```
1   # This program demonstrates passing two string
2   # arguments to a function.
3
4   def main():
```

Program 15-9   *(continued)*

```
 5       first_name = input('Enter your first name: ')
 6       last_name = input('Enter your last name: ')
 7       print('Your name reversed is')
 8       reverse_name(first_name, last_name)
 9
10   def reverse_name(first, last):
11       print(last, first)
12
13   # Call the main function.
14   main()
```

Program Output (with input shown in bold)

```
Enter your first name: Matt Enter
Enter your last name: Hoyle Enter
Your name reversed is
Hoyle Matt
```

Making Changes to Parameters

When an argument is passed to a function in Python, the function parameter variable will reference the argument's value. However, any changes that are made to the parameter variable will not affect the argument. To demonstrate this, look at Program 15-10.

Program 15-10   (`change_me.py`)

```
 1   # This program demonstrates what happens when you
 2   # change the value of a parameter.
 3
 4   def main():
 5       value = 99
 6       print(f'The value is {value}.')
 7       change_me(value)
 8       print(f'Back in main the value is {value}.')
 9
10   def change_me(arg):
11       print('I am changing the value.')
12       arg = 0
13       print(f'Now the value is {arg}.')
14
15   # Call the main function.
16   main()
```

Program 15-10   *(continued)*

Program Output
```
The value is 99.
I am changing the value.
Now the value is 0.
Back in main the value is 99.
```

The `main` function creates a local variable named `value` in line 5, assigned the value 99. The statement in line 6 displays `'The value is 99'`. The `value` variable is then passed as an argument to the `change_me` function in line 7. This means that in the `change_me` function, the `arg` parameter will also reference the value 99. This is shown in Figure 15-17.

Figure 15-17   The value variable is passed to the change_me function

```
def main():
    value = 99
    print(f'The value is {value}.')
    change_me(value)                          value
    print(f'Back in main the value is {value}.')

                                                        99

def change_me(arg):
    print('I am changing the value.')
    arg = 0                                   arg
    print(f'Now the value is {arg}.')
```

Inside the `change_me` function, in line 12, the `arg` parameter is assigned the value 0. This reassignment changes `arg`, but it does not affect the `value` variable in `main`. As shown in Figure 15-18, the two variables now reference different values in memory. The statement in line 13 displays `'Now the value is 0.'` and the function ends.

Control of the program then returns to the `main` function. The next statement to execute is in line 8. This statement displays `'Back in main the value is 99.'`. This proves that even though the parameter variable `arg` was changed in the `change_me` function, the argument (the `value` variable in `main`) was not modified.

Figure 15-18   The value variable is passed to the change_me function

```
def main():
    value = 99
    print(f'The value is {value}.')
    change_me(value)                          value
    print(f'Back in main the value is {value}.')

                                                        99

def change_me(arg):
    print('I am changing the value.')
    arg = 0                                   arg         0
    print(f'Now the value is {arg}.')
```

The form of argument passing that is used in Python, where a function cannot change the value of an argument that was passed to it, is commonly called **pass by value**. This is a way that one function can communicate with another function. The communication channel works in only one direction, however. The calling function can communicate with the called function, but the called function cannot use the argument to communicate with the calling function. Later in this chapter, you will learn how to write a function that can communicate with the part of the program that called it by returning a value.

Keyword Arguments

Programs 15-8 and 15-9 demonstrate how arguments are passed by position to parameter variables in a function. Most programming languages match function arguments and parameters this way. In addition to this conventional form of argument passing, the Python language allows you to write an argument in the following format, to specify which parameter variable the argument should be passed to:

   parameter_name=value

In this format, *parameter_name* is the name of a parameter variable, and `value` is the value being passed to that parameter. An argument that is written in accordance with this syntax is known as a **keyword argument**.

Program 15-11 demonstrates keyword arguments. This program uses a function named `show_interest` that displays the amount of simple interest earned by a bank account for a number of periods. The function accepts the arguments `principal` (for the account principal), `rate` (for the interest rate per period), and `periods` (for the number of periods). When the function is called in line 7, the arguments are passed as keyword arguments.

Program 15-11   **(keyword_args.py)**

```
 1  # This program demonstrates keyword arguments.
 2
 3  def main():
 4      # Show the amount of simple interest, using 0.01 as
 5      # interest rate per period, 10 as the number of periods,
 6      # and $10,000 as the principal.
 7      show_interest(rate=0.01, periods=10, principal=10000.0)
 8
 9  # The show_interest function displays the amount of
10  # simple interest for a given principal, interest rate
11  # per period, and number of periods.
12
13  def show_interest(principal, rate, periods):
14      interest = principal * rate * periods
15      print(f'The simple interest will be ${interest:,.2f}.')
16
17  # Call the main function.
18  main()
```

Program Output

```
The simple interest will be $1000.00.
```

Notice in line 7 the order of the keyword arguments does not match the order of the parameters in the function header in line 13. Because a keyword argument specifies which parameter the argument should be passed into, its position in the function call does not matter.

Program 15-12 shows another example. This is a variation of the `string_args` program shown in Program 15-9. This version uses keyword arguments to call the `reverse_name` function.

Program 15-12   **(keyword_string_args.py)**

```
 1  # This program demonstrates passing two strings as
 2  # keyword arguments to a function.
 3
 4  def main():
 5      first_name = input('Enter your first name: ')
 6      last_name = input('Enter your last name: ')
 7      print('Your name reversed is')
 8      reverse_name(last=last_name, first=first_name)
 9
10  def reverse_name(first, last):
11      print(last, first)
12
13  # Call the main function.
14  main()
```

Program Output (with input shown in bold)
```
Enter your first name: Matt [Enter]
Enter your last name: Hoyle [Enter]
Your name reversed is
Hoyle Matt
```

Mixing Keyword Arguments with Positional Arguments

It is possible to mix positional arguments and keyword arguments in a function call, but the positional arguments must appear first, followed by the keyword arguments. Otherwise, an error will occur. Here is an example of how we might call the `show_interest` function of Program 15-10 using both positional and keyword arguments:

```
show_interest(10000.0, rate=0.01, periods=10)
```

In this statement, the first argument, 10000.0, is passed by its position to the `principal` parameter. The second and third arguments are passed as keyword arguments. The following function call will cause an error, however, because a non-keyword argument follows a keyword argument:

```
# This will cause an ERROR!
show_interest(1000.0, rate=0.01, 10)
```

Checkpoint

15.13   What are the pieces of data that are passed into a function called?

15.14   What are the variables that receive pieces of data in a function called?

15.15   What is a parameter variable's scope?

15.16   When a parameter is changed, does this affect the argument that was passed into the parameter?

15.17   The following statements call a function named show_data. Which of the statements passes arguments by position, and which passes keyword arguments?
a. `show_data(name='Kathryn', age=25)`
b. `show_data('Kathryn', 25)`

15.6 Global Variables and Global Constants

  **A global variable is accessible to all the functions in a program file.**

You've learned that when a variable is created by an assignment statement inside a function, the variable is local to that function. Consequently, it can be accessed only by statements inside the function that created it. When a variable is created by an assignment statement that is written outside all the functions in a program file, the variable is global. A **global variable** can be accessed by any statement in the program file, including the statements in any function. For example, look at Program 15-13.

Program 15-13   (global1.py)

```
 1   # Create a global variable.
 2   my_value = 10
 3
 4   # The show_value function prints
 5   # the value of the global variable.
 6   def show_value():
 7       print(my_value)
 8
 9   # Call the show_value function.
10   show_value()
```

Program Output

```
10
```

The assignment statement in line 2 creates a variable named my_value. Because this statement is outside any function, it is global. When the show_value function executes, the statement in line 7 prints the value referenced by my_value.

An additional step is required if you want a statement in a function to assign a value to a global variable. In the function, you must declare the global variable, as shown in Program 15-14.

Program 15-14　　(global2.py)

```
 1  # Create a global variable.
 2  number = 0
 3
 4  def main():
 5      global number
 6      number = int(input('Enter a number: '))
 7      show_number()
 8
 9  def show_number():
10      print(f'The number you entered is {number}.')
11
12  # Call the main function.
13  main()
```

Program Output

```
Enter a number: 55 Enter
The number you entered is 55
```

The assignment statement in line 2 creates a global variable named number. Notice inside the main function, line 5 uses the global keyword to declare the number variable. This statement tells the interpreter that the main function intends to assign a value to the global number variable. That's just what happens in line 6. The value entered by the user is assigned to number.

Most programmers agree that you should restrict the use of global variables, or not use them at all. The reasons are as follows:

- Global variables make debugging difficult. Any statement in a program file can change the value of a global variable. If you find that the wrong value is being stored in a global variable, you have to track down every statement that accesses it to determine where the bad value is coming from. In a program with thousands of lines of code, this can be difficult.
- Functions that use global variables are usually dependent on those variables. If you want to use such a function in a different program, most likely you will have to redesign it so it does not rely on the global variable.
- Global variables make a program hard to understand. A global variable can be modified by any statement in the program. If you are to understand any part of the program that uses a global variable, you have to be aware of all the other parts of the program that access the global variable.

In most cases, you should create variables locally and pass them as arguments to the functions that need to access them.

Global Constants

Although you should try to avoid the use of global variables, it is permissible to use global constants in a program. A **global constant** is a global name that references a value that cannot be changed. Because a global constant's value cannot be changed during the program's execution, you do not have to worry about many of the potential hazards that are associated with the use of global variables.

Although the Python language does not allow you to create true global constants, you can simulate them with global variables. If you do not declare a global variable with the `global` keyword inside a function, then you cannot change the variable's assignment inside that function. The following *In the Spotlight* section demonstrates how global variables can be used in Python to simulate global constants.

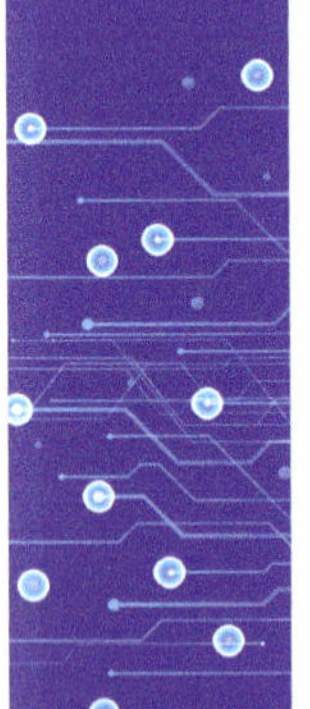

In the Spotlight:
Using Global Constants

Marilyn works for Integrated Systems, Inc., a software company. One of their benefits is a quarterly bonus that is paid to all employees. Another benefit is a retirement plan for each employee. The company contributes 5 percent of each employee's gross pay and bonuses to their retirement plans. Marilyn wants to write a program that will calculate the company's contribution to an employee's retirement account for a year. She wants the program to show the amount of contribution for the employee's gross pay and for the bonuses separately.

On Your Own: Working alone or with a partner, see if you can design an algorithm to solve the problem. You might also try writing the program code. When you have completed your work, continue reading to see a solution.

Here is an algorithm for the program:

    1. Get the employee's annual gross pay.
    2. Get the amount of bonuses paid to the employee.
    3. Calculate and display the contribution for the gross pay.
    4. Calculate and display the contribution for the bonuses.

The code for the program is shown in Program 15-15.

Program 15-15   (`retirement.py`)

```
 1  # The following is used as a global constant to represent
 2  # the contribution rate.
 3  CONTRIBUTION_RATE = 0.05
 4
 5  def main():
 6      gross_pay = float(input('Enter the gross pay: '))
 7      bonus = float(input('Enter the amount of bonuses: '))
 8      show_pay_contrib(gross_pay)
 9      show_bonus_contrib(bonus)
10
11  # The show_pay_contrib function accepts the gross
12  # pay as an argument and displays the retirement
13  # contribution for that amount of pay.
14  def show_pay_contrib(gross):
15      contrib = gross * CONTRIBUTION_RATE
```

Program 15-15   *(continued)*

```
16        print(f'Contribution for gross pay: ${contrib:,.2f}.')
17
18  # The show_bonus_contrib function accepts the
19  # bonus amount as an argument and displays the
20  # retirement contribution for that amount of pay.
21  def show_bonus_contrib(bonus):
22      contrib = bonus * CONTRIBUTION_RATE
23      print(f'Contribution for bonuses: ${contrib:,.2f}.')
24
25  # Call the main function.
26  main()
```

Program Output (with input shown in bold)
```
Enter the gross pay: 80000.00 Enter
Enter the amount of bonuses: 20000.00 Enter
Contribution for gross pay: $4000.00
Contribution for bonuses: $1000.00
```

First, notice the global declaration in line 3:

```
CONTRIBUTION_RATE = 0.05
```

CONTRIBUTION_RATE will be used as a global constant to represent the percentage of an employee's pay that the company will contribute to a retirement account. It is a common practice to write a constant's name in all uppercase letters. This serves as a reminder that the value referenced by the name is not to be changed in the program.

The CONTRIBUTION_RATE constant is used in the calculation in line 15 (in the show_pay_contrib function) and again in line 22 (in the show_bonus_contrib function). Marilyn decided to use this global constant to represent the 5 percent contribution rate for two reasons:

- It makes the program easier to read. When you look at the calculations in lines 15 and 24, it is apparent what is happening.
- Occasionally the contribution rate changes. When this happens, it will be easy to update the program by changing the assignment statement in line 3.

Checkpoint

15.18   What is the scope of a global variable?

15.19   Give one good reason why you should not use global variables in a program.

15.20   What is a global constant? Is it permissible to use global constants in a program?

15.7 Introduction to Value-Returning Functions: Generating Random Numbers

A value-returning function is a function that returns a value back to the part of the program that called it. Python, as well as most other programming languages, provides a library of prewritten functions that perform commonly-needed tasks. These libraries typically contain a function that generates random numbers.

In the first part of this chapter, you learned about void functions. A void function is a group of statements that exist within a program for the purpose of performing a specific task. When you need the function to perform its task, you call the function. This causes the statements inside the function to execute. When the function is finished, control of the program returns to the statement appearing immediately after the function call.

A **value-returning function** is a special type of function. It is like a void function in the following ways.

- It is a group of statements that perform a specific task.
- When you want to execute the function, you call it.

When a value-returning function finishes, however, it returns a value back to the part of the program that called it. The value that is returned from a function can be used like any other value: it can be assigned to a variable, displayed on the screen, used in a mathematical expression (if it is a number), and so on.

Standard Library Functions and the `import` Statement

Python, as well as most programming languages, comes with a **standard library** of functions that have already been written for you. These functions, known as **library functions,** make a programmer's job easier because they perform many of the tasks that programmers commonly need to perform. In fact, you have already used several of Python's library functions. Some of the functions that you have used are `print`, `input`, and `range`. Python has many other library functions. Although we won't cover them all in this book, we will discuss library functions that perform fundamental operations.

Some of Python's library functions are built into the Python interpreter. If you want to use one of these built-in functions in a program, you simply call the function. This is the case with the `print`, `input`, `range`, and other functions about which you have already learned. Many of the functions in the standard library, however, are stored in files that are known as **modules.** These modules, which are copied to your computer when you install Python, help organize the standard library functions. For example, functions for performing math operations are stored together in a module, functions for working with files are stored together in another module, and so on.

In order to call a function that is stored in a module, you have to write an `import` statement at the top of your program. An `import` statement tells the interpreter the name of the module that contains the function. For example, one of the Python standard modules is named `math`. The `math` module contains various mathematical functions that work with floating-point numbers. If you want to use any of the `math` module's functions in a program, you should write the following `import` statement at the top of the program:

```
import math
```

This statement causes the interpreter to load the contents of the `math` module into memory and makes all the functions in the `math` module available to the program.

Because you do not see the internal workings of library functions, many programmers think of them as **black boxes.** The term "black box" is used to describe any mechanism that accepts input, performs some operation (that cannot be seen) using the input, and produces output. Figure 15-19 illustrates this idea.

Figure 15-19   A library function viewed as a black box

We will first demonstrate how value-returning functions work by looking at standard library functions that generate random numbers and some interesting programs that can be written with them. Then, you will learn to write your own value-returning functions and how to create your own modules. The last section in this chapter comes back to the topic of library functions and looks at several other useful functions in the Python standard library.

Generating Random Numbers

Random numbers are useful for lots of different programming tasks. The following are just a few examples.

- Random numbers are commonly used in games. For example, computer games that let the player roll dice use random numbers to represent the values of the dice. Programs that show cards being drawn from a shuffled deck use random numbers to represent the face values of the cards.
- Random numbers are useful in simulation programs. In some simulations, the computer must randomly decide how a person, animal, insect, or other living being will behave. Formulas can be constructed in which a random number is used to determine various actions and events that take place in the program.
- Random numbers are useful in statistical programs that must randomly select data for analysis.
- Random numbers are commonly used in computer security to encrypt sensitive data.

Python provides several library functions for working with random numbers. These functions are stored in a module named `random` in the standard library. To use any of these functions, you must first import them. One way is to write this import statement at the top of your program:

```
import random
```

This statement causes the interpreter to load the contents of the `random` module into memory. This makes all of the functions in the `random` module available to your program.

The first random-number generating function that we will discuss is named `randint`. Because the `randint` function is in the `random` module, we will need to use **dot notation** to refer to it in our program. In dot notation, the function's name is `random.randint`. On the left side of the dot (period) is the name of the module, and on the right side of the dot is the name of the function.

The following statement shows an example of how you might call the `randint` function:

```
number = random.randint (1, 100)
```

The part of the statement that reads `random.randint(1, 100)` is a call to the `randint` function. Notice two arguments appear inside the parentheses: 1 and 100. These arguments tell the function to give an integer random number in the range of 1 through 100. (The values 1 and 100 are included in the range.) Figure 15-20 illustrates this part of the statement.

Notice the call to the `randint` function appears on the right side of an = operator. When the function is called, it will generate a random number in the range of 1 through 100, then **return**

Figure 15-20   A statement that calls the random function

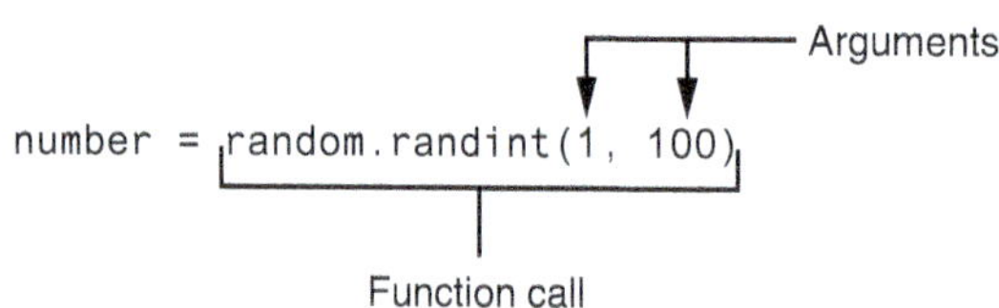

that number. The number that is returned will be assigned to the `number` variable, as shown in Figure 15-21.

Program 15-16 shows a complete program that uses the `randint` function. The statement in line

Figure 15-21   The random function returns a value

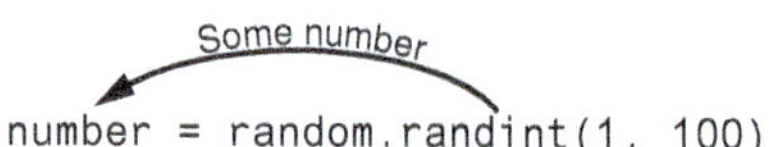

7 generates a random number in the range of 1 through 10 and assigns it to the `number` variable. (The program output shows that the number 7 was generated, but this value is arbitrary. If this were an actual program, it could display any number from 1 to 10.)

Program 15-16   (random_numbers.py)

```
 1   # This program displays a random number
 2   # in the range of 1 through 10.
 3   import random
 4
 5   def main():
 6       # Get a random number.
 7       number = random.randint(1, 10)
 8
 9       # Display the number.
10       print(f'The number is {number}.')
11
12   # Call the main function.
13   main()
```

Program Output

```
The number is 7.
```

Program 15-17 shows another example. This program uses a for loop that iterates five times. Inside the loop, the statement in line 8 calls the randint function to generate a random number in the range of 1 through 100.

Program 15-17   (random_numbers2.py)

```
 1   # This program displays five random
 2   # numbers in the range of 1 through 100.
 3   import random
 4
 5   def main():
 6       for count in range(5):
 7           # Get a random number.
 8           number = random.randint(1, 100)
 9
10           # Display the number.
11           print(number)
12
13   # Call the main function.
14   main()
```

Program Output

```
89
7
16
41
12
```

Both Program 15-16 and 15-17 call the `randint` function and assign its return value to the `number` variable. If you just want to display a random number, it is not necessary to assign the random number to a variable. You can send the `random` function's return value directly to the `print` function, as shown here:

```
print(random.randint(1, 10))
```

When this statement executes, the `randint` function is called. The function generates a random number in the range of 1 through 10. That value is returned and sent to the `print` function. As a result, a random number in the range of 1 through 10 will be displayed. Figure 15-22 illustrates this.

Figure 15-22   Displaying a random number

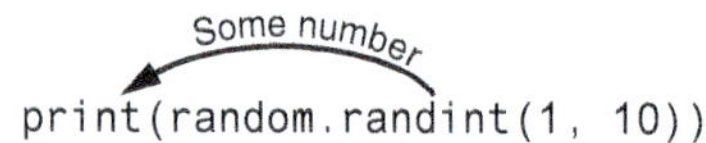


```
print(random.randint(1, 10))
```

A random number in the range of
1 through 10 will be displayed.

Program 15-18 shows how you could simplify Program 15-17. This program also displays five random numbers, but this program does not use a variable to hold those numbers. The `randint` function's return value is sent directly to the `print` function in line 7.

Program 15-18   (random_numbers3.py)

```
 1  # This program displays five random
 2  # numbers in the range of 1 through 100.
 3  import random
 4
 5  def main():
 6      for count in range(5):
 7          print(random.randint(1, 100))
 8
 9  # Call the main function.
10  main()
```

Program Output
```
89
7
16
41
12
```

Calling Functions from an F-String

A function call can be used as a placeholder in an f-string. Here is an example:

```
print(f'The number is {random.randint(1, 100)}.')
```

This statement will display a message such as:

```
The number is 58.
```

F-strings are especially helpful when you want to format the result of a function call. For example, the following statement prints a random number that is center-aligned in a field that is 10 characters wide:

```
print(f'{random.randint(0, 1000):^10d}')
```

Experimenting with Random Numbers in Interactive Mode

To get a feel for the way the `randint` function works with different arguments, you might want to experiment with it in interactive mode. To demonstrate, look at the following interactive session. (We have added line numbers for easier reference.)

```
1   >>> import random  (Enter)
2   >>> random.randint(1, 10)  (Enter)
3   5
4   >>> random.randint(1, 100)  (Enter)
5   98
6   >>> random.randint(100, 200)  (Enter)
7   181
8   >>>
```

Let's take a closer look at each line in the interactive session:

- The statement in line 1 imports the `random` module. (You have to write the appropriate `import` statements in interactive mode, too.)
- The statement in line 2 calls the `randint` function, passing 1 and 10 as arguments. As a result, the function returns a random number in the range of 1 through 10. The number that is returned from the function is displayed in line 3.
- The statement in line 4 calls the `randint` function, passing 1 and 100 as arguments. As a result, the function returns a random number in the range of 1 through 100. The number that is returned from the function is displayed in line 5.
- The statement in line 6 calls the `randint` function, passing 100 and 200 as arguments. As a result, the function returns a random number in the range of 100 through 200. The number that is returned from the function is displayed in line 7.

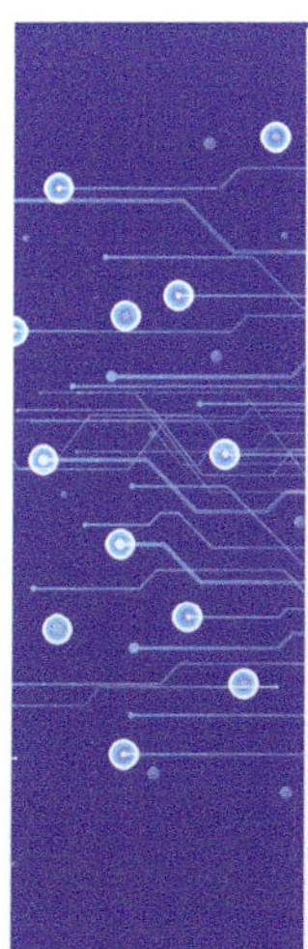

In the Spotlight:

Using Random Numbers

Dr. Kimura teaches an introductory statistics class and has asked you to write a program that he can use in class to simulate the rolling of dice. The program should randomly generate two numbers in the range of 1 through 6 and display them. In your interview with Dr. Kimura, you learn that he would like to use the program to simulate several rolls of the dice, one after the other.

On Your Own: Working alone or with a partner, see if you can design a program for Dr. Kimura. Try writing the pseudocode first, and then try writing the Python code. When you have completed your work, continue reading to see a solution.

Here is the pseudocode for the program:

While the user wants to roll the dice:
  Display a random number in the range of 1 through 6
  Display another random number in the range of 1 through 6
  Ask the user if they want to roll the dice again

You will write a `while` loop that simulates one roll of the dice and then asks the user if another roll should be performed. As long as the user answers "y" for yes, the loop will repeat. Program 15-19 shows the program.

Program 15-19   (`dice.py`)

```
 1  # This program simulates the rolling of dice.
 2  import random
 3
 4  # Constants for the minimum and maximum random numbers
 5  MIN = 1
 6  MAX = 6
 7
 8  def main():
 9      # Create a variable to control the loop.
10      again = 'y'
11
12      # Simulate rolling the dice.
13      while again == 'y' or again == 'Y':
14          print('Rolling the dice ...')
15          print('Their values are:')
16          print(random.randint(MIN, MAX))
17          print(random.randint(MIN, MAX))
18
19          # Do another roll of the dice?
20          again = input('Roll them again? (y = yes): ')
21
22  # Call the main function.
23  main()
```

Program Output (with input shown in bold)

```
Rolling the dice ...
Their values are:
3
1
Roll them again? (y = yes): y Enter
Rolling the dice ...
Their values are:
1
1
```

Program 15-19   *(continued)*

```
Roll them again? (y = yes): y Enter
Rolling the dice . . .
Their values are:
5
6
Roll them again? (y = yes): y Enter
```

The `randint` function returns an integer value, so you can write a call to the function anywhere that you can write an integer value. You have already seen examples where the function's return value is assigned to a variable, and where the function's return value is sent to the `print` function. To further illustrate the point, here is a statement that uses the `randint` function in a math expression:

```
x = random.randint (1, 10) * 2
```

In this statement, a random number in the range of 1 through 10 is generated, then multiplied by 2. The result is a random even integer from 2 to 20 assigned to the x variable. You can also test the return value of the function with an `if` statement, as demonstrated in the following *In the Spotlight* section.

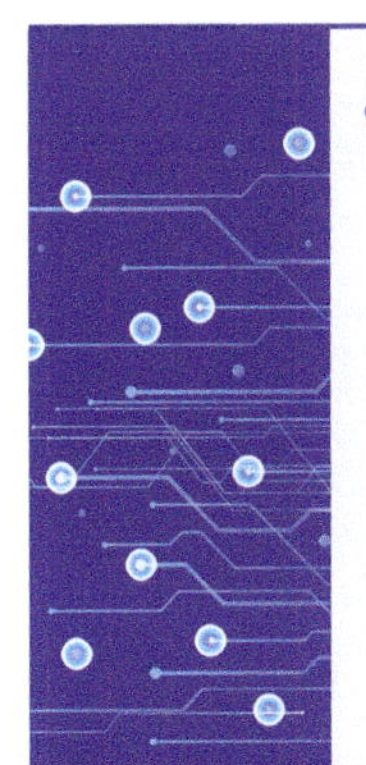

In the Spotlight:

Using Random Numbers to Represent Other Values

Dr. Kimura was so happy with the dice rolling simulator that you wrote for him, he has asked you to write one more program. He would like a program that he can use to simulate ten coin tosses, one after the other. Each time the program simulates a coin toss, it should randomly display either "Heads" or "Tails".

You decide that you can simulate the tossing of a coin by randomly generating a number in the range of 1 through 2. You will write an `if` statement that displays "Heads" if the random number is 1, or "Tails" otherwise.

On Your Own: Working alone or with a partner, see if you can write the pseudocode and code for the additional program. When you have completed your work, continue reading to see a solution.

Here is the pseudocode:

Repeat 10 times:
　　If a random number in the range of 1 through 2 equals 1 then:
　　　　Display 'Heads'
　　Else:
　　　　Display 'Tails'

Because the program should simulate 10 tosses of a coin, you decide to use a `for` loop. The program is shown in Program 15-20.

Program 15-20 `(coin_toss.py)`

```python
 1  # This program simulates 10 tosses of a coin.
 2  import random
 3
 4  # Constants
 5  HEADS = 1
 6  TAILS = 2
 7  TOSSES = 10
 8
 9  def main():
10      for toss in range(TOSSES):
11          # Simulate the coin toss.
12          if random.randint(HEADS, TAILS) == HEADS:
13              print('Heads')
14          else:
15              print('Tails')
16
17  # Call the main function.
18  main()
```

Program Output
```
Tails
Tails
Heads
Tails
Heads
Heads
Heads
Tails
Heads
Tails
```

The `randrange`, `random`, and `uniform` Functions

The standard library's random module contains numerous functions for working with random numbers. In addition to the `randint` function, you might find the `randrange`, `random`, and `uniform` functions useful. (To use any of these functions, you need to write `import random` at the top of your program.)

The `randrange` function takes the same arguments as the `range` function. The difference is that the `randrange` function does not return a list of values. Instead, it returns a randomly selected value from a sequence of values. For example, the following statement assigns a random number in the range of 0 through 9 to the number variable:

```
number = random.randrange(10)
```

The argument, in this case 10, specifies the ending limit of the sequence of values. The function will return a randomly selected number from the sequence of values 0 up to, but not including, the ending limit. The following statement specifies both a starting value and an ending limit for the sequence:

```
number = random.randrange(5,10)
```

When this statement executes, a random number in the range of 5 through 9 will be assigned to number. The following statement specifies a starting value, an ending limit, and a step value:

```
number = random.randrange(0, 101, 10)
```

In this statement, the randrange function returns a randomly selected value from the following sequence of numbers:

```
[0, 10, 20, 30, 40, 50, 60, 70, 80, 90, 100]
```

Both the randint and the randrange functions return an integer number. The random function, however, returns a random floating-point number. You do not pass any arguments to the random function. When you call it, it returns a random floating point number in the range of 0.0 up to 1.0 (but not including 1.0). Here is an example:

```
number = random.random()
```

The uniform function also returns a random floating-point number, but allows you to specify the range of values to select from. Here is an example:

```
number = random.uniform(1.0, 10.0)
```

In this statement, the uniform function returns a random floating-point number in the range of 1.0 through 10.0 (including 10.0) and assigns it to the number variable.

Random Number Seeds

The numbers that are generated by the functions in the random module are not truly random. Although we commonly refer to them as random numbers, they are actually **pseudorandom numbers** that are calculated by a formula. The formula that generates random numbers has to be initialized with a value known as a **seed value**. The seed value is used in the calculation that returns the next random number in the series. When the random module is imported, it retrieves the system time from the computer's internal clock and uses that as the seed value. The system time is an integer that represents the current date and time, down to a hundredth of a second.

If the same seed value were always used, the random number functions would always generate the same series of pseudorandom numbers. Because the system time changes every hundredth of a second, it is a fairly safe bet that each time you import the random module, a different sequence of random numbers will be generated. However, there may be some applications in which you want to always generate the same sequence of random numbers. If that is the case, you can call the random.seed function to specify a seed value. Here is an example:

```
random.seed(10)
```

In this example, the value 10 is specified as the seed value. If a program calls the `random.seed` function, passing the same value as an argument each time it runs, it will always produce the same sequence of pseudorandom numbers. To demonstrate, look at the following interactive sessions. (We have added line numbers for easier reference.)

```
 1   >>> import random Enter
 2   >>> random.seed(10) Enter
 3   >>> random.randint(1, 100) Enter
 4   58
 5   >>> random.randint(1, 100) Enter
 6   43
 7   >>> random.randint(1, 100) Enter
 8   58
 9   >>> random.randint(1, 100) Enter
10   21
11   >>>
```

In line 1, we import the `random` module. In line 2, we call the `random.seed` function, passing 10 as the seed value. In lines 3, 5, 7, and 9, we call `random.randint` function to get a pseudorandom number in the range of 1 through 100. As you can see, the function gave us the numbers 58, 43, 58, and 21. If we start a new interactive session and repeat these statements, we get the same sequence of pseudorandom numbers, as shown here:

```
 1   >>> import random Enter
 2   >>> random.seed(10) Enter
 3   >>> random.randint(1, 100) Enter
 4   58
 5   >>> random.randint(1, 100) Enter
 6   43
 7   >>> random.randint(1, 100) Enter
 8   58
 9   >>> random.randint(1, 100) Enter
10   21
11   >>>
```

Checkpoint

15.21 How does a value-returning function differ from a void function?

15.22 What is a library function?

15.23 Why are library functions like "black boxes"?

15.24 What does the following statement do?
x = random.randint(1, 100)

15.25 What does the following statement do?
print(random.randint(1, 20))

15.26 What does the following statement do?
print(random.randrange(10, 20))

15.27 What does the following statement do?
print(random.random())

15.28 What does the following statement do?
print(random.uniform(0.1, 0.5))

15.29 When the random module is imported, what does it use as a seed value for random number generation?

15.30 What happens if the same seed value is always used for generating random numbers?

15.8 Writing Your Own Value-Returning Functions

VideoNote
Writing a
Value-
Returning
Function

A value-returning function has a return statement that returns a value back to the part of the program that called it.

You write a value-returning function in the same way that you write a void function, with one exception: a value-returning function must have a `return` statement. Here is the general format of a value-returning function definition in Python:

```
def function_name():
    statement
    statement
    etc.
    return expression
```

One of the statements in the function must be a `return` statement, which takes the following form:

```
return expression
```

The value of the *expression* that follows the keyword `return` will be sent back to the part of the program that called the function. This can be any value, variable, or expression that has a value (such as a math expression).

Here is a simple example of a value-returning function:

```
def sum(num1, num2):
    result = num 1 + num 2
    return result
```

Figure 15-23 illustrates various parts of the function.

Figure 15-23   Parts of the function

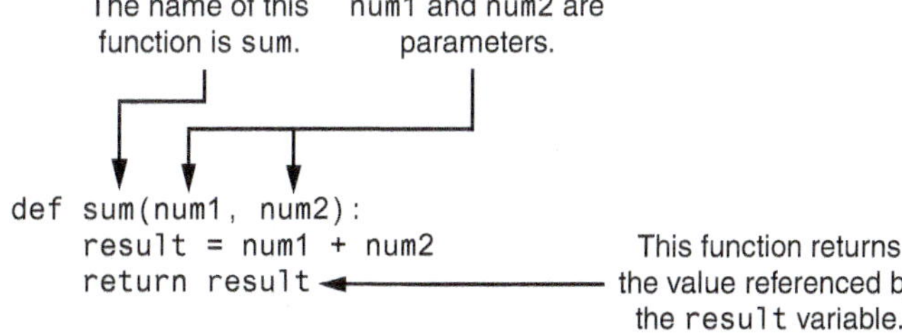

The purpose of this function is to accept two integer values as arguments and return their sum. Let's take a closer look at how it works. The first statement in the function's block assigns the value of num1 + num2 to the result variable. Next, the return statement executes, which causes the function to end execution and sends the value referenced by the result variable back to the part of the program that called the function. Program 15-21 demonstrates the function.

Program 15-21   **(total_ages.py)**

```
 1   # This program uses the return value of a function.
 2
 3   def main():
 4       # Get the user's age.
 5       first_age = int(input('Enter your age: '))
 6
 7       # Get the user's best friend's age.
 8       second_age = int(input("Enter your best friend's age: "))
 9
10       # Get the sum of both ages.
11       total = sum(first_age, second_age)
12
13       # Display the total age.
14       print(f'Together you are {total} years old.')
15
16   # The sum function accepts two numeric arguments and
17   # returns the sum of those arguments.
18   def sum(num1, num2):
19       result = num1 + num2
20       return result
21
22   # Call the main function.
23   main()
```

Program Output (with input shown in bold)
```
Enter your age: 22 Enter
Enter your best friend's age: 24 Enter
Together you are 46 years old.
```

In the main function, the program gets two values from the user and stores them in the first_age and second_age variables. The statement in line 11 calls the sum function, passing first_age and second_age as arguments. The value that is returned from the sum function is assigned to the total variable. In this case, the function will return 46. Figure 15-24 shows how the arguments are passed into the function, and how a value is returned back from the function.

Figure 15-24   Arguments are passed to the sum function and a value is returned

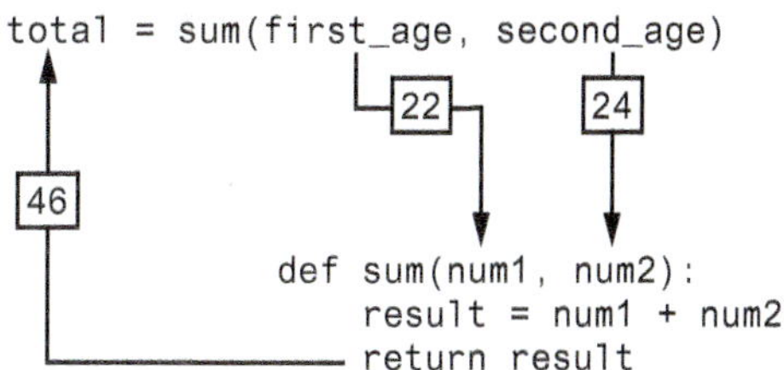

Making the Most of the `return` Statement

Look again at the sum function presented in Program 15-21:

```
def sum(num1, num2):
    result = num 1 + num 2
    return result
```

Notice two things happen inside this function: (1) the value of the expression num1 + num2 is assigned to the result variable, and (2) the value of the result variable is returned. Although this function does what it sets out to do, it can be simplified. Because the return statement can return the value of an expression, you can eliminate the result variable and rewrite the function as:

```
def sum(num1, num2):
    return num 1 + num 2
```

This version of the function does not store the value of num1 + num2 in a variable. Instead, it takes advantage of the fact that the return statement can return the value of an expression. This version of the function does the same thing as the previous version, but in only one step.

How to Use Value-Returning Functions

Value-returning functions provide many of the same benefits as void functions: they simplify code, reduce duplication, enhance your ability to test code, increase the speed of development, and ease the facilitation of teamwork.

Because value-returning functions return a value, they can be useful in specific situations. For example, you can use a value-returning function to prompt the user for input, and then it can return the value entered by the user. Suppose you've been asked to design a program that calculates the sale price of an item in a retail business. To do that, the program would need to get the item's regular price from the user. Here is a function you could define for that purpose:

```
def get_regular_price():
    price = float(input("Enter the item's regular price: "))
    return price
```

Then, elsewhere in the program, you could call that function, as shown here:

```
# Get the item's regular price.
reg_price = get_regular_price()
```

When this statement executes, the get_regular_price function is called, which gets a value from the user and returns it. That value is then assigned to the reg_price variable.

You can also use functions to simplify complex mathematical expressions. For example, calculating the sale price of an item seems like it would be a simple task: you calculate the discount and subtract it from the regular price. In a program, however, a statement that performs this calculation is not that straightforward, as shown in the following example. (Assume DISCOUNT_PERCENTAGE is a global constant that is defined in the program, and it specifies the percentage of the discount.)

```
sale_price = reg_price - (reg_price * DISCOUNT_PERCENTAGE)
```

At a glance, this statement isn't easy to understand because it performs so many steps: it calculates the discount amount, subtracts that value from reg_price, and assigns the result to sale_price. You could simplify the statement by breaking out part of the math expression and placing it in a function. Here is a function named discount that accepts an item's price as an argument and returns the amount of the discount:

```
def discount(price):
    return price * DISCOUNT_PERCENTAGE
```

You could then call the function in your calculation:

```
sale_price = reg_price - discount(reg_price)
```

This statement is easier to read than the one previously shown, and it is clearer that the discount is being subtracted from the regular price. Program 15-22 shows the complete sale price calculating program using the functions just described.

Program 15-22   (sale_price.py)

```
 1   # This program calculates a retail item's
 2   # sale price.
 3
 4   # DISCOUNT_PERCENTAGE is used as a global
 5   # constant for the discount percentage.
 6   DISCOUNT_PERCENTAGE = 0.20
 7
 8   # The main function.
 9   def main():
10       # Get the item's regular price.
11       reg_price = get_regular_price()
12
13       # Calculate the sale price.
14       sale_price = reg_price - discount(reg_price)
15
16       # Display the sale price.
17       print(f'The sale price is ${sale_price:,.2f}.')
18
19   # The get_regular_price function prompts the
20   # user to enter an item's regular price and it
21   # returns that value.
22   def get_regular_price():
23       price = float(input("Enter the item's regular price: "))
```

Program 15-22   *(continued)*

```
24       return price
25
26  # The discount function accepts an item's price
27  # as an argument and returns the amount of the
28  # discount, specified by DISCOUNT_PERCENTAGE.
29  def discount(price):
30      return price * DISCOUNT_PERCENTAGE
31
32  # Call the main function.
33  main()
```

Program Output (with input shown in bold)
```
Enter the item's regular price: 100.00 Enter
The sale price is $80.00.
```

Using IPO Charts

An IPO chart is a simple but effective tool that programmers sometimes use for designing and documenting functions. IPO stands for input, processing, and output, and an **IPO chart** describes the input, processing, and output of a function. These items are usually laid out in columns: the input column shows a description of the data that is passed to the function as arguments, the processing column shows a description of the process that the function performs, and the output column describes the data that is returned from the function. For example, Figure 15-25 shows IPO charts for the `get_regular_price` and `discount` functions you saw in Program 15-22.

Figure 15-25   IPO charts for the getRegularPrice and discount functions

The `get_regular_price` Function		
Input	Processing	Output
None	Prompts the user to enter an item's regular price	The item's regular price

The `discount` Function		
Input	Processing	Output
An item's regular price	Calculates an item's discount by multiplying the regular price by the global constant `DISCOUNT_PERCENTAGE`	The item's discount

Notice the IPO charts provide only brief descriptions of a function's input, processing, and output, but do not show the specific steps taken in a function. In many cases, however, IPO charts include sufficient information so they can be used instead of a flowchart. The decision of whether to use an IPO chart, a flowchart, or both is often left to the programmer's personal preference.

In the Spotlight:

Modularizing with Functions

Hal owns a business named Make Your Own Music, which sells guitars, drums, banjos, synthesizers, and many other musical instruments. Hal's sales staff works strictly on commission. At the end of the month, each salesperson's commission is calculated according to Table 15-1.

Table 15-1 Sales commission rates

Sales This Month	Commission Rate
Less than $10,000	10%
$10,000–14,999	12%
$15,000–17,999	14%
$18,000–21,999	16%
$22,000 or more	18%

For example, a salesperson with $16,000 in monthly sales will earn a 14 percent commission ($2,240). Another salesperson with $18,000 in monthly sales will earn a 16 percent commission ($2,880). A person with $30,000 in sales will earn an 18 percent commission ($5,400).

Because the staff gets paid once per month, Hal allows each employee to take up to $2,000 per month in advance. When sales commissions are calculated, the amount of each employee's advanced pay is subtracted from the commission. If any salesperson's commissions are less than the amount of their advance, they must reimburse Hal for the difference. To calculate a salesperson's monthly pay, Hal uses the following formula:

pay 5 sales 3 commission rate 2 advanced pay

Hal has asked you to write a program that makes this calculation for him.

On Your Own: Working alone or with a partner, see if you can design an algorithm to solve the problem and then write the code. When you have completed your work, continue reading to see a solution.

The following general algorithm outlines the steps the program must take.

1. *Get the salesperson's monthly sales.*
2. *Get the amount of advanced pay.*
3. *Use the amount of monthly sales to determine the commission rate.*
4. *Calculate the salesperson's pay using the formula previously shown. If the amount is negative, indicate that the salesperson must reimburse the company.*

Program 15-23 shows the code, which is written using several functions. Rather than presenting the entire program at once, let's first examine the main function and then each function separately. Here is the main function:

Program 15-23   (commission_rate.py) main function

```
 1  # This program calculates a salesperson's pay
 2  # at Make Your Own Music.
 3  def main():
 4      # Get the amount of sales.
 5      sales = get_sales()
 6
 7      # Get the amount of advanced pay.
 8      advanced_pay = get_advanced_pay()
 9
10      # Determine the commission rate.
11      comm_rate = determine_comm_rate(sales)
12
13      # Calculate the pay.
14      pay = sales * comm_rate - advanced_pay
15
16      # Display the amount of pay.
17      print(f'The pay is ${pay:,.2f}.')
18
19      # Determine whether the pay is negative.
20      if pay < 0:
21          print('The Salesperson must reimburse')
22          print('the company.')
23
```

Line 5 calls the get_sales function, which gets the amount of sales from the user and returns that value. The value that is returned from the function is assigned to the sales variable. Line 8 calls the get_advanced_pay function, which gets the amount of advanced pay from the user and returns that value. The value that is returned from the function is assigned to the advanced_pay variable.

Line 11 calls the determine_comm_rate function, passing sales as an argument. This function returns the rate of commission for the amount of sales. That value is assigned to the comm_rate variable. Line 14 calculates the amount of pay, then line 17 displays that amount. The if statement in lines 20 through 22 determines whether the pay is negative, and if so, displays a message indicating that the salesperson must reimburse the company. The get_sales function definition is next.

Program 15-23   (commission_rate.py) get_sales function

```
24  # The get_sales function gets a salesperson's
25  # monthly sales from the user and returns that value.
26  def get_sales():
27      # Get the amount of monthly sales.
```

Program 15-23   *(continued)*

```
28        monthly_sales = float(input('Enter the monthly sales: '))
29
30        # Return the amount entered.
31        return monthly_sales
32
```

The purpose of the get_sales function is to prompt the user to enter the amount of sales for
a salesperson and return that amount. Line 28 prompts the user to enter the sales and stores the
user's input in the monthly_sales variable. Line 31 returns the amount in the monthly_sales
variable. Next is the definition of the get_advanced_pay function.

Program 15-23   **(commission_rate.py) get_advanced_pay function**

```
33   # The get_advanced_pay function gets the amount of
34   # advanced pay given to the salesperson and returns
35   # that amount.
36   def get_advanced_pay():
37       # Get the amount of advanced pay.
38       print('Enter the amount of advanced pay, or')
39       print('enter 0 if no advanced pay was given.')
40       advanced = float(input('Advanced pay: '))
41
42       # Return the amount entered.
43       return advanced
44
```

The purpose of the get_advanced_pay function is to prompt the user to enter the amount of
advanced pay for a salesperson and return that amount. Lines 38 and 39 tell the user to enter the
amount of advanced pay (or 0 if none was given). Line 40 gets the user's input and stores it in
the advanced variable. Line 43 returns the amount in the advanced variable. Defining the
determine_comm_rate function comes next.

Program 15-23   **(commission_rate.py) determine_comm_rate function**

```
45   # The determine_comm_rate function accepts the
46   # amount of sales as an argument and returns the
47   # applicable commission rate.
48   def determine_comm_rate(sales):
49       # Determine the commission rate.
50       if sales < 10000.00:
51           rate = 0.10
52       elif sales >= 10000 and sales <= 14999.99:
53           rate = 0.12
54       elif sales >= 15000 and sales <= 17999.99:
55           rate = 0.14
```

Program 15-23   (continued)

```
56        elif sales >= 18000 and sales <= 21999.99:
57            rate = 0.16
58        else:
59            rate = 0.18
60
61        # Return the commission rate.
62        return rate
63
```

The determine_comm_rate function accepts the amount of sales as an argument, and it returns the applicable commission rate for that amount of sales. The if-elif-else statement in lines 50 through 59 tests the sales parameter and assigns the correct value to the local rate variable. Line 62 returns the value in the local rate variable.

Program Output (with input shown in bold)
```
Enter the monthly sales: 14650.00 Enter
Enter the amount of advanced pay, or
enter 0 if no advanced pay was given.
Advanced pay: 1000.00 Enter
The pay is $758.00.
```

Program Output (with input shown in bold)
```
Enter the monthly sales: 9000.00 Enter
Enter the amount of advanced pay, or
enter 0 if no advanced pay was given.
Advanced pay: 0 Enter
The pay is $900.00.
```

Program Output (with input shown in bold)
```
Enter the monthly sales: 12000.00 Enter
Enter the amount of advanced pay, or
enter 0 if no advanced pay was given.
Advanced pay: 2000.00 Enter
The pay is $-560.00.
The salesperson must reimburse
the company.
```

Returning Strings

So far, you've seen examples of functions that return numbers. You can also write functions that return strings. For example, the following function prompts the user to enter his or her name, then returns the string that the user entered:

```
def get_name():
    # Get the user's name.
    name = input('Enter your name: ')
    # Return the name.
    return name
```

A function can also return an f-string. When a function returns an f-string, the Python interpreter will evaluate any placeholders and format specifiers that the f-string contains, and it will return the formatted result. Here is an example:

```
def dollar_format(value):
    return f'${value:,.2f}'
```

The purpose of the `dollar_format` function is to accept a numeric value as an argument and return a string that contains that value formatted as a dollar amount. For example, if we pass the floating-point value 89.578 to the function, the function will return the string `'$89.58'`.

Returning Boolean Values

Python allows you to write **Boolean functions,** which return either `True` or `False`. You can use a Boolean function to test a condition, then return either `True` or `False` to indicate whether the condition exists. Boolean functions are useful for simplifying complex conditions that are tested in decision and repetition structures.

For example, suppose you are designing a program that will ask the user to enter a number, then determine whether that number is even or odd. The following code shows how you can make that determination:

```
number = int(input('Enter a number: '))
if (number % 2) == 0:
    print('The number is even.')
else:
    print('The number is odd.')
```

Let's take a closer look at the Boolean expression being tested by this `if-else` statement:

```
(number % 2) == 0
```

This expression uses the % operator, which is called the **remainder operator.** It divides two numbers and returns the remainder of the division. So this code is saying, "If the remainder of `number` divided by 2 is equal to 0, then display a message indicating the number is even, or else display a message indicating the number is odd."

Because dividing an even number by 2 will always give a remainder of 0, this logic will work. The code would be easier to understand, however, if you could somehow rewrite it to say, "If the number is even, then display a message indicating it is even, or else display a message indicating it is odd." As it turns out, this can be done with a Boolean function. In this example, you could write a Boolean function named `is_even` that accepts a number as an argument and returns `True` if the number is even, or `False` otherwise. The following is the code for such a function:

```
def is_even(number):
    # Determine whether number is even. If it is,
    # set status to true. Otherwise, set status
    # to false.
    if (number % 2) == 0:
        status = True
    else:
        status = False
    # Return the value of the status variable.
    return status
```

Then, you can rewrite the `if-else` statement so it calls the `is_even` function to determine whether `number` is even:

```
number = int(input('Enter a number: '))
if is_even(number):
    print('The number is even.')
else:
    print('The number is odd.')
```

Not only is this logic easier to understand, but now you have a function that you can call in the program anytime you need to test a number to determine whether it is even.

Using Boolean Functions in Validation Code

You can also use Boolean functions to simplify complex input validation code. For instance, suppose you are writing a program that prompts the user to enter a product model number and should only accept the values 100, 200, and 300. You could design the input algorithm as follows:

```
# Get the model number.
model = int(input('Enter the model number: '))
# Validate the model number.
while model != 100 and model != 200 and model != 300:
    print('The valid model numbers are 100, 200 and 300.')
    model = int(input('Enter a valid model number: '))
```

The validation loop uses a long compound Boolean expression that will iterate as long as `model` does not equal 100 *and* `model` does not equal 200 *and* `model` does not equal 300. Although this logic will work, you can simplify the validation loop by writing a Boolean function to test the `model` variable, then calling that function in the loop. For example, suppose you pass the `model` variable to a function you write named `is_invalid`. The function returns `True` if `model` is invalid, or `False` otherwise. You could rewrite the validation loop as follows:

```
# Validate the model number.
while is_invalid(model):
    print('The valid model numbers are 100, 200 and 300.')
    model = int(input('Enter a valid model number: '))
```

This makes the loop easier to read. It is evident now that the loop iterates as long as `model` is invalid. The following code shows how you might write the `is_invalid` function. It accepts a model number as an argument, and if the argument is not 100 and the argument is not 200 and the argument is not 300, the function returns `True` to indicate that it is invalid. Otherwise, the function returns `False`.

```
def is_invalid(mod_num):
    if mod_num != 100 and mod_num != 200 and mod_num != 300:
        status = True
    else:
        status = False
    return status
```

Returning Multiple Values

The examples of value-returning functions that we have looked at so far return a single value. In Python, however, you are not limited to returning only one value. You can specify multiple expressions separated by commas after the return statement, as shown in this general format:

```
return expression1, expression2, etc.
```

As an example, look at the following definition for a function named get_name. The function prompts the user to enter his or her first and last names. These names are stored in two local variables: first and last. The return statement returns both of the variables.

```
def get_name():
    # Get the user's first and last names.
    first = input('Enter your first name: ')
    last = input('Enter your last name: ')

    # Return both names.
    return first, last
```

When you call this function in an assignment statement, you need to use two variables on the left side of the = operator. Here is an example:

```
first_name, last_name = get_name()
```

The values listed in the return statement are assigned, in the order that they appear, to the variables on the left side of the = operator. After this statement executes, the value of the first variable will be assigned to first_name, and the value of the last variable will be assigned to last_name. Note the number of variables on the left side of the = operator must match the number of values returned by the function. Otherwise, an error will occur.

Returning None from a Function

Recall that in Python, a void function that returns no value actually returns None. Sometimes it is useful to return None from a function to indicate that an error has occurred. For example, consider the following function:

```
def divide(num1, num2):
    return num1 / num2
```

The divide function takes two arguments, num1 and num2, and returns the result of num1 divided by num2. However, an error will occur if num2 is equal to zero because division by zero is not possible. To prevent the program from crashing, we can modify the function to determine whether num2 is equal to 0 before we perform the division operation. If num2 is equal to 0, we simply return None. Here is the modified code:

```
def divide(num1, num2):
    if num2 == 0:
        result = None
    else:
        result = num1 / num2
    return result
```

Program 15-24 demonstrates how to call the divide function and use its return value to determine whether an error has occurred.

Program 15-24   (none_demo.py)

```
 1   # This program demonstrates the None keyword.
 2
 3   def main():
 4       # Get two numbers from the user.
 5       num1 = int(input('Enter a number: '))
 6       num2 = int(input('Enter another number: '))
 7
 8       # Call the divide function.
 9       quotient = divide(num1, num2)
10
11       # Display the result.
12       if quotient is None:
13           print('Cannot divide by zero.')
14       else:
15           print(f'{num1} divided by {num2} is {quotient}.')
16
17   # The divide function divides num1 by num2 and
18   # returns the result. If num2 is 0, the function
19   # returns None.
20   def divide(num1, num2):
21       if num2 == 0:
22           result = None
23       else:
24           result = num1 / num2
25       return result
26
27   # Execute the main function.
28   main()
```

Program Output (with Input Shown in Bold)
```
Enter a number: 10 Enter
Enter another number: 0 Enter
Cannot divide by zero.
```

Let's take a closer look at the main function. Lines 5–6 get two numbers from the user. Line 9 calls the divide function, passing the two numbers as arguments. The value that is returned from the function is assigned to the quotient variable. The if statement in line 12 determines whether the quotient variable is equal to None. If the quotient variable is equal to None, line 13 displays the message *Cannot divide by zero*. Otherwise, line 15 displays the result of the division.

Notice that the if statement in line 12 does not use the == operator. Instead it uses the is operator, as shown here:

```
if quotient is None:
```

When determining whether a variable is set to None, it is better to use the is operator instead of the == operator. Under some advanced circumstances (that we do not cover in this book), the comparisons == None and is None will not give the same result. So, as a rule, always use the is operator when comparing a variable to None.

If you want to determine whether a variable is not equal to None, use the is not operator. Here is an example:

```
if value is not None:
```

This statement will determine whether value is not equal to None.

Checkpoint

15.31 What is the purpose of the return statement in a function?

15.32 Look at the following function definition:
```
def do_something(number):
    return number * 2
```
a. What is the name of the function?

b. What does the function do?

c. Given the function definition, what will the following statement display?
```
print(do_something(10))
```

15.33 What is a Boolean function?

? Chapter Review

Multiple Choice

1. A group of statements that exist within a program for the purpose of performing a specific task is a(n) ___________.
   - a. block
   - b. parameter
   - c. function
   - d. expression

2. A design technique that helps to reduce the duplication of code within a program and is a benefit of using functions is ___________.
   - a. code reuse
   - b. divide and conquer
   - c. debugging
   - d. facilitation of teamwork

3. The first line of a function definition is known as the ___________.
   - a. body
   - b. introduction
   - c. initialization
   - d. header

4. You ___________ a function to execute it.
   - a. define
   - b. call
   - c. import
   - d. export

5. A design technique that programmers use to break down an algorithm into functions is known as ___________.
   - a. top-down design
   - b. code simplification
   - c. code refactoring
   - d. hierarchical subtasking

6. A ___________ is a diagram that gives a visual representation of the relationships between functions in a program.
   - a. flowchart
   - b. function relationship chart
   - c. symbol chart
   - d. hierarchy chart

7. The _______________ keyword is ignored by the Python interpreter and can be used as a placeholder for code that will be written later.
    a. `placeholder`
    b. `pass`
    c. `pause`
    d. `skip`

8. A __________ is a variable that is created inside a function.
    a. global variable
    b. local variable
    c. hidden variable
    d. none of the above; you cannot create a variable inside a function

9. A(n) __________ is the part of a program in which a variable may be accessed.
    a. declaration space
    b. area of visibility
    c. scope
    d. mode

10. A(n) __________ is a piece of data that is sent into a function.
    a. argument
    b. parameter
    c. header
    d. packet

11. A(n) __________ is a special variable that receives a piece of data when a function is called.
    a. argument
    b. parameter
    c. header
    d. packet

12. A variable that is visible to every function in a program file is a __________.
    a. local variable
    b. universal variable
    c. program-wide variable
    d. global variable

13. When possible, you should avoid using __________ variables in a program.
    a. local
    b. global
    c. reference
    d. parameter

14. This is a prewritten function that is built into a programming language.
    a. standard function
    b. library function
    c. custom function
    d. cafeteria function

15. This standard library function returns a random integer within a specified range of values.
    a. `random`
    b. `randint`
    c. `random_integer`
    d. `uniform`

16. This standard library function returns a random floating-point number in the range of 0.0 up to 1.0 (but not including 1.0).
    a. `brandom`
    b. `brandint`
    c. `brandom_integer`
    d. `buniform`

17. This standard library function returns a random floating-point number within a specified range of values.
    a. `random`
    b. `randint`
    c. `random_integer`
    d. `uniform`

18. This statement causes a function to end and sends a value back to the part of the program that called the function.
    a. `end`
    b. `send`
    c. `exit`
    d. `return`

19. This is a design tool that describes the input, processing, and output of a function.
    a. hierarchy chart
    b. IPO chart
    c. datagram chart
    d. data processing chart

20. This type of function returns either `True` or `False`.
    a. Binary
    b. `true_false`
    c. Boolean
    d. logical

True or False

1. The phrase "divide and conquer" means that all of the programmers on a team should be divided and work in isolation.
2. Functions make it easier for programmers to work in teams.
3. Function names should be as short as possible.
4. Calling a function and defining a function mean the same thing.
5. A flowchart shows the hierarchical relationships between functions in a program.
6. A hierarchy chart does not show the steps that are taken inside a function.
7. A statement in one function can access a local variable in another function.
8. In Python, you cannot write functions that accept multiple arguments.
9. In Python, you can specify which parameter an argument should be passed into a function call.
10. You cannot have both keyword arguments and non-keyword arguments in a function call.
11. Some library functions are built into the Python interpreter.
12. You do not need to have an import statement in a program to use the functions in the random module.
13. Complex mathematical expressions can sometimes be simplified by breaking out part of the expression and putting it in a function.
14. A function in Python can return more than one value.
15. IPO charts provide brief descriptions of a function's input, processing, and output, but do not show the specific steps taken in a function.

Short Answer

1. How do functions help you to reuse code in a program?
2. Name and describe the two parts of a function definition.
3. When a function is executing, what happens when the end of the function block is reached?
4. What is a local variable? What statements are able to access a local variable?
5. What is a local variable's scope?
6. Why do global variables make a program difficult to debug?
7. Suppose you want to select a random number from the following sequence:

   0, 5, 10, 15, 20, 25, 30

   What library function would you use?
8. What statement do you have to have in a value-returning function?
9. What three things are listed on an IPO chart?
10. What is a Boolean function?
11. Differentiate between local and global scope variable declarations.

Algorithm Workbench

1. Create a function, or subroutine, named `times_ten`. The function should accept an argument and return the product of its argument multiplied times 10.

2. Examine the following function header, then write a statement that calls the function, passing 12 as an argument.

   ```
   def show_value(quantity):
   ```

3. Look at the following function header:

   ```
   def my_function(a, b, c):
   ```

   Now look at the following call to `my_function`:

   ```
   my_function(3, 2, 1)
   ```

   When this call executes, what value will be assigned to a? What value will be assigned to b? What value will be assigned to c?

4. What will the following program display?

   ```
   def main():
       x = 1
       y = 3.4
       print(x, y)
       change_us(x, y)
       print(x, y)

   def change_us(a, b):
       a = 0
       b = 0
       print(a, b)

   main()
   ```

5. Look at the following function definition:

   ```
   def my_function(a, b, c):
       d = (a + c) / b
       print(d)
   ```

   a. Write a statement that calls this function and uses keyword arguments to pass 2 into a, 4 into b, and 6 into c.

   b. What value will be displayed when the function call executes?

6. Create a subroutine that generates a random number in the range of 1 through 100 and assigns it to a variable named `rand`.

7. The following statement calls a function named `half`, which returns a value that is half that of the argument. (Assume the `number` variable references a `float` value.) Write code for the function.

   ```
   result = half(number)
   ```

8. A program contains the following function definition:

```
def cube(num):
    return num * num * num
```

Write a statement that passes the value 4 to this function and assigns its return value to the variable `result`.

9. Create void functions, or subroutines. One should use parameters, one should use arguments, one should not use parameters, and one should not use arguments.

10. Write a function named `get_first_name` that asks the user to enter his or her first name, and returns it.

11. Create functions or subroutines that return typed values. One should use arguments, one should use parameters, one should not use arguments, and one should not use parameters.

12. Create functions that use calls to processes passing arguments that match parameters by number, type, and position.

Programming Exercises

1. Kilometer Converter

Write a program that asks the user to enter a distance in kilometers, then converts that distance to miles. The conversion formula is as follows:

$$Miles = Kilometers \times 0.6214$$

2. Sales Tax Program

Write a program that calculates and displays the county and state sales tax on a purchase. If you have already written that program, using functions redesign it so the subtasks are in functions. If you have not already written that program, write it using functions.

3. How Much Insurance?

Many financial experts advise that property owners should insure their homes or buildings for at least 80 percent of the amount it would cost to replace the structure. Write a program that asks the user to enter the replacement cost of a building, then displays the minimum amount of insurance they should buy for the property.

4. Automobile Costs

Write a program that asks the user to enter the monthly costs for the following expenses incurred from operating his or her automobile: loan payment, insurance, gas, oil, tires, and maintenance. The program should then display the total monthly cost of these expenses, and the total annual cost of these expenses.

5. Property Tax

A county collects property taxes on the assessment value of property, which is 60 percent of the property's actual value. For example, if an acre of land is valued at $10,000, its assessment value is $6,000. The property tax is then 72¢ for each $100 of the assessment value. The tax for the acre assessed at $6,000 will be $43.20. Write a program that asks for the actual value of a piece of property and displays the assessment value and property tax.

6. Calories from Fat and Carbohydrates

A nutritionist who works for a fitness club helps members by evaluating their diets. As part of the evaluation, the nutritionist asks members for the number of fat grams and carbohydrate grams that they consumed in a day. Then, the nutritionist calculates the number of calories that result from the fat, using the following formula:

$$calories\ from\ fat = fat\ grams\ x\ 9$$

Next, the nutritionist calculates the number of calories that result from the carbohydrates, using the following formula:

$$calories\ from\ carbs = carb\ grams\ x\ 4$$

The nutritionist asks you to write a program that will make these calculations.

7. Stadium Seating

There are three seating categories at a stadium. Class A seats cost $20, Class B seats cost $15, and Class C seats cost $10. Write a program that asks how many tickets for each class of seats were sold, then displays the amount of income generated from ticket sales.

8. Paint Job Estimator

A painting company has determined that for every 112 square feet of wall space, one gallon of paint and eight hours of labor will be required. The company charges $35.00 per hour for labor. Write a program that asks the user to enter the square feet of wall space to be painted and the price of the paint per gallon. The program should display the following data:

- The number of gallons of paint required
- The hours of labor required
- The cost of the paint
- The labor charges
- The total cost of the paint job

9. Monthly Sales Tax

A retail company must file a monthly sales tax report listing the total sales for the month, and the amount of state and county sales tax collected. The state sales tax rate is 5 percent and the county sales tax rate is 2.5 percent. Write a program that asks the user to enter the total sales for the month. From this figure, the application should calculate and display the following:

- The amount of county sales tax
- The amount of state sales tax
- The total sales tax (county plus state)

10. Feet to Inches

One foot equals 12 inches. Create a function or subroutine named `feet_to_inches` that accepts a number of feet as an argument and returns the number of inches in that many feet. Use the function in a program that prompts the user to enter a number of feet then displays the number of inches in that many feet.

11. Math Quiz

Create a program that gives simple math quizzes. The program should display two random numbers that are to be added, such as:

```
  247

+ 129
```

The program should allow the student to enter the answer. If the answer is correct, a message of congratulations should be displayed. If the answer is incorrect, a message showing the correct answer should be displayed.

12. Maximum of Two Values

Create a function or subroutine named `max` that accepts two integer values as arguments and returns the value that is the greater of the two. For example, if 7 and 12 are passed as arguments to the function, the function should return 12. Use the function in a program that prompts the user to enter two integer values. The program should display the value that is the greater of the two.

13. Falling Distance

When an object is falling because of gravity, the following formula can be used to determine the distance the object falls in a specific time period:

$$d = \tfrac{1}{2}\, gt^2$$

The variables in the formula are as follows: d is the distance in meters, g is 9.8, and t is the amount of time, in seconds, that the object has been falling.

Create a function or subroutine named `falling_distance` that accepts an object's falling time (in seconds) as an argument. The function should return the distance, in meters, that the object has fallen during that time interval. Write a program that calls the function in a loop that passes the values 1 through 10 as arguments and displays the return value.

14. Kinetic Energy

In physics, an object that is in motion is said to have kinetic energy. The following formula can be used to determine a moving object's kinetic energy:

$$KE = \tfrac{1}{2}\, mv^2$$

The variables in the formula are as follows: KE is the kinetic energy, m is the object's mass in kilograms, and v is the object's velocity in meters per second.

Write a function named `kinetic_energy` that accepts an object's mass (in kilograms) and velocity (in meters per second) as arguments. The function should return the amount of kinetic energy that the object has. Write a program that asks the user to enter values for mass and velocity, then calls the `kinetic_energy` function to get the object's kinetic energy.

15. Test Average and Grade

Write a program that asks the user to enter five test scores. The program should display a letter grade for each score and the average test score. Write the following functions in the program:

- calc_average. This function should accept five test scores as arguments and return the average of the scores.

- determine_grade. This function should accept a test score as an argument and return a letter grade for the score based on the following grading scale:

Score	Letter Grade
90–100	A
80–89	B
70–79	C
60–69	D
Below 60	F

16. Odd/Even Counter

In this chapter, you saw an example of how to write an algorithm that determines whether a number is even or odd. Write a program that generates 100 random numbers and keeps a count of how many of those random numbers are even, and how many of them are odd.

17. Prime Numbers

A prime number is a number that is only evenly divisible by itself and 1. For example, the number 5 is prime because it can only be evenly divided by 1 and 5. The number 6, however, is not prime because it can be divided evenly by 1, 2, 3, and 6.

Write a Boolean function named is_prime which takes an integer as an argument and returns true if the argument is a prime number, or false otherwise. Use the function in a program that prompts the user to enter a number then displays a message indicating whether the number is prime.

> **TIP:** Recall that the % operator divides one number by another and returns the remainder of the division. In an expression such as num1 % num2, the % operator will return 0 if num1 is evenly divisible by num2.

18. Prime Number List

This exercise assumes that you have already written the is_prime function in Programming Exercise 17. Write another program that displays all of the prime numbers from 1 to 100. The program should have a loop that calls the is_prime function.

19. Future Value

Suppose you have a certain amount of money in a savings account that earns compound monthly interest, and you want to calculate the amount that you will have after a specific number of months. The formula is as follows:

$$F = P \times (1 + i)^t$$

The terms in the formula are:

- F is the future value of the account after the specified time period.
- P is the present value of the account.
- i is the monthly interest rate.
- t is the number of months.

Write a program that prompts the user to enter the account's present value, monthly interest rate, and the number of months that the money will be left in the account. The program should pass these values to a function that returns the future value of the account, after the specified number of months. The program should display the account's future value.

20. Random Number Guessing Game

Write a program that generates a random number in the range of 1 through 100, and asks the user to guess what the number is. If the user's guess is higher than the random number, the program should display "Too high, try again." If the user's guess is lower than the random number, the program should display "Too low, try again." If the user guesses the number, the application should congratulate the user and generate a new random number so the game can start over.

Optional Enhancement: Enhance the game so it keeps count of the number of guesses that the user makes. When the user correctly guesses the random number, the program should display the number of guesses.

21. Rock, Paper, Scissors Game

Write a program that lets the user play the game of Rock, Paper, Scissors against the computer. The program should work as follows:

1. When the program begins, a random number in the range of 1 through 3 is generated. If the number is 1, then the computer has chosen rock. If the number is 2, then the computer has chosen paper. If the number is 3, then the computer has chosen scissors. (Don't display the computer's choice yet.)
2. The user enters his or her choice of "rock," "paper," or "scissors" at the keyboard.
3. The computer's choice is displayed.
4. A winner is selected according to the following rules:
   - If one player chooses rock and the other player chooses scissors, then rock wins. (Rock smashes scissors.)
   - If one player chooses scissors and the other player chooses paper, then scissors wins. (Scissors cuts paper.)
   - If one player chooses paper and the other player chooses rock, then paper wins. (Paper wraps rock.)
   - If both players make the same choice, the game must be played again to determine the winner.

16 Introduction to Object-Oriented Programming

TOPICS

16.1 Procedural and Object-Oriented Programming

KEY POINT: Procedural programming is a method of writing software. It is a programming practice centered on the procedures or actions that take place in a program. Object-oriented programming is centered on objects. Objects are created from abstract data types that encapsulate data and functions together.

There are primarily two methods of programming in use today: procedural and object-oriented. The earliest programming languages were procedural, meaning a program was made of one or more procedures. You can think of a procedure simply as a function that performs a specific task such as gathering input from the user, performing calculations, reading or writing files, displaying output, and so on. The programs that you have written so far have been procedural in nature.

Typically, procedures operate on data items that are separate from the procedures. In a procedural program, the data items are commonly passed from one procedure to another. As you might imagine, the focus of procedural programming is on the creation of procedures that operate on the program's data. The separation of data and the code that operates on the data can lead to problems, however, as the program becomes larger and more complex.

For example, suppose you are part of a programming team that has written an extensive customer database program. The program was initially designed so a customer's name, address, and phone number were referenced by three variables. Your job was to design several functions that accept those three variables as arguments and perform operations on them. The software has been operating successfully for some time, but your team has been asked to update it by adding several new features. During the revision process, the senior programmer informs you that the customer's name, address, and phone number will no longer be stored in variables. Instead, they will be stored in a list. This means you will have to modify all of the functions that you have designed so they accept and work with a list instead of the three variables. Making these extensive modifications not only is a great deal of work, but also opens the opportunity for errors to appear in your code.

Whereas **procedural programming** is centered on creating procedures (functions), **object-oriented programming (OOP)** is centered on creating objects. An **object** is a software entity that contains both data and procedures. It is a variable, but it has an **abstract data type**, which means its behavior is defined by its **data attributes**. An object's data attributes are simply variables that reference data. The procedures that an object performs are known as **methods**. An object's methods are functions that perform operations on the object's data attributes. The object is, conceptually, a self-contained unit that consists of data attributes and methods that operate on the data attributes. This is illustrated in Figure 16-1.

Figure 16-1   An object contains data attributes and methods

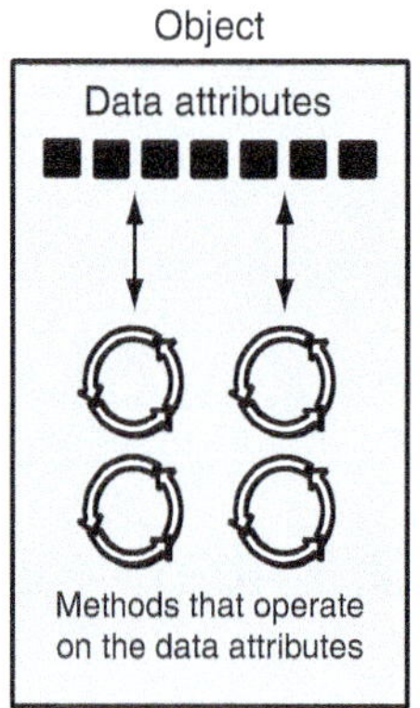

OOP addresses the problem of code and data separation through encapsulation and data hiding. **Encapsulation** refers to the combining of data and code into a single object. **Data hiding** refers to an object's ability to hide its data attributes from code that is outside the object. Only the object's methods may directly access and make changes to the object's data attributes.

An object typically hides its data, but allows outside code to access its methods. As shown in Figure 16-2, the object's methods provide programming statements outside the object with indirect access to the object's data attributes.

Figure 16-2   Code outside the object interacts with the object's methods

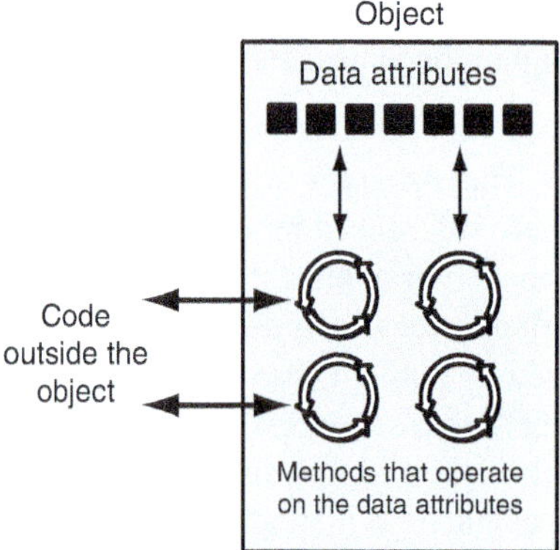

When an object's data attributes are hidden from outside code and access to the data attributes is restricted to the object's methods, the data attributes are protected from accidental corruption. In addition, the code outside the object does not need to know about the format or internal structure of the object's data. The code only needs to interact with the object's methods. When a programmer changes the structure of an object's internal data attributes, they also modify the object's methods so the methods may properly operate on the data. The way in which outside code interacts with the methods, however, does not change.

Object Reusability

In addition to solving the problems of code and data separation, the use of OOP has also been encouraged by the trend of **object reusability**. An object is not a stand-alone program, but is used by programs that need its services. For example, Sharon is a programmer who has developed a set of objects for rendering 3D images. She is a math whiz and knows a lot about computer graphics, so her objects are coded to perform all of the necessary 3D mathematical operations and handle the computer's video hardware. Tom, who is writing a program for an architectural firm, needs his application to display 3D images of buildings. Because he is working under a tight deadline and does not possess a great deal of knowledge about computer graphics, with permission, he can use Sharon's objects to perform the 3D rendering.

An Everyday Example of an Object

Imagine that your alarm clock is actually a software object. If it were, it would have the following data attributes:

- `current_second` (a value in the range of 0–59)
- `current_minute` (a value in the range of 0–59)
- `current_hour` (a value in the range of 1–12)
- `alarm_time` (a valid hour and minute)
- `alarm_is_set` (True or False)

As you can see, the data attributes are merely values that define the current **state** of the alarm clock. You, the user of the alarm clock object, cannot directly manipulate these data attributes because they are **private**. To change a data attribute's value, you must use one of the object's methods. The following are some of the alarm clock object's methods:

- `set_time`
- `set_alarm_time`
- `set_alarm_on`
- `set_alarm_off`

Each method manipulates one or more of the data attributes. For example, the `set_time` method allows you to set the alarm clock's time. You activate the method by pressing a button on top of the clock. By using another button, you can activate the `set_alarm_time` method.

In addition, another button allows you to execute the `set_alarm_on` and `set_alarm_off` methods. Notice all of these methods can be activated by you, who are outside the alarm clock. Methods that can be accessed by entities outside the object are known as **public methods**.

The alarm clock also has **private methods**, which are part of the object's private, internal workings. External entities (such as you, the user of the alarm clock) do not have direct access to the alarm clock's private methods. The object is designed to execute these methods automatically and hide the details from you. The following are the alarm clock object's private methods:

- `increment_current_second`
- `increment_current_minute`
- `increment_current_hour`
- `sound_alarm`

Every second, the `increment_current_second` method executes. This changes the value of the `current_second` data attribute. If the `current_second` data attribute is set to 59 when this method executes, the method is programmed to reset `current_second` to 0, and then cause the `increment_current_minute` method to execute. This method adds 1 to the `current_minute` data attribute, unless it is set to 59. In that case, it resets `current_minute` to 0 and causes the `increment_current_hour` method to execute. The `increment_current_minute` method compares the new time to the `alarm_time`. If the two times match and the alarm is turned on, the `sound_alarm` method is executed.

Checkpoint

16.1   What is an object?

16.2   What is encapsulation?

16.3   Why is an object's internal data usually hidden from outside code?

16.4   What is the difference between public methods and private methods?

16.2 Classes

VideoNote
Classes and
Objects

    **A class is code that specifies the data attributes and methods for a particular type of object.**

Now, let's discuss how objects are created in software. Before an object can be created, it must be designed by a programmer. The programmer determines the data attributes and methods that are necessary, then creates a **class**. A class is code that specifies the data attributes and methods of a particular type of object. Think of a class as a "blueprint" from which objects may be created. It serves a similar purpose as the blueprint for a house. The blueprint itself is not a house, but is a detailed description of a house. When we use the blueprint to build an actual house, we could say we are building an **instance** of the house described by the blueprint. If we so desire, we can build several identical houses from the same blueprint. Each house is a separate instance of the house described by the blueprint. This idea is illustrated in Figure 16-3.

Figure 16-3 A blueprint and houses built from the blueprint

Blueprint that describes a house

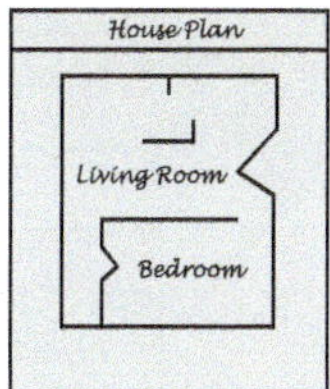

Instances of the house described by the blueprint

Another way of thinking about the difference between a class and an object is to think of the difference between a cookie cutter and a cookie. While a cookie cutter itself is not a cookie, it describes a cookie. The cookie cutter can be used to make one cookie or several cookies. Think of a class as a cookie cutter, and the objects created from the class as cookies.

So, a class is a description of an object's characteristics. When the program is running, it can use the class to create, in memory, as many objects of a specific type as needed. Each object that is created from a class is called an instance of the class.

For example, Jessica is an entomologist (someone who studies insects), and she also enjoys writing computer programs. She designs a program to catalog different types of insects. As part of the program, she creates a class named `Insect`, which specifies characteristics that are common to all types of insects. The `Insect` class is a specification from which objects may be created. Next, she writes programming statements that create an object named `housefly`, which is an instance of the `Insect` class. The `housefly` object is an entity that occupies computer memory and stores data about a housefly. It has the data attributes and methods specified by the `Insect` class. Then she writes programming statements that create an object named `mosquito`. The `mosquito` object is also an instance of the `Insect` class. It has its own area in memory and stores data about a mosquito. Although the `housefly` and `mosquito` objects are separate entities in the computer's memory, they were both created from the `Insect` class. This means that each of the objects has the data attributes and methods described by the `Insect` class. This is illustrated in Figure 16-4.

Figure 16-4   The `housefly` and `mosquito` objects are instances of the `Insect` class

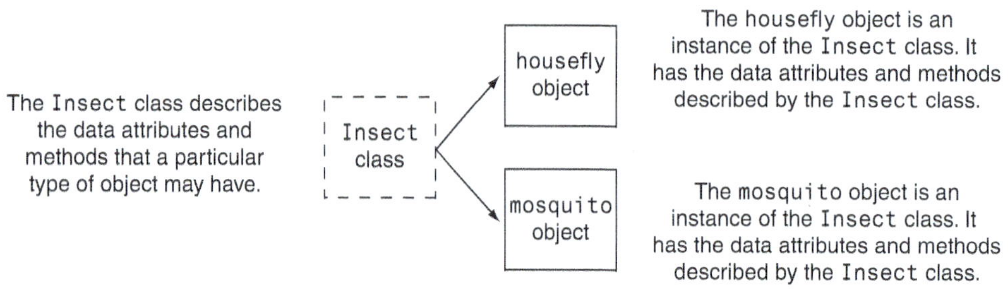

Class Definitions

To create a class, you write a **class definition**. A class definition is a set of statements that defines a class's methods and data attributes. Let's look at a simple example. Suppose we are writing a program to simulate the tossing of a coin. In the program, we need to repeatedly toss the coin and each time determine whether it landed heads up or tails up. Taking an object-oriented approach, we will write a class named `Coin` that can perform the behaviors of the coin.

Program 16-1 shows the class definition, which we will explain shortly. Note this is not a complete program. We will add to it as we go along.

Program 16-1   (`Coin` class, not a complete program)

```
 1   import random
 2
 3   # The Coin class simulates a coin that can
 4   # be flipped.
 5
 6   class Coin:
 7
 8       # The __init__ method initializes the
 9       # sideup data attribute with 'Heads'.
10
11       def __init__(self):
12           self.sideup = 'Heads'
13
14       # The toss method generates a random number
15       # in the range of 0 through 1. If the number
16       # is 0, then sideup is set to 'Heads'.
17       # Otherwise, sideup is set to 'Tails'.
18
19       def toss(self):
20           if random.randint(0, 1) == 0:
21               self.sideup = 'Heads'
22           else:
23               self.sideup = 'Tails'
24
25       # The get_sideup method returns the value
```

<table>
<tr><td>Program 16-1</td><td>(continued)</td></tr>
</table>

```
26          # referenced by sideup.
27
28      def get_sideup(self):
29          return self.sideup
```

In line 1, we import the `random` module. This is necessary because we use the `randint` function to generate a random number. Line 6 is the beginning of the class definition. It begins with the keyword `class`, followed by the class name, which is `Coin`, followed by a colon.

The same rules that apply to variable names also apply to class names. However, notice that we started the class name, `Coin`, with an uppercase letter. This is not a requirement, but it is a widely used convention among programmers. This helps to distinguish class names from variable names.

The `Coin` class has three methods:

- The `__init__` method appears in lines 11 through 12.
- The `toss` method appears in lines 19 through 23.
- The `get_sideup` method appears in lines 28 through 29.

Except that they appear inside a class, notice these method definitions look like any function definition in Python. They start with a header line, which is followed by an indented block of statements.

Take a closer look at the header for each of the method definitions (lines 11, 19, and 28) and notice each method has a parameter variable named `self`:

```
Line 11:    def __init__(self):
Line 19:    def toss(self):
Line 28:    def get_sideup(self):
```

The `self` parameter is required in every method of a class. Recall from our earlier discussion on object-oriented programming that a method operates on a specific object's data attributes. When a method executes, it must have a way of knowing which object's data attributes it is supposed to operate on. That's where the `self` parameter comes in. When a method is called, Python makes the `self` parameter reference the specific object that the method is supposed to operate on.

> **NOTE:** The parameter must be present in a method. You are not required to name it `self`, but this is strongly recommended to conform with standard practice.

Let's look at each of the methods. The first method, which is named `__init__`, is defined in lines 11 through 12:

```
def __init__(self):
    self.sideup = 'Heads'
```

Most Python classes have a special method named `__init__`, which is automatically executed when an instance of the class is created in memory. The `__init__` method is commonly known as an **initializer method** because it initializes the object's data attributes. The name of the method starts with two underscore characters, followed by the word `init`, followed by two more underscore characters.

Immediately after an object is created in memory, the _ _init_ _ method executes, and the self parameter is automatically assigned the object that was just created. Inside the method, the statement in line 12 executes:

```
self.sideup = 'Heads'
```

This statement assigns the string 'Heads' to the sideup data attribute belonging to the object that was just created. As a result of this _ _init_ _ method, each object we create from the Coin class will initially have a sideup attribute that is set to 'Heads'.

NOTE: The _ _init_ _ method is usually the first method inside a class definition.

The toss method appears in lines 19 through 23:

```
def toss(self):
    if random.randint(0, 1) == 0:
        self.sideup = 'Heads'
    else:
        self.sideup = 'Tails'
```

This method also has the required self parameter variable. When the toss method is called, self will automatically reference the object on which the method is to operate.

The toss method simulates the tossing of the coin. When the method is called, the if statement in line 20 calls the random.randint function to get a random integer in the range of 0 through 1. If the number is 0, then the statement in line 21 assigns 'Heads' to self.sideup. Otherwise, the statement in line 23 assigns 'Tails' to self.sideup.

The get_sideup method appears in lines 28 through 29:

```
def get_sideup(self):
    return self.sideup
```

Once again, the method has the required self parameter variable. This method simply returns the value of self.sideup. We call this method any time we want to know which side of the coin is facing up.

To demonstrate the Coin class, we need to write a complete program that uses it to create an object. Program 16-2 shows an example. The Coin class definition appears in lines 6 through 29. The program has a main function, which appears in lines 32 through 44.

Program 16-2   (coin_demo1.py)

```python
 1  import random
 2
 3  # The Coin class simulates a coin that can
 4  # be flipped.
 5
 6  class Coin:
 7
 8      # The __init__ method initializes the
 9      # sideup data attribute with 'Heads'.
10
11      def __init__(self):
12          self.sideup = 'Heads'
13
14      # The toss method generates a random number
15      # in the range of 0 through 1. If the number
16      # is 0, then sideup is set to 'Heads'.
17      # Otherwise, sideup is set to 'Tails'.
18
19      def toss(self):
20          if random.randint(0, 1) == 0:
21              self.sideup = 'Heads'
22          else:
23              self.sideup = 'Tails'
24
25      # The get_sideup method returns the value
26      # referenced by sideup.
27
28      def get_sideup(self):
29          return self.sideup
30
31  # The main function.
32  def main():
33      # Create an object from the Coin class.
34      my_coin = Coin()
35
36      # Display the side of the coin that is facing up.
37      print('This side is up:', my_coin.get_sideup())
38
39      # Toss the coin.
40      print('I am tossing the coin ...')
41      my_coin.toss()
42
43      # Display the side of the coin that is facing up.
44      print('This side is up:', my_coin.get_sideup())
45
46  # Call the main function.
```

Program 16-2   *(continued)*

```
47      if __name__ == '__main__':
48        main()
```

Program Output
```
This side is up: Heads
I am tossing the coin ...
This side is up: Tails
```

Program Output
```
This side is up: Heads
I am tossing the coin ...
This side is up: Heads
```

Program Output
```
This side is up: Heads
I am tossing the coin ...
This side is up: Tails
```

Take a closer look at the statement in line 34:

```
my_coin = Coin()
```

The expression `Coin()` that appears on the right side of the = operator causes two things to happen:

1. An object is created in memory from the `Coin` class.
2. The `Coin` class's `__init__` method is executed, and the `self` parameter is automatically set to the object that was just created. As a result, that object's `sideup` attribute is assigned the string `'Heads'`.

Figure 16-5 illustrates these steps.

Figure 16-5   Actions caused by the `Coin()` expression

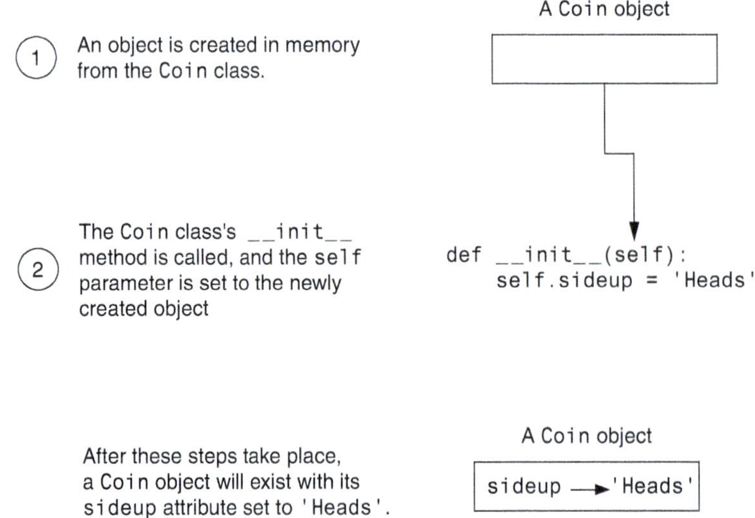

After this, the = operator assigns the `Coin` object that was just created to the `my_coin` variable. Figure 16-6 shows that after the statement in line 12 executes, the `my_coin` variable will reference a `Coin` object, and that object's `sideup` attribute will be assigned the string `'Heads'`.

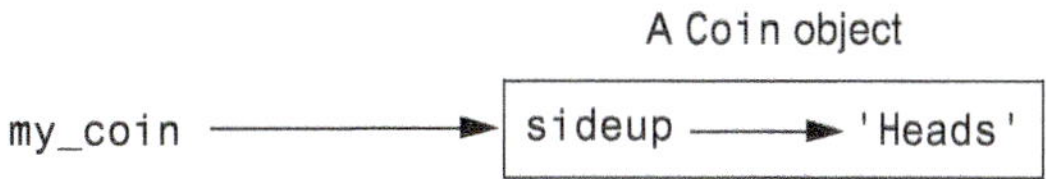

The next statement to execute is line 37:

```
print('This side is up:', my_coin.get_sideup())
```

This statement prints a message indicating the side of the coin that is facing up. Notice the following expression appears in the statement:

```
my_coin.get_sideup()
```

This expression uses the object referenced by `my_coin` to call the `get_sideup` method. When the method executes, the `self` parameter will reference the `my_coin` object. As a result, the method returns the string `'Heads'`.

Notice we did not have to pass an argument to the `sideup` method, despite the fact that it has the `self` parameter variable. When a method is called, Python automatically passes a reference to the calling object into the method's first parameter. As a result, the `self` parameter will automatically reference the object on which the method is to operate.

Lines 40 and 41 are the next statements to execute:

```
print('I am tossing the coin ...')
my_coin.toss()
```

The statement in line 41 uses the object referenced by `my_coin` to call the `toss` method. When the method executes, the `self` parameter will reference the `my_coin` object. The method will randomly generate a number, then use that number to change the value of the object's `sideup` attribute.

Line 44 executes next. This statement calls `my_coin.get_sideup()` to display the side of the coin that is facing up.

Hiding Attributes

Earlier in this chapter, we mentioned that an object's data attributes should be private, so that only the object's methods can directly access them. This protects the object's data attributes from accidental corruption. However, in the `Coin` class that was shown in the previous example, the `sideup` attribute is not private. It can be directly accessed by statements that are not in a `Coin` class method. Program 16-3 shows an example. Note lines 1 through 30 are not shown to conserve space. Those lines contain the `Coin` class, and they are the same as lines 1 through 30 in Program 16-2.

Program 16-3   (`coin_demo2.py`)

Lines 1 through 30 are omitted. These lines are the same as lines 1 through 30 in Program 16-2.

```python
31   # The main function.
32   def main():
33       # Create an object from the Coin class.
34       my_coin = Coin()
35
36       # Display the side of the coin that is facing up.
37       print('This side is up:', my_coin.get_sideup())
38
39       # Toss the coin.
40       print('I am tossing the coin ...')
41       my_coin.toss()
42
43       # But now I'm going to cheat! I'm going to
44       # directly change the value of the object's
45       # sideup attribute to 'Heads'.
46       my_coin.sideup = 'Heads'
47
48       # Display the side of the coin that is facing up.
49       print('This side is up:', my_coin.get_sideup())
50
51   # Call the main function.
52   if __name__ == '__main__':
53       main()
```

Program Output
```
This side is up: Heads
I am tossing the coin ...
This side is up: Heads
```

Program Output
```
This side is up: Heads
I am tossing the coin ...
This side is up: Heads
```

Program Output
```
This side is up: Heads
I am tossing the coin ...
This side is up: Heads
```

Line 34 creates a `Coin` object in memory and assigns it to the `my_coin` variable. The statement in line 37 displays the side of the coin that is facing up, then line 41 calls the object's `toss` method. Then, the statement in line 46 directly assigns the string `'Heads'` to the object's `sideup` attribute:

```python
my_coin.sideup = 'Heads'
```

Regardless of the outcome of the `toss` method, this statement will change the `my_coin` object's `sideup` attribute to `'Heads'`. As you can see from the three sample runs of the program, the coin always lands heads up!

If we truly want to simulate a coin that is being tossed, then we don't want code outside the class to be able to change the result of the `toss` method. To prevent this from happening, we need to make the `sideup` attribute private. In Python, you can hide an attribute by starting its name with two underscore characters. If we change the name of the `sideup` attribute to `__sideup`, then code outside the `Coin` class will not be able to access it. Program 16-4 shows a new version of the `Coin` class, with this change made.

Program 16-4   (`coin_demo3.py`)

```
 1   import random
 2
 3   # The Coin class simulates a coin that can
 4   # be flipped.
 5
 6   class Coin:
 7
 8       # The __init__ method initializes the
 9       # __sideup data attribute with 'Heads'.
10
11       def __init__(self):
12           self.__sideup = 'Heads'
13
14       # The toss method generates a random number
15       # in the range of 0 through 1. If the number
16       # is 0, then sideup is set to 'Heads'.
17       # Otherwise, sideup is set to 'Tails'.
18
19       def toss(self):
20           if random.randint(0, 1) == 0:
21               self.__sideup = 'Heads'
22           else:
23               self.__sideup = 'Tails'
24
25       # The get_sideup method returns the value
26       # referenced by sideup.
27
28       def get_sideup(self):
29           return self.__sideup
30
31   # The main function.
32   def main():
33       # Create an object from the Coin class.
34       my_coin = Coin()
```

Program 16-4   *(continued)*

```
35
36        # Display the side of the coin that is facing up.
37        print('This side is up:', my_coin.get_sideup())
38
39        # Toss the coin.
40        print('I am going to toss the coin ten times:')
41        for count in range(10):
42            my_coin.toss()
43            print(my_coin.get_sideup())
44
45   # Call the main function.
46   if __name__ == '__main__':
47        main()
```

Program Output
```
This side is up: Heads
I am going to toss the coin ten times:
Tails
Heads
Heads
Tails
Tails
Tails
Tails
Tails
Heads
Heads
```

Storing Classes in Modules

The programs you have seen so far in this chapter have the Coin class definition in the same file as the programming statements that use the Coin class. This approach works fine with small programs that use only one or two classes. As programs use more classes, however, the need to organize those classes becomes greater.

Programmers commonly organize their class definitions by storing them in modules. Then the modules can be imported into any programs that need to use the classes they contain. For example, suppose we decide to store the Coin class in a module named coin. Program 16-5 shows the contents of the coin.py file. Then, when we need to use the Coin class in a program, we can import the coin module. This is demonstrated in Program 16-6.

Program 16-5   (`coin.py`)

```python
 1   import random
 2
 3   # The Coin class simulates a coin that can
 4   # be flipped.
 5
 6   class Coin:
 7
 8       # The __init__ method initializes the
 9       # __sideup data attribute with 'Heads'.
10
11       def __init__(self):
12           self.__sideup = 'Heads'
13
14       # The toss method generates a random number
15       # in the range of 0 through 1. If the number
16       # is 0, then sideup is set to 'Heads'.
17       # Otherwise, sideup is set to 'Tails'.
18
19       def toss(self):
20           if random.randint(0, 1) == 0:
21               self.__sideup = 'Heads'
22           else:
23               self.__sideup = 'Tails'
24
25   # The get_sideup method returns the value
26   # referenced by sideup.
27
28   def get_sideup(self):
29       return self.__sideup
```

Program 16-6   (`coin_demo4.py`)

```python
 1   # This program imports the coin module and
 2   # creates an instance of the Coin class.
 3
 4   import coin
 5
 6   def main():
 7       # Create an object from the Coin class.
 8       my_coin = coin.Coin()
 9
10       # Display the side of the coin that is facing up.
11       print('This side is up:', my_coin.get_sideup())
12
```

Program 16-6 *(continued)*

```
13        # Toss the coin.
14        print('I am going to toss the coin ten times:')
15        for count in range(10):
16            my_coin.toss()
17            print(my_coin.get_sideup())
18
19   # Call the main function.
20   if __name__ == '__main__':
21       main()
```

Program Output
```
This side is up: Heads
I am going to toss the coin ten times:
Tails
Tails
Heads
Tails
Heads
Heads
Tails
Heads
Tails
Tails
```

Line 4 imports the `coin` module. Notice in line 8, we had to qualify the name of the `Coin` class by prefixing it with the name of the module, followed by a dot:

```
my_coin = coin.Coin()
```

The BankAccount Class

Let's look at another example. Program 16-7 shows a `BankAccount` class, stored in a module named bankaccount. Objects that are created from this class will simulate bank accounts, allowing us to have a starting balance, make deposits, make withdrawals, and get the current balance.

Program 16-7 (`bankaccount.py`)

```
1    # The BankAccount class simulates a bank account.
2
3    class BankAccount:
4
5        # The __init__ method accepts an argument for
6        # the account's balance. It is assigned to
7        # the __balance attribute.
```

Program 16-7   *(continued)*

```
 8
 9      def __init__(self, bal):
10          self.__balance = bal
11
12      # The deposit method makes a deposit into the
13      # account.
14
15      def deposit(self, amount):
16          self.__balance += amount
17
18      # The withdraw method withdraws an amount
19      # from the account.
20
21      def withdraw(self, amount):
22          if self.__balance >= amount:
23              self.__balance -= amount
24          else:
25              print('Error: Insufficient funds')
26
27      # The get_balance method returns the
28      # account balance.
29
30      def get_balance(self):
31          return self.__balance
```

Notice the __init__ method has two parameter variables: self and bal. The bal parameter will accept the account's starting balance as an argument. In line 10, the bal parameter amount is assigned to the object's __balance attribute.

The deposit method is in lines 15 through 16. This method has two parameter variables: self and amount. When the method is called, the amount that is to be deposited into the account is passed into the amount parameter. The value of the parameter is then added to the __balance attribute in line 16.

The withdraw method is in lines 21 through 25. This method has two parameter variables: self and amount. When the method is called, the amount that is to be withdrawn from the account is passed into the amount parameter. The if statement that begins in line 22 determines whether there is enough in the account balance to make the withdrawal. If so, amount is subtracted from __balance in line 23. Otherwise, line 25 displays the message 'Error: Insufficient funds'.

The get_balance method is in lines 30 through 31. This method returns the value of the __balance attribute.

Program 16-8 demonstrates how to use the class.

Program 16-8   (account_test.py)

```python
 1  # This program demonstrates the BankAccount class.
 2
 3  import bankaccount
 4
 5  def main():
 6      # Get the starting balance.
 7      start_bal = float(input('Enter your starting balance: '))
 8
 9      # Create a BankAccount object.
10      savings = bankaccount.BankAccount(start_bal)
11
12      # Deposit the user's paycheck.
13      pay = float(input('How much were you paid this week? '))
14      print('I will deposit that into your account.')
15      savings.deposit(pay)
16
17      # Display the balance.
18      print(f'Your account balance is ${savings.get_balance():,.2f}.')
19
20      # Get the amount to withdraw.
21      cash = float(input('How much would you like to withdraw? '))
22      print('I will withdraw that from your account.')
23      savings.withdraw(cash)
24
25      # Display the balance.
26      print(f'Your account balance is ${savings.get_balance():,.2f}.')
27
28  # Call the main function.
29  if __name__ == '__main__':
30      main()
```

Program Output (with input shown in bold)
```
Enter your starting balance: 1000.00 Enter
How much were you paid this week? 500.00 Enter
I will deposit that into your account.
Your account balance is $1,500.00
How much would you like to withdraw? 1200.00 Enter
I will withdraw that from your account.
Your account balance is $300.00
```

Program Output (with input shown in bold)
```
Enter your starting balance: 1000.00 Enter
How much were you paid this week? 500.00 Enter
I will deposit that into your account.
Your account balance is $1,500.00
```

<table>
<tr><td>Program 16-8</td><td>(continued)</td></tr>
</table>

```
How much would you like to withdraw? 2000.00 Enter
I will withdraw that from your account.
Error: Insufficient funds
Your account balance is $1,500.00
```

Line 7 gets the starting account balance from the user and assigns it to the `start_bal` variable. Line 10 creates an instance of the `BankAccount` class and assigns it to the `savings` variable. Take a closer look at the statement:

```
savings = bankaccount.BankAccount(start_bal)
```

Notice the `start_bal` variable is listed inside the parentheses. This causes the `start_bal` variable to be passed as an argument to the `__init__` method. In the `__init__` method, it will be passed into the `bal` parameter.

Line 13 gets the amount of the user's pay and assigns it to the `pay` variable. In line 15, the `savings.deposit` method is called, passing the `pay` variable as an argument. In the `deposit` method, it will be passed into the `amount` parameter.

The statement in line 18 displays the account balance. Notice that we use a f-string to call the `savings.get_balance` method. The value that is returned from the method is formatted as a dollar amount.

Line 21 gets the amount that the user wants to withdraw and assigns it to the `cash` variable. In line 23, the `savings.withdraw` method is called, passing the `cash` variable as an argument. In the `withdraw` method, it will be passed into the `amount` parameter. The statement in line 26 displays the ending account balance.

The `__str__` Method

You may need to display a message that indicates an object's state. An object's *state* is the values of the object's attributes at any given moment. Recall the `BankAccount` class has one data attribute: `__balance`. At any given moment, a `BankAccount` object's `__balance` attribute will reference some value. The value of the `__balance` attribute represents the object's state at that moment. Here is an example:

```
account = bankaccount.BankAccount(1500.0)
print(f'The balance is ${savings.get_balance():,.2f}'))
```

The first statement creates a `BankAccount` object, passing the value 1500.0 to the `__init__` method. After this statement executes, the `account` variable will reference the `BankAccount` object. The second line displays a formatted string showing the value of the object's `__balance` attribute. The output of this statement will look like this:

```
The balance is $1,500.00
```

Displaying an object's state is so common that many programmers equip their classes with a method that returns a string containing the object's state. In Python, you give this method the special name `__str__`. Lines 36 through 17 in program 16-9 show the `BankAccount` class with a `__str__` method added to it. It returns a string indicating the account balance.

Program 16-9 (bankaccount2.py)

```
 1   # The BankAccount class simulates a bank account.
 2
 3   class BankAccount:
 4
 5       # The __init__ method accepts an argument for
 6       # the account's balance. It is assigned to
 7       # the __balance attribute.
 8
 9       def __init__(self, bal):
10           self.__balance = bal
11
12       # The deposit method makes a deposit into the
13       # account.
14
15       def deposit(self, amount):
16           self.__balance += amount
17
18       # The withdraw method withdraws an amount
19       # from the account.
20
21       def withdraw(self, amount):
22           if self.__balance >= amount:
23               self.__balance -= amount
24           else:
25               print('Error: Insufficient funds')
26
27       # The get_balance method returns the
28       # account balance.
29
30       def get_balance(self):
31           return self.__balance
32
33       # The __str__ method returns a string
34       # indicating the object's state.
35
36       def __str__(self):
37           return f'The balance is ${self.__balance:,.2f}'
```

You do not directly call the __str__ method. Instead, it is automatically called when you pass an object as an argument to the print function. Program 16-10 shows an example.

Program 16-10   `(account_test2.py)`

```python
 1   # This program demonstrates the BankAccount class
 2   # with the __str__ method added to it.
 3
 4   import bankaccount2
 5
 6   def main():
 7       # Get the starting balance.
 8       start_bal = float(input('Enter your starting balance: '))
 9
10       # Create a BankAccount object.
11       savings = bankaccount2.BankAccount(start_bal)
12
13       # Deposit the user's paycheck.
14       pay = float(input('How much were you paid this week? '))
15       print('I will deposit that into your account.')
16       savings.deposit(pay)
17
18       # Display the balance.
19       print(savings)
20
21       # Get the amount to withdraw.
22       cash = float(input('How much would you like to withdraw? '))
23       print('I will withdraw that from your account.')
24       savings.withdraw(cash)
25
26       # Display the balance.
27       print(savings)
28
29   # Call the main function.
30   if __name__ == '__main__':
31       main()
```

Program Output (with input shown in bold)
```
Enter your starting balance: 1000.00 [Enter]
How much were you paid this week? 500.00 [Enter]
I will deposit that into your account.
The account balance is $1,500.00
How much would you like to withdraw? 1200.00 [Enter]
I will withdraw that from your account.
The account balance is $300.00
```

The name of the object, savings, is passed to the print function in lines 19 and 27. This causes the BankAccount class's _ _str_ _ method to be called. The string that is returned from the _ _str_ _ method is then displayed.

The _ _str_ _ method is also called automatically when an object is passed as an argument to the built-in str function. Here is an example:

```
account = bankaccount2.BankAccount(1500.0)
message = str(account)
print(message)
```

In the second statement, the account object is passed as an argument to the str function. This causes the BankAccount class's _ _str_ _ method to be called. The string that is returned is assigned to the message variable, then displayed by the print function in the third line.

Checkpoint

16.5   You hear someone make the following comment: "A blueprint is a design for a house. A carpenter can use the blueprint to build the house. If the carpenter wishes, they can build several identical houses from the same blueprint." Think of this as a metaphor for classes and objects. Does the blueprint represent a class, or does it represent an object?

16.6   In this chapter, we use the metaphor of a cookie cutter and cookies that are made from the cookie cutter to describe classes and objects. In this metaphor, are objects the cookie cutter or the cookies?

16.7   What is the purpose of the _ _init_ _ method? When does it execute?

16.8   What is the purpose of the self parameter in a method?

16.9   In a Python class, how do you hide an attribute from code outside the class?

16.10 What is the purpose of the _ _str_ _ method?

16.11 How do you call the _ _str_ _ method?

 **16.3** ## Working with Instances

Each instance of a class has its own set of data attributes.

When a method uses the self parameter to create an attribute, the attribute belongs to the specific object that self references. We call these attributes **instance attributes** because they belong to a specific instance of the class.

It is possible to create many instances of the same class in a program. Each instance will then have its own set of attributes. For example, look at Program 16-11. This program creates three instances of the Coin class. Each instance has its own _ _sideup attribute.

Program 16-11   (`coin_demo5.py`)

```python
 1   # This program imports the simulation module and
 2   # creates three instances of the Coin class.
 3
 4   import coin
 5
 6   def main():
 7       # Create three objects from the Coin class.
 8       coin1 = coin.Coin()
 9       coin2 = coin.Coin()
10       coin3 = coin.Coin()
11
12       # Display the side of each coin that is facing up.
13       print('I have three coins with these sides up:')
14       print(coin1.get_sideup())
15       print(coin2.get_sideup())
16       print(coin3.get_sideup())
17       print()
18
19       # Toss the coin.
20       print('I am tossing all three coins ...')
21       print()
22       coin1.toss()
23       coin2.toss()
24       coin3.toss()
25
26       # Display the side of each coin that is facing up.
27       print('Now here are the sides that are up:')
28       print(coin1.get_sideup())
29       print(coin2.get_sideup())
30       print(coin3.get_sideup())
31       print()
32
33   # Call the main function.
34   if __name__ == '__main__':
35       main()
```

Program Output

```
I have three coins with these sides up:
Heads
Heads
Heads

I am tossing all three coins ...

Now here are the sides that are up:
Tails
Tails
Heads
```

In lines 8 through 10, the following statements create three objects, each an instance of the `Coin` class:

```
coin1 = coin.Coin()
coin2 = coin.Coin()
coin3 = coin.Coin()
```

Figure 16-7 illustrates how the `coin1`, `coin2`, and `coin3` variables reference the three objects after these statements execute. Notice each object has its own `__sideup` attribute. Lines 14 through 16 display the values returned from each object's `get_sideup` method.

Figure 16-7   The `coin1`, `coin2`, and `coin3` variables reference three `Coin` objects

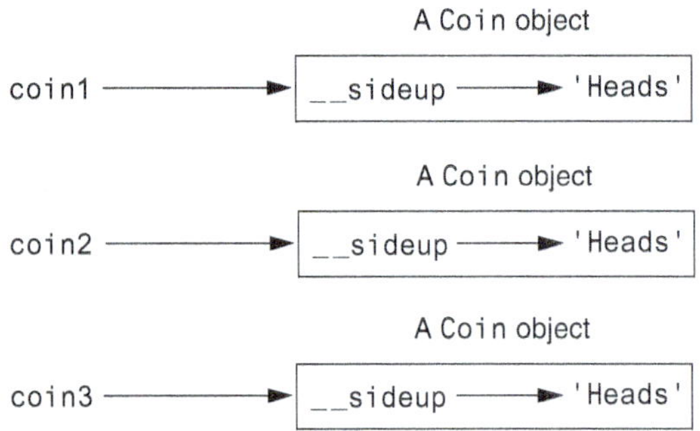

Then, the statements in lines 22 through 24 call each object's `toss` method:

```
coin1.toss()
coin2.toss()
coin3.toss()
```

Figure 16-8 shows how these statements changed each object's `__sideup` attribute in the program's sample run.

Figure 16-8   The objects after the `toss` method

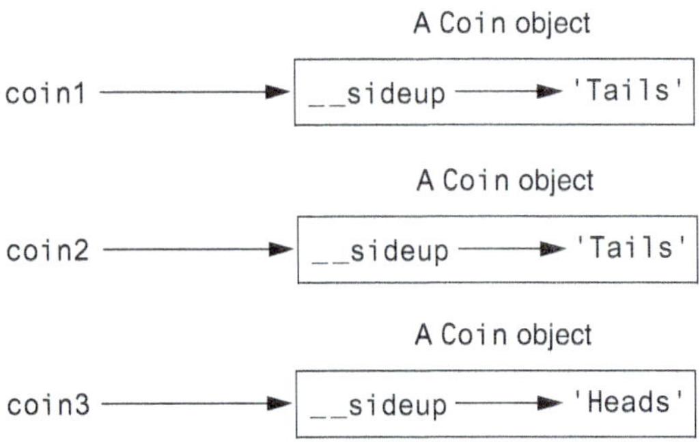

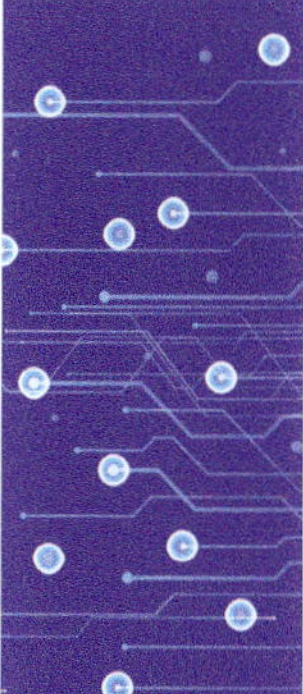

In the Spotlight:

Creating the **CellPhone** Class

Wireless Solutions, Inc. is a business that sells cell phones and wireless service. You are a programmer in the company's IT department, and your team is designing a program to manage all of the cell phones that are in inventory. You have been asked to design a class that represents a cell phone.

On Your Own: Working alone or with a partner, see if you can design and write a program to solve the problem. Use the skills you have learned in this chapter and in earlier chapters. When you have completed your work, continue reading to see a solution.

The data that should be kept as attributes in the class are as follows:

- The name of the phone's manufacturer will be assigned to the `__manufact` attribute.
- The phone's model number will be assigned to the `__model` attribute.
- The phone's retail price will be assigned to the `__retail_price` attribute.

The class will also have the following methods:

- An `__init__` method that accepts arguments for the manufacturer, model number, and retail price.
- A `set_manufact` method that accepts an argument for the manufacturer. This method will allow us to change the value of the `__manufact` attribute after the object has been created, if necessary.
- A `set_model` method that accepts an argument for the model. This method will allow us to change the value of the `__model` attribute after the object has been created, if necessary.
- A `set_retail_price` method that accepts an argument for the retail price. This method will allow us to change the value of the `__retail_price` attribute after the object has been created, if necessary.
- A `get_manufact` method that returns the phone's manufacturer.
- A `get_model` method that returns the phone's model number.
- A `get_retail_price` method that returns the phone's retail price.

Program 16-12 shows the class definition. The class is stored in a module named `cellphone`.

Program 16-12   **(cellphone.py)**

```
 1   # The CellPhone class holds data about a cell phone.
 2
 3   class CellPhone:
 4
 5       # The __init__ method initializes the attributes.
 6
 7       def __init__(self, manufact, model, price):
 8           self.__manufact = manufact
 9           self.__model = model
10           self.__retail_price = price
11
12       # The set_manufact method accepts an argument for
```

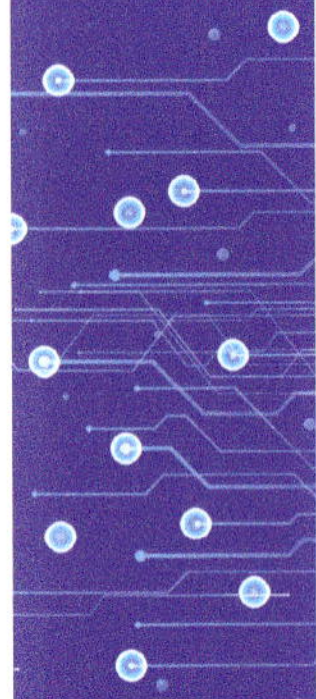

Program 16-12   *(continued)*

```
13        # the phone's manufacturer.
14
15        def set_manufact(self, manufact):
16            self.__manufact = manufact
17
18        # The set_model method accepts an argument for
19        # the phone's model number.
20
21        def set_model(self, model):
22            self.__model = model
23
24        # The set_retail_price method accepts an argument
25        # for the phone's retail price.
26
27        def set_retail_price(self, price):
28            self.__retail_price = price
29
30        # The get_manufact method returns the
31        # phone's manufacturer.
32
33        def get_manufact(self):
34            return self.__manufact
35
36        # The get_model method returns the
37        # phone's model number.
38
39        def get_model(self):
40            return self.__model
41
42        # The get_retail_price method returns the
43        # phone's retail price.
44
45        def get_retail_price(self):
46            return self.__retail_price
```

The CellPhone class will be imported into several programs that your team is developing. To test the class, you write the code in Program 16-13. This is a simple program that prompts the user for the phone's manufacturer, model number, and retail price. An instance of the CellPhone class is created, and the data is assigned to its attributes.

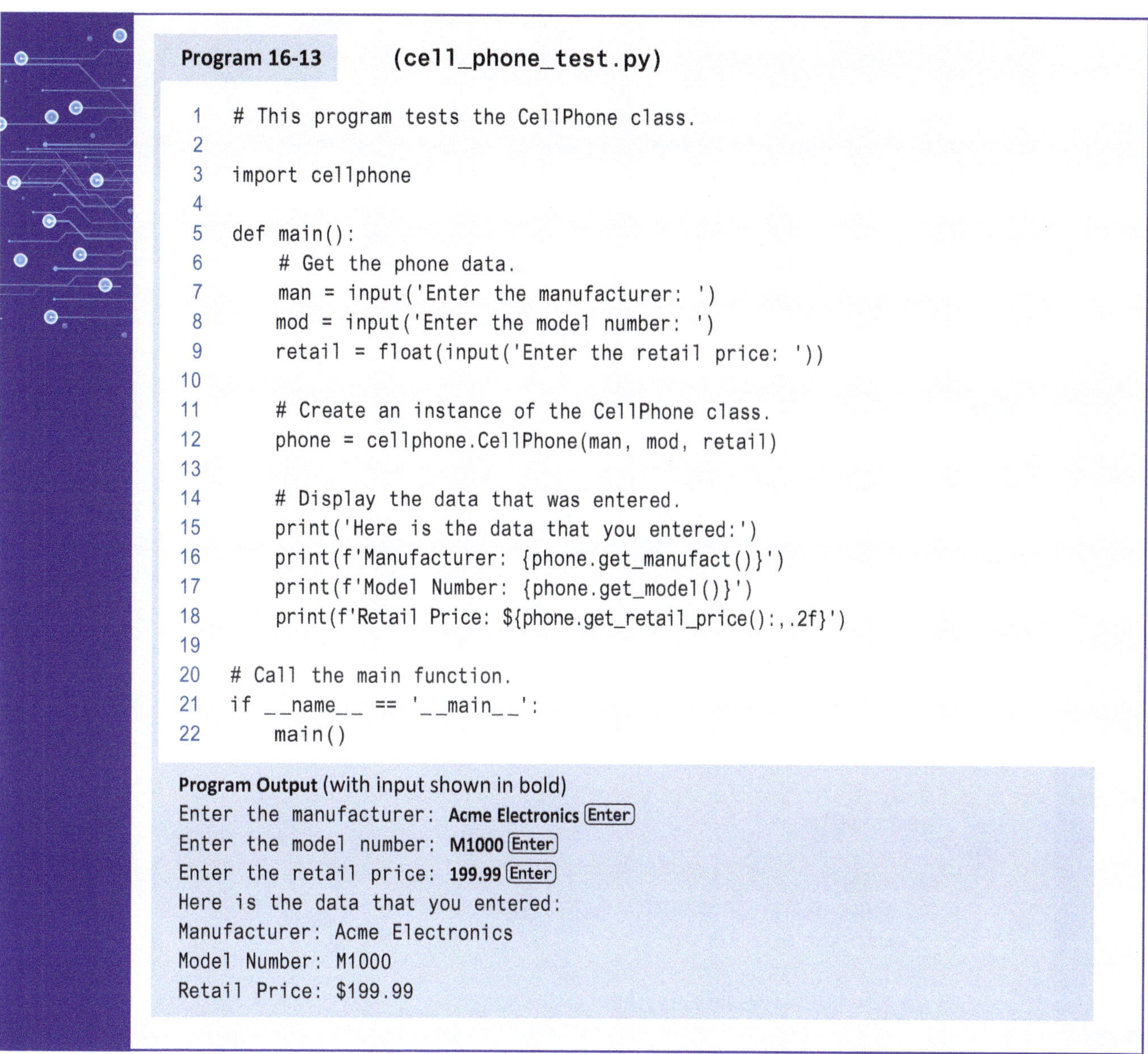

Program 16-13   (cell_phone_test.py)

```python
 1   # This program tests the CellPhone class.
 2
 3   import cellphone
 4
 5   def main():
 6       # Get the phone data.
 7       man = input('Enter the manufacturer: ')
 8       mod = input('Enter the model number: ')
 9       retail = float(input('Enter the retail price: '))
10
11       # Create an instance of the CellPhone class.
12       phone = cellphone.CellPhone(man, mod, retail)
13
14       # Display the data that was entered.
15       print('Here is the data that you entered:')
16       print(f'Manufacturer: {phone.get_manufact()}')
17       print(f'Model Number: {phone.get_model()}')
18       print(f'Retail Price: ${phone.get_retail_price():,.2f}')
19
20   # Call the main function.
21   if __name__ == '__main__':
22       main()
```

Program Output (with input shown in bold)
```
Enter the manufacturer: Acme Electronics [Enter]
Enter the model number: M1000 [Enter]
Enter the retail price: 199.99 [Enter]
Here is the data that you entered:
Manufacturer: Acme Electronics
Model Number: M1000
Retail Price: $199.99
```

Accessor and Mutator Methods

As mentioned earlier, it is a common practice to make all of a class's data attributes private and to provide public methods for accessing and changing those attributes. This ensures that the object owning those attributes is in control of all the changes being made to them.

A method that returns a value from a class's attribute but does not change it is known as an **accessor method**. Accessor methods provide a safe way for code outside the class to retrieve the values of attributes, without exposing the attributes in a way that they could be changed by the code outside the method. In the CellPhone class that you saw in Program 16-12 (in the previous *In the Spotlight* section), the get_manufact, get_model, and get_retail_price methods are accessor methods.

A method that stores a value in a data attribute or changes the value of a data attribute in some other way is called a **mutator method**. Mutator methods can control the way that a class's data attributes are modified. When code outside the class needs to change the value of an object's data attribute, it typically calls a mutator and passes the new value as an argument. The mutator can validate the value before assigning it to the data attribute. In Program 16-12, the `set_manufact`, `set_model`, and `set_retail_price` methods are mutator methods.

NOTE: Mutator methods are sometimes called "setters," and accessor methods are sometimes called "getters."

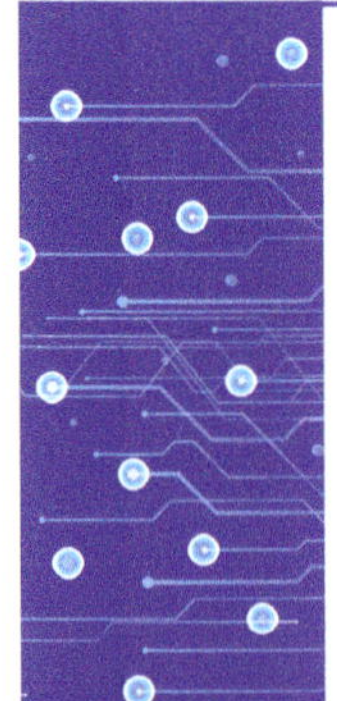

In the Spotlight:

Storing Objects in a List

The `CellPhone` class you created in the previous *In the Spotlight* section will be used in a variety of programs. Many of these programs will store `CellPhone` objects in lists. To test the ability to store `CellPhone` objects in a list, you write the code in Program 16-14. This program gets the data for five phones from the user, creates five `CellPhone` objects holding that data, and stores those objects in a list. It then iterates over the list, displaying the attributes of each object.

Program 16-14   (`cellphone.py`)

```
 1   # This program creates five CellPhone objects and
 2   # stores them in a list.
 3
 4   import cellphone
 5
 6   def main():
 7       # Get a list of CellPhone objects.
 8       phones = make_list()
 9
10       # Display the data in the list.
11       print('Here is the data you entered:')
12       display_list(phones)
13
14   # The make_list function gets data from the user
15   # for five phones. The function returns a list
16   # of CellPhone objects containing the data.
17
18   def make_list():
19       # Create an empty list.
20       phone_list = []
21
22       # Add five CellPhone objects to the list.
23       print('Enter data for five phones.')
```

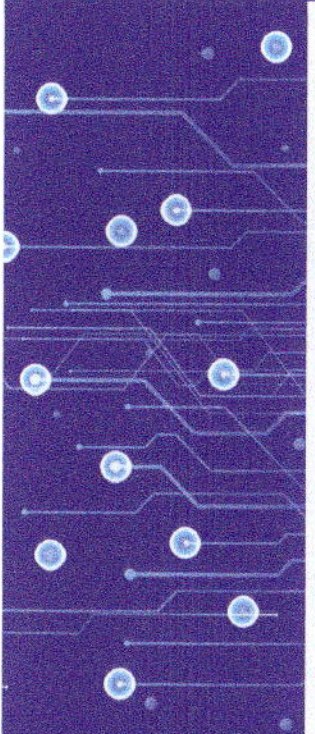

Program 16-14   *(continued)*

```
24        for count in range(1, 6):
25            # Get the phone data.
26            print('Phone number ' + str(count) + ':')
27            man = input('Enter the manufacturer: ')
28            mod = input('Enter the model number: ')
29            retail = float(input('Enter the retail price: '))
30            print()
31
32            # Create a new CellPhone object in memory and
33            # assign it to the phone variable.
34            phone = cellphone.CellPhone(man, mod, retail)
35
36            # Add the object to the list.
37            phone_list.append(phone)
38
39        # Return the list.
40        return phone_list
41
42    # The display_list function accepts a list containing
43    # CellPhone objects as an argument and displays the
44    # data stored in each object.
45
46    def display_list(phone_list):
47        for item in phone_list:
48            print(item.get_manufact())
49            print(item.get_model())
50            print(item.get_retail_price())
51            print()
52
53    # Call the main function.
54    if __name__ == '__main__':
55        main()
```

Program Output (with input shown in bold)
```
Enter data for five phones.

Phone number 1:
Enter the manufacturer: Acme Electronics [Enter]
Enter the model number: M1000 [Enter]
Enter the retail price: 199.99 [Enter]

Phone number 2:
Enter the manufacturer: Atlantic Communications [Enter]
Enter the model number: S2 [Enter]
Enter the retail price: 149.99 [Enter]
```

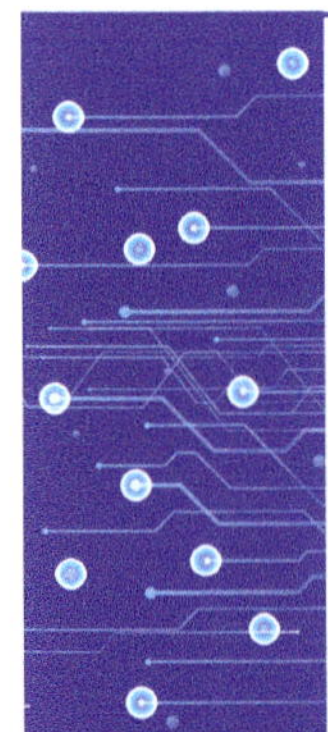

Program Output   *(continued)*

```
Phone number 3:
Enter the manufacturer: Wavelength Electronics (Enter)
Enter the model number: N477 (Enter)
Enter the retail price: 249.99 (Enter)

Phone number 4:
Enter the manufacturer: Edison Wireless (Enter)
Enter the model number: SLX88 (Enter)
Enter the retail price: 169.99 (Enter)

Phone number 5:
Enter the manufacturer: Sonic Systems (Enter)
Enter the model number: X99 (Enter)
Enter the retail price: 299.99 (Enter)

Here is the data you entered:
Acme Electronics
M1000
199.99

Atlantic Communications
S2
149.99

Wavelength Electronics
N477
249.99

Edison Wireless
SLX88
169.99

Sonic Systems
X99
299.99
```

The make_list function appears in lines 18 through 40. In line 20, an empty list named phone_list is created. The for loop, which begins in line 24, iterates five times. Each time the loop iterates, it gets the data for a cell phone from the user (lines 27 through 29), it creates an instance of the CellPhone class that is initialized with the data (line 34), and it appends the object to the phone_list list (line 37). Line 40 returns the list.

The display_list function in lines 46 through 51 accepts a list of CellPhone objects as an argument. The for loop that begins in line 47 iterates over the objects in the list and displays the values of each object's attributes.

Passing Objects as Arguments

When you are developing applications that work with objects, you often need to write functions and methods that accept objects as arguments. For example, the following code shows a function named show_coin_status that accepts a Coin object as an argument:

```
def show_coin_status(coin_obj):
    print('This side of the coin is up:', coin_obj.get_sideup())
```

The following code sample shows how we might create a Coin object, then pass it as an argument to the show_coin_status function:

```
my_coin = coin.Coin()
show_coin_status(my_coin)
```

When you pass a object as an argument, the thing that is passed into the parameter variable is a reference to the object. As a result, the function or method that receives the object as an argument has access to the actual object. For example, look at the following flip method:

```
def flip(coin_obj):
    coin_obj.toss()
```

This method accepts a Coin object as an argument, and it calls the object's toss method. Program 16-15 demonstrates the method.

Program 16-15   **(coin_argument.py)**

```
 1  # This program passes a Coin object as
 2  # an argument to a function.
 3  import coin
 4
 5  # main function
 6  def main():
 7      # Create a Coin object.
 8      my_coin = coin.Coin()
 9
10      # This will display 'Heads'.
11      print(my_coin.get_sideup())
12
13      # Pass the object to the flip function.
14      flip(my_coin)
15
16      # This might display 'Heads', or it might
17      # display 'Tails'.
18      print(my_coin.get_sideup())
19
20  # The flip function flips a coin.
21  def flip(coin_obj):
22      coin_obj.toss()
23
```

Program 16-15   *(continued)*

```
24   # Call the main function.
25   if __name__ == '__main__':
26       main()
```

Program Output
```
Heads
Tails
```

Program Output
```
Heads
Heads
```

Program Output
```
Heads
Tails
```

The statement in line 8 creates a Coin object, referenced by the variable my_coin. Line 11 displays the value of the my_coin object's __sideup attribute. Because the object's __init__ method set the __sideup attribute to 'Heads', we know that line 11 will display the string 'Heads'. Line 14 calls the flip function, passing the my_coin object as an argument. Inside the flip function, the my_coin object's toss method is called. Then, line 18 displays the value of the my_coin object's __sideup attribute again. This time, we cannot predict whether 'Heads' or 'Tails' will be displayed because the my_coin object's toss method has been called.

Pickling Your Own Objects

The pickle module provides functions for serializing objects. **Serializing** an object means converting it to a stream of bytes that can be saved to a file for later retrieval. The pickle module's dump function serializes (pickles) an object and writes it to a file, and the load function retrieves an object from a file and deserializes (unpickles) it.

You can pickle and unpickle objects of your own classes. Program 16-16 shows an example that pickles three CellPhone objects and saves them to a file. Program 16-17 retrieves those objects from the file and unpickles them.

Program 16-16   (pickle_cellphone.py)

```
1    # This program pickles CellPhone objects.
2    import pickle
3    import cellphone
4
5    # Constant for the filename.
6    FILENAME = 'cellphones.dat'
7
```

Program 16-16   *(continued)*

```python
 8   def main():
 9       # Initialize a variable to control the loop.
10       again = 'y'
11
12       # Open a file.
13       output_file = open(FILENAME, 'wb')
14
15       # Get data from the user.
16       while again.lower() == 'y':
17           # Get cell phone data.
18           man = input('Enter the manufacturer: ')
19           mod = input('Enter the model number: ')
20           retail = float(input('Enter the retail price: '))
21
22           # Create a CellPhone object.
23           phone = cellphone.CellPhone(man, mod, retail)
24
25           # Pickle the object and write it to the file.
26           pickle.dump(phone, output_file)
27
28           # Get more cell phone data?
29           again = input('Enter more phone data? (y/n): ')
30
31       # Close the file.
32       output_file.close()
33       print(f'The data was written to {FILENAME}.')
34
35   # Call the main function.
36   if __name__ == '__main__':
37       main()
```

Program Output (with input shown in bold)
```
Enter the manufacturer: ACME Electronics [Enter]
Enter the model number: M1000 [Enter]
Enter the retail price: 199.99 [Enter]
Enter more phone data? (y/n): y [Enter]
Enter the manufacturer: Sonic Systems [Enter]
Enter the model number: X99 [Enter]
Enter the retail price: 299.99 [Enter]
Enter more phone data? (y/n): n [Enter]
The data was written to cellphones.dat.
```

Program 16-17   (unpickle_cellphone.py)

```python
 1  # This program unpickles CellPhone objects.
 2  import pickle
 3  import cellphone
 4
 5  # Constant for the filename.
 6  FILENAME = 'cellphones.dat'
 7
 8  def main():
 9      end_of_file = False    # To indicate end of file
10
11      # Open the file.
12      input_file = open(FILENAME, 'rb')
13
14      # Read to the end of the file.
15      while not end_of_file:
16          try:
17              # Unpickle the next object.
18              phone = pickle.load(input_file)
19
20              # Display the cell phone data.
21              display_data(phone)
22          except EOFError:
23              # Set the flag to indicate the end
24              # of the file has been reached.
25              end_of_file = True
26
27      # Close the file.
28      input_file.close()
29
30  # The display_data function displays the data
31  # from the CellPhone object passed as an argument.
32  def display_data(phone):
33      print(f'Manufacturer: {phone.get_manufact()}')
34      print(f'Model Number: {phone.get_model()}')
35      print(f'Retail Price: ${phone.get_retail_price():,.2f}')
36      print()
37
38  # Call the main function.
39  if __name__ == '__main__':
40      main()
```

Program 16-17   (*continued*)

Program Output
```
Manufacturer: ACME Electronics
Model Number: M1000
Retail Price: $199.99

Manufacturer: Sonic Systems
Model Number: X99
Retail Price: $299.99
```

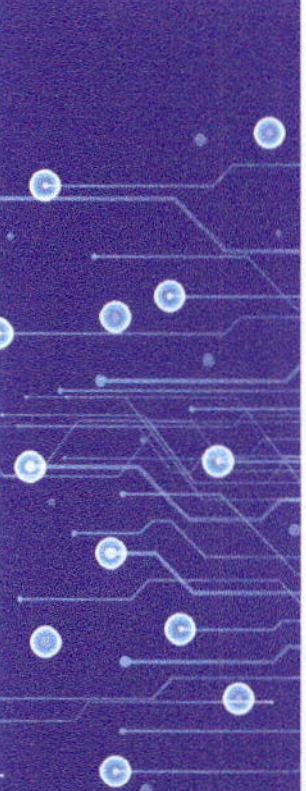

In the Spotlight:
Storing Objects in a Dictionary

Dictionaries are objects that store elements as key-value pairs. Each element in a dictionary has a key and a value. If you want to retrieve a specific value from the dictionary, you do so by specifying its key. Dictionaries are useful for storing objects that you create from your own classes.

Let's look at an example. Suppose you want to create a program that keeps contact information, such as names, phone numbers, and email addresses. You could start by writing a class such as the `Contact` class, shown in Program 16-18. An instance of the `Contact` class keeps the following data:

- A person's name is stored in the `__name` attribute.
- A person's phone number is stored in the `__phone` attribute.
- A person's email address is stored in the `__email` attribute.

The class has the following methods:

- An `__init__` method that accepts arguments for a person's name, phone number, and email address
- A `set_name` method that sets the `__name` attribute
- A `set_phone` method that sets the `__phone` attribute
- A `set_email` method that sets the `__email` attribute
- A `get_name` method that returns the `__name` attribute
- A `get_phone` method that returns the `__phone` attribute
- A `get_email` method that returns the `__email` attribute
- A `__str__` method that returns the object's state as a string

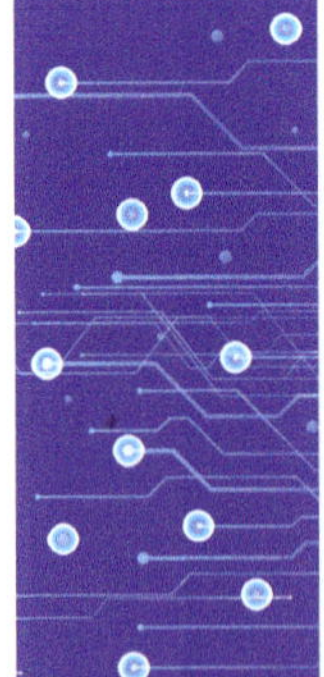

Program 16-18   (`contact.py`)

```python
 1   # The Contact class holds contact information.
 2
 3   class Contact:
 4       # The __init__ method initializes the attributes.
 5       def __init__(self, name, phone, email):
 6           self.__name = name
 7           self.__phone = phone
 8           self.__email = email
 9
10       # The set_name method sets the name attribute.
11       def set_name(self, name):
12           self.__name = name
13
14       # The set_phone method sets the phone attribute.
15       def set_phone(self, phone):
16           self.__phone = phone
17
18       # The set_email method sets the email attribute.
19       def set_email(self, email):
20           self.__email = email
21
22       # The get_name method returns the name attribute.
23       def get_name(self):
24           return self.__name
25
26       # The get_phone method returns the phone attribute.
27       def get_phone(self):
28           return self.__phone
29
30       # The get_email method returns the email attribute.
31       def get_email(self):
32           return self.__email
33
34       # The __str__ method returns the object's state
35       # as a string.
36       def __str__(self):
37           return f'Name: {self.__name}\n' + \
38                  f'Phone: {self.__phone}\n' + \
39                  f'Email: {self.__email}'
```

Next, you could write a program that keeps Contact objects in a dictionary. Each time the program creates a Contact object holding a specific person's data, that object would be stored as a value in the dictionary, using the person's name as the key. Then, any time you need to retrieve a specific person's data, you would use that person's name as a key to retrieve the Contact object from the dictionary.

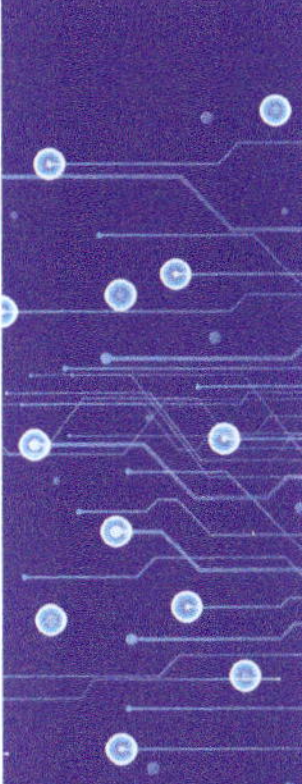

Program 16-19 shows an example. The program displays a menu that allows the user to perform any of the following operations:

- Look up a contact in the dictionary
- Add a new contact to the dictionary
- Change an existing contact in the dictionary
- Delete a contact from the dictionary
- Quit the program

Additionally, the program automatically pickles the dictionary and saves it to a file when the user quits the program. When the program starts, it automatically retrieves and unpickles the dictionary from the file. (Recall that pickling an object saves it to a file, and unpickling an object retrieves it from a file.) If the file does not exist, the program starts with an empty dictionary.

The program is divided into eight functions: `main`, `load_contacts`, `get_menu_choice`, `look_up`, `add`, `change`, `delete`, and `save_contacts`. Rather than presenting the entire program at once, let's first examine the beginning part, which includes the `import` statements, global constants, and the `main` function.

Program 16-19   (`contact_manager.py`: `main function`)

```
 1  # This program manages contacts.
 2  import contact
 3  import pickle
 4
 5  # Global constants for menu choices
 6  LOOK_UP = 1
 7  ADD = 2
 8  CHANGE = 3
 9  DELETE = 4
10  QUIT = 5
11
12  # Global constant for the filename
13  FILENAME = 'contacts.dat'
14
15  # main function
16  def main():
17      # Load the existing contact dictionary and
18      # assign it to mycontacts.
19      mycontacts = load_contacts()
20
21      # Initialize a variable for the user's choice.
22      choice = 0
23
24      # Process menu selections until the user
25      # wants to quit the program.
26      while choice != QUIT:
```

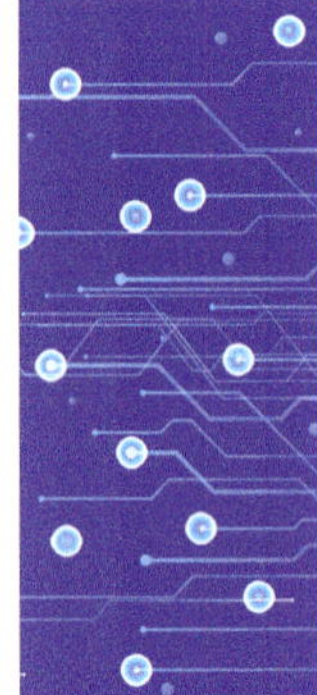

Program 16-19   *(continued)*

```
27              # Get the user's menu choice.
28              choice = get_menu_choice()
29
30              # Process the choice.
31              if choice == LOOK_UP:
32                  look_up(mycontacts)
33              elif choice == ADD:
34                  add(mycontacts)
35              elif choice == CHANGE:
36                  change(mycontacts)
37              elif choice == DELETE:
38                  delete(mycontacts)
39
40          # Save the mycontacts dictionary to a file.
41          save_contacts(mycontacts)
42
```

Line 2 imports the `contact` module, which contains the `Contact` class. Line 3 imports the `pickle` module. The global constants that are initialized in lines 6 through 10 are used to test the user's menu selection. The `FILENAME` constant that is initialized in line 13 holds the name of the file that will contain the pickled copy of the dictionary, which is `contacts.dat`.

Inside the `main` function, line 19 calls the `load_contacts` function. Keep in mind that if the program has been run before and names were added to the dictionary, those names have been saved to the `contacts.dat` file. The `load_contacts` function opens the file, gets the dictionary from it, and returns a reference to the dictionary. If the program has not been run before, the `contacts.dat` file does not exist. In that case, the `load_contacts` function creates an empty dictionary and returns a reference to it. So, after the statement in line 19 executes, the `mycontacts` variable references a dictionary. If the program has been run before, `mycontacts` references a dictionary containing `Contact` objects. If this is the first time the program has run, `mycontacts` references an empty dictionary.

Line 22 initializes the `choice` variable with the value 0. This variable will hold the user's menu selection.

The `while` loop that begins in line 26 repeats until the user chooses to quit the program. Inside the loop, line 28 calls the `get_menu_choice` function. The `get_menu_choice` function displays the following menu:

1. Look up a contact
2. Add a new contact
3. Change an existing contact
4. Delete a contact
5. Quit the program

The user's selection is returned from the `get_menu_choice` function and is assigned to the `choice` variable.

The `if-elif` statement in lines 31 through 38 processes the user's menu choice. If the user selects item 1, line 32 calls the `look_up` function. If the user selects item 2, line 34 calls the add function. If the user selects item 3, line 36 calls the `change` function. If the user selects item 4, line 38 calls the `delete` function.

When the user selects item 5 from the menu, the `while` loop stops repeating and the statement in line 41 executes. This statement calls the `save_contacts` function, passing `mycontacts` as an argument. The `save_contacts` function saves the `mycontacts` dictionary to the `contacts.dat` file.

The `load_contacts` function is next.

Program 16-19   (`contact_manager.py`: `load_contacts` function)

```
43   def load_contacts():
44       try:
45           # Open the contacts.dat file.
46           input_file = open(FILENAME, 'rb')
47
48           # Unpickle the dictionary.
49           contact_dct = pickle.load(input_file)
50
51           # Close the phone_inventory.dat file.
52           input_file.close()
53       except IOError:
54           # Could not open the file, so create
55           # an empty dictionary.
56           contact_dct = {}
57
58       # Return the dictionary.
59       return contact_dct
60
```

Inside the try suite, line 46 attempts to open the `contacts.dat` file. If the file is successfully opened, line 49 loads the dictionary object from it, unpickles it, and assigns it to the `contact_dct` variable. Line 52 closes the file.

If the `contacts.dat` file does not exist (this will be the case the first time the program runs), the statement in line 46 raises an `IOError` exception. That causes the program to jump to the except clause in line 53. Then, the statement in line 56 creates an empty dictionary and assigns it to the `contact_dct` variable.

The statement in line 59 returns the `contact_dct` variable.

The `get_menu_choice` function is next.

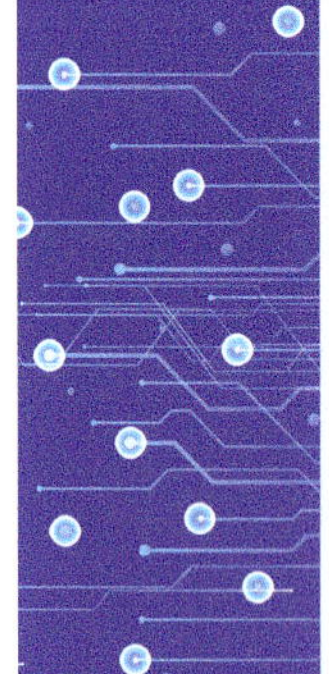

Program 16-19 (`contact_manager.py`: `get_menu_choice` function)

```
61  # The get_menu_choice function displays the menu
62  # and gets a validated choice from the user.
63  def get_menu_choice():
64      print()
65      print('Menu')
66      print('--------------------------')
67      print('1. Look up a contact')
68      print('2. Add a new contact')
69      print('3. Change an existing contact')
70      print('4. Delete a contact')
71      print('5. Quit the program')
72      print()
73
74      # Get the user's choice.
75      choice = int(input('Enter your choice: '))
76
77      # Validate the choice.
78      while choice < LOOK_UP or choice > QUIT:
79          choice = int(input('Enter a valid choice: '))
80
81      # return the user's choice.
82      return choice
83
```

The statements in lines 64 through 72 display the menu on the screen. Line 75 prompts the user to enter his or her choice. The input is converted to an `int` and assigned to the `choice` variable. The `while` loop in lines 78 through 79 validates the user's input and, if necessary, prompts the user to reenter his or her choice. Once a valid choice is entered, it is returned from the function in line 82.

The `look_up` function is next.

Program 16-19 (`contact_manager.py`: `look_up` function)

```
84  # The look_up function looks up an item in the
85  # specified dictionary.
86  def look_up(mycontacts):
87      # Get a name to look up.
88      name = input('Enter a name: ')
89
90      # Look it up in the dictionary.
91      print(mycontacts.get(name, 'That name is not found.'))
92
```

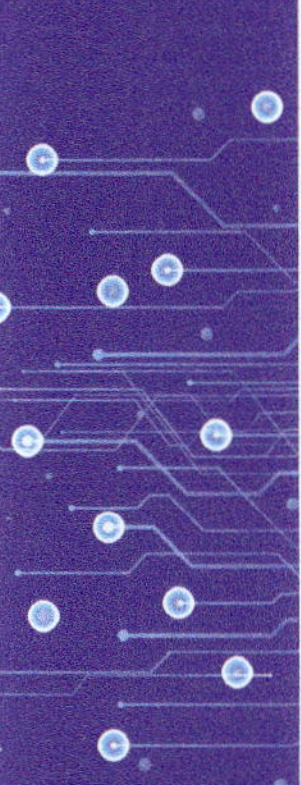

The purpose of the `look_up` function is to allow the user to look up a specified contact. It accepts the `mycontacts` dictionary as an argument. Line 88 prompts the user to enter a name, and line 91 passes that name as an argument to the dictionary's `get` function. One of the following actions will happen as a result of line 91:

- If the specified name is found as a key in the dictionary, the `get` method returns a reference to the `Contact` object that is associated with that name. The `Contact` object is then passed as an argument to the `print` function. The `print` function displays the string that is returned from the `Contact` object's `__str__` method.

- If the specified name is not found as a key in the dictionary, the `get` method returns the string `'That name is not found.'`, which is displayed by the `print` function.

The add function is next.

Program 16-19   (`contact_manager.py`: add function)

```
 93   # The add function adds a new entry into the
 94   # specified dictionary.
 95   def add(mycontacts):
 96       # Get the contact info.
 97       name = input('Name: ')
 98       phone = input('Phone: ')
 99       email = input('Email: ')
100
101       # Create a Contact object named entry.
102       entry = contact.Contact(name, phone, email)
103
104       # If the name does not exist in the dictionary,
105       # add it as a key with the entry object as the
106       # associated value.
107       if name not in mycontacts:
108           mycontacts[name] = entry
109           print('The entry has been added.')
110       else:
111           print('That name already exists.')
112
```

The purpose of the `add` function is to allow the user to add a new contact to the dictionary. It accepts the `mycontacts` dictionary as an argument. Lines 97 through 99 prompt the user to enter a name, a phone number, and an email address. Line 102 creates a new `Contact` object, initialized with the data entered by the user.

The `if` statement in line 107 determines whether the name is already in the dictionary. If not, line 108 adds the newly created `Contact` object to the dictionary, and line 109 prints a message indicating that the new data is added. Otherwise, a message indicating that the entry already exists is printed in line 111.

The change function is next.

Program 16-19   (`contact_manager.py`: change function)

```python
113  # The change function changes an existing
114  # entry in the specified dictionary.
115  def change(mycontacts):
116      # Get a name to look up.
117      name = input('Enter a name: ')
118
119      if name in mycontacts:
120          # Get a new phone number.
121          phone = input('Enter the new phone number: ')
122
123          # Get a new email address.
124          email = input('Enter the new email address: ')
125
126          # Create a contact object named entry.
127          entry = contact.Contact(name, phone, email)
128
129          # Update the entry.
130          mycontacts[name] = entry
131          print('Information updated.')
132      else:
133          print('That name is not found.')
134
```

The purpose of the change function is to allow the user to change an existing contact in the dictionary. It accepts the `mycontacts` dictionary as an argument. Line 117 gets a name from the user. The `if` statement in line 119 determines whether the name is in the dictionary. If so, line 121 gets the new phone number, and line 124 gets the new email address. Line 127 creates a new `Contact` object initialized with the existing name and the new phone number and email address. Line 130 stores the new `Contact` object in the dictionary, using the existing name as the key.

If the specified name is not in the dictionary, line 133 prints a message indicating so.

The `delete` function is next.

Program 16-19   (`contact_manager.py`: delete function)

```python
135  # The delete function deletes an entry from the
136  # specified dictionary.
137  def delete(mycontacts):
138      # Get a name to look up.
139      name = input('Enter a name: ')
140
141      # If the name is found, delete the entry.
```

Program 16-19   *(continued)*

```
142        if name in mycontacts:
143            del mycontacts[name]
144            print('Entry deleted.')
145        else:
146            print('That name is not found.')
147
```

The purpose of the `delete` function is to allow the user to delete an existing contact from the dictionary. It accepts the `mycontacts` dictionary as an argument. Line 139 gets a name from the user. The `if` statement in line 142 determines whether the name is in the dictionary. If so, line 143 deletes it, and line 144 prints a message indicating that the entry was deleted. If the name is not in the dictionary, line 146 prints a message indicating so.

The `save_contacts` function is next.

Program 16-19   (`contact_manager.py`: `save_contacts` function)

```
148  # The save_contacts funtion pickles the specified
149  # object and saves it to the contacts file.
150  def save_contacts(mycontacts):
151      # Open the file for writing.
152      output_file = open(FILENAME, 'wb')
153
154      # Pickle the dictionary and save it.
155      pickle.dump(mycontacts, output_file)
156
157      # Close the file.
158      output_file.close()
159
160  # Call the main function.
161  if __name__ == '__main__':
162      main()
```

The `save_contacts` function is called just before the program stops running. It accepts the `mycontacts` dictionary as an argument. Line 152 opens the `contacts.dat` file for writing. Line 155 pickles the `mycontacts` dictionary and saves it to the file. Line 158 closes the file.

The following program output shows two sessions with the program. The sample output does not demonstrate everything the program can do, but it does demonstrate how contacts are saved when the program ends and then loaded when the program runs again.

Program Output (with input shown in bold)
```
Menu
---------------------------
1. Look up a contact
2. Add a new contact
3. Change an existing contact
4. Delete a contact
5. Quit the program

Enter your choice: 2 [Enter]
Name: Matt Goldstein [Enter]
Phone: 617-555-1234 [Enter]
Email: matt@fakecompany.com [Enter]
The entry has been added.

Menu
---------------------------
1. Look up a contact
2. Add a new contact
3. Change an existing contact
4. Delete a contact
5. Quit the program

Enter your choice: 2 [Enter]
Name: Jorge Ruiz [Enter]
Phone: 919-555-1212 [Enter]
Email: jorge@myschool.edu [Enter]
The entry has been added.

Menu
---------------------------
1. Look up a contact
2. Add a new contact
3. Change an existing contact
4. Delete a contact
5. Quit the program

Enter your choice: 5 [Enter]

Menu
---------------------------
1. Look up a contact
2. Add a new contact
3. Change an existing contact
4. Delete a contact
5. Quit the program

Enter your choice: 1 [Enter]
```

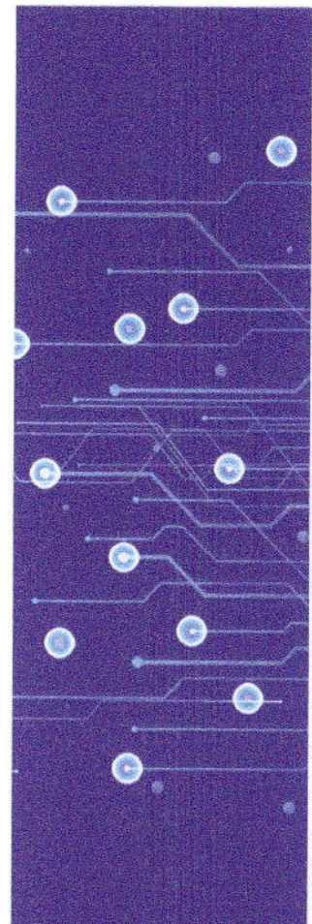

Program Output *(continued)*
```
Enter a name: Matt Goldstein Enter
Name: Matt Goldstein
Phone: 617-555-1234
Email: matt@fakecompany.com

Menu
--------------------------
1. Look up a contact
2. Add a new contact
3. Change an existing contact
4. Delete a contact
5. Quit the program

Enter your choice: 1 Enter
Enter a name: Jorge Ruiz Enter
Name: Jorge Ruiz
Phone: 919-555-1212
Email: jorge@myschool.edu

Menu
--------------------------
1. Look up a contact
2. Add a new contact
3. Change an existing contact
4. Delete a contact
5. Quit the program

Enter your choice: 5 Enter
```

 **Checkpoint**

16.12 What is an instance attribute?

16.13 A program creates 10 instances of the Coin class. How many `__sideup` attributes exist in memory?

16.14 What is an accessor method? What is a mutator method?

16.4 Techniques for Designing Classes

KEY POINT There are established techniques and processes that software developers use to design classes for object-oriented programming.

The Unified Modeling Language

When designing a class, it is often helpful to draw a **Unified Modeling Language (UML)** diagram. A UML diagram provides a set of standard diagrams for graphically depicting object-oriented systems. Figure 16-9 shows the general layout of a UML diagram for a class. Notice the diagram is a box that is divided into three sections. The top section is where you write the name of the class. The middle section holds a list of the class's data attributes. The bottom section holds a list of the class's methods.

Figure 16-9 General layout of a UML diagram for a class

Following this layout, Figure 16-10 and Figure 16-11 show UML diagrams for the `Coin` class and the `CellPhone` class that you saw previously in this chapter. Notice we did not show the `self` parameter in any of the methods, since it is understood that the `self` parameter is required.

Figure 16-10 UML diagram for the `Coin` class

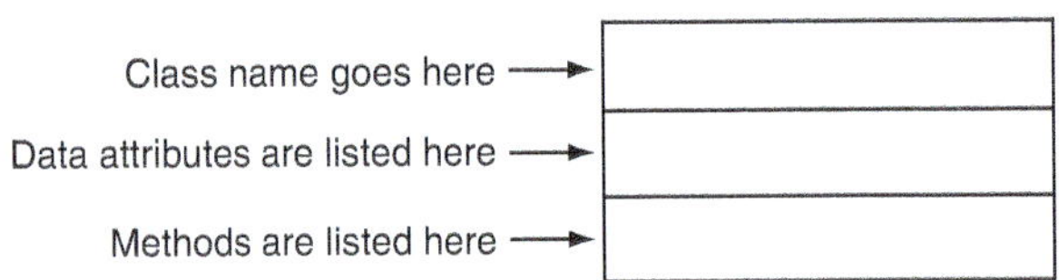

Figure 16-11 UML diagram for the `CellPhone` class

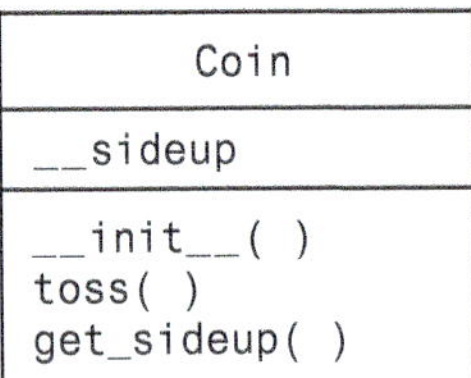

Finding the Classes in a Problem

When developing an object-oriented program, one of your first tasks is to identify the classes that you will need to create. Typically, your goal is to identify the different types of real-world objects that are present in the problem, then create classes for those types of objects within your application.

Over the years, software professionals have developed numerous techniques for finding the classes in a given problem. One simple and popular technique involves the following steps:

1. Get a written description of the problem domain.
2. Identify all the nouns (including pronouns and noun phrases) in the description. Each of these is a potential class.
3. Refine the list to include only the classes that are relevant to the problem.

Let's take a closer look at each of these steps.

Writing a Description of the Problem Domain

The **problem domain** is the set of real-world objects, parties, and major events related to the problem. If you adequately understand the nature of the problem you are trying to solve, you can write a description of the problem domain yourself. If you do not thoroughly understand the nature of the problem, you should have an expert write the description for you.

For example, suppose we are writing a program that the manager of Joe's Automotive Shop will use to print service quotes for customers. Here is a description that an expert, perhaps Joe himself, might have written:

> Joe's Automotive Shop services foreign cars and specializes in servicing cars made by Mercedes, Porsche, and BMW. When a customer brings a car to the shop, the manager gets the customer's name, address, and telephone number. The manager then determines the make, model, and year of the car and gives the customer a service quote. The service quote shows the estimated parts charges, estimated labor charges, sales tax, and total estimated charges.

The problem domain description should include any of the following:

- Physical objects such as vehicles, machines, or products
- Any role played by a person, such as manager, employee, customer, teacher, student, etc.
- The results of a business event, such as a customer order, or in this case, a service quote
- Recordkeeping items, such as customer histories and payroll records

Identify All of the Nouns

The next step is to identify all of the nouns and noun phrases. (If the description contains pronouns, include them too.) Here's another look at the previous problem domain description.

This time, the nouns and noun phrases appear in bold.

> **Joe's Automotive Shop** services **foreign cars** and specializes in servicing **cars** made by **Mercedes, Porsche,** and **BMW**. When a **customer** brings a **car** to the **shop,** the **manager** gets the **customer's name, address,** and **telephone number.** The **manager** then determines the **make, model,** and **year** of the **car** and gives the **customer** a **service quote.** The **service quote** shows the **estimated parts charges, estimated labor charges, sales tax,** and **total estimated charges**.

Notice some of the nouns are repeated. The following list shows all of the nouns without duplicating any of them:

address
BMW
car
cars
customer
estimated labor charges
estimated parts charges
foreign cars
Joe's Automotive Shop
make
manager
Mercedes
model
name
Porsche
sales tax
service quote
shop
telephone number
total estimated charges
year

Refining the List of Nouns

The nouns that appear in the problem description are merely candidates to become classes. It might not be necessary to make classes for them all. The next step is to refine the list to include only the classes that are necessary to solve the particular problem at hand. We will look at the common reasons that a noun can be eliminated from the list of potential classes.

1. Some of the nouns really mean the same thing.

In this example, the following sets of nouns refer to the same thing:

- **car, cars**, and **foreign cars**
  These all refer to the general concept of a car.

- **Joe's Automotive Shop** and **shop**
  Both of these refer to the company "Joe's Automotive Shop."

We can settle on a single class for each of these. In this example, we will arbitrarily eliminate **cars** and **foreign cars** from the list and use the word **car**. Likewise, we will eliminate **Joe's Automotive Shop** from the list and use the word **shop**. The updated list of potential classes is:

address	BMW
car	~~cars~~
customer	estimated labor charges
estimated parts charges	~~foreign cars~~
~~Joe's Automotive Shop~~	make
manager	Mercedes
model	name
Porsche	sales tax
service quote	shop
telephone number	total estimated charges
year	

2. Some nouns might represent items that we do not need to be concerned with in order to solve the problem.

A quick review of the problem description reminds us of what our application should do: print a service quote. In this example, we can eliminate two unnecessary classes from the list:

- We can cross **shop** off the list because our application only needs to be concerned with individual service quotes. It doesn't need to work with or determine any company-wide information. If the problem description asked us to keep a total of all the service quotes, then it would make sense to have a class for the shop.

- We will not need a class for the **manager** because the problem statement does not direct us to process any information about the manager. If there were multiple shop managers and the problem description had asked us to record which manager generated each service quote, then it would make sense to have a class for the manager.

The updated list of potential classes at this point is:

address	BMW
car	~~cars~~
customer	estimated labor charges
estimated parts charges	~~foreign cars~~
~~Joe's Automotive Shop~~	make
~~manager~~	Mercedes
model	name
Porsche	sales tax
service quote	shop
telephone number	total estimated charges
year	

3. Some of the nouns might represent objects, not classes.

We can eliminate **Mercedes**, **Porsche**, and **BMW** as classes because, in this example, they all represent specific cars and can be considered instances of a **car** class. At this point, the updated list of potential classes is:

address	~~BMW~~
car	~~cars~~
customer	estimated labor charges
estimated parts charges	~~foreign cars~~
~~Joe's Automotive Shop~~	~~manager~~
make	~~Mercedes~~
model	name
~~Porsche~~	sales tax
service quote	~~shop~~
telephone number	total estimated charges
year	

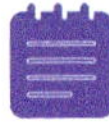

NOTE: Some object-oriented designers take note of whether a noun is plural or singular. Sometimes a plural noun will indicate a class, and a singular noun will indicate an object.

4. Some of the nouns might represent simple values that can be assigned to a variable and do not require a class.

Remember, a class contains data attributes and methods. Data attributes are related items that are stored in an object of the class and define the object's state. Methods are actions or behaviors that can be performed by an object of the class. If a noun represents a type of item that would not have any identifiable data attributes or methods, then it can probably be eliminated from the list. To help determine whether a noun represents an item that would have data attributes and methods, ask the following questions about it:

- Would you use a group of related values to represent the item's state?
- Are there any obvious actions to be performed by the item?

If the answers to both of these questions are no, then the noun probably represents a value that can be stored in a simple variable. If we apply this test to each of the nouns that remain in our list, we can conclude that the following are probably not classes: **address, estimated labor charges, estimated parts charges, make, model, name, sales tax, telephone number, total estimated charges**, and **year**. These are all simple string or numeric values that can be stored in variables. Here is the updated list of potential classes:

~~Address~~	~~BMW~~
car	~~cars~~
customer	~~estimated labor charges~~
~~estimated parts charges~~	~~foreign cars~~
~~Joe's Automotive Shop~~	~~make~~
~~manager~~	~~Mercedes~~
~~model~~	~~name~~
~~Porsche~~	~~sales tax~~
service quote	~~shop~~
~~telephone number~~	~~total estimated charges~~
~~year~~	

As you can see from the list, we have eliminated everything except **car**, **customer**, and **service quote**. This means that in our application, we will need classes to represent cars, customers, and service quotes. Ultimately, we will write a `Car` class, a `Customer` class, and a `ServiceQuote` class.

Identifying a Class's Responsibilities

Once the classes have been identified, the next task is to identify each class's responsibilities. A class's **responsibilities** are:

- the things that the class is responsible for knowing.
- the actions that the class is responsible for doing.

When you have identified the things that a class is responsible for knowing, then you have identified the class's data attributes. Likewise, when you have identified the actions that a class is responsible for doing, you have identified its methods.

It is often helpful to ask the questions "In the context of this problem, what must the class know? What must the class do?" The first place to look for the answers is in the description of the problem domain. Many of the things that a class must know and do will be mentioned. Some class responsibilities, however, might not be directly mentioned in the problem domain, so further consideration is often required. Let's apply this methodology to the classes we previously identified from our problem domain.

The Customer Class

In the context of our problem domain, what must the `Customer` class know? The description directly mentions the following items, which are all data attributes of a customer:

- the customer's name
- the customer's address
- the customer's telephone number

These are all values that can be represented as strings and stored as data attributes. The `Customer` class can potentially know many other things. One potential mistake is identifying too many things that an object is responsible for knowing. In some applications, a `Customer` class might know the customer's email address. This particular problem domain does not mention that the customer's email address is used for any purpose, so we should not include it as a responsibility.

Now, let's identify the class's methods. In the context of our problem domain, what must the `Customer` class do? The only obvious actions are:

- initialize an object of the `Customer` class.
- set and return the customer's name.
- set and return the customer's address.
- set and return the customer's telephone number.

From this list, we can see that the `Customer` class will have an `__init__` method, as well as accessors and mutators for the data attributes. Figure 16-12 shows a UML diagram for the `Customer` class. The Python code for the class is shown in Program 16-20.

Figure 16-12   UML diagram for the `Customer` class

```
                   Customer
      __name
      __address
      __phone
      __init__(name, address,
                      phone)
      set_name(name)
      set_address(address)
      set_phone(phone)
      get_name()
      get_address()
      get_phone()
```

Program 16-20   (`customer.py`)

```python
 1  # Customer class
 2  class Customer:
 3      def __init__(self, name, address, phone):
 4          self.__name = name
 5          self.__address = address
 6          self.__phone = phone
 7
 8      def set_name(self, name):
 9          self.__name = name
10
11      def set_address(self, address):
12          self.__address = address
13
14      def set_phone(self, phone):
15          self.__phone = phone
```

Program 16-20	*(continued)*

```
16
17        def get_name(self):
18            return self.__name
19
20        def get_address(self):
21            return self.__address
22
23        def get_phone(self):
24            return self.__phone
```

The Car Class

In the context of our problem domain, what must an object of the Car class know? The following items are all data attributes of a car and are mentioned in the problem domain:

- the car's make
- the car's model
- the car's year

Now let's identify the class's methods. In the context of our problem domain, what must the Car class do? Once again, the only obvious actions are the standard set of methods that we will find in most classes (an __init__ method, accessors, and mutators). Specifically, the actions are:

- initialize an object of the Car class.
- set and get the car's make.
- set and get the car's model.
- set and get the car's year.

Figure 16-13 shows a UML diagram for the Car class at this point. The Python code for the class is shown in Program 16-21.

Figure 16-13   UML diagram for the Car class

```
+---------------------------+
|            Car            |
+---------------------------+
| __make                    |
| __model                   |
| __year                    |
+---------------------------+
| __init__(make, model,     |
|              year)        |
| set_make(make)            |
| set_model(make)           |
| set_year(y)               |
| get_make( )               |
| get_model( )              |
| get_year( )               |
+---------------------------+
```

Program 16-21   (car.py)

```python
 1   # Car class
 2   class Car:
 3       def __init__(self, make, model, year):
 4           self.__make = make
 5           self.__model = model
 6           self.__year = year
 7
 8       def set_make(self, make):
 9           self.__make = make
10
11       def set_model(self, model):
12           self.__model = model
13
14       def set_year(self, year):
15           self.__year = year
16
17       def get_make(self):
18           return self.__make
19
20       def get_model(self):
21           return self.__model
22
23       def get_year(self):
24           return self.__year
```

The ServiceQuote Class

In the context of our problem domain, what must an object of the ServiceQuote class know? The problem domain mentions the following items:

- the estimated parts charges
- the estimated labor charges
- the sales tax
- the total estimated charges

For this class, we need an __init__ method and the accessors and mutators for the estimated parts charges and estimated labor charges attributes. In addition, the class will need methods that calculate and return the sales tax and the total estimated charges. Figure 16-14 shows a UML diagram for the ServiceQuote class. Program 16-22 shows an example of the class in Python code.

Figure 16-14   UML diagram for the `ServiceQuote` class

```
           ServiceQuote
 __parts_charges
 __labor_charges
 __init__(pcharge, lcharge)
 set_parts_charges(pcharge)
 set_labor_charges(lcharge)
 get_parts_charges( )
 get_labor_charges( )
 get_sales_tax( )
 get_total_charges( )
```

Program 16-22   (`servicequote.py`)

```python
 1   # Constant for the sales tax rate
 2   TAX_RATE = 0.05
 3
 4   # ServiceQuote class
 5   class ServiceQuote:
 6       def __init__(self, pcharge, lcharge):
 7           self.__parts_charges = pcharge
 8           self.__labor_charges = lcharge
 9
10       def set_parts_charges(self, pcharge):
11           self.__parts_charges = pcharge
12
13       def set_labor_charges(self, lcharge):
14           self.__labor_charges = lcharge
15
16       def get_parts_charges(self):
17           return self.__parts_charges
18
19       def get_labor_charges(self):
20           return self.__labor_charges
21
22       def get_sales_tax(self):
23           return __parts_charges * TAX_RATE
24
25       def get_total_charges(self):
26           return __parts_charges + __labor_charges + \
27                   (__parts_charges * TAX_RATE)
```

This Is Only the Beginning

You should look at the process that we have discussed in this section merely as a starting point. It's important to realize that designing an object-oriented application is an iterative process. It may take you several attempts to identify all of the classes that you will need and determine all of their responsibilities.

 **Checkpoint**

16.15 The typical UML diagram for a class has three sections. What appears in these three sections?

16.16 What is a problem domain?

16.17 When designing an object-oriented application, who should write a description of the problem domain?

16.18 How do you identify the potential classes in a problem domain description?

16.19 What are a class's responsibilities?

16.20 What two questions should you ask to determine a class's responsibilities?

16.21 Will all of a class's actions always be directly mentioned in the problem domain description?

Chapter Review

Multiple Choice

1. The _______________ programming practice is centered on creating functions that are separate from the data that they work on.
   - a. modular
   - b. procedural
   - c. functional
   - d. object-oriented

2. The _______________ programming practice is centered on creating objects.
   - a. object-centric
   - b. objective
   - c. procedural
   - d. object-oriented

3. A(n) _______________ is a component of a class that references data.
   - a. method
   - b. instance
   - c. data attribute
   - d. module

4. An object is a(n) _______________.
   - a. blueprint
   - b. cookie cutter
   - c. variable
   - d. instance

5. By doing this, you can hide a class's attribute from code outside the class.
   - a. avoid using the `self` parameter to create the attribute
   - b. begin the attribute's name with two underscores
   - c. begin the name of the attribute with `private__`
   - d. begin the name of the attribute with the @ symbol

6. A(n) _______________ method gets the value of a data attribute but does not change it.
   - a. retriever
   - b. constructor
   - c. mutator
   - d. accessor

7. A(n) _______________ method stores a value in a data attribute or changes its value in some other way.
   - a. modifier
   - b. constructor
   - c. mutator
   - d. accessor

8. The ________________ method is automatically called when an object is created.
   a. `__init__`
   b. `init`
   c. `__str__`
   d. `__object__`

9. If a class has a method named `__str__`, which of these is a way to call the method?
   a. you call it like any other method: *object.*`__str__()`
   b. by passing an instance of the class to the built-in `str` function
   c. the method is automatically called when the object is created
   d. by passing an instance of the class to the built-in `state` function

10. A set of standard diagrams for graphically depicting object-oriented systems is provided by ________________.
    a. the Unified Modeling Language
    b. flowcharts
    c. pseudocode
    d. the Object Hierarchy System

11. In one approach to identifying the classes in a problem, the programmer identifies the ________________ in a description of the problem domain.
    a. verbs
    b. adjectives
    c. adverbs
    d. nouns

12. In one approach to identifying a class's data attributes and methods, the programmer identifies the class's ________________.
    a. responsibilities
    b. name
    c. synonyms
    d. nouns

True or False

1. The practice of procedural programming is centered on the creation of objects.

2. Object reusability has been a factor in the increased use of object-oriented programming.

3. It is a common practice in object-oriented programming to make all of a class's data attributes accessible to statements outside the class.

4. A class method does not have to have a `self` parameter.

5. Starting an attribute name with two underscores will hide the attribute from code outside the class.

6. You cannot directly call the `__str__` method.

7. One way to find the classes needed for an object-oriented program is to identify all of the verbs in a description of the problem domain.

Short Answer

1. What is encapsulation?

2. Analyze and explain the concept of a variable as it relates to objects.

3. What is the difference between a class and an instance of a class?

4. The following statement calls an object's method. What is the name of the method? What is the name of the variable that references the object?

```
wallet.get_dollar()
```

5. When the `__init__` method executes, what does the `self` parameter reference?

6. In a Python class, how do you hide an attribute from code outside the class?

7. How do you call the `__str__` method?

Algorithm Workbench

1. Suppose `my_car` is the name of a variable that references an object, and go is the name of a method. Write a statement that uses the `my_car` variable to call the go method. (You do not have to pass any arguments to the go method.)

2. Write a class definition named Book. The Book class should have data attributes for a book's title, the author's name, and the publisher's name. The class should also have the following:

   a. An `__init__` method for the class. The method should accept an argument for each of the data attributes.
   b. Accessor and mutator methods for each data attribute.
   c. An `__str__` method that returns a string indicating the state of the object.

3. Look at the following description of a problem domain:

   > The bank offers the following types of accounts to its customers: savings accounts, checking accounts, and money market accounts. Customers are allowed to deposit money into an account (thereby increasing its balance), withdraw money from an account (thereby decreasing its balance), and earn interest on the account. Each account has an interest rate.

   Assume that you are writing a program that will calculate the amount of interest earned for a bank account.

   a. Identify the potential classes in this problem domain.
   b. Refine the list to include only the necessary class or classes for this problem.
   c. Identify the responsibilities of the class or classes.

Programming Exercises

1. Pet Class

Write a class named `Pet`, which should have the following data attributes:

- `__name` (for the name of a pet)
- `__animal_type` (for the type of animal that a pet is. Example values are 'Dog', 'Cat', and 'Bird')
- `__age` (for the pet's age)

The Pet class should have an `__init__` method that creates these attributes. It should also have the following methods:

- `set_name`
  This method assigns a value to the `__name` field.
- `set_animal_type`
  This method assigns a value to the `__animal_type` field.
- `set_age`
  This method assigns a value to the `__age` field.
- `get_name`
  This method returns the value of the `__name` field.
- `get_animal_type`
  This method returns the value of the `__animal_type` field.
- `get_age`
  This method returns the value of the `__age` field.

Once you have written the class, write a program that creates an object of the class and prompts the user to enter the name, type, and age of his or her pet. This data should be stored as the object's attributes. Use the object's accessor methods to retrieve the pet's name, type, and age and display this data on the screen.

2. Car Class

Write a class named `Car` that has the following data attributes:

- `__year_model` (for the car's year model)
- `__make` (for the make of the car)
- `__speed` (for the car's current speed)

The Car class should have an `__init__` method that accepts the car's year model and make as arguments. These values should be assigned to the object's `__year_model` and `__make` data attributes. It should also assign 0 to the `__speed` data attribute.

The class should also have the following methods:

- `accelerate`
  The `accelerate` method should add 5 to the speed data attribute each time it is called.
- `brake`
  The `brake` method should subtract 5 from the speed data attribute each time it is called.
- `get_speed`
  The `get_speed` method should return the current speed.

Next, design a program that creates a Car object, then calls the `accelerate` method five times. After each call to the `accelerate` method, get the current speed of the car and display it. Then call the `brake` method five times. After each call to the `brake` method, get the current speed of the car and display it.

3. Personal Information Class

Design a class that holds the following personal data: name, address, age, and phone number. Write appropriate accessor and mutator methods. Also, write a program that creates three instances of the class. One instance should hold your information, and the other two should hold your friends' or family members' information. Identify and employ any reusable components.

4. Employee Class

Write a class named `Employee` that holds the following data about an employee in attributes: name, ID number, department, and job title.

Once you have written the class, write a program that creates three `Employee` objects to hold the following data:

Name	ID Number	Department	Job Title
Susan Meyers	47899	Accounting	Vice President
Mark Jones	39119	IT	Programmer
Joy Rogers	81774	Manufacturing	Engineer

The program should store this data in the three objects, then display the data for each employee on the screen.

5. RetailItem Class

Write a class named `RetailItem` that holds data about an item in a retail store. The class should store the following data in attributes: item description, units in inventory, and price.

Once you have written the class, write a program that creates three `RetailItem` objects and stores the following data in them:

	Description	Units in Inventory	Price
Item #1	Jacket	12	59.95
Item #2	Designer Jeans	40	34.95
Item #3	Shirt	20	24.95

6. Patient Charges

Write a class named `Patient` that has attributes for the following data:

- First name, middle name, and last name
- Address, city, state, and ZIP code
- Phone number
- Name and phone number of emergency contact

The `Patient` class's `_ _init_ _` method should accept an argument for each attribute. The `Patient` class should also have accessor and mutator methods for each attribute.

Next, write a class named `Procedure` that represents a medical procedure that has been performed on a patient. The `Procedure` class should have attributes for the following data:

- Name of the procedure
- Date of the procedure
- Name of the practitioner who performed the procedure
- Charges for the procedure

The `Procedure` class's `_ _init_ _` method should accept an argument for each attribute. The `Procedure` class should also have accessor and mutator methods for each attribute.

Next, write a program that creates an instance of the `Patient` class, initialized with sample data. Then, create three instances of the `Procedure` class, initialized with the following data:

Procedure #1:	Procedure #2:	Procedure #3:
Procedure name: Physical Exam	Procedure name: X-ray	Procedure name: Blood test
Date: Today's date	Date: Today's date	Date: Today's date
Practitioner: Dr. Irvine	Practitioner: Dr. Jamison	Practitioner: Dr. Smith
Charge: 250.00	Charge: 500.00	Charge: 200.00

The program should display the patient's information, information about all three of the procedures, and the total charges of the three procedures.

7. Employee Management System

This exercise assumes you have created the `Employee` class for Programming Exercise 4. Create a program that stores `Employee` objects in a dictionary. Use the employee ID number as the key. The program should present a menu that lets the user perform the following actions:

- Look up an employee in the dictionary
- Add a new employee to the dictionary
- Change an existing employee's name, department, and job title in the dictionary
- Delete an employee from the dictionary
- Quit the program

When the program ends, it should pickle the dictionary and save it to a file. Each time the program starts, it should try to load the pickled dictionary from the file. If the file does not exist, the program should start with an empty dictionary.

8. Cash Register

This exercise assumes you have created the `RetailItem` class for Programming Exercise 5. Create a `CashRegister` class that can be used with the `RetailItem` class. The `CashRegister` class should be able to internally keep a list of `RetailItem` objects. The class should have the following methods:

- A method named purchase_item that accepts a RetailItem object as an argument. Each time the purchase_item method is called, the RetailItem object that is passed as an argument should be added to the list.
- A method named get_total that returns the total price of all the RetailItem objects stored in the CashRegister object's internal list.
- A method named show_items that displays data about the RetailItem objects stored in the CashRegister object's internal list.
- A method named clear that should clear the CashRegister object's internal list.

Demonstrate the CashRegister class in a program that allows the user to select several items for purchase. When the user is ready to check out, the program should display a list of all the items they have selected for purchase, as well as the total price.

9. Trivia Game

In this programming exercise, you will create a trivia game for two players. The program will work like this:

- Starting with player 1, each player gets a turn at answering 5 trivia questions. (There should be a total of 10 questions.) When a question is displayed, 4 possible answers are also displayed. Only one of the answers is correct, and if the player selects the correct answer, they earn a point.
- After answers have been selected for all the questions, the program displays the number of points earned by each player and declares the player with the highest number of points the winner.

To create this program, write a Question class to hold the data for a trivia question. The Question class should have attributes for the following data:

- A trivia question
- Possible answer 1
- Possible answer 2
- Possible answer 3
- Possible answer 4
- The number of the correct answer (1, 2, 3, or 4)

The Question class also should have an appropriate __init__ method, accessors, and mutators.

The program should have a list or a dictionary containing 10 Question objects, one for each trivia question. Make up your own trivia questions on the subject or subjects of your choice for the objects. Identify and employ any reusable components.

17 Digital Citzenship

TOPICS

17.1 Responsible Use of Technology

KEY POINT — A responsible user of technology respects the legal rights of individuals and corporations.

Using Software Legally

There are different types of software available for use. Some software is available for free, but most software requires a subscription or purchase. Table 17-1 lists types of legal software.

Table 17.1 Types of Software

Commercial software	Copyrighted software, also called proprietary software. The company or individual that developed the software owns the copyright. This means it is illegal for others to sell it, give it away, or even share it. When you buy commercial software, you are paying for the right to use the software, not necessarily for the right to the software's code. Software where the user doesn't gain access to the program's code is also called closed-source software.
Open-source software	A program, like proprietary software, and you may have to pay for it. Unlike proprietary software, it makes the source code available to the public. The idea is that the software will improve and benefit from the innovations of users, who troubleshoot weak points and expand features.
Public domain software	Software that the developers or authors allow others to use, copy, share, and even alter for free.
Shareware	Copyrighted software that you can use on a try-before-you-buy basis. If you decide to keep it, you must pay a fee.
Freeware	Copyrighted software that the copyright owner gives away for free on the condition that users do not resell it.

Proprietary, copyrighted software comes with a software license, which allows the buyer to use and install the program and sometimes entitles the buyer to receive free or reduced-cost support and updates. A **software license** is a legally-binding agreement between the software producer and the user. It specifies the terms of use and defines the rights of both the software producer and the user.

Individuals might buy a single-user license for one copy of the program or a single-seat license to install the program on a single device. Organizations such as schools or businesses usually buy a volume or site license, which lets them install on multiple systems or a network for multiple users. Network licensing generally costs less per user and allows users to share resources.

Copyright

Federal laws that involve **copyright** protect individuals and companies from the theft or misuse of their **intellectual property**, such as creative, literary, or artistic work. This includes software code.

Copyright exists as soon as a work is created, but the creator can register it with the U.S. Copyright Office. It is a crime to copy this kind of work without the permission of the person who owns the copyright to it. Penalties include paying a large fine and possibly jail time.

Copyright laws protect software developers from the misuse of their intellectual property by others. Someone who pretends that another person's work is their own has broken the law by committing copyright infringement. They have stolen another person's work. If you copy someone else's code and try to pass it off as your own or use it in your own product, you are breaking the law. If you want to use content created by someone else, such as software code, you must obtain permission from the copyright holder.

Plagiarism

If you do not cite your sources, you are guilty of **plagiarism**, which is the unauthorized use of another person's ideas or creative work without giving that person credit. Plagiarism is equivalent to stealing another person's work and passing it off as your own. The consequences of plagiarism can be quite significant. If you plagiarize work in school, you may have to redo the assignment or lose credit altogether. Your school may also take disciplinarian actions, like detention. In the professional world, the consequences of plagiarism are even more significant. A professional who plagiarizes work suffers a loss to their reputation and may face legal ramifications, such as a lawsuit. They may be liable for fines and other punishments.

To avoid plagiarism, you just need to properly cite your source. You should insert a citation when you quote, summarize, or paraphrase someone else, use someone else's idea, or reference someone else's work. In a works cited section or footnote, tell the reader the source of your credited information.

Software Piracy

People who copy copyrighted software to install on other computers, give away, or sell are guilty of violating federal copyright laws and stealing. This is called **software piracy**. Violating a copyright and pirating software are both morally wrong and illegal. These activities discourage the authors of good software from writing new and better programs because they may not get paid for their work. Pirated software cannot be registered, so users do not get the support services they may need.

Cite Your Source

If you want to use content created by someone else, make sure that you identify the source or owner of the content. If you use information you find on the internet in your work, you must give credit to the source. You do this by inserting a reference to the source called a **citation**, in a footnote, endnote, or bibliography. A proper citation gives credit to the source, and provides the tools a reader needs to locate the source on their own. Some websites have features that automatically generate citation information for you.

Fair Use Doctrine and Creative Commons

If the content is protected by copyright, you must have permission from the copyright holder to use the work. However, part of copyright law called the **Fair Use Doctrine** allows you to use a limited amount of copyrighted material without permission for educational purposes. For example, you can quote a few lines of a song or a passage from a book.

Similarly, an author may issue a **creative commons license** allowing others to use the work. The owner may set limitations on the usage, such as allowing students or teachers unlimited use but restricting commercial use. Some software developers create open-source software, which means they make the source code for their programs available to the public so users can change the way it works.

Trademarks and Patents

Some intellectual property is protected by a trademark or patent. A **trademark** is a symbol that indicates that a brand or brand name is legally protected and cannot be used by other businesses. A **patent** is the exclusive right to make, use, or sell a device or process. Many types of inventions can be patented. Using trademarked or patented property without permission is called infringement. The penalty is usually a large fine and a court order to stop.

Other Tools for Protecting Intellectual Property

Owners of intellectual property might also enter into an **intellectual property agreement.** This is a legal contract between or among various parties to buy and sell intellectual property rights. For example, if you create a program that you have agreed to sell to a specified buyer for a specified purpose, an intellectual property agreement with the buyer will ensure that it's used as intended.

Many business owners opt for **nondisclosure agreements** with employees to protect their intellectual property. With this type of agreement, employees are legally restricted from sharing certain types of information, even if they leave the company. These types of agreements are common in the computer science industry. Many software development companies require their programmers to sign nondisclosure agreements to bar them from sharing or reusing proprietary computer code outside of the company.

 **Checkpoint**

17.1 What is a software license?

17.2 What is the difference between commercial and open-source software?

17.3 What is software piracy?

 17.2) Evaluating Information for Accuracy and Validity

Critical thinking is your best tool for assessing whether information is true and accurate.

Whether you're doing schoolwork, working for an employer, or pursuing your own interests, it is important to use critical thinking to evaluate printed, spoken, and digital information for accuracy before you believe it or incorporate it into your work.

Consider news. Before the internet, most news was covered by professional news organizations. With the internet's easy access and global reach, anyone can post articles online or upload photos and videos. These people may give accurate reports of world events and fact-check the news in newspapers. However, they can also make things up or support others who spread information that may be based on rumors or lies.

When evaluating information, consider these criteria:

- **Author.** The author should be identified. If you can't locate this information, there may be a reason the author chooses to remain anonymous, or the work may be used without permission. If you do locate a name, conduct a search to find out more about the person or organization responsible for the content.

- **Purpose.** Evaluate whether the information is objective or designed for a purpose. Objective information is balanced and fair. Information designed for a purpose is presented to achieve the desired result, such as promoting a particular viewpoint, misleading, or supporting preconceived assumptions. An **assumption** is something that is accepted as being true even if there is no factual proof. Many people try to twist information or use it out of context in order to influence thinking. This type of misleading information is called **propaganda**. Always evaluate the content to determine if it is presented in a balanced, factual manner and supported by facts, or if it is biased or argumentative.

- **Content validity.** Does the author indicate the sources of the work? Do those sources appear to be respected, valid, and authoritative? Run a search on the references or other sources to see what you can learn. Determine if the information given is fact or just opinion. Also check for spelling and grammatical errors, which can indicate that the creator is not a professional.

- **Relevancy.** Evaluate the work to make sure it is relevant to your purpose before you choose to believe it or use it. Online, most search engines list results in the order of hits received. Thus, search engines sometimes place popular sites before relevant sites. Don't be fooled into thinking that a page is relevant simply because it appears at the top of a list of results. Also, commercial search engines allow advertising and sponsored links, which are paid for by companies hoping to get your business. Don't assume the first link on a results page is the best. It might just be for the company that pays the most.

 Checkpoint

17.4 Why is it important for an online article or website to provide information about the author?

17.5 What is an assumption?

17.6 What is propaganda?

17.3   Digital Etiquette

Each of us has a responsibility to be aware of the social and ethical ramifications of using technology, and to always treat other people and organizations as we want them to treat us.

Acceptable Use Policies

Organizations, including schools and businesses, have a right to expect people to follow certain rules when using their technology. These rules may address the ethical and legal use of computers, other devices, and networks.

Most organizations have an **acceptable use policy (AUP).** These policies spell out certain rules of behavior and explain the consequences of breaking those rules. An AUP may include the following ethical and legal guidelines:

- Do not visit websites that contain content that does not meet community standards.
- Do not use language that is profane, abusive, or impolite.
- Do not copy copyrighted material.
- Do not physically damage equipment.
- Do not access restricted information.
- Do not open suspicious links.
- Do not forward spam email.
- Do respect the privacy of other people.

Schools and businesses may restrict the content that users can access from internal computers. For example, they may censor, or block, specific sites that they determine are inappropriate.

They may also use a filter to block access to sites. Disabling the filters or otherwise accessing blocked sites is considered breaking the AUP and may result in punishment.

People who do not follow these rules may face consequences. They might lose privileges or be fired or suspended from school activities. Very serious violations, such as using the system to threaten or bully someone or to access and distribute confidential information, may require police involvement.

Social and Ethical Challenges of Technology

Technology provides many tools for communicating and interacting with others. In addition, advancements in technology may open the door to social and ethical challenges. For example, how will we communicate and interact with others in virtual and augmented reality environments? How will we use devices equipped with artificial intelligence?

As an ethical user of technology, you have a responsibility to use netiquette at all times. For example, email, social networking, and other forms of digital communication sometimes feel anonymous, which might make you think you do not have to be polite and respectful. When the time comes to meet with a team or with friends in a virtual situation, you must still behave as you would when meeting in the real world.

Some ways to practice **netiquette** in digital communication include:

- When writing, use correct spelling. Proofread before sending to make sure there are no errors. Also, be sure to use proper capitalization. Using all capital letters is considered to be shouting.
- Don't forward or send unwanted messages, or information, or spam.
- Don't flame, or insult, anyone, even as a joke. Using technology can result in a message being misinterpreted. A written joke might be taken seriously, even if it seems funny when you say it out loud.
- Don't be a cyberbully. Using technology to hurt, scare, intimidate, or otherwise bully others is a crime.
- Don't make false statements that might hurt someone's reputation. It's called libel, or slander, and it's illegal.
- Send emails only to people who really need to see the message.
- Avoid transmitting extremely large files.
- Do not use rude language.
- Do not pretend to be someone else.
- Do not use someone else's work without citing the source.
- Do not share files illegally.
- Do not share inappropriate pictures online.
- Do not meet in person with strangers who you've met online, especially if you have no way to verify the person is who they say they are.
- Do not download software or apps from unknown or untrusted sources.

In a company setting, netiquette might include rules for cyber safety and security, some of which may be mandated by your company's policy or even by law. These might include things such as:

- Following company policies or legal standards with regard to securing, storing, and disposing of client information and records.
- Using spam filters as directed by company policy, and disposing of any suspicious communication. Note that in some industries, companies are required by law to keep backups of email and private messages for a period of years, so keep your communication clean and ethical.
- Following company rules and procedures about what software and apps you can install on company devices.
- Following strong password practices. A secure password should have at least eight characters, including a mix of upper- and lowercase letters, numbers, and symbols. Store passwords in a secure location, and follow company policies for changing passwords when needed.
- Backing up work files and other information as required by company policy.

 **Checkpoint**

17.7 Give three examples of rules that might be part of an acceptable use policy.

17.8 What advances in technology might pose social or ethical challenges?

17.9 What is netiquette?

(17.4) Cybercrime Awareness

Cybercriminals use many attack methods to infiltrate personal and corporate systems. It is your responsibility to be aware of these methods to protect your data and the data of your employer and clients.

The internet has opened the door to new kinds of crime and new ways of carrying out traditional crimes. **Computer crime** is any act that violates state or federal laws and involves using a computer. The term **cybercrime** often refers specifically to crimes carried out by means of the internet. Many cybercrimes are based on the ability of people to tap illegally into computer networks. They may create a **virus**, **worm**, or **Trojan horse** program to infiltrate computers and damage or delete data. Or, they may use a variety of other criminal techniques.

More and more often, cybercriminals are trying to access corporate computer systems by targeting employees. As a computer science professional, you may have access to your company's most sensitive information. You may also have a responsibility for the security of the system. You must be aware of how criminals try to attack so you do not fall for their schemes and so you can warn others of the risks.

Cybercrime Tactics

Some intruders pretend to be network administrators. They call network users and ask for their passwords, claiming that the passwords are needed to solve a problem in the system. Users with access to the most data will likely be the target. With a password, the criminals have access to data stored on the network. They may be able to alter files or programs (Figure 17-1) or download data. They also may change user passwords to ones that only they know, so the real users cannot log in.

Figure 17-1   Once hackers gain access, they can alter files or programs.

Andrey_Popov/Shutterstock

Another method of gaining access is to use programs that try many different passwords until one works. This is called **scanning**, or probing. Networks can be blocked from scanners by limiting the number of failed attempts to log onto the system. After three password failures, for instance, the network can refuse access.

A program called a **superzapper** allows authorized users to access a network in an emergency situation by skipping security measures. In the hands of an intruder, a superzapper opens the possibility of damage to the system.

Some intruders **spoof**, or use a false Internet Protocol (IP) or email address to gain access. Intruders assume the IP address of a trusted source to enter a secure network and distribute emails containing **viruses**.

Phishing criminals try to lure victims into giving them usernames, passwords, bank account numbers, or credit card details, usually by sending an email that looks like it comes from an official and legitimate source. For example, in a typical phishing scam, a thief sends an email message that looks as if it is from your bank, asking you to verify or update your account information. The thief captures the information you enter and can then steal from your account. An employee who clicks a link in a phishing message while using a company device opens the entire system to the criminal.

Some criminals may use **packet sniffers.** A packet sniffer is a program that examines data streams on networks to try to find information, such as passwords and credit card numbers.

A **time bomb** is a program that sits on a system until a certain event or set of circumstances activates the program. For example, an employee could create a time bomb designed to activate on a certain date after they resign from the company. Although a time bomb is not necessarily a virus, these malicious programs are often categorized or described as viruses.

Some employees may create a **trap door**, or a secret way into the system. Once they quit working for the employer, they can use this to access the system and damage it. Not all trap doors are viruses, but some viruses are trap doors. Many Trojan horse programs, for example, act as trap doors.

Some criminals use advertisements and email messages to scam you into sending them money or gift cards. For example, they might claim you have won a lottery, and if you pay a tax or fee, they will send you the winnings.

A common criminal tactic is to use **social engineering** to trick you into clicking a link that will install a virus or capture your personal information. Social engineering is not technical. It relies on human nature and manipulation to convince someone to do something. A common social engineering hack would be a phishing scheme that sends an official-looking email notifying you about a problem with your bank account. When you click a link, you are sent to a fake bank website.

When a cybercriminal pretends to be someone else online, it is called **catfishing**. The criminal tries to trick the victim into revealing personal information or sending money.

Strong Passwords

Many computer crimes start when an unauthorized user hacks, or gains unauthorized entry, into a computer network. This often happens when the intruder learns the password to access the victim's computer and the network.

Too often, computer users choose passwords that are easy for them to remember, such as birthdates, names of pets, names of celebrities, and names of family members. Unfortunately, these passwords are also easy for intruders to guess. Surprisingly, the most common passwords used are "password" and "123456," both of which are extremely weak.

Always use a **strong password**. Don't use things like family names, nicknames, or birth dates. Random passwords are often the strongest, like S3nD3v?. Use a combination of at least six upper- and lowercase letters, numbers, and symbols. Often the site will let you know if your password is strong enough. Some sites require you to use a passphrase, which is similar to a password but is longer and includes a string of words, not just characters.

Other tips for a strong password or **passphrase** include:

- Change your password or passphrase every few months. Some sites may require this.
- Do not keep a record of your passwords or passphrases on your computer or on a piece of paper near your computer.
- Never give out your passwords or passphrases to anyone.
- Never type a password or passphrase while someone is watching

Most websites now offer **multifactor authentication**, which adds a second or even third layer of security to password access. Multifactor authentication requires you to use two or more verification factors to access a resource. It can be used for devices, like a smartphone, tablet, or computer, or for access to an online account or private network.

For example, instead of just entering a password, you might also have to enter a biometric identifier, such as a fingerprint or face scan, a code that you receive via text or email on a different, verified device, or the answer to a security question.

Protecting Data

In addition to strong passwords, one of the simplest and most important methods of protecting data and keeping your computer running efficiently is to install and use an **antivirus program** or **antimalware program**. These programs detect, quarantine, and remove viruses, spyware, and malware. These programs continually monitor your system for dangerous files so they can prevent them from getting into your system in the first place. Once they detect a virus, they block it. If they find a virus, they delete it or quarantine it so it can do no harm.

Simply installing an antivirus program is not enough to protect your computer. New viruses are created every day. Software publishers update their antivirus programs to defeat each new attack, and you must make sure you keep the program on your computer up-to-date. The easiest way to do this is to set your antivirus program to update automatically using an internet connection.

To help block unauthorized users from accessing your computer through a network, you can install and activate a **firewall**. A firewall is a program that restricts unauthorized network access to your computer. Most operating systems come with a firewall, and so do many antivirus programs.

In the Spotlight:

Securing Device Data

Imagine you are taking a picture of a sunset over a lake, and your phone slips out of your hands. You watch as it sinks to the bottom. Or, you put it down in the driveway and someone backs a car over it. What happens to your files, contacts, pictures, and videos?

Losing a device does not have to be a disaster as long as you have backed up your data. Backing up is simply creating a copy of the data that is stored separately in an off-site or remote location away from the original. You can back up data manually or use a program that performs the backup automatically on a set schedule. You can restore the data to a new device from the backup.

Now, think about what happens to your data when you trade in the device for a new one. Is your old data still stored on the old device? Who might have access to it? Deleting a file will not keep it secure. Hackers can easily find deleted files.

To make sure information is not left on a device, you must reformat or wipe the drive, which destroys all files. You can clear a smartphone or tablet by resetting it to its factory configuration or using the Erase All command, then removing the SIM card, if there is one. Before you do, however, make sure you back up your contacts, photos, and any other information you want to keep so you can install it on your new device.

Checkpoint

17.10   Why might cybercriminals want to target computer science professionals?

17.11   What is phishing?

17.12   Give an example of social engineering as a criminal tactic.

17.13   Explain how to create a strong password.

17.14   What does an antivirus program do?

17.5 Digital Privacy

KEY POINT   **Using technology responsibly protects personal and corporate privacy.**

Many people share personal information about themselves, their habits, and their finances. Sometimes, however, such information is gathered without a person's knowledge or approval. Personal information can be used for criminal activity such as identity fraud, phishing, and catfishing. The more you understand about how personal information is collected and shared, the better prepared you will be to protect your digital privacy and security.

Some businesses gather information from public records kept by the government. They may also access information that people volunteer about themselves. These are some ways businesses collect information:

- **Website registration**. Many websites require visitors to fill out registration forms.

- **Online purchases**. Some websites gather information about people who buy their goods or services.

- **Browsing**. A cookie is a small file that is saved to your storage device when you visit a website. Cookies give websites a way of storing information about you, so it is available when you return. Cookies are meant to make your web experience more pleasurable by personalizing what you see. However, they can also be used for navigation tracking and gathering data on your browsing and shopping habits without your consent.

- **Warranty registration**. To take advantage of a product warranty, you usually must register with the manufacturer. Some warranty registrations ask for a lot of personal information.

- **Sweepstakes entries**. Many people fill out sweepstakes entry forms hoping to win a prize. In doing so, they provide important personal information.

- **Social networking sites**. These sites gather information about their users from their profiles and posts, including where they live, what they like, and which products they use.

- **Search engines and messaging services**. Some of these sites collect data about users and their online search history to learn what interests them so they can target users with pop-up ads and recommendations.

Companies that gather personal information often sell it to other organizations, such as marketing companies, whose job is to sell products and services. As a result, marketing companies have access to enormous quantities of data about people. This information is stored in large computerized databases, which can be hacked, giving criminals access to your data without your knowledge.

Expectations of Privacy

Everything you post online or send by email is on record. Employees of a company have no right to privacy for any digital communication, stored files, or browsing history when they use their employer's computer system. Although the employer may not say so, every message might be read, every browser history checked, and every social media post analyzed by someone authorized to alert management if anything seems amiss. Even if you think you have deleted the file, you should assume the company has retained a backup.

Employees may face serious consequences if they disclose inside information to competitors, threaten or harass other employees, or spend company time and resources on personal business or entertainment. The best way to ensure privacy at work is to avoid using company systems for anything that is not related to your work.

You also need to make sure not to infringe or interfere with the privacy and rights of others. Do not share personal information about others online, via texts, or in emails. As an employee, you must never post or share confidential or private information about your company, coworkers, or managers.

In addition, you should expect potential employers will look for you online. A simple search will let them see a history of what you have posted on almost every internet site. These are strong reasons why you should always be respectful and polite online and never post items that may be embarrassing to you in the future.

Protecting Your Personal Information

You can protect your privacy by being careful to whom you give personal information about yourself. You can also select privacy settings on websites and social networks that limit who can access your personal information or view your posts.

Some basic actions you can take immediately to protect your privacy include:

- **Clear your browser history**, especially when accessing the internet from a public location, such as an airport or café (Figure 17-2).

- **Delete** bookmarks for sites that may store personal data.

- **Select settings on social networks** to only share your personal information with friends.

- **Set your status to invisible** so other people do not know you are online.

Figure 17-2   Accessing the internet from a public location puts your information at risk.

Иван Река/123rf.com

Following are some additional steps you can take for even more privacy and security.

Use a **virtual private network (VPN)**. A VPN uses encryption technology to make a public network, like the internet, more secure. Most companies provide VPNs for employees to access the company network. You can also use a VPN service for personal internet access.

Set your browser to reject cookies or warn you about them. Better yet, surf from sites that protect your identity. Anonymizer, Firefox Focus, and IDZap are examples of sites offering this service. Duck Duck Go is an example of an anonymous browser. Browsing anonymously can keep websites and browsers from tracking your history and may protect your personal information. These tools automatically delete your browsing history and default to high security levels.

Be careful of websites that require you to register. Do not fill out a registration form unless the site clearly says that the data will not be shared with other people without your permission. You can also sign up for a free email account from a website such as Outlook.com or Gmail. Use that address when you register at websites or participate in other public internet spaces. This will protect you from receiving unwanted mail, or spam, at your primary email address.

NOTE: Most browsers offer private mode browsing, including Chrome's Incognito or Edge's InPrivate. These modes affect your local privacy, meaning the privacy on your local device. They do not affect your online privacy. That means using Incognito or InPrivate will not hide your browsing from your employer, your internet service provider, or the websites you visit.

Checkpoint

17.15 What are three ways businesses collect personal information?

17.16 How do websites use cookies?

17.17 What is a VPN?

Chapter Review

Multiple Choice

1. What type of software is free to use, copy, share, and alter?
   a. public domain
   b. shareware
   c. freeware
   d. commercial

2. What type of software license lets you install a program for one user?
   a. site license
   b. network license
   c. single-user license
   d. volume license

3. If you do not cite your sources, you are guilty of __________.
   a. piracy
   b. plagiarism
   c. libel
   d. infringement

4. If you copy and sell software you do not own, you are guilty of __________.
   a. piracy
   b. plagiarism
   c. libel
   d. infringement

5. What is a clue that information online might not be accurate and valid?
   a. author is listed
   b. information is objective
   c. common words are misspelled
   d. sources can be verified

6. AUP stands for __________.
   a. authentic user program
   b. acceptable user problem
   c. authentic update program
   d. acceptable use policy

7. Which of the following is not a good netiquette practice?
   a. proofreading before sending
   b. pretending to be someone else
   c. never forwarding spam
   d. being polite

8. Trying different passwords until one works is called ___________.
   a. zapping
   b. spoofing
   c. phishing
   d. scanning

9. What security tool is similar to a password but includes a string of words?
   a. passphrase
   b. face scan
   c. fingerprint
   d. strongpass

10. What security tool requires you to use a password and a biometric identifier to access a resource?
   a. passphrase
   b. multifactor authentication
   c. access code
   d. firewall

True or False

1. Copyright protection does not cover software code.

2. The source code for open-source software is available to the public.

3. It is legal to use proprietary software without a license.

4. Software piracy is illegal.

5. Propaganda is balanced and fair.

6. Most organizations approve of people using their systems to access questionable websites.

7. One rule of netiquette is to never share files illegally.

8. Catfishing is when someone pretends to be someone else online.

9. A strong password should be easy to remember.

10. Antivirus software is not important for system privacy and security.

Short Answer

1. Explain intellectual property. Give at least three examples.

2. How does copyright law protect software developers?

3. What are three ways to evaluate information for accuracy and validity?

4. How might a technology such as virtual reality affect social interactions?

5. Explain the importance of keeping antivirus protection up-to-date.

6. Explain three ways to protect privacy online.

7. Explain how sharing information online can lead to cybercrime.

Exercises

1. With a partner or small group, review rules your school district may have for technology use as part of its acceptable use policy. Categorize policies based on appropriate use, vandalism or destruction, and consequences of violations. As a class, debate the benefits and drawbacks of items in the policy, such as censorship and filtering.

2. With a partner or small group, write a list of cyber safety and security rules and procedures you might be asked to follow as a computer science professional.

3. With a partner or small group, investigate intellectual property rights and copyright laws. When using technology, follow your school's AUP while demonstrating proper digital etiquette, ethical acquisition and use of digital information, and responsible use of software. Assess all sources for accuracy and validity, and record all sources of information. Write a summary explaining what you have learned about intellectual property and copyright laws, citing all sources. Discuss your findings about intellectual property with another group or with the class.

4. With a partner or small group, investigate online privacy and information sharing. When using technology, follow your school's AUP while demonstrating proper digital etiquette, ethical acquisition and use of digital information, and responsible use of software. Assess all sources for accuracy and validity, and record all sources of information. Write a summary explaining what you have learned about online privacy and information sharing, citing all sources. Discuss your findings about privacy and information sharing with another group or with the class.

5. With a partner or small group, investigate software licensing and piracy. When using technology, follow your school's AUP while demonstrating proper digital etiquette, ethical acquisition and use of digital information, and responsible use of software. Assess all sources for accuracy and validity, and record all sources of information. Write a summary explaining what you have learned about software licensing and piracy, citing all sources. Discuss your findings about software licensing and piracy with another group or with the class.

6. With a partner or small group, make a presentation explaining computer privacy and security. You should include information about strong passwords, passphrases, and other methods of authentication for safely accessing resources, as well as ways to detect and prevent computer viruses. Use the internet and other resources to investigate the topic. When using technology,

follow your school's AUP while demonstrating proper digital etiquette, ethical acquisition and use of digital information, and responsible use of software. Assess all sources for accuracy and validity, and record all sources of information. Create the presentation, citing all sources, and discuss it with another group or with the class.

7. With a partner or small group, investigate computing and computing-related advancements in technology. Pick one and write a report or news article, or create a website about it. Include a section on the social and ethical ramifications of your chosen technology and computer usage in general. When using technology, follow your school's AUP while demonstrating proper digital etiquette, ethical acquisition and use of digital information, and responsible use of software. Assess all sources for accuracy and validity, and record all sources of information. When you have enough information, write the report or article or create the website, citing all sources. Share it with another group or with the class.

A Installing Python

Downloading Python

To run the programs shown in this book, you will need to install Python 3.6 or a later version. You can download the latest version of Python from www.python.org/downloads. This appendix discusses installing Python for Windows. Python is also available for Mac OS, Linux, and several other platforms. Links to download versions of Python for these systems are shown on the Python download site at www.python.org/downloads.

> **TIP:** Keep in mind that there are two *families* of Python that you can download: Python 3.*x* and Python 2.*x*. The programs in this book work only with the Python 3.*x* family.

Installing Python 3.x For Windows

When you visit the Python download site at www.python.org/downloads, you should download the latest version of Python 3.*x* that is available. At the time this book was written, Python 3.10.6 was the latest version. Downloading puts the .exe file into your downloads folder.

Once you have downloaded the Python program, you should install it and set it up for use. Click the down arrow on the program name and select Open, or locate the program in your Downloads folder and double-click it.

If Windows prompts you with a message such as "Do you want to allow this app to make changes to your device?" or "The app you're trying to install isn't a Microsoft-verified app." click *Yes* or *Install* anyway to proceed. It is highly recommended that you check both options at the bottom of the screen: *Install launcher for all users*, and *Add Python 3.x to PATH*. Once you have done that, click *Install Now*. When the installation has finished, you will see the message "Setup was successful." Select the Close button to exit the installer. To launch Python, type py in the Windows search box and select the Python 3.x app.

B Introduction to IDLE

IDLE is an integrated development environment that combines several development tools into one program, including the following:

- A Python shell running in interactive mode. You can type Python statements at the shell prompt and immediately execute them. You can also run complete Python programs.
- A text editor that color codes Python keywords and other parts of programs.
- A "check module" tool that checks a Python program for syntax errors without running the program.
- Search tools that allow you to find text in one or more files.
- Text formatting tools that help you maintain consistent indentation levels in a Python program.
- A debugger that allows you to single-step through a Python program and watch the values of variables change as each statement executes.
- Several other advanced tools for developers.

The IDLE software is bundled with Python. When you install the Python interpreter, IDLE is automatically installed, as well. This appendix provides a quick introduction to IDLE and describes the basic steps of creating, saving, and executing a Python program.

Starting IDLE and Using the Python Shell

After Python is installed on your system, a Python program group will appear in your Start menu's program list. One of the items in the program group will be titled *IDLE (Python GUI)*. Click this item to start IDLE, and you will see the Python Shell window shown in Figure B-1. Inside this window, the Python interpreter is running in interactive mode, and at the top of the window is a menu bar that provides access to all of IDLE's tools.

Figure B-1   IDLE shell window

```
IDLE Shell 3.10.6                                                    —    □    ×
File Edit Shell Debug Options Window Help
Python 3.10.6 (tags/v3.10.6:9c7b4bd, Aug  1 2022, 21:53:49) [MSC v.1932 64 bit (
AMD64)] on win32
Type "help", "copyright", "credits" or "license()" for more information.
>>>




                                                                      Ln: 3 Col: 0
```

Python Software Foundation

The >>> prompt indicates that the interpreter is waiting for you to type a Python statement. When you type a statement at the >>> prompt and press the Enter key, the statement is immediately executed. For example, Figure B-2 shows the Python Shell window after three statements have been entered and executed.

Figure B-2 Statements executed by the Python interpreter

```
IDLE Shell 3.10.6                                              —    □    ×
File Edit Shell Debug Options Window Help
    Python 3.10.6 (tags/v3.10.6:9c7b4bd, Aug  1 2022, 21:53:49) [MSC v.1932 64 bit (
    AMD64)] on win32
    Type "help", "copyright", "credits" or "license()" for more information.
>>> name = 'Holly'
>>> favorite_food = 'spaghetti'
>>> print('My name is', name, 'and I like', favorite_food)
    My name is Holly and I like spaghetti
>>>
                                                                    Ln: 7 Col: 0
```

Python Software Foundation

When you type the beginning of a multiline statement, such as an `if` statement or a loop, each subsequent line is automatically indented. Pressing the Enter key on an empty line indicates the end of the multiline statement and causes the interpreter to execute it. Figure B-3 shows the Python Shell window after a `for` loop has been entered and executed.

Figure B-3 A multiline statement executed by the Python interpreter

```
IDLE Shell 3.10.6                                              —    □    ×
File Edit Shell Debug Options Window Help
    Python 3.10.6 (tags/v3.10.6:9c7b4bd, Aug  1 2022, 21:53:49) [MSC v.1932 64 bit (A
    MD64)] on win32
    Type "help", "copyright", "credits" or "license()" for more information.
>>> for x in range(10):
...     print(x, end='')
...
...
    0123456789
>>>
                                                                    Ln: 8 Col: 0
```

Python Software Foundation

Writing a Python Program in the IDLE Editor

To write a new Python program in IDLE, you open a new editing window. Select File on the menu bar, then select New File on the dropdown menu. (Alternatively, you can press Ctrl+N.) This opens a text-editing window like the one shown in Figure B-4.

Figure B-4   A text editing window

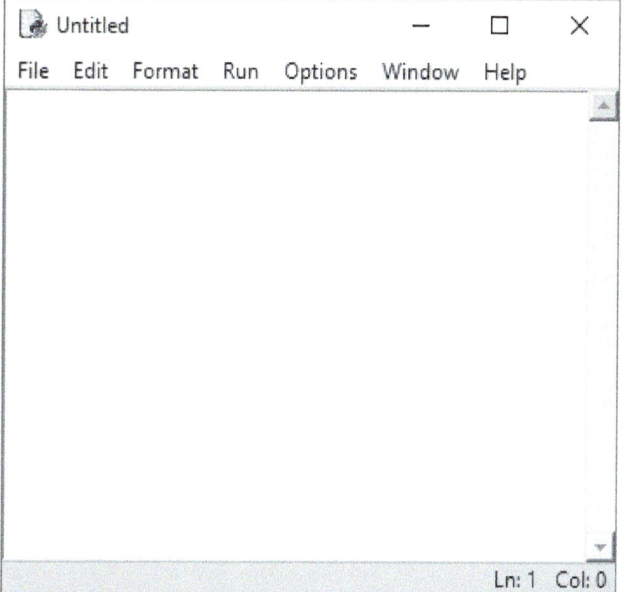

Python Software Foundation

To open a program that already exists, select File on the menu bar, then select Open. Browse to the file's location and select it, and it will open in an editor window.

Color Coding

Code that is typed into the editor window, as well as in the Python Shell window, is colorized as follows:

- Python keywords are displayed in orange.
- Comments are displayed in red.
- String literals are displayed in green.
- Defined names, such as the names of functions and classes, are displayed in blue.
- Built-in functions are displayed in purple.

TIP: You can change IDLE's color settings by clicking Options on the menu bar, then clicking Configure IDLE. Select the Highlighting tab at the top of the dialog box, and you can specify colors for each element of a Python program.

Automatic Indentation

The IDLE editor has features that help you to maintain consistent indentation in your Python programs. Perhaps the most helpful of these features is automatic indentation. The editor automatically indents after a function header, the first line of a loop, or any line ending with a colon (for example, an if clause).

For example, suppose you are typing the code shown in Figure B-5. After you press the Enter key at the end of the line marked ①, the editor will automatically indent the lines that you type next. Then, after you press the Enter key at the end of the line marked②, the editor indents again. Pressing the Backspace key at the beginning of an indented line cancels one level of indentation.

Figure B-5   Lines that cause automatic indentation

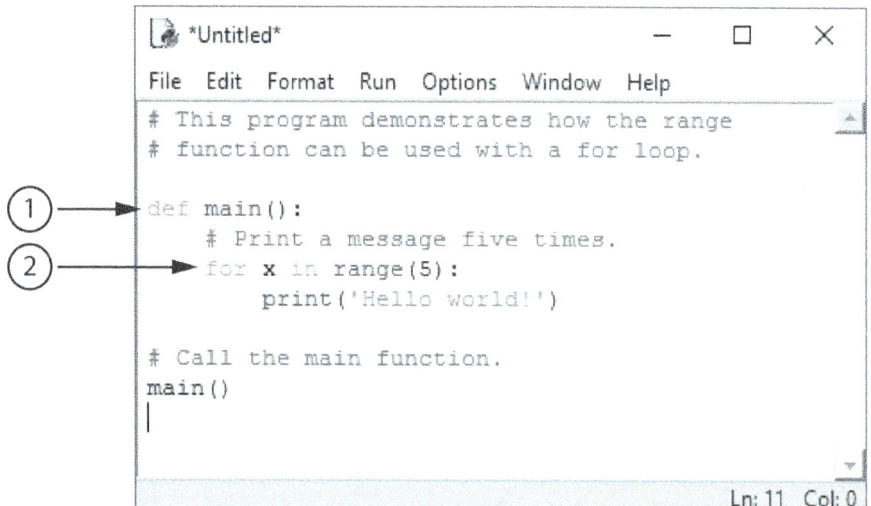

Python Software Foundation

By default, IDLE indents four spaces for each level of indentation. It is possible to change the number of spaces by clicking Options on the menu bar, then clicking Configure IDLE. Make sure Fonts/Tabs is selected at the top of the dialog box, and you will see a slider bar that allows you to change the number of spaces used for indentation width. However, because four spaces is the standard width for indentation in Python, it is recommended that you keep this setting.

Saving a Program

In the editor window, you can save the current program by selecting any of these operations from the File menu:

- Save
- Save As
- Save Copy As

The Save and Save As operations work just as they do in any Windows application. The Save Copy As operation works like Save As, but it leaves the original program in the editor window.

Running a Program

Once you have typed a program into the editor, you can run it by pressing the F5 key or by choosing Run on the editor window's menu bar, then choosing Run Module. If the program has not been saved since the last modification was made, you will see the dialog box shown in Figure B-6. Click OK to save the program. When the program runs, you will see its output displayed in IDLE's Python Shell window, as shown in Figure B-7.

Figure B-6   Save confirmation dialog box

Python Software Foundation

Figure B-7   Output displayed in the Python Shell window

Python Software Foundation

If a program contains a syntax error, you will see the dialog box shown in Figure B-8 when you run the program. After you click the OK button, the editor will highlight the location of the error in the code. If you want to check the syntax of a program without trying to run it, you can click Run on the menu bar, then click Check Module. Any syntax errors that are found will be reported.

Figure B-8   Dialog box reporting a syntax error

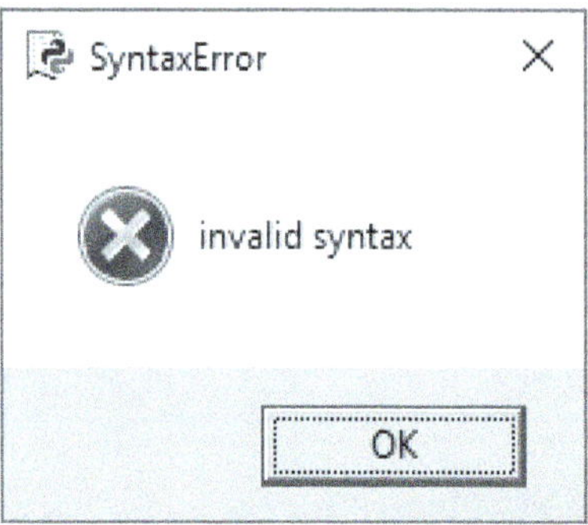

Python Software Foundation

Other Resources

This appendix has provided an overview for using IDLE to create, save, and execute programs. IDLE provides many more advanced features. To read about additional capabilities, see the official IDLE documentation at www.python.org/idle

C Python Keywords

These words in Table C-1 are reserved and cannot be used as a variable name, function name, or an identifier in a Python program.

> **NOTE: The list of keywords may change based on the current version of Python. You can display the list of keywords for the version of Python you are using by entering the following at the prompt:**
>
> ```
> >>> import keyword
> >>> print(keyword.kwlist)
> ```

Table C-1 Python Keywords

and	else	not
as	except	or
assert	False	pass
async	finally	raise
await	for	return
break	from	try
class	in	True
continue	is	while
def	lambda	with
del	nonlocal	yield
elif	None	

D Predefined Named Colors

These are the defined color names that can be used with the turtle graphics library, `matplotlib`, and `tkinter`.

'snow'	'ghost white'	'white smoke'
'gainsboro'	'floral white'	'old lace'
'linen'	'antique white'	'papaya whip'
'blanched almond'	'bisque'	'peach puff'
'navajo white'	'lemon chiffon'	'mint cream'
'azure'	'alice blue'	'lavender'
'lavender blush'	'misty rose'	'dark slate gray'
'dim gray'	'slate gray'	'light slate gray'
'gray'	'light grey'	'midnight blue'
'navy'	'cornflower blue'	'dark slate blue'
'slate blue'	'medium slate blue'	'light slate blue'
'medium blue'	'royal blue'	'blue'
'dodger blue'	'deep sky blue'	'sky blue'
'light sky blue'	'steel blue'	'light steel blue'
'light blue'	'powder blue'	'pale turquoise'
'dark turquoise'	'medium turquoise'	'turquoise'
'cyan'	'light cyan'	'cadet blue'
'medium aquamarine'	'aquamarine'	'dark green'
'dark olive green'	'dark sea green'	'sea green'
'medium sea green'	'light sea green'	'pale green'
'spring green'	'lawn green'	'medium spring green'
'green yellow'	'lime green'	'yellow green'
'forest green'	'olive drab'	'dark khaki'
'khaki'	'pale goldenrod'	'light goldenrod yellow'
'light yellow'	'yellow'	'gold'
'light goldenrod'	'goldenrod'	'dark goldenrod'
'rosy brown'	'indian red'	'saddle brown'
'sandy brown'	'dark salmon'	'salmon'
'light salmon'	'orange'	'dark orange'
'coral'	'light coral'	'tomato'
'orange red'	'red'	'hot pink'
'deep pink'	'pink'	'light pink'
'pale violet red'	'maroon'	'medium violet red'

```
'violet red'          'medium orchid'       'dark orchid'
'dark violet'         'blue violet'         'purple'
'medium purple'       'thistle'             'snow2'
'snow3'               'snow4'               'seashell2'
'seashell3'           'seashell4'           'AntiqueWhite1'
'AntiqueWhite2'       'AntiqueWhite3'       'AntiqueWhite4'
'bisque2'             'bisque3'             'bisque4'
'PeachPuff2'          'PeachPuff3'          'PeachPuff4'
'NavajoWhite2'        'NavajoWhite3'        'NavajoWhite4'
'LemonChiffon2'       'LemonChiffon3'       'LemonChiffon4'
'cornsilk2'           'cornsilk3'           'cornsilk4'
'ivory2'              'ivory3'              'ivory4'
'honeydew2'           'honeydew3'           'honeydew4'
'LavenderBlush2'      'LavenderBlush3'      'LavenderBlush4'
'MistyRose2'          'MistyRose3'          'MistyRose4'
'azure2'              'azure3'              'azure4'
'SlateBlue1'          'SlateBlue2'          'SlateBlue3'
'SlateBlue4'          'RoyalBlue1'          'RoyalBlue2'
'RoyalBlue3'          'RoyalBlue4'          'blue2'
'blue4'               'DodgerBlue2'         'DodgerBlue3'
'DodgerBlue4'         'SteelBlue1'          'SteelBlue2'
'SteelBlue3'          'SteelBlue4'          'DeepSkyBlue2'
'DeepSkyBlue3'        'DeepSkyBlue4'        'SkyBlue1'
'SkyBlue2'            'SkyBlue3'            'SkyBlue4'
'LightSkyBlue1'       'LightSkyBlue2'       'LightSkyBlue3'
'LightSkyBlue4'       'SlateGray1'          'SlateGray2'
'SlateGray3'          'SlateGray4'          'LightSteelBlue1'
'LightSteelBlue2'     'LightSteelBlue3'     'LightSteelBlue4'
'LightBlue1'          'LightBlue2'          'LightBlue3'
'LightBlue4'          'LightCyan2'          'LightCyan3'
'LightCyan4'          'PaleTurquoise1'      'PaleTurquoise2'
'PaleTurquoise3'      'PaleTurquoise4'      'CadetBlue1'
'CadetBlue2'          'CadetBlue3'          'CadetBlue4'
'turquoise1'          'turquoise2'          'turquoise3'
'turquoise4'          'cyan2'               'cyan3'
'cyan4'               'DarkSlateGray1'      'DarkSlateGray2'
'DarkSlateGray3'      'DarkSlateGray4'      'aquamarine2'
'aquamarine4'         'DarkSeaGreen1'       'DarkSeaGreen2'
'DarkSeaGreen3'       'DarkSeaGreen4'       'SeaGreen1'
'SeaGreen2'           'SeaGreen3'           'PaleGreen1'
'PaleGreen2'          'PaleGreen3'          'PaleGreen4'
```

```
'SpringGreen2'        'SpringGreen3'        'SpringGreen4'
'green2'              'green3'              'green4'
'chartreuse2'         'chartreuse3'         'chartreuse4'
'OliveDrab1'          'OliveDrab2'          'OliveDrab4'
'DarkOliveGreen1'     'DarkOliveGreen2'     'DarkOliveGreen3'
'DarkOliveGreen4'     'khaki1'              'khaki2'
'khaki3'              'khaki4'              'LightGoldenrod1'
'LightGoldenrod2'     'LightGoldenrod3'     'LightGoldenrod4'
'LightYellow2'        'LightYellow3'        'LightYellow4'
'yellow2'             'yellow3'             'yellow4'
'gold2'               'gold3'               'gold4'
'goldenrod1'          'goldenrod2'          'goldenrod3'
'goldenrod4'          'DarkGoldenrod1'      'DarkGoldenrod2'
'DarkGoldenrod3'      'DarkGoldenrod4'      'RosyBrown1'
'RosyBrown2'          'RosyBrown3'          'RosyBrown4'
'IndianRed1'          'IndianRed2'          'IndianRed3'
'IndianRed4'          'sienna1'             'sienna2'
'sienna3'             'sienna4'             'burlywood1'
'burlywood2'          'burlywood3'          'burlywood4'
'wheat1'              'wheat2'              'wheat3'
'wheat4'              'tan1'                'tan2'
'tan4'                'chocolate1'          'chocolate2'
'chocolate3'          'firebrick1'          'firebrick2'
'firebrick3'          'firebrick4'          'brown1'
'brown2'              'brown3'              'brown4'
'salmon1'             'salmon2'             'salmon3'
'salmon4'             'LightSalmon2'        'LightSalmon3'
'LightSalmon4'        'orange2'             'orange3'
'orange4'             'DarkOrange1'         'DarkOrange2'
'DarkOrange3'         'DarkOrange4'         'coral1'
'coral2'              'coral3'              'coral4'
'tomato2'             'tomato3'             'tomato4'
'OrangeRed2'          'OrangeRed3'          'OrangeRed4'
'red2'                'red3'                'red4'
'DeepPink2'           'DeepPink3'           'DeepPink4'
'HotPink1'            'HotPink2'            'HotPink3'
'HotPink4'            'pink1'               'pink2'
'pink3'               'pink4'               'LightPink1'
'LightPink2'          'LightPink3'          'LightPink4'
'PaleVioletRed1'      'PaleVioletRed2'      'PaleVioletRed3'
'PaleVioletRed4'      'maroon1'             'maroon2'
```

```
'maroon3'            'maroon4'            'VioletRed1'
'VioletRed2'         'VioletRed3'         'VioletRed4'
'magenta2'           'magenta3'           'magenta4'
'orchid1'            'orchid2'            'orchid3'
'orchid4'            'plum1'              'plum2'
'plum3'              'plum4'              'MediumOrchid1'
'MediumOrchid2'      'MediumOrchid3'      'MediumOrchid4'
'DarkOrchid1'        'DarkOrchid2'        'DarkOrchid3'
'DarkOrchid4'        'purple1'            'purple2'
'purple3'            'purple4'            'MediumPurple1'
'MediumPurple2'      'MediumPurple3'      'MediumPurple4'
'thistle1'           'thistle2'           'thistle3'
'thistle4'           'gray1'              'gray2'
'gray3'              'gray4'              'gray5'
'gray6'              'gray7'              'gray8'
'gray9'              'gray10'             'gray11'
'gray12'             'gray13'             'gray14'
'gray15'             'gray16'             'gray17'
'gray18'             'gray19'             'gray20'
'gray21'             'gray22'             'gray23'
'gray24'             'gray25'             'gray26'
'gray27'             'gray28'             'gray29'
'gray30'             'gray31'             'gray32'
'gray33'             'gray34'             'gray35'
'gray36'             'gray37'             'gray38'
'gray39'             'gray40'             'gray42'
'gray43'             'gray44'             'gray45'
'gray46'             'gray47'             'gray48'
'gray49'             'gray50'             'gray51'
'gray52'             'gray53'             'gray54'
'gray55'             'gray56'             'gray57'
'gray58'             'gray59'             'gray60'
'gray61'             'gray62'             'gray63'
'gray64'             'gray65'             'gray66'
'gray67'             'gray68'             'gray69'
'gray70'             'gray71'             'gray72'
'gray73'             'gray74'             'gray75'
'gray76'             'gray77'             'gray78'
'gray79'             'gray80'             'gray81'
'gray82'             'gray83'             'gray84'
'gray85'             'gray86'             'gray87'
```

'gray88'	'gray89'	'gray90'
'gray91'	'gray92'	'gray93'
'gray94'	'gray95'	'gray97'
'gray98'	'gray99'	

Character	Decimal Code	Binary Code
!	33	100001
"	34	100010
#	35	100011
$	36	100100
%	37	100101
&	38	100110
'	39	100111
(	40	101000
)	41	101001
*	42	101010
+	43	101011
,	44	101100
-	45	101101
.	46	101110
/	47	101111
0	48	110000
1	49	110001
2	50	110010
3	51	110011
4	52	110100
5	53	110101
6	54	110110
7	55	110111
8	56	111000
9	57	111001
:	58	111010
;	59	111011
<	60	111100
=	61	111101
>	62	111110
?	63	111111
@	64	1000000

(continued)

Character	Decimal Code	Binary Code
A	65	1000001
B	66	1000010
C	67	1000011
D	68	1000100
E	69	1000101
F	70	1000110
G	71	1000111
H	72	1001000
I	73	1001001
J	74	1001010
K	75	1001011
L	76	1001100
M	77	1001101
N	78	1001110
O	79	1001111
P	80	1010000
Q	81	1010001
R	82	1010010
S	83	1010011
T	84	1010100
U	85	1010101
V	86	1010110
W	87	1010111
X	88	1011000
Y	89	1011001
Z	90	1011010
[	91	1011011
\	92	1011100
]	93	1011101
^	94	1011110
_	95	1011111
`	96	1100000

Character	Decimal Code	Binary Code
a	97	1100001
b	98	1100010
c	99	1100011
d	100	1100100
e	101	1100101
f	102	1100110
g	103	1100111
h	104	1101000
i	105	1101001
j	106	1101010
k	107	1101011
l	108	1101100
m	109	1101101
n	110	1101110
o	111	1101111
p	112	1110000
q	113	1110001
r	114	1110010
s	115	1110011
t	116	1110100
u	117	1110101
v	118	1110110
w	119	1110111
x	120	1111000
y	121	1111001
z	122	1111010
{	123	1111011
|	124	1111100
}	125	1111101
~	126	1111110
DEL	127	1111111

Formatting Numeric Output with the format() Function

In this course we have used f-strings to format output. F-strings were introduced in Python 3.6. If you are using an earlier version of Python, you can use the format ( ) function.

You might not always be happy with the way that numbers display on screen. For example, when a floating-point number is displayed by the print function, it can appear with up to 12 significant digits. This is shown in the output of Program F-1.

Program F-1   (no_formatting.py)

```
1  # This program demonstrates how a floating-point
2  # number is displayed with no formatting.
3  amount_due = 5000.0
4  monthly_payment = amount_due / 12.0
5  print('The monthly payment is', monthly_payment)
```

Program Output

```
The monthly payment is 416.666666667
```

Because this program displays a dollar amount, it would be nice to see that amount rounded to two decimal places. Fortunately, Python gives us a way to do just that, and more, with the built-in format function.

When you call the built-in format function, you pass two arguments to the function: a numeric value and a format specifier. The **format specifier** is a string that contains special characters specifying how the numeric value should be formatted. Let's look at an example:

```
format(12345.6789, '.2f')
```

The first argument, which is the floating-point number 12345.6789, is the number that we want to format. The second argument, which is the string '.2f', is the format specifier. Here is the meaning of its contents:

- The .2 specifies the precision. It indicates that we want to round the number to two decimal places.
- The f specifies that the data type of the number we are formatting is a floating-point number.

The `format` function returns a string containing the formatted number. The following interactive mode session demonstrates how you use the `format` function along with the `print` function to display a formatted number:

```
>>> print(format(12345.6789, '.2f')) Enter
12345.68
>>>
```

Notice the number is rounded to two decimal places. The following example shows the same number, rounded to one decimal place:

```
>>> print(format(12345.6789, '.1f')) Enter
12345.7
>>>
```

Here is another example:

```
>>> print('The number is', format(1.234567, '.2f')) Enter
The number is 1.23
>>>
```

Program F-2 shows how we can modify Program F-1 so it formats its output using this technique.

Program F-2   (`formatting.py`)

```
1   # This program demonstrates how a floating-point
2   # number can be formatted.
3   amount_due = 5000.0
4   monthly_payment = amount_due / 12
5   print('The monthly payment is',
6         format(monthly_payment, '.2f'))
```

Program Output

```
The monthly payment is 416.67
```

Formatting in Scientific Notation

If you prefer to display floating-point numbers in scientific notation, you can use the letter e or the letter E instead of f. Here are some examples:

```
>>> print(format(12345.6789, 'e')) Enter
1.234568e+04
>>> print(format(12345.6789, '.2e')) Enter
1.23e+04
>>>
```

The first statement simply formats the number in scientific notation. The number is displayed with the letter e indicating the exponent. (If you use uppercase E in the format specifier, the result will contain an uppercase E indicating the exponent.) The second statement additionally specifies a precision of two decimal places.

Inserting Comma Separators

If you want the number to be formatted with comma separators, you can insert a comma into the format specifier, as shown here:

```
>>> print(format(12345.6789, ',.2f'))  Enter
12,345.68
>>>
```

Here is an example that formats an even larger number:

```
>>> print(format(123456789.456, ',.2f'))  Enter
123,456,789.46
>>>
```

Notice in the format specifier, the comma is written before (to the left of) the precision designator. Here is an example that specifies the comma separator, but does not specify precision:

```
>>> print(format(12345.6789, ',f'))  Enter
12,345.678900
>>>
```

Program F-3 demonstrates how the comma separator and a precision of two decimal places can be used to format larger numbers as currency amounts.

Program F-3   **(dollar_display.py)**

```
1  # This program demonstrates how a floating-point
2  # number can be displayed as currency.
3  monthly_pay = 5000.0
4  annual_pay = monthly_pay * 12
5  print('Your annual pay is $',
6        format(annual_pay, ',.2f'),
7        sep='')
```

Program Output

```
Your annual pay is $60,000.00
```

Notice in line 7, we passed the argument `sep=''` to the `print` function. This specifies that no space should be printed between the items that are being displayed. If we did not pass this argument, a space would be printed after the $ sign.

Specifying a Minimum Field Width

The format specifier can also include a minimum field width, which is the minimum number of spaces that should be used to display the value. The following example prints a number in a field that is 12 spaces wide:

```
>>> print('The number is', format(12345.6789, '12,.2f'))  Enter
The number is      12,345.68
>>>
```

In this example, the 12 that appears in the format specifier indicates that the number should be displayed in a field that is a minimum of 12 spaces wide. In this case, the number that is displayed is shorter than the field that it is displayed in. The number 12,345.68 uses only 9 spaces on the screen, but it is displayed in a field that is 12 spaces wide. When this is the case, the number is right justified in the field. If a value is too large to fit in the specified field width, the field is automatically enlarged to accommodate it.

Note in the previous example, the field width designator is written before (to the left of) the comma separator. Here is an example that specifies field width and precision, but does not use comma separators:

```
>>> print('The number is', format(12345.6789, '12.2f'))  Enter
The number is       12345.68
>>>
```

Field widths can help when you need to print numbers aligned in columns. For example, look at Program F-4. Each of the variables is displayed in a field that is seven spaces wide.

Program F-4   **(columns.py)**

```
 1  # This program displays the following
 2  # floating-point numbers in a column
 3  # with their decimal points aligned.
 4  num1 = 127.899
 5  num2 = 3465.148
 6  num3 = 3.776
 7  num4 = 264.821
 8  num5 = 88.081
 9  num6 = 799.999
10
11  # Display each number in a field of 7 spaces
12  # with 2 decimal places.
13  print(format(num1, '7.2f'))
14  print(format(num2, '7.2f'))
15  print(format(num3, '7.2f'))
16  print(format(num4, '7.2f'))
17  print(format(num5, '7.2f'))
18  print(format(num6, '7.2f'))
```

Program Output

```
 127.90
3465.15
   3.78
 264.82
  88.08
 800.00
```

Formatting a Floating-Point Number as a Percentage

Instead of using f as the type designator, you can use the % symbol to format a floating-point number as a percentage. The % symbol causes the number to be multiplied by 100 and displayed with a % sign following it. Here is an example:

```
>>> print(format(0.5, '%')) Enter
50.000000%
>>>
```

Here is an example that specifies 0 as the precision:

```
>>> print(format(0.5, '.0%')) Enter
50%
>>>
```

Formatting Integers

All the previous examples demonstrated how to format floating-point numbers. You can also use the format function to format integers. There are two differences to keep in mind when writing a format specifier that will be used to format an integer:

- You use d as the type designator.
- You cannot specify precision.

Let's look at some examples in the interactive interpreter. In the following session, the number 123456 is printed with no special formatting:

```
>>> print(format(123456, 'd')) Enter
123456
>>>
```

In the following session, the number 123456 is printed with a comma separator:

```
>>> print(format(123456, ',d')) Enter
123,456
>>>
```

In the following session, the number 123456 is printed in a field that is 10 spaces wide:

```
>>> print(format(123456, '10d')) Enter
    123456
>>>
```

In the following session, the number 123456 is printed with a comma separator in a field that is 10 spaces wide:

```
>>> print(format(123456, '10,d')) Enter
    123,456
>>>
```

G Glossary

A

acceptable use policy (AUP)
A policy—published by a school district, business, or other organization—that identifies rules of behavior that must be followed by anyone using that organization's telecommunications equipment, computers, network, or internet connection.

accessible color scheme
Colors that can be read and understood by everyone in accordance with the American with Disabilities Act (ADA).

accessor method
Accessor methods provide a safe way for code outside a class to retrieve the values of attributes, without exposing the attributes in a way that they could be changed by the code outside the method.

accumulator
A variable used to accumulate the total of the numbers.

active listening
A strategy for effective communication in which the listener pays attention to the speaker in order to hear and understand the message.

aggressive speech
Argumentative language that can lead to misunderstanding and resentment.

algorithm
A sequence of instructions. In programming, the specific steps the computer must follow in order to solve a problem or complete a task.

algorithmic solutions
Straight-forward solutions that can be solved using an algorithm or problem-solving approach.

alignment designators
A symbol used in programming to specify the horizontal alignment for a value.

alternate text
Text that is rendered by a web page or other digital document in place of an image or other element that cannot be rendered or viewed. Sometimes called Alt text.

American Standard Code for Information Interchange (ASCII)
A system that uses 128 numeric codes to represent English letters, punctuation marks, and other characters.

antimalware program
A software utility that detects, quarantines, and removes computer viruses, spyware, and other malware.

antivirus program
A software utility that detects, quarantines, and removes computer viruses.

app
An abbreviation for the term application, usually used for programs developed specifically for smartphones, tablet computers, and other handheld devices.

application software
A program or group of programs designed to perform specific tasks, such as create documents, store data, or edit graphics.

argument
A value sent to a function, subroutine or program.

array
A data structure consistence of a sequence of elements.

artificial intelligence
A branch of computer science that works to develop computers that can mimic human tasks such as heuristic problem solving and decision making.

assembler
A program that converts low-level code into machine language.

assembly language
A low-level programming language that provides machine instructions using language that people can understand.

assertive speech
Strong, positive language that supports effective communication.

assignment operator
An operator, such as an equal sign (=), that you use to assign a value to a variable.

assignment statement
A statement that creates a variable and assigns it to a piece of data.

assumption
Something that is accepted as being true even if there is no factual proof.

augmented assignment operators
A set of operators designed to assign a value to common programming operations.

B

binary
A format that has only two possible values: 0 and 1.

binary digit (bit)
The basic unit of data in computing that holds one of two possible values: 0 or 1.

binary numbering system
A base 2 numbering system in which all numeric values are written as sequences of 0s and 1s.

bit
The basic unit of data in computing that holds one of two possible values: 0 or 1.

black box
A term used to describe some library functions or other mechanisms that accept input, perform an unseen operation using the input, and produce output.

block
A set of statements that belong together as a group.

block comments
Comment that take up several lines and are used when lengthy explanations are required.

Boolean expressions
Expressions that are tested by an if statement.

Boolean functions
Functions used to test a condition, then return either True or False to indicate whether the condition exists.

branching
A term for moving to the next step in a problem or algorithm based on whether certain conditions are true or false.

by position
A term that describes the way arguments are passed to corresponding variables in a function; the first argument is passed to the first variable, the second argument is passed to the second variable, and so on.

byte
A unit of computer memory size usually consisting of eight bits.

C

call
To execute a function.

calling
When a program executes a function.

camelCase
A method of naming variables that uses a lowercase letter as the first character and an uppercase letter to start all other words within the variable name.

case-insensitive
Treating upper- and lower-case characters as being the same.

case-sensitive
Treating upper- and lower-case characters as different.

Cartesian coordinate system
A system used to locate the position of a point in two dimensions by referencing the x- and y- axes.

catfishing
When a cybercriminal pretends to be someone else online.

central processing unit (CPU)
The piece of computer hardware that processes and compares data, and completes arithmetic and logical operations.

character
A data type for text.

citation
A reference to a source that gives credit to the source and provides the tools a reader needs to locate the source on their own.

class
Code that specifies the data attributes and methods of a particular type of object.

class definition
A set of statements that define a class's methods and data attributes.

clause
An incomplete fragment of a statement.

cloud storage
Data that is stored and accessed on a remote internet server instead of on a local storage device. Sometimes called online storage.

code
The set of instructions written in a programming language.

code reuse
Reusing code written in one program in a different program, to perform the same task.

coding portfolio
An online resume that includes examples of coding programs.

comments
Short notes placed in different parts of a program, explaining how those parts of the program work.

commercial software
Copyrighted software that must be purchased before it can be used.

compile errors
Errors that are detected by the interpreter.

compiler
A program that translates a high-level language program into a separate machine language program.

components
The parts of a computer system.

computer crime
Any act that violates state or federal laws and involves using a computer.

concatenate
To join two things together.

concatenation
The operation of joining two things together.

condition
A statement that can be evaluated as being either true or false.

conditionally executed
A term that described how a statement will be performed only when a certain condition is true.

condition-controlled loop
A loop that uses a true/false condition to control the number of times that it repeats.

constructive criticism
Feedback that is delivered in a positive way, and includes advice for how to make improvements or solve problems.

contributor
A person who actively participants in a learning event by making suggestions and completing tasks.

control structure
A logical design that controls the order in which a set of statements execute.

cookie
A small file that is saved to your storage device when you visit a website.

copyright
The legal right to control the use of creative, literary, or artistic work, including software code.

count-controlled loop
A loop that repeats a specific number of times.

cover letter
A letter of introduction that you send with a resume.

creative commons license
A license that lets copyright holders make some of their work available for public use while letting them retain copyright for other parts of the work.

critical thinking
When you think critically, you are honest, rational, and open-minded about your options.

criticism
An analysis and judgement of the positive and negative aspects of something, such as a product, design, work of art, or project.

customer
The person, group, or organization that hires you to write a program.

cybercrime
Crimes carried out by means of the internet.

D

data attributes
Variables that reference data.

data hiding
An object's ability to hide its data attributes from code that is outside the object. Only the object's methods may directly access and make changes to the object's data attributes.

data type
The type of value a variable can store.

date
A data type for coding dates.

debug
The process of finding and correcting errors in a program.

decision structure
A logical design that controls the order in which a set of statements execute. Also called a selection structure.

definiteness
A property of an algorithm that specifies the sequence of operations for transforming input into output.

definition
The code you write to create a function and other elements.

deliverable
A product or segment of a product that can be provided to an employer, client, or the public.

desk checking
A debugging exercise in which you step through each of the program's statements one by one. Also called hand tracing.

development environment
The software and hardware tools that a programmer uses to create, modify, and test code.

dialog box
An area onscreen where a program prompts a user for input.

dictionaries
In Python, objects that store elements as key-value pairs.

digital
Anything that uses binary numbers.

digital data
Data that is stored in binary format.

digital device
Any device that works with binary data.

directory
A computer's filing system.

disk drive
A secondary storage device.

divide and conquer
A method of work in which a large task is divided into several smaller tasks that are more easily performed.

dual alternative decision structure
A decision structure that has two possible paths of execution— one path is taken if a condition is true and the other path is taken if the condition is false.

E

effective communication
Communication in which all participants understand the message.

effectiveness
A property of an algorithm that indicates that the steps can be accomplished without additional input.

element
An item that is stored in a list or array.

else suite
A block of statements that appears after an else clause.

employability
Having and using your life skills and abilities to be hired and stay hired.

encapsulation
Combining data and code into a single object.

end symbol
In a flowchart, the terminal symbol that marks the program's ending point.

end-line comment
A comment that appears at the end of a line of code.

escape character
A special character inside a string literal that is preceded by a backslash (\); when the string literal is printed, the escape characters are treated as a special command embedded in the string.

exception
An unexpected error that occurs while a program is running, causing the program to halt.

exception handler
Code that responds to exceptions when they are raised, and prevents the program from abruptly crashing.

exception object
An object created in memory when an exception is thrown that usually contains a default error message pertaining to the exception.

executing
When a computer is performing the tasks that a program tells it to do.

expression
A statement that represents a value or calls a procedure.

external documentation
Documentation designed for the user, such as a reference guide or tutorials.

F

Fair Use Doctrine
The use of copyrighted material in a review, in research, in schoolwork, or in a professional publication, which does not necessarily require permission from the material's owner.

fetch-decode-execute cycle
The process in which a CPU executes the instructions in a program by reading an instruction (fetch), determining which operation to perform (decode), and performing the operation (execute).

file extension
A short series of letters that indicate the application used to create the file and the file format, or file type.

file format
Standards that are used to write data to a disk so that the data can be read and used by a program.

file name
A series of characters that gives each file in a folder a unique name.

file type
The format that identifies the application that can open a file, usually identified by the file extension.

finally suite
A block of statements that appears after a finally clause.

finiteness
A property of an algorithm that specifies when the algorithm will end.

firewall
A program that restricts unauthorized network access to a computer system.

flag
A variable that signals when some condition exists in the program.

flash drives
Inexpensive, reliable, and small storage devices that use flash memory and a USB connection.

flash memory
Storage medium that has no moving parts and stores data in electronic cells.

float
A data type for real numbers that include a fractional part.

floating-point notation
An encoding scheme computers use to store real numbers in memory.

flowchart
A graphical representation of an algorithm or other step-by-step process.

format specifier
A specifier that causes a placeholder's value to be formatted when it is displayed.

formatted string literal
A type of string literal that allows you to format values in a variety of ways.

fraud
A crime in which deception is used for financial or personal gain.

freeware
Copyrighted software that the copyright owner gives away for free on the condition that users do not resell it.

f-string
A type of string literal that allows you to format values in a variety of ways.

function
A piece of prewritten code that performs an operation.

function header
The first line of a function definition.

G

Gantt chart
A horizontal bar chart developed by Henry L. Gantt in 1917 that shows a graphical illustration of a schedule.

garbage collection
A process the Python interpreter uses to automatically remove a value from memory when that value is no longer referenced by a variable.

global constant
A global name that references a value that cannot be changed.

global variable
A variable that can be accessed by any statement in a program file, including the statements in any function.

goal
Something you are trying to achieve.

graphical user interface (GUI)
An interface that accepts user input through graphical elements on the screen, such as windows, buttons, icons, and menus.

H

hand tracing
A debugging exercise in which you step through each of the program's statements one by one. Also called desk checking

handler
Code designed to focus on a specific type of data or task, such as an event handler or an exception handler.

hard skills
Skills used for a specific job that do not transfer to other jobs.

hardware
The physical parts of a computer.

heuristic solutions
Solutions that cannot be reached through a direct set of steps, like an algorithm, but require critical thinking or experience.

hierarchical
Multilevel organization, usually arranged in order of rank.

hierarchy chart
A chart used to illustrate a hierarchical relationship. Also called a hierarchy chart. Also called a structure chart.

high-level language
A programming language that uses words that are easy to understand, allowing the creation of complex programs without large numbers of low-level instructions.

I

identity theft
The fraudulent use of a person's personal information.

IDLE
The integrated development learning environment included with Python.

if statement
A single alternative decision structure that executes the statement following the if clause if the condition is true.

if-else statement
A dual alternative decision structure that executes the statement following the if clause if the condition is true and the statement following the else clause if the condition is false.

immutable
Unchangeable.

import
In Python, a keyword used to make code from one module available in another module.

index
In Python, an operator that refers to an element by its position within the list.

ineffective communication
Communication in which participants to not understand the message as it is intended.

infinite loop
A loop that continues to repeat until the program is interrupted.

informational interview
An interview at a company or organization to learn about career opportunities.

initiator
A person who starts a learning event, such as a discussion or activity.

input
Data the computer collects from people and from other devices.

input device
A computer component, or peripheral device, that collects data and sends it to the computer.

input error
An error that occurs when a user enters an invalid value.

input symbols
The symbol used in a flowchart to identify when input is received; usually a parallelogram.

instance
In object-oriented programming, an object created based on an existing class.

instance attributes
In object-oriented programming, attributes that belong to a specific instance.

instruction set
The entire set of instructions that a CPU can execute.

integer
A data type for whole numbers.

integrated development environment
A single program that provides all of the tools necessary to write, execute, and test a program.

intellectual property
Creative, literary, or artistic work.

intellectual property agreement
A legal contract between or among various parties for the purchase and sale of intellectual property rights.

interactive mode
One of two operating modes, in which the Python interpreter waits for the programmer to type Python statements.

internal documentation
Comments written for human readers in a program's code that are ignored by the compiler or interpreter.

internship
A position in a company in which you learn while you work.

interpreter
A program that translates and executes the instructions in a high-level language program.

IPO chart
A chart that programmers use to describe the input, processing, and output of a function.

"I" statement
A strategy for effective communication in which the speaker presents information from their point of view.

iterable
An object that holds a series of values that can be iterated over and over.

iteration
The execution of the body of a loop.

iterative
A description of a repetitive process.

J

job application
A standard form filled out when applying for a job.

job leads
Opportunities for employment.

job search resources
Resources that help identify job leads, including networking, online resources, career counselors, employment agencies, and job fairs.

K

keyword
Reserved words that have special meaning to the interpreter, and therefore cannot be used as an identifier, such as a variable name.

keyword argument
In Python, an argument written in accordance with syntax to specify which parameter variable an argument should be passed to.

knowledge base
A store of information or data a person or system can draw on.

L

leader
A type of manager who knows how to use available resources to help others achieve their goals.

learner
A person who is working to learn a new subject or skill.

learning community
A group of students, educators, and professionals who work together and support each other to achieve academic goals.

library
A collection of functions that have already been written and are available for use.

library functions
Functions stored in a library.

line comments
Comments that occupy a single line, and explain a short section of the program.

line continuation character
A character used to break a statement into multiple lines. In Python, it is a backslash (\).

list
In Python, a mutable comma-separated sequence of data items that are enclosed in a set of brackets.

local variable
A variable that can be used only within the function in which it is created.

logic error
A mistake that does not prevent the program from running, but causes it to produce incorrect results.

logical operators
Operators used to create complex Boolean expressions.

loop
A repetition structure used to make the computer repeat code as many times as necessary.

loosely-typed language
A flexible language that allows you to store data in variables without explicitly declaring the data type of the variable.

low-level language
A programming language that uses instructions that a computer can recognize without a compiler or interpreter.

M

machine language
Code that consists of binary or hexadecimal instructions.

magic number
An unexplained value that appears in a program's code.

main memory
The primary memory where the computer stores a program and the program's data while that program is running.

mainline logic
The overall logic of a program.

math expression
A mathematical statement that has at least two terms containing numbers or variables, or both, connected by an operator that performs a calculation and returns a value.

math operator
A symbol that identifies the mathematical operation you want to perform.

memory sticks
A type of inexpensive, reliable, and small USB secondary storage device.

mentor
A person who supports, encourages, and teaches someone with less experience.

metadata
Data about other data.

method
A function that belongs to an object and performs some operation on that object.

microprocessors
The integrated circuits that perform all the functions of a central processing unit.

mixed-type expression
An expression that uses operands of different data types.

mnemonics
In programming, short words used in place of binary numbers.

modularized program
A program that has been written with each task in its own function.

modules
In Python, files that hold related functions, stored in the library, and copied to your computer when you install Python.

modulus operator
A mathematical operator that performs division, but instead of returning the quotient, it returns the remainder. In Python, it is the % symbol.

multifactor authentication
Two or more verification factors required to access a resource such as a website, account, or device.

multiline string
A string on more than one line.

mutable
Changeable.

mutator method
In Python, a method that stores a value in a data attribute or changes the value of a data attribute in some other way.

N

named constant
A name that represents a special value.

navigation tracking
A technique websites and browsers use to gather data on your browsing and shopping habits.

nested function
A function that you define inside another function.

netiquette
Rules for acceptable online behavior.

networking
Sharing information about yourself and your career goals with personal contacts that might be able to help you identify career opportunities.

newline character
A command that instructs the computer to start a new line of output.

non-branching
A problem that is strictly sequential and therefore does not require condition evaluation in order to go through the steps to a solution.

nondegree certificate
A certificate program that allows you to learn skills that may help advance your career without attending a college or university.

non-disclosure agreement (NDA)
A contract that prohibits the signee from sharing proprietary information.

non-iterative
A process where you put in the effort of designing up-front, so when you finally create and test the algorithm, it works as intended.

nonverbal communication
Communication that consists of visual and physical messages that the receiver can see, such as a smile.

nonvolatile memory
Memory that stores data permanently, even when the power to the computer is off.

numeric
A data type for numbers or amounts used in calculations.

numeric literal
A number that is written into a program's code.

O

object
A software entity that contains both data and procedures.

object code
Source code translated by a compiler into binary form so it can be read and acted on by a computer.

object reusability
A practice in object-oriented programming in which objects are reused in any program where they are needed.

objective
A short-term goal used to keep a project on track for completion. Also, a way of evaluating information fairly, without emotion or prejudice.

object-oriented programming
A method of programming that provides rules for creating and managing objects.

online storage
Data that is stored and accessed on a remote internet server instead of on a local storage device. Sometimes called cloud storage.

open-source software
A program that you may have to pay for, but for which the source code is available to the public.

operands
Values on the right and left of a mathematical operator.

operating system
The software instructions that control the internal operations of a computer's hardware.

operator
In programming, an object that can manipulate a value or other operator.

output
Any data the computer produces for people or for other devices.

output device
Any piece of computer hardware that shows the result of computer processing.

output symbols.
The symbol used in a flowchart to identify when output is presented; usually a parallelogram.

P

packet sniffers
Programs that examine data streams on networks to try to find information, such as passwords and credit card numbers.

parameter
A special variable that is assigned the value of an argument when a function is called. Also called a parameter variable.

parameter list
In Python, multiple parameter variable names separated by commas, that appear inside parentheses in a function header.

parameter variable
A special variable that is assigned the value of an argument when a function is called. Also called a parameter.

parameter_name
In Python, the name of a parameter variable.

passed by position
In Python, when arguments are passed to the corresponding parameter variables in the function, based on position.

passed by type
In Python, when arguments are passed to parameter variables based on corresponding type.

pass by value
In Python, a form of argument passing where a function cannot change the value of an argument that was passed to it.

passive speech
Deferential language that shows respect for others without stating individual opinions or needs.

passphrase
A security tool similar to a password that uses a string of words, not just characters.

patent
The exclusive right to make, use, or sell a device or process.

path
A string of characters used to identify the specific location of a folder or file within the directory system.

peripheral
Input, output, and storage devices that can be connected to a computer.

PERT chart
A project management tool developed by U.S. Navy in the 1950s, which shows project tasks, the order in which they must be completed, and the time requirements. Stands for Program Evaluation Review Technique.

phishing
A scheme in which criminals try to lure victims into giving them user names, passwords, bank account numbers, or credit card details, usually by sending an email that looks like it comes from an official and legitimate source.

picture element
The basic logical unit in digital graphics, which are combined to form a complete image, video, text, or any visible thing on a computer display. Abbreviated as pixel.

pixel
The basic logical unit in digital graphics, which are combined to form a complete image, video, text, or any visible thing on a computer display. Abbreviation for picture element.

plagiarism
The unauthorized use of another person's ideas or creative work without giving that person credit.

portfolio
A collection of information and documents that demonstrate your academic and career skills and achievements.

precedence
Priority in terms of importance or order.

pretest loop
A loop that tests its condition before an iteration is performed.

primary memory
The main memory where the computer stores a program and the program's data while that program is running.

primitive
A designation meaning common or basic used for certain variables or data types, such as integer or float.

prioritize
Decide which tasks must be completed first.

private
In object-oriented programming, data attributes that can only be accessed by an object's methods.

private methods
In object-oriented programming, methods which can only be accessed in the class in which they are declared.

problem
Any barrier or obstacle between you and a goal.

problem domain
A set of real-world objects, parties, and major events related to a problem.

procedural programming
A method of programming that uses step-by-step instructions to tell a computer what to do.

procedure
A function that performs a specific task.

processing
The action of a computer executing the instructions in a program.

processing symbol
The symbol used in a flowchart to identify when the program is performing a process on data; usually a parallelogram.

productivity
A measurement of the amount of work accomplished.

professionalism
The ability to show respect to everyone around you while you perform your responsibilities to the best of your ability.

program
A set of instructions that a computer follows to perform a task.

program development cycle
The process of creating a computer program including designing, writing, testing, and correcting errors.

programmer
A person with the training and skills necessary to design, create, and test computer programs.

programming language
A set of instructions and rules used to create software programs.

programs
Algorithms customized to do a specific task.

project management
A process used to take a project from conception to completion.

propaganda
Misleading information.

proprietary information
Legally protected information such as copyrighted code, that is generally not available to the public, that has some degree of uniqueness, and that requires cost or effort to develop.

pseudocode
An informal language that has no syntax rules and is used to design programs not meant to be compiled or executed.

pseudorandom numbers
Numbers that appear random but are really produced from a starting set that is repeated over and over.

public domain software
Software that the developers or authors allow others to use, copy, share, and even alter for free.

public methods
Methods that can be accessed by entities outside the object.

Python interpreter
A program that can read Python programming statements and execute them.

Python program
A computer program written in Python and saved in a file with a .py extension.

Python script
A collection of commands in a file designed to be executed like a Python program.

Python shell
The Python interpreter running in interactive mode.

Q

query processor
A program that creates an ordered list of pages that hit on keywords in a search query.

R

random-access memory (RAM)
Type of volatile primary memory that stores data and instructions while the computer is working.

read-only memory (ROM)
Type of nonvolatile primary memory that stores instructions for starting the computer.

real number
A number that includes a fractional part.

reference materials
Documentation, guides, tutorials, knowledge bases, and other sources of information that users can access to learn about a program.

references
When a variable represents a value stored in the computer's memory.

relational operator
An operator that determines whether a specific relationship exists between two values.

remainder operator
The operator that performs division, but instead of returning the quotient, it returns the remainder. In Python, it is called the modulus operator.

repetition operator
An operator that makes multiple copies of a list and joins them all together.

repetition structure
A structure in which code for a sequence is repeated as many time as necessary.

reserved words
Words that have special meaning to the interpreter, and therefore cannot be used as an identifier, such as a variable name. Also called keywords.

responsibilities
Things others expect you to do or to accomplish. In Python, the things a class is responsible for knowing (data attributes) and the actions the class is responsible for doing (methods).

resume
A written summary of your work-related skills, experience, and education.

return
When, at the end of a block in a function, the interpreter jumps back to the part of the program that called the function and the program resumes execution from that point.

root directory
A main storage location.

running
When a computer is performing the tasks that a program tells it to do.

running total
A total that accumulates as each number in the series is read.

runtime errors
Errors that cause a program to terminate abnormally.

S

scanning
A method hackers use to gain access to a system by trying many different passwords until one works.

scope
In programming, the part of a program in which a variable may be accessed.

script mode
In Python, the mode in which the interpreter reads the contents of a file that contains Python statements.

secondary memory
Memory that can hold data for long periods of time, even when there is no power to the computer.

seed value
A value used to initialize a formula that generates random numbers. Also called a random seed.

selection structure
A logical design that controls the order in which a set of statements execute. Also called a decision structure.

sequence
An ordered set of logical steps. In Python, a sequence is a collection of items in a set order.

sequence structure
A set of statements that execute in the order in which they appear.

serializing
In Python, converting an object to a stream of bytes that can be saved to a file for later retrieval.

server
A computer that manages data and programs used on a network.

shareware
Copyrighted software that you can use for free on a try-before-you-buy basis. If you decide to keep it, you must pay a fee.

short-circuit evaluation
A technique used with Boolean operators in which evaluation is stopped as soon as the first condition which satisfies or negates the expression is found.

single alternative decision structure
A decision structure that provides only one alternative path of execution.

slice
A span of items that are taken from a sequence.

social engineering
A tactic used to try to influence and change societal behaviors. In cybercrime, it is used to trick people into clicking a link that will install a virus or capture your personal information.

software
A set of instructions that a computer follows to perform a task.

software developer
A person with the training and skills necessary to design, create, and test computer programs.

software development applications
Programs used to develop software.

software development tools
Programs and hardware that programmers use to create, modify, and test software.

software license
A legally binding agreement between a software producer and a user that specifies the terms of use and defines the rights of both parties.

software piracy
The act of enabling illegal access to software.

software requirement
A single task that the program must perform to satisfy the customer.

solid-state drives
A disk drive that stores data in solid-state memory. It has no moving parts and operates faster than a traditional disk drive.

solution
Actions for overcoming a challenge or problem.

source code
The software instructions that tell a computer what to do, written by a programmer in a high-level language.

spoof
To use a false Internet Protocol (IP) or email address to gain access to a device or account.

standard library
A collection of prewritten commonly-used functions.

start symbol
In a flowchart, the terminal symbol that marks the program's starting point.

state
In object-oriented programming, the characteristics or properties of an object.

statements
The individual instructions, consisting of keywords, operators, punctuation and other allowable programming elements, used to write a program in a high-level programming language.

string
A sequence of characters that is used as data.

string literal
A string that appears in the actual code of a program.

strong password
A password that combines random characters and symbols and is difficult for others to guess.

strongly-typed language
A programming language that requires programmers to explicitly declare the type of data that will be stored in a variable.

structure chart
A chart used to illustrate a hierarchical relationship. Also called a hierarchy chart.

style conventions
Recommended guidelines and best practices for writing code.

subjective
A way of evaluating information while influenced by existing opinions, feelings, and beliefs.

subroutine
A named block of code.

subordinates
People you supervise.

substring
A string that appears within other strings.

subtasks
Smaller tasks broken out of larger tasks to make a problem or project easier to complete.

superzapper
A program that allows authorized users to access a network in an emergency situation by skipping security measures.

syntax
A set of rules that must be strictly followed when writing a program.

syntax error
A coding mistake, such as a misspelled keyword, a missing punctuation character, or the incorrect use of an operator that is detected by the interpreter.

system software
Programs that control and manage the basic operations of a computer.

T

target variable
In Python, the variable that is used in the for clause that is the target of an assignment at the beginning of each loop iteration.

technical reading
A process that uses specific strategies such as highlighting and reviewing terminology to help readers understand technical writing.

technical writing
A process that uses specific writing strategies to convey technical information to a variety of people.

terminal symbols
The ovals, which appear at the top (starting point) and bottom (ending point) of the flowchart.

time bomb
A program that sits on a computer or network system until a certain event or set of circumstances activates it.

time management
The process of organizing a schedule to allow time to complete tasks and meet responsibilities.

tokenizing
The process of breaking a string into tokens.

top-down design
A technique for breaking down an algorithm into functions.

traceback
An error message that provides information about an exception error, such as the line number where the error occurred.

trademark
A symbol that indicates that a brand or brand name is legally protected and cannot be used by other businesses.

transcript
A record of the courses a student takes in high school and the grade earned in each course.

transferable skills
Skills such as problem solving and critical thinking that can be used in many careers and situations.

trap door
A system vulnerability that is well-hidden and provides access to a computer or network.

Trojan horse
A program designed to infiltrate a computer or network and damage or delete data.

traverse
A method of iterating over a set of data, such as a list or array, in order to locate individual elements in the set.

truncate
To shorten by cutting off the end; in programming it means to remove characters from the right end of some data types, such as digits from a float or characters from a string.

try suite
One or more statements that can potentially raise an exception.

tuple
In Python, an immutable comma-separated sequence of data items.

turtle graphics
A method for creating vector graphics using a cursor (called a turtle) on a canvas, included with Python.

two's complement
An encoding scheme computers use to store negative numbers in memory.

U

Unicode
An extensive encoding scheme that is compatible with ASCII, but can also represent characters and symbols for many languages.

Unified Modeling Language (UML)
A standard language for modeling real-world objects when designing object-oriented programs.

USB drive
A small storage device that uses flash memory and connects to the computer through a USB port.

utility program
A program that performs a specialized task that enhances the computer's operation or safeguards data.

V

value-returning function
A function that executes the statements that it contains then returns a value back to the statement that called it.

variable
A name that represents a value in the computer's memory.

verbal communication
The exchange of messages by speaking or writing.

virtual private network (VPN)
A network that uses encryption technology to make a public network, like the internet, more secure.

virus
A program designed to infiltrate computers and damage or delete data.

void function
A function that executes the statements it contains and then terminates.

volatile
A type of memory that is used only for temporary storage while a program is running.

W

whitespacing
Leaving blank lines in code in order to make the code easier to read.

work ethics
Beliefs and behaviors about what is right and wrong in a work environment.

worm
A program designed to infiltrate computers and damage or delete data.

wrap around
When an integer is too large or too small to fit within the range specified for the data type.

Index

Index

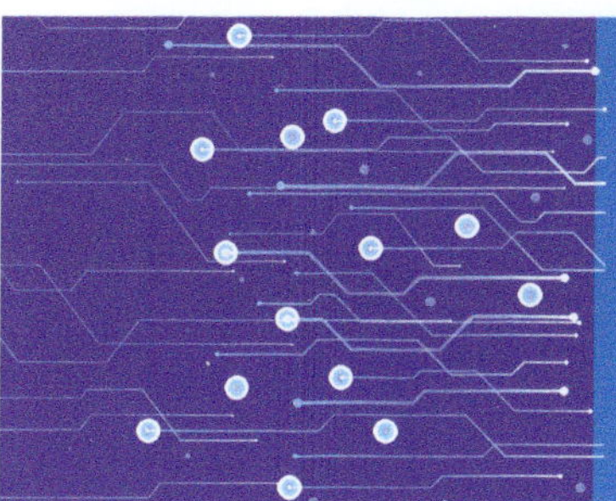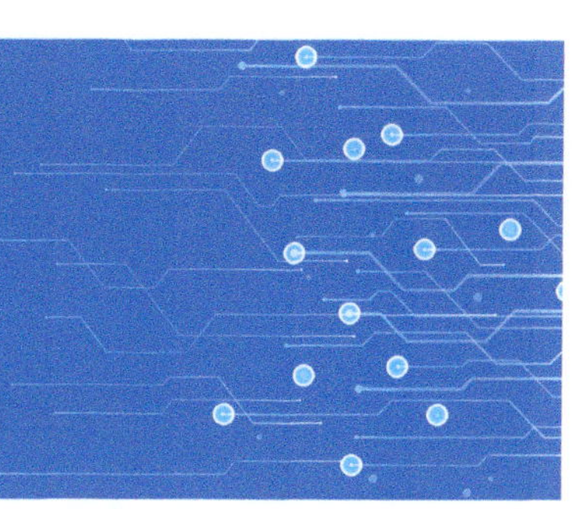

Index

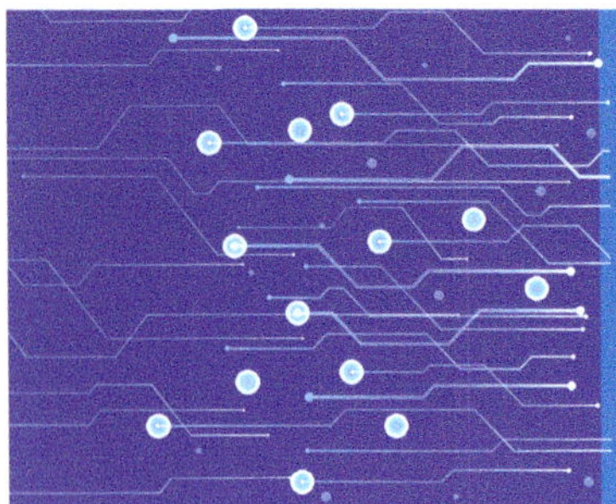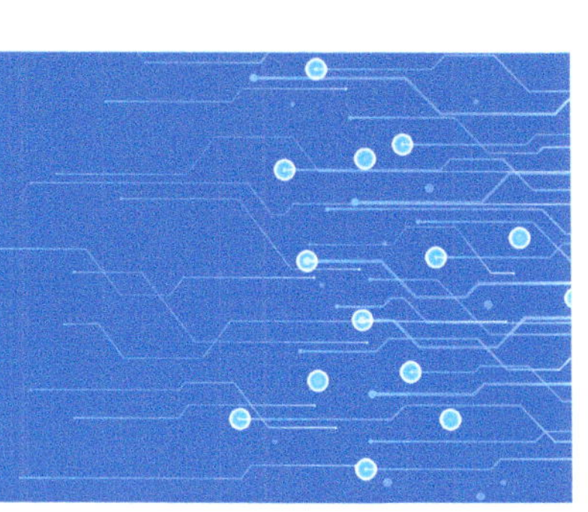

Index

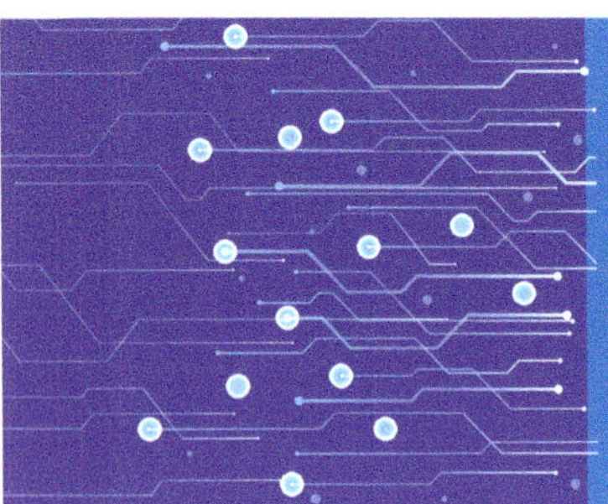
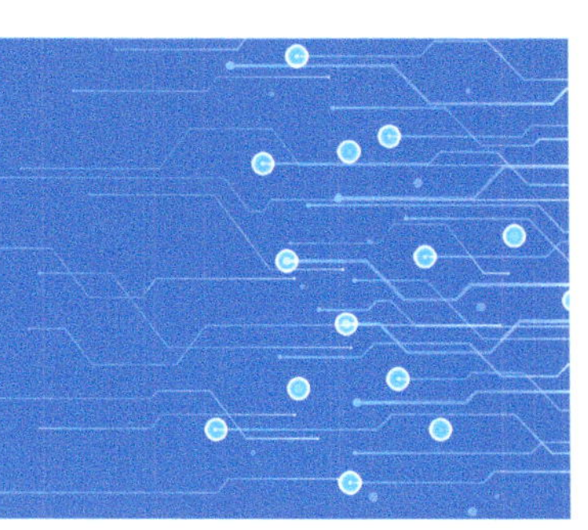

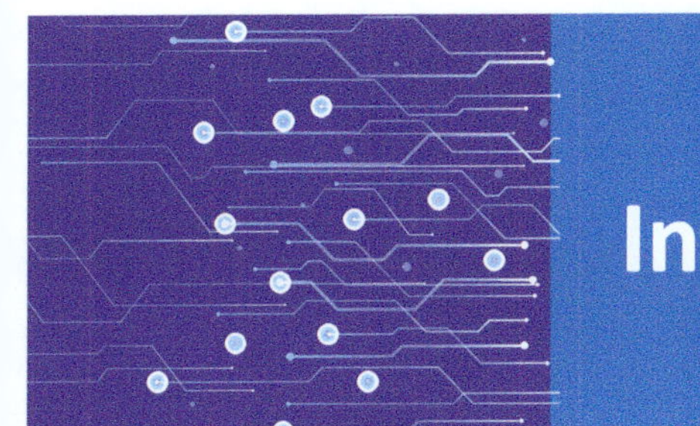
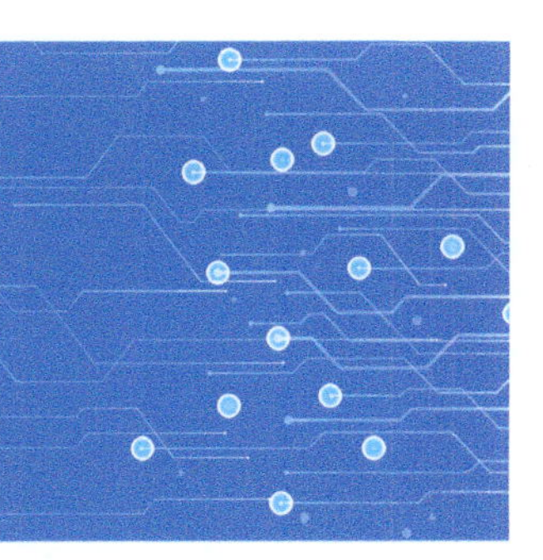

Index

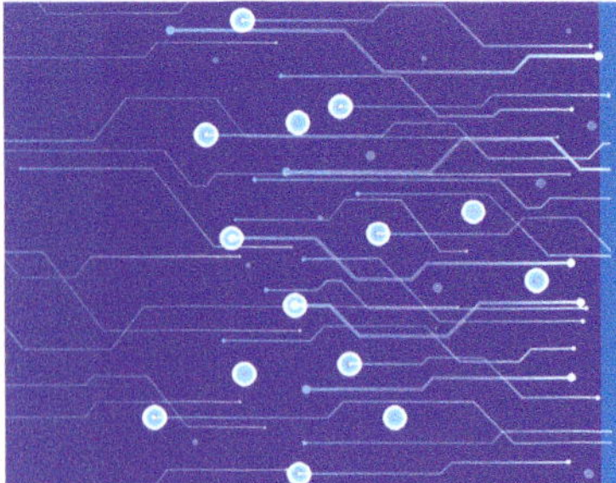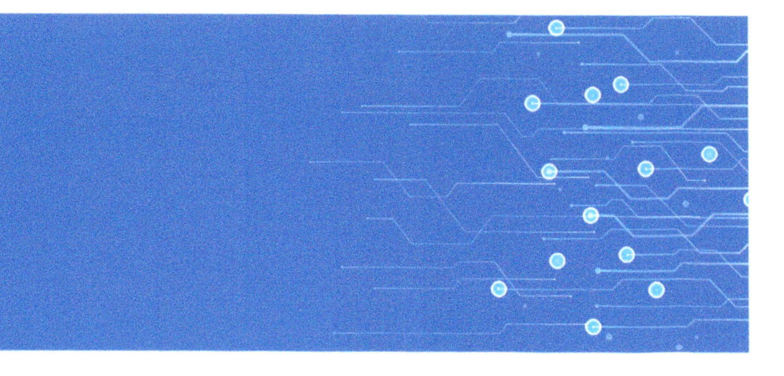

Index

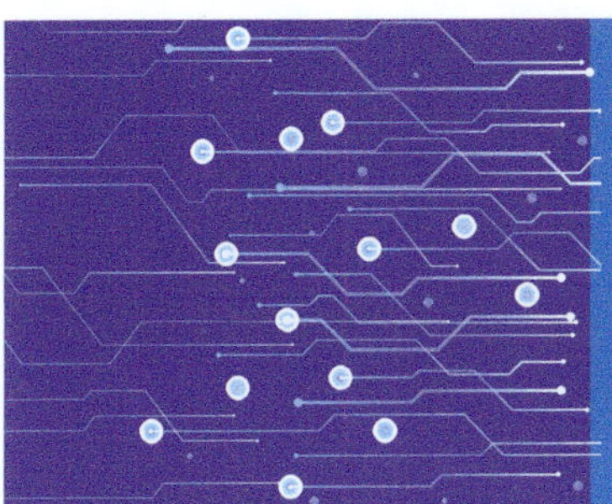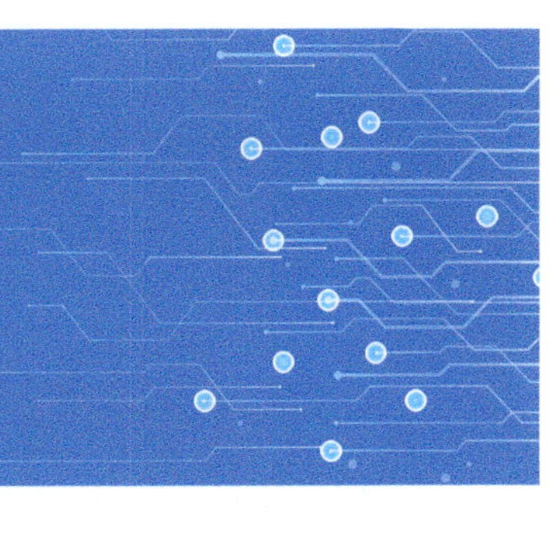

Index

nested decision structures, 245–251
nested function calls, 133. *See also* functions
nested loops exercise, 335
netiquette, practicing, 528
networking, 40–41
no_formatting.py, 561
nondegree certificate, 24–25
nondisclosure agreements, 525
None, returning from functions, 444–446
none_demo.py, 445
non-iterative solution, 200
nonverbal communication, 31
nonvolatile memory, 5
not equal to (!=) relational operator, 173
not logical operator, 254
not operator, 256
note-taking and listening, strategies for, 23
nouns
    identifying, 505–506
    refining list of, 506–509
Number Analysis Program exercise, 362
numbers. *See also* pseudorandom numbers;
    random numbers
    characters and codes, 557–559
    reading with input function, 132–134
    reading with input function, 224–225
    storing, 54–57
numeric data types and literals, 127–128. *See also*
    data types
numeric output, formatting, 561–565
numeric ranges, checking with logical operators, 259–260

O

object code, 8
object-oriented programming, 8
objects. *See also* classes
    data attributes, 462
    example, 461–462
    features of, 460
    passing as arguments, 489–503
    pickling, 490–493
    reusability, 461
    storing in dictionaries, 493–497
    storing in lists, 486–488
Ocean Levels exercise, 334
Odd/Even Counter exercise, 454
official transcript, 24
online resources, using for job search, 41
online storage, 6
OOP (object-oriented programming)
    hiding attributes, 469–472
    identifying nouns, 505–509
    instances, 480–482
    overview, 460–461
open-source software, 523
operands, 156
operating system, 7, 9
operator precedence, 159–160
operators, 73
opportunities. *See* job opportunities
or logical operator, 254–255
order of designators, 147
organization and planning, strategies for, 23
output, definition of, 6
output, displaying with print function, 116–117
output devices, 6
output symbols, 212–213. *See also* input and output
standards
output.py, 117, 222

P

PAC (problem analysis chart), 214–216
packet sniffers, 530
Paint Job Estimator exercise, 453
parameter, 408
parameter variable scope, 410
parameters
    making changes to, 414–416
    passing arguments to, 413
parentheses (()), grouping with, 160
Pascal language, 79
pass by position, 413
pass by type, 413
pass keyword, using, 405
pass_arg.py, 409
passive speech, 33
passphrase, 531
password.py, 241
passwords, validating characters in, 288–291.
    See also strong passwords
patents and trademarks, 525
path, specifying, 9
Patient Charges exercise, 519–520
pay calculation program, 115–116
payroll problem, PAC for, 215
pen, moving up and down, 97
pen size, changing, 98
Pennies for Pay exercise, 334
percent (%) symbol, 143
percentages
    calculating, 157–158
    formatting floating-point numbers as, 143, 565

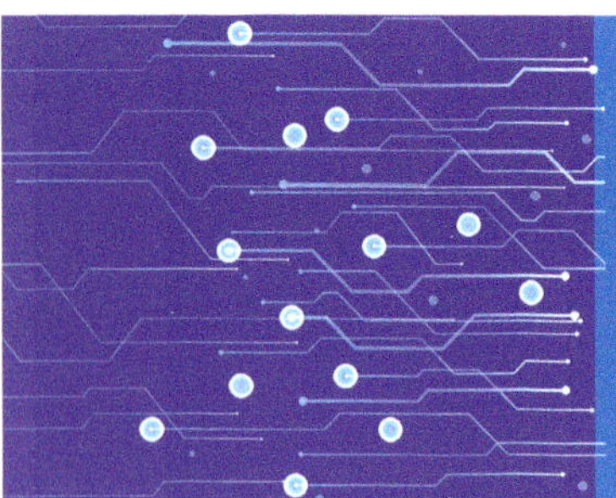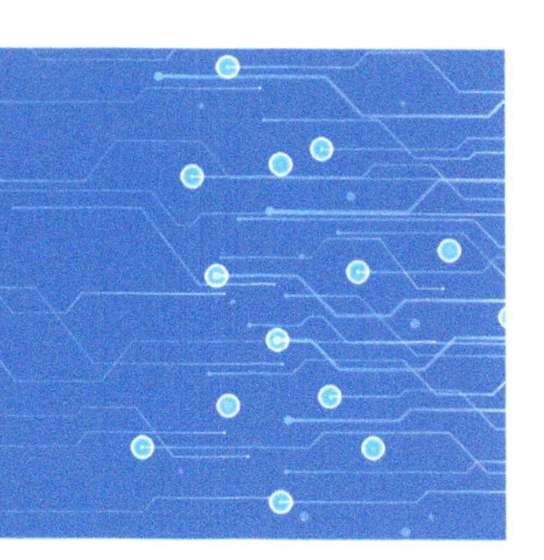

Index

peripheral devices, defined, 2
Personal Information exercise, 152–153
Personal Information Class exercise, 519
personal information, protecting, 534. *See also* information
Pet class exercise, 518
phishing, 530
pickle module, 490
pickle_cellphone.py, 490–491
Pig Latin exercise, 305
PL (programming language), 197
placeholder expressions, 141
plagiarism, 524
planning and organization, strategies for, 23
planning skills, 26–27
Planting Grapevines exercise, 184
Population exercise, 335
portfolio, 36, 38
postsecondary education, goals for, 23.
    See also academic planning; education
presentation program, 2
pretest loop, 313
primary memory, 5. *See also* flash memory; main
    memory; memory; secondary memory
Prime Number List exercise, 455
Prime Numbers exercise, 454–455
prime numbers, finding, 202–203
print function
    displaying items with, 126
    displaying output with, 116–117
    escape characters, 138–139
    item separator, 138
    suppressing ending newline, 137
print_multiple.py, 223
printing messages, 87
privacy, expectations of, 533–534
private methods, 462. *See also* methods; public methods
problem domain, writing description of, 505
problems
    analyzing, 214–216
    defining, 226
    finding classes in, 505
    solving, 26
problem-solving
    in action, 188–189
    with computers, 190
    difficulties with, 190–191
    six steps of, 187–188
    types of solutions, 189–190
procedural programming, 8, 459. *See also* programming
processing symbols, 212–213
professionalism, 28–29

program development cycle, 209–210
programmer, defined, 1. *See also* software developer
programming, procedural versus object-oriented,
    8. *See also* procedural programming
programming languages. *See also* Python language
    Ada, 78
    BASIC, 78
    C and C++, 79
    C#, 79
    COBOL, 78
    comparing, 76–78
    FORTRAN, 78
    Java, 79
    JavaScript, 79
    Pascal, 79
    Python, 79
    Ruby, 79
programs
    versus algorithms, 194–195
    compiling and executing, 74
    defined, 1
    executing, 3, 70
    hand tracing, 367–368
    instructions and commands, 70
    modularizing with functions, 393
    running in IDLE, 547–548
    running in script mode, 88
    saving in IDLE, 546
    storing, 70
    testing, 210
    writing, 88
    writing in IDLE Editor, 545
project management, 28
Property Tax exercise, 452
proprietary information, 45
proprietary software, 523
protecting data, 531
pseudocode. *See also* code
    describing steps with, 227
    overview, 212
    style conventions and comments, 219–220
pseudorandom numbers, 431. *See also* numbers
public domain software, 523
public methods, 461. *See also* methods; private methods
purpose of information, considering, 526
.py extension, 88
Python, downloading and installing, 541
Python code, variable declaration, 80
python command, typing, 86
Python interpreter, 86
Python language. *See also* programming languages

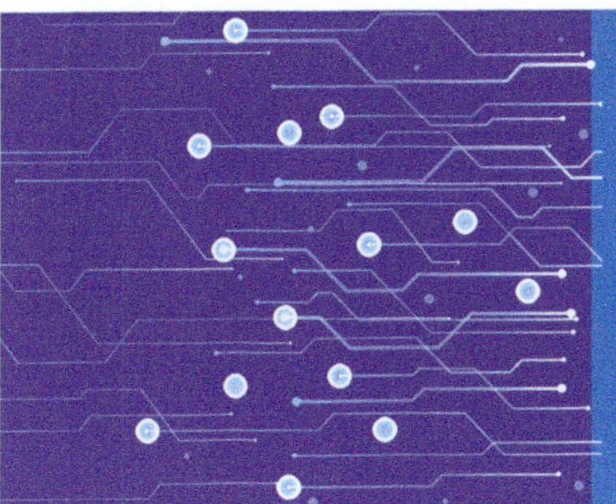

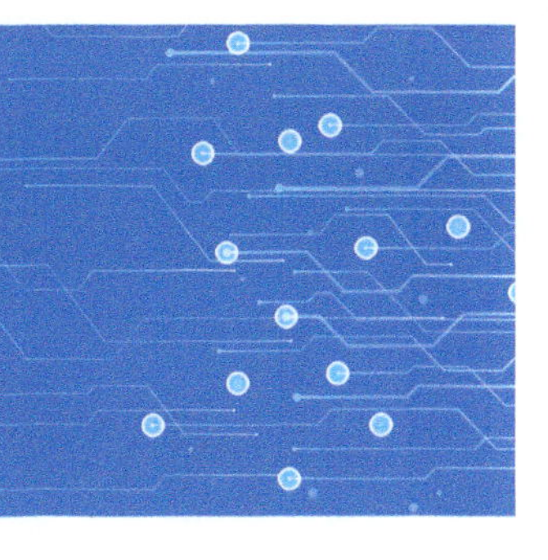

Index

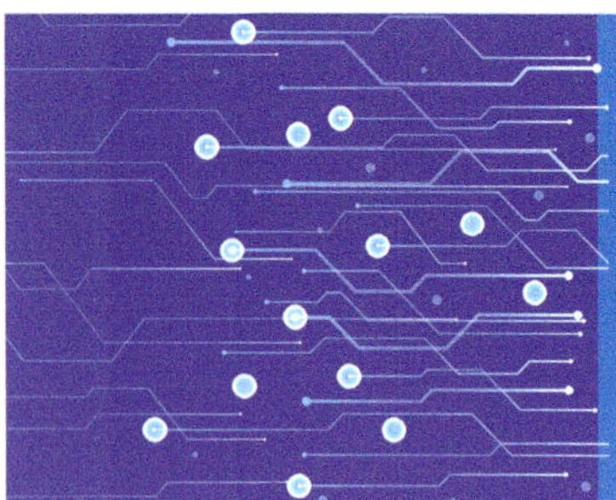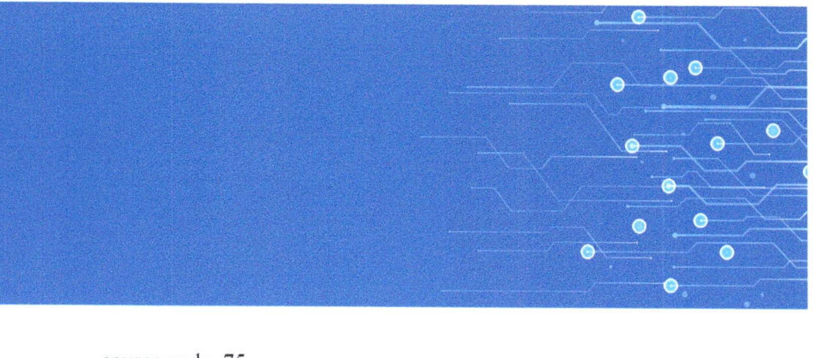

Index

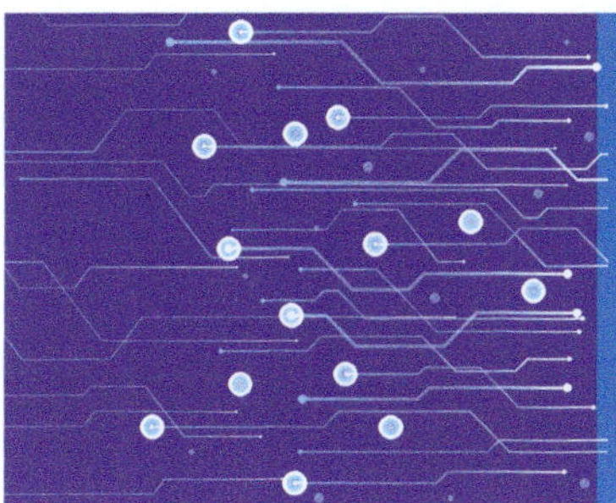

Index